# GOETHE: HIS LIFE AND TIMES

# GOETHE

## HIS LIFE AND TIMES

—

*Richard Friedenthal*

**WEIDENFELD AND NICOLSON**

LONDON

# Contents

# CONTENTS

# GOETHE

## HIS LIFE AND TIMES

# 1

# *In Praise of Ancestry*

It was a difficult birth, continuing over a period of three days. Goethe entered the world almost lifeless, 'quite black' as his mother said later. This meant, in fact, blue, through respiratory deficiency and interruption of the circulation; asphyxia is the medical term. There was no doctor present, only a midwife, who is said to have been clumsy, and the grandmother, who stood behind the blue check curtains of the bed; these curtains could be drawn. The child was shaken and rubbed under the heart with wine. 'Rätin, he is alive,' cried the old woman as the infant opened his eyes, very large dark brown, almost black eyes, as they were later described.

In his memoirs, *Dichtung und Wahrheit*, the fact and fiction of his life, Goethe sounds a more solemn note to record the date and hour of his birth: August 28, 1749, as the clock struck noon. He tells us the astrological constellation of the planets, which was favourable: the sun in the sign of Virgo, culminating, Jupiter and Venus favourable, Mercury not adverse, all of which had, for him, its secret and direct bearing on the course of his life. The full moon exercised its influence and opposed the birth until his planetary hour had passed.

A lying-in room in the eighteenth century, even in houses belonging to well-to-do middle-class families, was no very hygienic affair, quite apart from the absence of a doctor in this case. We must imagine the room as rather dark, with bull's-eye window-panes. The house was old; in fact, it consisted of two houses joined together, with many stairs and many 'Gothic' irregularities. The child was laid in an old family crib, made of brown wood with inlaid decoration; he was tightly swaddled, according to the custom of the day, and was probably subjected to other procedures which would shock us now. Infant mortality was high then, in the Goethe family as well. The birth was a miracle, but the boy was sturdy and lived to a great age, like Voltaire, whose life was also despaired of at birth. A wet-nurse was called in, the mother did not nurse the child herself.

At his christening the boy was given the names of his maternal grandfather, Johann Wolfgang Textor, who had just recently been made *Schultheiss*, the head of the judiciary, and the highest permanent appointment in the town. During the ceremony the infant was held over an old family heirloom dating from Gothic times, a bridal rug covered with a pattern of flowers and foliage. At Goethe's funeral in 1832, in the 'Prince's Vault' at Weimar, this rug was brought out once more and laid under the coffin.

The christening, at the Katharinenkirche, was performed according to the rites of the Protestant Church. Although the Emperors, who were strictly Roman Catholic, were elected and crowned in Frankfurt, the city was strictly Lutheran, and Goethe retained a formal adherence to this faith. He used to refer to himself as 'decidedly non-Christian', and even, to stress the fact, as 'pagan', or else he would profess to having a creed of his own; but occasionally when there was talk of protesting, he claimed to be a 'cheerful Protestant'.

The notice of his birth, in the Frankfurt weekly paper, was printed along with others announcing births of children to craftsmen and merchants, to a brewer, a potter, a joiner, a baker, a carpenter, a cobbler and a tailor. It ran: 'S(alvo) T(itulo) Hr. Joh. Caspar Goethe, Ihro Röm. Kayserl. Majestät würklicher Rath, einen Sohn, Joh. Wolffgang.'

Those were the old days: an old Imperial city, a republic of German nationality within the Holy Roman Empire, with its many crafts and trades, its old houses and crooked streets; a young mother of just 18, and an already ageing father of 39.

Bach and Handel were still alive. The memories passed on to the child by his parents and their circle went back to the beginning of the century and beyond. The wars against the Turks were no mere legend, nor were the wars of Louis XIV, traces of which were still clearly to be seen in the Palatinate and in nearby Heidelberg. On the city gates of Frankfurt, impaled on iron spikes, the withered and shrunken heads of rebels from times long past were still displayed. Frankfurt remained a medieval city, its houses and streets tightly packed within its walls; each morning the keepers of the city gates still had to collect the keys from the burgomaster before the gates could be opened. Membership of a guild was compulsory, there were regulations as to dress, there were patricians and plebeians. In the squares of the town, scaffolds were erected for the public execution of infanticides. The world of Goethe's *Faust* is no figment of his imagination, conjured up from a long-vanished age, it is the world in which he was born and bred.

His long life saw many changes: insurrections and wars; revolutions in the social order and living conditions, in science, art and literature. He lived through the Seven Years War, which among other things destroyed the old Empire; he lived through the American Revolution, and the French Revolution which followed, bringing twenty-five years of war in its train; he saw the rise and fall of Napoleon, the restoration of the monarchy and the reaction to it, and, as a very old man, the Paris Revolution of 1830 in which the proletariat made itself felt as a power for the first time. There were changes in art from baroque to rococo, and on to classicism and romanticism; German literature developed out of provincialism and insignificance into its noblest grandeur, with Goethe himself representing it to the world. Through him the tiny city of Weimar became the focal point of world literature, a place of pilgrimage for young Russians, Englishmen, Americans, Serbs, Poles, Scandinavians and Italians. Technical development made tremendous strides, and the aged Goethe dreamed of seeing the construction of the Suez and Panama Canals. His collections contained models of the first railways, while on the Lake of Constance steamers were plying in the service of Herr Cotta, his able publisher and a business man of great distinction. In science alchemy became chemistry, out of which whole new industries were already developing. The old theological picture of the world was dethroned and man given his place within the framework of natural evolution, a step in which Goethe, as a natural scientist, played a part. New branches of science were discovered, leading to ever-increasing intensity of specialization and refinement, while Goethe, the last of the old order, still attempted to combine in his own person the whole realm of science and research. Religious belief underwent changes from old-fashioned piety, as practised by Goethe's mother, to enlightenment, then back again to mysticism or strict orthodoxy, and then once more to whole-hearted materialism and scientific thinking. In all these changes Goethe participated, in his own way, maintaining his own belief in *Gott-Natur* and in a future life for his own powerful entity, whose destruction by death he was quite unable to envisage.

The origins of such a genius remain a mystery. The most extensive research into Goethe's ancestry has produced only a series of names and dates reaching back into the fifteenth century. But why this particular grandson of a ladies' tailor, this descendant of farriers and, on his mother's side, of lawyers, butchers, wine merchants and clerks, became the greatest German poet is a mystery as deep as that of the genius of Handel, whose pedigree, carefully traced for many generations, reveals not one single musically gifted forebear. Nor is much to be learned from an examination of the geographical origins of Goethe's family. Central Germany and Thuringia, the cradle of so many great men, are prominent on both sides. In his figure and in his features, however, with his commanding dark 'Italian' eyes, Goethe was in every way a child of the Rhine and Main districts. His origins were in the Roman Limes, the first great wall to divide the European world, and from behind which, for nearly four hundred years, the Roman legions kept their watch on German soil. The Roman blood, however, is open to question, for the legions were recruited not from Italy alone, but from Spain, Syria and the Balkans as well, and we are left only with the strange fact that Goethe felt completely at home in Italy from the moment he arrived, 'as though I had been born and bred there'. But this in itself proves nothing; the yearning for Italy is an old German tradition, dating back to the medieval marches on Rome, and to Albrecht Dürer. Goethe's father had made the pilgrimage, the only great event in his otherwise empty life.

We must content ourselves with a few pointers. The father's family came from Thuringia, where Goethe's great-grandfather was a farrier. His grandfather, Friedrich Georg, left his native village and turned to a more elegant craft; he became a ladies' tailor, going to France to study the finer aspects of his trade. Goethe would have nothing to do with this highly honourable calling of his grandfather's, and never once did he refer to it. In his old age, when discussing his title with the faithful Eckermann, he said: 'We Frankfurt patricians always considered ourselves the equals of the aristocracy, and the day I held the diploma of nobility in my hand I was not aware of anything that I had not already long possessed.' And this Goethe legend, invented by himself without the slightest compunction, for long received general acceptance. In the 'sixties of the last century Bancroft, the American Ambassador in Berlin and an eminent historian, once found himself in a dispute on the subject with a high Prussian official; Bismarck was also present. The official maintained the thesis of the patrician origin, Bancroft contradicted him. At their next meeting he referred to a sentence in Lewes' newly published biography: 'Goethe's grandfather was a tailor's apprentice who came to Frankfurt and became a master of the tailors' guild there.' Bismarck was asked his opinion. He declared: 'Of Goethe's origin I know nothing, but I do know that he had a tailor's soul; then, to roars of laughter, he quoted Goethe's poem *An den Mond*:

> *Selig, wer sich vor der Welt*
> *Ohne Hass verschliesst,*
> *Einen Freund am Busen hält*
> *Und mit dem geniesst ...*

(Blessed the man who stands aloof, unhating, from the world, clasping to his breast a friend with whom to share his joy ...) 'Anyone who can write that has a tailor's soul. Just imagine! No hatred! And clasping to his breast! ...'

Goethe's grandfather, the tailor, travelled far and wide, and was a man of great ability. At the time of Louis XIV's abolition of the Edict of Nantes, when, as a Protestant, he was driven out of France, he was working in Lyon, the centre of the silk industry; years later, in his foppish days, his grandson was to order an elegant silk frock coat from there. In addition to many able Huguenot manufacturers, soldiers and officials, Germany has to thank Louis XIV for her greatest poet.

Friedrich Georg went to Frankfurt. Throughout his life he called himself Göthé. In order to be accepted into the Guild, custom required him to marry a tailor's daughter or widow; he did so twice, in fact. On the death of his first wife he married a rich tailor's widow who bought him a prosperous inn, the *Weidenhof*, which for long remained one of the leading inns of Frankfurt. The business card of a subsequent owner shows an almost palatial building of four stories, with half pillars in the centre of the façade; the card also contains a list of distances from important towns, including places as far afield as Rome and St Petersburg, for the convenience of an international clientele. It was the wine trade that brought F. G. Göthé most of his business, and through it he amassed the greater part of the family fortune, from which his grandson was to defray his living expenses for very many years. A patrician the wine-merchant was not, but he left ninety thousand *florins* in land, mortgages and hard cash, this last contained in seventeen leather bags. The son, Goethe's father, made no addition to the fortune; he lived as a 'gentleman of means', with his title of Councillor—a meaningless sham, bought from the Emperor for three hundred and thirteen *florins*.

It is not easy to get an accurate picture of this Johann Caspar. Even Goethe's descriptions of his father are vague; they contain complaints of severity and lack of understanding but, at the same time, note his inner weakness, with its resulting awkwardness of behaviour. He studied law; the tailor wanted his son – the elder son was an imbecile – to better his social position by entering the influential ranks of the legal profession. After studying at the University of Leipzig he took his doctor's degree at Giessen, but without studying there; his thesis, a comprehensive affair, was published, and the cost of all this to his father was the not inconsiderable sum of 200 *florins*. He made the Italian tour, a very ambitious undertaking for a young man of no social standing, and afterwards, with the help of a language teacher, wrote an account of it in Italian. This Italian journey was the great experience of his life; anticipating his son's own journey to Rome, it exerted a considerable influence on Goethe. The strangest omens are to be found in the thick quarto volume: interest in the natural sciences and in mineralogy, including a detailed list of the types of stone used in Verona for building; observations on the evolution of all natural phenomena, from a speck of dust to the Creator, and, as an appendix, even the story of a love affair with a beautiful Milanese girl to whom he sends messages, from the window of his room at the inn, painted in large characters on a sheet of paper: 'When may I express my adoration in greater intimacy.' But the greater intimacy was never achieved, and in this it foreshadowed Goethe's affair, half a century later, with the Milanese Maddalena Riggi.

With this journey, however, the energy of Johann Caspar seemed to have spent itself. He dawdled, did not want to return home, and then, when he did so, presented himself as a haughty and overbearing young man, demanding, without further ado, a seat on the city council, for which he was prepared, initially, to forgo any salary. He received a curt refusal, probably because the city fathers did not like this rattling of the money-bag by the son of such a recent arrival as the tailor's apprentice. Out of spite he bought himself a title which, socially, placed him on a level with the higher Frankfurt circles, but which, at the same time, debarred him from any further attempted participation in the city government. Hurt and disappointed he withdrew into private life, before his public life had even begun. A further six years elapsed before he married, and then when nearly 40, a considerable age in those days, he took for a wife, but without a dowry, the 17-year-old Elizabeth Textor, a member of a highly respected family of lawyers. A year later the son, Johann Wolfgang, was born, followed by a daughter, Cornelia, and three other children who died young; after that, it seems, marital intercourse ceased. Henceforth the Councillor devoted himself exclusively to his collection of books, objects of natural history, paintings by Frankfurt masters and the education of his two children. His last major undertaking was the conversion of the two houses he inherited into a single building, containing a stately patrician staircase. His cultural interests were extremely catholic, the catalogue of his library covering a wide field; but one book in it he seems never to have read, a pamphlet by a Herr von Wondheim, *The Art of Being Always Happy*. The Councillor possessed a lute, which he tuned endlessly but which, as his son tells us, he almost never played. No characteristic is more significant of his life than this. Unsung melodies may have slumbered in his soul. They were never heard.

His father-in-law, Textor, was a man of very different calibre; sly and clever he had worked his way stubbornly up the tangled paths of city politics until he reached the top and achieved the leading position in the city republic of Frankfurt. But he was no patrician either. The Textors, the name latinized from Weber, were lawyers, and had lived in Frankfurt for only a few decades. His wife, a Lindheimer, came from a long line of butchers, who had also risen to the lawyer class in the person of her father. Textor had met his wife at the Reichskammergericht – The Imperial Supreme Court of Appeal – in Wetzlar, where the poet was later to be inscribed. Here, too, occurred the episode, immortalized by Goethe's little poem about his ancestry, in which 'one of them courted a lady fair'. Young Textor was summoned to answer a charge of adultery. As evidence the enraged cuckold threw onto the courtroom table the culprit's wig, which he had left in the bedroom on taking his hurried departure. Quite apart from this episode, however, he seems to have been fond of the good things in life. He was a gourmet, and his cookery book, which has been preserved, contains, among other things, complicated experiments in mixing together crabs and oysters. In his garden he cultivated peaches and carnations, and it was thus, as a patrician tending his trellised fruit trees, that Goethe remembered him.

With his son-in-law, Textor was soon on bad terms; they did not see eye to eye politically, and during the Seven Years War they nearly came to blows. The *Schultheiss* was a loyal supporter of the Emperor, as befitted an Imperial city official, while the Councillor was an admirer of Frederick the Great. The latter accused his father-in-law of dark deeds, saying he had been bribed by the French and had surreptitiously opened the city gates to them. The *Schultheiss* threw a knife at him, the Councillor drew his sword; a pastor, who was present, intervened and stopped the fight.

Subsequent relations between the two were cool. Cool too, in all probability, was the atmosphere in the father-in-law's home, which he kept overheated because he felt the cold.

With a cool head, and without standing on ceremony, he married off his daughters. He had spent little money on their education; they had grown up half wild and could barely read and write. The eldest got the elderly but well-to-do Councillor Goethe, the second a grocer named Melber, the third a pastor, and the youngest a lieutenant of the Frankfurt city garrison. The son became a lawyer and, later, a burgomaster. As he grew older Goethe virtually ignored this branch of the family. He lacked entirely the homely virtues of cultivating family relationships and of delving into his ancestry, let alone of actually engaging in research into his family pedigree. Once he had left Frankfurt he maintained a coolness even towards his own mother that is scarcely comprehensible. He visited her at long intervals, and then only when he could not avoid it; during the last eleven years of her life he neglected her completely, although he travelled often enough for other purposes. The references to her in his memoirs are meagre and tell us little. He intended to write a postscript to *Dichtung und Wahrheit* in praise of 'the best of all mothers', but it was never completed and was padded out with stories told him by Bettina Brentano, who had sat at his mother's feet and then created her own legend of the *Frau Rat*. Goethe quotes these stories reflectively, as though he were saying: well, it may have been like that, but I really cannot remember.

It is another example of his truly Olympian detachment, of his gift for leaving his past behind him 'like a sloughed snake's skin'. Never once did he accord his mother his highest encomium by referring to her as a *Natur*, an expression he was otherwise fond of using. And yet she deserved it more than many of those he considered worthy of this distinction.

Nature itself had already stamped her with the hall-mark of a Goethe character; poetry could not add to it, as it was able to do in the case of others he met. Goethe constantly transformed not only himself but everyone who came within the orbit of his life and work. His mother remained unchanging and unchangeable. He had to leave her as God had created her. She remained a mystery to him. And when Faust descends to probe the ultimate mysteries, 'the mothers', words fail him, he feels only a shudder. In these regions divination alone has validity; each individual must explore these depths for himself. And to Eckermann he says, quoting himself, '*Die Mütter, Mütter, s'klingt so wunderlich ...*' (Mothers, mothers, the word sounds so strangely).

Somewhat strange in many respects Goethe's mother may well have been, and possibly this quality in her was an embarrassment to him in his maturer years. Fortunately, we possess other evidence: first and foremost her letters, and then the testimony of her friends, of the 'sons' and 'daughters' in the wide family circle she created for herself, to replace the one and only

*Hätschelhans*, her own pet Hans, after he had vanished beyond recovery. She was a creative personality too, this mother of Goethe's, though not in the field of literature, despite the fact that her letters are better and more vigorous than those of almost all her contemporaries. Her life was her creation.

It was no easy life. If, in later years, she was able to declare that no one had ever left her presence without finding happiness and consolation, this was a claim to an active cheerfulness that she had richly earned. It was from his mother that he inherited his *Frohnatur*, his cheerful disposition, Goethe says in one of his poems, a thoroughly misleading statement, as his disposition was far from cheerful. But his mother's was, and it was a quality not merely inborn in her but one she consciously cultivated and developed. The art of relaxation, rare in anyone and particularly in the Germans, was understood by her to a quite remarkable degree. In one of her letters she elaborated on this, in her picturesque way, in the 'Fable of the Partridge', and sent it to her son, with hidden pedagogic intent, for the 'use and benefit of the family', who were in dire need of such advice:

> To St John there once came a stranger who had heard a great deal about the saint. He pictured to himself the man sitting among his manuscripts [with her quaint spelling she writes 'manuspricts] studying, sunk in profound meditation, etc. He visits him and to his great amazement finds the great man playing with a partridge, which is eating out of his hand – and the saint and the partridge are having tremendous fun together. John noticed the stranger's astonishment but behaved as though he had seen nothing. In the course of a discussion John said: 'You have a bow with you, do you leave it strung all day?' – 'Heaven forbid,' said the stranger, 'no marksman would do that, the bow would slacken.' – 'It is just the same with the human soul, it needs relaxation, otherwise it too will languish,' said John.

And this is what this old lady of 76 also does. Not when she is among her friends,

> then I laugh louder than the youngest of them, nor when I am at the theatre, where scarcely half a dozen people are likely to have so strong a feeling for beauty as I, or to find such delicious entertainment. I am speaking of the times when I am all alone at home, and my light is burning at half-past four in the afternoon – this is when I fetch my partridge.... So when it is five o'clock in the afternoon with you, think of her who is and remains

> Your faithful mother Goethe.    (14.12.1807)

She wrote many similar letters. A little catechism of the art of living could be compiled from them, if it were possible to learn such a thing from a book. The son experienced relaxation of this kind seldom, if ever. At times he played with a partridge too, but it immediately became a new problem to which he had to devote his whole attention – the word *heiter*, serenely happy, which, in his old age, became a standing formula, had a different ring, it was a demand. And yet this derived unmistakably from his mother's example, or was at least a maternal inheritance.

Her spelling was faulty; as she herself confessed it was not her strong point. Her writing was Gothic, with very bold strokes, and highly individual in punctuation. Reading she learned from Luther's Bible, which was printed in bold Gothic type, and she had a life-long aversion to Latin type. She regarded it as un-German, or 'classic', and on receiving from Goethe one of his classic works dressed in this garb, she warned him anxiously never to do it again; if things went on like this, soon no one would write German any more, 'and you and Schiller will become classics – like Horatz, Lifius – Ovid or whatever their names are . . . and then how the professors will tear you apart – interpret you – and ram your work down the poor children's throats. . .'.

In her lessons there had been no mention of Horace and Livy, not even of French, which was still considered indispensable. She grew up without corsets, as she wrote on one occasion, and it was thus, as the spirit moved her, that she wrote her Lutheran German. Her son's companion, Christiane, she called, in all innocence, his bed-fellow; and her husband's sculptures she called his 'bare arses'. She read a lot, everything that came her way, novels, Voltaire's *History of the World*, fashion magazines and almanacs. She loved going to the theatre: 'If in the storm and stress (*Sturm und Drang*) of watching *Hamlet* the feeling and turmoil within force me to gasp for breath and air, my neighbour may sometimes stare at me and say, but it isn't true, you know, they are only acting.' She understood the young geniuses of the *Sturm und Drang* movement, her 'sons', as though she were one of them; to Klinger, whose play gave the period its name, she wrote, when he whined about the miserable hole, Giessen, where he was studying: 'I have always imagined it must be child's play for you poets to idealize even the most horrid place. You are supposed to be able to make something out of nothing and it must be the devil's own doing if you cannot turn that Giessen into a fairy town. Anyhow, I have a great gift in that direction. It is a thousand pities that I don't write *dramatas*, I would astonish the world. . . .'

Also reminiscent of the *Stürmer und Dränger* is her outburst about the public, those

mugs and apes: they make a great song and dance about our century and the enlightened times, and yet – with the exception of a small number who are indeed the salt of the earth – everything about these ladies and gentlemen is so flat, so wretched, so perverse, so shrivelled-up, that they cannot so much as chew and digest a slice of beef – bread and milk – ice-cream – lollipops – *haut-gout* – this is their tack....

Perhaps it is a pity that she did not write any *dramata*, but she was a teller of stories, of fables, of anecdotes, of tales. It was in this that her strength lay. Here she is at the time of the revolutionary wars, when armies were marching to and fro: 'What do I say to the return of those twenty thousand Prussians? Only what a Cardinal once said to the Pope who – because he had lived in the seclusion of his cloister – looked with astonishment at the people assembled before him on the day of his elevation, and asked "How do they all live?" – "Your Holiness, the shits cheat one another." ' She is not going to worry her head about military matters, the outcome will show 'who has been cheated'.

This is in her son's style, the style of his farces and *Hanswursts Hochzeit*. On receiving and reading letters like this, the *Geheimrat* must have felt uneasy. Word had reached him that his mother, respected though she was, had the reputation of being somewhat eccentric, that her behaviour attracted attention. On Madame de Staël's visit to Frankfurt, Frau Goethe appeared very ostentatiously dressed, highly made up, with an enormous plume of ostrich feathers on her head, and declared in her few words of French: '*Je suis la mère de Goethe.*' So he always kept her at a distance, and when there was talk of her moving to Weimar he put his foot down firmly.

Lonely, with her partridge for company, she had to spend the greater part of her life in the large house, alongside her husband who, in the early days, treated her as a child and tried to educate her; then, becoming prematurely old, he ended up by leading a 'vegetable existence', as she put it. When Goethe was still a boy the Councillor, obeying a rather macabre whim, took as a paying guest a rich but deeply melancholy man of the name of Clauer, whose guardian he had become and who soon went totally insane. This guardianship was the one office in his life to which he obstinately clung. For twenty-five years the shadow of this idiot, who also raved at times, hung like a ghost over the Goethe home, side by side with the shadow of the portly Councillor. In the room next to this maniac the young Goethe wrote the first lines of his *Faust* and his *Goetz*. He forms a dark symbolic background to the mother's indestructible cheerfulness.

In the war years, at the end of the century, she sold the house, again cheerfully and without fuss. Remaining in Frankfurt when everyone else had fled, she said, 'All I wanted was for the cowardly poltroons to go away so that they would not contaminate the others.' Unhesitatingly she moved into a nice little flat, 'in the fifth act there should be applause and not booing'. All the papers, three hundredweight of them, went to the paper mill, to the eternal chagrin of Goethe scholars. We do not know much about Goethe's youth, and he recalls his mother only as a neatly dressed figure 'doing some dainty needlework', or reading a book, a picture that is hard to accept when we think of her five confinements, and the early deaths of three of her children. He even contrasts her with his vivacious aunt Melber, the wife of the grocer, who, so he says, took care of him and other 'neglected children', tending them, combing their hair and carrying them around, 'performing this service in my case for quite a time'.

With complete unconcern Frau Goethe sent the furniture, household effects and collections to be sold at auction, having first asked her son, who gave her no help whatever, to let her know what he wanted to keep. The new flat was nicely furnished, 'but all the trish-trash is being sold'. Finally, in 1808 she died, still cheerful and carefree, but with housewifely concern that friends and relatives should have a decent funeral repast. To a servant girl, who brought her an invitation to a party, she said: 'Say that Frau Goethe is unable to come, she is busy dying at the moment.' The son remained in Weimar; he did not go to Frankfurt for the funeral or for the division of the inheritance. He had not seen his mother for eleven years, and in the description of his travels there is not so much as a mention of his last visit to her in 1797.

And so for the greater part of their lives these two clearly defined, powerful personalities go their own ways, Goethe carefully, almost anxiously, preserving the distance between them. However much his mother liked to call him her own pet Hans, he was no mother's boy. But his mother's son he most certainly was, to a far greater extent than he ever admitted, to a greater extent, probably, than he ever realized. It is as a child of the people, with her origins in deeper, and more vigorous strata, that we see this daughter of lawyers and government officials. Her fresh, wholesome blood, however, could only partly clarify the dark strains in Goethe's heritage. The main stream was fed from other, less 'healthy' sources – to the benefit of his work, though hardly to his life. But all that is *derb und tüchtig*, sturdy and sound, to use the favourite words of his old age, and even of his youth, stems from her. From her he gets his sharp insight into mankind, his sense of humour, his open-mindedness, his ability to live and let live.

On the cultivation of Goethe's mind she exercised scarcely any influence. It is the uncultivated side of his nature, the side that constantly has to fight against a strong tendency to formulate, theorize and amass files and collections, which he owes to her. It is not the whole Goethe. Foreign to her nature are his qualities of doubting and questioning, his tendency to regard darkness as the necessary counterpart to light, all the antitheses out of which the synthesis that is Goethe is composed. She was a pious woman and believed in her God. The devil 'has to be swallowed without looking at him long'. Goethe never swallows the devil. He moulds him and makes him a partner in his world.

The most complete and the most powerful of all the figures in Goethe's life stands at its beginning, and even prior to its beginning. These two lives together, the one extending from 1731 to 1808 and the other from 1749 to 1832, may be said to constitute the full Goethe century.

# 2

# *Childhood*

Goethe was no prodigy; he was a quick-witted boy who learned easily, especially when an appeal was made to his love of games. This is a quality he retained. As an old man he could still say to his *famulus*, Riemer: 'Above all no professionalism. That is against my nature. I want to do everything I can as though it were a game, just as it occurs to me and for so long as the inclination lasts. In my youth I used to play like this unconsciously, now I want to continue to do it consciously for the rest of my life.' This is a somewhat dangerous principle to follow when one is trying to establish a scientific theory of colour, and is abusing all physicists as fools, which is precisely what Goethe was doing at the time he said this. As an element in children's education the love of games has long held an honoured place. In those days things were different, and it speaks very well for Goethe's father, regarded often merely as a pedant, that he went so far in condoning this propensity in his son. In any case, the father's pedantry, described by the son when he himself had already become fairly inflexible, should not be taken too seriously. The fact is that the boy's education, which was almost entirely in the hands of private tutors, proceeded quite unsystematically even for those days, and much of this left its mark on him. Almost everything in the father's large library seems somehow to have been brought into use: pictures, maps, engravings, travel books. And in his own old age Goethe, exactly like his father before him, never tired of displaying his treasures, and of explaining them to the 'little children', by whom he meant, more or less, everyone younger than himself.

A picture book was his first primer, the *Orbis pictus* of Johann Amos Comenius, one of the Moravian Brethren, and now rightly honoured as the father of modern education. In this, as it says in the Preface, the mind is 'lured', so that learning becomes 'no martyrdom but sheer delight'. To see and think in pictorial images – this made a strong appeal to Goethe's uniquely individual nature, even as a boy. 'Above all else you must learn the sounds known to the animals, of which human speech is composed – and your tongue knows how to imitate and your hand can draw. Here you have your living alphabet.' The text proceeds, with aids to easy memory: '*Cornix Cornicatur*, the crow caws *á á*, *Agnus balat*, the sheep bleats *bé é é*,

*Felis clamat*, the cat mews *nau nau*, *Serpens sibilat*, the snake hisses *s s'*, with appropriate pictures in coarse wood-cut. And thus it proceeds through the whole of creation, the crafts of mankind, its diversions and pleasures, through town and country and, as goes without saying, through the whole gamut of moral education and religion up to the Last Judgment.

Clean, careful handwriting was still regarded as a leading virtue, and Goethe, until the very end of his life, laid the greatest stress on this; an indistinctly or messily written letter he detested even more than a person with glasses or the barking of dogs. His own handwriting remained astonishingly clear, even into extreme old age, and it retained to the full, though with added touches of genius, the style he learned from his writing master, the *Magister artis scribendi* as he is called in his father's account book.

Spelling and punctuation, on the other hand, never interested him very much; later on he left these to his assistants in the Goethe chancellery. In his youth he wrote without bothering about them; his early letters in French rarely even have any accents. Grammar he liked equally little, 'the rules seemed ridiculous to me'. Composition and essay writing were his strong points. His Latin teacher, the son of a Turk who had strayed to Frankfurt, engaged in some lively dialogues with the boy. A number of these have been preserved and, as *Labores juveniles*, have given rise to speculation as to how far the first stirrings of his poetic imagination are manifest in them. In one of them the son goes down with his father to the cellar of their house, to look with awe on the foundation stone, which has been relaid in the course of rebuilding the two houses. Johann Wolfgang, as we learn, wears a mason's smock and holds a trowel in his hand:

> *Pater:* Was nothing else said on this occasion then?
> *Filius:* Oh, yes. The foreman was supposed to make his customary speech, but could not get it out, and began to tear his hair because so many of the onlookers laughed at him.

The *filius* may well have added this touch to the otherwise correct and schoolmasterly dialogue. But the father immediately takes a more serious line:

> *Pater:* What are your thoughts in looking at this stone you have been so eager to see?
> *Filius:* I am thinking and wishing that it may not be removed until the end of the world.
> *Pater:* That we must leave to God.

There is another dialogue which is characteristic of the boy, who was very much of a 'sensitive lad', something of a weakling, averse to any form of horse-play. Max – his school friend Maximilian Moors – and Wolf are talking together. Max is tough and quarrelsome, Wolf cautious and on the defensive. He has arrived late because he had to help lay the table. His parents are giving a large dinner party and he is not to be there.

25

*Max:* What do they mean by telling you to go out of the house?
*Wolf:* If a thing is of no importance to me, I don't bother my head about it.
*Max:* You are right, of course, but you will come off badly.
*Wolf:* What does it matter to me; let them eat their heads off.

To pass the time Max now suggests boxing with their heads:

*Wolf:* Not on your life; mine, at least, is not made for that kind of thing.
*Max:* What is the harm; let us see who has the hardest.
*Wolf:* Listen, let's leave this kind of game to the billy-goats, to whom it is natural.
*Max:* Coward! The exercise will give us hard heads.
*Wolf:* That would be no credit to us. I prefer to keep mine soft.

Nor has he any time for fencing, which Max now suggests:

*Wolf:* Suppose the teacher comes?
*Max:* No need to be afraid of that.
*Wolf:* Listen, listen, someone is knocking; what did I say? (Max wants to bolt the door.)
*Wolf:* Stop that. It is not seemly to shut out the teacher. Come in!

A model boy, and, if he composed that himself, in boys' language an absolute molly-coddle. We do not know who was the author of these little exercises, they may have been the combined efforts of teacher, *Pater* and *Filius*. It is a fact, however, that Johann Wolfgang, called Wölfchen by his mother, had a complete aversion to all rough games and fighting. His gait was given a slightly solemn look by his rather short legs; even later on they always hindered his movements to some extent. The children's dress itself, modelled on that of grown-ups, was solemn and clumsy, with long coat-tails; and at an early age they carried a sword, which made running about impossible. The 'coarseness' of the other children, with whom, for a short time and very much against his will, he had his lessons, still remained a source of irritation to him in his old age. The very style of his memoirs, otherwise so calm, becomes almost feverish at this point, and he describes with fury and satisfaction how he once seized some boys, who were tormenting him, and banged their heads together: 'Biting, scratching and kicking, they tried them all, but my thoughts and limbs were filled only with revenge.' He will strangle them, he says, yes, strangle them, if they molest him again. The children are separated. His father immediately discontinues the joint lessons.

For pages the old man is unable to calm down, and he tacks on elaborate observations about children of 'good breeding', about force that can only be met by force, about spite and malice against which an affectionate and sympathetic child has few weapons. He is also very sensitive to teasing and gibes. It seems that on one occasion he boasts a little about 'the high position held by his grandfather Textor, the *Schultheiss*'. At this one of the boys mentions the other grandfather, the inn-keeper – Goethe does not write 'tailor' which, if he were being teased like this, would have been the most likely epithet. He defends himself bravely: unfortunately, he never knew him, but the good thing about his home town is that all its citizens can consider themselves equal. Another boy murmurs something else, and when Goethe tells him to speak up the answer is that nothing definite is known about this grandfather at all. His parents, says the boy, claim that Goethe's father was really the son of a nobleman, and that the proprietor of the *Weidenhof* had proved willing to assume the role of nominal father. Strange indeed is the sequel. Far from feeling hurt by this, the boy is fascinated by the idea: 'It was not in the least displeasing to me to be the grandson of a nobleman, even if it had not come about in the most lawful way.' He even recalls having seen, in his grandmother's room, the miniature of a good-looking gentleman wearing uniform and medals; the miniature had disappeared after the rebuilding. And so, he says, one exercises 'at an early age that modern talent for poetry which, through an adventurous combination of the important circumstances of human life, is able to gain the sympathy of the whole civilized world'.

There were no childhood friends, only a few boys who allowed themselves to be ordered about. 'I like giving orders', he wrote when he was only fourteen, in the earliest letter we have of his. After his clashes with the 'coarse world', his only intimate relationship was with his sister, Cornelia, a year younger than himself. Until his student days in Leipzig she remained his sole confidante, his companion, his love. This had an effect on him for the rest of his life; it also had an effect on his love affairs. The image of his sister was always present, both consciously – he used the word often, especially in connection with Frau von Stein – and unconsciously. But in his writings this sister, whom he loved so dearly, finds no more place than does his mother. Cornelia was not exactly ugly, but she was far from pretty, with her long nose, high forehead and bad complexion, with its tendency to come out in spots, especially 'before any celebration or dance', which is easy enough to explain psychologically. She should have been an abbess, said Goethe later. More specifically he says, 'the idea of giving herself to a man was repugnant to her', and Eckermann notes this still more explicitly. She was at the same time tender and frigid, a not uncommon and very unfortunate combination. Under pressure and in conformity with the usage of her day, which had little understanding or patience for such dispositions, she attempted to stage a half-hearted love affair with a young Englishman; but nothing came of it. Under pressure, and against her will, she then married a very energetic, efficient man named Schlosser, a friend of the family. For her wedding she wore grey taffeta. Shivering and with a hot-water bottle in her lap, although it was mid-summer, she drove off to her married life. Sinking ever deeper into melancholy, she gave birth to a child, whose hearty screaming horrified her; at the birth of her second child, when she was twenty-six, she died. 'Her eyes were not the most beautiful I ever saw,' wrote the poet, 'but they were the deepest, the ones that seemed to conceal the most, and when they expressed liking or love, they had a lustre beyond compare.' Her love for her brother was the only love vouchsafed her; in it she found protection from the sensuality she hated so much. And, a fact that is not unimportant for Goethe's later love affairs, he too very often – though not always – cultivated similar 'abbesses', and it is striking how many of his loves were of the same type as Cornelia: a Charlotte von Stein, who had to submit to seven confinements in a reluctantly endured marriage; a Wilhelmine Herzlieb, who died, suffering from melancholia, after an equally unsuccessful attempt at marriage; an Ulrike von Lewetzow, who ended her life as a lonely old Sister of Charity. It is a strange list of sisters.

In their youth, however, things were by no means so dismal for the brother and sister; then it was all merely hinted at and in its infancy. They would run round happily, climbing up onto the city walls and looking down on the houses and gardens below. They explored the attics, where their father had carefully stacked his oak panels, which had to be well seasoned and rabbeted before being handed over to the painters; they were to last for ever and must not split. They ran on errands to the various craftsmen, to the colourful fair with its booths, gingerbread and toys. The Frankfurt toys competed with the famous Nuremberg toy industry in 'playthings' of every kind, and later, during the days of the French Revolution, Goethe's mother wrote furiously on one occasion of a toy guillotine which was on sale there: 'buy such an infamous instrument of murder – that I wouldn't do at any price – if I were in authority the makers would have been put in the pillory – and the machines themselves I would have had publicly burned by the hangman – What! Let the children play with such a horrible thing – put murder and shedding of blood into their hands as a pastime – no, no good can come of that.' It seems that the toy was wanted for her grandson, August, though whether by the silly mother or by the somewhat absent-minded father is not clear.

There were games with puppets, and the puppet theatre, a present from their grandmother to the children, achieved literary fame through *Wilhelm Meister*. The earliest version of the book begins with this glorious childhood memory, treated directly and in the most vivid and colourful way; in the finished novel the hero merely tells his sweetheart about it, somewhat verbosely and pedantically, and the lovely Marianne falls asleep over it. In the original version, however, the grandmother takes the threads firmly into her hands: 'Children must have comedies and puppets. It was the same when I was young; it cost me many a penny to see *Doctor Faust* and the Moorish Ballet. . . .' Goethe's *Faust* derives from the puppet theatre too, and it has retained not a few of its features.

This early version of the novel preserves more of the atmosphere of early youth than does the account written in his old age. In the former the boy, Wilhelm–Wolfgang, is not content with looking at the 'mystic veil' of the curtain. He is also conscious of the 'delight of observation and investigation', he wants to know how it is done, he wants to look behind the scenes. At the next performance he slips secretly into the room and lifts the curtain. Very aptly Goethe compares this behaviour with the first stirrings of puberty: 'Just as at certain times children become aware of the difference between the sexes, and strange and wonderful stirrings in their nature result from looking through the veils that hide the secrets, so it was with Wilhelm at this discovery; he was both quieter and less quiet than before, feeling that he had experienced something, and yet realizing that he did not know anything.'

This is all he ever says about these first stirrings of puberty; in later years he employs the term only to describe his own repeated 'puberties', which recur again and again far into his old age. Instead, and very characteristically, he transforms these early erotic impulses into a charming figure of romance to whom, in *Dichtung und Wahrheit*, he gives the ambitious name of Gretchen. We do not know who she was or what became of her. She seems to have been a waitress. The fourteen-year-old boy got to know her through a small group of young people whom he describes as 'fellows from the middle or, if you prefer, from the lower classes'; in any case they were older youths, with their schooldays behind them, who worked as solicitors' clerks or undertook commissions for merchants and jobbers. It is strange company for this young 'patrician', usually so reticent, and for his 'strict' father to allow, and the affair comes to a bad end.

Some of the youths try to use the boy's good connections for their own ends. In all innocence he introduces them to his grandfather, the *Schultheiss*. A little detective story unfolds, with the gang falsifying bills of exchange and records; it might have had serious consequences for Wolfgang had he not come from such a good family. Simultaneously there unfolds the little love affair with the waitress, who serves the gang their wine. They meet in the evenings at the tavern. Wolfgang has provided himself with a duplicate key to the Goethe house; this was the only offence to which he confessed. The father cannot have kept too strict an eye on him because there is talk of all sorts of parties, and of excursions by water to Höchst. Wolfgang acts as scribe for his companions, composing rhymed love letters, which he rattles off easily; one of these he slips into the waitress's hands. Here, too, a piece of trickery is intended; the youths' idea is to tease a rather timid swain by making him believe a girl is in love with him and wants to make his acquaintance. Goethe weaves their falsehoods together with great skill. But one day when he finds her alone in the tavern the Gretchen, whom he describes as endowed with 'incredible beauty', gives him a serious warning about acting in this way. 'What is a young man of good family, like yourself, doing letting himself be used as a tool like this?' she asks. This sounds like an authentic recollection, as does the 'No kissing!' when he draws near her. Less authentic sound the phrases added by the wisdom of old age, such as 'the stirrings of love in unspoilt youth always assume a spiritual form'. The affair was probably harmless enough. Easiest of all to accept is Goethe's account of his walk with his first 'sweetheart' during the coronation celebrations for Joseph II. Here the very thorough-going report on the processions of the ambassadors and the traditional customs of the people, done in his father's manner, is interrupted in the most delightful way. Wearing a light disguise, because after all it is better for the son of a good family to remain unrecognized, he strolls round with Gretchen. The town, normally so dark, is brilliantly lit. They go from one district to another. The ambassadors have vied with one another in the splendour and elegance of their illuminations. Ah! Esterhazy's is the finest: an illuminated gateway in colour, painted backgrounds, pyramids of lights, globes, festoons of lights hanging from one tree to the next. Bread and sausages are distributed to the people, wine is given out, there is laughing and talking. This strolling round in the sea of lights, gay, in high spirits, a little in love with the 'incredibly beautiful' waitress, to whom he has offered his arm, as befits a young cavalier – all this we can accept as true, as well as the farewell kiss on the forehead after enjoying a good supper and some wine with the gang.

Next day a representative of the authorities appears at the door, and only the action of a family friend, who intervenes on his behalf, saves the boy from very unpleasant enquiries. There is a threat of criminal investigations. The friend saves him from this. The forgers have been taken into custody, including those Wolfgang introduced to his grandfather. What becomes of them we do not know. Gretchen leaves Frankfurt, after clearing her name before the magistrates. Wolfgang discovers that she has looked on him as a mere child and claims to have saved him from further questionable pranks.

He seeks refuge from all these blows in illness, for the first, though not for the last, time. He storms when the enquiry threatens, he storms when he learns that Gretchen has not taken him seriously. He determines hence-forth to efface her image from his mind; he does not rest until he has 'divested her of every pleasing characteristic'. He claims also to have suf-fered severe convulsions and to have had difficulty in swallowing his food, which again is plausible. Finally he pulls himself together. He pulls himself together in his memoirs too, where he writes indignantly that he found it terrible to sacrifice his health for the sake of a girl, 'whom it pleased to regard me as an infant and to treat me as though I were in the nursery'. She is now well and truly forgotten, and for a long time to come. She comes to light again only during the composition of *Dichtung und Wahrheit*, where she is transformed into a figure of romance.

To this same period belongs the first direct documentary evidence of Goethe that we have, and it has a certain bearing on the Gretchen affair. Another group of young people emerges, of a somewhat finer and more virtuous type. Under the leadership of a Herr Buri, a young man of 17, they have formed a League of Virtue, called *Philandria*. Buri styles himself, slightly inaccurately, the Argon – for Archon – of this secret society. The members assume arcadian names, dabble a little in literature, adopt a very high code of morals, and observe a secret ritual somewhat reminiscent of freemasonry; later in fact, the Darmstadt lodge was formed from this society. Goethe applies for membership in the first letters of his that we possess. It is clear that a candidate was required to search his conscience and make some kind of confession. Goethe writes:

> One of my chief faults is that I am rather quick tempered. But you are familiar with choleric temperaments. On the other hand none is quicker to forget a slight than I am. Furthermore, I am very accustomed to giving orders, though when I have no authority I can refrain from doing so. But I am very willing to submit to leadership if it is conducted as your discernment leads one to expect. Right at the beginning of my letter you will find my third fault, namely that I write to you as though I had already known you for a hundred years.... One more thing occurs to me, it is that I am very impatient and do not like remaining in doubt. I beg you to reach your decision as quickly as possible.    (23.5.1764)

Even this rather demure petition is not enough. The Argon begins by collecting expert opinion on the candidate. The moral standing of the Philandrians must be beyond reproach. Meanwhile he writes a solemn letter to Goethe, protesting coquettishly against his encomiums, and requesting him to get in touch with Herr Alexis, the 'Monitor'. He is to make a report so that the Argon shall not be exposed to taking 'the cruel responsibility for the society'. All this in a very grave tone, complete with *Mein Herr*— half-childish nonsense, and a little grotesque.

But things get more serious. Alexis, the son of a Frankfurt lawyer, reports to Buri, the Argon, that he has rejected Goethe 'on account of his vices'; he makes a verbal statement as well. In the meantime Wolfgang has sent a second letter to the Argon, probably suspicious of what Alexis may have said: 'He should omit none of my faults, but nor should he conceal my good side. With all this, however, I beg you to examine me, for clever as Alexis may be, it is possible that something could escape him, and this you might find disagreeable. I am rather like a chameleon. Is Alexis to be blamed if he has not considered me from every point of view?' Innocently he writes yet again; he feels sure the interviewer has reported favourably to Buri and most obediently awaits 'the Society's verdict on me'. He is rejected. Buri has referred the matter to another member, Johann André, in Offenbach, the son of a silk manufacturer, later to become a musician and music publisher, warning him in advance that the said Goethe is 'prone to dissipation' and many other unpleasant faults. André's opinion is less harsh; he finds him simply too young 'to be a judge in matters of art'. They had a talk, over a cup of tea, about the Frankfurt theatre, and he found that he had a good flow of chatter rather than sound judgment; even in aesthetic matters the Philandrians seem to have set the highest standards. By his silence the Argon gives Goethe to understand that he is not wanted. Proudly he writes to Alexis: 'Herr Goethe maintains complete silence and I hope that he will not apply again.' He does not apply again.

Goethe's self-criticism, drafted in answer to a request, should not be taken too seriously as having a bearing on his early character. The good flow of chatter may well be true. The comparison with a chameleon, which always assumes the colours of its surroundings, is one he is to employ often. So far as his 'vices' are concerned, this word was used just as glibly in those days as the words virtue and love. Its use may have referred to the Gretchen affair. The likeliest conclusion is that his association with the gang of youths from the 'lower classes' was objectionable to the exclusive arcadians, especially as the affair had ended in a certain amount of notoriety.

More important is the fact that even this attempted contact with the outside world comes to grief and that, according to his memoirs, Goethe attaches himself more and more closely, almost passionately, to his sister. Opposition to his father is already acutely in evidence; 'incredible conclusion' and 'iron severity' are terms we meet with; we hear of 'strife' within the family, of his mother having to suffer too, and of a triad 'full of life and longing for enjoyment here and now'. Whether the father really curbed their enjoyment is hard to say. There were gay parties, excursions, boating trips with the usual pairing off, mock-marriages and banter, and we hear of a trip to the nearby Taunus mountains. By means of lessons in dancing, fencing and riding, the Councillor saw to it that his son acquired the necessary accomplishments. Later on Goethe rode a great deal, but of Herr Runckel's riding school he cherished only unpleasant memories. The very smell of the stables was offensive to him; Goethe always had a very sensitive nose, and he could not bear the smell of tobacco smoke, let alone the universal favourite snuff. Thoroughly characteristic is the fact that methodical riding instruction did not help him in the least. No doubt Herr Runckel taught the French school, then just coming into fashion, the somewhat stiffer school of Cavendish having been superseded by the newer method which still remains in vogue to-day. As Goethe peevishly remarks, 'they were for ever talking about the seat, and yet no one could say in what the seat consisted ...'. And the numerous petty fines if one let the crop fall or one's hat, if the curb chain did not hang properly, and so on, still irritated Goethe, even in retrospect. Later, as he says, he avoided the riding ring and he waxes indignant over the fact that such a pleasant art should have been taught in so discouraging a manner. Much pleasanter was Lisette, the riding master's pretty daughter, with whom he carried on a mild flirtation.

While the demand for a 'good seat' in riding seemed unnecessary to Goethe, there were no demands for final examinations of any kind in his tuition. One simply went to the university when one was old enough, provided one had first been to a 'Gymnasium' or had been privately educated; no certificate to this effect was required. The father had omitted nothing. The list of his son's subjects and languages is impressive, but how things stood in regard to his actual knowledge, in view of the irregularity of his lessons, is another matter. There is no need to play the schoolmaster, but it is not unimportant, for Goethe's life and work, to get some idea of his training. A mere catalogue tells us nothing; indeed it is misleading. Thus Goethe mentions mathematics, and speaks of geometry. This he immediately 'translated into practice' by making cardboard models and little boxes, and he recalls building pavilions, complete with pillars and steps; from time to time a friend of the family, with a bent for mathematics, helped him, and together they drew designs for architectural fantasies. This is not 'mathematics', but it is Goethe. Later in life he is to fight for many decades with his enemies, the mathematicians, when they accuse him, in his optical experiments, of knowing nothing about 'advanced arithmetic'.

In Latin, the main educational language of those days, he was sound; the Vulgate from his father's library still stood on his bookshelf in Weimar. Greek he read mostly with a parallel Latin translation. His French was adequate, though strangely enough it was less good than his sister's. He spoke it with a certain fluency, but with peculiarities of his own; even his year at Strasbourg, intended mainly for him to acquire the necessary elegance in this obligatory everyday language of polite society, brought no improvement. His early French plays, written, so he says, after listening eagerly to the actors in a visiting French company, have disappeared; he was 9 at the time. At Leipzig he wrote some French poetry, which is slightly better than his extremely amusing excursions into English verse. Italian, the father's special personal hobby-horse, was studied by him with the children, and with his wife as well, who, in the early days, shared their education. In history there were the great chronicles, and works with a semi-theological flavour, such as a multi-volume *History of the Popes* by the Scottish ex-Jesuit, Archibald Bower, which drove young Goethe to despair and produced in him a life-long aversion to all history; a 'hodge-podge of error and brute force' he calls it later. He speaks without warmth of the pastors' religious instruction, as he does in general of the cold, stiff Protestantism of his day; he never showed the slightest interest in dogma. On the other hand he was a passionate reader of the Bible, or of those parts of it which are picturesque and can be grasped in terms of characters, such as the world of the Patriarchs. Merian's huge illustrated Bible, dating from Frankfurt's great days of printing and engraving in the previous century, made an early impression on him, and continued to exercise an influence on him up to the very end, in *Faust*. For a while he studied Hebrew, but soon gave it up. English, still somewhat unusual, was taught by an itinerant language teacher who undertook to impart what was necessary in four months. So there grew up a small English speaking circle, which included a young Englishman, Lupton, the son of a cloth-merchant in Leeds, who was staying with a family in Frankfurt. Perhaps he may have been introduced through connections of Goethe's grandfather, the tailor, the one who was never mentioned. It was with him that Cornelia had her first, and only, rather wearisome love affair. For a time the young ladies called themselves 'Miss', instead of 'Demoiselle', and raved over Richardson.

Drawing was Goethe's greatest pleasure, and so it remained. In Italy, when he was nearly 40 and was preparing the first edition of his *Collected Works* for publication, he still dreamed of becoming 'really' a painter. Music was not entirely neglected: a little piano, some cello, both soon set aside. To sum up: a very comprehensive education, altogether unusual in its scope, embracing much, with much only touched on. The father may have been a pedant, but he indulged the boy's every wish, his every whim. The education of his son was the one fulfilled dream of his frustrated life. He could not foresee where it would lead.

Goethe's own judgment on himself, written when he was in Italy, is severer than that of any of his critics. In it he recapitulates his cardinal failings:

> One is, that I could never bring myself to learn the craft of what I wished or had to do ... either it was done by sheer force of mind, and succeeded or failed as luck and chance decreed; or, if I wished to do something well and with careful thought, I was apprehensive and could not complete it. The second, closely related, failing is that I never cared to devote as much time to a work or undertaking as it required. Since I enjoy the great good fortune of being able to think and combine a great deal in a short time, I find it boring and intolerable to work a thing out step by step.

At the time this was said primarily about drawing; but he had wider issues in mind as well.

With all its shortcomings it is difficult to conceive any education that would have been better suited to the unique gifts of this boy, and this human being, than precisely the universal and somewhat arbitrary one that he had, even though, from the standpoint of a strict educationist, it was almost slovenly. Luck and chance held sway. The constellation was favourable.

# 3

# *Gradus ad Parnassum*

We now reach the first steps to Parnassus. Even in poetry, Goethe does not follow an ordered *Gradus ad Parnassum*. He reads much, he sees much. During the period of occupation in the Seven Years War he hears French plays, catching the 'sound and tone' of the actors' voices in the same way as in the *Orbis pictus* of Comenius he had learned to listen to the twitterings of birds. He tells us that he once took a volume of Racine out of his father's library, memorized the lines, and recited them 'like a well-drilled parrot', without being able to understand them in their context. He makes friends with a rather precocious young boy in the company, whom he calls Derones, and studies French with him. Above all, armed with a free pass issued to his grandfather, the *Schultheiss*, he rummages round behind the scenes and in the dressing-rooms, 'where the behaviour was not always very decorous'; and he loses his heart a little to his young friend's sister, also a member of the company, though he complains of her behaving towards him 'like an aunt'. His father cannot have kept too strict an eye on these visits to the theatre, for they seem to have taken place almost every evening, over a period of two years, ending with late home-coming and a hasty supper.

A French play is concocted, which his young friend Derones proceeds to pull about and turn upside down. In *Dichtung und Wahrheit* Goethe gives us to understand that it was this episode which first awoke in him an aversion for the three unities of Aristotle and for the whole formalism of the French stage. He claims also to have read Corneille's essay on the subject, the controversies of the French classic authors among themselves and with their critics, the whole of Racine, and the whole of Molière. He was 9 years old.

Verse-making was practised at an early age in those days. Nearly every boy wrote verses, Latin ones at school, and so did parents; friends of the family wrote poems for weddings and christenings. Goethe's great uncle Loen described in verse the happenings on his estate, his mother used to write letters in verse. Wolfgang had to present himself to his grandparents at the New Year with carefully written greetings in verse – *Erhabner Grosspapa!* and *Erhabne Grossmama!* – which have been preserved; they offer no evidence of early poetic gifts, but are simply exercises in good hand-

35

writing. Some years later an ambitious verse picture of 'Christ's Descent to Hell', written 'by request', was actually published in a short-lived Frankfurt periodical. Most probably the poem was requested, or inspired, by Fräulein von Klettenberg, a distant relative of the Textors and one of the few patricians among the Goethes' acquaintances. She was not one of the haughty ladies of the aristocracy who strutted round, unapproachable, wearing an order on their breast. Truly pious, in contrast to most Sisters of Charity, she belonged to a pietist circle which had some affinities with the *Herrnhut* sect, noted for their calm serenity and meekness of spirit, and for a certain quiet pride. Goethe has left a memorial to her, in the *Bekenntnisse einer schönen Seele*, in *Wilhelm Meister*.

Of the spirit of pietism, however, there is no trace in this early poem, which is one of the longest he ever wrote. It is full of sound and noise and, in some of its short, concentrated climaxes, not without a certain strength and vigour; but it is a work in the already outmoded baroque style, a commissioned work.

The great German baroque poets were ignored by this ardent reader of his father's library; they were, indeed, scarcely represented there. The Councillor went with the times, with his own times not with those of his son. The list of his German authors, mostly names now forgotten, begins with Baron Canitz, who, although belonging to the seventeenth century, was regarded as one of the new writers and as an enemy of baroque 'bombast'. Goethe claims to have read all these masters on his father's shelves assiduously and even to have partially memorized them. Canitz may have appealed to the father because of his life story, printed as an introduction to the beautifully produced volume. In this he could relive once again the Grand Tour of France and Italy. Here were fine manners, distinguished company, lofty tone. Poetry was written in his spare time, as befitted a courtier. 'Poetry,' writes his biographer, 'which cost others so much trouble, time and thought, was for him a pastime; as a rule most of his poems were dashed off while just pacing up and down, sitting by the fireside over a pipe, or indeed while ensconced on that seat on which other people are least in the habit of working with their heads.' The formidable Swiss poet, Albrecht von Haller, also found a place on the father's shelves with his epic, *Die Alpen*, one of the first works to kindle enthusiasm for his native country and the 'unspoilt customs' of its people, though Haller could discern the latter only in the heroes of old. It is a poem of great spaciousness and of commanding, if somewhat unwieldy, force. Haller too was a spare-time poet. He was the foremost physiologist of the century and, with his research into the muscular system and the respiratory organs, a great innovator. Thinker, botanist, organizer of the Göttingen Academy and its periodicals, he was one of the universal minds of the Leibnitz era, an era he worthily continued.

All the poets whose works were in the father's library were great men of the world or great scholars; they all wrote poetry only 'on the side', and often with profuse apologies. Klopstock was the one writer who aspired to be poet and poet alone; the only one, indeed, in the whole of the eighteenth century fitted to play such a role, with his priestly and prophetic bearing; in later years he became cold and unapproachable. A friend of the family smuggled the first cantos of Klopstock's *Messias* into the Goethe household, for the Councillor rejected the verse as unsuitable. With an enthusiasm for new strains which kindled like wildfire, though it was soon to die out, the work was taken up and recited, and the master revered as a 'saint'. Klopstock communities were formed, small and often fanatical circles, the earliest literary cliques in Germany, which possessed no cultural centre and could offer only the example of religious sects. The Klopstock cult showed all the signs of such sectarianism: the private knowledge of an infallible truth, soon to be followed by the affectation of mystery as well, the passing from hand to hand of the founder's works under seal of secrecy, the pride of being counted among the initiates and the contempt for those who were not.

Goethe describes the eruption of this poem into the Goethe household in a grotesque scene: the father is having his shave, the two children are acting Satan and Adramalech from *Messias*, in subdued voices at first, while the barber is lathering the Councillor, then louder and with growing passion as Adramalech seizes Satan with his iron talons: Help me!... Vile, infamous criminal. ... Oh, I am being ground to dust!' The barber, startled, drops his mug; the Councillor, covered in soapy water, rises and once more bans the hexameters from the *Hirschgraben*.

'Thus do children and grown-ups transform the sublime into a game, into a farce,' adds Goethe, the *Geheimrat*. Klopstock was a sublime poet, even if later Goethe was prepared to admit his greatness only with many reservations.

Undoubtedly most of the verse the boy wrote at this time was done for fun; nothing of it has remained. As a pendant to his many-sided language study he wrote a novel in various languages, centred round six or seven brothers and sisters, scattered all over the world: there was French, Latin, English spoken by the merchant apprentice in Hamburg, while the youngest, 'a sort of cheeky little Benjamin', spoke the Frankfurt Yiddish of the nearby ghetto, with its narrow streets and red and black house signs, from which the Rothschilds and Schwarzschilds derived their names. There was also an epic on Joseph, there were verses written for friends in family albums, and there were letters in rhyme, which last he continued to write for a long time after this – it has all disappeared, mostly burned by Goethe himself, who liked *autos-da-fé*.

It is extremely rare for poetic genius to manifest itself convincingly at a very early age, and our knowledge of the early efforts of other great poets affords us no ground for regretting that Goethe has spared us his own. It is quite different with mathematics, or with music, which is akin to it; here the prodigy is almost the rule. Young Goethe himself saw just such a prodigy, and retained an indelible impression of him. On August 18, 1763, when Goethe was 14, the 7-year-old Mozart and his slightly older sister gave the first of four performances in Frankfurt. 'I still remember the little fellow quite clearly with his powdered hair and his sword', he wrote in his old age. It was a recital of clever tricks rather than a concert; the tickets cost a *thaler*. According to the advertisement puff the boy was to 'play the most difficult pieces by the greatest masters', perform on the clavecin, violin and organ, with the keyboard covered as well, determine from a distance, with his absolute pitch, the notes sounded by bells, glasses and clocks, and exhibit an aptitude scarcely ever before seen or heard. We know how much the boy earned on these journeys all over Europe, and how dearly he had to pay for this premature exploitation.

When, in conversation with Eckermann, the talk once turned to the subject of early death, Goethe, who had survived everyone, said:

> Do you know how I see it? Man must be brought to nought again! Every exceptional person has a certain mission he is called upon to fulfil. When he has accomplished it, he is no longer needed on earth in this form, and providence makes use of him again for something else. But since here below everything happens in a natural way, the demons trip him up over and over again until finally he succumbs. Thus it was with Napoleon and many others. Mozart died in his thirty-sixth year, Raphael at about the same age, and Byron was only a little older. But all had fulfilled their missions consummately, and it was probably time for them to go, so that something should remain for other people to do in the long-destined duration of this world's existence.

# 4

# *Leipzig Student*

It is as a small 'muffled up' boy, to use his own expression, that, in October 1765, the 16-year-old Goethe travels to Leipzig, to study law at his father's wish. He travels in the company of a publisher named Fleischer, a symbolic companion indeed, at a bad time of year and on 'wicked roads of which everyone had a tale to tell'. The German roads are frightful and long remain so, in the Duchy of Weimar as well. In Auerstädt, on the future battlefield of Napoleon's great victory over the Prussians, the carriage sticks. Night is falling and no one comes to their aid, so the delicate youth has to put his shoulder to the wheel, and in doing so strains the ligaments in his chest, a condition that is to trouble him for many years to come. In an abandoned quarry, countless lights are twinkling in the night; these 'by no means remained stationary but jumped to and fro. ... Whether this was a pandemonium of will-o-the-wisps or a company of luminant beings, I shall not attempt to decide', wrote the poet long afterwards, when he had already written *Faust*.

At any rate the boy does not sit still in the jolting chaise. Thought of what is in store keeps him restless and tense. Frankfurt he has left behind him like a sloughed snake's skin, to use one of his favourite similes for the repeated transformations in his life. He has left it without regret, indeed in decided ill-humour. The unhappy ending to the 'Gretchen affair', and the departure of the waitress, have 'wrenched out the heart' of this tender young plant, to use his own expression – an example of the gross exaggeration he used to employ in referring to his love affairs. He tells us, too, that the weaknesses in the government of his home town had become only too clear to him, through his association with the disillusioned cranks of his father's circle who spoke only of injustice, folly and madness; one of them, closing the lid of his blind left eye, used to say in a nasal twang, 'I detect faults even in God'. His father, having led an unsuccessful and lonely life, has become irritable. The boy is also uneasy about his education, which has resulted in a vague encyclopaedism. He has, as he says, quickly 'run through' a number of giant tomes from his father's library; but all this has only confused him, as he himself admits. As a solid *pièce de résistance* he carries with him in his trunk a little volume by Hoppe, a concise and useful

39

guide to law. His father has already taken him through the book thoroughly to his great dismay. But there is to be no more drudgery. To the end of his student days this little book by Hoppe remains his standby; he soon discovers that more is not necessary.

Very self-assured, very precocious, very critical towards everybody – the latter largely as a result of his association with elderly fogeys and cynics – the boy enters the new world that is opening before his eyes. 'Muffled up' he is literally, in the heavy, old-fashioned clothes which, for reasons of economy, his father had made for him by his servant; they were made of the very best English cloth, bought in quantity to last for many years. In his pocket he carries a particularly liberal letter of credit from his father. He is considered *trés riche* by his fellow students, who are often miserably hard up. He has good accommodation, has excellent meals at one of the best eating-houses in the town, and has the necessary letters of introduction to 'good families'. He goes frequently to the theatre, takes part in comedies, indulges in the prescribed flirtations and writes eagerly about them. He makes two little collections of his verse, soon forgets them and remembers them again only when he is an old man. During the first few weeks, or months, he attends the lectures fairly regularly, but quickly gives them up on discovering that his Hoppe is all he needs. It is not law but life that Goethe studies in Leipzig.

He takes up his residence in the spacious house *Zur Feuerkugel*, which, as its name implies, displayed a hand-grenade as its sign. It was an imposing building, of almost the same frontage as his grandfather's *Weidenhof*, and Goethe's accommodation consisted of no mere lodgings, but of 'a few nice rooms'. The poorer students were lodged in the barn-like students' homes, the *Bursen*, 'miserable holes, where no one else would want to live', half-timbered structures with external wooden galleries, connected by ladder-like staircases. In other respects Leipzig was considered a very modern city. To the young Goethe the houses seemed to tower into the air; the buildings, often built round small courtyards, where during the celebrated fair the merchants had their booths, seemed enormous, 'like miniature towns'. Coming from Gothic Frankfurt, with its narrow winding streets, he saw for the first time in his life a broad open city landscape, with modern suburbs beyond the walls, with avenues and promenades, much used for promenading, with street lighting and drainage, with famous book shops and publishing houses, and with a world-famous University, founded as an offshoot from that at Prague. Professors and students were divided into 'nations': the Meissen nation for Saxons and Thuringians; the Polish for those from Lausitz, Bohemia and Moravia; the Saxon for North Germans; and Bavarian-Franconian for South Germans, to whom Goethe belonged.

Leipzig liked to call itself 'Little Paris'. Its inhabitants cultivated elegant manners and elegant, up-to-date, clothes. It was here that the 'muffled up' boy first came into contact with the new world. People laughed at his old-fashioned Frankish clothes, with their heavy lead inlays sewn on to the coat-tails and cuffs; this was how country bumpkins were dressed on the stage, they pointed out to him. They took exception to his way of speaking, which was rough and provincial like that of his mother, and also contained solemn turns of phrase derived from Luther's Bible. The Saxons considered their German by far the finest and the most correct, a claim for which they were able to plead a certain historical and philological justification; but people in the rest of Germany sneered at the sound of their dialect in just the same way as the Saxons laughed at that of the young Goethe. He took all this very much to heart. He immediately sold his home-tailored clothes and bought new ones, *à la mode*. One of his young friends from Frankfurt wrote home about him:

> He is still the same haughty dreamer he was when I arrived. If you were to see him, you would either choke with rage or split your sides with laughter. I just cannot understand how anyone can change so quickly. All his manners and his whole behaviour now are poles apart from the way he used to be. Along with his haughtiness he is also a fop, and his clothes, fine as they are, are all in such crazy *gout* that they single him out among the whole university....

He delivers his letters of introduction. The wife of one of the professors, Madame Böhme, a kind woman in poor health, takes a motherly interest in the boy, still a little insecure, and for this he always remains grateful to her. She initiates him into the refined Leipzig *pli*, teaches him to sit still, at least for a time, and to listen. She gives him advice about his clothes, and earnestly recommends him to cultivate card playing as an indispensable introduction to polite society. With her husband, the Professor of Constitutional Law, he is less successful. Böhme is a strict jurist; the newly enrolled student speaks in all innocence of his literary inclinations. Stuff and nonsense, declares the professor, what would your parents say? There is a colleague of mine, Gellert, who writes verses and comedies; do you want to listen to him? Come to my lectures, stick to jurisprudence!

In the more abandoned students' activities Goethe takes no part; he takes just as little in the lectures on jurisprudence. At first, so he claims, he attended assiduously, but soon gave it up when it became too boring. The lectures in the faculty of law were held in an impressive auditorium: a large hall, its ceiling supported in the centre by two baroque spiral columns; on the walls hung portraits of kings and princes, and huge genealogical trees, a most important object lesson for students of Constitutional Law for whom, in the age of the Wars of Succession, it was a prime necessity to remember the family tree of every possible candidate for a throne. The students had to sit strictly according to rank, only the high nobility being allowed to sit on the raised podium round the sides of the hall, while below them, in the pit, sat the commoners, who had no benches and had to hire

41

chairs. But even ordinary law students considered themselves far superior to those in the other faculties, particularly to the theological students who for the most part were quite penniless. Two decades previously Lessing had been among these last, though he soon began moving from one faculty to the next, registering with the medical and then escaping very quickly into the faculty of literature. When Goethe began his studies Lessing was the rising star of the younger generation; his *Minna von Barnhelm* was to be seen on every stage, even at Leipzig, in spite of its pro-Prussian glorification of Frederick the Great and his Major Tellheim. In a town still suffering grievously from the ravages of the Seven Years War, saddled with an indemnity of ten million *thalers* for having been subjected to an unprovoked peace-time invasion and inflicted with six years of Prussian occupation, this amounted almost to high treason, coming from a native Saxon. In spite of this the play was performed. It was the age of tolerance. The nobility of the characters aroused people's enthusiasm; 'even the groom is noble minded ... the main characters vie with one another in a medley of fine sentiments ...', we read in a contemporary review. Not least in importance, the actors themselves eagerly accepted the challenge of their exceptionally well-written parts; and, finally, the heroine, Minna, was a Saxon. Her 'charm and amiability' overcame the 'worthiness, dignity and stubbornness of the Prussians', writes Goethe in retrospect, greeting, as it were, 'a happy marriage' that transcended the limitations of individual states, a coming national consciousness hitherto completely lacking. It was the chief literary experience of his Leipzig years, even though it was only later that he was able to see its more far-reaching importance.

He had as yet no idea that he might take part in this. His plans for his life and studies were quite vague. To set his father's mind at rest he wrote to Frankfurt: 'At the moment I do nothing but study Latin. And another thing. You cannot imagine what a wonderful thing it is to be a professor. I was quite enraptured when I saw some of these people in their glory, *nil istis splendidius, gravius, ac honoratius*'; he has a downright longing one day to walk about in similar professional splendour. The father may well have believed that one day his son would be a professor of law, though it is doubtful if this would have satisfied his ambition. He wanted to see him as a Frankfurt assessor, as a syndic, to see him one day as burgomaster or perhaps as *Schultheiss*, positions that had been beyond his own reach.

The Leipzig professors did in fact enjoy some splendour. They formed the patriciate of the town which, being a purely commercial centre, possessed no other ruling class and which, moreover, was overshadowed socially by the Court and Palace of nearby Dresden. For the most part they were well-to-do; in addition there were rich endowments. Goethe bore this in mind; when he was a minister, and Chancellor of the University of Jena, he saw to it that, so far as possible, his staff were financially independent or at least that they married wives with means. At Leipzig the Rector, who was elected yearly, had the right for life to the title *Hochedelgeborne Magnifizenz*, and he exercised this right. The *Magnifizenz* strode round in purple.

Of the gentlemen in their solemn wigs Goethe wrote less respectfully to his sister than he did to his father. There was Gottsched, a great man, even physically a giant. As a student he had barely escaped the press gang of Friedrich Wilhelm I, King of Prussia, who wanted to press him into service with his 'giant Grenadiers'. In the world of literature, too, Gottsched was – or rather had been – a giant, the first German literary pope, whose 'anathema' was feared all over the country. Of his true merits, which were very con-siderable, Goethe even later showed no grasp. At this period he was simply a butt for impertinent remarks in letters: 'Gottsched has married again. A virgin lieutenant-colonel. But you know about it. She is 19 and he is 65. She is four feet tall and he is seven. She is thin as a rake and he is fat as a pudding.' And still more merciless: 'The whole of Leipzig despises him; no one wants his society.'

Gellert was the other great name in *belles-lettres* at the university. His light was still shining, far afield and with a gentle glow; he was the only German poet of the day who already had something of an international reputation. His fables have been translated into French, Italian, Russian, Polish, Hebrew and Latin; his religious odes have been set to music by Philipp Emanuel Bach, Haydn and Beethoven. His well constructed, wise, pleasant verses survived as quotations for over a hundred years. A sentence from one of his comedies, *'die vernünftige Liebe ist kein grösseres ver-brechen als die vernünftige Freundschaft'* (rational love is no greater crime than rational friendship) encircled the globe for another hundred years as the operetta line *'Ist denn Liebe ein Verbrechen?'* (Must we then count love a crime?).

This sentence would have appealed to the young Goethe far more strongly than the lachrymose wisdom delivered by the ailing man in his lectures. These had an enormous vogue. Two attendants had the task of see-ing that the Professor was not mobbed. In his seminary, which Goethe attended, the poet warned all his students against dabbling in poetry. He insisted on prose, corrected in red ink, and asked with lowered head, 'Do you go regularly to church? Have you attended Holy Communion?' Goethe's gratitude was confined to the single fact that Gellert corrected his handwriting as assiduously as he did his style; and it is a fact that at this point his letters from Leipzig show a marked improvement in orderliness and clarity. 'A good hand leads to a good style' taught the poet of the fables.

Goethe, already very didactic, at once passes Gellert's words of wisdom on to his sister. She is still his closest confidante; she is also the only subject willing to submit meekly to his pedagogy. She is submerged by a flood of instructions: read this, read that, don't read the other. 'Write your letters on a folded sheet of paper and I will write my answer and my criticism on the other half. But do not get father to help you. That is no good. I want to see how you write. I shall start now. Bear in mind: write just as you would speak, and you will write a good letter.' This, too, is taken from Gellert, who had written an excellent little guide to letter writing.

For his own practice, as well as Cornelia's, they write in three languages, in French and highly comic English as well as in German.* There are quotations and lines of verse mixed with the prose; sometimes he jumbles up the languages in the middle of a sentence with an 'ich bin astonish'd, Schwester', or he will end one of his attempts at English verse with, 'Are they not beautiful, sister? Ho, yes, senza dubbio.' He boasts and hints at all kinds of flirtations, as befits a young cavalier: 'I wonder what you would say, sisterlet, if you could see me in my present room? You would cry out astonished: so tidy, so tidy, brother. There – open your eyes and look – here stands my bed. There my books. Yonder a table, all set out as your dressing-table will never be ... with lovely young w..., but what has that got to do with you? Away. Away. Away. Enough of girls.'

Enough it is not, and never will be. He flirts and casts his eyes in every direction; at least a dozen names flit through the pages of his letters. Some of the girls he has never seen, the mere name is enough and he is deeply in love straight away. Lisette – the riding master's daughter – what is she doing? Let her enjoy the letters too, he writes to his sister, 'it is for her as well that I am working'. 'Write me of my little one.' On his return home he wants to teach in a school for the fair sex; that would be better than law. 'Only the most beautiful ones, naturally, like my dear Lisette Runckel.' Often 'when I am in the right mood I go and call on pretty women and pretty girls. Sh! Not a word about this to Father.' Then he adds, 'Why should Father not know about it? It is a very good school for a young man.' A young gentleman, he means.

'Tirelireli! Chantons, chantons l'inconstance! Tirelireli!' he writes, probably quoting some operetta or other. The Singspiel was the great fashion, and Johann Adam Hiller, with his Der Teufel ist los and Liebe auf dem Lande, its chief exponent. The great Johann Sebastian Bach was already completely forgotten in Leipzig; his widow had died in miserable circumstances, supported by charity. It was in Hiller's weekly paper, Nachrichten

---

* Here is one of his poems (dedicated to his friend Behrisch) in its original 'English' version:

> What pleasure, God! of like a flame to born,
> A virteous fire, that ne'er to vice can turn.
> What volupty! when trembling in my arms,
> The bosom of my maid my bosom warmeth!
> Perpetual kisses of her lips o'erflow,
> In holy embrace mighty virtue show.
> When I then, rapt, in never felt extase,
> My maid! I say, and she, my dearest! says.
> When then, my heart, of love and virtue hot,
> Cries: come ye angels! Come! See and envy me not.

*und Anmerkungen die Musik betreffend*, that Goethe's first verses appeared
– if they are really his – along with the news of Telemann's death and the
appointment as his successor in Hamburg of Herr Philipp Emanuel Bach,
the 'great master of the clavecin', still so well remembered in Leipzig.

> Leipzig. On December 20 and 22 the Oratorio, *Sant 'Elena al Calvario*, by
> the excellent Kapellmeister of the Opera, Herr Hasse, was again performed
> at one of our concerts, and was heard by a numerous assembly with the same
> emotion and pleasure. Demoiselle Schröter, who sang the part of Helena, has
> had the following little poem composed in her honour by an unknown author;
> it has appeared in print:

> > *Unwiderstehlich muss die Schöne uns entzücken,*
> > *Die frommer Andacht Reize schmücken;*
> > *Wenn jemand diesen Satz durch Zweifeln noch entehrt,*
> > *So hat er dich niemals als HELENA gehört.*

> > (Endowed with all the charms of piety, devotion,
> > The fair one holds us in her thrall;
> > Whoever, doubting, calls this judgment mere emotion,
> > Has never seen thy HELENA at all.)

At all events the devil is loose in young Goethe; there is love-making
in the country and love-making in the town, in all its aspects but mostly in the
form of exercises on paper. His sister has merely to mention her new friend
Kätchen Fabricius, and Goethe writes back: 'My poetic imagination pictures Mlle Fabricius as even more beautiful and clever than she is, and in
future she is to be my Annette, my muse.' He had several Annettes, several
Kätchen. His student friend Behrisch tells him of his sister, Auguste, in
Dresden, and immediately we have: 'Hell! we have completely forgotten
the girl for four whole weeks' – four weeks was a long time for Goethe in
those days – 'and if ever a girl deserved to be remembered it is she. Make
a note of that. And when she comes here I shall fall in love with her, that is
already decided, if I have not done so already, and we shall have a romance
together, vice versa, and that will be nice. Good night, I am drunk as a
Lord.' This talk of getting drunk to a fellow student we can also probably
put down to poetic imagination.

For a long time the Dresden Annette, or Auguste, gives him no rest. His
friend Behrisch seems not to have taken the affair quite seriously. Goethe
protests: 'Auguste, what a funny thing it would be if I did not fall in love
with her. But to hell with it, I do love her very much.' She has written him a
note, the girls always enter into this game too: 'Forgive this liberty on the
part of someone unknown to you...' He places it, 'as one of my best *biglietti*,
in my treasure chest. If my girl were to know of it! – the Leipzig Annette
this time – *Ventresaint gris*, she would blow my head off!'

He has already started 'a treasure chest', a little Goethe archive, to house
all the *biglietti*. He never set eyes on the Dresden Auguste, just as later he

never set eyes on Auguste Stolberg, to whom he wrote his most ardent love
letters and confessions. All these little notes and poems of his Leipzig days,
all these Lisettchen, Lottchen, Kätchen, Fritzgen and the rest, only represent
love, or flirtation, in general, *toutes les filles ensemble*, and this distribution
of his love between a number of people is to recur frequently in the course of
his life. His student friend Horn, from Frankfurt, writes home that Goethe is
now slyly 'courting a certain Fräulein' – which in the terminology of the day
means a young lady of title – and gets teased about it in society; 'perhaps
she really thinks he loves her; but the good Fräulein is deceiving herself'.
In fact, Horn continues, he is in love with another girl, who is charming
but 'socially beneath him. ... Picture to yourself a girl well built though not
very tall; a round, pleasant, though not exceptionally pretty face; a frank,
tender, engaging air; great candour, no coquettishness; a very nice judgment, without having had the finest education.' She is virtuous, 'and innocent
as is his love, he none the less has misgivings over it. We quarrel about it
very often....'

To this day there are disputes over Kätchen Schönkopf's virtue. She has
the distinction of a little plaque on the Goethe Memorial in Leipzig, inspired by the charming portrait of her which Goethe included in *Dichtung
und Warheit*. Most probably this is a composite portrait of several people, a
quite legitimate poetic procedure: all the Leipzig love affairs culminating in
one Kätchen. There also exist contemporary letters of his about her, ardent
epistles anticipating the style of Werther; well composed, written in a
frenzy of passion, jealousy and anguish. The whole gamut of a lover's
feelings is unfolded and with incomparably more fervour than in the little
over-polished, pastoral, rococo poems he was writing at this time. The
*Sturm und Drang* is in full flood, long before it comes into existence as a
literary epoch.

'One more night like this, Behrisch, and I shall go to hell for all my sins!'
He describes the agonies of jealousy; he is told that Kätchen has gone to the
theatre, just when he wants to visit her: 'Ha! At the Comedy! At the very
moment when she knows her lover is ill! Oh God!' He rushes there, he sees
a gallant next her in the box, he sees it clearly from the gallery, short-sighted
though he is, he has taken opera glasses, he grinds his teeth, he is in the grip
of fever, 'in that moment I thought I should die ... I think I would have
taken poison at her hand ...'. He takes a new quill, the first one is worn down
by the grinding out of the sentences. 'Do you know an unhappier man than I,
with all my ability, with all my prospects, with all my advantages?... Ah! All
pleasure is within ourselves! We are our own devils, we cast ourselves out of
our paradise....' Heaven and hell, it goes on for pages, and finally, when
Kätchen's innocence is established, the 'memory of sufferings overcome is
pleasure'. It is all very innocent. The aftermath of the frenzy and the
paroxysm of fever is not lacking in humour: 'I tore my bed apart, devoured
a morsel of handkerchief and slept till eight o'clock on the ruins of the palace

of my bed.' He also mentions the characteristic nightmare that persists through his life: 'the beckoning at the door, the kisses in passing, and then suddenly – she had put me in a sack!' This terrifying idea of being put in a sack by a woman is to pursue him constantly; it is one of the basic themes of his life, the fear of being bound hand and foot by a woman in wedlock, the dark marriage sack. Here he can still make fun of it: 'A regular conjuring trick. One can imagine luring guinea-pigs inside, but a man like myself, it is unheard of.' Then the young man of letters adds: 'I philosophized in the sack and wailed out a dozen allegories in the style of *Schäckespear* when he breaks into rhyme.'

He has not yet read much of Shakespeare, only a few lines and extracts from an anthology, *Shakespeare's Beauties*, by the strange Reverend William Dodd of London, the 'maccaroni parson' and forger of bonds, who was horribly executed in spite of numerous petitions on his behalf, including one from Dr Johnson. His was a motley life and his book is a motley collection of Shakespeare's purple passages; it became the source of early German enthusiasm for Shakespeare.

The elegant quoting of the great name, then quite new, adds tone to the letter's composition. One allegory, a dozen allegories – what does it matter, it sounds fine. On another occasion he writes: 'My letter forms a nice basis for a little piece of writing.' He has read it through again and is alarmed at himself.

But it is love's labours lost to try to unravel these entanglements or to try to establish a clear-cut conclusion to the Kätchen affair. In *Dichtung und Wahrheit* Goethe himself calls her Ännchen: 'My previous attraction to Gretchen I had now transferred to an Ännchen...'; the verb alone is significant enough. As a 'little saint ... for a while' she finds a place in his heart, and here the adjective is telling.

Like Gretchen she leads us into the atmosphere of the inn. The Schönkopfs did not keep an inn, as such, but they took paying guests, kept a luncheon table and served wines. Goethe etched a very charming label for the father's wine bottles. Kätchen was already a somewhat mature young woman by the standards of the day and, in the miniature which was painted on Goethe's instructions, with the first suspicion of a double chin. She was not coquettish like the other Leipzig girls, about whom Goethe complained; the coquettishness and jealous tantrums were all on his side. She waited on the guests, and Goethe's tantrums were occasioned by the lodgers. 'What is your opinion, Behrisch, might it not be mere pride on her part, this love for me? It amuses her to see a proud man like myself chained to her footstool. So long as he lies there quietly she pays no attention to him; but let him try to break away and she becomes aware of him, her attention revives her love....' Breaking away, escaping, this is his main concern.

But it is not all jealous tantrums. Kätchen also has to be educated, because her parents have not paid much attention to this; she seems to have borne it patiently. Others were less docile: 'In the meantime I act as tutor to my girls here', he writes to his sister, 'make all kinds of experiments, some successful, some not. Mdlle Breitkopf I have given up almost completely, she has read too much and then there is no hope ... *plus que les mœurs se raffinent, plus que les hommes se dépravent.*' Kätchen has not read too much. She knits cuffs for him, looks after him a little, and sometimes lets him sit at her writing desk while she goes to the theatre with her future husband: 'You have always got some nonsense or other in your head, either in verse or prose, put it on paper at your leisure!' As a touching little symbol she leaves two apples, which he contentedly munches. She is already engaged, and soon after Goethe's departure from Leipzig she marries.

From the modest tavern of the Schönkopfs we cross the road to the distinguished publishing house *zum silbernen Bären*, and to this day the silver bear remains the signet of the music publishing firm of Breitkopf. The daughter, Demoiselle Konstanze, was too much of a blue-stocking for Goethe, as we have seen, but he formed a friendship with the family, and particularly with her brothers. The eldest, Bernhard, was something of a composer. He set Goethe's poems to music, and in 1770 a little oblong volume of these, *Neue Lieder mit Melodien*, was published, printed in the movable type press founded, or rather revived, by the father. It was the first collection of Goethe's poetry and for long remained the only one. Goethe's name was not mentioned.

In the attic rooms of the Breitkopf house lived an engraver named Stock, who, with his two daughters who later made names for themselves as artists, did vignettes for the firm. Here the young law student would sit and devote himself eagerly to a new passion. Since his Frankfurt days drawing had been his secret love; now he learned engraving, woodcutting and etching. With Stock's assistance he made an ex-libris for Kätchen Schönkopf, as well as two larger landscapes from paintings in Leipzig private collections. The private galleries of the well-to-do Leipzig merchants, which for their day were far from insignificant, remained very much more clearly in Goethe's memory than did the lecture-rooms.

More serious were his drawing lessons with the painter Adam Oeser, who ran an academy of painting and drawing high up in the attics of the Pleissenburg, the old castle. Even the climb up the winding staircase and the long passage past the granary, before he reached the studio and living-rooms, gave Goethe a sense of 'wonder and anticipation'; it was all incredibly modest, almost to the point of poverty. Modest to the point of poverty, too, were the master's method of teaching and his aesthetic maxims; *Edle Einfalt und stille Grösse* – the noble simplicity and serene greatness of Greek art – was his ideal. In this formula of a little man pupils like Winckelmann and Goethe found their inspiration. War was declared on baroque and rococo, with its ornamentation and rocaille work. To our eyes Oeser's own vignettes, such as his designs for Wieland's works, are purest rococo and feeble at that. The great influence of the man is almost incomprehensible to us. A confectioner had been his first teacher, and Court confectioners still went to the celebrated Director of the Academy for tuition; silversmiths, and designers for the Saxon textile industry, sought his advice; he was even consulted by planners of huge buildings, though he had never produced an architectural drawing in his life. His large paintings and ceiling designs are devoid of coherence, his drawings are vague; but his teachings determined the taste of an era. Formulae are often mightier than achievements, and, at a moment that was ripe for it, Oeser gave the tone, as with a tuning fork, for decades to come; even the poets and philosophers tuned in to him. 'The taste I have for what is beautiful, my knowledge, judgment, do I not owe them all to you?' is how Goethe rapturously expressed his thanks on his return to Frankfurt. It had been a turning point in his life and in his approach to art.

There exists, however, the phenomenon of what might be called creative error. Goethe's mighty creative power, feeding as it did on quite different sources, raised Oeser's teaching to incomparably higher levels. Yet much of it persisted throughout his life, and the pretty little vignettes we find in his work, or what is merely pleasant and attractive, involving no further effort, can be traced back to this teaching.

Antiquity! The ancients! 'The statues and larger sculptures of the ancients remain the foundation and summit of all artistic understanding!' This was drilled into him up there in the attic of the Pleissenburg. But what did he know of ancient art? One or two plaster casts stood in the studio; but for the rest the pupils had to rely on engravings and little reproductions of gems and cameos. These were considered as indisputable and authentic evidence of the genius of antiquity. They were easily accessible. They were collected in large albums and caskets. A dealer named Lippert sold them all over the world. The caskets opened like a book and one could imagine oneself spirited, as though by magic, back to Greece itself. The Greeks – this meant simply Lippert's little casts from so-called originals, mostly faked during the Renaissance and later. Lessing wore one of these cameos as a talisman on his finger, a gift from Lippert.

It was from such colourless outlines, or from empty and often grotesque engravings, that the ancients were re-created. When he wrote the most influential aesthetic work of the day, Lessing had never seen even a plaster cast of 'Laokoon'. We may smile, and yet our incomparably greater and sounder knowledge of what remains of antiquity has never again produced such enthusiasm, has never again exerted so profound an influence, as did these magic caskets with their faked gems. It was the compulsion to use the imagination, to reflect and think beyond the object seen, to improvise like a musician on a given theme, that evoked the creative energies. Granted that Lippert's pastes were forgeries – he himself was a thoroughly honest and touchingly industrious self-taught man – that the plaster casts and engravings were significant only of mistakes, that the whole faded, marble-white picture of antiquity seems to us to be completely false, nevertheless something emerged from it: a great movement, classicism, classic art and poetry. We have our own aesthetic slogans, our own forgeries and mistakes, and they can be just as fruitful.

Oeser, the weak, friendly man with the mild features, was in Goethe's eyes the great teacher; and so he remained till long past his Leipzig days. The pleasure Goethe derived from these small objects, these gems and cameos, was a constant source of delight to him, and when, in later years, a collection of these, like the one belonging to Princess Galitzin, came into his hands he cherished the 'priceless treasures' as though they had been jewels, and handled them over and over again. In Oeser's drawings, too, with their emphasis 'on the important, the allegorical, on what stimulates associated ideas', there was always something 'to ponder, the idea of completeness being created, although the works themselves were unable to achieve this by their art and technique alone'.

The tuition was only mediocre, as Goethe had to admit. Oeser had not much to impart. His figures were undefined, almost featureless, they had hands like fins, their movements were vague. But there was a magnetism about the man himself. A native of Austria, he knew how to get on with people. Wieland praised the 'beauty of his spirit and the goodness of his heart'. In the painter's family circle, with his two daughters, on his country estate, the young boy experienced the warmth of home life; to the daughter Friederike, the first of this name in his list of friends, he continued to write the most affectionate letters in verse and prose long after his Leipzig sweethearts had been forgotten. It was to her, and not to any of his Annettes, that he dedicated his *Leipziger Liederbuch*.

Oeser lived to a great age, to the same age as Goethe. In Weimar he was always a welcome guest, and paid many visits. There, too, he was appreciated as a stimulating influence; 'I have had a little bit of a hand in it', he used to say in Leipzig when some foreigner marvelled at the art treasures and objects of interest. 'All day long', Goethe wrote once from Weimar, 'the old man would potter about, finding some suggestion to make, something to change, to draw, to point out, to discuss, to teach, so that not a minute was wasted. The Duchess Anna Amalia was very pleased when he was there.' On one occasion she was very far from pleased, when the old man got one of her chambermaids pregnant; he had to stay away for a time, but was soon invited back again. In Goethe's description of this, one cannot help noticing his own predilection for the middle and lower walks of life.

In this way, with drawing, looking at paintings – he also made a short visit to Dresden and its famous gallery – flirtations, writing letters, and in a somewhat cynical contemplation of mankind, three years passed, a fairly generous allowance for a student. Apart from old Oeser and his daughter,

Goethe made no real friends at this time. He did not keep up with any of his fellow-students. The most important of them, Behrisch, soon disappeared out of his life; and when, in his old age, Goethe's letters to another friend of those days, Horn, were returned to him from the latter's estate, he destroyed them as an 'unpleasant memory of my youth', a reminder of a period in which he could not see a single redeeming feature.

Behrisch, older than Goethe, already tutor to some nobleman's illegitimate son, was his mentor, the confidant of his ardent epistles, as well as his abettor in all kinds of mischief with girls, 'who were better than they were reputed to be', as Goethe guardedly remarks. He strikes us as like a first sketch for Goethe's later friend Merck: slightly odd, with his partiality for grey clothes in every conceivable shade, slightly Mephistophelian in his advice on how to handle women, mischievous and melancholy, a good fellow and a jester. Behrisch was later dismissed from his post for neglecting his pupil, found a position as a very minor official at the indulgent Court of Dessau, and died there completely forgotten. At his request copies of the three odes which Goethe wrote for him in Leipzig, as well as Goethe's *Leipziger Liederbuch*, were placed in his coffin.

The mischief which cost Behrisch his post was partly a student's prank and partly of a rather less harmless nature. A small clique had been formed, to which Goethe also belonged. They composed somewhat insolent satirical verses about one of the university teachers, Clodius by name, who had replaced Gellert in the chair of poetry. A small, dumpy man with fidgety movements is Goethe's description of him, but in the town he had a high reputation as the official poet on all appropriate occasions. Morally he was above reproach, and on the walls of his study, as object lessons for the students, hung engravings extolling love of the fatherland, virtue and good manners.

Goethe had modestly submitted to him a poem he had been commissioned to write for the wedding of one of his Frankfurt relations, and Clodius had struck out with red ink what he considered the excessive mythological allusions. For six months Goethe had not dared to sit again on the tripod and dream. Now he took his revenge! Clodius himself could not manage without the use of the prescribed gods of mythology. So Goethe ridiculed him in a 'Paean' which he wrote in honour of the pastrycook, Händel, in whose restaurant, the *Kuchengarten*, the clique held their meetings; the Leipzig students on the whole did not indulge in the wild drinking and duelling of their colleagues at Giessen, Jena or Halle. The gay restaurant garden was like a fair, with its little green arbours; people smoked, though Goethe did not, drank coffee and consumed Samuel Händel's famous pastries. The clique had a club room, where they scribbled verses on the walls. In his 'Paean' Goethe underlined all the mythological words, 'Olympus', 'Cothurnus', and so on, in parody of Clodius. His friend Horn added some lines, and copies circulated; the matter in all its gravity was even reported to the government in Dresden. The father of Behrisch's pupil heard of the affair, and decided to look rather more carefully into this tutor of his.

At this point the girls 'who were better than they were reputed to be' come into the picture. In his letters to the 'skinny devil', Behrisch, Goethe names two of them:

> Yes, Behrisch, I have entertained my Jetty for half an hour quietly, without any witnesses, a good fortune I sometimes enjoy now though I never could before. This hand that is now holding the paper to write to you, this lucky hand, held her to my breast. Oh Behrisch, there is poison in these kisses! Why must they be so sweet? And it is you I have to thank for this, bless you! Your advice, your scheming. What an hour! What are a thousand of those shrivelled up, deadly glum evenings to this?

And, further on, the second one:

> I have been at Fritzgen's, who now lives in complete seclusion. So modest, so virtuous!... No bare throat any more, no longer without corsets, it was really laughable. On Sundays she is sometimes at home alone. A fortnight's preparation, and a Sunday like this should expel chastity from the castle, even though ten engineers had spent ten half years fortifying it ... if I could only do it with impunity....

He is afraid of the 'nails and cord' that Kätchen has ready should she hear of it. Otherwise, 'I should assume the devil's role and undo all the good work.' The elucidation comes at the end:

> Do you know me in this vein, Behrisch? It is that of a conquering young cavalier. And it and I together! It is funny. But without taking an oath on it, I'll guarantee to sed – how the devil shall I put it. Enough, Monsieur, this is all you can expect from the most tractable and diligent of your pupils.

It is not the vein of a conquering young cavalier. It is amusing to see him falter at the momentous word 'seduce'; there is no need to try to explain it. Goethe is very far from being the passionate young legendary hero he would so like to be taken for. In life he is cautious, it is on paper that he is bold; and this is true not only of these Leipzig days. It is for this reason alone that these otherwise quite insignificant Jettys and Fritzgen are worthy of notice.

Leipzig was far from being merely a town of professors' wives and decent burghers' homes, like that of the Schönkopfs. It was a celebrated fair town. For the diversion of visitors, and not only for visitors, the requisite numbers of 'nymphs' had to be maintained. It earned the name 'Gallant Leipzig', and there is a quite extensive literature on the subject. *Gallant Leipzig*, 'described according to its morals', was one of these books; it was by a theological student who was forbidden the pulpit as a result, and became a worthy professor of medicine. *Leipzig in delirium* was the most daring.

To what extent Goethe was involved in this we do not know. The ordinary student's life did not interest him in the least. He describes it only as a detached observer. He did not smoke, he seldom danced, he drank in moderation; he did not fight, though he carried a sword. Over-sensitive, he very quickly withdrew even from the social life, which soon became too much for him. His moods, as he admitted himself, must have been 'offensive' even to his friends. What he enjoyed most was being in some genial family circle, with children, or old maids who mothered him, such as he found at the Oesers and the Breitkopfs. More often still, being always in flight, he escaped into himself, into his

> chaotic, headstrong nature ... which became more and more pronounced the more dissatisfied I was with my surroundings, since I was under the impression that they were not satisfied with me. With the most arbitrary caprice I took offence at what I should have counted to my advantage, and thereby alienated many people with whom, hitherto, I had been on reasonably good terms ...

Finally comes the flight into illness, as the best way out. Sick-bed stories of bygone days are always extremely obscure. Goethe's malady in Leipzig has found the most varied explanations, from mere hysteria to syphilis. Its causes, as given by himself, are strange indeed. He mentions the ligaments he strained on the journey out, when he had to push the carriage, and a fall from a horse when out riding, and these are plausible enough. He accuses the 'heavy Merseburg beer', which was by no means so heavy, of having clouded his brain; the coffee – and Leipzig was not exactly famous for strong coffee – paralysed his bowels, even though drunk with plenty of milk. Further harm was done, he claims, by taking cold baths and sleeping on a hard bed, 'with only a light covering, so that all the usual perspiration was suppressed', which makes little sense to our way of thinking. In the end, his whole organism was 'goaded' to such an extent that the 'individual systems comprising it were finally forced to break out in conspiracy and revolt, in order to save the whole'. There is talk of a haemorrhage and then of an abscess on his neck. When the crisis is over, he feels free and relaxed, more cheerful than for a long time.

All his friends go to see him, even those he has offended through his ill-humour; suddenly he feels himself surrounded by friendship and care. He reads the Roman classics, debates the Bible with a student of theology, and finally travels home to Frankfurt. He had set out as a 'muffled-up boy', slight and delicate; he returns home, muffled up in his heavy overcoat, pale, with distended eyes, 'looking like someone who has been shipwrecked'.

# 5

# The Wayward Shepherd

The student of law did not have much to show his father as a result of his three years' study, and the latter cannot possibly have found any cause for rejoicing either in the appearance of the boy or in the bags full of drawings and manuscripts, with Hoppe's little law digest relegated to the bottom. There were scenes, but there was also a tacit agreement that, to begin with, there should be a rest and an interval. The sister, whom Goethe had rather neglected during his last year at Leipzig, now became his intimate companion again. She complained of her father's harshness, and opposed it with a hardness of her own. The whole of her pent-up love was poured out on her brother. She tried to cheer him up. They invented a private language between themselves, which no one else could understand, and boldly used it in front of their parents. It was a chrysalis state, a cocoon phase.

The boy had not been completely inactive in Leipzig. What he tells us in *Dichtung und Wahrheit*, however, about his cultural experiences and surveys of past literary history – much of it out of handbooks – is unconvincing. He certainly read a great deal during those years, most of it quickly, as was his habit. He went frequently to the theatre, in spite of Professor Boehme's admonition. He took part in comedies with the Breitkopf family and their neighbours, the Obermanns; this also gave him the opportunity to flirt with some of the girls in the cast. Lessing's *Minna von Barnhelm* was one of the plays they did, along with more fugitive pieces. The great name of Winckelmann was brought to his notice by Oeser, and remained permanently in his memory. But what of the great literary events of the time that took place in those years? Lessing's *Laokoon*, for instance. It is mentioned, certainly, and with due respect; it will also have been discussed at Oeser's, though not too favourably. Goethe's own comments have a later ring about them. Lessing paid a passing visit to Leipzig in Goethe's time, but Goethe avoided meeting him. The reason he gives in his memoirs, that he did not want to thrust himself forward, sounds a little strange – quite clearly he did not like the man and hid his dislike under the cloak of the respect due to a writer whose merits could no longer be denied. Lessing's mind was too caustic for his taste, too penetrating, too critical; he was also too quarrelsome, though this was equally true of Goethe. Only the little booklet on how the ancients portrayed death, *Wie die Alten den Tod gebildet*, really moved him. Goethe was enchanted by the 'beauty of the idea that the ancients regarded death as the brother of sleep.... Here at last it was possible truly to celebrate the triumph of the beautiful, and to relegate all that is ugly, since it cannot be banished from the world, to the lower sphere of ridicule'. Lessing concludes by calling on artists to replace the 'hideous crucifixion' with the ancient, serene and more cheerful image of death, and this, both at this time and later, was after Goethe's own heart.

Otherwise what Goethe writes in his memoirs is literary history; he himself remarks that enough has already been published on the subject. Satire is what appealed to him most, and as an old man he still recalled with pleasure a 'splendid epistle' by Rost in which the odious Gottsched had been pilloried as 'the devil', and 'clever people too sometimes enjoy seeing the devil let loose on the stage'. Everything else he recalls as insipid and shallow; the aesthetic controversy was confusing, the sum total worthless, 'a desperate state of affairs for anyone who felt within himself the urge to create.'

He did feel this urge. He wrote – whole volumes had they survived: volumes of letters, most of which we have, volumes of plays, of poetry, English and French verse, an Italian opera, a Biblical drama, *Belsazar*, of which some scraps have survived, and translations from Corneille. He also wrote some 'suites', small satirical pieces based on students' life, and we may feel a twinge of regret that he burned these. There was a tradition for this type of literature in Leipzig, dating from the beginning of the century when a dissolute student named Christian Reuter, in arrears with his rent, had taken revenge on his landlady and her daughters; he ridiculed them mercilessly, the woman as a glutton, and the daughters as wantons desperately seeking some nobleman as lover or husband. But Goethe had a partiality for funeral pyres which lasted for many years, until the establishment of the great Goethe chancellery in Weimar, where every smallest note was carefully filed.

There still exist from these Leipzig days, however, some small collections of verse, and two plays or playlets: the pastoral play *Die Laune des Verliebten* (*The Wayward Shepherd*) and *Die Mitschuldigen* (*The Accomplices*), not a pastoral at all, but a rather biting play of cunning intrigue, which he finished in Frankfurt, giving it a Frankfurt background. In the pastoral play his Leipzig jealousies are transformed into a graceful minuet for two couples: ribbons flutter, flowers are strewn, garlands are distributed, the characters suffer a little, tease each other a little, and it all ends with a kiss of reconciliation. There is something of Goethe in all the characters, in the girls too; indeed, the strongly marked feminine side of his nature led him always to portray women with more sympathy and charity than men. Above all the whole thing is a diversion, like a pretty tune played on a musical box; when someone stamps their foot, we hear a charming little bell ring.

The poems too, for the most part, are arcadian idylls, peopled by Ziblis, Lyda, Daphnis, Amin or Emiren. With very few exceptions Goethe soon forgot these verses, and the only copy he possessed he gave away. The little volume with young Breitkopf's music had a very small circulation; a few of the pieces were reprinted in almanachs. This 'young Goethe' was almost unknown to his contemporaries, and was only rediscovered after his death.

Nothing he wrote in Leipzig was originally intended for publication. Goethe always maintained a special attitude in regard to his lyric writings. He considered it unseemly to ask a fee for poetry, although in other respects he was far from shy in his dealings with publishers. A poem was something for his friends, for a prescribed circle of people with whom he felt in close touch.

In Leipzig he is still hesitant and vacillating. He writes to his sister in Frankfurt about the little collection of poems he has been forming, but he does not send them; he is afraid 'you will copy them out'. In August 1767 he writes of *douze pièces qui seroit écrites en pleine magnificence*', a typical example of his French; 'So far there have been twelve male and two female readers, and now my public is at an end. I have no liking for noise.' Seldom has a great writer started with such hesitancy. At the slightest criticism, even at that of the silly Professor Clodius, he loses heart immediately. His friend Behrisch, not only a droll but a penetrating critic as well, warns him: do not rush into print! He offers to make a fair copy of the little volume; he does so, with a raven's quill. The result is a small calligraphic masterpiece, with vignettes and tail-pieces copied from some contemporary book. This *Buch Annette* only came to light again at the end of the last century, when it was published.

The poems are charming enough, provided one does not expect too much, the rhymes flow easily, sometimes they are interspersed with simple prose. Much in them is very, indeed almost uncannily, well done for a boy of 18; at the same time they are very childlike. One of the poems depicts a wedding night; this is not licentiousness on the young Goethe's part but simply treatment of a favourite theme of the day, when it was the custom, among the family circle, for some small nephew of the bride and bridegroom to recite a marriage poem not so very different from Goethe's, in which the bridegroom is admonished:

> *Zum Zittern wird nun ihre Strenge*
> *Und deine Kühnheit wird zur Pflicht ...*

(Her scruples will receive a shaking, it is your duty to be bold ... )

A Poet had to 'serve', even though he had written a *Götz* or a *Werther*, and let us not forget that the great monarch, seated on his German Olympus, served all his life and served most deferentially. The 'occasional poem', which he regarded as the only legitimate one, was not always an occasion to express his innermost feelings. What is known as the 'anacreontic dallying'

of his Leipzig verses continues to recur from time to time; his development
cannot be explained solely in terms of strictly defined, constantly advancing,
stages. Sometimes he dallies on quite unsuitable occasions, as when, in the
midst of the 1814 War of Liberation, the *Amor* of his rococo years reappears, fluttering round the sickbed of a wounded warrior and the pretty
girl who tends him:

> *Der kleine Flügelbube hupft,*
> *Die Wirtin rastet nie,*
> *Sogar das Hemdchen wird zerzupft,*
> *Das nenn ich doch Scharpie!*

(The little cherub skips around, the hostess never rests, she even tears her vest
to shreds, what finer lint could be!)

Even the octogenarian can still write a graceful dedication, accompanied
by a little vignette of an eagle soaring with its lyre:

> *Sollen immer unsre Lieder*
> *Nach dem höchsten Aether dringen?*
> *Bringe lieber sie hernieder,*
> *Dass wir Lieb und Liebchen singen.*

(Must we always in our Lieder seek to reach the loftiest heights? Rather let
our singing humbly tell of love and love's delights.)

This strikes the same note as his Leipzig verses; in these there are no eagles'
wings, but the song is of love and loved ones, and the verses are written to
order 'at my maidens' command'. The plural predominates, there are
several Annettes. He wants to have them round him: 'Maidens, sit here by
my side, where no one will disturb us.' Wisdom beyond his age is revealed
to him, how to catch the coy ones, how to escape the marriage bond, the
'dark sack' of his nightmare; in her dreams the girl has seen him lead her
to the altar, he has stolen some kisses, and the bliss is over, 'the warmest
kisses pass like dreams, and every joy is like a kiss'. A little sadness is becoming. A dragon-fly flutters round the spring, its colour changing like a
chameleon; it whirrs and finally settles:

> I have her now! I have her now!
> And looking closely at her hue
> I see a sad and sombre blue –
> Thus too with thee, dismemberer of thy joys!

A charming face swathed in a moonlit silvery haze – a first attempt at
striking verbal imagery; a lock of hair is stolen, a 'living part of her given
to me, after slight demur, by my dearest…'. And then, lying in the flowing

waters of a brook, washed by the passing ripples, the memory of his sweet-heart returns:

> *Es küsst sich so süsse der Busen der Zweiten,*
> *Als kaum sich der Busen der Ersten geküsst!*

(So sweet is the kiss of the second one's breast, the breast of the first scarce so sweetly did kiss!)

There is still a trace of coquettishness, but it is already a leitmotif of his life that is constantly to recur.

*Lieder* in a strict sense most of these poems are not. Many of them are more like verse narratives, and the young Breitkopf had his work cut out in setting them in dialogue form to his tripping major and minor thirds. And yet how lightly, how brightly these verses dance on their way! How well the melancholy musing, the 'sad and sombre blue', suits the 'conquering young cavalier!'. We should not try to dismember, to analyse, these joys.

# 6

# *Twilight*

The next nine months of Goethe's life in Frankfurt are bathed in a strange twilight. And, he tells us, he has returned home ill and in good spirits at the same time. Letting himself slide completely, he hands himself over to the care of his sister and his mother. He is angered by the impatience of his father, who wants to see the 'weakling' quickly back at the University again and has no time for hypochondriac complaints. Under these circumstances the boy finds his illness a welcome protection, and he exploits it to the full. Medical research has failed to establish a clear picture of the nature of the illness, and Goethe's own statements, which are the only ones we have to go on, are themselves far from clear. He always complained a great deal about his health, about his teeth, a lifelong source of trouble for which there was no remedy in those days, about coughing and indigestion, which later were responsible for some of his serious crises. On the other hand he lived to a great age, was constantly described as a 'radiant Apollo' and, latterly, as a 'magnificent old man', the prototype of a near-immortal. Without any doubt there was a serious hypochondriac strain in him, and the word *heiter*, serene and cheerful, of which he was so fond, was first and foremost, an appeal to the gods.

In Frankfurt, in 1768, he was no mere *malade imaginaire*. Surgical treatment was necessary for the abscess on his neck, the surgeon asking the enormous fee of ninety-six *florins*; Frankfurt doctors lived in style. No expense was too great for the father where his only son was concerned. Another doctor treated the boy for lung trouble, and collected an only slightly lesser fee. The most plausible explanation of the case is that it was a tuberculosis of the lung, affecting the lymphatic glands of the neck. The boy was also attacked by severe constipation, a terrible affliction, for which no relief could be found until a 'puzzling, sly-looking, strange-speaking and generally abstruse doctor', as Goethe calls him, employed some mysterious secret remedy. He was one of Fräulein von Klettenberg's pietist circle, among whom there was a great deal of experimenting in alchemy and universal panaceas for body and soul. The strong solution of Glauber's salt, for it was nothing more, was effective. The mortal fear was allayed. Goethe's mother found comfort in her Bible: 'They shall plant vineyards again on the hills of Samaria, they shall plant and sound their pipes.' We must remember that in those days a person could die a miserable death from complaints such as this.

There is also another possible explanation for Goethe's illness, which should not go unnoticed. The leading role in this is played by a certain 'Don Sassafras', a part Goethe had played on several occasions in amateur theatricals at Leipzig. Sassafras was a well-known anti-luetic of the day. In a letter to his young friend Breitkopf, written shortly after his return home, Goethe sounds this warning note:

> But Saxony! Saxony! That is strong stuff. One can be as healthy and strong as you like, but in that damned Leipzig you burn up like a bad torch. Well, Well, the poor little fox will gradually recover. I will only say one thing: beware of dissipation! It is the same with us men and our strength as it is with the girls and their honour, sell your virginity once to the devil and you have said good-by to it. You can try all the quack remedies you like, but it will not do any good.

Goethe's sound state of health throughout his long life seems to preclude the possibility of venereal disease, though that is the conclusion we should otherwise have had to accept, as in the cases of so many of the great names in literary and artistic history. Once later, in his *Römische Elegieen*, he returns to the same subject, this time in solemn hexameters: this 'new phantom spawned in poisonous slime', unknown to the more fortunate ancients, which pollutes every spring and turns to poison *Amor's* life-giving dew'. He hails Hermes, the messenger of Zeus, as the God of Healing, in other words Mercury, quick-silver, the traditional remedy for syphilis. It is to him that the threatened lover must offer his prayer for thanksgiving for the protection of his little garden.

But let us be content with his lung and his lymphatic glands, and leave it at that. A period in bed is prescribed, with doses of ptisan and extract of quinine, which restore young gentlemen's relaxed nerves to strength. 'No stimulants.' The doctor removes Boucher's pink nude from the wall; from this we can see how deeply Oeser's doctrines of 'noble simplicity and serene greatness' have penetrated. A Dutch painting is substituted: a decrepit old woman, with furrowed face and half broken teeth, is how he describes it in a letter to the gentle Friederike Oeser, his sister-confessor during these months. He is bored to death in his sick-room and is driven to writing quantities of verse. In spite of his enormous and varied activities, Goethe was often bored, it is a word that recurs constantly. With daring audacity, he even hailed boredom as the 'mother of the muses'.

The Frankfurt girls seem to him stiff now, after the bright and sprightly Saxons, over whose coquettishness he had sighed when in Leipzig. Half-heartedly he attempts a little flirtation with another of his sister's friends, Charitas Meixner; after all a young gentleman should not be without his 'lass'. Frankfurt strikes him as being behind the times, old-fashioned; he writes of a 'dearth of good taste'. Oeser's vague teaching still exercises an influence over him. He calls Oeser, Shakespeare and Wieland his great teachers, in that order; Shakespeare, by the way, in Wieland's newly published prose translation, which contains far more Wieland than Shakespeare. But Boucher's nude also hangs on Wieland's wall. Goethe has come to the realization that 'wide scholarship, profound and subtle wisdom, rapier-like wit and a thorough knowledge of classroom subjects are quite heterogeneous to good taste'. Charm and deep pathos are heterogeneous to one another too. Then he cries: 'Make me aware of what I have not felt, think what I have not thought, and I will praise you.' What is Beauty? he asks. It is one of the questions of the century, though for the most part its concern is not too profound. 'Twilight' is his answer; 'a child of truth and untruth. An intermediate thing. Within its realm there is a cross-roads, so ambiguous, so misleading that a Hercules among philosophers might well be led astray.' He has no hesitation in seeing himself as Hercules: 'imprisoned, alone, with compasses, paper, pen and ink, and a couple of books, as my only tools. And yet with these simple means I often advance so far in the discernment of truth, further than others, with all their encyclopaedic knowledge.'

The 'couple of books', not specifically named, is worth stressing, because of the tendency to regard Goethe as the indefatigable reader of whole libraries. This concept of him derives to some extent from notes to be found in his first diary, named *Ephemeriden*, which starts at this time; this contains a confused mass of names, titles of books – books recommended to him, books he ought to read, books he may want to read – folk-lore and medical prescriptions, together with quotations from the Bible and living authors.

But his life at this time is not just a twilit reverie. He writes to friends in Leipzig; in Frankfurt he feels as though he were 'in exile' – another of his lifelong metaphors. Kätchen, of course, is married; in his letter of good wishes to her he looks back with emotion on the recent past. He has previously sent her a little parcel, carefully thought out, with scissors, knife and leather soles for a pair of slippers, which he hopes 'will last her as long as He [her husband] does ... for you deal cruelly with all that falls, or is placed, within your power'. After a little further reflection he sends a scarf and a pink fan as well, and then, finally, come the closing lines: 'You are ever the same dear girl, and will be a dear wife too. And I, I shall remain Goethe. You know what that means. When I speak my name, I speak the whole of me.'

And so this chapter in Goethe's life ends, to be re-opened only when he reaches it again in *Dichtung und Wahrheit*.

Carefully, and with a clear grasp of his craft, he continues to prune and polish his Leipzig *Lieder*. New and more powerful images are introduced. His illness has relaxed him. In high spirits he greets the new year in a ballad, which he distributes as a leaflet to his friends. It contains 'maxims for all stations in life', including the 'poor married fools'; there are maxims for youth, for young couples, who are advised not to be too faithful, not to observe the marriage conventions too strictly, and for his proud friends: 'You who count yourselves misogynists, may the wine give added zest to your great spirit....'

The biggest test of his talents is the completion of *Die Mitschuldigen*, a comedy of manners; in this there is no longer any trace of Oeser's artistic principles, of vague ideals of beauty or of hollow sentiment. Instead, with sure stage sense and relying on established theatrical tradition, he writes a clever, almost artful play. In many respects it is closer to the stage than almost all he wrote later. The verse, alexandrine *à la mode*, fits. The dialogue rings true. The plot convinces to a degree rare with him. On the basis of this play Goethe could have developed into a popular and successful playwright. But then he would not have been Goethe, who went on to erect his own stage, on which to enact the problems of being.

This play is not concerned with the problems of being. Everything is robustly physical. It is a sort of comedy thriller for which 'The Accomplices' might be a more appropriate title. There is no question of any guilt, no one feels guilty, no one feels the slightest scruple in deceiving anyone else. It is this skating along on the brink of villainy that gives the play its charm. In later years Goethe was often reproached on this score, but he never dissociated himself from the little drama. In his defence he remarked that at an early age he had 'observed a variety of criminal activities within the whitewashed circumstances of bourgeois society', the strange 'labyrinths by which bourgeois society is undermined'. He lists the bankruptcies, divorces, seductions, murders, burglaries and poisonings in his own outwardly conventional Frankfurt. To give vent to the feelings caused by these impressions, he tells us, he sketched a whole series of plays, mostly with tragic endings. Of these only 'this gay creature of burlesque, with its dark family background' survived.

Such words are far too pretentious for so slight a piece. The whole thing is plain unadorned roguery. The setting is an inn, like his grandfather's *Weidenhof*, where, we may hope, affairs proceeded in a more orderly way, although there too, during the fair or coronation celebrations, there was some lusty merrymaking. An inquisitive, blustering, old inn-keeper, his daughter as the soubrette, her rascally husband, and Alcest, her lover, who is staying at the inn – these are the four characters around whom the plot revolves.

Following time-honoured practice a theft takes place on open stage, only the audience being in the know. The young wife slinks off into the guest's room, with her father on her track; each character suspects the other, each thinks the other capable of anything. Alcest thinks the young woman, who at first has refused his advances, may yield if she is allowed to keep the money stolen from him by her husband. Finally Alcest returns his 'sweetheart' to her rogue of a husband, generously forgives the theft, and marches off. The thief has the last word in his address to the lover: 'Lust for the body or lust for gold, it is one and the same thing; if you do not deserve to be hanged, then neither do I...'; and addressing the audience: 'In short, do not take it all too literally, I stole the gentleman's money and he stole my wife.' The play must be brought to an end without further ado; the four actors advance to the footlights and take their bow. It has all been a game, in the style of the old-fashioned comedy, of which, as the dexterity of his writing shows, Goethe had made a careful study in Leipzig. This is really the only moral to be drawn from the little work, which points no moral of its own.

During this twilight period, side by side with this bright and shameless piece of roguery, an entirely different world exists in Goethe's life, the world of pietism, of the pious sect from Herrnhut, of mysticism and alchemy, with, at its centre, a fine, gentle, pure and nun-like woman. Even in his early days, the polarity of Goethe's nature can astonish us with the strength of its contrasts. At the very moment that he is striding the stage with the sure and certain steps of this impudent play, he betakes himself modestly and quietly to the devout Fräulein von Klettenberg. Here he finds a world very different from that of the inn, with its passages and mysteriously rattling doors. Here he finds quietness, a *'schöne Seele'*, as he later commemorates her in *Wilhelm Meister*, peace, and a certain serene determination which, for a time, proves beneficial to the somewhat unsteady young man.

The position of the pietists in the severely orthodox Lutheran city of Frankfurt was no easy one. The clergy resolutely opposed them. They had to meet in private, almost in secret. The aristocratic Fräulein von Klettenberg provided a welcome protection for them. But, in contrast to many of the other pietist communities, which were often composed of the poor and oppressed, this Frankfurt group was an affair of better class people. For a time, Goethe's mother also sympathized with these 'quiet ones'.

After very modest beginnings, pietism was already a power in Germany, and its importance for the cultural life of the country is not easy to overestimate. With its emphasis on feeling and sentiment it was a protest against the age of enlightenment; with its rejection of dogmatism, it was a protest against orthodoxy; with its disdain of class distinction, it was a protest against the excessively rigid social order of the day, when, even on entering a church, it was made quite clear where the upper and lower classes had to sit. In short, the pietists were Protestants in a very real sense. To the authorities, they were a subversive element, not least because, with their small groups and cells, their empire extended throughout the length and breadth of the country, thus breaking down the countless frontiers of state and petty state.

Even Goethe's mother had her private oracle, in the form of the *Golden*

*Treasure Chest*, by the pietist Carl Heinrich von Bogatzky; and she liked to turn to it. In the verses of this otherwise very weak poet are sounded some of the main themes of pietism: 'What am I on this earth, what is my state and calling? I am a beggar full of woes, a pilgrim in my fatherland.' Here too we find the blood of the lamb, the repentance and contrition, which were practised methodically to the point of a regularly conducted 'battle of repentance', the semi-erotic play between spiritual bridegroom and bride, and the cult worship of the wounds of the crucified Christ, which bordered on the abstruse: 'Let my table be set here in the hollow of Thy wounds, let Thy flesh, O Lord, be the food of my Soul', sang Bogatzky. All his life Goethe retained an abhorrence of this blood cult. The very image of the crucifixion was a thing he disliked intensely, and later he wrote blasphemous verses containing the line 'before Thy cross of woe, Thou blood-bespattered Christ', though admittedly he only showed these to very close friends. We may safely assume, however, that this aversion of his goes back to the imagery of the pietists.

The sect had other idiosyncrasies, which went deeper. Their probing of their consciences led them to acute self-observation; the best and most powerful autobiographical confessions of the time stem from this circle. In their 'realism' they usually go very much further than the professional writers. Nothing is overlooked. The earliest intimations of sensuality, even if caused by reading the Bible, are noted. In the confessions of a *Schöne Seele* – Fräulein von Klettenberg – which Goethe incorporated in *Wilhelm Meister*, the pilgrim girl tells quite innocently how her parents did their utmost to protect her from anything in the least seductive, 'nevertheless I knew more about the natural history of the human race than I would admit, and most of it I had learned from the Bible. Doubtful passages I compared with phrases and things that came to my attention, and in my thirst for knowledge I arrived successfully at the truth.' Still more uninhibited is her account of her first cooking lessons: 'To cut up a chicken or a sucking-pig was for me an occasion. I took the intestines to my father, and he talked about them as though I were a young student....'

Emotionalism was not everything with the pietists; they really did want to probe to the heart of things. Fräulein von Klettenberg was no prude or bigoted devotee, but a sensible woman, who had had her own experiences in life.

And it was experience, knowledge of life in all its aspects, that Goethe sought in these years, even when it came to him merely through the talk of others. He tells us that in his Leipzig days he remembers once sitting next to an old officer who told him things that were not to be found in books. In general people were very reticent, or else lived in a world of sentimental phrases borrowed from books, from Richardson's *Grandison*, for example, which was then the rage in Frankfurt. The pietists, on the other hand, opened their hearts freely the moment anyone was accepted into their circle.

It was a narrow circle, in which Goethe was only a guest, and from which he soon escaped to go his own way. Here again we can observe the duality in his nature: solitariness and the deep need for sociability. All his life he alternated between these two extremes. He was constantly searching for a group of people to whom he could attach himself, and his search took the most varied forms. Only when he was old and very famous did he find what he had been looking for, in the small Goethe communities that started to come into existence. Even then his demon made him very careful to avoid too close personal contact.

In the creation of a network of communities that disregarded territorial boundaries, pietism fulfilled a mission and paved the way for what Goethe regarded as his domain. But in place of religion he put his own creed: 'He who possesses science and art has religion as well – he who does not possess these two, let him have religion.' A genuine religious experience, let alone a conversion, this Klettenberg episode was not, but it was an experience of lasting importance.

Before long, personal contact with this circle inevitably led to disappointments. With Fräulein von Klettenberg, however, there was no fault to find, even in retrospect. Her conversation remained indelibly in his memory because of her 'charm, which amounted to genius', her cheerful confidence, and her humour, which would bring a rather heated discussion to an end with a kindly, 'You silly boy!' – Never well, she remained serene and confident even in death, which occurred shortly after this. Of her passing, Goethe's mother wrote to friends: ' "Good night, Rätin, I am dying.... Love one another", was her last loving injunction.' – The other members of the circle meant little to Goethe: the pompous doctor with his patent remedies, some gentlemen of the aristocracy, tedious ladies who analysed their feelings in great detail; a priggish group. Goethe also attended a synod of the Herrnhut communities in Marienborn, and claimed that they 'almost' converted him.

At this meeting he saw another side of the movement, the 'workings of piety', the 'craftsmanship', as he calls it, the methodical discipline. Despite their opposition to dogma, there was a strictly prescribed road to salvation, involving the obligatory 'battle of repentance' and 'break-through', that had to be recorded exactly according to the day and the hour. There was also constant talk of original sin which, even as a boy, Goethe was unwilling to accept, just as later he rejected Kant's ideas on the absolute evil inherent in mankind. And the people he saw at the synod were very different from the more refined, and socially more distinguished, members of the Frankfurt group. The Herrnhut communities, such as that at nearby Neuwied on the Rhine, were known, and hated, far and wide for their tireless industry and success as craftsmen. They lived in buildings run on strict monastic lines, with strict segregation of the sexes; these met only at the communal lovefeasts, on the model of the agape of the early Christians, where tea was served in the place of worship. They built up their own 'industry', with astonishingly high prices for their products. They sang their own hymns and they had their own pride.

Unconverted, Goethe returned to Frankfurt. But the pietist circle was still to provide him with one further encounter, and its consequences were more far-reaching. The pietists cultivated the early mystics such as Tauler, regarded as a forerunner of Luther, together with the cabbalists and alchemists, including mystic medicine. They sought a universal panacea for the body in the same way as they sought a universal method for the salvation of the soul. In 'feeling the pulse' spiritually, it was also necessary to keep the body under close observation. Everything unconventional and unusual was eagerly read. On questions of faith, Arnold's *History of the Church and its Heretics* was their great authority, and it acquired a decisive importance for Goethe too. In it those who had deviated from the official dogmas were recalled, vindicated and eulogized, their sufferings and steadfastness dramatically portrayed. Goethe never forgot it, and when, later, during his work on the *Farbenlehre*, he was accused of having founded his own sect in the realm of natural science, the figures in Arnold's *History* kept coming to his mind as comparisons. He proudly describes himself as a 'heretic' whom the orthodox would like to send to the stake.

The twilight continues to gather, following the broad daylight of Leipzig. With Fräulein von Klettenberg he reads Paracelsus, not yet the great name he has since become after long neglect, but nevertheless in print, and revered in this small group as one of the secret ancestors of unorthodox knowledge concerning the cohesion of the universe.

Still in poor health and given to morbid brooding, Goethe's thought is much occupied by medical questions. As though frightened by his precocious nature he copies down from the aphorisms of the great Dutch physician, Boerhave, the dictum that intellectual precocity may be a symptom of approaching rickets. He also writes out obscure prescriptions. He thumbs through the cabbalistic writings – it can scarcely have amounted to much more. These works consist, for the most part, of endless series of vast tomes, written in difficult, obscure language, much of it shrouded in mystery, with sentences in the form of cryptograms, pictorial riddles, symbols and emblems, one of the favourite conventions of the baroque. All these works rely as much on pictorial representation as on the written word, and the illustrations probably made a stronger appeal to Goethe than the text. Suns shine forth, surrounded by the signs of the zodiac and Hebrew lettering. The sun symbolizes gold, the great arcanum of the alchemists and the curse of their adepts, who often enough ended in prison or on the scaffold when they failed to deliver the promised treasure to some princely patron. We know that as sidelines they invented among other things, porcelain and the magnificent ruby glass we see in Kunckel, and discovered the element phosphorus. 'Transmutation' of base metal into precious, gold as the procreating power that was to create gold, the *prima materia*, the philosopher's stone, the red lion, the great elixir, the concept of *homunculus*, artificially produced man – all this was in the air at the time. '*Crepusculum matutinum*', the early dawn, of the old writers – there is no better motto for this daybreak mood of Goethe's. It is not *Faust*, but it is the atmosphere in which *Faust* originated.

One will search these endless rows of books in vain for actual words, phrases, or even images, appropriated by Goethe. The transmutations of his alchemy are of a far subtler kind. The frequently distorted and often desperately tedious allegories are scarcely recognizable in his poetry. But it is a world from which he draws his inspiration, a mover of dark and often turbid waters. Scientific history has only recently begun to sift this vast mass of literature, to separate the genuine from the fraudulent – and there was a great deal of fraud. This does not concern Goethe, however, who knew nothing of 'early chemistry'. To him alchemy was a thing of the present, not of the past, a still living survival from the middle ages.

The adepts did not only read, they performed experiments. The pious Fräulein von Klettenberg stood with the young Goethe in front of a wind furnace, with sand-bath and chemical flasks. They stirred up the 'ingredients of Macrocosm and Microcosm'. They tried to produce silicic acid by melting quartz pebbles from the river Main. They discussed mysterious salts, to be conjured up by unheard-of means, 'a virgin soil' with extraordinary powers. But the precipitate powder revealed 'no trace of any active quality in its nature'.

This whole range of experiments was not very productive and yet, for a Goethe, it was of far greater consequence than could have been any attempt to understand Kant or Lambert, for which, in any case, he lacked even the most elementary mathematical training. He became an alchemist in words. Even in his natural science he remained far truer to the world of *prima materia* and the *Chemical Marriage*, as the text-book of the Rosicrucians was called, than subsequent opinion has been willing to admit.

From the world of quartz pebbles, virgin soil and retorts, let us turn now to the world of spirits. The world beyond, now so close to the ailing Fräulein von Klettenberg, inevitably occupied a great deal of her thought. She conceived it as the purest happiness, and being of a sweet and loving disposition, the idea of permanent separation from those she loved on earth was well-nigh unbearable to her. Was there any communication with the dead? Were there spirits who could speak to us, communicate with us? This age-old idea had just found a powerful new advocate in the Swedish mining engineer Swedenborg. Swedenborg's *Secrets of Heaven*, and his *Heaven and Hell* – no time-honoured writings of ancient magicians, but works by a contemporary author – were studied by Fräulein von Klettenberg and her young friend. She meditated in the spirit of Swedenborg, whom Goethe considered the 'worthiest seer of our age, to whom the spirits spoke through every sense and limb, in whose bosom angels dwelt'. From him he got an inkling of the 'babbling of the prophets'. The children's word 'Lallen' – babbling – was a favourite expression of the pietists. There was a sort of pietist Dadaism.

In *Faust*, Swedenborg's spirit world, in which the whole universe, the planets and the earth, is peopled with inter-communicating spirits, is revived. The *Erdgeist* derives unquestionably from this source, and much else besides, even though in changed form; spirits are not so easy to document in terms of words. Visions, dreams and omens were things Goethe always believed in, and he repeatedly described his experiences at various stages of his life. In Fräulein von Klettenberg's notebooks there is a passage about a man's attempt to see the true picture of heaven: 'His innermost being was opened so that he might experience something of heavenly joy,' and when he was unable to hear it, 'his innermost being was closed again...'. This opening and closing, here still connected with pietist terminology, is to become one of Goethe's fundamental ideas of life, a constant rhythm in systole and diastole, inhaling and exhaling.

To use his own expression the young adept was now nine months' pregnant with all these figures and images, these experiments with virgin soil, with all this writing and drawing of 'nebulously outlined forms'. It was a veritable period of gestation, if we want to introduce a little numerical mysticism. At this point even the very indulgent paternal tyrant loses patience with his only son's sand-baths and retorts, with his excursions to pietist gatherings. He applies pressure. The boy's studies, hitherto scarcely begun, are to be completed. The father must be thinking that the landmarks in his own unfulfilled life are about to be repeated, and he hopes for better results than that. So he decides on Strasbourg, which he had visited on his own Grand Tour, as the next university. Strasbourg is the preparatory school for Paris; the boy is to perfect his French, still very indifferent, and acquire the social graces. Moreover, the climate is favourable: the boy's cough still persists, the universal elixirs of the alchemists have failed to cure it.

And so, as Goethe writes in *Faust*:

> *Die Geisterwelt ist nicht verschlossen,*
> *Dein Sinn ist zu, dein Herz ist tot,*
> *Auf! bade, Schüler unverdrossen*
> *Die irdsche Brust im Morgenrot.*

Faust, setting out on his great journey, is aware that, although his mind is numbed and his heart feels dead, the world of spirits is not closed to him; the time has come to shake off his torpor, to rise and bathe in a new dawn.

# 7

# *New Dawn*

Strasbourg represents the glow of dawn in Goethe's life or, in the language of the pietists, the 'break-through', though it was not preceded by any long 'battle of repentance'. 'Rose-tinted spring' or 'the whole world heady with the scent of flowers' is the imagery of his first mature poems. He finds himself in a new, rich, warm landscape and feels its glow as it suffuses the chillness of his being. The air, the clouds, the wide vistas, the mighty Rhine with its islands and islets, its sparkling waters not yet canalized: in his descriptions he has painted this with more love and care than any other landscape. There is a love affair, more serious now, with an Alsatian girl in long pigtails who wears the old national costume, and there are folk-songs and folklore that he has collected. This whole love affair is like a folk-song with its perfidy, parting and shunning of the loved one: after all it is Alsace, the country we meet even in German folk-song more often than any other. To all this we must add his first encounter with a mind superior to his own, one that 'scours' him unmercifully, as he puts it, that bears down on him until the proud young man feels himself to be no more than the humble satellite of some greater planet. Then he casts off the yoke, breathes again, and enters his first great creative epoch, an epoch that, in the exuberance of its genius, is to be the richest of his life.

The beginning is modest and restrained. He is still physically weak, the cough persists and he has occasional feverish attacks. Mentally, too, he is still somewhat numbed by his mystical excesses. His first lodgings are at the inn *Zum Geist*, and then he takes a room in the busy street *am Fisch-markt*. Luncheon he takes, as in Leipzig, at a very reputable establishment, where a group of ten to fifteen people, mostly medical students, meet. The group is presided over by a refined, well-to-do, elderly gentleman, an actuary by the name of Salzmann, who sees that the proceedings are conducted with good manners and decorum. A certain amount of pleasantry is allowed, within limits; but at times the conversation grows more animated and then Salzmann intervenes. He is a bachelor, with a far from exacting post in the administrative offices for wards in chancery, he also enjoys giving small parties for the children of his friends. Educational matters are his hobby-horse, and thus he also educates the young men round the luncheon table of the Misses Lauth. Goethe, as yet no titan, attaches himself closely to this cultured, spinsterish gentleman, who introduces him to his literary circle and, throughout this whole Strasbourg period, fathers him in an unobtrusive and discreet way, treatment hitherto quite unknown to Goethe.

Adopting the tone of a fatherly friend, he writes a letter, full of good intentions and advice, to a student acquaintance: in order to get a proper view of the world 'we must think of it as neither too bad nor too good; love and hate are very closely related, and they both cloud our vision'. But he pulls himself up, remarking ironically, 'it does not take much to start me off prattling'. Then didactically again, a subject rich in pedagogic possibilities:

> To see things as well as we can, to note them down in our memory, to be observant, and not to let a day pass without garnering something; and then to apply ourselves to those branches of knowledge which give a certain direction to our thinking, to compare things, to put everything in its right place and assess its value – a true philosophy, I mean, and a sound mathesis – this is what we have to do now. In doing it we must *be* nothing, but try to *become* everything, and in particular we must not rest and relax more often than the needs of a tired mind and body demand.

How does Goethe practise his true philosophy and sound mathesis? Very much after his own fashion; he does indeed garner, but not from the university and the lecture room. Through his luncheon circle he makes the acquaintance of an Alsatian, slightly older than himself, who hands over to him his note-books and coaches him a little. He also learns that in Strasbourg, following French principles, no particular store is set by a thorough study of the history of law and of age-old legal decisions. Here, on French soil, his coach assures him, he will only be asked questions on what exists and is valid now. It is only necessary to remember some simple rules; the rest is a matter of talent and circumstances. And so, after a few months, Goethe goes to the *Kapitelstube* and takes his 'candidate's examination'; he passes, and is henceforth freed from any further backbreaking study. To his friend and coach he writes, adopting the tone of a crier at the fair: 'Everyone has his place in the world, as in a peep-show. Has the Emperor passed with his army? But look, here comes the Pope with his retinue. Now I, too, have played my part in the *Kapitelstube*; herewith are your manuscripts, which have done excellent service.' So far as he was concerned this was the end of 'law' for the rest of his year in Strasbourg, though there was still a thesis to be written for his doctorship.

The jurists were not very strongly represented at the university; the medical faculty, on the other hand, was famous. His interest having been roused by the medical talk at lunch time, Goethe attends a few lectures on anatomy and gynaecology, as well as some on chemistry, 'still my secret love', as he writes to Fräulein von Klettenberg; these last were given by a medical man, who also lectured on botany. In those days the faculties were not so sharply divided as they are to-day, nor can all these activities have been pursued very seriously. The main reason for his interest in anatomy, Goethe tells us, was his desire to overcome his aversion for 'unpleasant things'. He was still delicate, and susceptible, to the point of fear, to noises, smells, the sight of illness and wounds, to say nothing of death. Because of this, he makes systematic efforts to harden himself. At the mounting of the guard he would march along-side to accustom himself to the sound of the drums 'which was enough to make your heart jump into your mouth', but he never overcame his dislike. All his life he had a horror of dogs barking. To combat his tendency to giddiness he used to climb the tower of the Strasbourg Minster and look down from the narrow platform just below the top. To conquer his fear of the dark he would visit lonely cemeteries and chapels at night. Having steeled himself in these ways, he was finally able to enjoy a 'free, sociable, active' life.

The young Goethe must, in fact, and for a considerable time, have been rather a delicate boy. But the extreme sensitivity of every organ of his body played the dominant part in this too, and that was a condition that persisted despite all his attempts to harden himself. Later in life, he made a thorough study of anatomy, but the sight of sick or dying people was something he never learned to bear, even though they were his nearest and dearest.

He studies and collects people. One of his luncheon companions, Lerse, reappears a year later as the 'honest Lerse' in *Götz von Berlichingen*, unaltered even down to his name; others re-appear in his memoirs. There is one by the name of Meyer, from Lindau on Lake Constance, who indulges in mockery and sarcasm. He is a medical student and is later to become a well-known physician in London. At Strasbourg he is more concerned with music than with anatomy; he plays the flute, writes a small opera, and is often seen at the theatre. In those days of no examinations the study of any faculty was easy and pleasant, provided one had sufficient means available. At table the rich and handsome young man sarcastically mimics the idiosyncrasies of his professors. With amusement in his eyes he evidently watches and makes fun of the young law student too, and Goethe, in his turn, takes revenge in his memoirs, calling him a 'slovenly fellow', dissolute and irresponsible. Meyer remembered the young Titan only as a slightly eccentric figure. In a letter to Salzmann, written soon after his Strasbourg days, a story about the crazy love affairs of some marquis or other, in which he quotes Vergil's '*O Corydon Corydon! quae te dementia cepit*', leads him to: 'following the chain by which our thoughts are supposed to be connected, Corydon and dementia remind me of the crazy Goethe. I take it he is back in Frankfurt once more?'

Meyer also behaves in an arrogant and overbearing way to an older man who now joins their luncheon circle. Simply and old-fashionedly dressed, his name is Jung. He has been a charcoal burner, a tailor and, having educated himself, has also done some schoolmastering. Latterly he has been performing operations for cataract, which anyone was allowed to do who had enough confidence in the steadiness of his hands and in God. Jung is not lacking in faith; he too belongs to the pietists, and is fully convinced that when he applies the knife the Lord will guide his hand. In Strasbourg he wants to take advantage of the celebrated faculty to improve his medical knowledge, although he scarcely knows from one month to the next how he is going to exist. But this again he is content to leave to God. Quietly he takes his place at table and looks round him. To his companions he murmurs that in this company one should not open one's mouth for the first fortnight. But Meyer rides roughshod over the newcomer. Goethe comes vehemently to the defence of the tormented man. Gratefully Jung moves closer to him, and an intimate relationship develops. Goethe can appreciate this kind of man, who is only waiting to unburden his heart. Jung talks and talks, telling him his whole life story.

This too is an experience. For the first time Goethe gets to know someone of the people. He hears the story of a family of charcoal burners in Siegerland, a story far more realistically told than most later tales of village life, a piece of nature itself. It is not the vaguely imagined natural state of man as described by Rousseau, but reality experienced, with its matchmaking, weddings and deaths. It is the fight for existence of a gifted but penniless boy. Jung trusts his new friend, and under these conditions he becomes uncommonly eloquent. His words are powerful and gripping; at times they are poetic as well. Some years later Goethe promoted the publication of Jung's memoirs, the story of his youth, and the book comes near to entering the orbit of his own works, even though he made but few alterations to the text.

This story of the youth of Heinrich Stilling, as Jung calls himself, is the most powerful among the confessional writings of the pietists. It had a long life as a popular book, mainly on account of its devout sentiment. But it is more than this. It is a book of the people, with folk songs and ballads; it also contains the tale of Jorinde and Joringel long before the brothers Grimm. The Germany of old comes to life again; the age of the knights and robbers. We meet the great robber Johann Hübner, the one-eyed highwayman: 'By day he used to sit with his men, strong men all of them, over there in the corner, where you can still see the broken window-frame; that is where they had their room, where they sat and gulped their beer....' With his one eye, he scours the countryside. ' "Hehloh!" he shouts. "There goes a rider! A fine horse. Hehloh!..." Then his men gave heed to the rider, took his horse and slew him dead.' Thus the one-armed Götz von Berlichingen, the robber-knight, is brother to the one-eyed Hübner, and the folk strain in Goethe's first play of consequence, the old German world with its life and customs, derives not so much from books and chronicles as from Jung's tales.

Jung's piety and his belief in strange dispensations did not disturb Goethe, at any rate not at this time; later the two became completely estranged. In his career as an oculist Jung fluctuated between successful and unsuccessful operations, of which he performed more than two thousand. He continued his memoirs in a long series of volumes, which grew progressively weaker and duller; he edited magazines, published a theory of spiritualism, and eventually became a professor of political science. The Duke of Baden made him a *Geheimrat*, expressly relieving him 'from all temporal obligations' and charging him, through his writings and correspondence, 'to promote religion and practical Christianity; to this end I summon and reward you'. When Jung died they wrote of him: 'In both the Indies, in the land of the Hottentots, in far-off Asia and Tahiti, he was loved and venerated; they offered up prayers for him.' Once, when they were both old, *Geheimrat* Goethe visited *Geheimrat* Jung. They had nothing to say to one another.

In his *Wanderjahre*, Jung describes the luncheon circle at Strasbourg, gratefully remembering Goethe as we like to think of him:

> In particular the attention of Herr Troost [Jung's companion] and Stilling was drawn to a beautifully built man, with large bright eyes and magnificent forehead, who boldly entered the room. The former said to the latter: that must be someone distinguished. Stilling agreed, but thought he would cause them both a lot of trouble as he had the appearance of being a wild fellow. He drew this conclusion from the independent manner the student adopted; but Stilling was very much mistaken....

We must remember that this was written after Götz and Werther had made Goethe famous. Meyer saw his erstwhile companion quite impartially as the 'crazy Corydon'. Both are probably right.

Following the earnest, devout, charcoal burner's son comes a small, nervous figure; fair, snub-nosed, with a strong Baltic accent and a slight stammer. Reticent at first, he soon becomes bold in conversation. Tutor to two aristocrats from his own province of Courland, son of a pastor and a poet of genius, his name is Jakob Michael Reinhold Lenz. We shall come across him again; Goethe only made his acquaintance towards the end of his Strasbourg days.

Another tutor now enters the picture, also from the Baltic provinces: Johann Gottfried Herder, preacher and travelling companion to a young prince. Coming of poor circumstances, his father being schoolmaster and choirmaster in a tiny East Prussian village, Herder, unlike Lenz, is a man of strikingly impressive appearance, with a leaning towards elegance, and of a somewhat proud and stubborn bearing. Goethe did not meet him in Salzmann's circle but on a chance visit to the inn *zum Geist*. 'Right at the entrance by the steps, I came across a man about to go up them; I could have taken him for a priest. His powdered hair was caught up in a ringlet;

his black clothes labelled him, too, and even more so did the long black silk cloak he was wearing, the ends of which he had gathered up and put in his pocket.' Herder was 26, barely five years older than Goethe, but already an established author, known through a series of writings, which he had called *Fragmente* and *Kritische Wäldchen*. Herder nearly always disseminated his ideas in the form of such miscellanies. Goethe addressed the striking figure in the soutane, and was courteously invited to have a talk.

Herder listened attentively. He was in pain. One of his eyes was inflamed through the closing of the lachrymal sac, and he was being treated by a series of painful operations which to us would seem beyond endurance: the sac was cut open, the bone pierced to create a lachrymal duct, and the hole thus formed threaded with a horse-hair, this last operation being repeated every day. The case was given to the great Strasbourg surgeon, Lobstein, but, after making repeated incisions, even he could not help. It is a marvel that Herder in his agony was able to give any attention at all to the prattlings of the young student with the large dark eyes. The meeting does great credit to both of them. Goethe, normally so impatient, remained in the sick-room for whole days at a time, and endured every mood of the invalid. Herder, who bore his suffering with great fortitude, displayed the range of his mind between the two extremes of attraction and repulsion. Wieland likened him to a great cloud charged with electricity. Something must have drawn him to the youth, who cared so patiently for him, and forthwith he set about educating him. Herder was a preacher and a teacher.

First of all he tries to get some idea of how much the young man in front of him knows, and Goethe brings out for him the motley collection of his odds and ends and notes. By means of a collection of seals he claims to have gained a knowledge of potentates, of the nobility and of their coats-of-arms, and hence of history. Herder brusquely declares that this is just toying with things. History does not consist of potentates and their heraldic poultry! It is a soaring of thought over wider spheres than your petty German princedoms and your Imperial cities. History means the peoples in general, my friend, each with its own indestructible *Volksgeist*. It means going back to their origins. It means studying their development and intertwined relationships, not just existing institutions, which are wretched enough anyhow. One has to plunge down even into the so-called dark ages; they are by no means so dark. Poetry exists at the genesis of history; poetry is the mother tongue of mankind. We need to discern this in the oldest writings; in the poetry of the Bible – the Bible is a work of poetry, the greatest of all time – in Homer, the myths, folk-poetry, *Lieder*, even in those of the so-called savage, or the despised and oppressed peoples, such as the Letts, Estonians and Lithuanians, the Wends, the Lapps, the Greenlanders and the old Icelandic heroes: each of these peoples has its own voice and we have to listen to it. Poetry is a living part of speech.

The young adept takes in what he hears, and contradicts, but with respect. For the first time he is face to face with a mind which he has to recognize as his superior. Hitherto he has been critical and precocious, and has only taken bites at things. Now he is being taken by the scruff of the neck and forced down until, once again, he finds himself sitting on the nursery chair. But childish things, he learns from Herder, are as little to be despised as in the childhood of nations. The very first stirrings of speech, the babblings, the inarticulateness, the first sensations! The sheer sense of touch! This sense of touch is really our truest guide. And then dancing, rhythm, music, all the senses combined! The whole man, with all his faculties.

A new name comes up, that of Hamann, in Königsberg, the 'Magus of the North', to whom Herder refers as his teacher and master. Goethe slaves away, trying to read Hamann's *Sibyllinische Blätter*; Herder mocks at his desperate attempts to grapple with it. He mocks unmercifully all the time. Goethe tells him of the classics which he has brought from home, and that are lying unread on his book-shelf. Herder writes him a note telling him to bring them along, and adds a triple pun on his name: 'You who are descended from the Gods, from the Goths or from the gutter, Goethe send them to me!' – which upsets the young man. Later, after a friendship which had lasted for decades, a similar pun brings to an end one of the most fruitful encounters in literary history. Herder scorns Ovid as a feeble imitation of the Greeks, whereas Goethe still clings to the beautiful imagery of the Latin poet. Herder sweeps away the whole of Oeser's world of little cupids, all that is over-civilized and merely elegant or pleasing. Only the really great are to be accepted: the poets of the Old Testament, Homer, Shakespeare and Ossian.

Here again, as in the case of Lippert's faked cameos, which Oeser praised as models, we come face to face with a creative blunder. Ossian, the faked 'ancient poetry' by the Scot Macpherson, who had used some scraps of old Gaelic songs round which to weave his 'age-old epics' – Ossian which, for half a century, was accepted as a work on the same level as Homer. The 'epics' were translated into every language, and when their genuineness was questioned, Macpherson translated them into Gaelic to prove their authenticity. Not only Herder, Goethe and Hölderlin, but a Napoleon, too, could wax enthusiastic over Ossian. To-day all that remains of this once worldwide fashion are the Christian names Oscar and Selma. Goethe made translations of Macpherson's Ossian while he was in Strasbourg. It was regarded as part of our oldest poetic heritage. *Ur-Poesie* to use the German term; whereas to our eyes there is not the slightest trace of epic in these hazy rhapsodic inventions. In the central poem the hero 'Fingal appears like a watery column of mist, surrounded by his heroes...'. Watery columns of mist in a moorland landscape – it was the misty mood, the primeval world as then conceived, that inspired the enthusiasm of the Ossian worshippers. Rarely has genuine poetry been so honoured by the great minds of the day as were these forgeries of Macpherson's. Even the fact that they contain remnants of ancient ballads cannot serve to reprieve them.

Supposition, deception even, can be more fruitful than reality. Poems were written in the style of Ossian; Goethe wrote them too, indeed he did so in *Werther*. Of Shakespeare, too, most people in Germany at this time had only the haziest notion; very few were able to read and understand him. It was in Dodd's anthology, consisting of extracts, that Goethe first met Shakespeare, and at once he sat down and wrote 'a dozen allegories' in his manner. In Wieland's translation, he had been introduced to a rococo Shakespeare, and now Herder, in terse and sombre phrases, presents him with a different Shakespeare, seen in a grey Nordic half-light, Macbeth on a desolate moor. Neither Herder nor Goethe had yet seen Shakespeare on the stage, and the stage, after all, is an essential element in Shakespeare. He has been experienced only through the written word:

> When I read him it is as though theatre, actors, scenery have disappeared! Single leaves only, tossed in the storm of time, taken from the book of events, of providence, of the world! – single impressions of peoples, classes, minds ... as we appear in the hands of the Creator – ignorant, blind tools in the totality of a single theatrical picture, of a single event of greatness that only the poet can survey.

The two friends do not spend all their time soaring in rarified atmosphere. The young adept in this new mysticism is learning something else. In Herder he meets for the first time a completely new type of literary man. This is no wretched, subservient tutor to some nobleman; he has already parted from his prince, and without too much scruple. He is not merely the disputatious scholar indulging in eternal wrangles with other scholars in the time-honoured, unholy tradition of theological polemics, which is how even Lessing had appeared to Goethe. In Herder he sees a man of the world, just returned from a journey to France, wearing the silk soutane of an *abbé*, but with its ends tucked carelessly into his pockets – not the stiff theologian with his starched collar and frills. A man who boldly aspired to be 'the Lycurgus of all Russia', if only they would give him the opportunity; an ambition that was not wholly fantastic, because Catherine the Great, the 'Semiramis of the North', had invited far lesser men than Herder to her Court to frame her laws for her. A ruler by nature, it is Herder's tragedy that he never achieved power, that he could sow, never reap. He was fated always to play a secondary role, under the shadow of a greater than himself.

But now, in Strasbourg, he is still the greater. He is in command, moulding the pliant young mind of his pupil. He gives him one more piece of advice: not to bury his nose in the hopeless maze of German petty principalities, whose day is past, with their seals and guaranteed rights. This man from the Russian steppes has very different ideas, and if he is not to be allowed to frame the laws of a nation, he can still rule over the spiritual realm of the mind. In the lives of nations there are ups and downs. The French have had their great days, now they are old; Voltaire is old, the whole of French literature is senile, its mission is fulfilled. Now it is the turn of others, the turn of ourselves, the Germans. The man from the extreme eastern border of Germany, now living in its western extremity, that is already half French, spans a wider arc than do the inhabitants of the centre, who still remain Saxons, Prussians, citizens of Lübeck–Eutin, like his former pupil the prince, or of the Imperial city of Frankfurt. However political frontiers may run or alter – and the Holy Roman Empire has no recognizable boundaries whatsoever – a new empire is arising.

With quick strokes he sketches his design; the idea takes root in Goethe's mind. It is the germ of his conception of a realm, independent of political frontiers; which he later created and over which he ruled.

The course, though it lasts only a few months, is not easy. At the end of it Goethe is tired; he has heard and absorbed enough. Herder in his suffering, which the doctors are powerless to cure, grows continually more caustic and aggressive. Goethe feels it wiser not to discuss his own literary plans with him, since Herder would only tear them mercilessly to pieces. Listening is not Herder's *forte*, he is a preacher. It is almost with a sense of relief that Goethe sees him leave, after a final, unsuccessful operation. Even a Herder, without a penny of his own, has to find a position. The independent writer does not yet exist. Lessing himself, the mighty 'conqueror', a European celebrity, has been forced to abandon the attempt, and has just found a modest position in Wolfenbüttel as librarian to the Duke of Brunswick. Another petty prince, Graf zur Lippe, formerly one of Frederick the Great's generals, has summoned Herder to Bückeburg, his capital, as ecclesiastical councillor. Thus the man, whose thought spans east and west, has now to pursue his researches into the 'oldest records of mankind' in the very centre of Germany, in the land of the ancient Cheruscans. He has to live among peasants, who still cling to their national costume, who house their cattle under their own roof, who fix a horse's skull from the times of Widukind to the gable, or nail a hawk to the door of the barn to ward off evil spirits. It is a land with scarcely more inhabitants than the city of Strasbourg, and there, discontented, he remains for five years until Goethe is able to offer him a position in the slightly larger principality of Weimar, where he has to remain for the rest of his life.

Goethe learns some practical lessons from Herder. Collect folk-songs! In the country here in Alsace, they still sing them; in the town, of course, people get more urban and more Parisian every day. Open your eyes and look around you, like the English Bishop Percy, who has just published his *Reliques of Ancient English Poetry*, the most magnificent ballads from the so-called 'Gothic' time, which is not Gothic and abstruse, as everyone says, but glorious. The book is a veritable treasure house. Take a thorough look at the Minster, there you have the old German art; one should write about it and the lamentable way in which it has been misunderstood. Herder speaks to him of literary connections and circles, of Darmstadt, another little court, where there is an enthusiastic group of Klopstock admirers, people of feeling and fine sensibility, amongst them a Demoiselle Caroline Flachsland, to whom Herder is engaged and whom he hopes to marry on the strength of his salary in Bückeburg. It is of such small groups that the German public is composed, there being no capital, no literary centre like Paris. Herder gives him an insight into the contemporary literary world and its tendencies, of which, in Leipzig, Goethe had formed but a very sketchy idea. There is still no thought, however, of a writer's or a poet's career; for German writers, as Goethe says, 'enjoyed not the slightest advantage in the world of bourgeois society; they had neither support, standing nor prestige'. But something is stirring within him. He tells us in his memoirs that he had already started to think of *Götz* and *Faust*, though this is probably an anticipation. The feeling of creative power is certainly present. Herder's lessons on creative genius have come at the right moment.

# 8

# *Strasbourg Wanderings*

Not all Goethe's time during these months is devoted to literature and cultural development. There is still something of the 'muffled-up' boy in him. He has to get himself unmuffled; and just as in Leipzig, where, chameleon-like, he changed his style of dress, so now in Strasbourg he adapts himself to his surroundings. Strasbourg is not Paris, but neither is it 'little Paris', like Leipzig; it is the vestibule to Paris. At the university there is a large number of aristocrats from all over Europe. They have come to 'perfect' themselves before they can be allowed on the floor of the great metropolis, where every step, every gesture, every slightest trait is observed and ridiculed. Public bearing and appearance is still a matter of vital importance in an age when even a man's entry into a room has to be performed like a minuet. A single clumsy, false move betrays the 'peasant', the 'bourgeois' or the 'bear', who has to be 'licked into shape', a saying derived from the old zoological notion of the newly born bear, which the mother had to lick into shape out of a formless lump of flesh.

Goethe's first move is to the hairdresser. The perruquier shakes his head; Goethe's hair has grown wild during his months of cabbalistic mysticism in Frankfurt. Ignoring his client's objections, the man cuts and crops and then, following the dictates of Paris fashion, sets on the hair a bag-wig and pigtail. Finally he powders it, and the impatient youth can now, as he says, 'always pass for the best groomed and wigged young man in town'. Of course he must move a little warily, so as not to betray his artificial adornment. Gingerly he sets off, in fine shoes, silk stockings and breeches, his hat tucked carefully under his arm as fashion decrees. As a special precaution he wears a pair of fine chamois leather under-stockings 'to protect me from the Rhine gnats'. Thus attired, or so we must imagine, he gazes up at the huge pile of the Gothic Minster, which he is shortly to describe as the archetype of German might and power.

Demurely, and dressed in his leather under-stockings, he goes out to play cards in society, an accomplishment as strongly recommended by Salzmann as it had been by Madame Boehme in Leipzig. The former introduces him to a few families, where he is accepted as a pleasant young man of good family; they will have been upper middle-class homes. With the higher strata of

Strasbourg society, already completely French in outlook, he scarcely comes into contact. Strasbourg, at this time, is in a state of transition. Many middle-class families, as well as some of the patrician families of the old Imperial city, still dress 'German', following the old custom: the girls in pigtails, caught up and held by a long pin, and with short skirts. The others, and above all the upper classes, follow the Paris fashion; this is constantly changing, and is very opulent and troublesome, with its long skirts, trains, complicated hair styles, beauty spots, ribbons, flowers and rosettes everywhere. They speak French too; the others speak German – Alsatian German which even people from other parts of Germany do not always understand.

Of opposition to France there is scarcely a trace. The Strasbourg people are proud of their ancient rights, and of their ancient constitution as a former Imperial city, which had been guaranteed by the French King on taking over the city ninety years before in a solemn capitulation. They are Protestants in a strictly Roman Catholic kingdom, from which Goethe's grandfather had been expelled shortly after the Strasbourg capitulation. If Goethe had wanted to pursue the study of constitutional law he would have found a fascinating curiosity: a republic, in the midst of a strictly absolutionist monarchy, with the whole ancient apparatus of the guilds, which elected their own committees and officials, the latter known as *Ammeister*. This city, nominally autonomous, existed within the framework of a province, called *'étrangère'*, which was itself separated from the rest of France and had its own customs barrier along the Vosges. To complete the confusion, there were numerous enclaves within the province which were under the rule of German princes beyond the Rhine; on his wanderings Goethe visited some of them. In Strasbourg itself there was a strong Royal garrison, and at the centre of the city, and dominating it, the citadel formed a Royal enclave. One regiment was called the 'Royal Allemand'; its soldiers sang *Zu Strassburg auf der Schanz* in German, its officers spoke French and were mainly German aristocrats. The king was represented by the *Praetor*, who more or less governed the city; he was often a native of Strasbourg. The whole situation was as confused as the old streets round the Minster. In his studies Goethe had been told not to worry himself over problems of legal history, he would only be examined on current procedure. The people of Strasbourg thought no differently. They regarded themselves as loyal German Protestant subjects of His Most Christian Majesty the King of France at Versailles.

From time to time they had to give proof of their loyalty in hard cash. According to the terms of the capitulation the city was exempt from national taxes. It had to make good the difference by *dons gratuits* on festive occasions. Goethe was present on one such occasion and saw the peep-show of world history pass by: 'Look! See!' an Emperor's daughter of the House of Habsburg handed over to the deputy of the heir to the French throne. All the splendour of military processions, illuminations, costly buildings specially erected for this one day; the city of Strasbourg had to dig deeply into its coffers. On this occasion, too, Goethe saw with his own eyes one of the leading players on the world's stage. It is remarkable how many of the great figures of history he saw, and even met personally, during his long life.

In this May of 1770 he saw Marie Antoinette, daughter of the Empress Maria Theresa, married to the Dauphin. It was an important move on the chess-board of European politics, France's reconciliation with her hereditary enemy, Austria. We know how it ended; in his memoirs Goethe pretends that even at that time he had melancholy forebodings. A *pavillon* was hurriedly built for the reception, with triumphal arches, state rooms and entrance halls, and with formal gardens in front, the whole thing a kind of Potemkin-like village, which was also intended to serve the purpose of hiding the slums down by the river. In the main state room, which Goethe visited frequently for the price of a small tip, the walls were hung with tapestries depicting Jason and Medea, the chariot of the furies and the slaughtered children. A favourite operatic subject, it was put up merely for decoration. Goethe, so he tells us, was horrified and protested vehemently at such thoughtlessness; he was just smiled at. All cripples, beggars, people with deformities, were rigorously excluded from the route of the procession; this inspired Goethe to write a poem in French on the subject of Christ and the halt and the maimed, but he laid it aside when a Frenchman criticized it on linguistic grounds.

Marie Antoinette entered the city in a glass state coach. Goethe saw her, chatting to her companions. He did not see the giving-away ceremony in the *pavillon* because that was a high act of state, performed with all the symbolic ceremonial of the *ancien régime* and reserved exclusively for the highest officials. The Austrian princess was required to undress completely before she was allowed to put on the French robes of state and cross the border into the country where, twenty-two years later, she was to be taken to the scaffold in a cart, and cast, naked once more, into the pit.

But in this warm spring of 1770, Goethe, untroubled by dark forebodings, strolls through the illuminated streets thronged with people in French and German national dress. The Bishop's Palace, belonging to the Rohan family, is brilliantly lit up in its heavy baroque outlines, the Prefecture also, the old Town Hall with its Gothic gables and crooked entrance corridors, and dominating everything the summit of the Minster tower, ablaze in the light of torches, which cast their brilliance high into the sky and far out across the river.

To Goethe the Minster is first and foremost a viewpoint from which he can gain a panoramic view of the countryside. On the terrace near the tower he drinks wine with his friends; his name is scratched on one of the huge sandstone blocks which in daytime have a soft rose-coloured glow. The Strasbourg Minster is the first great architectural masterpiece Goethe has seen. The Cathedral at Frankfurt, however much one might revere it as the place where the German Emperors were crowned, was not much to boast of; the building was never completed although, originally, it had been planned on as grand a scale as the Cathedrals at Ulm and Cologne.

Goethe enjoyed the building most in silhouette, in the evening, at dusk when 'the numberless parts fused into whole masses, and these stood before me in their simplicity and greatness, and my power to enjoy and perceive unfolded in wonder! Then was revealed to me, faintly discerned, the genius of the great master workman....' Some years later he commemorated the Minster and Erwin of Steinbach, whom he regarded as its builder, in a hymn-like essay, *Von deutscher Baukunst*, written in the style of his new-found genius. Erwin he places on a level with Albrecht Dürer, whose fame had never waned and to which some recent writings had just given new life. In his essay, Goethe fiercely extols pure feeling, careless unconcern, rugged-ness and wildness when allied to vitality, and these are the qualities he finds in the Minster's architecture. He goes so far as to praise the art of savages, 'with its grotesque features and hideous forms', as if he were an early fore-runner of the *Fauves*. He now rejects and abuses everything he learned from Oeser. He sounds a blaring nationalistic note, loudly proclaiming: 'This is German architecture, our architecture! Something of which the Italian can-not boast, far less the Frenchman.'

Of French Gothic not a word had reached him, but even the French themselves knew little of their great heritage. The Italians, indeed, called Gothic art 'German art'. The great and many sided complex, later crowned with the collective name of 'Gothic', was something that no one in that age could grasp in its entirety. At the most there were discussions as to how the pointed arch had originated, and it is significant that Herder, who pub-lished Goethe's essay in his collection *Von deutscher Art und Kunst*, also included in this, as an antidote, a sober mathematical paper by an Italian, which considered the statics of the pointed arch as compared with those of the rounded and the ancient vaulted arch. 'Gothic man' had not yet been discovered, and of the whole wealth of Gothic art scarcely more than the great tower of the Minster was known. The sculptures, for us the greatest treasure of Strasbourg Cathedral, Goethe failed even to notice, just as later he completely overlooked the *Stifterfiguren* at Naumburg. It is very much open to question whether he would have grasped the significance of the 'angel pillar' at Strasbourg, or indeed of the door-way figures, even had someone drawn his attention to them. Sculptures such as the *Ecclesia* and Synagogue, now regarded as the embodiment of Gothic art at its very great-est, were first recognized long after Goethe's time, and only became famous much later still. The complicated story of the building of the Minster, or of any Gothic cathedral, is a subject for academic theses. And the question as to how much of Strasbourg Minster is 'German', how much 'French', or even how much shows southern French influence, has become a matter of national interpretation and national prejudice. The thought of the Middle

Ages ran on different lines to these. Their concepts of loyalty were different; their loyalty was to a religious order or to a building tradition.

Goethe did not discover Gothic art. Here and there it was already beginning to be the fashion, especially in England, where, however, it was cultivated as one among many 'exotic' eccentricities, along with whims for the Chinese, the Japanese and the Persian: a Gothic ruin in a park, for example, or a complete Gothic mansion for a collector of taste like Horace Walpole, who wanted to be original. Goethe's enthusiasm for the Strasbourg tower was also due to the fact that he felt himself to be an original genius, a force capable of achieving something comparable. When he aggressively voiced the word 'German' he meant to convey what Herder had taught: now it is our turn!

In Strasbourg his thoughts will hardly have been as bold as this; at the most there will have been the first dim premonitions. Later, in a first draft of his memoirs, he noted down, as a watchword for the time, *Deutschheit emergierend* – German national feeling emergent – and it has a certain appositeness. But he does not emerge with a sudden, dramatic leap from the waters which are playing so pleasantly around him. He goes to the French theatre, which is very well represented in Strasbourg. They play Diderot or Rousseau's *Pygmalion*; he sees actors of standing in Racine and Corneille. In his diary he jots down verses from Voltaire, and passages from Rousseau, which comfortingly support his view that original sin is a senseless concept. He takes dancing lessons, which he had neglected in Leipzig but which are necessary here. There is a great deal of dancing in Strasbourg: in the pleasure gardens beyond the fortifications, at country houses, where they give private balls, and at the redoubts in winter. At these last the atmosphere is gay and unrestrained:

> Respectable women go there only masked and do not dance, but prostitutes and ladies of easy virtue, of whom there is an abundance in Strasbourg, wear no masks. Often one sees only these last; it is an abominable spectacle and one that fills anyone of a more refined nature with a loathing for vice. I had the feeling it produced the same effect on the Prince

– the young Karl August of Weimar, whose tutor wrote this hypocritical letter home to the young man's mother, the Dowager Duchess, when, some years later, the heir to the Duchy of Weimar also went to Strasbourg to receive the finishing touches to his education.

Goethe, however, is rarely seen at the large balls. In any case he never really masters the art of dancing, in spite of the fact that his dancing master's two pretty daughters take a great interest in him. After the lessons a certain amount of flirtation goes on, which ends in a jealous scene between the two girls and a piece of magical incantation: Lucinde goes up to him, takes his head in her hands and, kissing him, invokes a curse on whoever shall kiss him in the future, 'misfortune upon misfortune for ever'. Cheaply

83

romantic as it sounds, the curse was fulfilled: not one of Goethe's loves found happiness, except the hale and hearty Lotte Buff, and she only to a limited extent. And Goethe himself, if we are to believe him, never found happiness either: a mere four weeks in all he said, looking back over his life in his seventy-fifth year.

Of these 'four weeks', several months belong to his Strasbourg days. His letters bear witness to this. He enjoys the easy, pleasant life, the society of good companions, the lovely walks and public gardens. At the *Grüner Baum* the soldiers and their girls dance in the open. Even the garrison in Strasbourg is light of foot, and marches in a kind of dance-step to music from Grétry's operettas. Its commander, Prince Max of Deux-Ponts, has a dancer from the Paris Opera as his mistress and rewards her with the title of Comtesse de Forbach, the name of one of his scattered possessions in Alsace. On one of his excursions, which takes him into Lorraine, Goethe visits some of these princely castles. In Zabern he sees the enormous chateau of Cardinal Prince Rohan, where he is allowed, respectfully and from a distance, to watch the Cardinal, a famous gourmet, at dinner. To be admitted to see the great ones at table was one of the thoughtful customs of pre-revolutionary days; their subjects were thus allowed to participate in the pleasures of their rulers. Goethe visits mines and foundries. He hears the name of Dietrich, one of the great industrialists of the day, member of an old Strasbourg patrician family, who had forsaken politics for newer and more rewarding activities.

Such expeditions are made on horseback in the company of a few friends who have relatives in the neighbourhood. Goethe is already stronger; his contours have filled out into the youthful figure that, at first, had been a little beyond his reach. Thus, in writing of a journey to Saarbrücken, he strikes a very different tone:

> What good fortune it is to have a heart that is light and free! Boldness spurs us on to difficulty and danger; but great joy is only won through great efforts. And that is perhaps my main objection to love; they say it makes you bold. Never. As soon as your heart is tender it is weak. When it beats so warmly in your breast, when there is a lump in your throat, and tears come into your eyes and you sit in incomprehensible ecstasy as they flow! Ah, then we are so weak that daisy chains can bind us, not because some magic power gives them strength, but because we tremble to break them.

It is a presentiment, as it were, written to a girl, one of Cornelia's friends; but at the end there is a greeting to tell a 'Fränzgen that I still belong to her'. It is not possible to trace all those he cherishes as his distant loves; certain it is that he will not prove too weak and that the daisy chains will not bind him. It is all in the style of the day, a social game; from time to time a poem results. This description of a landscape sounds like an idea for a poem:

> Yesterday we went riding all day; night came on just as we reached the mountains of Lorraine, where below the Saar glides past in its lovely valley.

As I looked out to my right over the green depths beneath, with the river flowing so grey and quiet in the twilight, and to my left where the massive darkness of the beech wood hung down from the mountain above me, and as the shimmering birds quietly and mysteriously wove their way through the thickets surrounding the dark rocks – then in my heart it was as still as all about me....

With Goethe a love affair is nearly always ushered in by a phase of preparation. Frequently he prepares himself for it, tunes himself as it were, tightens the strings that they may sing. When he is older, with a great deal of experience behind him, he often tunes himself like this quite consciously. Here in Strasbourg he flirts a little at first, as he had done in Leipzig, or he writes non-committally to Frankfurt. Then things grow more serious.

# 9

# *Friederike in Sesenheim*

On one of their excursions Goethe is introduced by his companion, Weyland, to relatives in Sesenheim, a pleasant, prosperous village about a day's journey from Strasbourg. Weyland has described the household as very hospitable and friendly: the father is pastor in the village, the mother a kind woman who must once have been very pretty, as the daughters still are. The house is always full of cousins, nieces and other relations. It is not a stiff parsonage, very far from it, and they dance, play forfeits, tease one another, make love, dress up, sit together in the arbour or go for long walks through the woods and down to the river. The parents are very broad-minded and they keep a generous table. Indulging his passion for mystification, Goethe arrives disguised as a poor theological student. To the end of his life he presents this 'Sesenheim idyll' to his readers in countless disguises and games of hide-and-seek.

A long village street, a small church and the parsonage; this last has the appearance of a peasant's house, half-timbered like the barn alongside. When the visitors arrive, the family is at work in the fields. All except the father, who sits at his table musing over the re-building of the house, as Goethe's own father used to do; for him, too, it seems to have been a life-long dream, but one that was never realized. Pastor Brion comes from a Normandy Huguenot family, and it is to this that his daughter owes her fair tresses. The family had to leave France at the same time as Goethe's grandfather, the tailor, and settled here in the *province étrangère*. This meant their becoming Lutherans, as the Strasbourg theological faculty was strictly orthodox.

The visitors enter the house, and at once the father begins to speak on his favourite theme. The young man, ostensibly a theological student, listens attentively and takes up the subject. He is interested in architecture and drawing, and in a short time produces for the old man a detailed sketch for a fine new house. He thus becomes a great favourite, and remains so until his connection with the family is severed. The eldest daughter rushes in, gay and full of spirits, and rushes out again. The second one comes in from the fields, more slowly, dangling her straw hat on her arm; she is wearing 'German' folk costume, and the short skirt, fronted with a little black taffeta apron, reveals 'the prettiest feet'. She is no peasant girl but a quasi-city girl, a *demoiselle*; her long pig-tails reach to her knees, she has a pretty snub nose, and her blue eyes survey the scene with great composure. She has a greeting for her cousin Weyland and for his fellow student from Strasbourg too; she is used to visits and visitors. The mother comes in, the elder sister returns, and a still younger one arrives; the whole family is there; they eat, and drink a pleasant local wine. Friederike is told to entertain the young gentleman from the city, and sits down at the harpsichord. She plays and sings, though not very well; we can imagine her singing the song of the day that is on everybody's lips, *Ich liebte nur Ismenen, Ismene liebte mich*, with its charming tripping melody and its somewhat ominous phrase about parting and broken faith. The harpsichord is out of tune, and she soon closes the instrument, saying, 'Let's go outside and let me sing my Alsatian and Swiss songs there, they sound better!'

The visitors stay till evening and on into the night. Goethe strolls round with Friederike; she chats away, but there is 'no moonshine' in her talk, it is all as clear as day. Happily she describes her little world, accepting the slender youth immediately into the circle of her cousins and neighbours, while he grows quieter and quieter. He now stays the night, and sleeps fitfully in the spare room upstairs. The next morning he dresses carefully, discarding the mask of the poor theological student. He prefers to be the young Herr Goethe and appears 'spruce and elegant as you please'. With a burnt cork he extends his eyebrows so that they meet in the middle, copying the 'dissolute' Meyer, whose eyebrows do this naturally and who is considered to be a dare-devil.

This is how it starts, and this is how it continues. Goethe is accepted into the bosom of the family in the most friendly way, and for the young 'exile', as Goethe likes to think of himself, a pleasant home and family circle is always an important preliminary to a love affair. Friederike comes and goes, her cheeks the 'loveliest rosy red', without assistance from pencil or cork, and soon to be made famous in Goethe's poem as 'rose-tinted spring'. They play at hiding, dressing up, finding and granting pardon, there are all kinds of teasing and endless gaiety and merriment. Goethe describes how the wild Salome, the elder sister, once falls backwards on to the grass with laughter. It is certainly no stuffy parsonage.

In the evenings they sit round the large tiled stove and play forfeits, the debt always being redeemed with a kiss. One of the games is called the dying fox; as evidenced by the Leipzig verses, the fox is always one of the favourite love symbols, although apparently still undiscovered by psychoanalysis. The words are something of a riddle: 'When the fox is dead his skin is sold, if he lives long he will grow old; living he lives and dying he dies. He is not buried in his skin, all honour to him!' A newly extinguished candle, its wick still glowing, is passed round; on receiving the candle each person must quickly repeat these magic lines and pass it on, the one holding the candle when the glow dies out having to pay the forfeit. Goethe soon turns this game into a poem in which a girl called Dorilis hands the poet a candle that, instead of going out, flares up, scorches his eyes and his face, and engulfs his head in a sea of flame; 'with me the fox was found to be not dead but very lively'.

They dance the *Allemande*, waltzing and spinning round, the girls clasped tightly to their partners; it is regarded very much as a 'country bumpkins'' dance, and is one these country girls all enjoy. Friederike, however, who enjoys it too, is soon advised not to romp about so much, as she has a weak chest. So Goethe takes the elder sister, Salome, out; they walk over to the next village, where the music is good: 'On Whit-Monday I and the eldest one danced from after lunch, at 2-0 o'clock, till 12-0 o'clock at night without stopping, except for a few *intermezzos* for eating and drinking', he writes to Salzmann. 'You really should have seen it. The whole of me immersed in dancing.'

He also mentions a slight bout of fever, which he forgot in the excitement, and an attack of melancholy from which he is never quite free. 'If I could say I am happy, that would be better than all else.' And finally:

> Here I sit between two fires.... The world is so beautiful! So beautiful! If only one could enjoy it! Sometimes it makes me angry, and sometimes I give myself moralizing moral lectures on the *now*, on this doctrine that is so indispensable to our happiness, and which many a professor of ethics does not grasp, and which none of them can put into words.

Or, once more to Salzmann, his confidant,

> I am coming, or I am not, or – I shall know all this better when it is over than I do now. It is raining outside and in, and the beastly wind is rustling in the vine leaves outside the window, and my *animula vagula* is like the little weather vane over there on the church tower, turning, turning, and so it goes on the whole day long.... And I am four weeks older, too, and you know how much that means in my case....

Four or five weeks in all are spent with the pastor and his family; we do not know the exact details of his visits. Once he sends a note at Christmas time: 'I shall be with you soon, you precious children'; they will sit by the fire, make garlands, tie up posies, 'and be like little children'. He paints their *chaise* for them with bright flowers, and gets the faithful Salzmann to send sweets from Strasbourg, 'that produce sweeter looks than those we have been used to seeing lately'.

He does not say which faces could do with a sweeter look; the mother's, perhaps, whom Goethe describes as 'sensible' and who will already have formed her own opinions. The young student has been courting the girl for some time, even though it has not been too serious, and what is going to come of it? How far have things gone?

About this posterity has engaged in amusingly heated discussions. Goethe himself writes to Salzmann on one occasion: 'So far as I am concerned the outlook is not very bright, the little one continues to be very sad at being ill, and this gives the whole situation a false appearance. Not to speak of the *conscia mens*, and not I regret *recti*, that I carry around with me. But still we are in the country....'

This, indeed, is clear and youthfully natural enough, with its hint that, after all, in the country, there is no reason why one should not do as the country people do. Undoubtedly Goethe wrote more explicitly than this; but when Salzmann died, Goethe's letters to him went to the Strasbourg library, and much later still, the more 'damaging' ones were destroyed on the intervention of the Brion family. Richard Dehmel, the German poet, who heard about them from a friend, tried to save them. But there was nothing to be saved, apart from a quite superfluous family tradition and a legend. There is also the Goethe legend which would like to ascribe to him the severest pangs of conscience, long drawn out and extending even into *Faust*. His letters of the time contain nothing of all this. In these we read of his *animula vagula*, the little weather cock with its head pointing to 'changeable'....

But even in *Dichtung und Wahrheit*, in which Friederike is portrayed as the most enchanting and famous love of his early years, Goethe was not quite able to suppress the mystery. It is one of his most charming mystifications. 'They left us unobserved, as was the custom there in those days', at any rate in the country. Only in the open air is Friederike wholly herself. She skips around like a deer; the lightness of her movements remained the strongest impression in Goethe's memory. They stroll about in couples, or separately. They wander far afield. They visit friends and neighbours, even going beyond the Rhine. They make boating trips to the islands in the river, long, lonely and rather wild banks formed by the branches of the still uncanalized river. They fry small fish over an open fire and 'here in the cosy fishermen's huts we might have installed ourselves longer than was sensible, had it not been for the infernal Rhine gnats which drove us away again after a few hours'. The phrase, 'longer than was sensible' (*mehr als billig*), later became Goethe's standard formula in connection with love affairs he wanted to hush up a little.

He goes on to complain of 'this intolerable interruption of one of our happiest outings, on which the feelings of the lovers seemed only to increase with the success of the undertaking...'. On returning home, Goethe has a long and profane discussion with the pastor on the subject of the interruption. The gnats alone would have been enough to shake his faith in God, he says. The old man pulls him up and points out that midges and other vermin only came into existence after the Fall. Goethe parries, so he writes, by pointing out that there was no need for the angel with the flaming sword to drive 'the sinful couple' from the garden of Eden; there were certainly gnats on the Euphrates and Tigris.

The old man smiles, he 'had a sense of humour', and buries himself once more in the plans for his house. But what the point of this bold and furtive play on Adam and Eve and the Fall is, if it is not to transform Goethe's slight pangs of conscience into gnat bites, one cannot imagine. This kind of playing with fire was something that even the sexagenarian could not resist.

Almost unrepentant, but at the same time very revealingly, his memoirs continue: 'More serious and uplifting was one's pleasure in the seasons and the times of day in that wonderful country. One had only to surrender oneself to the present to enjoy the clarity and purity of the sky, the lustre of the rich soil, the mild evenings, and those warm nights at one's sweetheart's side.' He glows with increasing warmth as he paints this landscape, wedding it to Friederike's image and finally, after a short storm, allowing it to tower over her in a double rainbow, more splendid, more colourful, but at the same time more evanescent, than all else.

The storm, of whose approach his weather-vane nature has long been aware, is soon over. He sees the girls in Strasbourg, when they are visiting relations; in the city they look out of place in their short German skirts, 'like servant girls', as he says. He is already busy on his Doctor's thesis. His father has sent him a warning; he himself feels that he must finish with Strasbourg, and with this love affair, too, that can come to nothing. An engagement? And then marriage? Such an idea has never occurred to him; he makes his first and only proposal of marriage in his seventy-fourth year. He rides out to Sesenheim once more. 'I feared a violent scene.' From his horse, a very symbolic gesture, he gives Friederike his hand. More he cannot remember; 'they were painful days, of which I no longer have any recollection'. What has remained is the memory of the night ride, of the parting, in *Willkommen und Abschied*, his first really characteristic poem:

> *Ich ging, du standst und sahst zur Erden,*
> *Und sahst mir nach mit nassem Blick –*

(I went, you stood, your eyes cast earthwards, You watched me long with tear-filled eyes.)

In publishing the poem soon after the event, in his confusion, or else because he wants deliberately to mislead, he reverses the roles: 'You went, I stood, my eyes cast earthwards.' Later he restored the original version, which alone corresponds to what actually happened.

He wrote other poems too at this time. This first real love storm, short though it may have been, freed him and put an end to dallying with Oeser's cupids and with small boys peeping through the doors of marriage chambers. Only in one poem does he again play with the old rococo decorations; it accompanies a ribbon decorated with roses that he sends to Friederike from Strasbourg, a gentle reminder of city finery as it were and which he has painted himself with little flowers and leaves strewn playfully by young gods of spring gambolling on a fragile strip of silk. But the poem has a rather injudicious ending:

> *Reich mir deine liebe Hand,*
> *Und das Band, das uns verbindet,*
> *Sei kein schwaches Rosenband!*

(Maiden, you whose feelings are as mine, give me your dear hand, and may the bond uniting us be no fragile band of roses!)

This too, after some pin-pricks of conscience, he changes into 'Freely give me your hand!' But he makes no alterations of any kind to the *Mailied*, which is simply a song in praise of earth, sun, blossom on the boughs, love like morning clouds, and fresh fields bathed in the scent of flowers. The stanzas flow straight on to the end, which sings of youth, courage and joy in new songs and dances. To the girl, who has been the inspiration of all this, he says:

> *Sei ewig glücklich*
> *Wie du mich liebst!*

(Be ever happy in loving me!)

If Friederike Brion ever read that, it can only have been with bitter feelings. She found no happiness.

Nevertheless, she carefully preserved the many little verses which the faithless swain scattered around: lines cut into the trunk of a beech tree, memories of their games of 'forfeits', or a hail from the spare room in the morning. They are *biglietti*, as Goethe had called them in Leipzig, not true poems, and he never included them in his published verse. They only came to light much later, as the *Sesenheimer Liederbuch*, in a doubtful version, and interspersed with verses by the next lover and admirer.

For soon after Goethe's departure the poet Lenz enters Friederike's life. He has met Goethe in the Salzmann circle; he has heard about Friederike and has seen some of the letters and poems. A beginner of genius, in these early days he is scarcely inferior to Goethe. Indeed in some respects he is his superior, not least in the sensitiveness and sympathy of his insight into other people's feelings.

Lenz goes to Sesenheim and hangs around Friederike, who still has the other student very fresh in her memory; indeed Goethe even accuses Lenz of trying to seize his letters and estrange the girl. In the extravagance of his nature, over which the shadow of his later insanity may already have been cast, Lenz threatens suicide if she will not listen to him. In his letters to Strasbourg he boasts of a *veni, vidi, vici*. In the midst of all this he writes the most beautiful poems to the unhappy girl, which have often passed as Goethe's own.

In them the figure of the girl emerges unmistakably once more, but in a quite different reflection from any that Goethe could have seen. Goethe appears as the horseman riding suddenly away. From the clouds Friederike's spirit embraces him once more: 'Rest content, my Goethe, and know that now and only now I am thine!' Lenz sees her in her room before the mirror, still doing her hair to please 'him', and straightening her black apron, still thinking always and always 'of a man who came and stole her child's heart'.

Whatever the half-crazy Lenz may have done in Sesenheim – as a theology candidate he once delivered a sermon in Pastor Brion's church – his verses give us a more vivid picture of the girl than do Goethe's, who, in his own words, thought of these poems only as a 'prelude to new songs'.

Once more, and for the last time, Goethe returns, on his second visit to Switzerland in 1779. Strasbourg has been left far behind. It is not only four weeks that have elapsed, as in his student days, but eight years. In the meantime there have been many loves, and it is to the current one, Charlotte von Stein, that he writes about his impressions. Again it is significant how much more strongly the landscape impresses him than his meeting with the girl.

> ... the willows still in their silvery beauty. An air of gentle welcome breathes through the whole countryside. The grapes improve with each step, with every day. Each peasant's house with its vine up to the roof, each courtyard with its arbour hung with great clusters. The air like nectar, mild, warm and dewy; one ripens like the grapes, a sweetness fills one's soul. The Rhine and the clear mountains nearby, the changing pattern of woods, meadows and garden-like fields do one good and give me the sort of comfort I long have lacked.

Then, almost casually, he adds:

> The second daughter of the house once loved me, more truly than I deserved, and more than others on whom I have spent much passion and constancy. I had to leave her at a moment when it almost cost her her life; she passed over it lightly so as not to tell me how much of her former illness still remains. She behaved in the most charming way and from the very first moment, when we unexpectedly bumped right into each other on the doorstep, with such a warmth of friendship that I felt quite at my ease. I must say of her that not by the slightest move did she attempt to awaken any past feelings in my breast. She led me into each arbour, and there I had to sit, and all was well.

He stays the night and the parents, too, are welcoming. He takes his leave from friendly faces, so that 'Once again I can think contentedly on this small corner of the world, and live in peace with the spirits of the reconciled within me.'

Sesenheim is only a tiny corner of his world. For a lifetime he forgets it completely and Friederike is never mentioned again until his work on *Dichtung und Wahrheit* recalls her to his memory. Subconsciously, as in the case of many of his poems, which were born only after decades of gestation, he carries this experience around with him; 'for many years it wove pleasantly in and out of my thoughts'. Then he starts to create out of it a charming fiction, handled with much art.

Whatever he may have omitted, added, or changed, his *Friederike in Sesenheim* is one of the most charming portrayals of womanhood in his whole œuvre. And as such it immediately became popular. A Friederike cult started, Sesenheim became a place of pilgrimage, and finally, a hundred years later, operetta mongers took up the theme and we had Léhar's *Friederike*. In this, with sickening sentimentality, the girl voluntarily renounces her love for the genius Goethe, because she does not want to stand in the way of his career as a poet. And yet this is not so very far from the attitude of the early Goethe admirers and scholars. These appeared even in Goethe's life-time; they went to Sesenheim, although the family had all left, they searched and explored and uncovered some scraps of evidence.

When the first volumes of *Dichtung und Wahrheit* were published, containing the first part of the '*Sesenheim Idyll*', Friederike, unknown to Goethe, was still alive, a lonely old spinster in a small village in the Duchy of Baden. She had found refuge with her brother at the end of a very sad life. Its course we can no longer trace exactly; she is said to have had a child that was given into a foundling's home, and, with her sister, to have supported herself by means of a small business dealing in ribbons – a somewhat ironic touch when we think of the ribbon painted by Goethe. A few of her letters to a nephew have survived; in one of them she consoles him over some love affair, 'There are others with whom you can find solace – and you young men can do that so easily!'

It would have been possible for her to have read the book, but it is unlikely. In the last years of her life she never mentioned Goethe, and he knew nothing of her fate or death.

Now the first Goethe philologists arrive on the scene. A Strasbourg writer named Engelhardt wishes to publish a small volume about Goethe's youth in Strasbourg. He has seen the letters to Salzmann and writes to Goethe for permission to use them in his book. Goethe's answer is a masterpiece of diplomacy and the art of persuasion. He expresses his satisfaction that the task has fallen to such hands as these. Concerning the letters, however, he cannot give his consent to their publication, indeed he must formally protest against it.

> The way in which I have described my stay in Strasbourg and its surroundings [in *Dichtung und Wahreit*] has met with general approval, and this section, as I know, continues to find special favour with thoughtful readers. But this good effect would inevitably be disturbed by the interspersion of disconnected facts.

This does not allay his anxieties and he becomes still more persuasive. He can well understand an author not wanting to relinquish a project so full of promise for success. And so, as a bribe, he offers: 'a silver cup, gilded on the inside, and used daily by me at table for drinking my wine. This cup I am prepared to dedicate to you by having engraved on it the names of the recipient and the donor, together with the year of the event in question and the present year.' The gift was not sent. The letters remained in Strasbourg, unpublished, until the descendants of the Brion family were able to encompass their disappearance, assisted by a librarian who, being a theologian himself, understood their scruples.

Another pilgrim, a professor of philology at Bonn named Näke, tries to unravel the Sesenheim mystery at the same time as Engelhardt, and sends his notes to Goethe. The Olympian answers in the style of his extreme old age, using the simile of the 'repeated reflections', which he enumerates under nine headings as though it were an optical phenomenon. Going far beyond the image of the girl, which he now perceives only from a distance and only as reflected through other people's minds, he speaks of the things that now engage his attention.

> When one considers that repeated moral reflections not only keep the past alive but even raise it to a more exalted life, one is reminded of the entoptical phenomenon in which, similarly, the images do not grow weaker as they pass from mirror to mirror but only in doing so do they kindle into their full brilliance. In this we can find a symbol for the numerous recurrences that have occurred, and daily occur, in the history of the arts and sciences, of the church, and probably of the political world as well.

Friederike, however, is no mere phenomenon of the arts and literature, far less of the church. She is not to be regarded merely as the inspiration of Goethe's first truly independent poems or, as is often the case, as a highly stimulating experience that enabled him to write his *Faust* and to picture her, after some unavoidable pricks of conscience, as Gretchen. She is a complete and living human being. The curse of the dancing master's daughter is fulfilled, and far more terribly fulfilled, in her than Goethe's fictional account allows us to suspect. The sacrifices that accompany Goethe's life cannot be construed as an 'interspersion of disconnected facts' which disturb the picture for 'thoughtful readers'. Nor will he become more 'guilty' through our doing this, nor will he lose in stature. But, even though he may have been already slightly tainted by insanity, Lenz' vision was humanly true and accurate when he spoke of a man 'who came and stole her child's heart'.

# 10

# *Doctor Goethe*

The father has issued his warning; it is time for the boy's studies to come to
an end. He has cost his father a great deal of money, nearly half the very
considerable Goethe income over the past four years. Above all, the councillor is anxious for his son, following his own footsteps, to produce a nicely
printed Doctor's thesis. Goethe starts to work on it, if we can call it work;
Herder's ideas on original genius are very much in his mind. In a few
weeks, with someone to help him, in particular to help him polish his Latin
style – elegant Latin was still of much greater importance to a thesis than
its content – he manages to put together something on the subject of ecclesiastical law. The little work has been lost, and almost all we know about it is
what Goethe himself has told us: it dealt with the problem of to what
extent the authority of the State is entitled to establish the form of worship,
and thereby bring to an end all religious disputes. This should have pleased
the professors, who all had a great respect for State authority. Obviously,
however, Goethe incorporated in his thesis various unorthodox ideas: that
the Ten Commandments, for instance, were not the real laws of the Children
of Israel but a form of ceremony. At any rate the Dean refused to accept
the work and deposited it, as not suitable for publication, in the official files.
Goethe was far from inconsolable. He was told that he could get the
degree of 'Licentiate' merely by debating a number of themes in public.
With the help of friends he quickly put together fifty-six *positiones juris*.
They sound almost like a students' rag: 'The study of law is by far the most
distinguished of all studies' and 'Uneducated people and those unversed in
the law cannot be judges', along with some others slightly less naïve. The
public 'disputation', conducted in Latin, was also an amusing affair, held
among friends, with the good Lerse as his opponent. Lerse harassed Goethe
a little, until the latter laughingly called out to him in German, which was
out of order: 'Methinks, brother, you are trying to bully me!' And so instead
of the 'Doctor's feast', they held a fraternal celebration for his Licentiate.
The *positiones* were printed by the university printer, Heitz – the firm still
exists – and sent to the father; in ill humour the latter put the little thing on
his shelf, alongside his own imposing quarto volume. The Strasbourg Licentiate, so Goethe consoled himself, should be 'as good' as a Doctor's degree

in Germany, and, in any case, it permitted him to practise law. So he now happily assumed the title Doctor Goethe, and kept it until he became 'Geheimrat Goethe'. No one bothered; even the first edition of his collected works, published four years later by the pirate firm of Himburg in Berlin, bore the title *D. Goethens Schriften*. They were not so scrupulous about academic titles in those days.

The day following the 'disputation' one of Goethe's Strasbourg professors wrote to an ex-colleague in Marburg that a student from Frankfurt, named Goethe, had tried to get his Doctor's degree there. The faculty had made it clear to him, however, that they knew the regulations.

> The young man, his head swollen with his learning, above all with his knowledge of certain sophistries of Monsieur de Voltaire, tried to submit a work under the title *'Jesus autor et judex sacrorum'*. In it he proffered the ideas that Jesus Christ was not the founder of our religion, it having been created by other sages in his name, and, further, that the Christian religion was nothing more than sound practical wisdom, and so forth. We were good enough to forbid him publication of this *chef-d'œuvre*; whereupon, as a small mark of his contempt, he submitted the most utterly primitive theses such as, for example, 'the law of nature is what nature teaches all living creatures' He was laughed at, and departed. ...

Not all the Strasbourg professors thought so scornfully of the young man. Following his excursions into anatomy and chemistry, Goethe had also attended some lectures on local history. He skimmed through Schoepflin's *Alsatia illustrata*, one of the enormous and greatly esteemed volumes of the day dealing with countries and cities; in Italy he came across another work of this kind, in Maffei's sumptuous history of Verona. The volumes had a richness of text and illustration, and were produced with an opulence, which have never since been equalled. Schoepflin was held up to Goethe as a model of what a *savant* could achieve. The French authorities were interested in young men of ability with a good family background, and certain people in Strasbourg encouraged the elegant young 'patrician' from Frankfurt to consider a career in the French government service: they needed intelligent young men for the chancellery at Versailles. His student friend Lerse did in fact work there later.

Goethe declined. This was not only because of his feeling of 'German nationalism emergent'. He was sensitive. He was constantly hearing that, apart from a fashionable hair style and impeccable clothes, *à la mode*, the most perfect and elegant French, without a trace of dialect, was stipulated for such a career. Even the great Schoepflin, who was always in and out of Versailles, was said to be not entirely faultless in this respect, and that decided the matter for Goethe. Furthermore he did not want to be tied, either by marriage to a pretty country girl or by vague prospects of a position. He wanted to be an original genius, as defined by Herder. This was no career, admittedly, but it was a feeling about life, and Goethe was now entering a period in which feelings, frames of mind, whims and even what the philistines called eccentricities determined his existence.

Without any very deep feelings of emotion he took leave of his friends, of Salzmann, of Lenz, of Wagner, the young Strasbourg writer and lawyer. In his portfolio were his diary notes, containing the titles of large numbers of books for future reading and trailing off at the end into phrases intended for dramatic works he was planning. One of these was a Caesar tragedy, in which Sulla says of a rising young genius, emerging as his rival: 'There is something damnable about having a youngster like this grow up in your vicinity and to feel in every fibre of your being that he is going to outdistance you', which can be taken as a reference to Goethe's relationship with Herder. Or: 'He is a devil of a fellow. At the right moment he can stand there and listen respectfully and quietly, and at the right moment lower his eyes and nod significantly.' It is thus, more or less, that we are to picture to ourselves the young Licentiate, attentive but fully aware of himself.

There are a few poems, carefully selected; his little *biglietti* he has left in Sesenheim. There are a few sheets of folk-songs 'snatched from the throats of the most ancient grannies' on excursions. *Heideröslein* is copied out and passes, only slightly altered, into his works. The alteration had some hidden meaning, for originally the last lines ran:

> *Das Röslein wehrte sich und stach,*
> *Aber er vergass darnach*
> *Im Genuss das Leiden.*

(The little rose defended itself and pricked him, but in his pleasure he – the cruel boy – forgot the pain.)

There is the ballad of the young count, which also has faithlessness as its theme, the song of the jealous lad, of the chatterbox, of little dark Anne – a dozen in all. Rarely has so small a collection exercised so wide an influence. Herder later included some of them in his *Volkslieder*, a volume which created a surge of enthusiasm for folk-verse a quarter of a century before Romanticism unleashed the romantic cult with its volumes of *Des Knaben Wunderhorn*. These harked back to the past, to the Middle Ages; often the material was altered arbitrarily and included contemporary poems written in "folk" style. Goethe, on the other hand, wrote down what he heard, or adapted his own *Lieder* to the old tunes. They became singable, whereas previously they had been conceived as recitations with graceful gestures. It is from this time that the German *Lied* can probably be dated, with its unique flowering both in music and in poetry. The very name has been adopted by other languages, by French and English, to denote a lyric form for which no equivalent could be found.

In August 1771 Goethe returns home to Frankfurt, brown and healthy, proud and in high spirits; there is no longer any trace of his cough. In Mainz he picks up a lost young harpist, as though he were a pet marmot, and arrives with him at the *Grosser Hirschgraben*, explaining that he wants to adopt the child, care for him, and feed him; he can be given one of the attic rooms. The mother has to intercede because the father is not very pleased at the sight of this vagabond boy. Goethe would often yield to his weakness for stray children of this kind, educate them – generally without much success – and spoil them; it was a deep-seated urge, a compensation for his profound aversion to the idea of marrying and having children of his own.

The councillor, however, is pleased that, at last, a regular career for his son is in prospect. A career in the city government, unfortunately, is out of the question because Goethe's grandfather, Textor, has just died and his own son has succeeded to a senator's post. Politics in Frankfurt are run on a strictly controlled basis where families are concerned, and the statutes decree that there is now no place for the cousin. Goethe applies for admission as an advocate. In his application he states proudly that he is prepared to undertake 'those transactions of a more important nature for which one day he might be graciously commissioned by some high and respected authority.'

A sort of office is set up in which the father, overjoyed at having at last found something to do again, takes over the leading role. An efficient clerk looks after the clerical side. Friends and relations put some cases in the way of the young lawyer; about thirty suits are listed, in many cases on behalf of Frankfurt Jews. The first case concerns the defence of a son against charges by his father. The opposing counsel is his boyhood friend Max Moors, who had once wanted to box with him and had called him a coward for refusing; now the roles are reversed. With ferocity, irony and sarcasm, Goethe makes an onslaught on his opponent, and is rebuked by the Court. But he very soon loses his taste for the law, and passes the files to his father, and then to others as well. Thus ends Goethe's career as a lawyer.

In his attic room, next to that of his father's insane ward, who from time to time does some clerical work for the advocate's office downstairs, Goethe has opened another office of his own. The father, however, also takes an active interest in his son's new activities; it is touching to see the ageing man assume a new lease of life. Without so much as a hint about the business of earning his living, he sorts out the manuscripts his son has brought from Strasbourg and has them stitched together and filed, all with the same care that he bestows on the legal documents. Wolfgang's drawings, too, are mounted and ruled round with finely drawn lines. As a cultivated side-interest befitting an elegant young man is how all this will have appeared to the father at first. But why should one not have the things published? Goethe hesitates. He is dissatisfied, both with himself and with the city of Frankfurt which is a nest 'fit for hatching birds but otherwise, figuratively speaking, a pot-house, a wretched hole. Heaven preserve me from this misery. Amen.' The figure of Herder still looms over him. 'My whole being is shattered', he writes in answer to one of the master's biting, sarcastic letters; or again almost imploringly, 'Herder, Herder, remain for me what you are.... If I am destined to be your planet I will be so, willingly, loyally. A friendly moon to its earth....' Herder continues with his reproaches, speaks of Goethe's 'sparrow-like' nature, calls him a woodpecker, who merely pecks at everything. 'A woodpecker is not a vulgar bird', writes Goethe in his defence. He has still not been released from Herder's stern tutorship.

His Strasbourg schemes are in a tangle of disorder: plays, a speech in honour of Shakespeare's birthday, his essay on the Minster, translations from Ossian, poems, a drama on Socrates, a Caesar, a Prometheus, perhaps even preliminary sketches for *Faust*, writings about the ancients, writings in their style and in the old German style. He chances on an old book, a life of Götz von Berlichingen of the iron hand: *Lebensbeschreibung Herrn Götz von Berlichingen, zugenannt mit der eisernen Hand*, published forty years previously in Nuremberg.

The real Götz of the sixteenth century is rather a sorry figure, a robber knight or, at best, a man fighting in a feud for his own, or some other feudal lord's, 'rights'. He lives in the darkest days of the degenerate small nobility, scarcely better than the honest robber, Johann Hübner, in Jung's memoirs: 'Hehlo! A rider and a horse!' – and then they slaughter the rider and take the horse. In like manner Götz waylays the merchants, the *Pfeffersäcke*, who have grown rich through the spice trade, while the honest knights have become impoverished and have sunk almost to the level of peasants: 'Hehlo! A wagon and riders!' Then they hurl the riders to the ground and make off with the wagon. Götz is outlawed, twice, but the law no longer has much force; the Empire itself is half ruined by the constant feuds between the innumerable petty princes, both temporal and spiritual. The Emperor is powerless and squanders his resources in extravagant schemes for world conquest, in Hungary, in Italy, in Scandinavia. Everybody fights everybody else, archbishops, dukes, counts, mostly in small skirmishes; even a sturdy man with a few trusty servants is a force to be reckoned with, and is welcome everywhere. In one of these skirmishes Götz has his right hand shot away; fire-arms, the powder invented by the devil and a monk, now begin to play their role and throw the knights in armour from their saddles. But Götz lives to stand again, the last of the knights, a name given also to his Emperor, Max. He has an iron hand forged, to his own design, by a smith and fixed to the stump; he lifts it high in the air or else strikes some obstinate fellow across the mouth with it. He becomes a legend, as the knight with the iron hand, and it is thus that Goethe sees him: a sturdy figure, a 'true German' of the right stamp, with simple features, as though carved out of wood, and a block of a head as hard as iron. The word *'einfältig'* – simple-minded as well as simple – has for Goethe at this period a noble sound, it means to him primal, primordial, just as the word *dumpf* – inarticulate – conveys to him feeling and instinct, something stronger than reflection, intention, discretion. He delves into this story at random, which tells only of random deeds; but in its telling it is not without a certain skill, and it has the deep ring of sincerity of a man who feels aggrieved and injured in his age-old hereditary 'rights'. Ostensibly Götz even fights in a good cause, such as the Empire or the Emperor. Seen over a distance of two hundred and fifty years the story is colourful and robust, as is the language of the man, who abuses his opponents in the German of Luther. In one of his letters of defiance he calls a certain count a wine-bibber, a liar, a scoundrel, a braggart, and a coward to boot, who crawls under his bed-clothes and feigns illness when he fears that Götz may seek him out. The defiant obstinacy of the man fascinates Goethe, who is himself in a very defiant mood and up in arms. The background is an age in ferment: the monks running out of the monasteries, the blazing signals of the peasants' revolt. The rebellious peasants of Odenwald elect the impoverished knight as their leader. Götz stays with them so long as the rising has prospects of success, and then, when things go wrong, slyly maintains he was only there under duress. His fellow knights pass sentence of honourable detention on their peer, while the dishonourable peasants are bloodily beaten back into their former serfdom, which is theirs by divine decree.

This whole colourful world Goethe now re-creates, in his own bright colours, from the remains of it that surround him: the ancient splendour of the coronations, the crooked streets, with their gabled houses dating from Maximilian's day, the anxiety about the maintenance of the Holy Roman Empire. 'How does it still hold together?' we read in *Faust*. Its colour and picturesqueness, its vigour, its robustness, its many-sidedness excite Goethe. He has learned from Shakespeare, or so he imagines, that nothing is to be gained from formal classification and design, let alone from the categories of Aristotle and the French. Scenes can be changed at will, and may consist merely of a few lines. 'Historical truth' is unimportant, more especially as no one can say in this case what the truth is. There is no need to concern himself with the fact that the real Götz, as an old man and in his own castle, sat down peacefully to write his own vindication with his good left hand. Goethe transforms him into a hero who dies young and gloriously, his iron fist held aloft and pointing prophetically to the future: Freedom! Freedom! – Noble, noble man!, murmur his faithful followers, Woe to the century that rejected you! Woe to posterity if it fails to understand you!

The whole thing is written down in one burst, in the space of a few weeks. He reads it to his sister. It is a chronicle in dialogue form. The 'epic theatre' has not yet come into existence, but Goethe quite logically calls his play *Geschichte Gottfriedens von Berlichingen mit der eisernen Hand, dramatisiert* (The Story of Gottfried von Berlichingen with the iron hand, dramatized.)

Personal experiences of his own are incorporated and a love story invented with a fatally lovely woman of a type Goethe himself always sedulously avoided. There is a vehmic court with masked judges, poison and murder, a gypsies' chorus such as we so often find later in opera, domestic scenes, and children who prattle like the little harpist, who has already been quietly dispatched from the Goethe household. It would be easy to enumerate the many faults in the work. It is rather long, though it is still only a first draft, there is nothing final about it. As a result of criticism, especially that of Herder's, Goethe very soon rewrites it. Later in life he alters it again in an attempt to produce a version for the stage, as he understands it. In the theatre itself there have been countless versions.

An important point, demonstrated even in this first of his great writings, is that he never really regards a work as finished. He always prefers to think of his things as 'coming into existence' rather than as 'existing'; he always has the feeling that he has unlimited time at his disposal, that one day, at an opportune moment, he will be able to take the work up again. 'You speak as though you think we shall both live to be three hundred', his friend Lavater once said to him. And, in spite of all his depressions, this is the feeling that runs through his life. In writing his *Götz* the idea of living to be a hundred does not enter his head, but he sees a long vista opening out in front of him.

There is another point: from the very outset he pays no heed to the theatre, to the public, or to the problems of aesthetics. He creates his own stage. This has always weakened the effectiveness of his theatrical works, but at the same time it is what gives them the unmistakable Goethe stamp. And in his *Götz* there is so much life, strength and plasticity that the play has never been off the stage. Nor has Goethe been sparing of the most striking effects, the 'great and small lights of heaven' he speaks of in *Faust*: night scenes in the forest, singing, battle scenes, sinister revenge, intimate family scenes – he runs through the whole gamut. He may have had no 'grasp of the stage' but even at the age of 24 he has an infallible instinct for what is right.

His instinct for the mood of the day is equally sure; *Götz* is an immediate success. This was by no means always so with him, and some of his greatest works had long to wait before they found their public. But at the decisive moments of his life he was able to grasp the mood of the day with unerring certainty and power. This was no accident, any more than was the fact that he always met the right people at the right moment, the right people to further his interests, such as teachers, assistants, collaborators, the right 'loves'; it was all an essential part of his genius. He knew how to select and how to reject, the two criteria of a great artist. It is idle to regret the loss of his possible 'Caesar' or his 'Mahomet'; his choice fell on *Götz*, and he was right.

It was an age which liked to see the 'rescue' of great misunderstood figures of the past, or even of whole epochs. Lessing had started his career with a whole series of literary salvage operations. Everywhere, in England and in France as well, the Middle Ages were being discovered, seen in a new light. Even superstition, feuds, *Faustrecht* – club-law – long held in

101

derision as signs of the Dark Ages, found their defenders in the reaction to the cold clarity of enlightenment. Even *Faustrecht*? Indeed, yes. A highly respectable man named Justus Möser, a syndic of the diocese of Osnabrück, had just published an essay on the subject. 'The cowardly historians', he wrote, 'behind their monastery walls, and the easy-going scholars and sleepy dullards can despise and decry (those times) as much as they like, but every good judge must admire the *Faustrecht* of the twelth and thirteenth centuries as a work of the highest art, and our nation should study this period fairly.' This in itself was an invitation to write a *Götz*; the difference of a few centuries did not matter, the Middle Ages, anyhow, were seen as a single period of some thousand years. Möser continues: 'We should become acquainted with the genius and the spirit that worked, not in stone and marble, but in human beings, and ennobled man's feelings and powers in a manner that we to-day can hardly conceive.' And yet the man was no romantic, but a practical and considerable politician in his own limited sphere. He adds: 'The isolated robberies that occurred from time to time are as nothing in comparison with the devastations caused by our wars of to-day....'

The manuscript of *Götz* is complete. Copies are made and sent to his friends. Herder is critical and out of humour; he feels that Shakespeare has corrupted his pupil, though fundamentally this is a criticism of Herder's own concept of Shakespeare, which he had impressed on the receptive young Goethe. The latter, still unsure of himself in the presence of his 'sun', immediately starts to re-write the play. At the same time he feels hurt; he dislikes being called a sparrow and a woodpecker. Always very quick to drop people when they have fulfilled their role in his life, he now replaces the stimulus and patronage of Herder by that of another mentor, the Darmstadt writer Johann Heinrich Merck. He, too, has a sharp tongue. He, too, can contradict ruthlessly and, like Herder, is also unable to resist cutting or witty remarks, however damaging they may be. He has often been portrayed as a sort of Mephistopheles and even as his prototype. This is misleading; Mephistopheles is Goethe himself, or rather one side of him. Goethe, in his old age, remembered Merck as a tall, lean, sharp-nosed man with penetrating grey eyes; there was something 'tigerish' about him, he said. In his Memoirs Goethe is a little unkind to this friend and mentor of his youth, as he is to everyone who has failed to make a success of his life. Merck's life was a failure. He advanced no higher than the ill-paid position of paymaster to the forces, a post he filled inadequately enough. He also wrote essays and poetry, and acted as an agent for princes and princesses, purchasing engravings and small paintings for them. He corresponded with Goethe, Wieland and Herder, collected objects of natural history, and speculated extremely unsuccessfully in all sorts of business enterprises. Finally, ill, in debt and in despair, he shot himself. It is probable that Goethe burned the best and most valuable of his letters. He said that, while they were 'uncommonly bold, blunt and Swiftian in their venom', and remarkable for the originality of their viewpoints, 'they were, at the same time, written with such power to offend that I would not care to publish them at the present time, but must either destroy them or preserve them for posterity as striking documents of the secret schisms in our literature.' Unfortunately he destroyed them.

Enough has survived, however, to give us a fairly clear picture of Merck. He is the *raisonneur* of the old plays, and his *raisonnement* is usually more to the point than the sentimental tirades of the chief actors. In an age of inveterate sentimentality he is the one to say, 'Bah!' at the first sign of effusiveness. At the same time he shows the most acute perception of real worth, in both men and art. He is no sovereign *manqué* like Herder. He knows his is not really a creative talent. He is the helper, the collaborator, the promoter, prepared if necessary to use obstetric forceps; he is the born obstetrician in the Socratic sense. Literature often owes more to such men than to the disseminators of Sibylline oracles. They are rarely given their due, and even Goethe rewarded his old friend with but barren gratitude. In later life he regarded Merck merely as a rather tiresome purveyor of news, as his Darmstadt correspondent, who supplied the ducal family and their friends at Weimar with a mass of gossip and piquant stories, *pudenda and scandalosa*, to assuage their prevailing boredom. 'More of the splendid *pudenda*', urged the 'Musenhof'.

Merck and Darmstadt: the first station on the road to Goethe's fame. A little court, a little town, built round the turreted red sandstone castle of the 'great Landgravine' Karoline, a little cultural centre in a Germany that possessed neither a political nor a spiritual capital; the tradition still exists, in Darmstadt as elsewhere. The country was poor, the court indigent. The five princesses went about in *Zitz* – little cotton dresses; one of them, Luise, later to become the Duchess of Weimar, accompanied the course of Goethe's life into his extreme old age. The Landgravine acts as regent, the Landgrave being an 'absentee landlord', who preferred to live in the small town of Pirmasens, in the distant Palatinate, which, in those days of incredibly scattered possessions, somehow managed to belong to Hesse-Darmstadt. There he maintained one of the strangest households of an era which condoned many strange things in its princes. He composed military marches with two fingers on his spinet, sometimes writing as many as three hundred in one day, as Merck relates, and reaching a grand total of 52,365 in all; he kept a strict account. His passion, apart from ghosts, was playing soldiers. The national income, transferred to him in Pirmasens by his councillors, was largely devoted to this, and as he could not afford sufficient real soldiers he surrounded himself in ghostly fashion with a vast collection of paintings of the uniforms of all nations. By the absent Landgravine, whom he visited from time to time, he had five daughters and three sons. For his amusement in Pirmasens he imported a series of mistresses from France, and these swallowed up the rest of the national revenue. When they had to be fitted out he sent them to Darmstadt. One of them, waking up early one morning and absentmindedly reverting to her former occupation, put a basket of laundry on her head and took it out to the bleaching lawn.

'The food at the Darmstadt Court is bad', one visitor, the future Prince Hardenberg, wrote, 'and everything looks very shabby. The officers are turned out in a very slovenly manner in boots, etc. There are no gentlemen-in-waiting; all the duties are performed by officers, some of whom look like old corporals.' But, as in Weimar, this very indigence had its advantages. Darmstadt could not maintain an opera like Dresden, Berlin, Vienna or Mannheim; when there was a lack of musicians the Landgravine's children played in the orchestra. There was no large theatre; instead the Landgravine corresponded with Voltaire, Helvétius, Grimm and the Francophile Frederick the Great. This last expressed his respect and esteem for her, she was probably the only woman to be thus honoured, and gave her a funeral urn on which her manly soul was praised. It is known that otherwise, and with world-wide political repercussions, he spoke only of the 'whores' who ruled Europe, including among these Maria Theresa.

It was in this town and at this Court that 'Kriegsrat' Merck worked as general factotum. He came from an old established apothecaries' family which later – though, alas, too late for the permanently impecunious Johann Heinrich – was to found the world-famous chemical firm of Merck. In the life of a small town the apothecary was a person of importance. He was a centre for local and outside news, adviser and confidant in many, and often delicate, situations; people used to meet at the apothecary's for a glass of home-made wine and a chat. Like an alchemist he made his experiments, often in new and untried methods, and was receptive to new ideas; in most cases he was in opposition to the physicians, who were very conscious of their standing. Something of the apothecary always remained in Merck.

He had also, as his countryman Kasimir Edschmid says of him, the 'double sight' of many distinguished Darmstadt people; he could see 'close to as an interested party, and from a distance as a disinterested one'. With one of these sides of his nature, and deeply involved, he writes to his wife: 'I am beginning to fall seriously in love with Goethe. He is a man close to my heart, such as I have seldom found.' With the other, which was more speculative, he tried to win over his new acquaintance, as a member of Herder's circle, for a literary enterprise. A certain Hofrat Deinet, who had been Master of the Pages at the Darmstadt Court, had relinquished this badly paid position to marry a well-to-do Frankfurt widow, owner of a printing firm. Deinet was an active man, with vision. He sensed something in the wind, a new generation knocking at the door. He wanted to turn the Frankfurt *Gelehrte Anzeigen*, an old-established and dull paper which he had bought, into an organ for the new writers. Herder, already an established name, was enrolled and Merck was to be the editor. The idea was to criticize, thoroughly and without mercy, everything – the whole of European literature. The paper was to be a counterpoise to Leipzig, which was considered hopelessly out of date and professorial, and to Berlin, where Nicolai was editor of the *Allgemeine deutsche Bibliothek*, with Lessing, to begin with, as his collaborator; but this periodical had already lost the charm of novelty. Literary fashion changed then as quickly as it does to-day. 'A group of men, free from all attachments as authors, and with no private ends to serve, who hitherto have watched the literary situation as observers', is how Merck introduced his contributors in the announcement. His contributors, of course, were all good friends and really formed a clique, as is always the case when new periodicals are launched.

In Darmstadt the project was discussed in more detail. Immediately there was great enthusiasm. Darmstadt was a hot-house of the most passionate feelings, a nursery in which friendships, love affairs, intimate confessions, luxuriated. Karoline, the great Landgravine, herself provided the framework for this with her imaginative gardens. In the *Herrengarten* she erected little Greek temples, a hermit's cottage disguised with bark, and near it, connected by an underground passage, the family vault; in the vault was a couch, lit by a tiny window to enable her to read there quietly, and next the couch her future grave, dug by her own hands. The younger people wandered further afield and consecrated rocks and trees with their names, names such as Psyche, Lila, Urania. They walked arm in arm, embraced, kissed – often only by letter – tears flowed and bosoms quivered with emotion. The girls, all from the Court or higher circles of society, were tightly laced, and to this fact were due the frequent, and often welcome, fainting fits.

From the letters and confessions of the time, let alone from the novels, it is not easy to tell how much is fact and how much romantic fiction. All these girls and young men had their very real worries; the girls wanted to, and indeed had to, find husbands – it was very difficult to place even the five princesses – and the young men had to find positions, which, in view of the prevailing poverty, was just as difficult. But it would be wrong to regard the effusive sentiment merely as a mask; there was much genuine feeling, and even sentiment culled from a novel can break out into real tears and real despair.

It is into this circle that Goethe now enters, the least burdened of them all. He has no desire to snatch a job or tie himself to any girl. 'And I, I shall remain Goethe', he had written to Kätchen Schönkopf. So he plays around and flirts a little with them all, and all are enchanted by him. He recites his latest poetry and reads Sterne's *Tristram Shandy* to them.

Petty jealousies play a big role among the men too. They rush into each other's arms even if they have only just heard of one another and are meeting for the first time; 'Is't you, brother? – T'is!' The panting, abbreviated style, intended to express superabundance of emotion, is the fashion.

The men weep on each other's shoulders, and take offence at once if they fancy they detect any coldness. They complain endlessly about the absence of letters, which flutter back and forth ceaselessly. In a letter to Merck even the seignorial Herder groans: 'To all my letters, requests, implorings, no one answers!'; or more forcefully still, when he suspects a weakening in their bond of friendship: 'This slackening of the fibres is to me the most woeful evidence that all is vanity and that there is no purpose in our existence here, because the noblest bond between men, friendship, is filled with dung and rotting, decaying, human flesh.' Herder, too, came from a strictly pietistic family, as his metaphors reveal.

Klopstock is the idol of the 'Community of Saints', as they call themselves. In Darmstadt there is a small group of his adorers; his odes are passed from hand to hand. It is a great distinction to possess a manuscript copy because, apart from isolated ones in almanacks, the odes have not been published. The Landgravine arranges for a private edition of thirty-four copies, and again it is a high honour to belong to this exclusive circle; even Herder has to ask to be admitted, which piques him somewhat. God, his maiden and his fatherland is the trinity proclaimed by Klopstock. There are great, sweeping flights of imagination in Klopstock, and these are considered 'Pindaric' – once more a 'creative error'. Pindar is now set by the side of Homer. Nothing is known of the severely formal poetry of the Greek poet, of the construction of his verse in triads of strophe, antistrophe and epode. 'Pindaric' means unfettered, free-flowing, with streaming tresses as it were, whereas in Pindar one has to imagine, not these at all, but the compact and far from streaming, locks of archaic sculpture. But above all it is sentiment that they see in these 'Pindaric' odes, something for which the Greek poet had not even a verbal equivalent.   Goethe now writes Goethe odes, invoking Pindar in his *Wanderer's Sturmlied*. Anacreon, the poet of rose garlands and flowers, and the 'mellifluous' Theocritus are discarded. In their stead we hear the 'whip cracks of young men drunk with victory'; from the mountains they come, the rattling wheels of their chariot raising an avalanche of stones in the valley below, 'thy soul glowing, Pindar – danger, courage!' Here truly is a new sound, announcing itself with the crack of a whip. It is not only Pindar who is invoked; Goethe's own genius, too, encircled by the muses, soars until, like a god, it bestrides the waters and the land. The age of genius is announced, and Goethe is its prophet.

He walks and wanders much at this time, but not like the 'saints' of Darmstadt, whose only words are 'wandering' and 'pilgrimage'. He makes his way from Frankfurt to Darmstadt on foot, through the woods and through snow storms. Forgotten are the chamois under-stockings, his protection against the 'infernal Rhine gnats'. With the wind in his face he sings; 'half nonsense', as he describes it in his old age. He murmurs dark gypsy sayings, with imprecations that sound like the howling of wolves and end in the hooting of owls: *'Wille wau wau wau ... wito hu!'* He kneads words and images together, and they yield to him as they scarcely ever do again in the hands of his followers, who pile words on words and babble in mere sounds. He is in excellent health, still slim, his face rather hard and stubborn, with its strong, sharp nose between the large dark-brown eyes. Thus he reaches Darmstadt, sits down on the stone bench outside Merck's house, and grants an 'audience befitting a genius' to the assembled young ladies, as they later told.

Two things stand in immediate juxtaposition: the wild sweep of his wanderings, and the Darmstadt sentimentality, with its little Greek temples and little bark cottages. And these latter are the stage properties that find their way, often strangely, into the streaming flow of his 'half-nonsense' poems. Again and again we meet with the 'little cottage', where he takes shelter in the storm; we meet a young woman, nursing her baby in her arms, to whom he dreams of coming home in the evening, to the 'little cottage', golden in the dying rays of the sun: 'May such a woman greet me too, and in her arms her boy!' In another poem Psyche – Karoline – is hailed by the 'errant wanderer', in others Lila and Urania, all in verses which far transcend these ladies of the court and fiancées of court preachers, and which really have nothing to do with them, even though the poems speak of eternal flames, loving arms, the ecstasy of a kiss, or Elysium,! Ah! 'Why but Elysium!'

As a young eagle amongst doves is how the poet sees himself; the wounded eagle lies in a thicket; a pair of doves pass by, look at him complacently and try to console him by pointing out the blessings of silvery springs, moss and quiet happiness – 'Oh Wisdom! Thy voice is like a dove!' His only cure is the *'allgegenwärtger Balsam Allheilender Natur'* (the ever-present balm of All-healing Nature).

Nature! This is the magic word, and Goethe is not the first to utter it. It is the watchword of the day, announced by Rousseau and passed on by every sentimentalist, and by many serious teachers as well. The term embraces all manner of things: natural man, noble and upright; the natural state of mankind, the golden age, without war or hunger; nature as seen in the landscape, the English park with its willows and shrubs, uncut and unspoilt, though with well laid-out paths, and little huts in which to rest from one's excesses in nature worship. The most usual expression is the 'bosom' of nature – rounded, feminine and pleasant. Nature is also thought of as a book in which one has only to read – Goethe uses this simile often. The pious see 'God's handwriting' in nature, clearly written in rock and mountainside. The impious fancy they can read the writing without God's help. Thus Goethe writes to Merck:

> *Sieh, so ist Natur ein Buch lebendig,*
> *Unverstanden, doch nicht unverständlich ...*

(Observe, how nature is a living book, Unfathomed although not unfathomable.)

And the following day: 'I feel I know thee, Nature, now – And thus I have to grasp thee!' It is not so much with his hands that he grasps as with his eyes. Sight is Goethe's dominant sense.

His feeling for nature and his faith in nature are to pass through the most varied stages; they are also to lead him to natural science. At this period, however, they constitute a vague defiance, an escape from the narrow confines of the attic room in Frankfurt, that 'wretched hole'. Often, too, he sees nature, not in images of his own creating, but in the recollection of paintings he has seen in various galleries. With Merck he visits Madame de la Roche at her home on the Rhine, a lovely house with a view over the river: 'The rooms were lofty and spacious and the walls like those of a gallery, hung tight with paintings. Each window, with its view in all directions, formed the frame to a natural picture that stood out very vividly in the glow of a gentle sun.' This was written from memory, but this practice of seeing nature 'framed', of hunting out pictorial motifs, was for long a favourite with Goethe. In Italy, looking at a waterfall in the mountains, he sees an 'authentic Everdingen'; during the campaign in Champagne, in the midst of a battle, he sees a burning village as a Van der Meulen. It is nature seen, not 'through a temperament', as the impressionist painters expressed it, but through the temperament of an old master.

But on the way to Madame de la Roche he finds himself still in doubt whether to become a painter or a poet. So he appeals to an oracle. A willow bush by the river is a fine motif that attracts his painter's eye. He decides to throw his best pocket-knife into the river: if he sees it fall into the water he will be an artist, if the bush hides the knife he will give up painting. The oracle's answer is ambiguous, as always. He sees the splash, but the knife is hidden by the furthest branches of the willow. He remains a writer.

At Madame de la Roche's, whom Merck also wants to win over for his paper, Goethe immediately finds himself in the active world of literature. As a boy at school Wieland had admired her and had written verses to her; they have kept up this contact and now the master has just published her novel, *Die Geschichte des Fräuleins von Sternheim*, which, so its title page claimed, was 'based on original papers and other reliable sources'; in fact it was based on the then fashionable Richardson. Herder, the merciless critic, considered the work a masterpiece, and ranked it above Richardson's *Clarissa*. Goethe reviewed the book in the newly formed periodical, also recommending it, and he took its epistolary form, including even the 'original papers', as a model for future novels of his own.

It is as a journalist that he begins his writing career. As a poet he is already a genius, but few people are aware of it. A young *attaché*, Jerusalem, very soon to reappear as the original of Werther, writes: 'He was in Leipzig during our time, and was a fop; now he also writes for a Frankfurt newspaper.'

Thus Goethe's first excursion into print is a very modest one. He is a member of the editorial staff of a small journal. The staff discuss the books, with mingled laughter and sarcasm, and throw the ball back and forth between each other; it would be hopeless to try and attribute the unsigned contributions to individuals. Goethe himself, when he was old, made the most sweeping claims about what he had written, and in so doing made many mistakes; the fact that a number of articles look like 'Goethe' does not necessarily mean that he wrote them. The contributions, for the most part, were team work. The whole thing lasted only a year; the publisher then took fright and appointed another editor.

The tone of the paper was militant. From the outset the intention was to shock. Merck was the *spiritus rector*. Herder was regarded as the intellectual suzerain. Whole piles of trashy English novels were summarily disposed of: 'very modest and demure, but insipid' – one line; 'malicious convent stories' – one line; *'The Brother*, by a lady': 'Let us hope this brother remains his father's only son, for the work is beneath criticism' – one line.

Much of it is amusing enough and the editorial staff must have had their fun out of it. Much of it is childish, such as a eulogy of Oeser: 'We can only stammer an indication', because there are no words to express all the emotions aroused by this 'most deeply felt work of art'. The watchword is rebellion. The *Sturm und Drang*, as this whole epoch has been christened, is in full spate.

Goethe, who thus began as a critic, never had much patience in reviewing the writings of others. He read carelessly and, as he once said later, felt he knew the contents of a book from its title-page. His interest was only awakened when some theme, phrase or word touched a subject that was near his heart at the time; then what he wrote usually went far beyond the chance cause that had aroused his interest. In the Frankfurt paper he reviewed a small volume of poems by a Polish Jew in this way; it is his only really Goethean review. He makes fun of the young man who has turned from business to belles-lettres, hums other people's tunes, and complains bitterly that the girls are so 'prim' that he is only allowed deferentially to nibble at their gloves, instead of taking them by the head and giving them a 'good round kiss'. Then he parts company with the Jewish boy and launches out into an invocation to the genius of the Fatherland:

'Let a young man arise, full of youthful strength and feeling, boldly to voice for us all his follies, joys and victories! Let him, O genius of our Fatherland, find the maid who is worthy of him, full of sweetness and homely gifts, her mother's right hand, virtuous, young and warm. Let them find each other, these two! At the first encounter they will sense dimly yet powerfully what a wealth of happiness each is to find in the other. There will be truth in his singing and living beauty, not the coloured soap bubbles that pass for ideals and float about in hundreds of German songs! But does such a maid exist?'

He sets out to find her – and succeeds.

# 11

# *Lotte in Wetzlar*

Goethe's father makes one more attempt, his last, to determine his son's career. He has observed Wolfgang's new friends amiably enough and has extended hospitality to them. One of these, Schlosser, a colleague on the editorial staff of the Frankfurt paper, is a prosperous advocate, in addition to his literary activities, and has assigned a number of cases to the Goethe office; he is courting the daughter, Cornelia, whom he subsequently marries, a step that brings happiness to neither of them. But writing unpaid literary reviews and making sentimental trips to Darmstadt form a poor basis for a sound and settled existence, and, in view of Wolfgang's inadequate legal training, the law practice does not hold out any permanent prospects either. So the father decides to send his son to Wetzlar, to the *Reichskammergericht*, the Supreme Court of Appeal of the Holy Roman Empire. There are family connections in Wetzlar. Grandfather Textor once worked there and, indeed, left his wig there when he had to beat a hasty retreat from some amorous visit. The grandson also is to leave his wig there, finally and for ever, in making his escape from a love affair.

Goethe welcomes any opportunity to get away from Frankfurt. He enrols, in May 1772, in the list of young attorneys in Wetzlar, in the only document we possess relating to his legal activities, and looks around him. The town is a warren of crooked houses and narrow streets, littered with great piles of dung; its inhabitants are mostly smallholders. It is all up and down hill, and steep; the roofs are steep, and gabled. Wetzlar boasts the title of a free Imperial City, its coat of arms bears the Imperial eagle on its breast; but at this period anything connected with the word 'Imperial' has a somewhat hollow ring about it. The *Reichskammergericht* is the pride of Wetzlar, and for many their main source of income. Accommodation is difficult to find, and Goethe has to be content with a room in a dark, closed-in house in a narrow side street.

In his zeal for reform the Emperor Joseph II has decided to reform this highest court of appeal, as well as other institutions of his tottering empire. Conditions at the court are a public scandal. Sixteen thousand two hundred and thirty-three cases await hearing, most of them deliberately shelved; they were still unheard when the court and the Empire expired together in 1803.

But at this moment there is a great influx of people; the court is to be inspected and revised. Bribery of the judges, who are badly paid and live mostly off perquisites, is common practice. Among the law suits Goethe entrusted to his father's care was one of these cases of bribery, and not a very pleasant one. Twenty-four deputations from the various German states have been dispatched to bring order out of chaos; but they only increase the disorder and confusion. They each have different viewpoints, especially on questions of rank and status, which in Wetzlar, following long tradition, have always been the main preoccupation of all concerned.

A local Wetzlar preacher-poet, a Jesuit and a man of the stamp of Father Abraham a Santa-Clara in Vienna, has left a very vivid description of conditions as they were in the days of Goethe's grandfather, and times had not changed. Here is a conversation between two lawyers:

> Herr Collega, how is my lawsuit going? The grass must be growing over it. – That may well be because it is already over one hundred and fifty years since the suit was filed, good things take time ... *Justitia*, poor thing, is so gouty that she limps and hobbles unless she is shod with silver shoes. – Sir, you are speaking double dutch. – I am speaking of things as they are, of your duplicating, triplicating, quadruplicating, *ad infinitum* ... to such an extent that the client is sometimes legally ruined, sometimes he dies or rots in the process.

Councillors are concerned only with questions of precedence and ceremony; one says to another: 'One step back, Sir, do not step in front of me, your place is a few inches behind me. ... – Very well then, as we cannot agree, my commission is herewith terminated.' ... Such disputes over questions of precedence form the background of Wetzlar society at the time of Goethe's *Werther*.

The valiant days of the ancient Emperors and heroes are revived for Goethe by his company at the inn *Zum Kronprinzen*. It is where the young assessors meet. They none of them take their work very seriously. They squander their allowances or they borrow; they write poetry or do other literary work, carry on flirtations, and form a 'Band of Knights', with old German names and solemn regulations. Goethe, who has shown them his play, is called 'Götz the upright'; others have names taken from French dramas of the age of chivalry, St Amand the Stubborn or Lubomirski the Valiant. Among the members are a few officers from the small town garrison. They have a Grand Master and a Chancellor, they hold ceremonies for the conferment of knighthoods, and partake of knightly picnics in the surrounding countryside. The cock of the walk is a secretary from one of the legations named von Goué, a 'genius' – a word used very freely – a droll and a mystagogue; later he founds another circle, an 'Order of Transition', and later still a number of masonic lodges. He is soon dismissed from his secretary's post, for neglecting his duties, and finally, after many vicissitudes, ends his life wretchedly as a gentleman-in-waiting and court fool to some Lilliputian count.

Goué's Order of Transition, in which there were four degrees, the final one bearing the mystic name of Transition of Transition to Transition of Transition, sounds like a symbolic prelude to the next stages of Goethe's development, the knights' masquerade like a postlude to *Götz*. Goethe very soon gets tired of playing at knights, but draws closer to one of the members, Gotter, almost a namesake, and likewise secretary to one of the legations. He is a man of refined and sensitive nature, with a taste for French literature, and he has close connections with Göttingen, where another Klopstock circle has been formed. This group of young people want to go back beyond the age of chivalry to the very earliest times, to the Bardic age. They too have a secret society, the *Hügel und Hain* – the hill and the coppice – soon to be known as the *Göttinger Hain*. They meet by moonlight, their heads garlanded with oak sprays, and solemnly process round an old oak tree. They inscribe their poetry in a black leather volume. They have also found a publisher in Göttingen who produces a *Musenalmanach* on the model of the Paris *Almanach des Muses*. Gotter is one of the editors and prints in it Goethe's 'Pindaric' odes. All over Germany are now to be heard the first chirpings of almanachs, anthologies, keepsakes, all attacking and pirating each other, but offering to young poets their best chance of publication. For decades Goethe's poetry is known to the world at large mainly through almanachs.

This we may call the first transition. The second leads out into the countryside. The ugliness of Wetzlar is matched by the beauty of its surroundings. And it is the month of May. Goethe was always very dependent on the seasons of the year and even on barometric changes which, later on, he carefully recorded. But now, in Wetzlar, he roams carefree around. 'Every tree, every hedgerow, is a bunch of blossoms; one would like to be a cock-chafer and hover in the sea of fragrance.' In the nearby village of Garbenheim he sits down under a lime tree outside the inn, drinks some milk and plays with the children. A flock of children brings us to the third stage in his transition, the house of the bailiff, Amtmann Buff; and his daughter, Lotte, leads to the fourth, to *Werther*.

Goethe has some distant relations in Wetzlar on his grandfather's side; he has also brought with him some letters of introduction but has made little use of them. Through one of these channels, however, he finds his way into the *Deutsches Haus*, a complex of buildings belonging to the Order of Teutonic Knights, the great Order that had played an historic role in the crusades, and later in East Prussia. It was now not much more than an aristocratic society, though it still owned very extensive and widespread possessions. Amtmann Buff was responsible for the administration of the Order's properties in the Wetzlar area. He was in his sixties; his wife was dead and his daughter, Lotte, kept house for him. She looked after her younger brothers and sisters, there were twelve of them in all; she herself later had a round dozen children by her marriage to Councillor Kestner of Hannover, at this time her fiancé, and holding a diplomatic post in Wetzlar.

Lotte is a pretty, healthy girl, a 'desirable creature', as Goethe calls her, one of those 'who, even if they do not arouse violent passions, are intended to create a good general impression'. Above all, she is already pledged, and this is an important safeguard for the young Goethe, as indeed it is for the older Goethe as well. He feels relaxed in her company. And how she mothers that army of children! She cuts their bread and butter for them, and Lotte cutting bread for the children is to become the most famous figure in the most famous novel of the day, celebrated in engravings, and dearer far to sentimental readers than Werther's questionable end, with its pistols and suicide. In these engravings, however, she looks more like a worthy young matron, her curls piled high and topped with a rose, wearing a full skirt with many flounces and little bows; her small brothers are in children's tail coats, the tails reaching to their knees, with carefully plaited pig-tails, and even the tiny ones are dressed in long garments like the grown-ups, with feather headdresses or little crimped caps. Lotte's costume is not the 'simple white dress with pale pink bows' described by Goethe. She is, in fact, not the Lotte of *Werther* at all, who is drawn from quite different sources, but she is just what Goethe needs at this moment.

And now begins the friendship and love that is to be idealized through the novel and made the object of a Lotte cult, in which even the protagonists participate, and that at a very early stage. Fiction and reality, *Dichtung und Wahrheit*, are inextricably intertwined. We shall make no attempt to reduce these to their elements, let alone construct an *Ur-Erlebnis* as the original motivating experience. It is Springtime – let that suffice. Goethe finds himself in a pleasantly domesticated family circle, an important preliminary to love for a man without a home, a self-styled exile. He befriends Lotte's fiancé sincerely; Kestner is a very solid, hard-working man, one of the few diplomats in Wetzlar who really works and does not waste his time on trivial things or wrangle over questions of precedence. To Goethe, Kestner means security; at the same time his ceaseless activity provides Goethe with ample opportunities for walks and flirtations with Lotte. It was at a dance that they first met. Later Kestner proudly recorded: Goethe did not know Lotte was not free, 'Lottchen completely conquered him, the more so since she made no attempt to do so, but simply surrendered herself to the enjoyment'. The next day Goethe went to enquire after her and 'then for the first time got to know her from the side where her strength lay, from the domestic side'.

More important, because still quite unprejudiced, is Kestner's description of his new acquaintance in a letter to a friend:

In the spring a certain Goethe, by profession a Doctor of Law, twenty-three years old, only son of a very rich father, arrived here from Frankfurt, for the purpose of gaining legal experience – such was his father's intention; his own, however, was to study Homer, Pindar and others, and whatever else his genius, his way of thinking, and his heart chose to provide him with. From the outset the local prigs announced him *in publico* as a colleague, and as a contributor to the new Frankfurt intellectual paper, and as a philosopher as well, and went out of their way to associate with him.

Kestner meets him on a walk:

lying on his back in the grass under a tree, conversing with some bystanders, one of them an epicurean philosopher, one a stoic, and a third a cross between the two; he was very much at his ease. He has a great many talents, is a true genius, and a man of character; he has an exceptionally lively imagination and as a result generally expresses himself in terms of images and similes. He is vehement in all the emotions, yet he often shows great self-control. His way of thinking is noble; he acts without preconceived notions, as the mood takes him, without concerning himself whether other people like it, whether it is fashionable, or whether good manners permit it. All compulsion is hateful to him. He loves children and can become very absorbed in them. He is bizarre, and there are various aspects of his conduct, of his outward behaviour, that could render him disagreeable. But with children, women and many others his stock stands high. He has a great respect for the feminine sex. *In principiis* he is not yet sure of himself and is still searching for some definite system.

This is also a piece of self-characterization on Kestner's part, who, *in principiis*, already has both feet very firmly planted on the ground. He also adds that Goethe does not go to church or pray, that he is interested in Rousseau and is searching for truth, though he places a feeling for truth higher than he does its demonstration. 'He has already achieved much, and has great knowledge and has read widely, but has thought and reasoned out for himself still more. He has made belles-lettres and the arts his chief concern, or rather all branches of knowledge except the so-called workaday ones.' Kestner's letter is the first comprehensive testimony we have of the impression Goethe made on an intelligent and thoughtful observer; it is also the last to be completely unprejudiced, because all later ones, consciously or unconsciously, portray the famous author of *Werther* or *Faust*.

The summer is spent with Kestner and Lotte, or with Lotte alone, a 'truly German idyll for which the fertile land provided the prose and a pure affection the poetry'. We can also reverse this order. Goethe's feeling for nature as described in *Werther*, which is based on his Wetzlar experiences, is for us much more powerful and has a much greater immediacy of perception than the love story, which still wears its little bows and flounces. His love for children we can readily believe. Back in Frankfurt he still continues to request a 'complete weekly chronicle of all the seven boys' scratches, bumps and squabbles', which the eldest has to send. But he falls in love too, though not to the point of heartbreak; Goethe's heart is completely unbreakable. He toys with the idea of seeing just how inviolate is the attachment of this pretty, fair, homely girl for her honest Kestner, for whom a great passion is scarcely imaginable. Should not a young genius, to whom all compulsion is hateful, be entitled to certain claims? Do not other girls cast passionate glances at the handsome young man?

Merck visits him and finds his attentions engaged, rather too deeply so for his taste. What is the meaning of it? he asks, with his habit of going straight to the point with the younger man. What is wrong with Demoiselle so-and-so opposite? She is a striking creature, plump, voluptuous, with a 'Junoesque figure' – the highest praise in those days. She is unattached. Why do you not make advances to her, instead of sighing around forlornly for this nice girl who is already engaged?

But Goethe does not want a girl who is free and may try to tie him down. He derives a sense of inner well-being from his grief, his indecision. He is perfectly happy to love unhappily and to be spared the final consequences. This intermediate state alone is true freedom, and it is highly poetic.

Nevertheless, from time to time the situation becomes a little uncomfortable. He writes to Kestner: 'I shall expect you to-morrow, sometime after five, and to-day – you ought to know me well enough by now to guess – to-day I was in Altspach. To-morrow we go there together, and then I hope to get some pleasanter looks.' The co-actors in the drama of his life pull sour faces from time to time, as they did in Sesenheim. 'In the meantime I was there and must tell you that to-night in the moonlit valley Lotte deeply enjoyed herself, and is going to say good night to you.... To-morrow morning we shall drink coffee under the tree in Garbenheim where to-night I sat in the moonlight. Alone – yet not alone.'

Kestner is not the man for moonlight. He curtly tells Goethe not to fill his head with silly nonsense. 'He grew pale and very downcast', he notes in his diary. To his fiancée he also sends a warning: 'As a friend I must tell you that all is not gold that glitters, that words, which perhaps are taken from some book, or are spoken only because they have a fine sound about them, are not to be relied on.' He even gets a little angry: 'There is no art in being gay and entertaining when one is entirely one's own master, when one can do or leave undone exactly what one likes.'

Then comes autumn; the seasons play their role too. One September evening there is a long and very autumnal conversation about what happens after death, and about meeting again in the hereafter. Lotte speaks of her mother's death, and then reminds Goethe that it is time to go. The next morning Goethe has flown. He leaves a note for Kestner: 'He has gone, Kestner; by the time you get this note he will have gone. Give the enclosed note to Lotte. I was quite composed, but what you said rent me asunder. At the moment all I can say to you is "farewell". Had I remained with you a moment longer I could not have contained myself. Now I am alone, and to-morrow I go. Oh, my poor head.'

The note to Lotte refers to their last conversation about the hereafter: 'Ah, I was concerned with this world, with your hand, that I kissed for the last time....' He also once gave her a kiss on her lips, for the first and only time; Lotte confessed it immediately to her fiancé. Above all she was to give his greetings to the boys, to the children. Children he always liked to have round him, so long as there was no wife to go with them.

After the poetry the prose; Kestner notes down everything faithfully and prosaically in his diary. All these people write everything down all the time. The diary becomes a novel, the novel a diary or a collection of letters. Letters in any case are a form of publication; they are handed round, read aloud and copied out. Goethe vanished! Secretly and without a word! That is not right; especially when you are such close friends. Goethe's great aunt, *Geheimrätin* Lange, who introduced him to the Buffs and who lives just round the corner, sends her maid across: it was very ill-mannered of Goethe to go off like that without saying good-bye! Lotte gives the girl a message for her mistress: why did she not bring her nephew up better? The *Geheimrätin* replies that she will write to Goethe's mother about his behaviour. The Buff children groan in chorus: Dr Goethe has gone! Lotte reads the note in tears. Kestner writes in his diary: 'We spoke only of him; I too could do nothing but think of him.'

Kestner, the 'philistine', the hard-working office man, is no less affected than the principal actors in the play. Writing to a friend, everything has to be communicated at once to some sympathetic soul, he reflects on the young man: he might well be dangerous to a woman's heart; Lottchen, thank heaven, kept him on a tight rein; Goethe suffered under the treatment. Kestner suffers in sympathy, marvelling 'how love can transform even the strongest and most independent people into the strangest creatures. For the most part I felt sorry for him and was a prey to inner conflicts: on the one hand I thought I might not be able to make Lotte as happy as he could, while on the other I could not bear the thought of losing her. The latter got the upper hand'.

This is the cardinal point, if we really want to delve into this medley of feelings. Goethe takes to flight the moment he feels that Kestner might retire and leave the field to him – to what end? Marriage? Not that, above all not that. The image is what he wants to preserve.

This, in the form of Lotte's silhouette, he straightway hangs on the wall of his room, on his return to Frankfurt. The Lotte cult begins, the transition to the written novel, though this still requires time and further experience to mature.

And Lotte? She, too, is relieved that the young assessor has left, even though the manner of his going was unfortunate – people are talking about it. They probably also talked about their numerous walks together, the dances, picking beans in the garden, his playing with the children and sitting at their little foster mother's feet, fingering her bows and flounces. Who is this young Goethe anyway? she muses. A young lawyer; son of a wealthy father admittedly, but what else? He writes for Frankfurt papers and is said to be a genius, but all young men are geniuses to-day. Should one get oneself talked about for someone as unreliable as this? But as fiancée to a man held everywhere in such high esteem as Kestner, with a safe career?

She marries her Kestner, lives happily with him and bears him twelve children. Later she is to apply to her old friend, by then very famous and not least through herself and Wetzlar, for his friendly patronage for one of her sons, who wishes to settle as a doctor in Frankfurt, to which end he is required to marry the daughter of a Frankfurt family. She also makes one rather ill-fated visit to Weimar, which Thomas Mann has described with irony and a deeper significance in his *Lotte in Weimar*. It is to be the grief and pride of her life that she is indeed 'talked about' – in Wetzlar, in Frankfurt, throughout Germany and far beyond.

# 12

# *Genius in Exuberance*

The Wetzlar summer lasted four months. Goethe endures Frankfurt for another four years and then he breaks away for ever. But these four years are not years of inactivity; they constitute a period of ceaseless wandering, in the countryside and on paper, of constant meetings with new acquaintances, friends, patrons and young talents, of new loves and new escapes from these loves. It is the most tumultuous period of Goethe's life; it is also the richest in creative activity. Much of this never got beyond plans or fragments, much has been lost, and some of it saw the light of day only after long wrestlings. Within the period the main themes of his *œuvre* are already in existence, *Faust*, *Tasso* and possibly *Wilhelm Meister*; *Götz* and *Werther* are completed and published, along with *Singspiele*, dramatic works, shrovetide plays, daring parodies and pamphlets, and poems. At the end of it his *Collected Works*, in three volumes, begin to appear, not collected by himself but in pirated editions, as was then the custom.

Goethe's flight from Wetzlar takes him, first of all, into the world of literature, to Madame de la Roche, whom, in point of fact, he cannot endure. He finds this already ageing lady coquettish, pretentious, as a result of her fame as a young author, and very far from the fine, simple person her novel, *Fräulein von Sternheim*, would have one expect. But her house at Ehrenbreitstein, with its view over the river, is beautiful and a flock of angels circle round their mother. One of these, Maximiliane, is *petite* and dainty, with very lively black eyes, in strong contrast to the homely blue ones of Lotte. The transition to transition, in the jargon of Goué's esoteric teachings, is quick and easy. 'It is a very pleasant feeling when a new passion begins to stir within us before the last one has quite died away' is Goethe's comment on the meeting, and it is a maxim that guides him throughout his life. To bask in the light of the sun and the moon at the same time, as he is doing at the moment, is not only pleasurable but it is a safeguard against too violent and too passionate entanglements. Goethe needs a great deal of protection, and in Wetzlar he may have committed himself a little too far.

And so he yields to this new fascination and endows the figure that is taking shape within him with the deepest black eyes, instead of with blue ones, uniting these to a particularly clear and fresh complexion.

At the house of Madame de la Roche he also enters for the first time a higher social environment. In Leipzig he had spent his time with bourgeois people and professors, in Strasbourg with his luncheon companions and young writers. Here he finds the elegant tone of the great world, and Goethe's initial ill-humour may have been due to the fact that he did not feel at ease in this atmosphere. Monsieur de la Roche, the illegitimate son of a count, is minister to the Archbishop of Treves, a follower of Voltaire and a man of the world. Living in an age when etiquette is no longer quite so rigid, he can happily make fun of the clerics, although he derives his salary from them. He has even published a book, in the form of letters, about the dubious lives of the monks, which created something of a sensation. The sentimental ways of his wife, which as he well knows do not go very deep, he regards with amusement. For her daughters' marriages she has eminently realistic plans, in which sentiment plays no part. Other high officials visit the house and mix with the sentimentalists. A sort of 'congress of sentiment' has been formed and Madame de la Roche wants to give it the status of a permanent institution. The previous year she had invited her old friend Wieland to take part; they renewed their friendship with many tears, and in a calm and businesslike way discussed the publication of her novel.

It is with deep emotion that Goethe takes his leave of this sanctuary of the tenderest sentiments, of maternal happiness, and of angels. In the letters he writes he can scarcely find words to express what he feels; for a considerable time he is at pains to cultivate this new acquaintance. He continues his friendship with Kestner too, tells him how he has dreamed of Lotte and feigns annoyance that she does not dream of him; her silhouette hangs on his wall. He hears a strange story from Wetzlar: one of his former companions at the inn *Zum Kronprinzen*, young Jerusalem of the Brunswick legation, has shot himself. An unhappy love affair and wounded pride were the reasons. Goethe had known him slightly in Leipzig, and had met him again at the luncheon table in Wetzlar. Used he not to wander around in the moonlight, obviously in love? Lotte will remember the smiles it caused. That damned clergyman, his father, must have been the cause of it; Goethe would like to see him break his neck. He thunders on about idolatry and idolatrous sermonizing, which fetter a good disposition and plunge us into misery, about the vanity of mankind that destroys the best in us.

But Jerusalem's father, court preacher in Brunswick and well-known throughout Northern Germany, was scarcely to blame; he was, it is true, a somewhat haughty gentleman who, as Boswell tells us, boasted that he would convert even Frederick the Great to true Christianity if he could but meet him once in private. It is unlikely, however, that the delicate, finely-wrought son, whose posthumous writings Lessing later edited and spoke highly of, was other than a sensitive, touchy young man who took insults too much to heart. In his work he was treated harshly by his superior; at some proudly aristocratic gathering he had been cut, because it was rumoured that he had wrongly presented himself as an aristocrat in Wetzlar; the husband of the object of his adoration had forbidden him the house. He borrowed pistols from Kestner and shot himself. Goethe, likewise very sensitive, was horrified at the young man's fate: 'God knows, it was loneliness that undermined his heart....'

But he does not yet write, he draws – landscapes and portraits. It is as though he feels the need to exercise and loosen his hand in some other medium. He hesitates. His friend Merck spurs him on. He has seen *Götz*, which has been re-written; Goethe wants to improve it yet again. 'Hang out your nappies on the line and let them dry!' cries Merck impatiently with his Darmstadt candour. But what is to be done with the child? Goethe has already published, at his own expense, a few little writings on religious themes, echoes of his pietist days, intermingled with Herder's teachings and ideas suggested by Rousseau. One of the pieces is called *Brief eines Pastors*, a letter in which he imagines himself as a simple village clergyman, proclaiming: 'When you examine it closely everyone has his own religion.' Another is called *Zwo biblische Fragen*; in this he is bolder and satirizes his supposed fellow clerics, who, so he alleges, after a short spell of duty sit down to cards, heavy drinking and dirty stories. He wants to show them how biblical questions should be handled, for example the problems as to what was written on the twelve tablets of Moses, and what did speaking 'with other tongues' mean? Here again, in the vein of his review of the young Jew's poems, he ends by bursting into an invocation to a chosen vessel who shall come forth proclaiming: Blessed art thou, whencesoever thou comest! Thou who art the light of the gentiles! Thou that makest the hearts of the people to glow with warmth!

These little pamphlets, published only in small editions for distribution among friends, produce no glow of warmth in Merck. Here and there people prick up their ears. The famous preacher, Lavater, in Zurich is reported to have said that he longed, nay more, his soul thirsted, to learn theology from a Doctor of Law. But Merck is of the opinion that the time is ripe for something bigger, for *Götz* in fact and for *Götz* alone. But who is going to publish it? With his strong speculative strain, Merck persuades Goethe that they should publish the crazy thing themselves, Merck to undertake the printing, through the Darmstadt Court printer, and Goethe to defray the cost of the paper. Thus it is that *Götz* is launched on the world, the two friends making their own publicity, packing and posting the copies, writing out the accounts. Business is bad. At the cost of untold efforts they have to try to persuade friends to take the packets because meanwhile the booksellers have made their own arrangements by pirating the book. Once, twice, three times the pirates have reprinted it, the printing and lay-out becoming worse with each printing. Their knowledge of the trade, however, has brought the book into circulation. From this first great success, which made him famous at one stroke, Goethe reaped nothing but debts.

But as his contemporary, the poet Bürger, said, 'It is not the worst fruit at which the wasps gnaw.' In the eighteenth century pirated reprints meant fame and circulation. The graph of Goethe's public success can be drawn with a considerable degree of accuracy from those of his works which were pirated and, later on, from those that were not. And the greatest proof of his present success is that an astute publisher immediately approaches the hitherto unknown author with a request for another dozen plays about knights and chivalry, as fast as he can write them. Laughingly Goethe declines the offer. Other writers take over, and for the rest of the century there is no end to the spate of plays, novels and stories about knights and fair ladies, Gothic castles and gloomy dungeons. None is of any importance, Goethe never founded a school in the narrower sense of the word.

In the wider sense, however, modern German literature starts with *Götz*. In his old age Goethe expressed himself in a very wise and detached way on this phenomenal success of his youth: his own youth, he said, coincided with the youth of German literature; it was not all that difficult in those days, to write something that gave birth to an epoch. Subsequent writers had a more difficult task.

The younger generation is jubilant. The critics call the play a monstrosity; so much the better. It is a magnificent monstrosity! After all the snivelling, docility and good behaviour, here is vigour! German strength! A noble, unfettered hero who tramples the whole wretched code of aesthetic rules under his feet! Older people, too, are captivated by the national spirit expressed in the play. The wider public, as Goethe himself remarks, is thrilled by the material effects: by the dungeons, the cellars, the ruined castles and above all by the gypsy scenes in the woods at night and the secret vehmic judges. Lessing, on the other hand, who had just held up his own newly published *Emilia Galotti* as a model of how a stage-play should be constructed, was bitter; he exclaimed angrily that Goethe had filled sausage skins with sand and sold them as rope. And Frederick the Great, who heard that the monstrosity had been performed in Berlin itself, wrote, in French, in his polemic, *De la littérature allemande*, that *Götz* – which he had not seen – was only a pitiful imitation of the bad English plays, by which he meant Shakespeare. In his magnificent library there was not a single book by a German writer.

Not the least of the reasons for the play's success was its language, and the coarse tone of *Götz* became the fashion in that exuberant age. It is no mere chance that the most famous of all Goethe quotations is the passage in *Götz* where the hero slams the window in the truce-bearer's face with the injunction to tell his captain to go and lick his arse. Goethe himself at once makes use of it in sending a poem about his newborn child, an allusion to the 'nappies on the line', to Merck. Having poured scorn and derision on all philistines and all critics and their like, he ends by saying that one should express his scorn and derision by 'sticking one's arse out of the window' at them. To his more sensitively minded friend, Gotter, however, he writes another poem advising him, for the ladies' sake, to tone down the nasty words into politer language.

In shrovetide plays and satires this coarseness is given even freer rein. In these Goethe is closer to the times of *Götz* than in the play itself. The old *Fastnachtspiele*, by the Nuremberg barber Hans Rosenplüt and others, which literally teem with obscenities, he is scarcely likely to have read. They are the forerunners of the comparatively mild Hans Sachs, ridiculing the swinish peasants with swinish delight for the amusement of the burghers; there is often this kind of social arrogance in ribaldry. The Dutch genre painters too, whose pictures of drunken peasants fighting and relieving themselves were known to Goethe, worked for a clientele of wealthy merchants who delighted in such scenes. Goethe, however, has no public of any sort in mind. He writes for himself, and perhaps for a few friends like Merck. He is testing his strength in every direction, on every plane. He is liberating himself, or, to use his own favourite simile, which he uses for other functions too, he is inhaling and exhaling. To a parody of *Werther* he writes a counter parody, which ends with the original parodist relieving himself on the suicide's grave: 'Delighted by his excrement, with freer breath away he went.'

Such things should not be taken too seriously; they were only included in his 'works' at a late date. Much of the obscenity is delayed puberty. Mozart also wrote obscene letters to his Augsburg cousin, his *Bäsle*; these letters, which he signed 'Sauschwanz Wolfgang Amadeus Rosenkranz', were for long a source of horror to his pious admirers. And Goethe wrote a *Hanswursts Hochzeit* in which obscene names and situations fall as easily from his pen as from that of some sixteenth-century Grobian.

The wealth of curious names in Goethe's writing, and his whole vocabulary of obscenities, derives directly from his Frankfurt surroundings. The *Grosser Hirschgraben*, where his father's patrician house stood, belonged to, or at least was immediately adjacent to, the *Rosenthal* which, since the Middle Ages, had been a famous district of brothels. Its denizens had a vocabulary of their own, and there are records of a Frankfurt lawsuit in which a man is accused of abusing his opponent 'in language fouler than that of a Rosenthal whore-master'. There is no need to imagine Goethe as a regular visitor there, but undoubtedly his vocabulary was greatly enriched by his proximity to this neighbourhood.

Throughout his life he makes full use of the whole range of his vocabulary; in later years he does it mostly in private, in talking to certain very intimate friends, or in secret additions to *Faust*, that he called his *Walpurgisbag*. It would be stupid to ignore this strain in his nature, and equally silly to exaggerate it. But he never indulges in the sniggering, prurient obscenities so beloved of many writers of his day. He called a spade a spade, as his mother did too, whose language also often shocked nineteenth-century readers.

If there had been a public in Germany such as existed in Greece at the time of Aristophanes, he might have written Aristophanic comedies. As it was he had to confine himself to farces, parodies and the like, on the model of the old *Fastnachtspiel*, known to him through Hans Sachs, whose works had never quite sunk into oblivion. The doggerel verse of the old shoemaker, derisively known as *Knittel-Vers* because its rhythm sounds as though beaten out with a stick, proves a surprisingly apt medium for the expression of everything, from the lowest to the highest. With a sure eye Goethe picks on subjects that lend themselves to satire: a mawkish clergyman who hovers round the women and gets put in his place by a stouthearted warrior; another cleric who practises the new doctrine of natural love; a dry-as-dust professor who explains the Bible along the most up-to-date lines. He also attacks Wieland, one of the most popular writers of the day, daringly and by name. The others remain anonymous, and identification is difficult. They are types, figures that turn up constantly and everywhere.

The cult of sentiment produced its exploiters. In Darmstadt a Hofrat Leuchsenring, a Court physician, spread consternation among the 'saints'. He maintained an enormous correspondence, exceeded only by that of Lavater. He also collected other people's love letters and intimate confessions, such as those by one of Rousseau's mistresses. Leuchsenring travelled round with strong-boxes carefully packed full of such letters; he would open them, untie the bundles and read them aloud. It was a social entertainment. In private the master used to take the pulses of the ladies and demoiselles, and then let his hands wander further afield. Herder's fiancée Karoline, Psyche, was one of this satyr's faithful adherents until his activities forced him to leave Darmstadt.

Goethe seizes on this theme and transfers Psyche to his play *Satyros*, or 'The Faun Deified'. The faun comes limping down from the mountains, where he has drunk his fill from the udders of wild goats. He is a child of nature, and Goethe – the Mephistopheles in Goethe – is already ridiculing the nature cult in whose midst he himself is still active. The goat-footed creature sounds an almost Faustian note: *'Natur ist rings so liebebang'* (all round us nature yearns for love), he sings, and plays his flute to the girls by the well; they listen eagerly and he embraces the simple-minded Gretchen-like Psyche; he kisses her and she stammers of ecstasy, of woe and death. Relatives and neighbours come, the whole village, and Satyros bewitches them too. He founds a new cult based on ecstatic frenzy, the joy of living and loving, and vegetarianism. He condemns clothes as burdensome and Psyche wants to tear hers off her back. He preaches of the *Urding*, the elemental, all-pervading, and always with sly looks at the girls.

It is a parody, an antistrophe to *Faust*, of which Goethe has as yet scribbled down but a few lines. As the plot develops, it borders on the weird and on the political: in a temple the satyr sits enthroned, the villagers on their knees; blasphemers are to be sacrificed to him, the crowd roars blood and death to all non-believers. The *dénouement* is farcical: a courageous man rends the veil from the Holy of Holies and God appears in his primal faun-like being, leaping on one of the girls. A beast! A beast! they cry. He is chased from the village, and goes off to join a new community of saints.

Of all his works of this period it shows Goethe's genius at its most luxuriant, although it is but a sketch for a larger work, a work that was never to be realized or, at any rate, only in a quite different form. Satyros is Mephistopheles and Faust compressed into a single figure, pointed ears and universal comprehension in one. The characters are interwoven. There is a pious hermit, for instance, who introduces the play and represents true religion as opposed to the cult of nature. But then he, too, sings a pantheistic paean to Spring, to the stimulus and impulse welling from creative force, to the beasts that mate before his very eyes, 'on leaf and bud, on every hand, one sees a marriage- or a child-bed stand'.

'Welling from creative force' is the most significant phrase. Goethe seizes on the greatest themes: Prometheus, Mahomet, Socrates, Caesar, Christ and Ahasuerus, the wandering Jew. They all remain fragments; a few lyrics are incorporated in his poems. Some are fragmentary in concept, such as his Ahasuerus which bears the superscription 'First Scrap of the Wandering Jew'. This epic was intended to embrace the whole history of church and religion. In keeping with the spirit of this age of exuberance, this *Geniezeit*, Goethe leaps out of bed at midnight like a madman, as he tells us later, and ploughs out the lines across the paper, snatching up a pencil because a pen is too refractory for his mood. In the fragment itself he declares that he would even have written with a broomstick. In his frenzy to be original much of what he writes is blasphemous: God the Father calls His Son, 'The Son then made his stumbling way athwart the stars, in disarray'. The characters become entangled, and, just as in Satyros, it is always Goethe and not Christ who speaks. On returning to earth, and recalling his earthly sufferings, Christ lapses into the metaphor of flying into the arms of a girl 'who sucked our blood for long years past and then deceived us at the last'. But, in and among all this, we find magnificent imagery and scraps of genius.

Mahomet is chosen by Goethe as an act of defiance against the times; he is the great and long neglected figure for whose reinstatement the time is now ripe. The notorious book, *De tribus impostoribus*, on the three great impostors, Moses, Jesus and Mahomet, clandestinely reprinted and constantly reread, had surrounded his name with a Lucifer-like glitter. In a polar reversal of fact Goethe turns the great lawgiver of the desert races into a deity of the sea, singing a mighty psalm of sea and river that is one of his most powerful songs, though it has nothing whatever to do with the Koran.

A Caesar drama, dealing as it did with a man of action, was the first to be discarded. Goethe never created heroic men of action, not even when Napoleon pressingly urged him to write a play on the death of Caesar. Prometheus, the titanic figure who defies the gods, engaged his attention time and time again, and in the most varied transformations. At this stage in his career he creates his own myth, very far removed from that of the Greeks. It begins defiantly, with Prometheus refusing to recognize father, mother or the gods. They are mere vassals of fate, heroes do not respect such as they. He turns to his children, formed by him from clay – it is primarily as a sculptor-creator, forming men, that Goethe sees him – and the poet summons Minerva to assist Prometheus in bringing his creations to life, she is his muse. The figures live, the heavens are in uproar, high treason stands at the threshold. At this point, however, Goethe – true to his own nature, for even at this early stage he always favours conciliation – avoids the dramatic by making Jupiter, a wise though somewhat cynical figure, declare: they shall live; this race of worms will increase the number of my servants. Their sufferings begin as soon as they scatter, and at this point Goethe, for the first time, makes whole epochs of human history pass before our eyes in the space of a few lines: strife, violence, war; the children of Prometheus are both cruel and kind, both beasts and gods. And he ends very beautifully, and very much in keeping with his mood at this time, with an 'Ode to Death' -- death, the fulfilment of all we have dreamed of, hoped for, feared. When the senses fade into oblivion and we embrace a whole world, this is dying. And after death? Resurrection, to fear, to hope, to desire anew!

From heaven and resurrection back to earth again, he writes about everything; he writes literary satires as well. In the full consciousness of his power he launches into an attack on Wieland, the most important of the German masters. From Wieland he has learned much, he has a high regard for his gifts and when Wieland dies he delivers a fine funeral oration in memory of his old friend. But at this moment fierce opposition to Wieland is rife. The *Göttinger Hain*, excessively Teutonic and bardic, has outlawed him as French in outlook, a corrupter of morals and a purveyor of eroticism; its members are very virtuous. At the celebration for Klopstock's birthday, their pure-moraled and pure-minded master, they place a chair for their absent idol in their meeting-room and garland it with roses and gilly-flowers and with his complete works. Under the chair, in tatters, lies Wieland's latest book. The torn-out pages they use as spills to light their pipes and they trample on what is left. They drink the health of Klopstock, Luther, Hermann the Cheruscan, and Goethe, whose *Götz* they have just read. At the end they burn Wieland's portrait.

One Sunday afternoon, a bottle of claret at his side, Goethe scribbles down a little satirical pamphlet, 'Götter, Helden und Wieland'. He is in a pugnacious mood. 'The lad is bellicose, he has the spirit of an athlete', writes Knebel, who is shortly to become his friend. 'Goethe lives in a state of constant inner war and turmoil, since all objects affect him in the most violent way. His spirit forces him to make enemies with whom he can do battle, and for this purpose he is certainly not going to select the worst.' Wieland was not among the worst, and he behaved with great generosity when the insolent affair was printed, reprinted and circulated. He had an exceptionally good nose, and it told him that a new generation was arising, which disposed of forces to which he could not lay claim. Of all the writers of his day Wieland was always the most generous in his understanding of others, however strongly their natures contrasted with his own; later on the extremely difficult Heinrich von Kleist was to provide an example of this. Still only in his forties Wieland saw himself already as an old man, as Papa Wieland, who let the children rampage. Of Goethe and his *Götz* he wrote in his paper, the *Teutscher Merkur*: 'Young, spirited men of genius are like young, spirited foals; they abound with life and vigour, romp around like mad things, snort and neigh, roll and rear, snap and bite, jump up at people, lash out fore and aft, and will not suffer themselves to be caught or ridden. So much the better!'

All this was of little concern to Goethe. He had read articles by Wieland in the *Teutscher Merkur*, and in one of these the master had imprudently made some disparaging remarks about Euripides and his *Alcestis*. Herakles, in particular, he found unsatisfactory, and not without reason; Wieland was an excellent connoisseur in ancient literature. In Euripides, Herakles does in fact play a strange role in the otherwise essentially tragic play: glutton, rowdy, upstart, his place is in a satyric play rather than in high tragedy. This very early work of Euripides is not easy to classify and has found the most varied interpretations; it has been called a tragi-comedy or a 'hybrid' play. But Goethe did not know this. For him it was sufficient that Wieland had found fault with the sacred Greeks.

And so he presents him in his night-cap. Who is this Wieland? ask the Greek giants. He is Hofrat and tutor to the Princes in Weimar. But he does not understand their language. 'We are speaking Greek', they reply. Herakles appears, very much the braggart of Euripides. Wieland remarks that such a colossus had never entered his head, he had conceived him as a well-built man of medium height. 'Medium height! Me!' snorts the mighty creature. The Princes' tutor now has the temerity to speak of virtue. Herakles bursts into a wild eulogy of the new age, but transferred back to antiquity and the Middle Ages. He jeers at the worthy citizens who cross themselves at the very thought of *Faustrecht*, he lauds the strong and lusty demi-gods who, in the excess of their virility, give a sound hiding to the others or, like himself, give the women all the children they desire, or do not desire. 'I myself have fathered fifty boys in a single night.' Goethe did not find this in Euripides, but in one of the dictionaries of mythology of which he made use. It is the story of Herakles' visit to Thespios, who was anxious for his fifty daughters to have progeny by his famous guest; in one night, or, according to a more guarded version, in seven nights, the hero performed this most Herculean of his deeds. Goethe storms on about the servitude of ethical codes: can they not understand that a demi-god gets drunk and is a boor? Pluto rises from the under-world and calls a halt: can one not even go to bed quietly with one's wife, if she has no objection?

Since *Götz* nothing of Goethe's had met with such success, short-lived though it was, as this 'piece of malicious infamy', as he himself described it. The younger generation saw themselves as Hercules, older people were not going to grudge a little humiliation to the darling of the public. In his *Merkur* Wieland proclaimed the little work a masterpiece of persiflage and witty sophistry. Goethe was embarrassed when he read the review. He thought that as a result Wieland would gain much and he would lose in public estimation. 'I have been prostituted.'

He had no need to worry over the public, *Werther* was about to appear.

# 13

# *The Sufferings of the Young Werther*

*Die Leiden des jungen Werthers* was the title of the book which appeared, in two small volumes, in Leipzig in 1774, without its author's name; the pages were adorned with delicate little rococo vignettes by Goethe's old friend Oeser. On the title-page was a small candle in front of a mirror – what did it symbolize? The flame of genius? By the side of the candlestick was a book. Whatever the symbolism, the mirror became a burning-glass, kindling a fire, a fire of instantaneous combustion and destruction, such as no German book had ever caused before or was ever to cause again. There was a *Werther* epidemic: *Werther* fever, a *Werther* fashion – young men dressed in blue tail coats and yellow waistcoats – *Werther* caricatures – *Werther* suicides. His memory was solemnly commemorated at the grave of the young Jerusalem, his original, while the clergy preached sermons against the shameful book. And all this continued, not for a year, but for decades; and not only in Germany but in England, France, Holland and Scandinavia as well. Goethe himself noted with pride that even the Chinese had painted Lotte and Werther on porcelain; his greatest personal triumph was when Napoleon told him at their meeting, that he had read the book seven times. The Emperor, who liked to air his knowledge, pointed out in criticism that he regarded the double motive of warped ambition and passionate love as a fault; he had a tidy mind.

*Werther* was no mere best-seller, if only for the reason that it was written by a poet, a circumstance otherwise virtually unknown with books in this category. And in any case it is doubtful whether, in spite of all its printings, reprintings and translations, the book would rank among the 'biggest sellers' even of its own day. Its influence was of a different nature. Its success was due in only small degree to its poetic merits and in far higher degree, as always with great fame, to misunderstandings. That the flame of genius burned within it, however, was unquestionable. The word 'genius' in those days was used frequently and indiscriminately, and it had a derisive secondary meaning: a 'genius' was a rather bizarre, haughty young man who made great claims for himself without having proved whether or not such claims were mere arrogance. Goethe's work was his proof. Henceforth the word 'genius' was to have a richer sound.

This new fame had its effect on Goethe's personal life. From now on, whatever else he might publish, he was 'the author of *Werther*'. This persisted almost throughout his life; it was only later that he became known as 'the author of *Faust*', and still later as the 'Olympian' of *Weimar*. He suffered as a result; he protested often, very angrily and very bluntly too, but to no avail. The descriptions we have of him from now on have also suffered, none is any longer unprejudiced. Visitors and correspondents all see in him the author of *Werther*, not Goethe; they are enthusiastic if their preconceived idea is confirmed, disappointed if he does not correspond to their idea of Lotte's lover. In those days the public had a very personal attitude towards an author, and towards the characters of a novel too; its likes and dislikes were highly personal. Young girls wanted to be Lotte, or Julie in Rousseau's *Heloïse*. As a student in Leipzig Goethe had seriously resolved to experience, or contrive, his life as '*un roman*'. The originals of famous fictional characters were tracked down with the utmost zeal, and, once found, their private lives were subjected to the most unrestrained and shameless intrusions. As Lotte, Frau Hofrat Kestner was the first victim of this treatment, to her sorrow and satisfaction; next came her husband, who entered into the game and complained in all sincerity that, as 'Albert', Goethe had not given him sufficient integrity and dignity. The grave of the unhappy Jerusalem became a place of pilgrimage. The pilgrims cursed the parson who had denied him an honest burial, put flowers on the grave, sang sentimental songs and wrote home about their moving experience.

It was the heyday of letter writing and sentiment. The *Werther* literature fills the shelves of a whole library. It is mostly trash, consisting of street songs, parodies, gruesomely illustrated ballads for the fair, with pictorial sequences of Werther's suicide – the forerunner of the film. 'The ball has almost reached his brain now', wrote Goethe in a counter-parody. A sentimental trifle *Ausgelitten, ausgerungen* (now the struggle and the pain is o'er) became the rage. Tirades from the clergy only increased the sales of the book; the suicide was their main stumbling block. One preacher showed some understanding of Goethe's knowledge of the most subtle shades of feeling of the soul and of its 'mechanism' – even the theologians could not avoid metaphors from physics. Others inveighed against the tide of atheism: 'At least Spinoza and the Socinians wrote as scholars, but these present scoffers dance like monkeys. As for reason and the Bible – these are mere drivel to them.' To the highly logical ecclesiastics reason and the Bible were synonymous.

When the epidemic was at its height some officer said: 'A fellow who shoots himself for the sake of a girl he cannot sleep with is a fool, and one fool, more or less, in the world is of no consequence.' There were many such fools. One 'new Werther' shot himself with particular *éclat*: having carefully shaved, plaited his pigtail, put on fresh clothes, opened *Werther* at page 218 and laid it on the table, he opened the door, revolver in hand, to attract an audience and, having looked round to make sure they were paying sufficient attention, raised the weapon to his right eye and pulled the trigger.

In Berlin, Nicolai wrote *Werther's Joys* with a happy ending; it was this that inspired Goethe to write the counter-parody which ended with the man relieving himself on Werther's grave. Goethe also wrote another parody on the book, in a scene showing Werther and Lotte as a married couple, very much like Nicolai; the suicide only blinds himself and singes his eyebrows, Lotte fusses over the wound caused by the 'beastly shot at the head', and, after enjoying a little fun at the expense of Kestner, the Albert of the novel, the two of them go off quietly to bed. The piece, which fortunately the real Kestner never saw, shows Goethe's double nature once more; only one side was engaged in the pursuit of the sentimentalist cult. By writing the book he had dispossessed himself of his drunkenness and his frenzy, which were now committed to paper. These were the actual words he used, as taken down by his valet who, from now on, is to be his constant companion, both at home and on his travels. Goethe dictates to him and carries on nocturnal conversations with him, while the valet looks after his master and apes him a little.

A young lad, Philipp Seidel, quick and with a very clear brain, had gone to Goethe's father as a clerk at the age of 17; previously he had been in the service of Goethe's rather jolly Aunt Melber. The poet now adopts the wide-awake young man, and of all his attempts at 'adoption', this is the most successful. Seidel makes the fair copies of *Götz* and *Werther*, he and Goethe travel together and share the same bedroom, continuing to do so long after Goethe's move to Weimar. He contradicts his master freely when the latter says something with which he does not agree; he looks after his correspondence, soon to become very voluminous, keeps the diary, and notes down conversations with visitors. Here, for example, is a conversation between Goethe and one of the town syndics, who declares that the thing, *Werther*, is too extravagant. Goethe asks if he has never been drunk. Well, perhaps; after all even an honest fellow always has something he is ashamed of. – Good, replies Goethe, the only difference is that your drunkenness was slept off, mine is on paper! The man still maintains that *Werther* is a dangerous book. Goethe begins to lose patience: 'Dangerous! What do you mean, dangerous? It is beasts like you who are dangerous, who contaminate everything round you with putrefaction, who beslobber and besmirch everything that is beautiful and good, and then try to convince the world that nothing is any better than their own excrement!'

Seidel is a careful listener. We can hear Goethe speak, without the somewhat dubious medium of letter or literature, and this was his style of speech, more or less, at this period, and remained so until a lady at the Weimar Court took him in hand.

The book did indeed contain much that was beautiful and admirable, and Goethe had just cause to be angry that the whole affair was made merely a theme for buckles and ivory sweetmeat boxes, for *Werther* fans and *Eau de Werther* perfume, for decorating tea cups or for stimulating drawing-room tittle-tattle. It is true he did not set himself too hard a task. A novel compiled from letters was an accepted form; Madame de la Roche had used it, following the famous models of Rousseau and Richardson. In this way it was possible to create the impression of a 'true story', based on original papers and reliable sources. Goethe, too, starts in this way by claiming that he has collected all the evidence he could lay his hands on. Among the original papers are, in fact, his own letters to Kestner, as research has established, Kestner's reports on the death of Jerusalem, pages from diaries, confidential notes to Merck and to his sister. And so he now presents these letters and diary entries as a novel. Without the slightest hesitation he uses Lotte's name and, in the course of his work on the book, writes in high spirits to the young couple: 'If it should enter your heads to be jealous, I reserve the right to present you on the stage, and with the most telling strokes!' At first he has a play in mind: 'I am working out my situation as a play, in defiance of God and mankind.' Then it becomes a novel, interspersed with lyric scenes. The portrayal also changes. Little Lotte, of the homely blue eyes, acquires characteristics of Maximiliane de la Roche – deep black eyes, rather more disquiet, rather more temperament. Quite unmoved by sentiment Madame de la Roche had married off her daughter to an elderly, dull, but very wealthy, merchant in Frankfurt, named Brentano. Goethe continued to hang round the couple, flirt with the none-too-happy young wife, and to play the cello to her sketchy accompaniment on the spinet. The husband became jealous; he was no Kestner, had no intention of giving way to a young genius, and forbade Goethe the house. All these are original papers and sources. In addition Goethe had eagerly studied Homer in Wetzlar, and one of the finest passages in the novel is a paraphrase of Homer, the scene at the well where the girls come to fetch water from the cool vault, the most everyday activity and the most necessary, and one which, in olden times, the daughters of kings performed themselves. The scene harks back to the days of the Bible patriarchs, who met and wooed at the well, because round it hovered benevolent spirits. We hear the sound of folk-song and popular ballad too, as well as invective against the stuffiness of Wetzlar society, with its constant bickerings about precedence and status: 'Now enters the over-gracious Lady von S... with her husband and well-hatched gosling of a daughter, with her flat chest and pretty corsets; they make the traditional play, *en passant*, with their aristocratic eyes and nostrils....' He tacks on a malicious sketch of an aristocratic old aunt, who has nothing left of her former beauty but her sixteen nobly born ancestors, with whom she has struck fear into many a young heart, and into her husband too, whom she bought and then plagued to death for a 'brazen age'; 'she now finds herself alone in the iron age, and no one would cast a glance at her were it not for her charming niece.'

A militant note like this makes as great an impact on his contemporaries as does the charming and sentimental one of Lotte cutting bread for the children, or the sweeping psalms to nature: 'Huge mountains surrounded me, abysses lay before me, rivulets plunged headlong, and beneath me flowed the rivers, and forest and mountain resounded; and I saw their play and interplay upon the earth, and under the heavens the teeming species of manifold creation.'

This goes beyond the rococo scenery of the vignettes, or the little bows on Lotte's breast. It is an interplay of everything, a mythical primeval landscape in which the microcosm of Wetzlar finds a place too, even the disputes about rank and precedence on the part of the 'hero', who is no hero. The description of his death has a precision that sounds like the blows of a hammer on the coffin: 'At twelve noon he died. The presence of the bailiff, and the precautions he took, prevented a riot. At night, at about eleven, he was buried in the place he had chosen. The old man followed the coffin with his sons, Albert could not. They feared for Lotte's life. Workmen bore him. No priest accompanied him.'

Scarcely ever again did Goethe write short sentences of such force or, as elsewhere in the novel, periods with such a span of lyric flow, anticipating his finest poems. We can believe him when he tells us that he wrote the book down in a few weeks, as though in a state of somnambulism, after long months of carrying it round and remoulding it in his head. There is also already at work a high degree of artistic understanding, or, at any rate, of intuition for what is artistically necessary. Longing for death, indeed the morbid infatuation with death, one of the basic themes of German writing, is evident early in the work. At first only the word 'pistols', no louder than a faint bugle call, and then it grows with increasing insistence up to the final clear and shattering: 'A neighbour saw the flash of powder and heard the shot ring out', with which the action closes.

Not quite so convincing is Goethe's description, written in his old age, of his mood at the time of the novel, of his own thoughts of suicide, of how he played with a dagger, placed it against his bare skin, and then laid it aside. It is possible that he played with such thoughts; in any case he took up his pen. He wrote *Werther* and his *Werther* parodies. To the very end of his life his own longing for death always presupposed resurrection, a resurrection, as he wrote in *Prometheus*, 'to fear, to hope, to desire anew...'.

# 14

# *Sturm und Drang*

With his *Götz* and his *Werther* Goethe has become the leader of a 'movement', of the younger generation of writers, one of whose plays, *Sturm und
Drang*, is later to give the movement its name. Klopstock is still the undisputed great poet and master, Lessing the clearest and most penetrating
mind, greatly feared as the supreme arbiter in the arts. Wieland remains
the most popular author, with an extensive and varied output. Herder, for
a short time the leader of the younger generation, has already had to cede
this position to the young adept, who only recently had seen himself as his
'moon'; it is from this moment that the great bitterness in Herder's life
begins. Goethe is seen as a man of unlimited possibilities; there seems to be
nothing beyond his power to achieve. He is sought out on every side, sent
invitations, urged to write; people flock to him from everywhere, either by
letter or in person, and the house on the *Hirschgraben* is turned into an
headquarters and an hostelry for writers. His father bends over his legal
briefs and, with tolerable good grace, lets his son's activities roar over his
head. His mother, on the other hand, enters into it all delightedly; meals
are prepared and beds made ready. She takes enthusiastic part in everything, sparing neither the grandfather's precious wines nor her own advice.
Before long she is mother to many; 'Frau Aja' as they call her, after a character in the popular old chap-book, *The Four Children of Hemon*. The
older her husband gets, the younger she feels. This is the great moment of
her life. She basks in the new-found fame of her darling Hans, her *Hätschelhans*, a sunshine that seems all the warmer for the coldness of her daughter
and the sorrow of her unhappy marriage. But now she has other children,
naughty ones, good ones, needy ones, proud ones, dejected ones, aristocratic, and soon even princely, ones, and plebian ones. She mothers them
all, though only for a time, because the whole *Sturm und Drang* movement
is not to last for very long. Goethe is the first to sever himself, after a few
years. He soon tires of movements as well as of people. There are still
many metamorphoses for him to undergo.

At this period of his life new works are quickly finished. Never again does
he commit them to paper in this way, in one breath as it were, and then
rush them into print. Fame and the pressure of demand prevent his putting

things aside for revision, as he normally does, waiting for a favourable wind. Thus, as soon as *Götz* is out of the way, a new play, *Clavigo*, is hewn out, in eight days. He has been criticized for his inability to write for the stage; at once he announces 'a drama for the stage, so that these fellows can see that the observance of rules is entirely up to me'. Lessing's *Emilia Galotti* has been held up to him as a model; very well then, he will take it as a model. At a Frankfurt party, to which he is invited, they play the marriage game, basically only a development of the all-pervading business of match-making; for the third time Goethe finds himself paired with a pretty, homely girl, and is declared her temporary husband. She charges him to write a play based on Beaumarchais' memoirs of his Spanish experiences, which Goethe has been reading aloud to them. He agrees; any stimulus to write is welcome.

Beaumarchais, not yet the author of *Figaro* or *The Barber of Seville*, had published a series of *Mémoires*, dealing, for the most part, with his some-what dubious lawsuits and his various 'calumniators'. In one of them, how-ever, and with a total lack of scruples, he had inserted an intimate family matter: a Spanish journalist, Clavijo, had broken a promise of marriage to Beaumarchais' sister and this was the author's revenge. Such things in those days were written and published in order to reach a wide public, just as letters on the most delicate family matters were handed round and circu-lated. Beaumarchais' description of the whole affair is exceptionally vivid: he compels the faithless suitor to make honourable amends, and succeeds in getting him dismissed from his influential position in Madrid. Goethe needed to do little more than turn the narrative into dialogue, which he proceeded to do. He also made some additions: he turned Beaumarchais into a knight and a nobleman, which he was not, although he used the form 'de Beaumarchais'; he invented a tragic ending in which Clavigo, who has been faithless once more, meets the funeral procession of the girl he has deserted and who has died of a broken heart. By these means he created a play that was theatrically effective, and which was, in fact, successful. His mentor, Merck, however, pronounced it 'rubbish'; other people could write stuff like that. Annoyed, Goethe later declared that there was no need for everything to be beyond compare, that, if he had had a little more en-couragement at the time, he might well have gone on to write a dozen such plays of which, perhaps, three or four would have kept their place in the repertoire.

The faithlessness, the vacillation, of the unheroic hero has been inter-preted, not without some hints on Goethe's part, as subsequent remorse for his own breach of faith in Sesenheim, just as it has been in the case of the similarly vacillating Weislingen in *Götz*. In Goethe's letters of the day there are only a few fleeting lines to his friend Salzmann in Strasbourg, asking him to send a copy of *Götz* to 'poor Friederike', so that she can console her-self with the fact that the faithless Weislingen is poisoned.

Goethe learns to skate. He is introduced to the sport by Klopstock, on his visit to Frankfurt, and takes it up delightedly. The carefree sensation of floating lightly over the thin surface of ice appeals to him and, like the gay tinkle of sleigh bells, is soon to find its metaphorical application. He includes a sort of skating waltz in his *Concerto dramatico*, a secular cantata text written for his Darmstadt friends: 'in the air, on the ground, on the water, on ice, one may well break one's neck and Lord knows what besides'; there is a threat of danger from one of the host of 'Sibyls', an imminent threat, but the seasons whirl swiftly by, didli di dum. Remorse? There will be plenty of time for that later.

He writes little operettas. Composers are also beginning to seek him out, among them his former friend André in Offenbach, who had described him as having 'a good flow of chatter rather than sound judgment'. He takes a ballad by Oliver Goldsmith, one of his favourite authors, whose *Deserted Village* Merck had had privately printed for him in an edition of a few copies; out of it Goethe creates his play with music, *Erwin und Elmire*. It is a success, and receives more performances than any other of his stage works of this period. One song in it, *Das Veilchen auf der Wiese*, has been set to music by some thirty composers: from it Mozart created his only *Lied*, which is really a miniature operatic scene in itself; reversing the theme of *Heidenröslein* it is here the shepherd girl, not the uncivilized boy, who tramples on the violet. There is quite an old-fashioned arcadian quality about the plot of *Erwin und Elmire*, which concerns the reunion of a loving couple, after some misunderstanding; the boy disguises himself as a hermit, the girl comes and confesses to him, and then they recognize one another. 'It is I – It is you'; to which Goethe adds a production note: 'The music should try to express the feeling in these pauses!'

In another operetta, *Claudine von Villa Bella*, Goethe expresses his personal feelings more distinctly. He presents himself as Crugantino, a Bohemian, singing a student song: *'mit Mädeln sich vertragen, mit Männern rumgeschlagen, und mehr Kredit als Geld, so kommt man durch die Welt!'* (be popular with girls, engage in fights with men, use credit not hard cash, success you'll then attain!). His first *roman* is over – after all, it has lasted three weeks. If one wants to look for Goethe's own experiences in his works, personal confessions can be read into all this. After sundry cloak and dagger scenes Crugantino finds himself in prison; when a fatherly friend reproaches him, he flares up with the authentic voice of this new age: 'What do you know of the needs of a young heart like mine? A young mad cap, am I? Can you provide me with a stage on which to play out my life? Your bourgeois society is intolerable to me! If I want to work I must be a slave, if I want to enjoy myself I must be a slave. Is not anyone who is worth anything at all bound to prefer to go out into the world?' Crugantino does not go out into the world, he gets his Claudine. Both, it transpires, are of the old nobility, and the play ends in eternal bliss for the happy couple.

In *Stella*, the most important of these plays, the bourgeois setting is completely abandoned. In this little five-act drama Goethe writes one of his life's dreams. He is never able to tie himself wholly to a single woman; he almost always loves two at the same time, or one right after the other, with his feelings mingling during the transition. He often feels the need of a dear *Nebengeschöpf* – a complementary being – as he later calls the companion of his Christiane; or else he has to tell his beloved Charlotte von Stein of Corona, the other one, and Corona of Charlotte. Once he planned a novel, *Der Sultan wider willen*, in which four different women, with varying characteristics, were in love with the same man; each, when he was with her, alone seemed lovable. Goethe's secretary, Riemer, who tells the story, adds: 'just as in his own younger days his feelings were engaged by this one and that at the same time, even though his feelings in each case were not the same'.

In *Stella* Goethe attempts to handle this theme. A man is caught between two women, one of them high-minded, the other with only her love; he has forsaken them both, but to both he returns. Meanwhile they have formed a sisterly affection for one another. Once again the sister motif, his constant preoccupation, plays a role. The two women now want to live as sisters, along with their Fernando, the most feminine of all Goethe's male portrayals.

The theme of the double marriage is an old one. There is the story of Count von Gleichen, quoted by the high-minded Cäcilie in Goethe's play when she makes known her noble resolve. In this medieval tale the Count, a prisoner during the crusades, has won the love of the beautiful coloured daughter of the Arab prince who took him prisoner. She helps him to escape and together they return to his castle. The Countess, deeply moved, embraces her, and the three of them live happily together, indeed even with a dispensation from the Pope. Their tombstone in the cathedral at Erfurt shows the three of them united. Martin Luther himself gave a similar dispensation to one of the princes who supported him and whose support he needed, though he did so with a heavy heart. And among the rulers and great ones of Goethe's day there were few who did not maintain a double relationship, openly and with princely pomp. To the bourgeois world from which Goethe came it was an abomination.

But Goethe gives no thought to such bourgeois ties. Nor does he set out to state a thesis, play the part of reformer, or announce the gospel of free-love, which haunts the minds of many of his companions of the *Sturm und Drang*. He is moved solely by overwhelming feelings of love, which recognize no boundaries. It would be pointless to look among the circle of his acquaintances for the originals of these two women, even though his personal experience, or his experience of literature, embraced such labyrinthine and many-partnered affairs of the heart. His heroine's name he takes from Swift's dark and confused affair with his Stella and Vanessa; he knew little else about this pitiful relationship. Goethe's play, however, exhibits only a passionately surging labyrinth of feelings; the point made by Riemer, that a man may love two women at the same time though not in the same way, finds no place in it. All three feel the same similarly vague love and, in the course of it, even the difference of the sexes becomes almost lost. Fernando is feminine; the high-minded Cäcilia is more manly than he is.

Crugantino's protest from prison acts like a battle-cry on the young members of the *Sturm und Drang* movement, who now flock round Goethe. They all want to escape from their narrow lives, where they are mere 'slaves', condemned to drudgery and servitude, and get out into the world at large, to America if need be, to war, anywhere. The bourgeois world has become intolerable, the aristocratic world is closed to them and detested, the princes and tyrants are a disgrace. Nearly all these young men came from very poor and oppressed backgrounds. Voss, the translator of Homer, came from a family of serfs, others were the sons of desperately poor country pastors, like Lenz, or of equally poor village schoolmasters, like Herder. Klinger of Frankfurt, whose play gave the movement its name, was brought up by his mother, widow of a member of the town constabulary, through her untiring labours as a washerwoman. Even the great scholars of the day were often sons of craftsmen and labourers: Winckelmann's father was a cobbler, Heyne, the greatest Greek scholar of his day, was the son of a starving weaver. It is remarkable that circumstances such as these should form the social background to the enthusiasm of the Greek and Roman revival, the new classicism. Interwoven among all this was an active revolutionary element. Heyne tells us in his autobiography that even at school his hero was Brutus, the prototype of those who fight against the oppressors of the poor, such as his own father. Hero-worship of the great figures of antiquity was permitted even to those who took their meals at aristocrats' free tables or acted as tutors to their sons; their names were hallowed by convention. The word 'freedom', which otherwise rendered one suspect, was allowed in reference to the Greeks. Even the sons of aristocrats were allowed to express enthusiasm for the republican ideas of the ancients; Montaigne's aristocratic young friend, La Boëthie, had already written his impassioned discourse, *In Tyrannos*, which was actually reprinted during the French Revolution. Schiller later printed this as a motto on the title page of *Die Räuber*, by far the most powerful play produced by the whole *Sturm und Drang*, though it only appeared after the movement had already passed its zenith.

Young noblemen have often sympathized with revolutionary movements. Two Counts, the brothers Stolberg, turn up in the movement as twin poets. They also share the common enthusiasm for antiquity, and Friedrich, the older one, has made a translation of Homer that is even better than that of his friend Voss. They share, too, the enthusiasm for freedom and independence and enjoy shocking the bourgeoisie. They cause a sensation among the Darmstadt sentimentalists by stripping off their well-cut aristocratic tail-coats, diving naked into the lake, and splashing about in it. The Psyches and Uranias are horrified, the provincial Darmstadters even more so. The Stolbergs' activities consist largely of splashing about, to the accompaniment of wild oaths and imprecations; the *Götz* tone is the fashion, like the Werther dress, which they also copy faithfully, with their blue tail-coats, yellow waistcoats and top-boots, in protest against the courtly knee-breeches, silk stockings and buckled shoes. There is a vast amount of drinking, or at any rate of clinking of glasses, and Goethe's mother brings up from the cellar the grandfather's best vintage and christens it 'tyrants' blood', a term that survives in the family until the end of the century, when real blood flows. At this time it is just boastful rhetoric, like most of the Counts' talk. Friedrich is soon to become a diplomat, his country's envoy, and president of some chamber or other; finally he becomes a convert to Roman Catholicism – an act that inspires his old friend Voss to a bitter polemic: 'How did Fritz Stolberg become a bondsman?' – and writes a fifteen-volume history of the Christian religion. Now, however, he is writing odes in the style of Klopstock, ballads, *Lieder*; he addresses nature in the much quoted lines, '*Süsse heilige Natur, lass mich gehn auf deiner Spur*'. He has written better verses than these, if one wants to take the trouble to look for them. But most of all this is only a veneer. He dons the garb of the *Sturm und Drang* just as, later, he dons the uniform of a diplomat; even when he goes naked it is fancy dress.

Goethe enjoys a short and passionate friendship with the two brothers, and plots a love affair with their sister, Auguste, as well. 'To hell with the fact that she is a Countess!' he exclaims angrily. He is determined to love her, as he loved the other Auguste, Behrisch's sister, in Leipzig. As in that case he never sets eyes on 'Gustchen', but he writes her his finest and most passionate love letters, a novel in letters. If we did not know that she remained in far-off Holstein, separated from him by half Germany, she would certainly share first place among those he loved – a true first place does not exist. Goethe's letters to her are *hingewühlt*, dashed out in a turmoil of agitation, as befits a young genius, and they are well composed. They are magnificent in their graphic power; never again does Goethe portray himself, his moods, activities and aspirations, with so much colour and vitality. We seem to hear him breathe in the pauses – indicated by dashes – that are meant to express what cannot be put into words. 'I make these dashes for you because for a quarter of an hour I have been sitting lost in thought, while my spirit has flown round the whole inhabited world. Oh, unhappy fate, that will allow one no middle course. Either I am clinging, clasping tight to one place, or I roam off to all four quarters of the globe!'

He clings to this new sweetheart, his angel: My love! My love! Farewell, no you must have the original, what good is a copy of a kiss in replica! Then it is dear sister, angel sister, wipe my brow with your dear hand. In his imagination he travels to Copenhagen, where she is at the Court, and falls in tears at her feet: Gustgen, is it you? Oh! my darling! He immediately has to tell her of another sweetheart, a Lili, and of the agonies and joys he has to endure with her. He has written a scene of his *Faust*, he tells her, and then: 'Idled away a few hours. Dallied a few more with a girl your brothers will tell you about, a strange creature.' She is another Lotte; in Offenbach she has set up a sort of 'bar of all the talents' in the basement of an inn, very shabby and very gay, with silhouettes of young members of the *Sturm und Drang* stuck on the walls. Goethe carries her silhouette round with him, until he gives it away to a friend. She is a pretty thing; Goethe writes her a poem, 'caught in the tumult of many joys', calls her a true, good child, worthy of someone's love, and calls down heaven's blessing on her. We do not know what became of her. But who knows how much of this child of the people has found its way into other writings of Goethe's, mixed, perhaps, with characteristics of others of his acquaintance?

In his letters to Auguste he gives precise descriptions of himself, and not merely of his states of mind. We see him sitting at a card-table under a chandelier, dressed in a coat trimmed with braid, his hair carefully dressed, and with impeccable mien. He goes to a ball, where he pays court to a 'pretty little blond'. From Lyon, where the grandfather he never mentions worked as a tailor, he has ordered a special coat with blue trimmings. The perruquier works for a whole hour on his head, and then Goethe, in his impatience, tears the whole thing apart again. For the masked ball he orders an old German costume in black and yellow, with wide breeches, doublet, cloak and feathered hat, but he puts it aside when he learns that Lili is not coming to the ball. He dreams heavily and then wakes up in the most cheerful mood, with the sun streaming into the room: 'Gustgen! This is the moment for us to be happy, this is the moment when I must see my Gustgen, the only girl whose heart beats truly in my breast.'

Then he describes the other Goethe, the one in the beaver-grey coat, brown silk neckerchief, and boots; still elegant but more casually dressed. This Goethe roams about, already senses the spring in February, 'striving and working, at one moment putting the innocent feelings of youth into little poems, at another turning the strong spice of life into sundry dramas'. He draws and paints, without asking his way to right or left, 'because in his work he is always climbing a step higher, because he is not leaping after ideals, but, fighting and playing, wants to let his feelings develop into faculties'. Here we have another maxim of his life: fighting and playing.

The playing, even trifling, is still more important than the fighting. Gustgen's silhouette hangs on the wall of his room, alongside that of the Wetzlar Lotte; in his pocket case he carries the picture of the Offenbach Lotte. He writes: 'Oh! If I don't write plays now, I shall perish', a remark that should not be taken out of its context. Nothing more is to be published, he declares; in future these joys and children of his are to be buried quietly in some corner; he is sick and tired of this eternal dissecting of his *Werther*. Even while saying this he is publishing more than at any other period of his life. He boasts a little about his distinguished friends: Gustgen is the daughter of a *Hofmarschall* and is staying at the Danish Royal Court in Copenhagen. Goethe spends a pleasant afternoon with the 'great ones' – 'I had the pleasure and honour of the company of two princesses in the same room'.

From everywhere people now seek out the author of *Werther*: 'Another thing that makes me happy is that so many fine people from every corner of my fatherland, admittedly along with many insignificant, intolerable ones, come here to see me, sometimes on their way through, sometimes for a longer visit. It is only when one recognizes oneself in others that one discovers one's own existence.'

A quite astonishing period of travel has started, in spite of the terrible roads and high costs. Even the completely penniless young adherents of *Sturm und Drang* are always on the move, and not only in their writing. They come to Frankfurt, to the Goethe headquarters and hostelry, with their projects and their manuscripts. Their writings are often so similar in style and content that they are scarcely distinguishable and are often confused by the public. Goethe becomes involved in this too. His Strasbourg friend, Lenz, has had Goethe's impudent satire on Wieland published, behind his back the author assures us; he even hints that Lenz did this in order finally to alienate him from the master. Heinrich Leopold Wagner, another Strasbourger whom Goethe met in the Salzmann circle, pours scorn on the critics of *Werther* in another satire, *Prometheus, Deukalion und Seine Rezensenten*, and Goethe is forced to deny the authorship, energetically and in public. Mistakes were easily made, not only because almost everything, including *Werther* itself, was published without the author's name, but because the highly refined methods of stylistic comparison, which have since been developed, were not available to contemporaries, who were much more inclined to see a single style, that of the *Originalgenie*, the product of this exuberant age.

These young people were looked upon as a clique, a 'sect' they called it in those days. They did not have very much in common, really, beyond a feeling of youth and a desire to wipe out the past and start again with a clean slate. The fact that they themselves looked back to the most ancient times, or to the dark ages of the *Faustrecht*, did not concern them in the least; they also had their feet firmly planted in the present. They had no programme, these young talents, only a common enthusiasm: it might be for Shakespeare, who was regarded as the progenitor of all that was wild and unruly, or some ancient destroyer of tyrants.

Heinrich Leopold Wagner came to Frankfurt from Strasbourg, where his father had been a merchant. He had taken his degree as Doctor of Law and wished to settle down in the Imperial city as an advocate. In accordance with guild regulations, which applied to the liberal professions as well, he had to marry a Frankfurt citizen. Like grandfather Göthé he took a widow eighteen years older than himself who, nevertheless, still managed to survive him; Wagner died a few years later of consumption. As a writer Wagner was a vigorous talent, in spite of his physical weakness. His few plays are well written for the stage and show a strong feeling for the theatre, they are 'naturalistic' and provide good parts for the actors; they were immediately taken up by Schröder, the great actor-manager, for his Hamburg theatre.

In the *Kindermörderin* Wagner anticipates the Gretchen tragedy; Goethe took this very much amiss and accused his former table companion of plagiarism, quite oblivious of the fact that he himself had just taken over whole pages of Beaumarchais word for word and, what is more, had put Beaumarchais himself, who was still alive, on the stage. Comparison of the two works, naturally, is very much to Wagner's disadvantage, who wrote a robust stage play on a very well-worn theme, that of the seduced girl who has to kill her child because she can see no other way out.

In Wagner's play the seducer is an officer, and Lenz follows this with his play *Die Soldaten,* which should really be called, not *The Soldiers,* but *The Officers.* His own experiences in Strasbourg, as tutor to two young barons from the Baltic provinces who were on military service at Fort St Louis, provide the background. It is a tragedy of manners: seduction of respectable girls, lack of scruples, on the part of the girls as well, one of whom, the heroine Marie, sinks lower and lower until her own father, stumbling across her in the shadows, accosts her. His own daughter, a wanton!

But Lenz, in short colourful strokes and with a sure hand, presents a sharply critical satiric portrait. The plot, which is hopelessly involved, leads finally to Lenz's proposal for military reform, made in all seriousness: a corps of amazons, composed of voluntarily enlisted harlots, is to be formed in the hope of thus protecting the daughters of respectable bourgeois families from the insatiable lust of the officers. To understand such a proposal we must realize that officers in the mercenary armies were compelled to remain single in order to be without ties and 'on immediate call'; should an officer contract a marriage, however, as happened from time to time, his wife was not allowed to live where the regiment was garrisoned. The type of man they looked for was an utterly reckless dare-devil, a lady-killer, gambler and brawler; if he caused a certain amount of unrest among the pious lambs of the neighbourhood, this was a risk that had to be accepted in the interests of the State.

Another type of the day was portrayed by Lenz in his *Hofmeister* (The Private Tutor), a play often attributed to Goethe, though with great lack of perception as the well-to-do 'patrician's' son was very far removed from a calling that was reserved for penniless students. For these, however, to become a private tutor was the only prospect open on the completion of their studies, while they were waiting in hopes of finding some position which, again, was only procurable through patronage and influence. Almost all the writers and men of genius, until well into the nineteenth century, served their time as private tutors. In doing so they had to accept all the humiliations such a post entailed, with its enforced obeisances, mental and physical, and the inevitable catastrophe should the young man develop a passion for the lady of the house, as Hölderlin did, or fall in love with one of the daughters. With merciless logic and symbolism, Lenz sees no other solution for his tutor, Läuffer, after he has seduced or been seduced by the aristocratic daughter, than to castrate himself, not merely mentally, as was usual, but physically. Bert Brecht, with the eye of the great adapter and producer, attempted to revive the play, presenting the tutor as an example and warning of German servility.

The fact that Lenz, after many wanderings, and after much imposing on people's hospitality, always with unhappy results – on the Goethes in Frankfurt, on Goethe's sister and brother-in-law in Baden, in Weimar, and elsewhere – finally went insane and ended his days miserably, damaged his reputation in the eyes of his contemporaries, but has enhanced it in the eyes of posterity.

Contemporaries saw in the slight, nervous and very boyishly good-looking Lenz a 'little younger brother' of Goethe. 'A delicate, tapering face', is the description of one of his circle, 'a keen, quietly observant expression, with the goodness of mother nature in his heart and on his tongue'. Lenz, too, thought of himself as Goethe's twin brother. He brought with him from Strasbourg a manuscript entitled *Unsere Ehe* (Our Marriage), about his relationship to his greater friend, which has disappeared. He wrote ardent poems to Goethe's sister, the 'abbess' Cornelia; his attentions were engaged in a constant groping from one hopeless object to another. People treated him as a sick child, as indeed he was, most probably suffering from syphilis which, after long agony, brought him to his death in his native Russia.

In strong contrast to Wagner, with his weak chest, and Lenz, with his disordered brain, was Maximilian Klinger, a powerful fellow with broad shoulders and long legs, the only one among these lively young talents who 'did something' with his life; nearly as old as Goethe, he died in Moscow, a Russian general, ennobled and greatly esteemed. Not least because of the admirable way in which he conducted his life, Goethe preserved a kindlier memory of him than of any of his other friends of these days, and kept up a correspondence with him until quite late. As a young man Goethe helped him in many ways; Klinger's mother helped with the laundry in the Goethe household, the boy helped by carrying wood and fetching water. He went with the poor students, singing from door to door, and was given a school and university education. Goethe helped him with introductions, with money, and by letting him have little manuscripts to publish and earn the fees from. Goethe made a portrait of him; it is one of his best drawings, and shows a strong, firm profile, bearing some resemblance to his own. He never showed the slightest trace of jealousy, even when his *protégé* began to write on his own and his plays brought him a fame that, for a short while, eclipsed Goethe's.

Klinger's literary success was not long-lived. He wandered around with groups of itinerant actors and then, as everyone was advising the well set-up young man to do, he tried military service. A letter of introduction, the usual means in those days, brought about the turning point in his life; he was appointed 'reader' to the Grand Duke Paul, heir to the Russian throne, in St Petersburg. The wild young man of *Sturm und Drang* adapted himself with surprising rapidity to the atmosphere of Court life. He married an illegitimate daughter of Catherine the Great. Slowly but surely he climbed the ladder of success, starting as a teacher at the School for Cadets, and eventually becoming its Director, with the rank of Lieutenant-General and with the personal title of nobility. When the reaction set in after the great wars he was honourably retired and, to the end of his life, lived comfortably in his house in St Petersburg, maintaining numerous connections with the progressive literary world in Russia.

*Sturm und Drang* was the name of the play by Klinger which gave the whole movement its name. Originally it was to have been called *Wirrwarr* (Hurly-burly). Prior to this he had written, among other things, a tragedy, *Die Zwillinge* (The Twins), which received a drama prize from the Hamburg theatre, the leading stage in Germany. In it he had sounded one of the basic themes of his generation: the younger son who, by an accident of a few minutes at birth, finds himself disinherited in favour of his elder brother, the weakling, the pretty one, who gets everything – the fortune, the title and the bride. It was as disinherited younger sons cheated of their patrimony that all the men of the rising generation saw themselves. 'With one proud blow I will tear him down, seize him and dash him to the ground! He shall crawl on the ground and I will soar into the air!' Fratricide and a son's death at his father's hand; a well-constructed horror play, set out in short scenes, and effective on the stage.

But where is there an outlet for all this fire and frenzy? The old continent of Europe is too small, too confined. America! is the cry, where there is fighting, where there is space. 'Hurrah for the tumult and uproar, when the senses reel like a vane in the storm!' With these words Klinger's *Sturm und Drang* opens, and the imagery of the weathercock also occurs in Goethe's writings of the time. The heroes' names are Wild, La Feu and Blasius the Blasé. The plot is nonsensical, an old family feud between rival British nobles, with eventual mutual recognition between the hostile older generation and happy reunion among the younger – all this on American soil against a background of fighting, shooting and embracing. It is in fact a hurly-burly of confusion, as though taken from one of the 'Gothic novels' of the day. The only innovations are the characteristic phrases of the new generation: 'War,' cries Wild, 'the only happiness I know!' A feeling of emptiness, of hollowness, comes over him: 'I shall have myself stretched out over a drum so that I can acquire a new dimension! I feel so wretched again. Oh that I could exist in the barrel of this pistol, till someone fired me off into the air. Oh, indecision! How far, how awry dost thou lead one!'

It is a caricature of Goethe's moods of the time, and has the significance of any exaggeration. Even in their love-making they wail, pant, sigh and languish: 'Cheerful indeed!' says Blasius. 'I am bored to death. My heart is so cold, so dead, and the girl is so pretty and gay.' We even meet the old arcadian pastoral tradition in this wild setting, complete with hut, shepherd's cloak and staff. 'I am your shepherd,' sings Blasius. 'In marriage too, my Lord?' asks the shepherdess coyly. 'Heaven forbid! Only in spirit, only in imagination. There lies the charm!'

Klinger wrote a great deal during his long life, later on mostly fantastic novels, including a life of *Faust* with satirical and sometimes rather coarse skits on contemporary life. The Russian censor, unobservant or careless, passed the book without comment, perhaps because it was the Germans rather than the Russians who were castigated in it:

> Lazy blockheads, slavishly bowing to appearance and wealth, to all the differences among men, believing that their princes and counts are made of nobler stuff than they are and thinking themselves splendid fellows when they kill each other on their behalf or allow themselves to be sold as cannon fodder to other princes. Are they not perfectly content with their lot under this feudal tyranny, no matter who flays them or how? Do you hear one word of rebellion against tyranny coming from that country?

The general and teacher of military youth is speaking from St Petersburg to his former countrymen, and in Russia, a country of the grossest feudal tyranny, they feel themselves sufficiently secure to allow such passages into print. The great Catherine herself loved to flirt non-committally with daring modern ideas, and she had her grandson Alexander brought up on Rousseau's *Emile* and the Swiss republican La Harpe.

Klinger, Lenz and Wagner – these formed the 'inner circle' of *Sturm und Drang,* with lesser figures scattered round the periphery. They travelled hither and thither, visited each other, quarrelled and were reconciled, admired, criticized and parodied one another. And all this activity centred round various women and girls, who acted as peacemakers or created new disturbances. The whole movement was like a large, rambling family. Much of what they wrote, and much of what they published, has the air of private utterance; only later did it achieve literary rank.

Goethe quarrelled with the two Jacobi brothers; both had very sentimental dispositions and both were very active men of letters, a frequent combination. They had taken offence at his parodies and reviews, which they called 'infamous'. Goethe's confidante at this time was a Johanna Fahlmer in Frankfurt, whom he called 'Aunt', although she was only five years older than himself; she had taken the place of his sister who was fretting out her soul in marriage. Soon after Cornelia's untimely death Johanna married the widowed Schlosser, and this brought her short friendship with Goethe to an end. The little 'aunt' acted as intermediary between Goethe and her relatives, the Jacobis. A visit was arranged, no excuses were necessary for the parodies, no introduction even, 'I just dropped down from the skies at Fritz Jacobi's feet. And there we were, I and he! And before any sisterly eye had spied us and done the preliminaries, we were together and had become friends.' It was a strangely mixed company that was gathered there: a large group of pietists, among them his friend Jung-Stilling from Strasbourg, the famous Lavater from Zürich, and the young writer Wilhelm Heinse, author of the novel *Laidon*. Goethe said of this book that it was 'written with the voluptuous graces' richest ardour' and contained the best stanzas of *ottava rima* in the German language. Like the rest of them Heinse was a penniless lad from Thuringia, who was forced to act as travelling companion or tutor in order to make two ends meet. He took refuge in passionate erotic fantasies instead of in revolutionary dreams of tyrannicide and greatness. Of all this group of young talents he was the most sensual, and consequently their best writer on art; his descriptions of the great Rubens paintings in the Düsseldorf gallery are almost without parallel in their feeling for the master's rendering of skin and flesh.

Goethe now joins this circle, dancing around like a will-o'-the-wisp, a 'genius from tip to toe', as Heinse describes him. He pulls faces, recites ballads, his own and Scottish ones, horrifies the devout pietists and bewitches Fritz Jacobi. The latter writes to Wieland that Goethe is a man possessed, but that one only has to spend an hour with him to see how ridiculous it is to expect him to think or behave other than as he does. Jacobi even tried to convince himself that this encounter was at last going to give real strength and stability to his own character. But in this he was deceived, for throughout his life he remained a sensitive, eclectic, philosophical dilettante, although he managed to rise to the position of President of the Bavarian Academy in Munich. His brother, Georg, also overwhelmed by the magnitude of Goethe's mind, noted in his diary that he would have liked to record Goethe's table-talk verbatim.

With Heinse, Georg Jacobi edited a small periodical in Düsseldorf called *Iris*, an attractively got-up little publication, 'for the ladies'. Goethe's *Lieder* and Lenz's poems appeared in it alongside Jacobi's own effusions and a weak novel by his brother, which quite unconcernedly romanticized the members of his circle in a series of letters from Sylli to Clerdon. A fiery translation of Sappho by Heinse was printed side by side with a discourse on the dance for demure young demoiselles by Georg Jacobi, a moving lament for the barbarism of modern dancing, citing Madame de la Roche and

145

Goethe's *Werther*, who also never wanted to let his girl dance with anyone else. Are we to see, the author cries, 'our wives, daughters or sweethearts clasped in men's arms, breast to breast, whirled around to the strains of wild music, their true characters completely numbed?' He is referring to the Waltz or 'German dance', then new. He continues:

> Even if some innocent creature, pressed to the bosom of an ardent youth, remains uncontaminated herself, what a thought it is that she should serve to awaken the play of his voluptuous imagination, the excitement of his desires, and that she should be the object of sensual pleasure to a man she does not love! Our fair ones, if they still maintain a semblance of innocence, should hide in a corner now and then and listen to the conversations of some of those to whom they yield in so frivolous a manner....

All these things go on side by side, both in the *Iris* and when the bright young talents meet; arcadian pastorals as they have existed for centuries and lyric verse of the most modern kind coining new and powerful word images, flashes of genius side by side with tame advice and vague religious feeling. Nature is invoked incessantly, and they strut about well dressed and carefully coiffured. They inveigh against tyrants, and look furtively round for a position in some petty court. There is Promethian defiance, or a prayer meeting at Lavater's where Goethe is to be seen as well. *Sturm und Drang* is not merely an affair of literary documents; it was a very human and very active movement, comprising the most diverse and contrasting elements.

# 15

# *Physiognomics*

The Zürich preacher Lavater, eight years older than Goethe, was already famous when he wrote his first letters to the young poet; shortly afterwards he visited him. In a period of vivid contrasts he was, perhaps, the figure with the most disparate characteristics, both in his outward appearance and in himself. Goethe's opinions of him reflect these contrasts: at first Lavater is the best, the greatest, the wisest, the most profound of mortals, and he forms a close attachment to the prophet, even sharing the same bed with him on their travels; in later years he disposes of him as though he had been a swindler, 'he deceived himself and others'. There was something of all this in Lavater; he was like a piece of patchwork, woven with the most varied strands: there are fine, delicate threads, a deep understanding of the spiritual conditions of others, side by side with a down-to-earth industriousness; there is humility coupled with the arrogance of the sectarian; the unassuming domesticity of a family patriarch, in which everyone who visits him sees the ideal of the unspoilt Swiss way of life, and a vast correspondence which proudly embraces the Empress of Russia, duchesses, marchionesses, and the mistresses of princes. His face, with the long, pointed nose of a man on the track of souls, has, at the same time, fine eyebrows and a delicate mouth, though this latter can be very firm on occasion. His flat chest and his stiff ungainly walk, which reminded Goethe of a crane, do not prevent him from moving nimbly and with a sure step among the most reluctant of his admirers and winning them over by his charm of manner. His small eyes give the impression of candour but, in fact, they see virtually nothing, or only what he has already made up his mind about, or what, by clever questioning, he extracts from the person in front of him, this last one of his greatest gifts. He was one of the very first to recognize Goethe's greatness, and bestowed extravagant praise on him before ever he saw him or had read *Werther*. But he was equally extravagant in his praise of a rogue and swindler like Cagliostro, refusing to alter his opinion even when irrefutable evidence of the man's villainy came to light; he simply declared stubbornly that that was a different Cagliostro, the miracle worker of the same name was a saint.

Endowed with these characteristics the preacher now set about teaching the art, or science, of physiognomics, and thereby became world famous. It was really the reversal of the pietists' procedure: instead of analysing the soul in all its facets and 'excrescences', even the gravest of them, he proposed to work from the outward appearance inwards, to deduce the qualities of a man's soul from the shape of his head and the features of his face. It was in his face, and primarily even more simply in his profile, that a man's inner-most being was revealed: this was the gospel and Lavater was its prophet. He believed himself capable of so grasping a person's essential nature at a glance that he could both tell his past and prophesy his future.

There is a story of the physiognomist meeting a modest, unassuming man in the stage coach, on his way from Zürich to Schaffhausen. Lavater was fond of demonstrating his art to any and everyone. He immediately em-barked on an exposition of the man's character: gentleness above all, and an understanding of other people's needs, caring affectionately for them, taking them by the hand, leading them on their way.... 'The public hang-man of Schaffhausen at your service, Sir', came the answer.

Lavater's book *Physiognomische Fragmente zur Beförderung der Men-schenkenntnis und Menschenliebe* (Physiognomic Fragments for the Pur-pose of Promoting the Knowledge and Love of Mankind) began to appear in 1775; publication of the four large volumes, copiously illustrated with engravings and sumptuously produced on beautiful paper, occupied four years. Goethe eagerly collaborated, contributing both to the text and to the illustrations; he also supervised the printing. French, Dutch and English editions followed, in some cases even more elaborately illustrated than the original; there were extracts and pocket editions as well, and the names Lavater and Physiognomics remained synonymous until far into the nine-teenth century. The book was jeered at, imitated and parodied. Lichtenberg wrote his *Fragment von Schwänzen*, predicting from the rings in a pig's tail the spiritual qualities of a promising young piglet; in his Aphorisms he also made the more serious observation that lack of symmetry in a face often denotes exceptional talent, and he claimed to have remarked this in Vol-taire. Goethe's head, too, as can be seen from the life mask taken when he was in his fifties, had a fairly strongly marked asymmetrical form.

With finesses of this kind Lavater was not concerned. He amassed a prodigious amount of raw material, and carried on a huge correspondence. He employed draughtsmen and engravers, in particular the numerous dile-tantes who had taken up the fashionable hobby of silhouette making. There were even special chairs for this equipped with a frame, and the business was pursued with all the eagerness of latter-day amateur photography. Fail-ing the costly miniature, a silhouette was the first gift expected by the lover of his sweetheart, and by friend of friend. Profiles of almost all Goethe's contemporaries, including their children and servants, have been preserved for posterity in large albums. Before long itinerant silhouette cutters made their appearance at fairs, working free-hand and adding 'characteristic touches'; one especially clever artist trained his dog to bite the famous profile of Monsieur de Voltaire out of a slice of bread, thus earning much applause.

The silhouettes published by Lavater in his great work are documents of great reliability; the drawings, on the other hand, are mostly of only limited value, being often stylized to conform to literary taste or, in the case of famous men of Greek and Roman times, inventions pure and simple and paraphrases of preconceived ideas.

Brutus, for example, is depicted as a youth with defiant bosses on his forehead to denote the tyrant killer, like some hero out of one of Klinger's plays. Goethe contributes a hymn in prose to the mighty rebel, which contains some reminiscences of Ossian: 'A mind of iron is entrenched behind this high forehead, gathering its forces it then projects itself in these protuberances, each, like the bosses on Fingal's shield, pregnant with desire for battle and for deeds. . . .' 'No master can he suffer, nor master can he be. No pleasure has he ever had in slaves. To live among his fellows was his need, as free men and as equals. In a world of free and noble beings he would find his own fulfilment.' These are the moods of the new age, they are not physiognomic interpretations of a head; for Brutus' head no historical portrait existed, it was pure fantasy.

Lavater's interpretations often strike a jarring and comically impudent note. Before he had seen either Goethe or his portrait he boasted that he could describe his head: 'Domed forehead, blue eyes, very small nose; many features, muscles, zigzags and pictorial criss-crosses throughout the whole face.' He could hardly have been wider of the mark. The zigzag is characteristic of Lavater's method, which consisted of hit-or-miss fortune-telling and which sometimes showed the fortune-teller's gift of putting two and two together quickly.

Goethe's interest in physiognomics is aroused in the first instance because he sees in it an aid to his drawing, which he now starts to work at seriously. He assists in drawing some of the heads. He contributes to the text and in so doing discovers 'characters', a literary genre that Theophrastus and La Bruyère had made popular. He describes the head of an 'idiot': 'The pattern of this insane person is like the leaf of a tree which blight has caught only in a single spot; radiating out from this locality the form is distorted, leading into it the lines contract, and in the same way here all the other features twitch convulsively towards the disordered brain.' This is a sketch for a character in a novel.

Interpretations are attempted from the skulls of animals too, and here Goethe makes his first contact with a sphere of activity that is to occupy him far into the future. His interpretations are still very tied to the old zoology of authorities like the sixteenth-century Konrad Gesner, who describes the fox as a stinking evil beast, cunning and at enmity with all the rest. To Goethe the skull of the tiger is the 'seat of a slight imagination and greedy cruelty', the mouse exhibits 'appetite and timidity', the lion, the heraldic beast, is noble in the curvature of its skull, and the cat discriminatingly fond of dainties. In his contributions to the prefaces he remarks cautiously that the whole thing is only fragmentary, and that physiognomic speculation and endeavour, too, 'amount in the last resort to a mere stammering'.

It is a game, and to most of those who read the book it becomes a party game of making comparisons, teasing one another and pensive meditation. But it stimulates observation too, and herein, for Goethe, lies its source of profit. With his accustomed habit of always proceeding to a more comprehensive view, he drafts a programme showing how the term physiognomics can be applied in a much broader sense. It is not only the build, the mien, the outward appearance of a man that are important, but also his social position, his habits, his dress and his possessions. Is it possible, he asks, to penetrate all these husks and arrive at a man's innermost being and formulate his character. Be of good cheer! he cries. He is confident of his ability to do so. 'Nature forms the individual, he transforms himself, and this transformation is again natural; seeing himself set down in the great wide world, he fences and walls off a small piece of it for himself and furnishes it after his own image.' Goethe, as he is often to do later, invents his own terminology, and in this instance is already close to his later concept of natural science. Basically this is nothing but an aspect of his urge to form and create, the attempt to recreate, like a god, the world and all its phenomena.

Precise observation interests him less. In his contributions to Lavater's book one is struck by how rarely he describes actual physiognomic features; and in his own writings we notice the same trend, which enhances his characterization. It has long been realized that detailed descriptions of a hero or heroine in a novel only disturb and bore the reader and paralyse the all-important co-operation of his imagination.

But physiognomics, provided one does not accept Goethe's highly personal definition of the term, was something different. Nor was it discovered by Lavater, who only gave new life to an old art. It was a kind of soothsaying, and in the older writings, which were still in circulation in numerous editions in Goethe's day, a *physiognomica* was generally included among tracts on astrology, palmistry and magic. It is to this that Goethe refers when he says that people speak of physiognomics in great awe as though it were some mysterious science; to hear about a wonderful physiognomist gives them as much pleasure as hearing about a magician or a conjurer.

A great magician had already compiled a book on physiognomics in the Middle Ages for the Emperor Friederich II of Hohenstaufen, mostly from Greek and Arabic sources. He was Michael Scotus, the Emperor's personal physician, who was also said to have invented a means of flying. In the dedication Scotus proudly declared that with this knowledge the Emperor would be able infallibly to recognize people's vices and virtues, and with the same accuracy as if he himself inhabited their bodies. It was a teaching that must have appealed to a ruler who was always suspicious. The book was reprinted many times during the Renaissance, until Scotus was superseded by another physiognomist, the Neapolitan Porta, whom Goethe came across in his work on the *Farbenlehre*. It is from Porta that the still current physiognomic comparisons between men and animals derive: an aquiline nose, a hawk-like profile, a foxy face. It is the translation of medieval zoology into the language of physiognomics: the eagle is bold, the noblest heraldic beast, and a man with an aquiline nose is therefore a noble man; to have the face of a wolf indicates cruelty and greed. As an antidote we can remind ourselves of an old judge's words of wisdom, as reported by Theodore Fontane: 'My murderers all looked like young girls.'

Like Michael Scotus, Lavater claimed to be able to deduce people's vices and virtues from their profiles, not to serve a tyrant who wanted a quick means of distinguishing traitors from loyal servants, but to promote faith and morals. He claimed to be able to recognize by his face the man who was suited to be a proselyte for his own very distinct form of faith in Jesus. In his practical activities he found a quite astonishing number of adherents and believers from every class of life. Whatever can be said against his book, and this is much, he exercised an influence during his life such as is given to few. Goethe was fascinated by him, almost to the point of feminine devotion; Goethe's mother, solid and undemonstrative as she was, attached herself with fervour to the prophet. Women formed his main audience and there was no lack of the painfully grotesque scenes that commonly abound among the devotees of the founder of a sect. The beautiful Branconi, mistress of the Duke of Brunswick and courted from far and near, wrote a letter to the master asking for some material token of his favour, a handkerchief, a few hairs from his head, something 'that will be to me what my garters are to you'; she had evidently sent these to him. There is a hidden erotic element in most ecstasy of this sort, though in Lavater's case it was probably platonic; his family life was exemplary. With other miracle workers, who appeared frequently, it assumed more tangible form.

But what interest did this man, whose character was in many respects so alien to his, hold for Goethe? What was it that attracted him so strongly, and then repelled him until he brusquely severed the bond between them? First and foremost it will almost certainly have been the influence that such a prophet has over people which fascinated him; the word *würken*, to have an effect or to exert an influence, was one of Goethe's favourite expressions at this time. He learned, gleaned and studied on all sides. He was open-hearted to the point of surrender, and then he had to withdraw into himself to the point of hardness. It was in such alternations that his life consisted.

Thus he travels round with the prophet, who is awaited everywhere either with longing or with curiosity. A second prophet joins them, the educationist Basedow, a man of very different stamp. Squat and heavily built, he smokes his pipe incessantly. In a rough voice he preaches his new educational gospel, based on the principles of Rousseau mixed with un-orthodox religious views and heresies concerning the Trinity, all of which he throws at the heads of his listeners in blunt language. To Goethe, the 'child of this world' caught between two prophets, the journey is like a continuous fair and he enjoys himself thoroughly as they travel to Bad Ems, the river Lahn and then on to the Rhine. As the author of *Werther* he, too, is awaited everywhere; people want to hear more about Lotte and Jerusalem. Instead of which he evasively tells them fairy tales, and argues throughout the night with Basedow on the subjects of the church fathers and the early councils; he even shares a room with him, in spite of the stench of tobacco which is anathema to him. At other times he dances all night long at the Kursaal, disguised as a country parson – it is significant that on these fancy-dress occasions, he generally adopts the disguise of a poor theologian, as though goaded by a bad conscience – and he plays practical jokes on his travelling companions. He observes them closely, and the physiognomic studies he made of them are the clearest evidence in the whole of his *œuvre* of the interest he took in this new hobby.

Lavater's observation was less acute. He thought he could detect in Goethe's head another adept for his faith. But this was the parting of the ways. Goethe was prepared to recognize the gentle, pious nature of his companion, as well as the simplicity of a man who could tap an excited opponent on the shoulder with a 'Come along now, be good!' He compared favourably Lavater's clean and tidy appearance with that of the uncouth, tobacco-stinking Basedow, his childlike faith in the Bible with the educationist's heretical ravings. Further he was not prepared to go. Lavater long hoped to be able to convert Goethe; in his correspondence he constantly returns to the subject, and in the most naïve way. Goethe was not cut out to be a disciple of any sect or faith at all. He had his own faith. And when Lavater, in his devout fervour, grew more and more insistent until finally he reached the inevitable, high-handed 'he that is not with me is against me', the break came and with unnecessary harshness.

But Goethe's interest in physiognomics remained with him for life. Other prophets appeared, such as the phrenologist Gall, who again created a new epoch in the art and described Goethe's head as that of a great popular orator. When Schiller's skull was disinterred, long after his death, Goethe holding it pensively in his hands, wrote a poem, significantly choosing the *terza rima*, the strictest of all verse forms, to discipline the streaming flow of his emotions. In this 'withered shell' permeated with sacred meaning he sees a vessel, proclaiming oracles of the *Gott-Natur* and its manifestation:

> *Wie sie das Feste lässt zu Geist verrinnen,*
> *Wie sie das Geisterzeugte fest bewahre.*

See how it (nature) melts, and turns to spirit, matter, how tightly guards what spirit hath begotten.

This is his answer to Lavater's attempts to convert him, this is his way of creating a physiognomics of his own, in poetry.

# 16

# *Lili*

Having broadened his experience with prophets, uncouth and tender, with his talented friends and with pietists, and with a visit from the great Klopstock – with whom he discussed skating, Klopstock emphatically recommending the low, flat Dutch skates – Goethe finds his way, in Frankfurt as well, into social circles very different from those in which his parents move. His father, the Councillor, the private gentleman, does not mix with the Frankfurt *élite*. The son has fewer scruples. He dresses very fashionably, in his blue-trimmed tail-coat from Lyon. He is a celebrated author, and the friend of other celebrities. In spite of this the patricians and sons of the great banking families do not really regard him as their equal; they know about the tailor and wine merchant grandfather. None the less he has now become a well-known personality. A friend introduces him to the Schönemanns, one of the foremost banking families in the town and reputedly very rich. They live in great style and entertain lavishly, and at their receptions the gambling is for fairly high stakes. There is music, both serious and gay, as well as dancing.

A pretty fair girl of 17 is playing the clavecin as Goethe enters the house; she plays with charm and skill. Goethe goes over and watches her. When she has finished what she is playing the girl gets up and greets him with the easy manners of a young society lady. Meanwhile a quartet has started to play. The two take careful stock of one another, and even forty years later Goethe could still feel 'that I was very much under inspection!'

As a very old man he said of her: 'She was, in fact, the first I deeply and truly loved. I can also say that she was the last; for, in comparison with that first one, all the little attractions I felt during my life were slight and superficial.' This is not just senile forgetfulness and Olympian remoteness, hard as this may be to accept for those whose research or interest has led them to study the many 'slight attractions' that came afterwards. But Goethe's statement can be understood only if we do not regard the words 'love' and 'loved one' as constant and invariable, as is so often done. Goethe's love takes many different forms. Here, it seems, he meets for the only time in his life a member of the opposite sex to whom he is in complete subjection and from whom he is unable, or able only with the greatest difficulty, to tear him-

153

self away. Lili Schönemann is no 'sister' type. Nor is she already married, engaged, altogether too young, or easy to handle. Demoiselle Schönemann is extremely difficult to handle. Goethe's love for her is an ardent, burning, tormenting affair, a genuine fire, not the kind at which one can warm oneself and then move away when it gets too hot. To say this is not to detract from his other loves, which had a different significance. In this case, however, for the first and seemingly for the only time in his life he feels himself caught, tied up 'in the sack', of which he had dreamed so frighteningly in Leipzig. The comparison is a little too crude. This is a net with strands of silk. But they hurt.

The mother invites the young advocate to pay them another visit. Lili's brothers, older than she is, are less taken with the visitor. To them his bearing seems too self-consciously casual, and in any case they have very definite plans for their pretty sister. She is an important piece on their chessboard, with whom it is imperative to make the right moves. For the truth is that the Schönemann splendour is now only a façade. The sons have inherited none of their father's ability. Like many of the Frankfurt bankers, such as Bethmann and Willemer, he had made a great deal of money during the Seven Years War, but he died shortly after peace was declared. His partner, Heyder, has left the firm; a merchant of the old school, he does not like the new methods; his own pretty daughters have to work in the office. They sit at the counter changing the innumerable different types of currency; in these days of great monetary confusion, with the full-weight and clipped thalers and ducats, this brings in very good business. The father makes no objection if the clients are distracted by the charms of the pretty cashiers. Frau Schönemann, on the other hand, has very strong objections to her daughter being so vulgarly exploited. She is to be an accomplished claveciniste, an elegant horsewoman, a good dancer, a fluent conversationalist, and above all she is to present the family with a wealthy son-in-law. The new mansion, the 'Palais Schönemann', has swallowed up a large proportion of the family fortune, with its large stables, its special salon for the receptions, its costly painted wallpapers and its gaming tables. The company is partly aristocratic and, in the case of rich merchants connected with the banking business, partly very wealthy; there is also a sprinkling of more lightweight guests. The malicious Frankfurt chronicler, Senckenberg, even speaks in his diary of 'easy morals' at the Schönemanns, which probably does not signify more than that their parties were less straitlaced than elsewhere in Frankfurt.

It is in this company that Goethe finds himself, proud and yet ill at ease, for he immediately senses the family's opposition. The drama of his love affair is played out between Frankfurt and nearby Offenbach, where Frau Schönemann's brother, Herr d'Orville, has his house. The d'Orvilles are partners in one of the largest snuff businesses in Germany; they make the famous 'Marokko' snuff, and employ several hundred workers. As the residence of Count Isenburg – one of more than three hundred independent German princes – Offenbach has a style of living very different from that of the much stricter Imperial city of Frankfurt. Industry, and not only the snuff industry, flourishes, the rich families entertain with the greatest hospitality, and many well-to-do people from Frankfurt have their summer villas there or rent accommodation for the season. In Offenbach there is music making everywhere, and dancing too; the town takes advantage of the fact that the Frankfurt authorities very rarely sanction public balls and masquerades. On Saturdays whole caravans of people come from Frankfurt to go to the theatre, which provides entertainment of an elegance quite unlike anything to be found in the Imperial city.

And so there now begins for Goethe a period of cheerful coming and going between the two towns, of gay social life, a perpetual carnival with intervals spent in the family circle of the d'Orvilles, from whom he receives a very warm welcome. He plays with the children, for whom he buys toys at the Frankfurt toy fair; once again we see, as in Wetzlar, how important a background of children is to any love affair of Goethe's. He thanks his hosts in a charming letter in verse in which the children appear with Arab nicknames, Mufti, Ali Bey, Abu Dahab – an allusion, perhaps, to the 'Marokko' snuff – climb onto his knee and are told to give Lili, who has a headache, a kiss in his name; the old servant enters and asks the ladies what they would like for dinner, they choose capon and venison; André hums a song and from the next room the calls of the card players can be heard; the poet also refers to the bad mood which drove him away, but, 'Pliz! Plaz! and here I am again.'

Lili keeps a menagerie, which occasions another poem. He is a bear sitting at her feet, held by silken bonds. He growls, he struggles, she gives him playful slaps and from time to time gives him a morsel of honey. He sighs for freedom, stretching his limbs – 'I still have strength.'

'Goethe is in a gay mood at present,' we read in one letter, 'he goes to balls and dances like one possessed! He also plays the gallant with the fair sex, which he used not to do.' But in the middle of a conversation he will suddenly run off, and on festive occasions he appears dressed in the most slovenly way. At the same time he spends large sums of money with his perruquier, on gloves, with his swordsmith, on silver buckles for his shoes, and on flowers, sweetmeats and other presents. He goes riding with Lili and writes about it to his distant Auguste: 'You should see the angel in her riding-dress!' Lili gives him a little golden heart which he wears round his neck, under the lace frills of his jabot. In his eyes she coquettes with him: in reality she is no more of a coquette than any other girl, and probably less so because fundamentally she is a serious and extremely sensitive person. Goethe is always complaining of coquettishness in others, while he himself behaves in the most feminine way, gossiping and broadcasting news of his latest love affair to all and sundry, to Auguste Stolberg, to his Aunt

Fahlmer, and even to people he knows as slightly as the poet Bürger in Göttingen, or Frau Karsch, the Prussian 'Sappho', in Berlin, about whom he cares even less but who has started a correspondence with him about his writings. Little notes fly back and forth between Frankfurt and Offenbach, and poems too; of all this only scraps remain, but these are sufficient to make us realize that he was tormented. He is constantly trying to leave, but is always forced to go back. 'I cannot stand it here for long, I must go away again – where?'

In the freer atmosphere of Offenbach, where Goethe stays with his friend André and where Lili is not under the suspicious eyes of her brothers, their relationship is more intimate. Goethe sits in Lili's room, among all her hat-boxes and riding clothes, while she goes into the next room to dress. Sitting at her writing-desk he writes to his other sweetheart in Copenhagen; it is both amusing and revealing to note how he always sits at 'his girl's' writing-desk to write to some other girl.

These other girls continue to swirl round in his head. The black eyes of Maximiliane Brentano, whom he has seen at the play and of whom he writes to her mother, 'I have seen those eyes again, I do not know what it is about those eyes'; Maximiliane has now been promoted to the position of 'sister'. Then there is the Offenbach barmaid, alongside the Offenbach Lili and the distant Auguste. In his later autobiographical notes we find only a short sequence of words: 'Adventure with Lili. Prelude. *Verführung*. Offenbach.' The word *Verführung* can mean almost anything; it can mean seduction, or it can mean simply that he felt he was being lured away from his true path.

Neither family takes a favourable view of the affair. Goethe's father does not want a *Staatsdame*, a society woman, for a daughter-in-law. In any case, where is such a couple to live? His son has the little attic room, where he lives among his easels, with his drawings and silhouettes stuck up on the wall; the other rooms on that floor are occupied by the mad lodger and the servants. Furthermore the Schönemanns are Calvinists, the Goethes Lutherans. They have no friends in common. Frau Schönemann wavers. Her financial worries are uppermost in her mind; the young advocate, with his very modest practice, hardly seems a very good match, and while writing may bring fame it does not earn bread and butter. The two sons are openly hostile.

A friend of the Schönemann family now takes a hand, a Fräulein Delph, a business woman who engages in a wide variety of business dealings in Heidelberg, such as financing loans, dabbling in secret political intrigues, and match-making. She is a determined, masculine-looking person. She takes to the irresolute Goethe and manages to bring the affair to the point of a formal engagement. 'Your hands on it', she orders, the parents having given their reluctant consent. 'I stood in front of Lili', Goethe tells us in his memoirs, 'and held out my hand; slowly, but without faltering, she placed suppressed eroticism Goethe writes a passionate translation of the *Song of Solomon*, converting it into his own personal idiom. He tells Auguste in Copenhagen, what he has told Merck, that he feels 'stranded' – poor, and gone astray:

And yet, my dearest, when I feel once more that in the midst of all the nothingness so many skins are once more peeling off my heart, that the convulsive tensions in my foolish little constitution are abating, that my outlook on the world is more cheerful, my relations with people surer, firmer and on a broader basis, and yet that deep within myself I remain for ever dedicated only to the sacred love, which little by little expels all that is alien through the spirit of purity which is its very essence, and which finally will become pure like spun gold – then I leave things as they are – perhaps I am deluding myself. – And thanks be to God. Good night. *Addio.* Amen: 1775.

These are outpourings, and we must not press them too closely in our endeavour to extract a clear-cut meaning. But looking back over his whole life, as we are able to do, one thing emerges clearly and that is his devotion, his dedication, to 'sacred love', to love in general, rather than to some particular individual who has happened to cross his path. Lili is the 'alien' thing that must be cast off, sloughed like a snake's skin, to use his own constantly recurring simile. The new skin is already there, underneath, and this is the manifestation of the 'spirit of purity'. To his fiancée, who was willing to follow him even to America, this skin changing must have appeared in a very different light. He takes flight, for the second and last time, not only from his relationship with Lili but from his parents' house and from his native town – for ever.

There are still a few echoes of his love for Lili in poems, and then for more than a quarter of a century she fades into oblivion. As Baroness von Türckheim, wife of a Strasbourg banker, Lili, now calling herself Elise, writes once more after twenty-seven years to her 'revered friend' and *Geheimrat* asking for his intervention on behalf of a young protégé of hers who wishes to enter government service in Thuringia. At the same time she tells him, though very guardedly, something of her family story during the intervening years. Although she does not tell him so, she has been through very difficult times. The business went bankrupt soon after Goethe's departure from Frankfurt, and her elder brother, who apparently had falsified the accounts, shot himself. The elegant furniture, including the clavecin at which Goethe had first seen her, was all sold at auction. Shortly before the catastrophe, however, Lili had married the banker, Baron Türckheim. Her marriage was neither happy nor particularly unhappy; like so many, she poured out her sorrows to the father confessor, Lavater. During the revolutionary days, when her husband, as Mayor of Strasbourg, was in danger of his life, she behaved with great courage: disguised as a peasant woman, with her youngest child on her back and leading the others by the

hers in mine. We each took a deep breath and then, overcome with emotion, fell into each other's arms.'

In his old age he admitted he had never been so near to happiness as at that moment. But in his biographical notes he writes: 'Presentiment of a false conclusion, one suppresses the doubt, admits what is propitious, feels outwardly reassured after wavering inwardly, without any lessening of the passion. Complete submission had supervened.' The last sentence is the decisive one. Goethe promptly takes flight in a journey, one of his well-tried methods of escape.

The Stolberg brothers have arrived in Frankfurt and have been given some of the 'tyrants' blood' from the Goethe cellar. They want to go to Switzerland, the land of the free, the land of the honest defiant peasants, of unspoilt ancient customs, of high peaks. Goethe immediately decides to join them, his father will look after the legal practice and his mother will keep an eye on his fiancée. They don their Werther uniforms and then take them off again to plunge naked into some stream or other. Between whiles they go to Court; in Karlsruhe they are presented to the Margrave of Baden and meet the young Prince of Weimar, Karl August, who has also just become engaged to one of the five Darmstadt princesses, Luise. She is an 'angel', writes Goethe, a word he uses as often as the words love and loved-one; the glittering star at her breast does not deter him from 'picking up some flowers which fell from her bosom and which I still have in my pocket-case'. Thus begins a lifelong association with yet another 'abbess'. Goethe had already met Prince Karl August a short time previously, when the latter was passing through Frankfurt; the Prince's equerry, Herr von Knebel, had called on Goethe in his attic room, and with this began another lifelong friendship.

'I have seen a great deal', writes Goethe to his Aunt Fahlmer. 'A magnificent book, the world, to make one wiser – if only it were any good. Enough for the present from the escaped bear, from the runaway cat.' He goes to see his brother-in-law, Schlosser, bailiff to the Margrave of Baden in Emmendingen, and his sister. The sight of this unhappy pair is not conducive to the furtherance of marriage plans. Cornelia hates the unborn child she carries, and the mere presence of her able and successful husband, overseer, in the name of his Prince, of a considerable district, makes her shudder. To Cornelia Goethe confesses his relationship to Lili. She warns, implores, beseeches him: 'Do not marry! Not this girl! Nor anyone, ever, promise me!'

On to Zürich now, by way of Strasbourg, where he sees Lenz again. He has already parted from the Stolbergs; 'it is stupid of you to go around with these fellows, you won't stay with them long', had been Merck's warning. The silly pranks of their extrovert way of living soon got on his nerves: bathing naked, smashing their glasses against the wall at the inn, the imprecations against tyrants. In addition to this, Fritz Stolberg was involved in a painful love affair of his own with a beautiful English girl, and insisted on talking about it; but he refused to listen to anything about Lili.

In Zürich Goethe discusses physiognomics with Lavater. The preacher introduces him to two strange and interesting characters, the peasant poets and philosophers Bosshard and Kleinjogg, the latter known as the Swiss Socrates. They are said to represent the unspoilt natural wisdom of the people. Goethe listens to them tolerantly. He is prepared to welcome any human being who can enrich the world of his experience. Goethe is the 'most charming, friendly, lovable person towards those with no pretensions', Lavater writes to Wieland, but 'the most crushing Hercules to all pretentiousness...'.

This refers to Bodmer, the Grand Old Man of Zürich literature, to whom Lavater also introduces Goethe. Everybody wants to meet the author of *Werther*. Bodmer, a patrician with a beautiful estate, is now not much more than a name, an old man of almost eighty living on a reputation gained in the early years of the century, when at one time he was a rival of Gottsched's for the German literary leadership. He still remains enormously active, pugnacious and inquisitive. He insists on seeing the young man, in spite of having written to a friend that 'young people find sophisms for the most dissolute passions' in his work. He has been told that the young man is going to write a *Faust*, and comments scathingly: 'A humbug could turn it into a farce easily enough.' Goethe for his part knows as little about Bodmer as he did about Gottsched. He is unlikely to have read any of the hundred and more books that line the old man's shelves, or to know about his attempts to re-edit the *Nibelungenlied* and the *Minnesänger* and introduce Milton to the German-speaking world. All he sees in front of him, as he did with Gottsched, is a half-forgotten figure, an old man in his dotage, who gesticulates with alarming vigour while he paces up and down the room jerking his small narrow head. Soon afterwards Goethe parodies him as the 'Owl', who wants to scare the happy birds.

At their meeting, however, Goethe is restrained and almost stiff, as he always is at Court; he is, after all, in audience with intellectual royalty. He does not say a word about his own writings. He speaks with great respect of Klopstock. He puts on a mask, as he so often does.

In Lavater's house he meets a young theologian from Frankfurt named Passavant, and in his company he continues his journey. They climb up the Rigi, go on the Lake of Lucerne and climb the well-known St Gothard road to the hospice at the top. Italy lies below them. Passavant wants to continue down. Goethe hesitates. He makes a sketch, as though to clear his thought, and writes in the corner: 'farewell glance at Italy'. There is nothing to prevent him going on. His father would willingly agree and give him the money, they have discussed it together. Goethe takes flight once more, this time back in the direction he has come from.

On his way back through Zürich he forms a new acquaintance in the

Lavater circle, with the 30-year-old wife of a manufacturer, Barbara Schul hess. The sensitive, but calm and very level-headed, Barbara, a lover ( beauty, though by no means beautiful, and with an interest in literature ar religion, listens patiently to his confessions. Goethe has constant need ( women of her type to whom he can unburden his heart and to whom he ca complain. They keep up a correspondence until the relationship betweer Goethe and Christiane Vulpius, incomprehensible to the devout Swiss woman, puts an end to it. Goethe used to send her his new works long before they found their way into print, and these then lay forgotten among her papers; some are lost, but in 1910 the first version of *Wilhelm Meister*, whose existence even Goethe forgot, came to light among her things.

From this cool soothing friendship he now has to return to the purgatory of Frankfurt. To Lili he has written no more than a short farewell on leaving – he makes great demands on his partners. She is recalled in a few verses during his wanderings, and there is a brief reference in his diary, in his best lawyer's manner: '*vide* the personal archives of the poet, letter L'; L stands for Lili, but there is no mention of anything under any other letters of the alphabet. She may possibly have been sent some scraps of verse, or there may have been some letters which have since disappeared. In the meantime her family has taken good care to impress on her the hopelessness of the engagement. She is still not convinced. Indeed friends tell Goethe on his return that she has remained constant, and that she has even declared herself willing to go to America with him.

But, to borrow a phrase from one of his letters, Goethe has already 'ordered the horses' for the next stages of his journey. He is seriously thinking of going to Italy after all. To his friend Merck he writes in his *Götz* style:

I am shittishly stranded, and could give myself a thousand boxes on the ear for not cutting loose when the going was good. Now I am on the look out for a new opportunity to cut adrift, but I should like to know whether, in such an event, you would be willing to help me out with a little money, only to see me over the first fence [perhaps in the spring]; but I shall scarcely survive till then, boating around on this reservoir and going off on frog and spider hunts with great solemnity.

This is the tone he affects in order to counteract the violence of his feelings; he still cannot free himself, however hard he tears at the silken strands. He is back again in her room in Offenbach, or sitting at a card table in the drawing-room in Frankfurt, jealously eyeing the Schönemann's wealthy merchant friends as they give Lili an avuncular pat on the cheek or ask for a kiss. He learns of other suitors, more serious ones, and of the plans of her brothers. He sends fresh tokens of his love, 'trinkets, ornaments, the latest, and smartest', but Mama must not know about them. To Lili's mother the breaking off of the engagement must have seemed long overdue. In his

hand, she escaped from the inferno in the town and rescued her children. She has grown into a distinguished woman, both mentally and physically, with a 'classic' profile that reminds those of her friends who know their Goethe of *Iphigenie*; at all events the fresh and slightly voluptuous beauty of her youth has given way to something different. She is a good mother, a solicitous wife, a woman of sophistication and a person of fine and serious outlook, as her letters show. She may well have pondered reflectively on the news she heard from Weimar of the uncouth little creature, a former worker in a flower factory, who now shared the life of her childhood sweetheart.

Goethe replies in his formal, Geheimrat style, saying how pleasant it is to hear from his '*verehrte Freundin*' after such a long time; unfortunately there is nothing he can do for her friend. In a second letter he kisses her hand a thousand times 'in remembrance of those days which I count among the happiest of my life'. In the interval he has heard of Lili's courageous behaviour, and adds: 'May you enjoy peace and contentment after the many sufferings and trials you have been through, news of which has only lately reached us; they have often given me cause to think of your steadfastness and greatness of endurance. Once more may all be well with you and may I find a place in your thoughts' (14.12.1807). Ten years later she died.

It was only in the very last years of his life that Goethe could bring himself to describe in *Dichtung und Wahrheit* these 'happiest days'. The correspondence between the two has disappeared; it is not known to what extent it ever existed. The fact that there are few traces of Lili in his poetry is no indication of any weakness of his attraction, rather the contrary. Many observers have regretted that Goethe let slip this unique opportunity of finding a life partner worthy of him. But for him there never was any such person, least of all a woman of the type of Lili; there were only new loves, new relationships, new changes of skin and transformations, right up to the end of his life. It may well have been the very inner strength of this girl, which Goethe must have felt, that caused him to run away, rather than the superficial pretext of family opposition, which could easily have been overcome. But he would have had to overcome a great deal in order to give himself, not alone to his Sacred Love, but to this particular human being with her particular claims – social claims perhaps as well, but above all her claim to be treated as an individual in her own right. It was his destiny to remain solitary, with a limitless need for warmth and intimacy.

# 17

# *Weimar*

Seen in retrospect Goethe's flight from Frankfurt and his journey to Weimar have often been regarded as a particularly significant step in his endeavour to mould his life as a 'work of art'. He himself, at the time, gives a much simpler explanation, ascribing it to chance. The young prince and heir to the little Thuringian Duchy of Weimar, having been attracted by the young man during their short meetings, invites Goethe to visit him. People in the most varied places and positions have now become aware of Goethe. The Prince of another of these Thuringian Duchies, that of Meiningen, also met him in Frankfurt, and the author of *Werther* made a very good impression: 'he talks a lot, and his talk is good, striking, original, ingenuous, and it is astonishingly amusing and gay. He is tall and well built ... and has his own very individual way of behaving, just as in general he belongs to a quite special type of human being. He has his own ideas and opinions about everything. For people, and he understands them, he has his own language, his own expressions.' On their cultural tours young heirs to these princedoms were expected to cast their eyes round for useful people. Such men were greatly in demand, and if they had original ideas, this was no drawback. Reform and innovation were in the air, and even these princes read their Rousseau and the encyclopaedists. They knew something of mercantilism, of Turgot and his physiocratic system, which the Margrave of Baden was trying to introduce in some of his possessions. They were all poor, with small impoverished territories in which there was pressing need for improvement. They all had loyal subjects and native born officials of limited ability in whom they had little faith. They preferred to recruit their officials from outside, as did the great Courts as well. In Prussia a very high proportion of the leading posts was held by Frenchmen, Italians, Scotsmen, or Germans from everywhere else but Prussia. If someone 'with brains' was also good-looking, a point on which they set great store, and was gay and amusing and a social asset, so much the better. It was a time of great opportunity for young men of the calibre of Goethe.

By the time he left Frankfurt Goethe had gained the reputation of being one of Germany's leading writers, but this was no career, and not only in his father's sense of the term. It did not bring him in enough to cover his living expenses, though admittedly these were on a somewhat generous scale; he was in debt, for small amounts, to Merck, Madame de la Roche and others. The legal practice was going badly and it bored him; he would leave letters unanswered for months and put his cases on one side. Attempts were made to find him other employment. The competent Fräulein Delph had plans for him, after the Schönemann affair came to grief. She wanted to launch him in Mannheim in the service of the Elector of the Palatinate, once more in connection with marriage plans. Service in some court, of which there were fifty odd, or in commission with some prince, of whom there were several hundreds, seemed the only prospect for the poet.

And there was no doubt about his being a poet. During these Frankfurt years he had planned and sketched more than he ever brought to completion. In this very year of 1775 two editions of his Collected Works appeared, in Switzerland and Berlin, both pirated and therefore without fee; others followed, also without fee. In his portfolios and paper bags – he liked to keep his sketches and fragments in such containers and would sometimes empty them out in front of a visitor – lay the opening scenes of *Faust*, a *Tasso*, *Egmont*, epic and lyric poems, satires, essays, fragments of novels. He was at the peak of his creative powers. He wrote easily and fast, in a very clean hand; even in his passionate letters to Auguste Stolberg there are few corrections. He had already started to dictate a great deal – later it became his constant habit – to his young servant Seidel, who went everywhere with him, even to Offenbach. From the viewpoint of a later day it is possible to imagine a work of Goethe's with an appearance quite different to the one it actually has, and this has in fact been done; such musings are idle. He would break off, and then start again quite differently. His flight from Frankfurt is also a flight from the responsibility implied in these literary plans. Every work rebels against its creator, and the greater the creator the more stubborn the rebellion. We shall see how often Goethe took flight from the completion of his great works, or sidestepped into other, lesser, works, or into other activities altogether.

The young Prince of Weimar, who at the age of 18 has just succeeded to the Dukedom, returns once more to Frankfurt on the way to his marriage with Princess Luise of Darmstadt. Together with the Prince of Meiningen he invites Goethe to the hotel where he is staying. The poet is at his most agreeable: adroit, serious, courteous. He speaks of Justus Möser and his *Patriotische Phantasieen*, essays which seem to him to be a model of the lines on which a small state should be ruled. The man, whom he never met, fascinates him. He sees in Möser's writings the same partiality for the old Germanic way of life as exists in his own *Götz*, and an understanding of the 'organic growth' of a state, developing naturally, like a plant from root to flower; religious tolerance he sees too, and far-seeing proposals for reform in finance and trade, often of a most unexpected nature. Above all he recognizes a 'good brain', such as his own, directing this little state of the

Bishopric of Osnabrück. He has full confidence in his own ability to do something similar; perhaps in Weimar, perhaps elsewhere, that is still quite undecided.

The young Duke repeats his invitation to Weimar. Goethe promises to come. At first everything goes wrong. The carriage sent to fetch him does not arrive. Goethe has already packed, and is dressed for the journey. His father, always suspicious of princely connections, which he considers most unreliable, persuades his son to undertake the journey to Italy instead. Heidelberg is his first stop. He starts a diary, but soon discontinues it, to our lasting regret; never again does he keep a diary with such freshness and vividness. He makes us feel his joy at getting away from Frankfurt, 'that hole, that den'. He is in great spirits, referring to fate, not in solemn words, but calling it 'the dear, invisible thing that guides me', as though it were a girl. He has packed to go north, he turns south. 'The gate-keepers come jangling from the burgomaster and, before it is day and my neighbour the cobbler has opened his workshop and his shutters, I am off! Adieu mother!' Even in the free city of Frankfurt the city gates have to be opened in the morning, the gate-keepers fetching the keys from the Burgomaster. Lili receives another farewell greeting, the second, 'the first time I left, still hopeful of uniting our destinies. The decision is taken – we must play our roles separately. At this moment I feel no anxiety for you or for myself, however confused the outlook appears. Adieu!' His dual nature must needs remember his other sweetheart in Copenhagen too; sweet flower is to be her name and how is he to bid her farewell? 'It is time – high time indeed. A few days longer – and then – O, farewell! Am I only in the world to writhe in eternal guiltless guilt?' He continues the epistolary romance for a few more lines, sends a greeting to Merck, and then: 'everything else is in the hands of the dear thing who made the plan for my journey'.

In the village of Weinheim he drinks some good wine, and muses:

> But what is the political, moral, epic or dramatic purpose of all this? The real purpose of the affair, gentlemen, is that it has no purpose at all. This much is certain, the weather is excellent, the stars and a half-moon are shining, and the afternoon was excellent. The giant bones of our forefathers on the mountains, the rows of vines running downwards at their feet, the avenue of nut trees and the valley of the Rhine going away into the distance filled with fresh sprouting winter crops, the leaves still quite thick on the trees and a clear view of the setting sun to boot!

The landlord apologizes for the house being crammed full of wine butts and vats. It is a good harvest. Nothing puts Goethe out: 'This evening I am in a communicative mood; I have the feeling I am talking to people as I write this ... I intend giving free play to every whim. ...'

In Heidelberg he stays with Fräulein Delph, who explains her latest plans for another marriage. An express letter from the Weimar Chamberlain, Herr von Kalb, who has been sent to accompany him, overtakes him, brought by a postillion with much blowing of his horn. The carriage is there. Fräulein Delph begs him to continue his journey south. The postillion sounds his horn impatiently. Goethe turns back to Frankfurt and goes to Weimar. It is to the accompaniment of caprice and confusion such as this that the greatest turning point of his career is achieved. In his memoirs he describes the moment as the work of a demon, and adds a quotation from his *Egmont* about the chariot of fate, whose sun-steeds race by as though whipped on by unseen spirits. Whither? Who knows? 'He scarce remembers whence he came.'

Very soon he too will no longer remember whence he came. Of all his many transformations the quickest and most emphatic is this from the provincial Frankfurter to the cosmopolitan, the world citizen, who chooses little Weimar as his residence. He never really becomes a true citizen of Weimar. From Frankfurt he retains a few idiosyncrasies of speech, and that is all he takes with him from his home, apart from his grandfather's fortune which long continues its flow to Weimar and helps him to maintain his independent way of life.

This is a cardinal point for Goethe's position in his new surroundings. The young Duke, still completely inexperienced, has not invited him as a poet, to found a *Musenhof*. He has taken to this lively, vigorous, original person and would like to have him in some capacity or other; in just what capacity he will have to find out. To start with Goethe is to be a Court 'favourite'. These exist everywhere, both men and women; he is only one amongst countless others. The great difference is that he is independent. The others, even if they are of noble birth, are seeking their fortunes, as adventurers, sword in hand, as diplomats, or merely as gamblers; the commoners are without exception impoverished creatures, who have to be satisfied with whatever post or pension they can pick up. The writers, one and all, are the poorest of the lot. Not one of them can live by his pen. The most famous of them, the universally idolized Klopstock, has to rely on a pension from the Danish Court as the mainstay of his existence. Lessing, having tried to establish himself in Hamburg as an independent writer and failed, has had to accept employment as librarian in Wolfenbüttel. Wieland, the most popular German author, holds the post of tutor to the Weimar Princes. Herder is an ecclesiastical commissioner. The young talents of *Sturm und Drang* roam the country looking desperately for some position; soon they are to flock in droves to Weimar, where they hang on to Goethe's coat-tails, and he has his work cut out to get rid of them.

As the Duke's guest and accompanied by the Chamberlain, von Kalb, Goethe enters the little town of Weimar, the Ducal seat of a country of whose size and structure he has but the vaguest idea. It is only when he starts his practical work as an official that he learns how complicated this structure is and how little it conforms to Mösers' concept of 'organic growth'. For these small Thuringian Duchies, twenty-seven in number at the beginning of the century and at this time slightly fewer, have not developed organically but have been cast like dice in the gamble of rights of succession and divisions of inheritance. The larger Thuringian principalities had been splintered off from the electorate of Saxony; they in their turn had again been divided up by the disastrous German laws of succession, according to which each son of a prince, or an aristocrat, inherited the title and a certain part of the possessions. Thus these became carved up into little scraps of land, often no bigger than private estates, a 'state of confusion' similar to that of the peasant properties, and as economically unproductive. Peasants are the country's main economic asset. The whole style of living, until high up in the social scale, is basically peasant. The town of Weimar itself, which Goethe approaches along field tracks that can scarcely be called roads, is little more than a village. The peasants are supposed to keep these roads in repair, but they do so very reluctantly. They are harassed and oppressed enough as it is, and when a carriage gets stuck they may be able to earn a few *groschen* helping it out. The little town has about six thousand inhabitants, roughly the same number as the Frankfurt suburb of Sachsenhausen. At the town gate the Ducal carriage, even though carrying the Chamberlain, is inspected like any other; its occupants' names, standing and places of origin are taken and the Duke is notified at once. The houses are modest or humble, pigs and chickens roam the dirty streets, farmers' carts cross the path of the carriage. The castle, which with its outbuildings occupies almost a third of the town, had been burned down two years previously; it is now a ruin with charred, crumbling walls. The Ducal family has been accommodated elsewhere. Goethe alights at the house of the Chamberlain's father, the Finance President, with whom he is to stay. The von Kalb family have been eagerly awaiting his arrival, in the hope that he will strengthen the von Kalb faction at Court, for even this diminutive Court is divided into factions, all engaged in bitter feuds among themselves.

It is as Court favourite that Goethe spends his first year, and particularly his first winter, in Weimar. He arrives in November 1775, he is to remain until March 1832. At first everything is very indefinite; he has no fixed plans and starts by taking a look round.

Weimar has no castle – it is another fifteen years before its reconstruction can be contemplated – but there are two Courts: that of the young Duke and his wife, and that of the Dowager Duchess, Anna Amalie, who until recently has been acting as Regent. There are, indeed, several buildings in the town graced with the name of 'castle', but they are scarcely more than rather imposing private houses. The Duke and Duchess occupy the *Fürstenhaus*, originally intended to house Court officials and offices, and hurriedly rebuilt with bad materials; after a few years the beams rot, the rafters decay and the ceilings either sink or collapse altogether. Weimar can boast very few craftsmen, and these few none too competent, and not a single architect. The rooms are neither large nor sumptuous, the furniture is simple; the kitchen is housed in a building across the street, and the meals have to be brought over, because the ground floor of the *Fürstenhaus* is needed for the pay offices, accommodation for Court officials, and some reception rooms. The Duchess, who in Darmstadt used to go about in little cotton dresses, occupies the first floor, the Duke the second. In one of the rooms the Council of Ministers, the *Conseil*, holds its meetings; there is no government building.

The Dowager Duchess has moved into a house which her Prime Minister, von Fritsch, originally built for himself; after the fire he handed it over to her. It is called, somewhat pretentiously, the *Palais*, though it is barely as large as the *Weidenhof* of Goethe's grandfather. It is a building such as in Würzburg – where at this time they were adding to the great Residence for the archbishop – would have been allocated to one of the higher Court officials. No greater contrast can be imagined than that between the splendour of this huge palace, with its three hundred rooms, decorated in the finest stucco, the walls inlaid with tortoiseshell or covered with mirrors, and with the most magnificent hall and stairway in the world, its ceiling painted by Tiepolo, the whole building a feast of sensuous pleasure, and the almost monastic simplicity at Weimar. No greater contrast in sheer workmanship either: in Würzburg they built so well that the walls and marvellously daring vaulted ceilings, designed by one of the greatest German architects, withstood even the bombs of the Second World War, whereas in Weimar the walls started to scale off almost before the occupants moved in. But in Würzburg the creative energy spent itself exclusively in architecture and the applied arts; in Weimar, in impoverished surroundings and around the small and ugly figure of the Duchess Amalie, a *Musenhof* was born.

The two exist side by side, at the same time, in the same Germany. It is also worthy of note that in spite of his interest in architecture, and everything to do with building, Goethe never showed the slightest interest in any of the baroque or rococo architecture in his own South German homeland, nor in any of the subsequent developments. All that he has left behind him, like the crooked streets of medieval Frankfurt; he has now entered the village of Weimar, and here he remains.

First mention must be accorded the Dowager Duchess, Anna Amalie, for it was she who founded the Weimar *Musenhof*. Her son had other interests, such as hunting, his army, and women. Amalie was a Guelph; an unattractive little Princess, badly treated by parents and governesses alike, she had a miserable upbringing at the brilliant Court of Brunswick. Her parents were relieved to find even a tolerable match for her, and she was relieved to get away from her home. The young heir to the Dukedom of Weimar, whom she married, was the son of a coarse and brutal father, an insatiable huntsman, a merchant in his own soldiery, whom he hired out, a great builder of flimsily erected little castles, and an impatient man who signed death warrants readily. The son was a delicate, consumptive, lanky youth; he died two years after succeeding his father, leaving the young Amalie, with two sons, to act as Regent of the little state, which was in debt and under pressure from all sides. The pressure was exerted by the other Thuringian Princes, who had already had hopes of inheriting the Duchy, and, by no means least, by Amalie's famous uncle, Frederick of Prussia, who used Weimar as though it were occupied territory, marching his armies through it, foraging freely, and pressing young men there into his own military service, as he did in Goethe's time too. Amalie could do very little more than bridge over this interim period as best she could, and she did it with a large assortment of feminine ruses and caprices. The financial situation was pitiful: sixty thousand *thalers* a year for everything, her Court and general administration included, no more than the income of an English or French landlord. The country was poor, the nobility was poor and its younger members sought positions outside. The officials were so badly paid that they could support their families, generally with from five to ten children, only by earning extra money on the side. One of the teachers at the 'Gymnasium', Weimar's only grammar school, was a Professor Musaeus: he lived in a tiny house in which he let off every single room except one, in which he, his wife, and two children lived. The wife spun, while the Professor wrote marriage and funeral odes at a *thaler* apiece; later he became famous through his fairy tales, which he had picked up from the children and old women, and these earned him redemption from his lodgers.

From the Court at Brunswick Amalie had brought with her a number of cultural interests. She painted, and by no means badly if her pictures are really all her own work. She was very fond of music, and composed as well, this last probably with the help of some *Kappellmeister* – her settings of Goethe's *Erwin und Elmire* is no worse than large numbers of contemporary *Singspiele*. She had a troupe of good actors in her service, and the Weimar theatre in her day was of a higher standard than it was under her son, at any rate for the first ten years of his reign. She engaged Wieland as tutor to her son, and in so doing brought to Weimar the first member of the future *Musenhof*.

The real tutor was a Count Görtz, like almost all the leading personalities in the little state, a 'foreigner'; her Prime Minister, von Fritsch, came from outside too, from Saxony. Görtz, who regarded Weimar merely as a step in his career – he later became a Prussian Minister – soon began to intrigue: he tried to get the young Prince declared of age at 15, with the intention of taking over the reins of government himself. A sort of *coup d'état* was planned and the boy was involved in the plot against his mother. All this would be quite irrelevant if it were not for the fact that it provides the background for the state of affairs in which Goethe found himself as Court favourite.

Amalie, not without the use of feminine aids, had warded off the threatening situation by sending her son, along with his Görtz, on the Grand Tour to

Paris and by arranging his marriage. It was on this tour that Karl August first met Goethe. Paris it was to be then as his introduction to the great world, with Strasbourg as the first stage – even the heir to the Duchy of Weimar was awkward and clumsy, a little 'bear'; Görtz also had the task of attending to the boy's necessary preparation for marriage. This was undertaken by a little French woman who, in return, received a pension for life, which she happily consumed in Epernay; the grateful State of Weimar later transferred this pension to the charge of the State.

The selection of the bride, one of the five penniless Darmstadt Princesses, was not without political significance. Catherine the Great had sent for three of these daughters of an obscure ruling house as candidates for the hand of her son. As the girls stepped out of their carriage she observed them carefully from a window, and immediately rejected Luise; one of her sisters was accepted and became the Grand Duchess. Thus Darmstadt and, through Luise, Weimar had prospects of being related to the rich and mighty Court of Russia; the third sister married the Prussian Crown Prince, later King Friedrich Wilhelm II. As compensation for the expense and fatigues of the journey, Catherine made royal gifts to the Darmstadt ladies, the presents being largely in cash. The greater part of the small dowry Luise brought to Weimar consisted of Catherine's roubles: otherwise she did not have much to bring. Goethe, it is true, described her as the 'angel Luise', but she was thin and lanky, sentimental, and unsensual to the point of complete frigidity; another of Goethe's abbesses.

Now let us turn to the main character, Karl August. Goethe spoke and puzzled much about him; the 'incommensurable' in the nature of this man, with whom he spent a lifetime and to whom he owed so much, was a matter of constant concern to him. He even tried to see in Karl August a 'demoniac' quality, a fiery spirit, for whom his tiny land was too small, and who, like Napoleon or one of his paladins, might have wanted to win for himself a larger. But Karl August was no fighter; he was not even a good soldier, although he had a passionate love of soldiering, and became in turn a Prussian general, a French general, and a Russian general, and took part in several campaigns. In none of his campaigns did he achieve anything worthy of note, and senior officers and future leaders who met him were unimpressed. By far the greater part of the achievements of his long reign stands to the credit of his extremely able ministers and officials. But here we can already see a leading trait in his character: he understood people, or at any rate men; with women he was less successful. He was what Goethe used to call a *Natur*, a character, a term indicative of his highest praise, and he had an instinct for other such characters. This instinct had already enabled the 18-year-old boy to select a Dr Goethe of Frankfurt from a whole host of other young people suggested to him; and having selected him he achieved something still more remarkable in a stubborn loyalty that, surviving many vicissitudes, remained steadfast from the beginning to the end.

When he first came to power, however, the young Duke was an unruly, obstinate, pleasure-seeking boy; certain boyish traits he retained into his old age. He was small and stocky, although his health was by no means good in his early years. His face bore no trace of the aristocratic distinction evident in his decadent father. With his short head, small firm nose and powerful chin he looked more like one of his huntsmen or foresters, who were his favourite companions in roaming the woods, hunting and living rough. He was rough and simple in all his tastes, not least in his taste for the rough village girls, by whom he had a considerable number of children; the latter, if they were boys, were always placed among the huntsmen and foresters, and were recognizable through the fact that the Duke addressed them with the familiar second person, *Du*, instead of the third person, *Er*, which he used for all the others. His marriage to the pale, thin Luise was a failure from the outset; it could hardly have been otherwise. On the day after her wedding the Princess wrote to her Russian brother-in-law, the Grand Duke: 'Permit me, Sir, to inform you of my marriage to the Duke of Sachsen-Weimar. You would have taken pity on me, had you seen me on the day; I was in the most violent state. And I thank God that it is over.'

It was far from over. The mother of her people was expected to be a mother herself in the shortest possible time, and above all the mother of a son and heir; as Frederick the Great put it, in his inimitable, terse style, in a letter to Luise's mother, she was expected to have the virtues of 'gentleness, distinguished bearing, and fecundity'. Distinguished bearing was Luise's great asset, but because of her shyness and lack of selfassurance it degenerated into stiffness and the most pedantic insistence on etiquette; in this too she was the opposite of her informal husband. With the fecundity there were many set-backs: miscarriages, baby girls too weak to survive, and husband and State continually disappointed until finally, after seven anxious years, a son was born. It was only then that the hitherto extremely precarious situation, both of her marriage and of the future of her land, was to some extent stabilized. Goethe had to act as matrimonial counsellor and mediator, even to the extent of including such counsel in his plays, and this was not the least onerous of his tasks as Court favourite.

Thus it was a small Court with a small staff of officials. The high-sounding titles, copied from the great Courts, need not deceive us; the Weimar Court attracted for the most part only minor figures. Anyone with ambition looked for a position in one of the wealthier Courts in the larger countries. Once when his friend Charlotte von Stein's son, and Goethe's pupil, wanted to try his luck elsewhere, in Prussia, Goethe wrote to her: 'For my part Fritz is quite forgiven. Anyone desirous of living, having a definite sense of purpose within him and an untrammelled outlook on the world, must shudder at the thought of a petty service as if it were the grave. Such narrow circumstances can only become interesting as the result of an extreme consistency, whereby they assume the form of a large household.'

These words, spoken after long and thorough experience of 'petty service', may serve as an introduction to the narrow circumstances of the Weimar Court, and as an indication of the iron consistency with which Goethe established his position there. The interesting, and in his eyes the only interesting, thing about Weimar was that it was, in fact, a sort of 'household', like one of the ancient communities and city-states of Greece, which were no longer; it could be taken in at a glance almost from one's window, the people were like members of a family whom one knew personally, and not merely as anonymous ciphers. A small world, but a self-contained world, and as such the right soil for a poet, who is concerned with human beings and not with institutions.

For Goethe's life the members of this Weimar society have another important significance. Quickly as he changes his 'loves', whose precise number it is impossible to calculate, his friends and his confidants, especially in his younger days, the main figures of this Weimar society remain constant, and accompany his life almost to its end. The Duke, in spite of his early weak health, lived to a great age, as did the frail Luise. Von Knebel, the Chamberlain, who arranged Goethe's first meeting with the Duke, the *Ur-Freund*, as he was later called, survived the poet; the Dowager Duchess Amalie accompanied him well into the new century, while with the Prime Minister, Fritsch, who also lived into his late eighties, he collaborated for a lifetime, and, after his death, continued to work with his son. There were many whose lives accompanied his own in this way, and younger ones grew up from the same families. This Weimar 'family' is his real 'household'; but his own household, which he established much later, was of a questionable nature, as we shall see. It may have been chance that took him to Weimar; it was no chance that kept him there. And it was certainly no chance that out of it he created something that was destined to remain in the memory of mankind.

# 18

## *Sleigh-Ride*

'My life is like a sleigh-ride, quickly away with bells jingling, and parading up and down', writes Goethe shortly after his arrival in Weimar. The whole first winter is a carnival. Goethe has brought his skates, the kind recommended by Klopstock, and teaches the new sport to members of the Court. The Duke is enthusiastic, as he is about all physical exercise. There are dances, masked balls and other kinds of gaiety – the 'gay time in Weimar' it was called later. The gaiety is short lived; soon the little town will become gloomy and ill-humoured again. But to begin with the people are cheerful, or rather one faction is cheerful, that of the young Karl August and his favourite. The other faction, that of the older officials and older residents in general, views these activities with sullen, anxious eyes. Have they not been told to save? Is not the country in debt? Did not the wedding and the Duke's assumption of government involve them in exceptional and painful expenditure, and in special taxes? And now at Court money is being frittered away, taken from empty coffers, borrowed, given away to foreigners and outsiders who will soon move on elsewhere. Is the young Duke sitting at his desk and acquiring some knowledge and insight into the plight of his land? He is doing nothing of the kind. He is fooling about with his friends, these young men who call themselves geniuses, he is off hunting, play acting, sleigh-riding or dancing with the village girls. One of these days he is going to break his neck, galloping round at full tilt the way he does; he is not a very good horseman anyway, and he has fallen off three times already. Is he leading a well-conducted married life with his young wife? Far from it, everyone knows that things are not well between them. There is no prospect even of an heir. The country will be annexed by Gotha, or Meiningen, or Coburg, a menace that has often threatened. Officials will lose their posts, or be paid even less than they are now, and that is little enough.

Side by side with all this the sleigh-ride continues. Six years later Karl August writes:

> Man, and especially if he does not belong to the common people, has to wear the 'Spanish boots' the gods have provided for him and, regardless of everything, to jump and dance in them to the tune of every whim of fate. To the citizens it is not given to shake off their princes, even if, with their own

hands, they write in the records malicious, stupid, inconsequent votes and resolutions. To us it is not given [i.e. to the princes!] to probe fate and its whims, and to oppose it – therefore *fiat voluntas*, and we wrap ourselves up as best we can in our little bit of position, and our capacity to enjoy life, and let the heavens – rain cats and dogs.

They let it rain cats and dogs. Even their capacity to enjoy life is not particularly great. One of the courtiers, commenting on the ceaseless dancing and play acting, writes: 'I do not know what obstacles stand in the way of merriment. The intrigues, the uncertainty about the future, the hidden jealousies, give a forced air to everything in the midst of the amusements, and deprive the festivities of life and vigour. People tell each other they are enjoying themselves, but there is probably scarcely one in ten who is not bored to death.'

It is no grumpy old gentleman who writes this, but a young nobleman of about Goethe's own age, Herr von Seckendorf, who started by trying his luck in service in Sardinia and who is now hoping for some post in Weimar; he writes, composes, translates *Werther* into French, and finds the Weimar way of life rather empty. When Goethe arrives he is wearing the famous Werther uniform, and immediately the young men all begin to appear in blue tail-coats and yellow breeches, and above all in the half-length boots, the most important mark of a strong, masculine bearing. They model their talk on *Götz*, and even at table at Court Goethe swears disgracefully, even if the soup is too hot – Blast! Damnation! Hell! Duchess Luise, brought up on Klopstock, is horrified; but she is powerless to stop it. At least she insists on keeping the long-hallowed seating tradition; only the nobility may take their meals at the Duke's table; the others have to eat at a side table, known as the 'Marshal's table', and it is at this that the otherwise almost omnipotent favourite, Dr Goethe, sits, even after he becomes *Geheimrat* Goethe. It is only when his friend Karl August gets the Emperor in Vienna to bestow on him the order of nobility that he is finally allowed to sit at the Duke's table.

Such details aside, nothing interferes with the close intimacy of the two young men. Soon they are calling one another by the familiar *Du*, though not, of course, on official occasions. They arm themselves with large hunting whips, and ride round the market-place cracking them before galloping off. They tear off into the woods, with a few huntsmen or hussars, and there they sit round their camp fire and talk all night long, about people, about nature, about women. They sleep in some village or hunting lodge, sometimes sharing the same bed or couch. Karl August has many of the habits which, throughout his life, infuriate Goethe. He is an inveterate smoker, his pipe is never out of his mouth, and Goethe's hatred of tobacco smoke is as great as his hatred of syphilis. The Duke is always surrounded by his dogs, large, big-mouthed, yelping hounds, and Goethe could never stand dogs. On this he is at one with the Duchess; nothing disturbs the peace and quiet of their marriage so much as the fact that Karl August takes his pack of hounds with him into his wife's boudoir. The Duke and his companions engage in endless practical jokes and banter at the expense of others, and the victims are forced to respect His Highness' dignity. This is not really to Goethe's taste either, but for a time he joins in everything. In fact they behave like the 'tough' university students at Jena or Giessen. Hitherto Goethe had known only the refined university manners of Leipzig, and in Strasbourg he went round beautifully groomed, and wearing his chamois leather under-stockings to protect him from the 'infernal Rhine gnats'. Now he is embarking on a belated wild period, and finds himself enjoying the freedom from restraint. There is no ageing father to make wry faces at him, no stiffly respectable Frankfurt society, no one in fact to stand over him; there is only the young friend at his side, who finds all his proposals wonderful and, if possible, tries to outdo them. All his life Karl August remained a student at heart, a trait that his fellow princes disliked in him; they deplored his lack of princely dignity. Even after the Congress of Vienna, during which he was elevated to the rank of Grand Duke, Gentz still called him just an 'eternal student'.

They perpetrate all kinds of pranks and practical jokes, some in extremely doubtful taste. Because of the dignity of the poet's name, later generations have tried to dismiss these as 'mere gossip', but they are well documented, even Goethe's friends and admirers bearing witness to them. The cracking of their hunting whips is only symbolic; everything is done headlong, and they scour the bewildered countryside as though on the *wilde Jagd* (the wild chase) of German legend. Putting the fear of death into honest citizens is one of the chief amusements of student life. Laukhard, a ne'er-do-well ex-university student, has left us, in his memoirs, a description of this kind of thing from his own days at Giessen. A poor devil, a former theological student, who earns a miserable pittance by teaching in a girls' school is driven almost to suicide by having stones systematically flung through his window. Then there is the repulsive face: a repulsive mask on the end of a long pole is held up in front of someone's window at night; he is brought to the window by loud knocking and the students derive great amusement from this means of scaring the Philistine rabble to death. Should the Rector of the university intervene, the entire student body withdraws to the neighbouring villages, and returns only when the very citizens they have tormented, terrified of losing their livelihood, intercede for them. Another favourite is the *Generalstallung*, the chief retaliation against an unpopular citizen: a large crowd of students collects in front of his house at night and, at a word of command, neighing like horses, they relieve themselves against the wall and door; they then go off singing their coarse songs.

The pranks in Weimar are not as crude as this, but they are not so very different. The Duke and his companions ride at night, 'through wind and mist' like the *Erlkönig*, swathed in white sheets, and are amused when the peasants cross themselves. Or there is the case of Amalie's lady-in-waiting, the humpbacked little Fräulein von Göchhausen: they have the door of her room secretly bricked up and concealed; when she returns home in the evening she wanders round in despair, beginning to doubt her normally very active reason, until finally she spends the night on a friend's sofa. There is the merchant in Stützerbach one of the neighbouring villages: while he is out they roll all his barrels and packing-cases down the hill-side, and then feast themselves and tipple in his parlour; a portrait of him in oils, which they think rather pretentious, hangs on the wall, so Goethe cuts out the face and, when the owner returns, substitutes his own, grinning at him and rolling his large brown eyes. It is all grotesque and farcical, and not quite free from an unpleasant after-taste: the perpetrators of these jokes are gentlemen of the Court and include His Serene Highness himself; there can be no question of retaliation or even of grumbling, the victim has to submit and, in the merchant's case, quietly haul his packing-cases up the hill again.

One of Goethe's favourite words at this time, and one immediately adopted by Karl August, is *dumpf* – inarticulate; to feel something in a *dumpf* way is a sign of the inspiration of genius. Goethe had already given an indication of this in *Werther*:

> Oh, you sensible people! Passion! Drunkenness! Madness! You stand there so calmly, you moral people, and abuse the drunken, abhor the insane, passing by like priests and thanking God, like the Pharisee, that he did not make you like one of these.... Why is it that the river of genius so seldom bursts out, so seldom roars by in full spate, convulsing your astonished souls? Dear friends, the sensible fellows live there on its banks, on either side; their summer-houses, their tulip beds, their vegetable plots would be destroyed, and so they know in good time how to dam and divert the threatening danger and ward it off.

The building of dams is not yet Goethe's concern. He is raging. The first piece of news he sends home is that he has caught himself in the eye with his large whip while out sleigh riding, and hurt himself badly. Karl August is continually hurting himself by falling off his horse or being kicked by one, or else he suffers a severe attack of rheumatism through sleeping out in the damp woods. There is a vast amount of drinking. The Stolberg brothers turn up, the first of Goethe's *Sturm und Drang* companions to do so. They eat at the *Fürstenhaus*, throw their wine glasses out of the window, and order some funeral urns to be brought from a cemetery. Fritz Stolberg delivers a drunken funeral oration over these vessels, praising them as though they held the ashes of ancient Teutons; the urns are filled with wine and passed round, and they drink the health of their forefather Thuiskon. They have another drinking bout at the house of the Duke's younger brother, Prince Konstantin, where the Dowager Duchess Amalie joins them, with Frau von Stein, wife of the Duke's Master of the Horse; the two ladies carry ancient swords from the armoury and dub the young men knights. 'We remained seated at the table', writes Stolberg, 'and the ladies went round pouring us out champagne. After dinner we played blind-man's-buff, and during the game kissed Frau von Stein, who was standing at the Duchess's side. At what other Court could one do that?'

Karl August straightaway offers Fritz Stolberg a post as Chamberlain. The tyrant-hater accepts with alacrity, but he never takes up the post. Before doing so, he has to go and consult his master, Klopstock; Stolberg's fiery language is matched by his tameness in action, where matters affecting his life are concerned. Klopstock is shocked by the reports that reach him from Weimar. His ideal of the poet, as someone enthroned far above the common things of life, is in danger. News of the mad escapades in Weimar has spread far and wide. The Duchess Luise has complained bitterly in letters to her relatives. Count Görtz, cheated of his hopes of getting the reins of government into his hands, paints the Court 'in colours of filth', to use Wieland's phrase. The clergy are raising an outcry because neither the young Duke nor any of his favourites ever goes to church. The Lord Chamberlain, Herr von Putbus, complains of the wildness, the swearing, the shouting, the stamping into drawing-rooms in riding boots. The lady-in-waiting Frau von Stein writes to one of her friends:

> Goethe has provoked a veritable revolution here; if he can create some order out of it again, so much the better for his genius. Undoubtedly his intentions are good, but he is too young and has had little experience. We shall see how it turns out. But all our happiness has vanished, our Court is no longer what it was. A dissatisfied ruler, dissatisfied with himself and the whole world, who hazards his life every day, and has little in the way of health to spare; his brother still more delicate; a discontented wife; all of them good people, yet nothing goes right in this unhappy family.

Her friend thinks she is too lenient to Goethe and has some bitter words to say about the wild set, these 'gentlemen who exercise their power without regard for time, place or circumstance', who look down contemptuously on the others, the 'dogs'. Johann Heinrich Voss, one of the members of the *Göttinger Hain*, writes his fiancée a letter full of righteous indignation: 'Alarming things are happening in Weimar. The Duke chases round the villages with Goethe like a wild student; he gets drunk and enjoys his girls with him like a brother. One of his ministers, who had the temerity to advise him to stop these excesses because of his health, got the answer that he had to do it to build up his strength.'

Excesses in reigning princes were far from unusual, indeed they were the rule. The only unusual thing in Weimar is the 'new note', and the participation of a young writer who has just become famous. Klopstock, who regards himself as the doyen of the poets, decides to take a hand. He starts by forbidding Stolberg to accept the Court post, a ruling to which the latter obediently submits. Then he writes to Goethe, couching the letter in friendly terms. He is not going to interfere – and then he proceeds to do so, forcefully. What is the outcome of it all going to be?

> If the Duke continues to drink to excess and makes himself ill, he will succumb to it, instead of strengthening his body as he says, and he will not live long…. For the time being the Duchess may be able to suppress her grief, for she has a very masculine way of thought. But this grief will turn into melancholia. And will she then still be able to suppress it? Luise's melancholia! Goethe! – No, do not pretend that you love her as I do!

In a sense the whole world of German poets is a family too, and Klopstock sees himself as its head.

For two months Goethe does not reply. Then he writes coldly: 'In future spare us letters such as this. …' He does not wish to recite any *pater peccavi*, and casually goes on to say that, if he were to answer all such letters and warnings, he would have no time at his disposal. This was the greatest blow to the master's pride: 'And as you go so far as to include among "all such letters" and "all such warnings" – for you express yourself as forcibly as this – the letter containing this proof (of my friendship), I declare to you herewith that you are not worthy that I should bestow it on you.' It is the strongest rebuff Goethe ever had in his life. The breach with Klopstock was complete, it was never healed. At the end of his letter the master had added peremptorily: 'Stolberg shall not come.' Stolberg did not come.

Others come, however, attracted rather than repelled by the stories of wild living. Lenz saunters in, already rather lame and unsteady; he had been hovering around Friederike Brion, and then went on to pay court to Goethe's sister, the most unsuited object conceivable for such attentions. 'The lame crane is here', he writes on a scrap of paper from the inn, 'and knows not where to set his foot.' They all put themselves out for the charming snub-nosed little poet, whose fame is scarcely less than that of Goethe himself. They all find him enchanting – and soon impossible. The wild tone may be the fashion, but nevertheless a certain code of social behaviour is still observed in the town – not outside in the woods and village inns. Lenz walks boldly into one of the Court balls in fancy-dress, and has to be told it is completely out of place. He sulks. He addresses verses to the pale Duchess Luise, once more a totally unsuitable object for his muse; he is said to have gone down on his knees to her. To the Duke he presents his plan, as outlined in his play *Die Soldaten*, for reforming the army by creating a corps of amazons, composed of honest whores, and takes offence when the idea is turned down as the harmless nonsense of an amiable scatter-brain. To keep him away from the Court they find him accommodation in the outlying village of Berka, where he writes a satire on Goethe and one of the ladies at Court. Goethe's patience, not his strong point anyhow, is now exhausted. Lenz' bill at the inn is paid, he is put on the stage coach, and leaves Weimar for ever.

Klinger is the next to arrive, no lame crane, but a well-built handsome young fellow; he wants to become an officer in the Duke's army, of which he has somewhat exaggerated notions. The Weimar armed forces total some six hundred men in all, mostly old, with a certain number of hussars who serve at Court as footmen; the officers' posts are all filled and by the nobility. What kind of post does Klinger want? He reads Goethe his latest play of *Sturm und Drang*, but his friend listens absentmindedly, finally mutters something about 'foolish stuff' and leaves the room. 'Deuce take it,' says Klinger calmly, 'he is the second one who has done that to me to-day.' He stays on a little while longer, under increasing strain. 'Klinger is festering', Goethe writes of this troublesome thorn in his flesh, 'and will soon fester himself off.' The Duke once more pays the bill at the inn, and thus brings Klinger's visit to an end.

Goethe wants no young talents or men of genius round him, and this is not confined to his present phase as Court favourite. He is sufficient genius in himself and, apart from this, Weimar is a small and insecure foothold. He does not know himself how long it will all last. He has friends and enemies, and the latter far outnumber the former. The Court – and after all it is to a Court that he has been appointed – is against him, as can well be imagined. Fortunately Karl August is also against the Court, which bores him, and whenever he can he escapes into the country. The officials, and the government, are naturally against the new-comer, being afraid he may stay. The Duchess has her doubts about him, and appreciates only that he sometimes acts as peacemaker between her husband and herself.

One friend whom he has gained, and during his first days in Weimar, is Wieland, the very man he has been ridiculing so insolently. At the age of 42 Wieland has resigned; or one might put it that he has retired with the graceful and elegant gesture of a man of the world. Unlike Klopstock, his long keen nose very much more sensitive, he realizes that a greater figure than himself has arisen. Unhesitatingly he takes Goethe's part, and in so doing disappoints his many correspondents, who had been looking forward eagerly to a bitter and entertaining struggle between the two men. Far from it. Wieland sings Goethe's praises from the moment of his arrival, and he knows how to praise. No one has said such fine, noble, prophetic things about Goethe during this highly problematical phase of his life as Wieland. Above all he never tires of stressing Goethe's kindness, his goodness and the warmth of his humanity. The others need to be told this because Goethe has the reputation of being biting, haughty and arrogant. His face at this time is still hard, strained, with prominent cheek-bones and a strong prominent nose, the fine lips giving an expression of irony to the mouth; it is the head of a handsome favourite, who is forging his way and cannot afford to be too considerate in the process.

Wieland had renounced all this. He too had once hoped to play his role in the little *teatro mundi*. He had written his *Fürstenspiegel*, as a result of which

Amalie appointed him tutor to the Princes; he had played a modest part in the intrigues surrounding the succession of Karl August, but soon realized that this kind of thing was not his *métier*. It is to cost Goethe ten years, and the expenditure of much energy, to reach the same conclusion. Wieland foresees this too: 'How much more could, indeed would, this splendid spirit achieve if he were not submerged in this chaos of ours, out of which – with all his will-power and all his strength – he will never create a tolerable world.' Wieland had also allowed himself to become entangled in this 'impossible adventure, as the light of day shows it to be'. A few months after Goethe's arrival he writes: 'Goethe is only 26. How, in the awareness of such powers, can he be expected to withstand a still greater fascination?'

Wieland, with smaller powers and less inner tension, withstands it. He is a good housekeeper and knows how to economize, as a writer as well as in life – his novels are models of economy. He has a pleasant, comfortable home, deriving additional income from his successful magazine; and a very simple wife, who bears him a child every year; he is proud of the fact that, even up to an advanced age, his paternal virility keeps pace with his abundant literary output. The author of – according to the jingoists of the Göttinger Hain – the 'lewdest and most Frenchified' works in German literature is a good German family man. In his home children peep from every corner. In the intervals between his wild escapades Goethe also likes to go and sit there quietly, patting the children on the head and chatting with 'Papa Wieland', who sits, with a little skull cap on his balding head; with his feet stretched out under the table, Goethe enjoys Frau Wieland's homely fare.

Winning Wieland over to his side is Goethe's first victory on this difficult ground, and it has far-reaching consequences. To put it crudely, Wieland means publicity. He is the editor of the *Merkur*, one of the most influential papers, and in it he at once sides with Goethe. He maintains a private correspondence that is one of the widest and most important of the day, and in those days letters were the chief means of fostering and spreading reputations. Wieland's opinion is respected; he is known to be extremely cynical and malicious at times. There is not a trace of this in what he says about Goethe. He lauds and praises Goethe without reservation, even writing verses, which spread far and wide: 'of a sudden there was a magician in our midst ... a handsome sorcerer ... a true monarch of the spirit ... and in God's world was never seen his like among the sons of men!' He is a Proteus, he writes, capable of an infinity of transformations, 'and each of his thousand forms so natural, so completely his, that one is forced to accept it as the true one...'.

Goethe's next conquest is the Dowager Duchess. She has not resigned, although she has had to relinquish the reins of government, probably without much regret. It is as a woman that she has had to learn resignation, at a very early age, after two years of marriage to a sick husband. For this plain little woman, with sharp features resembling those of her uncle Frederick the Great, is by nature very sensual. Schiller, who was sensitive in this respect, later said of her: 'She is interested in nothing unless it is connected with sensuality.' He has also preserved for posterity a rather embarrassing affair the ageing lady had with one of her Court musicians: 'She is making herself ridiculous through an attachment she has formed for one of the singers, a miserable dog.' The poor devil had to accompany her on her tour through Italy and, in despair, threw himself into the sea near Naples, and was drowned. But in the main this strain in Amalie's nature finds an extremely beneficent outlet, in her love for art and artists, though much is mere play. She likes dancing and loves the masked balls, at which she appears bedecked with diamonds. Faro is played at her *Palais*, and she knows how to lose her Louis d'or with grace. The atmosphere in her circle is easy and natural, not in the wild unbridled manner of her son, but none the less in very sharp contrast to the stiff ceremonial of her daughter-in-law, with whom she cannot get along at all. With feminine adroitness she has chosen for her lady-in-waiting the hunchback Fräulein von Göchhausen, in comparison with whom even she can appear to advantage; at the same time she is entertained by the witty little creature, who never takes offence at a joke and always 'joins in'. There is a great deal of music making at Amalie's, and for this she has considerable understanding. The theatre occupies an important place, with amateur performances. There are readings and recitations, poems are written for every occasion, and they tease each other in verse; the slightest sign of a love affair is severely dealt with in verse. It is a gay circle that surrounds the 36-year-old dowager; she now comes to life for the first time and is quite determined to spend the coming years as pleasantly as possible, free from the cares of government. And out of all this, though not without encouragement on her part, unexpectedly develops the celebrated *Musenhof*, whose fame soon spreads throughout Germany.

Amalie takes to Goethe immediately. To what extent she is aware of his importance as a poet is open to question, but the man she finds as sympathetic as does her son. She even overlooks his excesses in these early days; she is amused by his grimacing and his large gestures, and if he chooses to roll about on the floor, as he does from time to time, well, after all, it is a sign of genius and at least it is not boring. Weimar can be intolerably boring – and in her letters to Goethe's mother, who, as an exceptionally entertaining correspondent, is very soon drawn into the circle – Amalie is constantly complaining that nothing ever happens in Weimar, there are no visitors, no opportunities for processions, no market, no fair as there is in Frankfurt, let alone any coronations. All one's resources have to be found within oneself or in a small circle of friends. It is Amalie's fame and glory that she possessed these resources.

At the same time it is Goethe's fate that during this decisive period of his life, when he is young, ardent and vigorous, he remains captive within this narrow circle. For eleven years it is the only public he knows. He publishes nothing. The publishers, who are still busy pirating and reprinting his earlier works, have given him up, convinced that as a writer he is finished. For Amalie's circle he writes little plays for their amateur performances, acts as *maître de plaisir* in arranging festivals, masquerades and balls, and writes little New Year verses, sometimes in conjunction with von Seckendorf and others. He gives readings from his *Faust*, of which he has brought fragments in one of his paper bags from Frankfurt. Fräulein von Göchhausen writes down these scenes, and it is only through her that this *Ur-Faust*, as it is somewhat misleadingly called, has been preserved.

Goethe's thought is now occupied by very different things from plays and novels, however much these may be quietly germinating in the recesses of his mind. He wants to play a part on the stage of the world. His friends are saying that he has handed over the literary sceptre to his 'little younger brother' Lenz. This new role of statesman he conceives at first, like everything else, as a game. There is no suggestion that, aware of his heavy responsibility, he now sets about governing the tiny country and educating its small, unruly Duke. In his most casual tone, the one he employs in talking to people and which so annoys the courtiers and officials in Weimar, he writes to his confidante, his Aunt Fahlmer: 'I contrive to find myself in the most desirable position in the world. I soar over the most intimate and most important situations, I exercise a happy influence and I enjoy myself and I am learning and so on. But at the moment what I need is money....' Would she please tell his parents that they should 'give two hundred *gulden* on account of the brilliant splendour of their son'; if his father refuses, his mother might try borrowing it from Merck, which is what she does. In his letter of thanks to Merck he writes: 'I am now completely involved in all the business of Court and politics, and it will be hard for me to extricate myself again. My position is favourable enough, and the Duchies of Weimar and Eisenach are, after all, a stage on which one can see how a role in world affairs suits one.' Or again to his aunt: 'I shall probably remain here and play my part as well as I can and for as long as it pleases me and fate wills. Even if it is only for a year or two it is always better than the life of inactivity at home, where with the best will in the world I can do nothing. Here at least I am confronted with a duchy or two.' Soon after this he tells his mother that in Frankfurt he would have 'perished'. Here in Weimar he feels a new life before him. 'The girls here are very pretty and nice, and I am on good terms with everyone. Frau von Stein is a splendid person, and to her, as one might say, I am tied hand and foot.' With the Duchess Luise, the angel, his intercourse is confined to glances, and a word here and there; with Amalie he enjoys himself and plays all sorts of pranks. It is hard to believe how many splendid young people and good brains there were then in Weimar. 'We stick together, get on famously and dramatize one another, and we keep the Court at arm's length.' Sleigh-rides, amateur performances of French plays by Voltaire or Destouches and of German ones like Lessing's *Minna von Barnhelm*, *Singspiele*, ballets and masked balls. Goethe arranges a masque, *The Temptation of St Anthony*, who is tempted by avarice, greed, lust and pride; Goethe himself plays the devil of pride, striding about on stilts and bedecked with peacock's feathers.

Goethe is soon to find himself in harness. He is called upon to govern. And he himself is taken in hand by a lady at Court, to be educated, groomed and governed by her.

# 19

# *Government*

'To govern!' writes Goethe in his diary. His first move is to persuade the young Duke to bring Herder to Weimar. The highest ecclesiastical post in the Duchy, that of General Superintendent, has been vacant for some years; ten elderly pastors, from old-established local families, have applied for it. Karl August wants young men around him; Herder is just 30, and that suits him perfectly. He has the reputation of being sarcastic, with a sharp pen and a sharp tongue – so much the better. Karl August has no use for 'priests'; he hardly ever goes to church, later on he never goes at all. He knows the clergy disapprove his new way of life. It is a relatively uncontroversial post, he wants to begin asserting his authority and this is a good opportunity; at first, on his mother's urgent advice, he had left everything in the government and administration as it was. No serious objections can be raised to Herder; he is Court preacher in Bückeburg, and his edifying sermons are greatly esteemed. *Fiat voluntas!* Goethe takes over the correspondence. He is going to 'round up the fellows with hunting whips', he writes to Herder. The latter, after some hesitation, comes.

Karl August takes a further and bolder step. He decides to appoint his favourite to high office. He does not dare dismiss his Prime Minister, Fritsch, who has proved his worth during the days of the Regency. Fritsch is an independent man; he has possessions in Saxony, where, before the sons were promoted into the nobility, his grandfather had been a successful bookseller and publisher. He has a great many connections everywhere, and has the reputation of being completely incorruptible, a high distinction at this time in any Court, great or small. He has uncontested authority over the other councillors, who are poor and industrious and keep the records in order, because Herr von Fritsch does not concern himself with the minor details of administration. He is conscientious and indolent at the same time. Calmly he writes to his young master and, in a half-hearted way, tenders his resignation, recommending a reshuffling of the main posts. He finds himself a somewhat unpolished diamond and too abrupt in manner, 'inflexible and not sufficiently tolerant of the prevailing taste' at Court. The letter is intended both as a criticism and a warning. For some time the matter is passed back and forth; the Duke even tries to bring in a Prime Minister from outside, but the man takes one look at Weimar and goes away again. Fritsch it must be then, although now he has submitted his resignation in earnest. Karl August has announced that he wishes to have Herr Goethe as a member of his Privy Council, the *Conseil*, the supreme instrument of government, consisting of four councillors. He also wishes to have young Herr von Kalb, in whose father's house Goethe is living, as President of the 'Chamber', the department of finance. Fritsch explains his misgivings with great dignity. He pleads for men of integrity and experience, men better suited to these posts than the young gentlemen in question, but possibly unknown to His Serene Highness on account of their modesty; it would be unjust to pass them over. He does not deny that Herr Goethe may well be imbued with 'true devotion and love' for His Serene Highness, qualities he would indeed show to be near his heart were he to decline the gracious favour now bestowed on him. In any event he no longer wishes to serve on a council of which the said Dr Goethe is a member.

Karl August replies with fire and spirit:

If Dr Goethe were a man of doubtful character, everyone would approve your decision. Goethe is a man of integrity, however, and possesses an exceptionally good and sensitive nature; not only I myself, but men of discernment, consider that I am fortunate in the possession of such a man. His intellectual ability and genius are well known. You yourself will appreciate that a man of this stamp would not endure the dreary and mechanical process of working his way up through the ranks of our administration. Not to make use of a man of genius where his exceptional talents will have scope is to misuse him. I trust you are as convinced of this truth as I am.

In his whole reign, this is Karl August's most significant act of government, and his defence of Goethe is to prove justified. In itself his action was dictatorial and arbitrary; in the case of von Kalb it was also extremely unfortunate, because Kalb was incompetent, and a few years later was forced to resign under embarrassing circumstances. Fritsch remained – for another twenty-five years. He too was right. We cannot judge his attitude solely from the standpoint of Goethe-worship. He was prepared to go. What concerned him was the position of his colleagues, whom Karl August dismissed as boring and all too limited. With gravity and dignity he begged his young master to gain 'a different and more favourable opinion of their work and not to disclose the fact that His Highness regards it as mechanical, boring and easy'. These are frank words to use under the conditions of an autocratically governed state. Some years later Goethe would have subscribed to them. He worked with Fritsch for almost a generation, as well as with the officials whom Fritsch had trained.

Fritsch decides to remain when Amalie, too, takes Goethe's part. Very feminine, she appeals to her old servant's sense of duty: even if her son has taken a hasty step – and she is not certain that this is not the case – he cannot forsake him now. There are all kinds of rumours about Goethe, she tells him, and he should endeavour to get to know the man; he is no toady or place seeker, if he were she would be the first to oppose him. 'I do not wish to speak to you of his talents, of his genius; it is only of his morals that I am talking. His religion is that of a true and good Christian, a religion that teaches him to love his neighbour and to try to make him happy.' Fritsch has also expressed misgivings on religious grounds, and Amalie dispels these with a light touch.

His ministerial colleagues also implore Fritsch to remain. If he, the only aristocratic and independent one among them, were to go, the government would become a mere spineless cabinet, a mere office whose sole function would be to receive the Prince's orders. Goethe is certainly better than Kalb, and the latter might well become President should they succeed in persuading the Duke to drop his Frankfurt favourite.

The waves calm down. On June 11, 1776, barely six months after Goethe's arrival, the 'new establishment' is announced. Goethe is appointed a member of the *Conseil*, with the title of *Geheimer Rat*, or Privy Councillor; Kalb becomes President of the Chamber. A rain of titles descends on officials of the middle and lower ranks; Herr von Fritsch's warnings have not been without effect. Goethe receives a salary of twelve hundred *thalers* a year, the second highest in the country; in addition the Duke back-dates it by six months, that is to the time of Goethe's arrival in Weimar. In order to strengthen still further his hold on his wavering friend, the Duke has also bought a pretty garden, with a little garden house in it, on the outskirts of the town, and given it to Goethe. Their relationship is a true friendship, almost a love, and now, as Goethe writes, it becomes a marriage. For the first and, as it turns out, for the last time in his life Goethe is tied, and this tie is lasting.

Undoubtedly there is an erotic element involved in all this, but it is not necessarily of a physical nature. Karl August is the masculine partner, who does the courting; Goethe the feminine, who is courted. The way they lead their lives is unusual in itself and excites comment everywhere. It is not only that they ride together, camp out together, drink together, and dance with the village girls together, Goethe is continually sleeping 'at the Duke's', in other words sharing a room with him, even in Weimar. Almost every night before any important decision has to be taken there is an entry to this effect in Goethe's diary. In long talks, sometimes lasting half the night, they discuss everything that touches their hearts and their heads. They discuss their love affairs; and in Goethe's letters to his new love, Frau von Stein, we often find sentences or little verses added by Karl August – *Liebe Frau*, he addresses her. Goethe gives counsel to his friend on his own many amours, as well as on the very much more vexed question of his marriage. Appointments and vacancies in the establishment are discussed, relations with neighbouring Courts, as well as with the great powers, especially closely related Prussia, the constant threat. It is the strangest ministerial council imaginable, carried on from bed to bed, or side by side on a big settee.

But all this must be seen in the context of the time. Goethe is a favourite, and all over Europe favourites, men and women, are in power. One speaks of cabinet policies, but in the eighteenth century it would be just as true, or even truer, to speak of bedroom policies. Catherine the Great, and there is indeed a strange *greatness* about her, disposes of whole countries in favour of her bed-fellows, presenting one of them with the crown of Poland, while others receive as payments 'only' domains, but of a size to make Weimar look like some outlying farm. In France the reign of the great mistresses is open and unchallenged, and the smaller Courts copy France in this as faithfully as they imitate the architecture of Versailles. Frederick the Great, who scathingly calls Europe a 'household of harlots', has his valet Fredersdorff, a source of embarrassment to nineteenth-century historians, who usually ignore the relationship. Of all these things, and of the conversations which took place from bed to bed, there are no official records; we have only gossip, letters, memoirs and a great number of *on-dits*. And yet it is these bedroom activities, substantiated if scarcely believable, that largely – though not entirely – govern the politics, great and small, of the time.

Many may find it unpleasant to see a Goethe in such surroundings, and he soon extricates himself, but there is no denying that for a considerable time he is quite happy living this life of a favourite; the public records as well as Goethe's private diaries clearly prove it. In Weimar they hope that, as the older of the two, he will exert a restraining influence on the wild young Karl August, and he does so again and again. His admonishments are couched in cautious terms and in parables. In the guise of 'Sebastian Simpel', a small peasant, he points out to the Duke, in a poem, that loyal peasant blood is a ruler's finest possession, more important than the horses and studs amongst which Karl August spends most of his time. To avoid too serious a tone he adds some lines about a good fairy who reigns in a magic castle close by, and Karl August probably reads these more carefully than the passage about the peasants. In looking at the portrait of the Duke's grandfather, from whom Karl August has inherited his addiction to hunting and playing with soldiers, Goethe sees in the old man's eyes a certain 'inflexibility and fear', and traces of the tyrant – a further warning. He quotes from the Bible, from Isaiah: 'Behold, the Lord maketh the earth empty, and maketh it waste, and turneth it upside down, and scattereth abroad the inhabitants thereof.... The new wine mourneth, the vine languisheth, all the merry-hearted do sigh.' This is somewhat obscure; perhaps it is a very personal mood, for Goethe suffers frequent attacks of melancholy. It may also be intended to portray the situation in the country, which is not so very different.

These are veiled warnings. In general Goethe is happy and enjoys the new life. Karl August, away on one of his unavoidable visits to relatives'

Courts, this time to Gotha, writes to his friend, very much in Goethe's own style:

> Dear Goethe, I have received your letter, it has given me enormous pleasure; how greatly could I wish to see, free in heart and soul, the sweet sun rise and fall in those Jena crags, and to see it with you. I see it here every day, but the castle is so high, its situation so unpleasant and flat, and it is filled with such a host of servile spirits, who have cloaked their light and airy beings in silk and velvet, that I feel quite sick and giddy, and would like to surrender myself to the devil every evening.

In his love of nature he is at one with his friend. All stern and boring notions of governmental duties are set aside, by Goethe as well as by Karl August, for some time to come.

Goethe is now *Geheimer Rat* and a member of the *Conseil*; he is sworn in according to the evangelical articles of the Schmalkalden Convention, one of which requires him, under oath, to inform the authorities should he feel leanings towards Roman Catholicism, Calvinism, or any other 'important sect'. He swears to preserve the secrets of his office and to preserve the State institutions, of which he still has to acquire any detailed knowledge. He attends his first meeting wearing a silver sword and silver buckles on his shoes, but dressed in black mourning, which has been ordered for the Duchess' sister, the Russian Grand Duchess, who has died in childbirth, the occupational death of women in those days. With her death one of Weimar's most important political connections has vanished into nothingness.

Goethe is presented to the other councillors, who cast anxious and expectant glances at their new colleague as he takes his seat at the council table, third in order according to the official listing but first in order in the Ducal favour, as everybody knows.

Will he now immerse himself in the State records, set about orientating himself, and take part in the sittings regularly and permanently? Will he request his colleagues to initiate him into the complicated situation in Weimar? Does he even know the size of the country, or rather the combined area of Weimar, Eisenach and Jena, with the autonomous district of Ilmenau? The other councillors themselves, try as they will, do not know it exactly; nor do they know the precise number of their subjects, there may be a hundred thousand, there may be more, there may be less, they have never been counted. They know only that the four territories have become united through claims of inheritance, that each has its own 'government', its own diet, which scarcely ever meets, its own system of taxation, which produces but little revenue; and they know that each engages in involved, long-hallowed, traditionally worded correspondence, with the others. Over all this stands the *Conseil*, the supreme authority, whose function is to control it with the requisite tact and knowledge of its personnel. Will the new man adapt himself to this procedure? Above all will he at last persuade His Serene Highness, his friend, the all-supreme authority whose decree is absolute, to participate in the work?

There is little to be gleaned about this from Goethe's diaries, detailed though they are. Following his enrolment the leading State officials are invited to dinner at Court. A few days later there is another meeting. Then he is off again, to Ilmenau, and there are notes of sketching, dancing and hunting; and on to Stützerbach, where the unfortunate merchant has to be teased again. There is target shooting, bathing in the streams, inspection of a mine, skittles; '*Gesang des dumpfen Lebens*', he notes. '*Mit Miseln gekit-tert*': the word *Misel*, from *Mäuschen* (mouse) or *Mamsell*, Goethe picked up in Alsace; it serves to describe any flirtation or any passing, amusing, acquaintance, and crops up constantly in his letters and diaries, without necessarily having any deeper significance. We read of solitary walks in the rain among the crags, a sketch for a play, *Der Falke* (The Falcon), games of faro. After about a month another meeting of the *Conseil* is noted; later there are others, but scarcely more than a dozen in the whole of the first six months. Goethe has been represented as an official with a touching devotion to duty, dedicating the whole of his mighty resources to his country; this is legend. We shall see later how the task gradually stirs his imagination, and how he comes to grips with it; it is a matter of several years.

Goethe has his own very personal ways and means of getting to know the country, the ways of a poet and of a genius, and they are to enrich his work with a vast wealth of impressions of nature and of human characterization. If the state of Weimar gains something in the process, this is simply a by-product; for, in spite of his commitments, Goethe has made certain reservations from the beginning, even towards his friend and patron. To Merck, his constant admonisher, he writes, on taking over his part on the world stage, his *Weltrolle*: 'Freedom and satisfaction are to be the two main conditions of the new arrangement, albeit I am in a better position than ever to recognize the absolute shittiness of this passing glory....'

So out into the country it is, mostly on horseback; the roads and tracks are so bad that driving is impossible. Goethe rides a horse from the Duke's stable, a fairly good goer though apt to shy rather easily; it is white and is called *Poesie* in honour of the poet. On this beast he roams around, either alone or with a few companions from the inner circle of the Duke's friends. It is the period in his life when he takes hold of nature with every faculty he has; hitherto his homage has been mostly in terms of literary reminiscence. He rides through the woods in all weathers, he wanders over the hills, he camps by a fire under the pine trees. As if to get even closer to the elemental forces of nature he is always plunging into the water, bathing in the streams and rivers, or in the Ilm that runs past his little garden-house. In the hitherto shamefully neglected district of Ilmenau he comes upon an old, disused mine, and immediately explores it. A fantastic Faustian plan emerges. The old mine must be worked again. It had been a silver mine and was said to contain vast treasure. At a single stroke the impoverished country's financial troubles would be ended! It was with the silver mines in the Harz mountains that the Saxon Emperors had established their country's dominant position in Germany in the early Middle Ages; it was thanks to this wealth that they built their palace at Goslar, their churches round the Harz, and dominated the other princes who had no such mineral wealth behind them.

This mining project is Goethe's greatest practical scheme; he devotes himself to it for tens of years, enthusiastically and at the cost of great effort. It is also his first active intervention in his country's destiny. A Mines' Commission is set up with Goethe at its head. Unexpectedly he stumbles on the study of geology and in doing so finds a new love. He reads books on mineralogy, chemistry and alchemy in which Luna, the silvery moon, connotes silver. He busies himself with silver tests and ore-hammers. A few technical experts are brought in from Saxony, where there is the famous mining college at Freiberg. In the company of the young mining engineers there is some gay drinking, and they drink to the success of the enterprise. The journeys Goethe undertakes over the next few years to the Harz mountains have as their objective visits to the still flourishing mines and smelting houses.

Eight years later, at the inauguration of the new shaft, the 'Johannes' shaft, Goethe speaks of the undertaking as though it were his child: 'I have helped to nurse it, to protect it, to educate it, and now to my joy it is to continue for posterity.' He breaks down in the middle of his speech, but no one laughs or interrupts. Solemnly, with his large eyes, he surveys the assembled crowd without a trace of embarrassment and, after a long pause, continues as though nothing had happened.

Alas, the little episode is symbolic. The great undertaking comes to grief. Flooding, insufficient skilled manpower, inadequate funds, disputes over mining rights, despondency, lead finally to the shaft becoming slowly waterlogged. The project had devoured a great deal of money and yielded nothing. Goethe had as little success with this plan as Balzac had with his grandiose mining project in Sardinia, which was to have made him a millionaire; but at least Balzac's dream was realized after his death, the Ilmenau mine has never been reopened.

At the very outset of the experiment, however, Goethe learns much and gains a great deal of experience. In the first place he discovers the complicated constitutional position into which he has got himself. All the Thuringian principalities descending from the 'Ernestine' line of the House of Wettin exercise rights in this dormant and unproductive mine, as does also the Electorate of Saxony, through an overlordship of several centuries earlier. He has to negotiate with Gotha, Meiningen, Coburg, Hildburgshausen; when Ilmenau was added to Weimar, as the result of the partition of the County of Henneberg, the other heirs prudently retained their rights and interests in this subterranean treasure house. Goethe, who has never seriously studied law, now has to study the laws on mining. There is also a private family which, in years gone by, had sunk a considerable sum of money in the necessitous undertaking, and the heirs now want compensation. The people of Ilmenau look to the new venture with touching and joyous expectancy; the place is desperately poor and looks forward to a new lease of life from it. The Weimar Department of Finance has claims on the mine of many years' standing, and is extremely reluctant to invest more money, which in any case is not available. The worst aspect of all is that skilled workmen and engineers of ability are not to be had. A mining surveyor, who undertakes to survey the place, soon departs, to mines with better prospects. To entice so much as a foreman with some knowledge of the work is a triumph for Goethe, and he mentions him with pride in his report. Here in Ilmenau Goethe comes face to face with practical realities for the first time, with the indolence of the masses, the spitefulness of the rock, the incalculable behaviour of water, the slowness of the people. It is only in his *Faust*, where the treasures of the earth are mobilized by a stroke of magic, that he is able to master these problems. All he needs is a devil.

The simpler tasks of government Goethe fulfils with a light and elegant touch. The Duke's younger brother, Konstantin, has fallen in love with one of the ladies at Court, a Fräulein von Ilten, and wants to marry her. It is not possible, for she is not of equal birth. Because of the uncertain state of the Duke's health – at this period he is constantly dogged by broken bones, rheumatism, jaundice, fever, and there is still no heir – the succession must not be endangered. Goethe acts with energy and makes, as can be imagined, two new enemies. The Prince is sent to Paris and returns with a French girl. He does not want to marry her, but she is already pregnant. Goethe, as minister, has to ensure that the birth takes place in an outlying village; the child, a son, is handed over to the foresters, like Karl August's own offspring. The mother, however, does not give in so easily; Goethe has to ride over several times himself to try to persuade her to leave. Finally he sends her away and, as a precaution against her return, sends his servant, Philipp Seidel, to accompany her as far as Frankfurt. He can also take the opportunity of telling Goethe's parents how things are going on in Weimar. The son's letters to his father and mother are brief. Usually they are to ask for money, through his mother, who is to raise the subject with his father: 'Now that I am brother and everything else to a prince, I cannot economize', or 'Father owes me an endowment!'

At the same time he really lives very modestly, at any rate so far as his lodgings are concerned. He has a small apartment in the town, for which he pays only a tiny rent, and, as his main home, the garden-house which Karl August gave him. In this latter he sleeps on a straw mattress, in a room just big enough to hold a pinewood couch. Philipp Seidel often shares the same room with him. They talk far into the night, after Goethe has returned from a ball or one of the amateur theatrical performances. Seidel has noted down some of these conversations, but only a few unfortunately; he also notes down his own remarks, and these are occasionally revealing. Soon after their arrival in Weimar Seidel writes to a friend in Frankfurt:

In our talk we passed from one thing to another, and included everything under the sun. Imagine the startling turn: love stories on the island of Corsica, and there we continued in the most tremendous and heated set-to until nearly four o'clock in the morning. The question we fought out with such vehemence and learning was this: whether a nation is not happier when it is free than when it is under the authority of a sovereign lord. I said: The Corsicans are truly unfortunate. He said: No, it is a stroke of good fortune for them and their descendants, they will become more refined, less savage, they will learn the arts and sciences instead of being uncouth and savage as they were before. Sir, I said, to the devil with all the refinements and improvements, and leave me my freedom, which is our real happiness. The Corsicans cannot be savage, the mountain dwellers excepted, otherwise they would not have so strong a feeling for freedom nor be able to display such bravery. They were happy. They satisfied their needs easily, and were able to do so because they created no unnecessary ones. Now their needs grow daily greater and they cannot satisfy them, for none of us can dress, eat, drink, enjoy society and so forth as he wishes. They had everything they asked, because they did not ask much, and they had that much in freedom.

The Corsicans' fight for freedom against Genoa and the French was in everybody's minds at that time, and Paoli, the Corsican leader, was a hero whose praises Hölderlin still continued to sing in his Odes. Seidel will scarcely have known of Boswell and his book on Corsica, or of Rousseau's intervention in the islanders' cause, although the young man was a great reader. But his argument with Goethe is also significant as showing how free the relationship between master and servant was. Goethe is a whole-hearted supporter of 'enlightened despotism'. Only thus, he thinks, can morals be improved, the arts and sciences promoted; this is a view he never relinquished.

A servant at this time had great liberty to express his opinion, even if he was not always the equal of Beaumarchais' Figaro. For the most part, however, it was only a sort of jester's freedom; the master could send the impudent wretch packing at will, and in other respects too he could do what he liked. But Goethe treats his Philipp like a confidant. He is the only person who knows all his secrets; he is his agent and secretary, he is allowed to open his letters, he looks after Goethe's financial affairs and deals with part of his correspondence. It is to Philipp that Goethe, when he is in Italy, sends his *Iphigenie*, the first great work in which he makes his re-appearance as a poet. About this, too, Seidel expresses his opinion freely. Goethe replies:

> What you say about my *Iphigenie* is, in a sense, unfortunately true. When, on artistic and technical grounds, I had to decide to re-write the play, I foresaw that the best passages would have to be lost if the bad and the less good ones were to gain. You have quoted two scenes that have clearly lost. But when the thing is published, read it again in a quite detached way, and you will feel what it has gained as a whole. [On another occasion:] Moreover stick to what you are doing, because this is what I want you to do, to tell me your opinion frankly, without preface or apology, about everything that concerns me or about anything else you feel you want to. I have always looked upon you as one of my guardian spirits; please do not tire of fulfilling this small office in the future either.

We have, unfortunately, only a very few glimpses into this unique relationship; in all probability much of what Seidel saw and heard he was prevented by his loyalty and discretion from writing down. After his return from Italy Goethe found him a position as a revenue official, and at this point the intimacy ceases. But for the first ten years that Goethe was in Weimar we must regard Philipp Seidel as his closest confidant. He could have told us more about the poet than all the letters and diaries can ever reveal. He kept his silence.

What more can we glean on the subject of government from the letters and diaries? Very little, apart from brief entries such as *'Conseil'* or 'Commission', this latter referring to the mining project. There is much talk of fires. There are fires everywhere, in the little town of Weimar and in the villages. The houses and cottages are roofed with thatch or shingles. There is no organized fire service; fires are put out with the aid of water and a few buckets, or the burning houses are torn down. As often as not the people just stand helplessly by, bewildered in the face of the raging elements. Goethe jumps on his horse and gallops to the spot.

> The whole village was razed by the time we got there, it was only a question of saving wreckage, and the school and the church. [There follows a description of the blaze, which casts its light into *Faust* itself:] Behind and in front and at my side a fine glow but no flames, the deep, hollow-eyed glow of the caved-in village, and the wind in its midst, and then somewhere a flame leaping up again, and the magnificent old trees round the place aglow within their hollow trunks, and the red smoke in the night, and the stars red, and the new moon hiding in the clouds. It was two o'clock in the morning before we got home.

On another occasion he almost burns the soles of his feet giving assistance at very close quarters.

It is this getting to grips that affords him pleasure and satisfaction, and it satisfies too his poet's eye and ear. In talking with the peasants, with the village headman at the fire, he gets to know the people, from whose 'marrow we really live', as he notes down reflectively one day. But redress? How? Fire insurance exists, but the peasants do not pay their premiums. They have no money. They are always in arrears with the wretched taxes, and only pay them off when threatened with seizure. Fire engines! There is no money for these either, and where are the craftsmen to build them? In future houses are to be roofed with tiles, the government has issued orders to this effect over and over again. But the peasants shrink from the expense, which seems to them exorbitant, and the brick-yards cannot supply sufficient tiles; there are disputes between the guilds, the tilers complaining that bricklayers are secretly laying tiles, contrary to rules and against all guild tradition. Everywhere Goethe finds himself up against the delicate obstacles of reality. They are living in a feudal, absolutist state, why cannot they simply issue orders, *fiat voluntas*? He has to learn that the feudal lord is tied to the self-same traditional order of things, of which in the last resort he represents but the feudal summit.

For Goethe it is always the same story, he must get out into the country. It is there that the peasants, the backbone of the country, are to be found, honest folk, 'industrious and simple. Smocks without buttons – only little straps', he notes. They are too poor to buy buttons, and the straps they make themselves; this Goethe did not know. 'Complaint about deficiencies in cattle breeding and the extensive pasturage of the tenants.' The pasturing rights of the landlords and tenants who, according to old tradition and vested 'rights', are allowed to let their cattle graze on the peasants' land, are one of the deep-rooted evils of the country. Here Goethe can only observe, he cannot change the social structure of the country; the Duke himself, the absolute monarch, would find it hard to do this, even supposing he wanted to. But he is not greatly interested in reform; in fact he himself contributes greatly to the deterioration. His mad passion for hunting devastates the land, and the peasants are forced to act as beaters to drive the game over their own fields. Black game is the Duke's great passion, and the huge preserve he has had fenced in for his boars is his proudest possession of all. Goethe has constant arguments with his friend on this subject, but to no avail. He admonishes, warns and even accompanies him on one of his boar hunts, almost getting stuck by a wild boar when his spear breaks. Hunting, the passion of princes, the jealously guarded privilege of the great lords, and the subject of the bitterest uprisings since the peasants' revolt of Götz' day, is Karl August's privilege – on this point he remains adamant.

There is a visit to the little town of Apolda, where a certain amount of weaving is carried on; it is the only town in the Duchy with any pretence to an industrial life. Goethe notes – among the first sketches for his *Iphigenie* – 'Stocking-makers idle at a hundred looms since the New Year. The manufacturers' council does not help. Poor start for these people. Hand-to-mouth existence. The manufacturer saddles them with their looms. Marry easily....' None of this was in the records of the *Conseil*.

There is an inspection of recruits. Goethe has taken over this rather unpleasant task. He paints the scene in one of his most vivid sketches. The Commission takes down particulars of the unfortunate wretches. A woman forces her way up the stairs in a desperate attempt to save her son or her sweetheart. The sergeant pushes her roughly down again. The clerk glances indignantly over his shoulder; the business has been going so smoothly. Goethe scribbles down another sketch: a recruit entering through the 'Gate of Glory', above it a gallows crowned with a wreath. The President of the War Commission has no very high opinion of military service.

He has a high opinion of agriculture, however. They have brought in an Englishman named Batty with some knowledge of irrigation, dyke construction and amelioration of the soil; English agriculture at this time, on the eve of the Industrial Revolution, had reached its zenith. Batty is a man after Goethe's own heart, the only one, in fact, to whom in his diary he gives unstinted praise: 'When something needs to be done, he immediately sees what is necessary and does it.' Batty's relations with the difficult landlords are excellent, although there is much strife and opposition. Why build a dam which may also benefit the people in the next village, or even those across the border in Gotha? The tenants obstinately resist the dividing up of estates, which has been mooted. Land reform, envisaged in vague outline, does not materialize. But Goethe is delighted with his Batty: 'He is almost my only beloved son, in whom I am well pleased! So long as I live he shall lack neither food nor drink.' Batty remains in Weimar, where he dies at a ripe old age.

Observing Batty's fight with the fields and meadows, Goethe writes reflectively: 'What a beautiful thing this cultivation of the land is, the response is always so clear whether what I do is stupid or sensible.... But I can feel in advance that it is not for me. I must not stray from my prescribed path; my existence is no simple one.'

# 20

# *Minister of State*

After several months of amateur playing at it, Goethe now finds himself caught up in earnest in the business of government. Karl August's need for him increases daily. New duties are constantly being entrusted to him, and he never refuses. He even rejoices on one occasion: 'The pressure of business is very good for the soul; when it is released it has freer play and enjoys life. Nothing is more wretched than the man who lives in comfort without work.' (Diary entry: January 13, 1779.) He has assumed the Presidency of the War Commission, 'my mind firm, my senses keen'; to use his own expression, he 'wallows' in it.

A mere list of the offices held by Goethe and his titles, such as we usually find appended to his biography, does not get us very far. Nor can we be satisfied to regard his official activities merely in relation to their importance for his writing or his experience of life and people. He did not see them in this light. For a time, at least, he took them extremely seriously and they made a decided mark on his character. We may regret that he expended so much time and effort on them. Merck, always the adviser, had already warned him that he ought 'to leave the dirty work to others', he was too good for that. Herder, ever ill-humoured, had ridiculed Goethe's activities as Director of Roads and Services from the very beginning, calling him *Pontifex maximus*, 'in plain German road-inspector and crossing-sweeper'. Later, Goethe himself wrote: 'In our youth we think ourselves capable of building palaces for people, and when it comes to the point we find we have our hands full merely disposing of their excrement. Great resignation is required for this loathsome task, nevertheless it has to be done.'

A few dates are necessary here. In June 1776 Goethe becomes a member of the Privy Council, the *Conseil*, with the title *Geheimer Legationsrat*; in August 1779 he is promoted to *Geheimrat*, and twenty-five years later to *Wirklicher Geheimer Rat* when he receives the title 'Excellency'. The period of his real ministerial activity, however, is the decade from 1776 to 1786, the year he leaves for Italy. After his return he enters into a new relationship with his Duke and his country, one tailored entirely to his own personal requirements; he becomes general supervisor for arts and sciences,

195

in other words he becomes a sort of Minister of Culture. But, despite many fluctuations, he still remains Karl August's personal adviser on matters of importance.

So we see that his serious official activities cover a period of ten years. The term 'Minister' is not the official one, but it was used by his contemporaries. Officially Goethe is one of the members of the *Conseil*, the committee of councillors whose duty it is to advise the Duke. Individually, their duties are not confined to specific departments. They meet, deliberate, vote and submit the final vote to the Duke, who then announces his decision in a rescript to his 'dear and trusty servants', the councillors; they, in their turn, pass on the supreme decision to the governments of the four territories composing the Duchy. A certain division of duties does, of course, exist, though not consistently: thus Goethe deals in the main with questions of foreign politics, home affairs, road building, for which he is chairman of a special committee, and the war commission of which he is president; later on, when the incompetent and unscrupulous Kalb is dismissed, he takes over finance as well. To bring order into the country's financial affairs becomes his chief preoccupation and his finest achievement. In these early days cultural matters concern him only occasionally; that comes later.

The documents in the Weimar archives relating to Goethe's official activities have recently been published. They present a strange picture. The official style of writing – and the whole business of government was carried on by means of memoranda, addresses or letters – in the normal baroque style of the day, consisting of old-established and complicated formulas. The Duke is always referred to as *Serenissimus* or, if the matter in hand is a little more troublesome, as *Serenissimus clementissime regens*. The vote of the councillors is always an *untertänigstes Promemoria*, a most humble submission. Goethe, who on their wild riding and dancing escapades calls Karl August *'Du'*, naturally adheres to these forms; in fact he is the one who observes them most scrupulously, to the point of extreme pedantry. It is not the elderly Excellency but the young man of under 30 who casts an adverse vote when one of his colleagues makes some very sensible proposals for simplifying the almost grotesquely involved formalities. The Duke himself, we can imagine, would also have been in favour of such a simplification; he never set much store by ceremony. Goethe's vote is an energetic 'No!' He considers any such change pernicious, 'since such apparently arbitrary forms involve so wide a range of related circumstances, which will now be severed'. Nothing is severed. And the same Goethe who has just written his *Harzreise im Winter* in free *'Pindaric'* verse, gravely inscribes his corrections in the margins of the documents: not 'S. Durchlaucht Herrn Karl August' but 'Herrn, Herrn Karl August'; in the case of other Serene Highnesses not *'Fürstlicher'* but *'Hochfürstlicher Durchlaucht'*, and if there is any doubt about the addition of *hoch* to *fürstlicher* some paraphrase should be found. Peculiarities of this kind belong to Goethe's protean nature.

The very term pedantry finds in him an energetic defender. In his view it stands for order, tradition, law. 'Anyone having to observe and deal in forms and ceremonies finds a degree of pedantry necessary. Take away the pedantry from garrison duty – what remains?'

It also has importance for him in aspects of life other than government work. At Karl August's wish he joins the Weimar Freemasons' Lodge. He returns from one of their meetings indignant, and writes to his friend: 'No midsummer's day can ever have produced more blunders in ritual and ceremony. As Master of the Lodge a deputy, unrehearsed, two principals chosen on the spur of the moment, etc.... And as soon as this kind of thing is divorced from pedantry, then good night!' He has just been introduced to the masonic ritual, and immediately it becomes for him something fixed and immovable; to tamper with it is negligence or sacrilege.

So far as the meetings of the *Conseil* were concerned there could really be no question of strict procedure. They met in one of the rooms of the Duke's suite, chosen and provided with a table and chairs only at the last minute. There were no standing orders. No minutes were taken, notes being made of the arguments and voting only in important cases. It is significant that at first Goethe is almost always represented only by a brief *accedo*. His colleagues usually explain their reasons *pro* and *contra* in more detail; often, indeed, in very much more impassioned, or even heated, terms. Goethe censures this as 'invective'. He is extremely cautious, which is not to say that he does not generally impose his will with great determination. His colleagues are forced to respect his wishes because they know he has the Duke's ear. He governs, in the name of *Serenissimus regens*. 'In my circle I have few if any obstacles other than myself. In myself there are still many.' (May 1780.)

The other ministers were no geniuses, but they were men of ability. The decisions had to be taken as a committee; the other members submitted to this, and Goethe submitted to them. There is no mention in the records of any considerable differences; for these we have to look in Goethe's diaries. There we read: 'Pierced the thick skin of several people', or 'ugly light cast on Fritsch as a result of many of his actions, which for a time I allowed to pass'. Fritsch remained as aloof as ever; at first he pointedly withdrew and requested leave, which Goethe authorized on the Duke's behalf when on one of his hunting trips, or else visited his estates in Saxony. His other colleagues were not in a position to adopt such an attitude. They were miserably paid, at the rate of two hundred or three hundred and fifty thalers a year, and most of them had anything from six to ten children. And in Weimar, certain emoluments and perquisites apart, there were almost no opportunities for earning additional income. Of corruption, except in the case of Kalb, there is hardly a trace. They cut their coats to fit the cloth, of which there was very little. It is astonishing that, in spite of everything, they were so honest and upright.

Of what then did this whole business of government consist? Petitions and suggestions were submitted in writing, discussed, and presented to *Serenissimus* for signature, the resulting instructions being sent to the governments of the four territories. The oddest trivialities came up, just as they did in the larger states; Frederick the Great, for instance, made his own entirely personal decisions about marriages, civilian as well as military, or about the eviction of some undesirable – 'Let him go to the devil!' Goethe finds himself involved with the leather breeches of a deserter from the Hussars, the Duke's *Corps d'élite*. His attention has been drawn to the differences arising between the *Conseil* and the Captain of the Hussars, von Lichtenberg, concerning the leather breeches to be issued to the recruit who is taking the place of a deserter. Detailed instructions follow as to how long the leather breeches issued to the Hussars are to be worn: 'Every two years one pair of leather breeches, each pair to be worn for four years, will be issued to the Corps.' It was Karl August's wish that his *Corps d'élite* should be suitably equipped, and he had replaced the old cloth breeches by these new leather ones.

The Hussars formed the Weimar guard, and they had their tradition. Karl August's great-grandfather, the pomp-loving Wilhelm Ernst, had introduced the uniform; for a number of years he had employed Johann Sebastian Bach as his *Konzertmeister*, and on festival occasions Bach and the entire orchestra had to appear in the uniform of the Hussars.

But soldiers, even Hussars of the *Corps d'élite*, were beneath all social grading. The Weimar Hussars consisted of thirty to forty men. They served as a bodyguard and as the Duke's postillions, as torch-bearers at balls and on other festive occasions; they also delivered Goethe's love letters to Frau von Stein. Sometimes they had more serious tasks to perform, such as tracking down deserters or accompanying prisoners. Desertion was common in every army and was often practised on a very large scale. It was the sole means of procuring one's release from a service that lasted for life and in which the only legal provision for release was in cases of total physical incapacity. There were constant desertions even from the world-famous Prussian army, and in the orders issued by Frederick the Great to his generals the first and most important section deals with means of preventing desertion. In this the Hussars played a leading role: they had to accompany marching columns, stationed on both sides like watch-dogs, especially in terrain where observation was difficult.

All this was by no means divorced from Goethe's own activities; he was involved in it. Prussian deserters used to escape into Weimar territory, and Frederick the Great then demanded that they be handed over or, if that was refused, some others in their place. The Weimar Hussars had to escort these unfortunates. But Prussia now goes even further and sends its recruiting officers on to Weimar soil. The *Conseil* has to advise on the problem: is the Prussian recruiting to be allowed to continue or are they themselves going to hand over some people? 'An unpleasant and shameful business', Goethe writes in his appreciation. 'If we choose the first alternative, these dangerous people [the recruiting officers] will establish themselves and take root everywhere'; eventually they will even rob the Duke of his own soldiers. All at once Goethe finds himself involved in the high politics of a tiny state. The Emperor demands the same facilities for his Austrian recruiting officers. To whom are they to turn? To the Reichstag, the Imperial Diet, in Regensburg? It still exists, but it is a completely powerless body; at the most, as Goethe points out, they will get only empty words of sympathy from that quarter. To the other member states? They have their own worries and fears. It would be a good thing, in Goethe's opinion, if the princes of the Empire were to wake up. There is talk of a Prince's League, a sort of 'third force' between Prussia and Austria. Karl August, supported by Goethe, has worn himself out over the project, but to no avail. The Empire is already in a state of dissolution.

But at least an attempt is made to bring some sort of order into the little state of Weimar. To begin with a national budget must be introduced. The rewards offered for capturing ravens and magpies can be terminated as unnecessary expenditure. A reserve of ten thousand *thalers* – about £1,500 – is to be created, a figure that enables us to form some idea of the country's financial position. The Duke's civil list, out of which the Court and travelling expenses have to be paid, is just over twenty-five thousand *thalers* a year, a sum that young aristocrats at a London Club, such as Brooks or Whites, gamble away in a single bet. The ministers humbly, but with a sort of desperate courage, beg *Serenissimus clementissime regens* to try to maintain a household within his means. The Duke promises to do so.

It is wise not to form too idyllic a picture of peaceful Weimar. Petitions from districts ravaged by fire or damaged by flood are legion, as are complaints about ruthless seizure of tax arrears. The Hussars have to assist the tax collectors in such cases. Goethe votes constantly for leniency and tax reduction; existing duties and taxes are far too high in his opinion. One of his colleagues remarks that none the less barely one-sixth of the subjects pay without a threat of execution; the remaining five-sixths would immediately cease to pay if the writs of attachment were discontinued. The indulgent tax collection of modern times was unknown under absolutist rule.

Goethe has a document of two hundred pages in front of him concerning the town of Ruhla, once famous for its manufacture of arms and now fallen on bad times, its inhabitants eking out a miserable existence with pipe-making and farming. The tax-collector has described them as agitators and inflammatory rebels. They are resisting a new assessment of their houses on which they are to pay one chicken and a quantity of poppy seed for each chimney stack; there is a ground rent in addition. Goethe notes 'passionate harshness' against the tax-collector who, in any case, is not to be blamed. The ground rent should remain, 'on the other hand the surrender of pullets, cockerels and poppy seed should not be demanded of them'. The people of Ruhla are under-nourished, at least they should not be deprived of their courage. 'Where are the arrangements for giving them hopes and prospects? If these cannot be provided, at least leave them unmolested with what they have, their progress should not be hindered by weighing them down still further....'

The total sum involved for the whole town of Ruhla – the pullets being assessed at three *groschen* each – amounts to three *thalers*, twenty-three *groschen* and ten *pfennigs*. The demon of bureaucracy and pedantry takes its revenge on all who approach its domain. After careful study of this mountain of documents, the paper for which alone cost several times the sum involved, Goethe himself begins to wonder whether the work he is doing makes any sense. But he patiently adds still more paragraphs to the pile.

Finally a loan is decided on to help the country out of its constant financial plight. Goethe negotiates for this in Switzerland, and a journey he undertakes with the Duke, known in Weimar as a *Geniereise*, has as its main object this transaction. Their goal is Bern, an enormously wealthy republic until the day when Napoleon plunders its coffers to the last dreg in order to finance his Egyptian expedition. The Frankfurt banking house of Bethmann, friends of the Goethe family, initiates the negotiations. Bern grants the princely sum of fifty thousand *thaler* against collateral of some of the Duke's estates. The *Conseil* gives its approval with a sigh of relief. It is hoped to get the money very shortly, preferably at the time of the Frankfurt fair, when escorted convoys will provide a safe opportunity.

They are no longer living in the days of the robber knights, like Götz, but nevertheless bands of robbers make the roads in Weimar, and throughout Thuringia, unsafe, and the thirty Hussars have too many other tasks to be able to get to grips with them. It is not only in Schiller's great play that robbers make their appearance; there are robbers in Goethe's *Wilhelm Meister*. Merchants have to travel with an escort, and then often find they have to defend themselves against the escorting soldiers, who are not much better than the highwaymen. Goethe has a case to deal with where an escorting soldier has had a row with two Jewish merchants. He insulted them, they abused him in return, whereupon he put them under arrest and exacted a fine. Goethe rules that the merchants have been sufficiently punished by the detention, from which they can longer be absolved, but the fine is to be returned; the soldier is to be detained for the same length of time as the Jews, and is to bear the costs. As chairman of the road commission Goethe is very concerned 'to make the journey through Weimar safe and pleasant for each and every traveller'. Weimar lay completely outside the normal travel routes, there was not even a post road leading to the little capital; Erfurt was the nearest post station.

Throughout Goethe's life the roads remained poor, and any journey was regarded as a hazardous undertaking; it was easy to break one's neck, the usual thing being for the carriage to overturn. Forty years after this, travelling south to a rendezvous with some new love, Goethe's own carriage overturned, his companion was badly hurt, and the journey had to be abandoned. In his present position he was unable to effect any great improvement. It was the peasants, always the peasants, who were responsible for the upkeep of the roads, and they never did more than they could possibly help. Road planning on any large scale was out of the question because every few miles the road would reach the frontier of another state.

Thus Goethe continues to find himself face to face with realities. Foreign territory intermingled with Weimar territory. Desire for independence on the part of the four constituent territories. Quarrels among the guilds. A further stack of documents relating to the collection of sparrows' heads. Provision of a Weimar contingent of one hundred and eleven men for the army of the Empire: *Serenissimus*, always receptive to questions of military importance, is prepared to pay these troops out of his own pocket. Even smaller contingents than the Weimar one exist in this army of the Holy Roman Empire: an independent Imperial abbey at Gutenzell in Swabia is scheduled to provide three and a half infantrymen and half a cavalryman. A League of Princes with such partners has little prospect of becoming a power, a 'third force'.

Questions of a *pfennig* on beer, a *pfennig* on meat are discussed; it is always *pfennigs* – a microcosm. Even the provision of a map and survey of the country, with the object of at last providing a basis for assessing the size, frontiers and population of the Duchies of Weimar, Jena, Eisenach and the District of Ilmenau, poses considerable difficulties, first and foremost that of finding even one man qualified to do the job.

What has Goethe learned in this Lilliputian world? He has learned moderation, and to concentrate on some one particular task. Among his official duties, and in complete opposition to his natural inclinations, he has taken upon himself that of finance; as the Duke's friend and favourite he is the only person who can handle the problem with sufficient authority. He has urged strict observance of budgeted expenditure, he has threatened to resign unless the steward of the Duke's privy purse will comply with his demands for economy, and, following the dismissal of Kalb, who had been lining his own pocket, he has taken over his duties as well. He has also carried through a resolute policy of disarmament, in spite of the army being Karl August's hobby horse, and this reduction of the armed forces is the main basis of his attempt to put the country's finances on a sound footing.

The word 'army' is as great an exaggeration as is the title 'War Minister' for Goethe's presidency of the War Commission. The military strength of the Duchy of Weimar consisted of five hundred and thirty-two infantry, an artillery force of eight men and one officer, and the thirty Hussars. Goethe reduces the infantry to two hundred and ninety-three, most of those dispensed with being veterans whose loss is not too serious even for Karl August. The artillery disappears completely. The Hussars have to remain because they are indispensable as postillions, attendants at Court functions, escorts for deserters and collectors of tax arrears. In future if Karl August wants to play at soldiers he will have to go abroad and serve in a real army, which is what most of the petty princes do. The Duke admires his great-uncle, Frederick; at the same time he has every reason to fear him because he knows he regards rulers like himself as mere 'brats', diplomatic nonentities. Karl August's hopes are pinned on the Prussian Crown Prince, his brother-in-law. Meanwhile he has to steal across the border like a naughty boy, and very much against Goethe's advice, in order to feast his hungry eyes on parades in the Prussian garrison town of Halle. It is a tragicomic outcome of Goethe's most sensible measure, the reduction of the army, that it has the effect of driving the Duke out of his own country. He feels an almost desperate need to command, and to command something bigger than his own miserable little force. Immediately after Frederick the Great's death he leaves his inherited lands without a qualm and takes over the command of a Prussian regiment of Cuirassiers stationed at Aschersleben. There he lives in a Prussian garrison and rules his country from outside, in the same way as the Landgrave of Hesse ruled Darmstadt from Pirmasens. But Karl August is no mere fool like the Landgrave. Equally certainly he is no demon either, and if he appears to Goethe as such it is because he, and he alone, is the person, the power, with whom Goethe has to struggle, like Jacob with the angel; in fact Goethe himself uses this comparison, in speaking of his desperate attempts to achieve results: 'even if I had to put my thigh out of joint'.

Goethe loses the struggle. Karl August's wild boars, in their preserve behind the Ettersberg, break out time and time again and devastate the fields and pastures; as Goethe bitterly complains in a letter of protest to the Duke, the beasts even uproot and overturn the young trees, stakes and all, which Batty has just planted. The infantrymen are demobilized and the Duke goes off and puts on the uniform of a Prussian major-general. The finances are put on a healthier basis and there are now three civil lists: that of the Court in Weimar, with the Duchess Luise, that of the Duke in Aschersleben, surrounded by his brother officers, and that of the Dowager Duchess Amalie. The free and independent League of Princes, of which there has been talk, becomes dominated by Prussia almost at its inception and so loses all meaning. At the end of his years of duty in the service of his country, all that is left to Goethe is a feeling of utter resignation: 'Anyone who meddles in administration, without being the ruling Prince, must either be a philistine, a knave or a fool.'

In the same letter in which he says this he goes on to speak of the vegetable kingdom. What a different effect this has on him! Here everything falls into place, he scarcely needs even to reflect,

> the vast kingdom becomes so simplified in my mind that I am able to solve the most difficult problem straight away. If I could only convey to anyone the vision and the joy, but it is not possible. And it is no dream, no figment of the imagination; it is an awareness of the essential form with which nature, so to speak, plays all the time, and in so playing generates life in all its variety. Had I but time in my short span of life I would make bold to extend it to include every realm of nature, its entire kingdom.

His researches into nature are an escape. It was almost impossible to get the better of the Holy Roman Empire and its quarrelling member states; he was never able to get beyond trivialities, of which the Weimar sparrow heads were a symbol, and everywhere he found himself up against frontiers. Yet to govern is Goethe's desire and his intention. So he turns to nature. In nature there are no frontiers. In nature there is no one to raise objections. On the contrary he finds ready agreement everywhere. Everything manifests itself to his poet's eye in the beauty of its essential form. With such forms of creation one can live, in this realm government is possible.

But before he can indulge this new passion he still has to pass through another school, a school situated not far from his office, and one that is to re-mould him as decisively as the 'pressure of business', which at first seemed so sweet to him. The two operate side by side: his ministerial service and his relationship with Charlotte von Stein. They begin together and they end together. A completely changed Goethe emerges as a result.

# 21

# *The School of Frau von Stein*

Eight days after his arrival in Weimar Goethe is introduced to Charlotte von Stein, one of the ladies-in-waiting, whose silhouette he has already seen and tried to interpret. She is 33, small, no beauty, but with finely wrought nervous features; her hair is black and she has large dark eyes. Her complexion is 'Italian brown' and her cheeks bright red, the colour probably artificially heightened. 'Her body slim, her whole being a combination of elegance and simplicity' is how Zimmermann, the physician, describes her, after meeting her at Pyrmont where she was taking the waters. She suffers a great deal, largely as the result of her seven confinements in the eleven years of her marriage; four of the children are dead, leaving her with three sons. Zimmermann, whose correspondence is as extensive as his practice, immediately informs Lavater of his new acquaintance; it was also he who showed Goethe the silhouette of this interesting woman. It is a strange way of life that is in vogue among the sentimentalists of the day, a constant getting together or bringing together of other people. They try forming endless combinations, they spin threads and sever them again, they instigate friendships, love affairs and marriages, and then discuss them with a total lack of restraint. Zimmermann spins a thread between Goethe and Frau von Stein, who have not yet met, and Goethe takes up the game. In Lavater fashion he indulges in fancies about the profile: 'It would be a glorious spectacle to see how the world is mirrored in this soul. She sees the world for what it is and yet through the medium of love. And thus gentleness is the pervading impression.' To this he adds: 'traps with nets'. Zimmermann gives a circumstantial report of all this to Frau von Stein, who can only have shaken her head, for trapping with nets was utterly foreign to her nature. But she is curious, and wants to know more about this Goethe, some of whose books she has read, such as *Werther*, which probably did not greatly appeal to her, and *Götz*, which almost certainly was even less to her taste. For this new wildness and aggressiveness she has no use. Zimmermann spins a new thread over to Weimar: he has been staying in Frankfurt at the Goethes, 'and if you should happen to see him one day remember that, because of all I told him about you, he was unable to sleep for three nights'. In a further letter he becomes still more insistent: 'You want me to tell you more about

Goethe? You want to see him? My poor friend, you do not know how very dangerous this charming man could become for you?' If there is to be any talk of nets, it is the indefatigable doctor who has set them.

And so from the outset the meeting between these two is enacted before a private audience, and there is a certain group of people, both in Weimar and elsewhere, who never tire of observing them. 'Goethe and Frau von Stein' – this well-known parlour game is no invention of subsequent fanaticism and silliness about Goethe. Every element of Weimar society plays its part. Schiller, on his arrival in Weimar ten years later, repeats the general opinion. He meets her among a number of other ladies, 'insipid creatures' for the most part, one day when he is out for a walk:

> The best of them all was Frau von Stein, a truly singular and interesting person, and I can understand Goethe's tremendous attachment to her. She can never have been beautiful, but there is a gentle seriousness in her face and a candour all her own. Sound intelligence, sentiment and truth are contained in her nature. This woman has in her possession possibly over a thousand letters from Goethe and even when he was in Italy he still wrote to her every week. Their relationship is said to be completely pure and blameless.

> (August 12, 1787.)

At the time of writing this Schiller's attitude to Goethe was still distinctly cool, even hostile. His letters teem with every sort of intimacy, some of a very embarrassing nature, and there was plenty of scope for gossip in Weimar. The *chronique scandaleuse* of the little town is rich in content, and Goethe is not exempt. They could look into each other's windows, quite literally, in the narrow streets, and most of the houses had no curtains. Every step could be watched, by night as well as by day because the streets were unlit and people had to grope their way along with lanterns. Everybody knew everybody and the Court society was the object of the most unbridled curiosity. Servants, cooks and lackeys recounted every detail; everybody knew exactly when the Duke slept with his pale Duchess, and, much more important, they knew he did so only rarely. The life stories, and the love stories, of every lady and gentleman were known, and some were romantic indeed. The people at Court wrote and gossiped about all these things with complete lack of restraint and enormous enjoyment. Every slightest love affair and flirtation was the object of poems and verses, masquerades and amateur theatricals, a game from which Goethe by no means held aloof. If one were to exclude from his work the verse and plays in lighter vein, its volume would shrink very considerably. It can be done, but the great works among his poetry, novels and drama are built on the broader basis of these *pièces d'occasion*. He himself tells us repeatedly that all his poetry is *Gelegenheitsdichtung*: he needs an occasion before he can write at all, some person, some situation, must first engage his interest. Thus it is not surprising that there has been a constant search for the 'originals' of his characters, and he himself was not above encouraging these researches. He casually let fall innumerable hints of this nature. He was sufficient of an author to realize that his readers enjoyed recognizing people they knew or knew about in his writings.

But a search for 'originals' that is too ingenuous and blind involves a misunderstanding of the nature of writing and of its creation. This holds true in a special degree of Goethe. It holds true even though we can call his own words in witness to the contrary. He often has his reasons for misleading us, and he enjoys mystification and disguise. He blends his characters or divides them, just as he divides himself into Faust and Mephistopheles, both of whom are Goethe. He mixes the sexes, often putting more of himself into his feminine characters than into his masculine; he also invents characters such as a Helena or a Mignon, for whom one can discover no 'original' of any kind among the people he knew. Then again he ignores completely some of the most important people in his life, his sister, for example, or his mother, although in each of these cases he expressly stated that one day he might want to treat them at length. If he did not incorporate his beloved sister Cornelia, the 'abbess', in a novel, the reason may have been that her fate was an experience he never quite mastered. His instinct will also have told him that such a pitiful tale of woe was more than he could expect his readers to accept; in those days there was no public for the problems of a frigid woman, and Goethe was always very much aware of his public, even though it might consist only of his close friends.

All this holds good to a remarkable degree of his relationship to Frau von Stein, and of the work he dedicated to her, his seventeen hundred letters. The work admits of no precise description. There are letters, confessions, diary entries, descriptions of nature, prose poems, preliminary studies for other works, monologues. There is passion and realism; he raises his partner's hopes and then dashes them again, he runs through almost the whole gamut of the emotions, makes promises, breaks them and then renews his assurances of eternal love. In his Leipzig letters, and in his correspondence with Auguste Stolberg, Goethe had already practised this kind of writing, for which the term 'letter' is misleading. It is an interweaving of *Dichtung und Wahrheit*, as in his later memoirs, and as in that work nothing is pure fiction yet nothing is described quite literally, 'just as it was'. In any case the reality of love feelings, of emotions, evasions, self-deceptions or deceptions of the partner, is a complex that defies 'exact' description. Goethe writes his letters as a poet, condensing, sublimating, merging things and then separating them again. The more ardent his words, the more convincing their passion, the more certain it is that he is writing as a poet. This does not mean that in such cases his words have no basis in fact and are mere literary invention. Everything Goethe writes to Frau von Stein is born of experience, and of suffering too. The letters are genuine documents of a great passion, but they are not what those readers look for who want the feeling of 'being there', of knowing 'what really happened' In such longing for tangible evidence there is an unpleasant element of the peep-show, and people's minds have been quite unduly occupied by the question of whether Goethe did or did not sleep with the woman.

Nevertheless we cannot afford to ignore this question, because it has a certain importance for Goethe's psychography. We have already seen what Weimar society, whose curiosity was insatiable, thought about it. But there are other and more important considerations. Once again, as so often in his life, Goethe chooses a type of woman who is a sister rather than a wife. It is a necessary safeguard for him, and particularly in this case because he soon begins to feel himself greatly endangered by this life. Over and over again in his letters and poems he uses the word 'sister': 'You must once have been my sister in a former age'; as an afterthought he adds 'or my wife'. He calls her his Madonna. He speaks of the need of finding 'some way of living to- gether' – some very indefinite way, but never the definite and practical way of divorce and marriage. Weimar was full of divorced people; no stigma was attached to divorce among the aristocracy. There were many free associa- tions as well. Schiller, whose fame when he went to Weimar did not approach that of Goethe, reported with pride that he was received everywhere with his declared mistress, Charlotte von Kalb. But Goethe paid not the slightest attention to the opinion of Weimar society; later he forced on it, and for decades, his association with a simple, rough, uneducated girl.

It will certainly never have occurred to Frau von Stein to permit herself such extravagances as did her social equal Charlotte von Kalb. She was a lady-in-waiting, and not only in name. At the Weimar Court, in company with the Duchess Luise with whom she had much in common, she was the avowed champion of good breeding, of exquisite manners, and of decorum in speech and bearing. In nothing else did she have so much to teach Goethe as in these arts. She hated the *Genieton*, with its swearing, its cracking of hunting whips, its noise, its violence, its storming in and out of rooms. We no longer possess her letters to Goethe, she burned them. There is no doubt they contained many warnings and admonitions – complaints and lamentations, too, perhaps; they were written in French. These are guesses, but there is no guess-work about her influence over Goethe; she groomed him, tamed and moderated him. '*Tropftest Mässigung dem heissen Blute*', he wrote later in a poem: she dispensed moderation drop by drop to assuage his savage blood, and this medicine must often have had a bitter taste. A steady hand and a cool head were necessary.

Charlotte was a cool woman, even if she was not a cold one like the Duchess. She almost always dressed in white, elegantly, but with no touch of colour; this too was characteristic. Throughout the whole of her life there is not a single trace of passion discernible; feeling there is, in rich measure, and later on irritation and a feeling of having been wronged when Goethe 'betrayed' her, as it must have seemed to her. Her marriage can remain entirely out of the picture. She was married off by her parents, according to the custom of the day: the wealthy, good-looking Herr von Stein, the Duke's Master of the Horse, was a good match for a poor girl at Court. She bore him seven children and then became a prey to illness. She treated her husband with patience and consideration, but she was not often called upon to exercise these virtues: he did not take his meals with her, but at Court, and for a great part of the year he was away on official journeys, buying horses, visiting the stud, Karl August's other great hobby. He cut a good figure wherever he went, and at Court was popular as a good dancer. He was an excellent horseman, and sometimes gave exhibitions of horsemanship. A sufferer from violent headaches, he died of paranoia. Goethe treated him in a friendly, though distant way, in so far as he ever saw him; his diaries and letters rarely mention him.

Charlotte's attitude to her children was cool, too, cool to the point of iciness. She sent them all away; the eldest as a page, the second to Brunswick, and the youngest she handed over to Goethe, who took him into his own house to educate. Cool, intelligent, with a very good head for the affairs of life – she was a true daughter of her Scottish mother, who was an Irving – she wends her way, dressed in white, through Weimar society. It is the 'half-tones' in her nature that make the strongest appeal to Goethe, and although he is always trying to paint a portrait of her he never succeeds; she remains a riddle for him. The 'half-tones', however, give us a valuable hint. Her character is not a simple one, and even her lack of sensuality cannot be described simply as frigidity. Goethe woos her with the utmost tenderness and ardour, and even a woman who recoils from the ultimate contact feels a need for tenderness, affection and the little intimate tokens of love. It is a strange and, frankly, rather atrocious game that Goethe plays, because under no circumstances does he want to accept the final consequences either. But he is attracted by the idea of awakening this shy, retiring member of the nobility who, to all intents and purposes, has already finished with life, of seeing her unfold, at his side, their lives interwoven but in some indefinite way, as his mistress, his mother, his sister, and even, if need be, as his wife, but a wife of long ago, in some previous existence.

Goethe even attempted to treat this problem, in a half veiled form, in his one act drama, *Die Geschwister*, which he wrote for amateur performances by members of the Court; to-day we cannot help being somewhat taken aback at the idea of such highly personal matters being presented on the stage to an audience well aware of the relationship between the two main protagonists. The play deals with a couple, Wilhelm and Marianne, who are in love but who cannot consummate their love because they are brother and sister, or so Marianne believes. Wilhelm, however, knows that, in fact, she is the daughter of his former love, by her first marriage, a woman he had loved very dearly but who was unable to marry him because 'circumstances' prevented it; she died, 'too precious for this world'. Goethe naïvely gives her the name Charlotte, and Wilhelm tells a friend how through this Charlotte he 'became a completely different person'; he quotes one of her letters in which she confesses her love for him, and it is not impossible that Goethe is here inserting one of Charlotte von Stein's own letters, in the same way as he included original letters in his *Werther*. In any case the letter describes her feelings authentically: 'The world was dear to me again – I had already severed myself from it completely – and it was dear to me through you. My heart reproaches me, and I feel I am going to be the cause of torment to you and to myself. Six months ago I was so ready to die, and now I am no longer. ...' Wilhelm, having lost sight of Charlotte, is able to find happiness again in her *'rejuvenated likeness'*, her daughter.

Goethe regarded this little play as so intimate a piece that, in handing it to Charlotte von Stein, he expressly asked her to show it only to very close friends, such as the Duchess Luise, who was in a position to understand the meaning of resignation. He also stipulated that it was always to be returned to her: 'it is to remain our own.'

How Charlotte felt when she saw the play performed, we do not know, nor do we know whether she hoped that she herself might become the 're-juvenated likeness'; perhaps she felt simply confused. She was often forced also to be witness to another kind of Goethe play. Goethe constantly tells her in his letters of his 'Misels', his flames: there is a Christel with whom he skylarks around, or there is the beautiful singer Corona Schröter, whom he brings to Weimar and of whom he writes to Charlotte: 'If only God would grant me a wife like this, so that I could leave you in peace.' *Ein Weib*, a wife, a woman – never is this word used in relation to Charlotte. She is the lady, the *Frouwe* of medieval poetry, in which the minnesingers used to sing of the same double game: adoration of a noble lady, and love in the 'lower regions' to a country lass.

Finally, there is the difference in their ages. Charlotte is 33 when he first meets her; she will soon be 40, and that is an advanced age at a time when girls marry at 14, and at 40 are already grandmothers. If in her relationship with Goethe, in her love for him, she begins to unfold – and it seems, that even physically this was so – there is something terrible and tragic about it. It is a flowering that comes too late, that is without hope or prospect, that can never develop into anything; and it never does. All his life Goethe made enormous demands on his partners of both sexes; it was part of the economics of his life, which was geared to an unlimited consumption. The erotic needs of his body were served by other loves and love affairs.

Of Frau von Stein's suffering there can be no doubt. One woman commentator has suggested, as an explanation, that at the last moment, when she felt he was slipping from her grasp, she decided in desperation to submit to the final surrender, as result of which Goethe then fled. This is a problem with which we need not concern ourselves, but should we feel inclined to do so it is as well to remember that there are also 'half-tones' in eroticism, and manifold stages in the last and final surrender, particularly in a Goethe. The decisive fact is that Goethe remained single, alone in his little garden-house, and that Charlotte von Stein remained alone in her apartment over the Duke's stables. Here she lived until her death, impoverished as a result of the war years, brave, always dressed in white, aristocratic and lonely. One of her last instructions was that her funeral procession was not to pass Goethe's house, which would have been the normal route; she knew it might disturb his peace of mind.

When he came to her he was disturbed, bewildered, wild, restless, and unmannerly to the point of boorishness. She took him in hand and educated him. First of all, to put it bluntly, she taught him manners. In this field the 'half-tones' in her nature were able to take effect in the most beneficial way. Whether she was aware of his true greatness is open to question. But the biographer should not make too great demands on this woman; he can view the scene with a knowledge of Goethe's whole life and work. Charlotte saw in front of her a young man from Frankfurt, of bourgeois stock, who had become famous through a number of works of genius, as a result of which he had clearly lost his head a little. Whether he would ever write anything more was something Goethe himself was not sure about at that time. 'Am I not really a writer?' he notes casually in his diary, among entries about hunting, balls, masquerades and committee meetings.

She sees him as a young man who has been appointed to the Court through the favour of the Duke, another unmannerly boy. Goethe attaches himself to the lonely woman with the whole vehemence of his nature. She alone, so he assures her and others too, can save him, without her he will perish. Court society hates him, officials fear him, the populace stares anxiously at the mad escapades which this young South German intruder perpetrates daily with the Duke. With the women, as Charlotte writes, he is nonchalant and coquettish; he is without respect for the whole sex. For the most part their behaviour is such as to preclude his respect. He receives offers on all sides and seizes them indiscriminately, pressing a hand here, putting his arm round a waist there, or whispering to a dancing partner: 'Could I but spend the night with you, no qualm should I be caused; one day I'll take you in my arms and slake my long desire. ...' He dances everywhere, but with the village girls; on the ball-room floor at Court his feet feel tied. Charlotte is an excellent dancer, in the minuet and *contre-danse*, that is, not in the bucolic waltz of course. She is light on her feet and performs the complicated set figures with delicacy. This is something Goethe cannot do, despite his dancing lessons, something he never learns to do. He stands glumly up against the wall or else makes caustic remarks. He does not know how to make an entrance, how to bow, where to put his feet, all matters of the greatest importance. He has no knowledge of the subtleties of rank and behaviour, and princes, other than his friend Karl August, are apt to take it amiss when they are not shown the respect due to their rank. This boy, with his bourgeois Frankfurt background, is as likely as not, on leaving a room, to turn his back on some reigning prince. Or he will lean stiffly and awkwardly against a pillar without saying a word; he is unable to make light, easy conversation. It is only in an atmosphere of intimacy that his conversation flows, and then it does so wildly, like his writing, and mixed with coarse and unseemly expressions, or with exaggeratedly high-sounding ones, or with strange old-fashioned biblical turns of speech that no one uses any more.

Frau von Stein takes him in hand and teaches him these things, in so far as a Goethe can be taught. He never becomes a courtier. He never masters the easy elegance of aristocratic poise and bearing, not even when he becomes Excellency; he can only admire it in others, which he often does with exaggerated respect. His bearing remains stiff, or clumsily deferential, in front of his superiors. Nevertheless the lady-in-waiting 'licks' his bearishness sufficiently into shape for the Duke to be able to send him, without too great misgivings, on missions to the neighbouring Thuringian Courts. Even so he is always making *faux pas*. In Gotha he pats the flaxen heads of the young Princes and says casually, 'Well, you little tow-heads,' an outrage that was not forgotten for very many years. When the formalities of Court life get too much for him, 'the wanderings about up there athirst in the desert', as he haughtily calls it, he simply goes off, without even taking his leave, and withdraws into solitude. After a time he returns and complains that everyone has forgotten him.

His very way of life is strange and must seem quite impossible to Charlotte. There he sits in his little garden-house outside the city walls, with his odd servant Philipp, who copies his master's walk, opens his letters, sleeps in the same room with him and with whom, of a night, he chats as with an equal. The roof of the little house is half rotten and needs repairing, the furniture is of the very simplest, and one has to sit on bone-hard wooden chairs. When weather permits Goethe sleeps in his overcoat out on the verandah, which he has built on. He bathes in the river at the bottom of the garden, and, when people pass, looks at them laughing and dripping wet, with his hair hanging down over his face. The approaches to this strange abode he barricades jealously, putting gates, to which only he and possibly Philipp have keys, on the little wooden bridges which span the river. In the town he has a couple of other rooms, low-ceilinged attic rooms, which he uses when he attends the Court. These are cluttered up with trunks, drawing-boards – he draws ceaselessly and talks of becoming a painter – sketch-books, paper bags containing fragments of poetry, quantities of half-read books, rolls of engravings, boxes of letters to his old sweethearts, whom he likes to talk about but mostly in a way that confirms Charlotte in her conviction that he has little respect for the opposite sex.

Then suddenly he is gone, and Charlotte gets a note from Ilmenau, where he is busy with his mine, or from the Wartburg near Eisenach, where he crawls around among old ruins and vaults. On another occasion he goes off on a trip incognito, like some travelling journeyman, and returns dishevelled and in high spirits: now at last, like Haroun al Rashid, he has found out what the people are thinking.

What the people in Weimar think is apparently a matter of complete indifference to him. Toads and basilisks are his names for the people at Court, and yet these are the people with whom he has to live and mix. The moment one puts one's foot out of the house one steps 'on nothing but dung' – he always expresses himself in the strongest terms. In his intercourse with Karl August and their companions on their trips into the woods the language is stronger still and such language sometimes finds its way to table at Court. If the 'silent fury' of Court society makes things too uncomfortable for him, as he often feels, he declares quite openly that he is prepared to go, it is only a matter of harnessing the horses. Charlotte alone, so he keeps on telling her, can hold him there; she is the anchor that holds his little ship fast. 'If it had not been for you I would have shaken it all off long ago.' 'Finish your work,' he implores her on his knees, 'make something worthy out of me!'

It is a labour, this love, a task, and that is certainly no lesser thing than passion which, in Goethe's case, never lasts long. It demands all their energies, on both sides. Charlotte gives, from her by no means inexhaustible resources, and Goethe accepts what she gives – his resources are still immense. When their relationship comes to an end the woman is completely worn out, old, tired and bitter; Goethe, in his Olympian aloofness, is not even aware of this at first, and is astonished, indeed offended, by her 'coldness'. The intimacy, the love, lasts ten years. This is a long time in Goethe's life, the longest, at this intensity, that he ever devotes to a woman. In the course of these years he is transformed. If *dumpf*, inarticulate, is his watchword at the beginning, by the end it has become *hell*, clear and bright. If, at the beginning, his pleasure, and his strength, is in formless exuberance, by the end his interest is focused on shape and form. In the process much is undoubtedly lost. But lifelong *Sturm und Drang* is a manifest and embarrassing absurdity; there are examples. It is undeniable that, at this ageing woman's side, Goethe himself ages remarkably early; the man of 30 frequently speaks in retrospect, as though his life were nearing its end. In learning manners he becomes stiff and dry. Merck notes in pained surprise on one of his visits that Goethe has become completely the *Geheimrat*; his reception was distant and official, there was no sign of the rough Götzian familiarity of old. In this process of concentration his old friends die away; though he still writes occasionally it is with increasing coolness, and then the correspondence ceases altogether. His sister, on his own testimony the greatest love of his life, has died; during the last year of her life he sent her scarcely a line. Without immediate contact Goethe is unable to maintain any intimacy of relationship. It is a period of contraction; in many respects he grows narrower, but he rises to the heights. His good fortune and his genius see to it that he does not remain tied to this one contraction, although it is the most powerful of his life. Numerous transformations still lie ahead of him.

The outward forms of this love, this semi-marriage, are the strangest imaginable. Goethe lives in his little garden-house. Frau von Stein in her apartment over the Duke's stables, and from time to time on her husband's country estate at Kochberg, some four hours' journey from Weimar. Goethe generally has lunch with her, Herr von Stein taking it at Court. Letters and presents pass to and fro between them, carried by the Hussars. Goethe takes Fritz, the youngest son, into his house, neither Herr nor Frau von Stein showing any interest in him or, indeed, in any of their children. He educates him according to his own ideas which, he says, are based on those of the Greek sailors, the Hydriots, who took their sons to sea with them at a very early age and let them scramble round on board doing odd jobs; if they accomplished anything they got a share in the profits and so, very early on, began to take an interest in trade, exchange and booty, thus developing into able seamen and most daring pirates. It is a somewhat daring theory and in Fritz' case it was not very successful. Goethe lets the boy take part in all his activities; he acts as messenger, reader, audience, copyist and later as Goethe's assistant, treasurer and factotum. He develops into a weak and vacillating character who only late in life, after two unsuccessful marriages and long after leaving Weimar, begins to feel solid ground beneath his feet.

Goethe's feeling for children is very strong. This unmarried man feels a constant urge to surround himself with children, whom he likes to entertain in his garden, giving little parties and, at Easter, dispensing coloured eggs and sweets. He has his protégés too, as we have already seen. One of these, a thoroughly unsatisfactory youth to whom he gives the name Kraft, he has placed with a family at Ilmenau. He is always sending him money, and writes him long letters, the longest he wrote during these years, full of practical wisdom, solicitude and forbearance. He continues to do this even though the wretched young man becomes increasingly impossible and rejects every suggestion for any activity whatsoever; Goethe continues to support him until the young man's death some years later. Then there is a little Swiss boy who suddenly turns up in Weimar, and causes Goethe endless trouble. The rumour goes round in Weimar that he is an illegitimate son of the *Geheimrat*'s, or of the Duke's, or possibly of Anna Amalie's. The boy's name is Peter. A romantically inclined officer found him in the Swiss mountains, under some trees in a garden, and christened him 'Peter im Baumgarten'.

He sent out a circular: 'Devout children of nature! ... Open the way of life to this child, you sons of nature!' A 'plan of resurrection' was drawn up and Goethe sent a contribution. The officer went to America where he was killed, serving as a lieutenant in one of the Hessian regiments of mercenaries. Before leaving he had sent Peter to a boarding-school from which he ran away. He must have found out Goethe's address, and one day he turns up on his doorstep, a long pipe in his hand, a little dog at his heels.

It is touching to see how Goethe accepts the child. 'The lad is now mine,' he writes. 'I want to see if what I have in mind for him succeeds. If all goes well, he shall be dependant on no one should I die, or should I leave him or he me.' Here we have this man of 30 planning for his death. There are soon scenes. Peter daubs Goethe's plaster casts with ink, and is always running off into the town. Goethe takes him out to Frau von Stein at Kochberg. Here he shares a bed with young Fritz von Stein – how odd the sleeping arrangements of the day now strike us. Fritz complains bitterly that the boy insists on taking his little dog to bed with him as well, saying that he cannot sleep without it. Fritz gets bitten by the fleas and Peter has to find another home. Goethe sends him to Ilmenau, to his other protégé Kraft, who is to look after him, then to Berka; Peter is to become a forester. The head forester throws him out: the boy is lazy, slovenly, never up before ten, a toper, and in addition to all this has got the pastor's daughter with child. Goethe has no luck with his protégés, just as later he has none with his own children. Peter has to marry the pastor's daughter, because of the scandal, and has five more children by her; Goethe stands godfather to one of them. He keeps on trying with the boy, who is not untalented; he can draw, and Goethe sends him to the Weimar academy of drawing. In some way Goethe seems to see his own dreams of becoming an artist, and of breaking away, crystallized in this wild, unruly, ungrateful boy. One day Peter is gone, leaving his wife and six children to be a burden on the parish of Ilmenau; where he went or what happened to him no one knows, perhaps he followed his first patron to America.

Thus for a time Goethe has a little family out at Ilmenau and Berka which he supports, Kraft, Peter and Peter's children. Fritz von Stein he has in his own house. Philipp Seidel shares his bedroom. He has two homes, or really three, because lunch-time, afternoon and evening he spends at Charlotte's. Friends he has none, apart from the Duke, and the prematurely care-worn Knebel, who does not like Weimar, wants to leave and does not know where to go – eventually he goes to Jena. Herder, of whom Goethe had such high hopes, is irascible and almost hostile. Charlotte is his only refuge. Only when he is with her can he relax and unburden his mind, and to her are addressed his seventeen hundred letters and notes. At Charlotte's he often meets the Duke, and many of the most important decisions are discussed there between the three of them. Goethe's appointment to the *Conseil* is to a great extent due to her. Together they read: Homer, Voltaire, books on natural science. Goethe writes out his earlier poems for her, and adds new ones addressed to her. He does not think of any other public, it is enough that the verses are in her hands. They sketch and draw together; Charlotte is quite a gifted amateur artist, and a self-portrait sketch in profile is the only authentic likeness we have of her: tender and, at the same time, severe, with thin lips and a determined look, charming and desperately unhappy. She also writes, some of her things being published even in her lifetime; others were not published until later. In a little entertainment for the amateur performances, written at the beginning of her friendship with Goethe, she already expresses doubt as to the genuineness of his feelings for her and remarks sarcastically that she does not know whether it is 'he or Werther' who speaks out of the parcel of letters she possesses. After the break she writes bitterly and helplessly, in a 'Dido' drama, on the subject of deserted womanhood, including in the play her friend the Duchess Luise. In it she quotes Goethe's own remarks on his transformations, distorting his words to make them more brutal: 'True human nature is snake-like, after a certain number of years the old skin must be cast off; this one I have rid myself of at last.'

She should not be taken to task for such utterances; she had cause for bitterness. Thus embittered she also re-writes the finest of the poems he dedicated to her, the Lied *An den Mond*: '*Breitest über mein Gefild, Lindernd deinen Blick, Wie der Liebsten Augen mild, Über mein Geschick*' (Soothingly thy glance is cast over my domain, as my dear one's tender eyes cast theirs upon my fate). Charlotte altered this to: '*Da des Freundes Auge mild Nie mehr kehrt zurück* (Since my dear friend's tender gaze will ne'er return again) – and then added: '*Lösch das Bild aus meinem Herz …*' (Efface the image from my heart).

# 22

# *Courtier and Poet*

In a letter of July 1782 to his friend Hamann, Herder writes this about Goethe:

> So he is now Wirklicher Geheimer Rat, President of the Chamber [of finance], President of the War Commission, Inspector of Building, down to the building of roads, and in addition *directeur des plaisirs*, Court poet, author of pretty festivities, Court operas, ballets, costumes for masked balls, inscriptions, works of art, etc., Director of the Academy of Drawing, where during the winter he has been giving lectures on osteology, leading actor everywhere, leading dancer, in short the Weimar factotum and, with God's bounty, soon to be the Major-domo of all the Courts of the Ernestine succession, which he visits to receive their adoration. He has been ennobled and his elevation is to be announced on his birthday. He has moved from his garden into the town where he holds court in the grand manner, has readings, which will soon be transformed into assemblies, etc., etc.... With all this, government affairs have to look after themselves....

This is not a very charitable way of looking at things, but it gives an idea of Goethe's position. He is expected to be ready with his pen on any and every occasion, and to place his gifts for organization and embellishment at the disposal of all Court festivities. Far from declining such tasks Goethe welcomes them. He continues to retain this enjoyment of masquerades and pageantry into his extreme old age. If some 'deeper significance' is involved, there is no harm in that; if there is no 'deeper significance', someone will probably invent one. These writings later find their way into his Collected Works, where they present a somewhat strange appearance. Most of them are rather like subjects for improvisation in music, or little casual sketches for some *commedia dell-arte*, in which the actors are left to supply the wit and the gestures. There are countless allusions which no longer have any meaning for us, or which can only be unravelled after the most painstaking research. Much of the material was written in collaboration with others, or by others at Goethe's instigation. And, unless we are among those who regard every line written by Goethe as a stroke of genius, the greater part of it is poor stuff.

Everyone in Weimar writes, Frau von Stein, Anna Amalie, even the

Duke, the chamberlains and the keeper of the privy purse. Verse writing and play writing is not a profession, it is a social accomplishment, like playing cards. And the results are often written down on little cards, or pieces of paper, and passed round. Everyone takes part in the amateur theatricals, the Court is too poor to afford a professional theatre. The Duke acts, although he finds learning the parts irksome, and his brother Konstantin is drawn in too, although he is surly about it and soon has to be replaced by someone else; Goethe takes over the main roles. But he, too, dislikes learning parts and prefers to extemporize. All ideas are welcome, mythology, arcadian and pastoral scenes, Greek subjects, Roman subjects or contemporary subjects.

We must not allow the presence of a Goethe to deceive us into overestimating these activities and productions, his own included, although he may well have felt stimulated by the fact that all his tastes and inclinations, including those for painting and drawing, could be indulged. The plays are produced with natural scenery and artificial lighting effects. In Weimar 'Rembrandt' signifies violent contrasts of light and darkness, and they arrange Rembrandtesque night scenes by the river banks. Goethe writes an operetta, *Die Fischerin*, which the beautiful singer Corona Schröter sets to music and in which she sings his ballad *Erlkönig*, the only number that has survived from this light piece. Goethe does not over-tax himself in it; the whole plot is contained in a scene of jealousy between the young fisherman and his Dortchen. In order to frighten her fiancé Dortchen hangs her hat on some bushes by the river and hides; they think she is drowned and search the river for her. The setting is the river Ilm; they search the banks with torches and in boats, and finally comes reconciliation. 'I have rarely seen a more beautiful effect', writes Goethe of this *tableau* in his old age. His pleasure in such *tableaux* and picturesque effects is a lasting one, and it finds expression again in *Faust*. In this way quite unimportant works, written for a single day or evening, are connected intimately with his great works and can hardly be separated from them.

And so it goes on all the time, with plays and allusions involving all the members of this little circle. The Duchess meanwhile grieves because the Duke neglects her. Goethe writes a playlet, *Lila*, in which he plays the role of a sort of pre-Freudian mental healer. The Duke is quite openly portrayed as an 'ogre', who spends all his time hunting. The evil demon is exorcised with the aid of fairies and spirits, but towards the end the poet loses interest and simply declares that the fourth act can be left to the discretion of the ballet master. From this playlet, too, only one poem has survived in Goethe's collected poetry: *Feiger Gedanken, bängliches Schwanken, Weibliches Zagen, ängstliches Klagen, Wendet kein Elend, macht dich nicht frei* (Cowardly thinking, timorous doubting, feminine trembling, nervous lamenting, undo no misery, ne'er make you free). No one would imagine that this was originally intended as advice in matrimonial difficulties, nor were such resolute words the cure for the Duchess' sorrows. It was only when, after seven long years, the son and heir was finally born that Luise's position became secure and she herself began to feel some inner security. Ready to use any subject that came to hand, Goethe tried to make even this dynastic event the theme of a play, *Elpenor*, the Boy Hope. Inadvertently he was led by this theme into high tragedy: the boy's father became a tyrant, with murder on his conscience; it could only lead to a tragic ending, and the play remained a fragment. Later, when he showed it to Schiller, Goethe himself cited it as an example of 'incredible misapplication' of material.

At this period his grasp of the writer's craft, normally so sure and certain, is often very uncertain and wavering, a circumstance that finds a ready explanation in the extraordinary diversity of his life. Thus he inserts the monodrama 'Proserpine', a scene of great beauty in the grand manner, into a farce, *Der Triumph der Empfindsamkeit*, intended to ridicule the cult of sentimentality. Later he himself described this as a 'crime'. The reason for the crime was simply that he needed an important solo scene for the beautiful Corona Schröter, the only professional taking part in these amateur performances. It is an extremely strange play, containing many remarkable personal features and veiled allusions. In many respects it is very 'modern' and anticipates the 'romantic irony'. The characters talk among themselves: the fifth act is coming to an end and we've got ourselves into a fearful mess! – Well, let's go on to the sixth, on the German stage one can do anything. – The audience might think we were trying to make fun of them! – Would they be so very far wrong? – No, indeed! really we are only playing ourselves!

And in amongst all this we find the most daring Aristophanic insertions. There is to be a monodrama, added for reasons we have already seen, and the girls ask what a monodrama is. – It is a play with only one character, as you would know if you understood Greek. – But whom does this character act with? – With himself, of course. – We would like to do that one day, say the girls. – Leave that to others, and thank Heaven that you have not come to that yet! If you want to act, then at least act with one other person; after all, since the days of the Garden of Eden that has been the most usual and the most sensible way of doing it!

Even as Court poet Goethe cannot quite conceal the Mephistophelean side of his nature; he suddenly tires of speaking in a dead voice and uses quite a different one. But this passage also throws a strange light on the interpolated monodrama. The lovely Corona is to play the part of Proserpine. Having first admired her as a student in Leipzig, Goethe has now brought her to Weimar and courted her; Karl August has fallen in love with her and so has every visitor to the little town. Her coolness and detachment are well known, and her only appearances in the streets of Weimar are in Greek costume, walking majestically by the side of her stout Sancho Panza-like woman companion. Is Goethe in the above passage mocking her a little, taking a little secret revenge on a woman who has unsettled him considerably and for quite a time?

Whatever the answer, the scene that follows is a night scene in Tartarus, dark and gloomy. It is an opportunity for Corona to display all her gifts, and she is a gifted actress with a penchant for tragedy. Wife of the hated Pluto, Proserpine has been banished to the underworld. By eating of the pomegranate she has made herself guilty. All the horrors of the Greek hell are invoked. Corona points to the Danaides who vainly seek water to fill their cask, but it is empty, always empty, not a drop to moisten their parched throats. Ah! thus it is with her heart, whence can it draw, whither can it seek? For but a single moment love opened her heart, and then it closed for ever. In a fury of hatred for her husband, for his detested embraces, for the agonies of this night of banishment, from which there is no escape, the strange scene comes to an end. In his old age Goethe himself no longer quite understood it, and tried to re-write it in a more agreeable form.

Even in ancient times the myth of Proserpine had often been re-written and altered. Virgil transplants her, not to the underworld but to Elysium, which would have pleased Goethe as an old man better than his own merciless earlier version. Her momentary tasting of the pomegranate, the fruit of love, from which she derives only passing enjoyment and which leads to her damnation, may well be a personal allusion to Corona's short relationship with Goethe. And when her thoughts go back to the youth she loved, when 'no night was too deep for us to talk together, no time too long' – may this not be intended as Corona's own lament at her banishment to the underworld of her self-sufficiency?

We can only pose the question. Goethe scarcely wrote a line at this time that was without some personal significance. On the other hand it is possible that he intended nothing more than a solemn solo scene, a *lamentoso*, such as had been a favourite device in opera since the time of Monteverdi. The stimulus to write such a scene at all may have come from the operatic stage of the day, where melodramas and solo scenes were fairly common. Goethe's friend Gotter had written a *Medea* as a solo scene, and the form was a subject for discussion in contemporary journals. Goethe's own moods, his feelings of emptiness and frustration, may have played their part. And finally, as so often, the theme he chose was 'incommensurable', it lays itself open to many interpretations.

Many interpretations, too, can be put on his relationship with this beautiful singer and actress. It is not only the roles of Proserpine and the fishergirl that she takes, or of Iphigenie, a masterpiece that also made its first appearance in this motley procession of amateur performances. Ghostlike she moves through these early Weimar years, aloof and little understood by Goethe's contemporaries. Corona was the daughter of a musician, a poor oboist in some military band, and was produced as a child prodigy. Her brothers and sisters were also musicians, one brother emigrating to London, where he became famous as a pianist; Burney praised his playing for its cool detachment and classical refinement. While still too young she was compelled by her father to sing, to practise long hours, to force her voice too high and to make her stage debut. By the time she was 20, after great initial success, she had almost completely lost her voice. She was beautiful, cultured, fluent in four languages, and able to draw, compose and recite with striking expressiveness. She dressed beautifully, and with great taste, in the Greek style, still uncommon in her day. Very soon after his arrival in Weimar Goethe, remembering her from his Leipzig days, mentions her to the Duke; the offer of an engagement follows immediately. Goethe travels to Leipzig. Meanwhile letters have passed back and forth. With the exception of a single note from Goethe, the correspondence between them has disappeared. Goethe also destroyed Corona's autobiography, which she gave him. All that remains are entries in his diaries, and references in his letters to Frau von Stein, in which he speaks of the 'beautiful Misel'. There are also reports of Weimar contemporaries, who stared wide-eyed at the performance being enacted in front of them.

An actress in those days was regarded first and foremost as the mistress of some prince or Court notable; at many Courts this leading role was tacitly understood, or even incorporated in writing in the terms of her engagement. When Goethe arrives on the scene Corona has already had a bitter experience with a Saxon count who tried to win her as his mistress by vague promises of marriage. After this, as a protection, she acquired a woman companion, and in Weimar was never seen without this massive individual. Proud and aloof she rejected every suitor, an attitude the suitor was apt to regard as totally misplaced in a woman of her calling. Goethe prepares his visit to Leipzig by sending costly presents, an expensive gown and some fine Dutch linen handkerchiefs, which he has asked one of his Leipzig friends to buy for him. On his arrival he is able to offer Corona the post of *Kammersängerin* to the Dowager Duchess, involving only light duties and with a salary of four hundred *thalers*. Having already lost her voice she sings only in concerts and oratorios or takes ordinary stage parts.

Goethe writes to his friend the Duke in his usual familiar manner but, to amuse him, adopts the style of Johann Fischart, the sixteenth-century translator of Rabelais. He talks about the 'quivering, grinning, billing and cooing girls' in Leipzig, and the 'whore-like, strutting, tail-wagging, mincing wenches' of servant girls there. In contrast to these horrors, however, Demoiselle Schröter is an angel and he does not trust himself to say too much about her: 'For the last twenty-four hours I have not been myself, in other words too much myself. The true story must wait till my return, because it contains pp....'

To his friend Charlotte he writes more guardedly: 'a noble creature in her way – ah, if only she could spend six months with you'. He calls her an angel again, but a woman at the same time and one such as he would like for a wife, 'so that I could leave you in peace'. To the Duke once more: 'the Schröter is a dear good thing'. A week is spent playing in this way. Whether it was really a *veni, vidi, vici*, as has so often been rather credulously taken for granted, or whether it was only a sort of amusement, is unclear, as is everything to do with this relationship. The idea of Goethe for once in his life having a love affair with a really beautiful woman is an attractive one; certainly moral scruples would not have stood in his way. But he also regards Corona as 'over-beautiful' and from this type of woman he always recoiled as strongly as he did from marriage. On one other occasion he was to meet a similarly over-beautiful woman, Frau von Branconi, former mistress of the Crown Prince of Brunswick, one of the great beauties of her day and, when Goethe met her, leading a sad and lonely life. She corresponded with Lavater about her emotional troubles, and visited Goethe in Weimar, apparently having sought him out. The two of them went for walks together, and the ever ready Weimar gossip coupled their names in a love affair. Goethe wrote to Lavater, however, and significantly said that such a woman might well 'prize the soul out of my body...'. He takes flight into solitude, to the woods near Ilmenau and then up to a lonely hunters' lodge called the Gickelhahn, on the wall of which, a few days later, he writes his poem, *Uber allen gipfeln ist Ruh....*

It takes longer than this before peace and quietness reign in his relationship with Corona. For six months things are in a state of flux: they meet at rehearsals, there are visits to Goethe's garden-house, masked balls, heart-throbs and moments of ardour, too, as his diary tells us. The Duke joins in, and the three of them go for walks together, and take their meals in the open in full view of everyone, with the actress, for once, in a rather daring costume with flesh-coloured tights under her flowing Greek drapery. Wieland, who sniffs around – this whole thing has to be 'seen and sniffed' he says – writes to Merck that in the refinement of her dress and the extraordinary nobility and Attic elegance of her figure she looked like a nymph in some charming rocky landscape, and it was all 'so openly done under God's clear sky and in sight of all the people, who from morning till night were wending their way past'.

Corona has become the cause of serious tension: Goethe reproaches Karl August, and the Duchess her husband. When the Prince and heir is born, and Luise's position is thereby restored, she insists that she will never again set eyes on 'that person'. Frau von Stein, who is otherwise very indulgent towards Goethe's open confessions of his flirtations with his various *Misels*, or even welcomes them as distractions, is apprehensive and displeased over this one – it is significant that Goethe himself always uses this term in reference to Corona, because it normally denotes his 'lesser loves'. Charlotte does not attend the performance of *Iphigenie*, in which Corona plays the title role; Corona, for her part, indignantly puts the blame on Goethe, as is clear from his one remaining letter to her, and then he puts an end to a situation that has become impossible. He asks her forgiveness; if he has erred, well, to err is human: 'Let us live together as friends ... we cannot bring back the past but it is less difficult to control the future, if we are sensible and good.'

And so this situation, too, is mastered. He has already developed the characteristics of the great master. He now has to disentangle the threads: his love for Charlotte, his adoration of the Duchess which is beginning to assume the aspect of a cult, Corona's plans for a liaison with Karl August, and finally the demands of the theatrical performances, for which the beautiful actress is indispensable. All comply and everything is smoothed out. He writes a poem in homage to Corona. The Court carpenter, Mieding, Goethe's main support in constructing and preparing the stage and sets for the theatrical performances, dies; excellent at his job, and almost as indispensable as Corona, he was long missed. To him Goethe addresses the longest poem of these years, sings his praises, almost extravagantly, as 'director of nature' – a word of endless shades of meaning where Goethe is concerned – and interweaves some verses about the various actors and actresses: 'sisters' who ride on Thespis' cart, 'from hunger scarce, dishonour never, free, in every haunt exposed for eyes to see'. From among these Corona steps forward, pleasing, decorous, her beauty artless yet displayed with art, an ideal that only artists can perceive. She speaks the farewell to the carpenter, and it is Goethe's farewell to her, the homage of a Court poet, who hands her a carefully composed wreath, bound with a black mourning ribbon and with an allusion to her name, Corona.

After this dismissal, her life is a sad one. She stays on in Weimar, appears at Anna Amalie's, where she sings songs by Rousseau and Gluck with what is left of her voice, and writes songs, of which she publishes two collections; she also paints, and does some teaching to augment her meagre stipend. At Court she has been forgotten, and long since by Goethe also. For many years she carries on a halting and hopeless affair with the courtier, Einsiedel, a gambler and spendthrift, one of the many half-talents whose lives foundered in Weimar. They exchange letters in code, with assurances of a 'late and friendly love'; it all leads to nothing. She dies in loneliness at Ilmenau at the very moment when Goethe's *Iphigenie*, her great role on the amateur stage, is receiving its first public performance at the Court theatre. No one attends her funeral except her old companion. There is no wreath from Weimar with the name Corona on it. Only Goethe's old friend Knebel, himself half-forgotten, concerns himself over her memory. He persuades the young Princess Karoline to defray the cost of a gravestone, but she asks him to keep it secret, one has 'to be a little politic and submit to the current trend at Court'. A small memorial is erected, with a laurel wreath, a butterfly and a little tear-vase. In a letter to his sister, who has been the Princess's intermediary over the gravestone, Knebel complains bitterly of the callousness of Weimar society. She says in reply: 'Here in Weimar, where the pulse of life is so strong and deeds and action rise to such intensity, it is not the custom to speak of death, let alone of burial.' She is referring to Goethe and says so explicitly. When another of his 'loves', the pretty Englishwoman Elise Gore, died, he flatly refused to discuss the matter, remarking that there could be no interest in discussing a fairy-tale that was always the same. 'Nothing must be allowed to disturb his enjoyment of life to the full.'

Such things are not said by his enemies but by his friends. The icy coldness that people so often remarked in him is no legend. So far as he is concerned, what is past is past, be it a sweetheart, a friend, or his own mother. Decades later, in his annals, he writes quite casually of Corona's death that, at the time, he was not in the right frame of mind to erect a well-deserved memorial to her; he sees it as 'agreeably wonderful', however, that he had bequeathed a memorial to her so many years earlier, namely in the poem addressed to the Court carpenter Mieding.

Of such stuff are great poems and writings made. There is scarcely a doubt that, at least as regards the Greek outlines, the costume and the gestures, the fair Corona contributed her share to the creation of Goethe's *Iphigenie*. Her share, indeed, may have been greater than that of Frau von Stein, who is always cast for the heroine's part. Whatever the truth of this, it is an irony of creative genius that this particular play, this song of songs of humanity, should be bound up with such human sacrifices.

Human sacrifice is the original, underlying theme of the Iphigenie myth. Human beings are slain on the altar of Artemis, the goddess of hunting, to ensure the hunt's success on which, in ancient times, the whole nation or tribe depended; Iphigenie is to be sacrificed to this goddess to ensure the success of the great hunting expedition against Troy. This is *Iphigenie in Aulis*, known to Goethe's contemporaries from reminiscences of the Greek plays, from Racine, and above all from its recent revival in Gluck's opera. The Greeks themselves, however, had already substituted for the actual sacrifice a symbolic treatment: the virgin is carried away by the goddess to Tauris in the Crimea. Here her brother, Orestes, discovers her serving as a priestess to a barbaric tribe; by ruse and robbery he abducts her and brings her home, together with the image of the goddess, which is to be set up on the shores of Attica. This is *Iphigenie in Tauris*. Just how familiar Goethe was with previous versions of this great theme, those of Euripides, Racine or Gluck – whose opera was first performed in Paris almost at the same time as Goethe started work on his play – we do not know. With profound wisdom he once told Riemer that his very lack of knowledge of the classic models had been his great advantage: *'das Unzulängliche ist produktiv'* (incompleteness stimulates). 'I wrote my *Iphigenie* as a result of a study of the Greek masters that was incomplete. Had it been complete my play would have remained unwritten.'

No cries are heard in Goethe's work. There is only a hint at contrasts.

All the characters are noble, even the lesser ones. The barbarian king is noble and forgives. There are no storms, scarcely a breeze to rustle the tree-tops in the grove of Diana. All outward effects are avoided.

'May the concept of what is pure, which extends to the morsel of food I place in my mouth, grow ever brighter within me', writes Goethe in his diary at the time he is working on the play. Iphigenie herself is a 'pure soul' and, quite frankly, nothing else. She is so incorporeal that her representation on the stage is almost always somewhat embarrassing and quite absurdly so when, as used often to be the case, the part is played by some stout, majestic, ageing actress. She is a priestess and a sister, and the memory of his dead sister, Cornelia, may have exerted quite as strong an influence on him as the presence of his living 'sister', Charlotte. She purges her brother by her purity, by her presence alone, and so atones for the age-old curse on the House of Atrides. She is an idealized figure rather than one based on some 'real' original, something to be aimed at, hoped for. She is not en-dowed with a single womanly characteristic nor with any trace of minor human frailty. Her mould is cast on the severe lines of classic architecture; but even this comparison is too coarse, she is soul, pure soul and nothing but soul. She speaks a language that is almost in the Christian tradition, the heart must be 'immaculate'. With her immaculate heart she purges her brother's sin, turns her back on all ruse or stratagem, in complete contrast to the Greek drama, and conciliates the barbarian king – they part in peace.

Peace, purity, freedom from sin, understanding, and forgiveness: these are the soft ethereal tones sounded by Goethe's play. When he was writing it he had soft chamber music played in an adjoining room; the savage stormy sounds of Gluck's opening are an infinity away and, indeed, are un-likely to have reached Weimar, which knew of the opera's European success only by report. But having sounded the note with his chamber music, how does Goethe proceed? Even in Weimar classical themes were not new; many of the plays performed there had had for their subjects Medea, Alcestis or Polyxena. Orestes and Pylades had long been well-known figures on the German stage. Goethe has also done a certain amount of reading. He con-stantly finds the incentive to further work by writing a few sentences in the style of the ancient classics, in much the same way as Bach would seek in-spiration by playing works of other composers: 'A useless life is a pre-mature death', or 'Woe to him who leads a lonely life, far from his parents, his brothers and his sisters.' Quite apart from Charlotte and Corona, Goethe's life is far from lonely while he is writing this play. The most im-probable conditions surround the creation of this masterpiece. It is written between February 14 and March 28; he records the dates precisely. During this same period he has to inspect roads and attend the impressment of re-cruits. 'Only one foot in the stirrup of the poet's hippogryph,' he remarks, and this is no mere metaphor. He rides, he gallops off to the most diverse places; there is no such thing as a study desk for the composition of this play, these scenes of unparalleled quietness are written down in little towns and villages, in way-side inns. For a few days he retires to lonely Schloss Dornburg, near Jena, and complains: 'always sketches, only sketches! We shall have to look to the colouring.' He works only in outlines, as he does in his drawings which he always colours later; but the question of colour hardly arises, his figures in this play are clothed in white. He has to rush off to Apolda on business: 'Thoas must speak as though there were no starving stocking weavers in Apolda', he writes. One of the scenes is 'tormenting' him, a day is 'spent without much dramatic success'. Four days later the play is finished.

The performance of the play is prepared and rehearsed at the greatest speed and takes place barely a week after its completion. Corona plays the title role, Goethe Orestes, the silly Prince Konstantin, replaced for the next performance by his brother, Pylades and Goethe's old friend Knebel the King. The costumes are Greek, with Corona in long flowing white draperies; while Goethe himself wears a sort of Roman emperor's costume, with high sandals, hair waved round his head and a coat of mail. One had the impression of an 'Apollo', one of the small circle of spectators said in after years. On the evening of the performance Goethe notes: '*Iphigenie* played. Very good impression, especially on the pure-minded.' The following day: 'War Commission.' Further rides on horseback and journeys, interspersed with one, and then another, repeat performance for visitors from outside. Then, once more in strange contrast to all this activity, he notes down his thoughts on the instinctive aspect of doing anything:

> Every activity engaged in by man has what I might call a certain odour. Just as in the crude sense the horseman smells of horses, the bookshop slightly musty, and the huntsman of hounds, so it is in the more refined activities. The material with which one moulds, the tools one uses, the limbs one employs, all this together produces something like a feeling of domesticity and wedlock between the artist and his instrument. This sense of quietness between him and all the strings of his harp, the certainty and assurance with which he touches them, indicate the master whatever his métier. When he sees a thing he goes straight to the point, as Batty does on an estate, he does not dream in generalities as we ourselves have done in the past in the fine arts. When he has to act, he tackles precisely what is necessary at the time.

Only in this way, by his tackling what was necessary in the full consciousness of his mastery, amidst all the smell of horses and hunting, is the completion of this work explicable. Moreover, in common with all his works, *Iphigenie* was never regarded by Goethe as finished. The first version was in prose, then he turned the rhythmically flowing lines into a kind of verse, and finally, when he was in Italy and at Herder's suggestion, he recast the lines into true iambics. The adaptation of the play for the stage he left to Schiller; he very quickly felt remote from the work and even termed it ironically 'confoundedly human'. It was a long time before it made its way into the consciousness of its readers, and still longer before it made its way on the stage. It then became a *Bildungserlebnis*, part of people's education, a subject for school essays and university papers, and sometimes for penetrating commentaries of great distinction. Perhaps it needs to be put aside for a time before entering a new phase of its influence.

Goethe also writes scenes for a *Tasso* at this time, but the play is not worked out until he goes to Italy. There are some literary satires, and a literary comedy, *Die Vögel* (The Birds) which, however, has only a very slight connection with Aristophanes' great comedy, merely making use of the attractive bird costumes; it is intended as a skit on Klopstock or Bodmer, or both. They do shadow plays, masques, there is a procession of Laplanders, and ballets in pantomime; in one of these last the mountain opens and reveals all its treasures, in pious anticipation of the mine at Ilmenau. Alas, no magic formula can make the real mountain yield its treasure. In a little farce a doctor is cheated by Scapin and Scapine, comedy figures of long tradition. 'I am taking almost too much upon myself', writes Goethe to Lavater in February 1781, referring to his duties at Court and as Court poet,

> but again I cannot do otherwise. A man who is embroiled in State affairs should devote himself entirely to them, and yet there is so much else I am loath to forego. The closing days of last week I spent in the service of vanity. Through masquerades and brilliant inventions one often deadens one's own and others' needs. I treat these matters as an artist, so it is all right still. You adorn the festivals of Godliness, I decorate the pageants of folly.

Flight is the only thing that can rescue him from all this excessive activity, which devours the ten long years of his early manhood. During these years he never devotes himself entirely to anything, in the way that he himself says one should to State affairs, not to any woman, not to any writing. Indeed he is in doubt as to whether his true vocation is writing or painting, and when he notes in his diary that he was 'really' born to be a writer he sounds almost surprised. On one occasion, when out riding, he feels the horse running away with him, spreading its wings like the wings of Pegasus. His publishers and fellow writers have abandoned hope of his reappearing as a poet. Apart from reprints of his earlier works only a few poems are published, and one or two scenes from *Iphigenie* in an obscure Swabian periodical. We look in vain elsewhere for a parallel to the circumstances that surrounded the writing of *Iphigenie*, and we look similarly in vain for another great writer who spent a decade such as this after beginnings such as Goethe's, a pause for which no illness, no dire need, and no other stroke of fate can be held responsible. It is of his own free will that he dallies and delays. He knows this and he takes to flight.

# 23

# *Flight*

Goethe's privileged position in Weimar gave him frequent opportunity to take to flight. Sometimes he travelled in company with the Duke and not infrequently this was in the nature of a flight for both of them. In 1777 he writes in his diary, 'projects for a secret journey', while Karl August and his companions are off boar hunting again. His journey to the Harz mountains he calls a 'dark move', or a vagary, undertaken in the depth of winter. He conceals himself under a new disguise, takes the name of Weber, pretends to be a painter, and enjoys the incognito. 'So far I have had nothing to do with women', he writes to Frau von Stein. He travels in the simplest manner, and is delighted to find how small a man's needs really are. He enjoys talking to simple people, the 'so-called lower classes', in whom he finds a combination of all the virtues: loyalty, contentment, endurance, perseverance. The Mephistopheles in him gets fun out of his disguise too: 'No one gives me more enjoyment than the dirty old scamps, whom I can now permit to do just what they like and to go through all their tricks at their ease in front of me.' He feels as he did when he was a boy, and that, after all, was not so very long ago. When the weather turns mild, and there is a gentle rain, he notes down the first lines of one of his most beautiful poems on nature and the countryside, *Dem Gleier gleich* ... (Like a vulture's flight). He visits the mines and smelting works, so that he can have something useful and practical to report when he gets back. 'Went over the whole mine to the very bottom', and the next moment he is climbing to the very top, to the summit of the Brocken, the highest peak. This is also a sporting achievement, and it is only with difficulty that he manages to persuade the forester, who regards the venture in snow and ice as risky, to go with him.

The following year he goes to Berlin with the Duke; with the exception of those in Italy it is the only large city he ever visited in his life. The mission is a political one. There is a threat of another war of succession, due to the extinction of the main line of the Wittelsbach dynasty in Bavaria, and Frederick the Great is preparing to intervene, in order to prevent Austria from reaping the harvest and seizing Bavaria. In the bustle of this military and diplomatic activity Goethe feels completely out of place; his notes reveal how ill-suited he was to play the role of statesman in any wider field. What this Weimar minister of state sees is 'how the great play with men and how the gods play with the great', or 'the greater the world the more disgusting the farce becomes, and I swear that no Hanswurst ribaldries and obscenities are as nauseating as the way the great, the lesser and the small figures behave among themselves'. To him the whole thing is like looking at a peepshow at the Frankfurt fair. The King himself Goethe does not see, but he meets his brother, the leader of the secret opposition to Frederick; and at table he meets the generals, all in a mutinous and angry mood because the great and terrible old man refuses to die. After a visit to Potsdam and Sanssouci he writes to Merck that he felt very close to the old King there: 'I saw his *milieu*, his gold, silver, marble, monkeys, parrots and his tattered curtains, and I heard his own shabby rascals grumbling about the great man.' For the rest he maintains a determined silence and wins the reputation of being proud and aloof.

The very size of Berlin, its 'splendour', modest though it is, oppresses him. He never goes back although, especially in later life, he often receives pressing invitations to do so; Vienna, or even Hamburg, he never saw, let alone Paris or London. In Berlin he is alarmed by the teeming throngs of people, by all the business of mobilization, by the Prussian orderliness; he is astonished at the 'thousands upon thousands of people ready to be sacrificed for it'.

After a few days he is back in Weimar again, determined to fortify the inner recesses of his being, trustingly left exposed for too long, to enlarge the 'citadel of his heart' – he is still thinking in military terms. Henceforth the citadel is to be a symbol for him, a refuge. Even at this time, although he is not yet 30, he is already preparing himself for solitariness and expressly says so in a letter to his beloved Charlotte.

In Weimar difficulties pile up on all sides. To escape them, as well as to extricate his friend the Duke from his own manifold entanglements, they undertake a journey to Switzerland together in September 1779; not the least important reason for the journey is to try to find a solution to the country's financial problems. This time it is Karl August who travels incognito. In Frankfurt they stay with Goethe's parents, where Goethe has peremptorily ordered accommodation: the Duke will sleep in the little room, he likes a clean straw mattress covered with a linen sheet and a light blanket; 'for me it will be upstairs in my old room, also with a straw mattress'. No banquet, 'but your best homely efforts'; in the morning fruit, if possible. Shortly before leaving Weimar, he is promoted to *Wirklicher Geheimer Rat*: 'it seems wonderful to me that in my thirtieth year, as though in a dream, I have reached the topmost degree of honour to which a citizen in Germany can attain. One gets furthest when one does not know where the road is leading, said one of the great climbers of this world.'

Jubilantly Goethe's mother reports to the Dowager Duchess on the visit of her *Hätschelhans* as the *Geheimrat*, on the gaping neighbours and on

Frankfurt society: 'What airs our silly little geese of aristocratic misses gave themselves, what efforts to make a conquest, with nothing coming out of it all.' Goethe uses the journey to visit his former loves once more. Friederike in Sesenheim is quiet and peaceful. Lili Schönemann, now Frau von Türkheim and living in Strasbourg, the 'pretty little monkey' as he calls her or that 'good creature', plays with her seven weeks' old little girl. He is filled with benevolence. 'Unclouded by any limited passion' is how he sees his relationship with these people. The mountains lie ahead.

An extensive and, for those days, exacting expedition into the mountains is embarked on as soon as the loan negotiations in Bern have been successfully concluded and this great load has been taken off their minds. They climb up into the Bernese Oberland and cross a number of glaciers, though not without moments of tension between them; Karl August, who always 'wants to lard the bacon' as Goethe puts it, is continually pressing Goethe to make senseless detours, or else stopping like a child to roll chunks of rock down into the valleys below. There are moments when Goethe thinks of taking flight from the flight itself; he never regards his role of favourite as that of a mere servant, which is the normal attitude of those serving at Court. His is a guest performance, and at any moment he may move on to another stage. He draws, and indulges his interest in art. Goethe gets restless whenever he sees a landscape painted by another artist, 'the toes of my feet begin to twitch in my shoes as though they wanted to grip the earth, and the fingers of my hands move convulsively'. Physical possession is not only a desire, it is a necessity for him: 'I try to take hold of things with my eyes, to pierce them.' At the same time he is fully aware that his drawing is only scrawling and botching, to use his own words. 'What is it, this strange striving from art to nature, and from nature back to art? If it is indicative of the artist, why am I lacking in constancy?' In a private collection he sees a 'Danäe', which unsettles him, though in a different way. What does he know of the human body, he asks himself. He gets a friend, a young man, to bathe naked in the lake, derives enjoyment from the forms of his body, and peoples the woods and meadows with Adonis-like figures. In Geneva he gets a *procureuse* to produce a girl for him, and thus sees, apparently for the first time in his life, a naked woman. 'What is it that we see in women?' he cries. 'What kinds of women do we like? How confused all our ideas are! A small shoe looks nice and we cry, what a pretty little foot! There is elegance in a tight corset, and we praise the lovely waist.' We can already see the Goethe of the *Römische Elegieen*, especially in the final scene of this set-piece. After a series of carefully posed attitudes, the girl lies down on a couch and pretends to fall asleep, to dream; she stretches out her arms for her dream lover, and finally, very matter of fact, says: 'Come on, my friend, before I really fall asleep.'

Goethe's remarks on Switzerland and its people are now sharply critical, his eye trained by observation of people and social conditions. Nothing is left of the romanticism of his first visit to Switzerland, that saw in every peasant the personification of Rousseau's free, natural man. The Swiss, as he now sees it, have freed themselves from a tyrant, through the Wilhelm Tell of legend, and 'now the warm sun has produced a swarm of little tyrants out of the carcass of the oppressor'. They still continue to tell the same old fairy-tale, and ensconce themselves with their Philistinism behind their walls, or outside on their rocks, imprisoned for six months of the year like marmots in the snow. The little towns look black to him, heaps of stone and shingles. And the dirt! the dungheaps! all the gaping idiots, all the people with goitre!

He describes the countryside with topographical precision and then suddenly takes wing again with descriptions of glaciers, of Mount-Blanc, of ice-bound passes. They walk over the Furka pass up to the St Gotthard, in those days still a daring undertaking in winter, although Switzerland had already been discovered by those indefatigable travellers, the English, who had even built huts and shelters here and there. But the Duke's party is travelling with servants and guides and mostly on horseback; it is no wild student expedition. In Zürich they make a halt to visit Lavater: Karl August is to be shown a picture of what a model, patriarchal, family life can be. The pastor, having been instructed by Goethe, takes the Duke severely to task, and Goethe rejoices, prematurely, at the success of this educational journey. Lavater is once more the salt of the earth. Observing this peaceful family scene Goethe meditates: 'What a moral death is this life that we usually live, that results in the drying up and freezing up of the heart, which in itself is never dry and never cold.' He is already dreading 'the sirocco of discontent, ill-will, ingratitude, indolence and pretentiousness' that await him in Weimar.

On the way home they visit some south German Courts. In Stuttgart Duke Karl Eugen presents the pupils of his *Karls Schule*, among them a tall, slim boy named Schiller who, as one of the prize winners, is allowed to kiss the lapel of his Duke's coat. Goethe already feels very remote from Court life, although his ministerial career has lasted just four years and he is thus still only in the middle of it. He sees the pettiness and wretchedness of these small Courts, the boredom; even the food and drink is bad. The people are nervous of talking during visits by foreign potentates; such princes are 'usually surrounded by simpletons and rascals', writes Goethe in his diary.

The journey has lasted four months; Goethe's duty as minister and favourite is to last another four years. The Duke, showing signs of gratifying improvement, is received back with great hopes; but very soon he reverts to his old life, a little tyrant in an all too little state, though with very human traits. He can be very frank and friendly, as he is to Knebel, for example, to whom he writes an extremely warm and far from ducal letter on hearing that the disappointed man wants to leave his service. This also has its significance as a background to Goethe's own constant desire to break away from the narrowness of Weimar life. There are very few who feel contented in Weimar; everyone tries to find a better position elsewhere, only those unable to do so remain. Karl August himself is always furtively on the look-out, and as soon as his great and menacing uncle Frederick dies he is off. Until this happens, however, he has to content himself with hunting and love-making, the latter mostly of a very low order. Goethe breathes more freely when a love affair of a better kind starts to develop.

A Countess Werthern, sister of the future statesman Freiherr vom Stein, is the object of the Duke's love. Even this very proud, independent and aristocratic family evidently raised no objections to a relationship between one of their members and a petty prince. Goethe's admiration for the lady is boundless, to the point of idolatry: for the first time in his life he sees a true lady of the world, perfectly composed, sure of herself and with the greatest ease of manner. 'What is known as genius in the arts, she has in the art of living', he says rapturously. 'She knows the greater part of the nobility, wealth, beauty and intelligence of Europe, partly on her own account, partly through others ...'; in a word she knows the great world. Charlotte, to whom he wrote this, must have read it with feelings of distress and jealousy. She is an aristocrat herself, but she is provincial. She can improve Goethe's manners and perhaps train his heart, but of the great world she knows nothing. There is also something provincial about Goethe's admiration; he extols the Countess in his *Wilhelm Meister*, and henceforth the aristocracy plays a dominant role in his novels. But the great world in this sense has no place in his works, which are staged in the Goethe world. And when, later on, he comes face to face with high society, in the spas of Bohemia, he can only pay court in elegant poems of devoted homage. His aristocrats are ladies and gentlemen of noble birth who follow their inclinations, whether towards *belles lettres* or something else, and whose lives are remote from all the unpleasant problems of day to day existence; only the men, if things become too difficult at home or the financial position too embarrassing, escape to some form of military service. Of the honest and vigorous country gentry, who also existed and who often hardly knew where to find the means to raise their large families, Goethe says scarcely a word. Of the penniless aristocracy, which in Weimar formed the majority, he says nothing at all.

In one of his quick transformations Goethe's scorn of the 'aristocratic little geese' in *Werther* has become admiration for the established order, an order which he describes with bitter sarcasm again on his visits to other Courts. He himself is now ennobled. Karl August, who as a petty prince is unable to bestow such honours, has applied to the Imperial Court in Vienna, and on April 10, 1782 the diploma receives the Emperor's signature. The Dowager Duchess has played an energetic part in this move. The ranking at Court needs to be revised. Goethe is required for missions to other Courts and the indispensable favourite and minister can no longer be allowed to eat at the 'inferior marshal's table'. The honour is not intended primarily for Goethe the poet, although the application mentions his importance in the intellectual field. Goethe accepts the news as a matter of course, like any other dispensation of fate. For his coat of arms he chooses, with some significance, the morning star.

*Geheimrat* von Goethe departs at once, as planned, to the neighbouring Courts. He takes a firmer hold of the reins of government. From the keeper of the Duke's privy purse he demands strict accounts; hitherto private and public expenditure have been confused: 'As agreed, you will draw nothing this quarter. At the beginning of April you can obtain the money for the whole month of April. But subsequently, in May, I wish you to wait until the end of the month. You will be so kind, my dear Councillor, to make your arrangements accordingly, for I must have everything in order by mid-summer's day or resign.' He warns the Duke against foreign political adventures; he is doubtful about the plans for a League of Princes. He is opposed to playing at soldiers and reduces the Weimar army by half. He sides increasingly with the Duchess Luise in her sad marriage. When, finally, after seven barren years, an heir is born and the continuance of the dynasty is assured, a culminating point in Goethe's role as advisor is reached. Simultaneously he feels that his governmental activities have come to an end. He retires gradually. He no longer takes part in the hunting, for which Karl August has now found other companions, he appears rarely at Court, administrative work becomes increasingly irksome. In conscious or unconscious preparation for his great flight he detaches himself from everything, even from his beloved garden-house.

He rents a house in the town, which later becomes the famous Goethe house on the Frauenplan. It is a spacious building for which he needs a staff: a cook, two servants, a boy, and Philipp Seidel as personal servant, secretary and confidant. Formal and rather stiff tea parties are given once a week, and with these his social obligations are fulfilled 'in the cheapest way', as he writes. He puts his papers in order and has them stitched together, or bound in volumes, by the book-binder, in future his constant practice; Goethe's own correspondence, in so far as it is not burned, is always prepared with a view to ultimate publication. To Knebel he writes to say that even in his Frankfurt days he never had any idea of combining his legal practice with his intellectual life; and, in the same way now, he keeps the *Geheimrat* and his other self separate. 'It is only in the innermost secrets of my plans and intentions and undertakings that I remain mystically true to myself and thus bind together again in a secret knot my social, political, and moral and poetic life.' As a summing-up he addresses a long poem to his friend the Duke. It begins lightly and pleasantly with recollections of Ilmenau and the camp fires in the woods, and then grows increasingly serious up to the final lines: '*Wer andre wohl zu leiten strebt Muss fähig sein, viel zu entbehren*' (If others we would seek to guide, we must ourselves learn self-denial).

Goethe's oud friends fade away. Merck, as he bitterly remarks, is received like a suppliant. With Lavater, he breaks off relations abruptly, indeed brutally at the end; when the pastor sends him one of his books with the fulsome dedication, 'Noble, guileless, dear, dear one!', Goethe notes down: 'You come to the wrong person with your silly prattling. Be off, you sophist, or you will get a kick!' Goethe can be merciless to those whose roles in his life are played out. But he can forget an estrangement equally quickly. Living in his dark house under the shadow of the church, Herder has spent seven years at Goethe's side, alienated from him, embittered and neglected, even in official matters, especially educational and school affairs, which are very close to Herder's heart and over which Goethe has made no effort to help him. Now they become reconciled, but on a new basis. Goethe is no longer the pupil, playing moon to Herder's sun. Like Wieland Herder has had to step down, but unlike Wieland he never quite gets over it. Goethe needs him now, as a stimulus for his plans and researches, as a helper and colleague, because from know on it is Goethe's constant habit to surround himself and his projects with a staff of assistants, to advise him on technical matters, to correct his manuscripts, a task he always hated, and to look after the correspondence with publishers. He also needs a deputy, endowed with full powers, to take over in his absence.

In doing this he is also preparing his separation from Charlotte von Stein. She has started to complain that when they are together he is insufferable, that they can no longer talk to one another. This is no mere feminine touchiness; her role, too, is finished. Only in their correspondence is the famous love still kept alive, in words and pious exclamations: 'Your presence never leaves me.' Then he writes: 'Since it seems as if our verbal conversation is reluctant to develop again, I am taking my leave in writing, so that I shall not become completely estranged from you.' This was written a year before the final break; it is already the end, in spite of renewed protestations of love: 'I am leaving and my heart stays here. ... I love you beyond words and do not want to go away from you, I want to find you again wherever I am. ...'

A new love has emerged, since people, business, writing always bring disappointment: his interest in natural science. Here all the responses are 'pure', as he says: clean and tidy Linné's botany, which he studies eagerly; distinct and clear the human bone structure, as the anatomist, Professor Loder, in Jena demonstrates to him. Immediately he feels stimulated to think, to explore, to synthesize. The scientific theories and teachings, however, seem to him inadequate, in so far as he has become acquainted with them and understands them. As he sees it they are concerned only with collecting information and listing it under headings; everything is detached and separated, but the great inner connection, the concatenation of all things, is overlooked. He had already adopted Herder's idea of organic development in his youth. Herder is now working on his *Ideen zur Philosophie der*

*Geschichte der Menschheit* (Ideas on the Philosophy of the History of Mankind) and speaks prophetically of the natural evolution of all existence. Herder's concern is the progression of mankind towards the goal of humanity; Goethe is interested in the evolution of the kingdom of minerals, plants and animals up to man, but no further. The development of mankind, which is a thing he always doubts, is of little interest to him. The progressive organic evolution of the human race and its conditions he does not believe in; so far as he is concerned this has always been obscure and chaotic and will remain so. Natural phenomena, on the other hand, seem to him clear and definite, and for him they are forms, *Gestalten.*

His interest in mining has introduced him to geology. He singles out granite and terms it the *Ur-Gestein.* This prefix *Ur*, which denotes original, primal, the very first, now begins a long career in Goethe's usage; he feels an imperative need to penetrate to the ultimate origin of things. He endows granite, his favourite stone, with a sort of royal splendour and dignity; with disdain he points out that for some time it has been 'degraded' by false interpretations on the part of scientists. His way of looking at the phenomena of nature is always personal, poetic and anthropomorphic. Thus, later, he ordains purple the 'royal colour', because it was used by the Greeks for the mantles of their kings. In botany he speaks of certain species of plant as 'unprincipled', because they lose their entity in countless sub-species, and such multiplicity is confusing. 'I have sometimes taken the liberty of calling these species dissolute (*die Liederlichen*), and have ventured to apply this epithet to the rose, though needless to say this cannot detract from its charm. ...'

Goethe bestows names on natural phenomena and they respond. As he grows older he sometimes addresses them in person, greeting some rare and long sought stone on the roadway with a 'there you are, at last!' In his younger days he saw nature as a lovely young girl, with a full firm figure, a sort of muse; later on he bestows on it the more respectful name of mother, but he always sees it as a figure, a *Gestalt* to use his own term, and he tries to recreate these *Gestalten.* He reconstructs them physically, too, and fusses tirelessly with his own hands over his favourite models, plans, charts and tables. This sensuous contact is an essential element of his approach to nature, of his philosophy of nature, and any wild, disorderly offshoots and tendrils disturb him in this approach. Even at this early stage he constructs for himself, though only tentatively, a complete universe, in which everything is interconnected, interwoven and organically developed; there are no jumps or gaps in nature, *natura non fecit saltus*, as he has learned from the ancients. He has a hatred of all violence and breaks in continuity; consequently he wages a lifelong and almost desperate war against the Vulcanists. Everything should evolve gently, flowingly, without noise or violence.

The seeds of plants, fulfilling these conditions as they do, arouse his interest. He is assisted by a young botanist in Jena, by herbalists, by the

Weimar apothecary, who has a garden containing medicinal plants. Goethe's method of learning is through living contact with people, not from books, and although he reads in Linné, he soon grows tired of it; his memory is bad and the infinite variety of species confuses him. He prefers to listen to what those who know have to say, and as soon as he has taken the first steps in any new field he, in turn, wants to communicate his discoveries to others. He notes with satisfaction in Rousseau's botany that the author had lectured on his researches to cultured ladies, that it is possible for an amateur to contribute so much of benefit to science. Frau von Stein copies out his botanical studies. A group of ladies from the Weimar Court forms the audience when, assisted by diagrams on a blackboard, he gives his lectures on the subject.

Having attended Loder's lectures on anatomy in Jena, he immediately gives lectures himself, at the academy of drawing in Weimar, on the importance of the human bone structure as a basis for correct drawing of the human body. His urge to teach is insatiable, and in teaching he always learns himself. He begins to make comparisons, to criticize, to investigate, and his observations can be very penetrating, his conclusions very sharply drawn. In a state of tremendous excitement he tells Herder of a great discovery:

I have discovered – neither gold nor silver, but something that affords me unspeakable joy – the human *os intermaxillare*! With Loder I compared the skulls of men and animals, came on the track, and lo! there it is. Only, I beg of you, not a word about it because it has to be treated as a secret. You, too, should be cordially delighted, because it is like a human keystone: it is there, there is no doubt whatever! I have also thought of it in connection with your (concept of) wholeness, how well it will look there!

The keystone in the human edifice: for him it is something of limitless significance. This small jaw-bone, the *os intermaxillare*, was supposed, according to the view generally held at that time, to exist only in animals, and this fact was regarded as constituting an essential difference between man and beast. That man was completely separate from the animal kingdom was primarily a religious demand; even Darwin still had to contend with this. Goethe has no theological inhibitions; he wants to find the uninterrupted continuity of all creation, and he finds it. It is his first discovery and it has remained undisputed.

The bone in man is not, as in animals, distinct and separate; it is joined to the upper jaw-bone, from which it is separated only by fine, almost invisible, sutures, and it was these delicate lines that Goethe saw. He plunges at once into further experiments and comparisons. He has an elephant's skull sent from Cassel, secretly and at considerable expense. He hides it away in one of the furthest rooms, 'otherwise people may think I am crazy. My housekeeper thinks the enormous chest contains porcelain.' He makes drawings of the bone and writes a paper on his discovery. Everything has to be done secretly, because he lives in constant fear that someone may contest his magnificent discovery or even steal it. Loder translates the paper into Latin, still the normal language of scholarship, and in 1784 Goethe sends a copy to the famous Dutch anatomist Camper, who welcomes his observations without being able to accept his final conclusion; Camper, himself a celebrated anatomical draughtsman, is also critical of the illustrations. Some other scientists, whom Goethe approaches, remain equally unconvinced. Loder, however, is completely convinced and four years later, in 1788, announces Goethe's discovery in one of the plates of his *Manual of Anatomy*. Goethe's own paper is not published until 1820, when he prints it in his journal, *Zur Morphologie*.

In the meantime, to Goethe's dismay, it had become known that the French anatomist, Vicq-d'Azyr, had already made the same discovery in 1780, in Paris, publishing it four years later. When he published his own paper in 1820 Goethe did not mention this, although otherwise he gave a full survey of the literature supporting his discovery. That priority in the discovery belongs to Vicq-d'Azyr there can be no doubt; Goethe quite independently, and almost simultaneously, made the same observations and drew the correct conclusion. In the course of scientific history questions of priority have often caused great bitterness, and precise dates are decisive.

Questions of priority in this new field were vastly more important to Goethe than the first editions of his *Werther* and his *Götz* which, soon after publication, he no longer even possessed, being quite satisfied to have some later, nondescript, pirated edition. It was only here, in this new field of conquest, that he was so jealous and exacting, and later, in his desperate fight with Newton, dogmatic and fanatical. To have been the first, a Luther or a Columbus, and this is his own comparison, was his vanity and affliction. When he meets opposition, as he does now with his 'little bone', as he affectionately calls it, he withdraws embittered and disillusioned. A hatred for the whole guild, the whole tribe, of scholars, for the scientific priests of Baal. wells up within him, and remains till the end of his life.

Such hatred is comprehensible as a reaction and on grounds of disappointment. Nothing ever touched his heart as did these discoveries: 'I am so full of joy, that my very bowels are stirred', he writes to Charlotte about his little bone. When as a very old man he remarked, with scant gratitude, that in the whole of his life he had known scarcely four weeks of true contentment, he was not including his joy over these discoveries. But, Sisyphus-like, he may well have been thinking of the 'eternal rolling of a stone, which has always got to be taken up from the bottom again'.

Ill-humour, caused by the feeble echo produced by his magnificent discovery, contributes further to his discontent with life in Weimar. The Duke is impatient to start military service; this eagerness for war is itching under his skin 'like scabies', says Goethe. The business of government has grown boring, his beloved Charlotte has become difficult. He has finished with his friends, as he says of Lavater. In the last three years he has scarcely written a poem, apart from Mignon's songs of longing for Italy, *Kennst du das Land?*, or *Nur wer die Sehnsucht kennt.* ... A new edition of his Collected Works, authorized this time, is to be prepared; but he has very little new work to include, apart from fragments and one or two of the trivialities he wrote for the Weimar Court. He no longer gets any fun out of his *Misels*, the word virtually disappears from his diary. He lives a solitary life in his stately mansion, with his five servants. But most important of all, he feels a new skin growing beneath the old, withered one.

With a secrecy like that surrounding his discovery of the little bone he prepares his flight. No one is to know of it, least of all Charlotte. He goes with her to Karlsbad, where she takes the cure. She returns to Weimar and he writes to her there 'You should always be with me; we would have a good life', To Karl August he addresses a formal application for leave of absence, but for no definite period: he can be spared in Weimar now and he wants to disappear to some corner of the world where he is quite unknown. Italy is never mentioned. To the faithful Seidel alone he entrusts his address, and this under a pseudonym: Jean Philippe Möller, painter, Rome. At 3 o'clock on the morning of September 3, 1786, Goethe steals secretly out of Karlsbad by the mail-coach. A small travelling bag and a portmanteau are his only luggage.

# 24

# *Italy*

Goethe's visit to Italy is usually known as his *Italian Journey*, from the title he gave in his old age to the book describing it. But his life in Italy would be a truer description of the time he spent there, most of it in Rome. It was no mere holiday tour or pleasure trip, and sightseeing occupied but a relatively small place in it; although he took 'Volkmann' with him, a digest of English and French travel books and the *Baedeker* of its day, he rarely used it, and when he did it was mostly to contradict it. He called on very few people, although it was then the custom to do so, and he did not take with him a single letter of introduction. Of Italian society, the chief goal of visitors in those days, he saw virtually nothing, nor did he ever go to any of the famous *conversazioni*, where visitors were always welcome; it was only in Naples that he mixed a little in the higher circles of society. Most of the time he spent, true to his pseudonym of Filippo Möller, as a painter among painters, living in the simplest conditions. He drew a great deal, talked with artists and dreamed once more of becoming a painter. At the same time he continued to work on his poetry and edited the first volumes of his *Collected Writings*. But above all he lived, loved and enjoyed life, delighting in the Italian sun and the brilliance of its light as he wandered round. In Italy he felt at home, for the first and last time in his life; elsewhere he always regarded himself as an exile. On returning to Weimar he felt more of an exile than ever, 'a victim of despair', cast out without hope, living in an alien land.

The truth is that for him there was no home anywhere; he could not have remained permanently even in Rome, and the attempt to repeat his Italian experience on his visit to Venice three years later, resulted only in ill-humour. A third attempt foundered in Switzerland, and it was with a feeling of relief that he turned back to study, in the peace and quiet of Weimar, the drawings and priceless notes amassed in Italy by his artist friend Meyer. Even Italy, the greatest love of his life, could hold him only for a time.

The *Bildungsgehalt*, the cultural experience, of these months is all that remained, and this continued to grow and occupy an increasingly prominent place in his writings. His *Italienische Reise* would probably have been even more strongly impregnated with this experience but for the fact than in his old age he developed the lazy habit of putting together his works from old papers, with the help of his staff of assistants and a pair of scissors. His old letters he cut literally into little strips, and many invaluable notes may have been lost to us in this way; the editing was so carelessly done that the seams often show through. It is only from the journey in its original form – and this is a matter of reconstruction, though the many splendours of the book continually recall it to us – that we can obtain a true picture of this deepest experience of his life.

We can see how, in the course of this journey, his whole constitution is transformed: his figure becomes fuller and broader, in the end almost majestic. The portraits and busts done at this time show him as a noble Apollo with a profusion of curls, or else as a painter looking out on the world with large eyes from under the brim of a Rembrandt hat. Consonant with his doctrine of anticipation, he sees things as he has always imagined them; everything seems familiar, a re-encounter. 'I have made many conquests towards my recreation of the world, but nothing has been wholly new or unexpected,' he writes as he climbs up the mountains on his way. The motionless rock begins to stir under his feet; it is as though he can feel it throb. The mountains condition the weather, producing atmospheric tension, and this is none other than the tension in his own breast. He sees a mountain peak spinning a cloud like a woman with her distaff. Of the early morning sun, in the valley between Bolzano and Trento, he says, 'it makes one believe in God again', or of the gentle air at sundown, with the crickets singing, 'one feels at home in the world once more, and not as though loaned out or in exile. I enjoy this country as though I had been born and bred here, and had just returned from a whaling expedition in Greenland.' Everything is welcome, down to the primitiveness of the Italian inns and the dust on the roads.

Goethe draws and sketches ceaselessly; by the time he returns home he has filled nearly a thousand sheets of paper. On the Austro-Venetian frontier he is almost arrested as a spy because of his sketching, as Hogarth was when he tried to paint the Calais Gate. The Venetian Republic, not without reason, is concerned over the Emperor Joseph's plans for annexation. The Emperor's Chancellery is also suspicious of Goethe, but for different reasons. His pseudonym does not hide his identity for long, and the 'artist's journey' is trailed by secret reports from the Austrian Ambassador to the Vatican; a secretary from the Embassy in Rome even steals one of his mother's letters from his room, though it contains nothing but expressions of joy that this great wish of his to see Italy has at last come true. To the government in Vienna Goethe is not the painter Möller but the minister who had participated in the secret negotiations over a German 'Princes' League' and may well be engaged in conspiracies against the Emperor and the Empire.

Of this spying on the part of the 'reforming Emperor' Goethe knows nothing, and to the Holy Roman Empire, from which he has just escaped, he is completely indifferent. He is in search of ancient Rome. In Verona he finds his first evidence of antiquity, the Roman amphitheatre, which he immediately sees filled with people. He feels a constant need to create microcosms and give them life and movement, and so here, in his imagination, he fills the large, empty building with an audience: 'that beast of many heads and many minds, swaying and roving hither and thither and yet united as one noble body – *one* being animated by *one* mind'. He sees an ideal audience in front of him.

Looking at pictures he regards more in the nature of a duty, which he fulfills in order to be able to report to those at home. He says himself: 'I understand but little of art, of the painter's craft.' He pays respect to a Veronese, praises the light touch of Tintoretto's brush, or declares: 'Eve is the prettiest wench in the picture and, as from time immemorial, a little wanton into the bargain.' The reason his artistic judgments are so insignificant is that in looking at paintings he is unable to participate as a creator. Therefore he nearly always confines himself to expressions of veneration and respect, or to remarks about the great benefits bestowed on the onlooker by such treasures. The monuments of antiquity, on the other hand, he almost always sees as ruins, as incomplete, and in this lies their attraction. His remark about his *Iphigenie*, 'incompleteness stimulates', is valid in this context too. To reconstruct a picture from fragments, the image of a whole people from an empty amphitheatre, to read into the mutilated relief figures of a sarcophagus the forms of Greek gods and heroes: this is his way of seeing, the way of the poet. Connoisseurship and archaeology concern him too, but only secondarily; he feels a little uncertain of himself in these fields, and prefers to trust some well-known authority like his revered Winckelmann, or to try and find someone with reliable factual knowledge to assist him, which he soon does in the person of the invaluable Meyer.

In Vicenza he discovers another master, Palladio. Since the sixteenth century Palladio had been a guide to generations of architects and amateurs, especially in England; and now to Goethe he becomes more than a guide, his four volumes become the gospels of architecture. In Palladio he does not see late Renaissance or early Baroque, terms unknown not only to Goethe but to his times, he sees the truth, something divine. The great master's solution of the difficult problem of combining walls and pillars, that age-old contradiction, has for Goethe 'the force of the great poet who, out of truth and untruth, creates a third entity, whose borrowed existence enchants us'.

Overjoyed, he acquires a de luxe edition, with engravings, of Palladio's works, edited by the British Consul, Joseph Smith: 'One has to admit that the English have long known how to value what is good, and that they dispense their knowledge in the grand manner.' Deeply moved Goethe stands at the 'splendid' Consul's graveside in Venice, thinking how richly he deserves a monument. He knows nothing of the picaresque story of the man's life, of his dubious money transactions, his pandering to aristocratic visitors, and his art dealing, with its modern touch of supplying his wares with historic puffs.

This aside, Goethe is restless in Venice; Rome is his goal. The mosaics in St Mark's mean nothing to him, his roots do not go back far enough. In a collection of antiquities he sees a fragment from a Greek temple and, quite forgetting the enthusiasm of his Strasbourg days, cries out: 'Here is something very different from the owlish saints of our Gothic decoration perched in layers on their little corbels, very different from our pillars that look like pipe stems, from our little pointed doors and flowered finials; from this, thank heavens, I have rid myself for ever!'

On the Lido he collects seeds and little crabs, enjoying his newly won knowledge of nature: 'What a precious, wonderful thing a living creature is! How precise its status, how true, how actively it exists!' But now he must hurry on. Venice, so often described and praised by his father, has confirmed the picture he had formed in his mind; he has not been seeing it for the first time. He races through Bologna with a hired guide, allows himself three hours in Florence, and finally, coming in from the north, enters Rome, so impatient these last few days that he has scarcely taken his clothes off to sleep, and has left again each morning at the first stirrings of dawn.

He does not even notice the Campagna, that waste of neglect almost unique in Italy, nor does he spare a thought for the bands of robbers, the main subject of conversation among travellers, whose presence is very much in evidence in the rotting arms and legs displayed on the roadside by the Papal authorities. All he sees is the dome of St Peter's in the distance, clear in the November light. It is the ancient approach to Rome, when the city was gradually rising from the dark background of its surroundings to unfold in triumphant splendour. The Ponte Mollo with its towering Roman arches, far outside the town, is the first landmark; the Tiber, still uncanalized, with its yellow sandbanks; the Via Flaminia, a wilderness without houses, honoured only in its classic name; and finally, fortress-like, the Porta del Popolo, through which he drives into the piazza, known to him from boyhood from his father's engravings. Everything is just as he had imagined it: the twin-domed churches to right and left, the oval square, and in its centre the Corso, the street leading up to the Capitol. He takes rooms in a modest and very ancient inn on the banks of the Tiber, where Montaigne had stayed two hundred years before. He is visited by a German painter named Tischbein, for whom he has been able to procure a grant from one of the princes of his acquaintance. Goethe is standing by the fire in his green travelling coat; it is cold at this time of the year in Rome. The painter, awkward and unsure of himself, looks up at Goethe enquiringly. 'I am Goethe', says the traveller and holds out his hand. He enquires about cheap, simple lodgings, he does not want to stay at the inn. Tischbein suggests a room at the place where he is living, along with other German artists; but will it be good enough for the *Geheimrat*? The house is run by an elderly couple, a coachman and his wife, a sort of Philemon and Baucis. The son, who works as a servant, is a handy fellow and will be able to look after him. Goethe is satisfied with everything. He takes the room, which is almost empty apart from a low couch, puts his valise in the corner and hangs some silhouettes on the bare walls. The house is on the great thoroughfare, the Corso, near the Rondanini Palace. The 'German painters at the Rondanini' is what the local people call the little colony. For Goethe there now begins a peaceful student's life. The local priest, who has to keep the records of the district for the authorities, enters 'Filippo Möller, *tedesco, pittore,* 32' next the others, Tisben (Tischbein) 28, Bir (Bury) 24, Zicci (Schütz), whose names he cannot spell properly, all Protestants, which he also has to enter, and all young people. Goethe feels at home as he has never done in his life. The old couple look after their guests as though they were their own children. The food is simple, onion soup, perhaps, or *polenta*. 'How comforting this is after living in those Italian inns only he can know who has tried them', writes Goethe. When he opens his shutters in the morning he looks out on to the pine tops of the Pincio. A little way along the Corso and he stands on the Capitol. In a few hours he has seen everything: 'Everything is as I imagined it, and everything is new.'

Only now does the faithless wanderer write to Weimar; they imagine him still somewhere in Bohemia. Charlotte realizes that this is the end of her educational labour, and all Goethe's subsequent letters cannot eradicate this feeling, although he writes as lovingly as ever and tries to let her share his great experience as if nothing had happened. To him the distant friend is now a recipient for his impressions and ideas, as well as a public for the reports of his journey. He also writes to the Duke and to Herder. In his mind he is already dividing everything into chapters, and his drawings are to be used for an illustrated record of his travels; he later intended to publish this, but it came to nothing. The young painters round him are to help. Goethe sends a few chapters to Wieland, which are published in the *Merkur*.

The eternal city seems immense and the attempt to grasp it almost hopeless. He bemoans the fact that he was unable to come when he was younger, and that he has no mentor to guide him. And, as always happens with him, he finds the very man he is looking for within a few days of his arrival. He hurries off to the Quirinal, at that time the residence of the Pope, sees him celebrate mass, and is disappointed; his 'Protestant original sin' stirs within him, to whom original sin is otherwise anathema, and the whole ceremony seems superficial and worldly. How different the picture gallery! The German painters are all there in a group, eagerly discussing the paintings. Goethe joins them, he asks the name of a master whose painting he admires but no one can enlighten him. A small, modest man, with a round face, small eyes and firm features, looking more like an artisan than an artist, steps forward;

his name is Meyer, he is Swiss. Precisely and unhesitatingly he supplies the facts: it is a Pordenone, one of his best paintings. Goethe is delighted. Here is a guide after his own heart. He does not want grandiose ideas and flights of imagination; what he wants is reliable information. Meyer becomes his 'living encyclopaedia', as he is later called, always ready for consultation, hard working, a provider of material. He becomes Goethe's intimate confidant in all matters of art, living in his house in Weimar for many years; until his death Meyer remains the nearest to him of all his inner circle of friends. He dies in the same year as the poet, a few months after him.

For antiquity Goethe has to rely on Winckelmann, or on his successor as cicerone in Rome, Reiffenstein, a man of many activities who, like most guides, does some art dealing, gets commissions for young painters, dabbles a little in pastels as well as in the latest fashion of experimenting with 'encaustic' wax colouring after the manner of the ancients; with his habit of leaving nothing untried, Goethe also joins in this last activity. For the rest he complains of the labour involved in 'picking out' the ancient city from the ruins. He complains also about the later architects – this means the entire Renaissance and Baroque – for 'laying waste' all that was left. He complains a great deal, even about the 'endless distractions' of his almost monastically cloistered life 'at the Rondanini'. Much of his complaining may be due to a bad conscience, to the feeling that he ought not to appear too favoured to those he has left at home.

But joy predominates. He is free from ties, in good health, and without financial worries; his minister's salary is to continue, as Karl August generously assures him. Rome, so long dreamed of, stands before him; he is free to study natural history, write poetry, enjoy himself, and all of these he does. He absorbs information in his own way, without guide or guide book. He roams about. Rome at this time is still small and easy to take in; it is only the ruins, towering up out of the rubble and refuse, that are huge. No longer is it the 'capital of the world', and even as the seat of the Pope its importance has become almost neglible. In the sacred city itself sceptics are saying that 'all this' cannot go on much longer. The present Pope's predecessor had dissolved the all-powerful Society of Jesus, and Pius VI himself has had to suffer the humiliation of travelling to Vienna, a step unprecedented in Vatican history, to implore the Emperor to modify his measures of reform and, what is worse, has achieved nothing thereby. The Pontifical State has reached the nadir of its power.

The Papal States are poor, the city of Rome is poor; with its 160,000 inhabitants it lags far behind some other Italian cities. Barely a third of the space enclosed by the walls of the Imperial Roman city, large stretches of which still stand, is built up; the rest consists of gardens, their villas often in ruins, and pasturage for cattle. Many of the inhabitants are engaged in some kind of agriculture, others are artisans or small tradesmen. They live in tiny hovels and display their wares on the street outside. The palaces of the great form islands in a sea of huts and hovels, and give their names to the surrounding districts; Goethe lives 'at the Rondanini'. The Vatican forms a city of its own, on the other side of the river; here too a maze of wretched and appalling slums surrounds Christianity's greatest architectural splendour. The foreign legations, again, form districts in themselves, exercising their own jurisdiction and rights of asylum. The same contrasts are apparent in the priesthood. There are a few immensely rich Cardinals and dignitaries and relatives of the Pope: a nephew of Pius VI has just built himself one of the very few new buildings of consequence, his palazzo on the Piazza Navona. And then there are the hordes of penniless monks and *abbés*, most of them in tatters, who offer their services to visitors for whatever they may require. The people are indomitable, despite the harshest punishments and the gallows that stand by the bridge of St Angelo. Goethe notes the many homicides that are calmly accepted by the people; an act of violence is admired, 'the murderer reaches a church, and all is well'.

Indomitable the lust for pleasure too. The poverty of existence is offset by the abundance of festivals. Until far into the night crowds surge down the Corso talking, singing, playing mandolins and guitars. Life is lived in the streets; trade, crafts, discussions on art, and ordinary talk all take place there. The children play in the streets half naked, mothers nurse their babies on the doorsteps, craftsmen plane their wood and hammer their pots, housewives roast and fry in the street. Wares are laid out in the open on benches, shops hardly exist. In the squares fairy tales are told by itinerant rhapsodists, songs and ballads are performed in language that is coarse and frank. The Roman is forceful and candid to a degree that astonishes the northern visitor, in so far as he understands what he hears. Love is the great theme of all conversation and song. Of an evening lovers stand in the street, in full view of everyone, voicing their love and devotion to the windows above. The whole city is one great market and the market in love its most popular section; everyone takes part in it, by no means only the harlots. These, in fact, lead a harassed life, mostly round the Piazza d'Espagna where the foreigners are to be found; if they are caught by a *sbirro*, and cannot buy their release with a heavy tip, it means a ride on the wooden donkey through the length and breadth of the district – a spectacle for the children and young married women, who mercilessly pelt them and shout abuse.

All sections of society take part in this love-market. At the elegant *conversazione* some *abbé* or young nobleman will introduce the foreign visitor to a lady, as Goethe's father described in his Viaggio. In the churches – there are strict ones, and 'galant' ones like St Carlo on the Corso – the beggar women act as *procureuses*. Servants perform the same service, or else one merely follows the lady of one's choice. The German painters tell the story of one of their number who followed a pretty, bourgeois woman to her house; on arriving she thanked him pleasantly for his attention, regretting that nothing was possible that day as her husband was at home, but *'venite domani'* (come to-morrow!).

In the story of his travels Goethe does not mention love; in fact, for the benefit of those at home, he lets drop a few chilly sentences to indicate that his time is spent entirely in study and on 'matters of substance'. Only at the end of his book, knowing his public, does he insert, fictionally, an episode concerning a pretty Milanese girl, which ends on a most honourable note: the lady is engaged and he renounces her. Research has revealed her name; it was Maddalena Riggi, and she married a well-known engraver. Her portrait shows a typical Lombardy face, full, with a strong nose and powerful chin. No amount of research, however, has been able to trace, with any degree of probability, the name of Goethe's real love. In his poems he gives her the ancient Roman name of 'Faustina'; in keeping with his lifelong habit, there may even have been two Faustinas.

Whoever she may have been, this Faustina is no mere gallant adventure or episode in his life. It is only here in Rome, at the age of 40, that Goethe finds complete erotic freedom, only now that his experience of love is complete. Whatever the significance of his many *'Misels'* (or flames) – in all probability they were often harmless flirtations, eagerly pounced on by an expectant society in Weimar – Goethe had never had a mistress in the full sense of the word. Whatever forms his frequent dallying with village girls may have taken, it was at the most a here to-day and gone to-morrow. The quite indescribably inquisitive Weimar gossip, and the countless intimate letters to which it gave rise, have brought to light nothing on the subject. Nor would Goethe's garden-house, with its cell-like bedroom and straw mattress, have proved inviting to any mistress, had she been ever so modest. In his flat in town he was under constant observation by the whole population. It may seem strange that the great poet of eroticism had to reach the full maturity of his manhood before experiencing love as the ancients understood it, not the adoration of a noble woman nor yet the rococo sporting with a wench, but so it was. And Goethe himself fully and clearly admits it.

For him Faustina is the personification of antiquity. He looks at things differently now, more sensuously; the marble becomes skin beneath his fingers, it comes to life. The very fact that for the first time in his life he can look at ancient originals, instead of the plaster casts and poor engravings with which he has hitherto had to be satisfied, is important. The fact that they are mostly Roman copies of Greek originals, as we now know, is irrelevant, as is the fact that the works which excite his greatest wonder, as being the supreme masterpieces of all time, are now relegated to a very different category. He enjoys, discovers and forms his lasting ideal. He has found truth and beauty, his own truth and beauty. His room is filled with casts; the Juno from the Palazzo Ludovisi is his especial favourite. Tischbein has made a drawing of Goethe's room, with its over life-size plaster heads, the round valise, the pile of books supporting a shelf and clearly never read; drawings are stuck onto the bare walls, there is a small table on which stands an oil lamp, and in the centre is the low couch, with a second pillow for Faustina. Gently he taps out his hexameters on her back, as he tells us in his Elegies. He is writing in the metre of antiquity and is still not quite sure of himself in the new medium. Security and peace he finds only in the possession of his young mistress.

An entirely new element now enters his life: a sense of ease and well-being. This is something he has never known before, least of all in his relationships with women. His Roman mistress asks for and expects nothing beyond the usual presents, such as a dress or a small necklace. Even society ladies take it for granted that a lover expresses his appreciation tangibly; a marchesa will look doubtfully at a bouquet of roses, and only favour her admirer with a smile when she discovers the hidden diamond ear-ring. Goethe is happy that he does not have to economize; the girl that he loves is not close like her countrymen; the mother, too, is pleased with the generous guest. They all know it will not last, but while it lasts it is good. Never for a moment is Goethe tempted to feel trapped – the greatest fear of his life; there is no one to watch over him, criticize him or spread gossip about him. He lives in Rome as one does live in Rome – Filippo Möller, *pittore*. The fire his sweetheart lights outside his room in the morning warms him as no fire of love has done before. It has always meant restlessness, a flaring and flickering, trouble, and renunciation or flight. Here he can inhale and exhale in peace. Whoever the nameless Faustina was, her place in Goethe's life is as important as that of others of whom we hear so often and of whom too much has been written. She represents neither a 'sacred' nor a 'profane' love, and she cannot be judged by moral standards which, in this Rome and for this Goethe in Rome, do not exist. When Goethe, in his *Römische Elegieen*, decides to clothe her in ancient dress, it is only a thin covering as a protection against criticism. The 'true naked love', as he calls it, recognizes only man and woman.

Love-making does not occupy all his time, 'there is also sensible talk'. With his mistress he talks of simple things, of her childhood, of the attractions of Roman life, of her former admirers; with the young painters he discusses art. A new helper enters the scene to advise Goethe over questions of prosody. He is a young scholar from Berlin named Carl Philipp Moritz, who has earned a reputation with an autobiographical novel, *Anton Reiser*, describing his hard and tormented youth. To Goethe he is like a younger brother, 'but abandoned and hurt by fate, where I have been favoured and preferred'. Moritz has come to Italy to escape an unhappy love affair. Goethe seeks his advice in putting his *Iphigenie* into blank verse, happily without being influenced too deeply by Moritz' theories. They discuss problems of aesthetics, a field in which Moritz also has his own ideas. Goethe's mind just now is very open, he wants only to learn, listen and look. When

Moritz breaks an arm in falling from a horse, Goethe looks after him like a brother, sitting for weeks on end in his sick friend's room.

In such intimacy does he live with his young artist friends in the little colony 'at the Rondanini' that others grow jealous. The German painters in Rome, some two dozen in all, are almost without exception hard up; they live on allowances from great lords, by copying famous paintings in the galleries, or by painting travellers' portraits, as Ingres had to do for years. But nevertheless they are split into factions. One of them, Friedrich Müller, who in the days of *Sturm und Drang* had made his appearance as a poet with a *Faust* fragment, writes scathingly about Goethe and his 'body-guard': 'Whenever I saw the powerful Goethe marching round with those unsavoury kiss-me-quicks, I always had the impression I was watching Achilles among the women of Skyros.' Bury really did look like a young girl with his plump cheeks, Tischbein had a rather deprecating air about him, and with his snub nose and troubled expression, Moritz resembled Goethe's other 'younger brother', the unfortunate Lenz; Goethe always preferred to surround himself with insignificant, docile companions. They persuade him to read his *Iphigenie* to the artists' circle. It is his first resounding failure in front of an audience. The majority, like Müller, are expecting something striking, another *Götz* – and they are confronted with a quiet landscape of the spirit. Goethe is immersed in classicism, and this means nothing to them; they are surrounded by it anyway. Goethe is deeply hurt by their rejection of him. The period of alienation is beginning. For ten years he has been silent; for the next ten years his readers remain aloof.

His first stay in Rome lasts three months, and then he goes on to Naples. A new city opens up before him, three times the size of Rome, with a colourful life, and a colourful society into which he now enters. He no longer travels as Filippo Möller but as Herr von Goethe. Instead of the white marble figures of Rome he now sees colour, and Naples is still enormously colourful: the outside of the churches gaily painted, the people with their silk ribbons and flowers, the carriages a brilliant red, the horses decked with gold, the women dressed in scarlet jackets trimmed with gold and silver; the ships in the harbour are brightly painted and the butchers even dress their legs of mutton in gold. In the chapter he sends to Wieland for his *Merkur* Goethe energetically defends the Neapolitans against the charge of laziness levelled against them by travellers; on the contrary they are industrious and ceaselessly active, quite tiny children carrying wood, water and fruit. Even the famous lazzaroni, he declares, are not idle. And lastly these people do not work merely to earn a living but for enjoyment, to get the best out of life. With secret yearning he watches this gaiety, which is something that has not been vouchsafed to him.

Of the Court he sees but little. King Ferdinand spends most of his time on giant hunting expeditions; in an hunt-crazy age he is the greatest Nimrod of them all. The government he leaves in the hands of his English Prime Minister Lord Acton; the British Ambassador, Sir William Hamilton, in whose house Goethe is welcomed, is the leader of the city's social life, with his magnificent villa on the Posilippo where he entertains lavishly. Goethe casually looks over the art treasures of this great collector, who is one of the first to discover the artistic value of Greek vases, and buys them up by the hundred; sometimes he has them dug up secretly in some remote corner, or finds them in a cottage, standing forgotten on a shelf or even still in daily use. The Neapolitans watch in amazement as they see the distinguished gentleman coming straight from Court, resplendent in his full Court uniform, with its blue ribbon and star, helping a lazzarone to carry a basketful of these pots back to his villa. Hamilton publishes his finds in large folio volumes illustrated with engravings, and in so doing inaugurates a whole new fashion, *alla greca* or *all'etrusca*, that anticipates by decades the 'Empire' style; Tischbein, who has accompanied Goethe to Naples, is engaged by Hamilton to help with the illustrations. The Ambassador is a connoisseur in other fields too. He has set his heart on the famous beauty, Emma Hart, from London, whom later he graciously passes on to Lord Nelson. In private performances he presents this famous 'Greek' beauty, to his specially chosen guests, in a series of classic attitudes. Goethe describes her performance, clad in veils, a wealth of expression and a variety of head-dresses – these last her main article of clothing – while Sir William Hamilton rediscovers in her the figures on his vases, seeing in her the reincarnation 'even of the Apollo Belvedere himself'. There is excellent music at his house and the young Mozart once played there. Hamilton is a sportsman too and has climbed and explored Vesuvius twenty-two times, reporting his findings in detail to the Royal Society. Spurred on by him Goethe makes the ascent as well and finds the celebrated volcano not especially dangerous.

Goethe has long conversations with Filangieri, a lawyer of great culture, who is at work on an eight volume *Scienza della legislazione*, based on the ideas of Montesquieu and Beccaria. He is impressed by the man's delicate moral feeling, and agrees with him in seeing in the Emperor Joseph the 'image of a despot' – he has never liked the 'reforming Emperor' anyway; this talk, in the midst of a land of unbridled despotism, has a strange irony about it. Here Goethe is completely the child of the Age of Enlightenment, when it was universally accepted that a book written in a spirit of fatherly benevolence could change the world. He sees in this young jurist the 'will to good' actively at work; the social and political conditions of the kingdom of Naples he does not notice, while those in Germany are infinitely remote.

He has received news that, following the death of Frederick the Great, Karl August, who has been waiting for this moment, is going to leave Weimar and its three hundred soldiers to take command of a regiment of Prussian cuirassiers under Frederick's successor, his brother-in-law Friedrich Wilhelm II. This is the very thing Goethe has always advised him against, but now he accepts it calmly. The Duke will be as happy among his cuirassiers as he is among his ancient marbles, and will no longer be so anxious for the return of his minister. The little Duchy of Weimar can govern itself; and in fact things there do run of their own accord, without the Sovereign and without his recently indispensable *Geheimrat* Goethe. Schiller, who has just arrived in Weimar, writes of Goethe, with all the trenchancy at his command: 'While he is painting in Italy the Voigts and the Schmidts have to sweat for him like pack horses. He squanders a salary of 1,800 *thalers* in Italy for doing nothing while they have to carry twice the burden for half the money.'

This does not worry Goethe in the least; on the contrary he contemplates further travel. Sicily, still relatively unknown, calls him. Tischbein remains in Naples working for Sir William Hamilton, and in his place Goethe engages a young, very modest and very hard-working artist by the name of Kniep. Goethe has noticed with satisfaction how carefully the young draughtsman sharpens his English pencils, and with these pointed instruments Kniep makes his large landscape drawings; very clean and tidy, they have a certain dry charm of their own. Goethe himself has grown a little tired of drawing, and he is anxious to take home some topographically exact views of these little-known regions. He has made another attempt in Naples to master the difficult art, with Philipp Hackert, Court painter to King Ferdinand, but the latter has warned him that he will need at least a year's study with him if he is to have any chance of becoming a painter. Goethe doubts the wisdom of this. But he continued to remember Hackert with gratitude and, after the painter's death, devoted a little monograph to him, compiled mostly from the artist's reminiscences.

On their way down they stop at Paestum. Here Goethe sees an authentic Greek temple for the first time, and the building strikes him as totally strange, disturbing and even frightening, with its heavy, stumpy columns and its tightly packed masses. His eye has been trained on late Roman art and the classicism of Palladio. He has to take himself in hand to be able to assimilate this alien style, and it is wonderful to see what pains he takes to rid his mind of impressions formed by the more slender style, how he struggles to overcome his earlier feelings, until he can sing the praises of this ancient Greek architect. He spends a whole day wandering round the place. In those days great works of art still had to be explored, discovered and made into an experience; the traveller knew he would never see them again. Goethe knows this and, as he sagely remarks, reproductions can give no idea of a building of this kind. He must, and does, preserve it in his memory, even though his conception of a classic temple always remains closer to the models of later times.

They now take ship to Palermo, and then cross the whole length of the island on horseback, over lonely tracks and paths, to Messina – in those days a journey through Sicily was still an expedition. After the giant forms of Paestum, a temple at Girgenti once more comes nearer to 'our criterion of what is beautiful and pleasing'. But another passion has been awakened, a phantom, as he puts it, that has been shadowing him for several days. In the botanic garden at Palermo he has seen plants growing in the open air that normally one sees only in pots indoors. They seem to him to bloom more freely out of doors, to unfold with greater clarity. And so he finds himself possessed once more by his 'old whim', and wonders whether among them he may not discover the *Ur-Pflanze*, the primal plant. 'There must be such a thing! Otherwise how could I recognize the fact that this or that formation was a plant, if they were not all created after one pattern?' He has been intending to write a *Nausicaa*, under the Greek sky, but this has disturbed his poetic plans; instead of the garden of Alkinoos a 'world garden' has opened up before his eyes. 'Why,' he asks, 'are we moderns so easily distracted, why are we provoked to demands which we can neither attain nor fulfil!' His *Nausicaa* remains a fragment, the *Ur-Pflanze* becomes his dream and torment for many decades.

More distractions follow: in a park belonging to a Prince Pallagonia an array of distorted, mis-shapen sculptures, the work of some whimsical nobleman that to-day would frighten no one, completely horrify Goethe – distortions, and even caricatures, were things he could not stand. He pays a visit to the family of the great swindler, 'Count' Cagliostro, poor people with the more genuine name of Balsamo; he is able to help them a little. After a four-day sea crossing from Messina, including a storm off Capri, he returns to Naples. Here he takes leave of Kniep, who has completed a whole portfolio of large and often excellent landscapes of their journey. This unassuming man spends the rest of his life in Naples, occupying the most humble positions, half forgotten and growing forgetful himself; when, many years later, some German artists visit Goethe's former travelling companion, the old man asks absentmindedly what the *Geheimrat* has been writing.

Goethe spends almost another year in Rome. He lives a fuller life now, his mask of Filippo Möller, *pittore*, has been discarded. But his room at the elderly couple's is the same, perhaps with a new Faustina, perhaps with the same one, or perhaps it is only now that she enters his life. He even accepts a few honours, and is elected a member of the 'Arcadians' Society; on one occasion he gives a small party, with music. While staying in Castel Gandolfo at the country villa of the Englishman Jenkins – painter, art dealer, artists' patron and a kind of unofficial consul – Goethe makes one last attempt to become a painter. With his young painter friends he goes off looking for motifs, and in the evenings they expend much time and effort reading Sulzer's voluminous work on aesthetics, which, as a young man, Goethe had angrily ridiculed. Then he renounces this dream finally and for ever. Renunciation is the outcome of his love affair with the Milanese

Maddalena Riggi, too, as it had been of his father's window to window infatuation with an earlier Milanese.

His chief companion in Rome is Angelica Kauffmann, the 'inestimable' as he calls her, renowned in London as in Italy as the greatest woman painter of her day. When she died her funeral was a triumphal procession such as has rarely been accorded any artist: attended by one hundred clergy of every denomination, by the aristocracy and by painters, the cortège was led by girls dressed in white bearing two of her pictures. Her whole life was a triumph, from her early years as a child prodigy. She was the darling of London society, where a misfortune she suffered served only to make her more popular: a footman, posing as a foreign aristocrat, persuaded her to marry him; fortunately he did not survive long and she was then able to marry a Venetian painter named Zucchi. Known to visitors and the world of art as Madame Kauffmann, she lived a delightful life with her husband in Rome entertaining visitors from all over the world. It was for her soulfulness that 'this poetess of the brush' was acclaimed, for the very qualities, in fact, that make her paintings and the innumerable engraved reproductions, mostly done in insipid stipple engraving, well-nigh unbearable to our taste. Like many sentimental people, however, she had a very practical side to her nature and, with her husband, carried on an extensive business as an art dealer. She painted Goethe's portrait which, in the softness of its lines makes him look like the brother of her own self-portrait; despite his admiration for her 'really enormous talent', even he declared a little irritably that it was 'the face of a charming boy and nothing more'. She designed illustrations for Goethe's works, which were shortly to be published, and took him through the art galleries. Instructive as he found it to look at pictures with people 'who were trained in theory, practice and technique', it is very questionable whether his discussions with her and Zucchi added anything to his understanding of art. When Goethe sees with the eyes of others he becomes small, when he uses his own, as he did at Paestum, he is great.

To some extent this habit of conforming to the views of others is a kind of laziness. He already feels a constant need for assistants and suppliers of information, and is all too ready to accept, as a welcome simplification, such instruction as Angelica can provide. Simultaneously, as is his nature, he himself now wants to teach and lecture. Tischbein is too self-willed for him, so he turns to others. For a long time he interests himself in a young musician named Kayser, with whom he tries to write opera or operetta, but it comes to nothing; Kayser himself never composes anything worth while. Goethe employs him to copy out old church music, and once goes to hear the famous choir in the Sistine Chapel. Of the rich musical life in Italy, and of opera in particular, he is scarcely aware; his participation is limited to collecting a number of librettos to take home and adapt for his little theatre in Weimar, work which other people do better. In complete contrast to his attitude during his shorter first visit to Rome, he now becomes harsh and domineering towards his young companions: 'I am merciless and intolerant to all who loiter or lose their way.... I subject them to jest and mockery until they change their lives or part company with me.' The majority of these young painters are nice young men who want to get a little enjoyment out of life, which otherwise is drab and difficult. But Goethe has become stern, his thought exalted; he demands peremptorily that others should follow him.

In any case he is already in a different realm. He finds that drawing has stimulated his poetic faculty. The new edition of his works is taken in hand. *Egmont* has to be completed and additions made to *Tasso*; *Faust*, however, resists his attempts to continue it, and he writes only one scene. So far as art is concerned Meyer is his greatest acquisition: 'It was he who first opened my eyes to detail, to the characteristic features of individual forms'; and it was he who introduced him to the real 'construction' of a painting by 'describing the only true line'. Goethe speaks only of form and line, not of colour. His eye is centred on plastic form, and so it remains all his life. With Moritz, who in his brooding indolence has degenerated into evolving etymological fantasies, he indulges in a kind of 'chess game', as he calls it: an alphabet of reason and sensation. Again and again one is amazed at the way Goethe wanders off and allows himself to be distracted – he himself constantly refers to it – and then one is equally amazed at the way he pulls himself together and proceeds to his goal.

Once more he is beset by a great temptation: he is offered a journey to Greece. One imagines that to such an enthusiastic admirer of antiquity this would have been the most wonderful opportunity, but he turns it down unhesitatingly. He contents himself with examining the drawings brought back from Athens by Sir Richard Worsley, in which he can see, in very poor outline, the sculptures on the Parthenon by Phidias and his school. It was only as a very old man that he received from London a cast of one of the horses' heads, and marvelled at this *Ur-Pferd*. Another traveller brings back sketches of the ruins of Baalbeck and Palmyra. Excavations and discoveries are being made everywhere, in the near East, in Southern Italy, and in Rome itself. The surge of interest in the classic age, and in classicism, mounts daily. Publications pour forth. Winckelmann's great *History of Art*, published only twenty years previously, has already been superseded in many respects. Every day brings to light new treasures, new knowledge. But Goethe stands firm on the ground he has already won. He has created a certain order in his mind, a ritual even; his canon is established, he does not intend to hazard it.

Now he wants to start collecting and gathering things together. Threads are already being spun across the Alps to Weimar. He buys some works of art for Anna Amalie, and some portfolios of engravings for himself; his thoughts go to his house and how he is going to fill it with his new treasures. He buys casts of ancient cameos, 'the most beautiful examples we have of ancient workmanship'. The carnival, which he experiences a second time, is now only a horrible nuisance, and he is glad when the fools are finally laid to rest. He gives a painstaking description of it, however, for those at home, and after his return issues this, with Schütz' drawings, as a little booklet for private distribution.

In a murky corner of Rome, surrounded by a wooden hoarding and half-forgotten, lies one of the great Egyptian obelisks; not long after Goethe left it was erected on Monte Citorio. Goethe examines it carefully, admiring the beautiful granite, and the hieroglyphs with which it is covered and which, in those days, no one could decipher or even attempt to explain. Deeply moved he notices that the apex itself, intended to point towards the sun and invisible to any human eye, is also decorated with sacred signs and pictures, for these were carved with no thought for any material effect. He has casts made of these, and takes them with him. For him they are symbols of his own signs and images.

Solemnly he takes his leave. There are three nights of full moon at the time of his departure, and he sees the ancient monuments once more all grouped together in great blocks of light. For the last time, as he feels, he wanders round alone through the familiar streets and open places, along the Corso and up to the Capitol. In front of the Colosseum he stops: it is closed by iron gates and in a little chapel inside lives a hermit. Goethe turns away and goes back to his room. He never sees Rome again.

Quickly now he takes his departure, making only short stops in Florence and Milan, where he sees the remains of Leonardo's 'Last Supper'. He does not even stop in Frankfurt, where his mother is eagerly awaiting him. Impatiently, as he had come, he returns north and 'into exile'.

# 25

# *Erotikon*

Goethe has already outlined his future position in Weimar in letters to the Duke from Rome. In these he writes as one sovereign to another, and Karl August displays the nobler side of his character in accepting this. The correspondence between them, which hitherto has often been almost school-boyish in its *camaraderie*, and coarse as well – the coarsest of their notes, in which they exchanged experiences in the lighter forms of love, have been lost – now takes on a completely different tone. During these months the correspondence reaches a level unique in the annals of princely relations with a poet, and as a result this petty Weimar Prince has rightly earned his own small share in the immortal fame of his Court. In other respects he remains as he always has been, and soon reverts to his senseless hunting, both on horseback and on foot through the woods. Goethe is no longer his companion in these activities. He is now only a 'guest', as he himself defines his role: 'Whatever else I am is for you to judge and make use of.' Above all, however, he is now an artist, as has become clear to him in Rome. By this he does not mean a painter, that is a dream he has given up; he wants to be a poet, a writer, an explorer among all the phenomena of life, nature and the sciences – in a word Goethe the *uomo universale*, who has selected modest Weimar as his residence.

There has never been a position such as this, and there never will be. With a noble and symbolic gesture Karl August intimates what he understands to be Goethe's new position. His friend has expressly asked to be relieved of all the 'mechanics' of government; he decides, therefore, that in future the Ducal chair is to be reserved for Goethe at meetings of the *Conseil*. Goethe hardly ever makes use of it; if and when he acts as adviser he does so, as formerly, in private conversation with the Duke. But the awareness of this friendly support and protection is a vital safeguard to him and also, let us not forget, to his material existence. His salary, the second highest in the land, continues undiminished; indeed it is even increased from time to time, and constitutes his main source of livelihood until he is well on into old age. Goethe's income as a writer is just about adequate to maintain his modest garden-house, and to finance an occasional journey, but it is quite inadequate to maintain his more expansive style of living in the large

254

house on the Frauenplan. And it is this ampler life that he now wants, with his collections, assistants and secretaries, and with comfort in all the things of life, such as he tasted in Rome. He has grown heavy, purely physically, as well as intellectually under the weight of material he has collected and which he now wants to assimilate for future use. He has become sensuous, as his old friend Charlotte notices at once, and it is a sensuousness that embraces not one but all his senses. He sees things differently now. He has returned as a stranger, and is astonished at being received as such.

With all his wisdom in matters concerning mankind and human activity in general, Goethe can be touchingly naïve in matters concerning himself. He had taken to flight without even saying good-bye, withdrawn into solitude, transformed himself and become a new person, and now he expects to be received back, without further ado, as though nothing had changed and he were still the Goethe of old. He has amassed a vast wealth of material and experience, and now he expects everyone to listen eagerly to what he has to say. He has passed the most delightful nights with a Roman mistress; he wants to tell Charlotte about these 'pleasant secrets' and is disappointed when she does not want to hear about them. He has seen, or at any rate almost caught a glimpse of, the *Ur-Pflanze*, the primal plant, in Palermo and immediately takes it for granted that everybody is now interested in botany and morphology and is anxious to follow him on this still untrodden path. He is lonely and seeks company, friendless and craves friends. He has grown cold and longs for warmth. He is to spend long years dogged by these inner schisms. He might well have collapsed under the strain, or have become embittered and barren, had he not at this very moment, as always in his life, found the person he needed.

A young girl, or really a young woman, as she is 23 and therefore almost past the marriageable age of those days, comes up to him in the park. With a respectful curtsy, she presents the *Geheimrat* with a petition on behalf of her brother, a young man by the name of Vulpius, who is in dire need of help; formerly a university student and now secretary to a German baron in Nuremberg, he is in imminent danger of losing his job because, badly paid though he is, the baron has found someone else willing to accept even less. The young man supports his two sisters; the parents are dead and the children have been left without any means whatsoever. Vulpius is a hard worker and has written numerous books for the cheaper booksellers, who pay just as badly as the baron; there have been novels on the age of chivalry, *The Adventures of Prince Kalloandro, The Story of Blondchen*, comedies, a glossary of the eighteenth century, and now he is at work on a four-volume collection of 'sketches from the lives of amorous ladies'. He is active, he is a good boy, but he simply cannot get on and is in urgent need of patronage – is there any chance of some work for him in Weimar?

Quite unaffected, the girl looks up at the great man expectantly. She is not tall, she is not exactly beautiful – Goethe does not like excessive beauty

– but she is pretty: rather dark, with fresh lips, a well-rounded chin and plump cheeks, her low forehead half-hidden by the loveliest curls which, unplaited and undressed, wreath her whole face. Her dress too is very simple. How do you live, my child? She works at Bertuch's flower factory.

Goethe remembers visiting the place, which is not a factory but a large attic room in Bertuch's imposing house; formerly keeper of the Duke's privy purse he has now become a highly successful entrepreneur in many fields of business. With his wife he has set up a sort of sewing room in his attic, where a staff of some thirty to forty girls sit cutting flowers out of remnants of taffeta and silk and sewing them together. In this way Bertuch hopes to satisfy the large demand of the Court, and perhaps even of the whole country, for trimmings for hats and costumes, which need a wealth of floral ornament. Bertuch insists on strict order being kept in the work-room. Goethe does not really like the man, although he is by far the most efficient employer in the whole Duchy, and the only one to provide any employment at all in the town itself; in his diary Goethe describes him as a 'shockingly easy-going lout'. Wieland also made fun of him and his sewing girls in one of his poems: 'young and chaste this maiden band, pure of morals, clean of hand'. The *Geheimrat* promises the girl his sympathetic interest in her petition.

He sends out letters of recommendation, having first made some enquiries. The father, who had been a scribe in one of the Weimar offices, is said to have died of dipsomania; the son has written a great deal, and 'that is not exactly the best recommendation', as he writes to his old friend Jacobi. 'We are horrified at our own sins when we see them in others.' Vulpius, however, had made an honest attempt to get an education, at Jena University, and Goethe now makes an honest attempt to find some employment for the young man. The sister he takes to his garden-house and she becomes his mistress, in much the same way as his Roman 'Faustina' whom, as a type, she may have resembled.

For a while he is able to keep the relationship a secret, and he writes a fine elegy on discretion, the cherished goddess who has led him safely through life. It is only to his hexameters that he feels he can entrust his feelings about his loved one: *'Wie sie des Tags mich erfreut, wie sie des Nachts mich beglückt'* (How she delights me by day, how she transports me by night). Weimar is not Rome. People see the girl in the garden, they talk, they gossip, they become indignant. Young Fritz von Stein, whom his mother had made a point of taking back into her house when Goethe was away, is the first to report the presence of this new guest in the garden-house. Charlotte, long since disillusioned, in spite of Goethe's long letters from Italy, and suspicious of his constantly reiterated protestations of inviolable love, now rebels openly and in front of everyone. She is approaching her fifties, undergoing her change of life, a sick woman, and exhausted by the many changes in her relationship with Goethe. Her life has lost the meaning that he had given it and she has become embittered. It is not just jealousy of the girl, as has been supposed; she has overlooked or condoned many of Goethe's affairs. She senses that her role is over, indeed has been for a long time, and that things will never again be as they were. She feels too, otherwise she would not be a woman and a lady, that she has been made ridiculous and cheapened in the eyes of '*tout* Weimar', which had looked with admiration and envy on the two of them, on their almost legendary relationship which recalled to many the famous love stories of the past. To reproach her with not stepping down with a big gesture of generosity, or of not being willing 'to understand' and resign herself to the new situation, is to ask too much. She knows only too well, seeing things much more clearly than Goethe, that this is no mere infatuation, another *Misel*, but a 'solid relationship', no matter whether this 'Mamsell Vulpius' remains or whether she is replaced by someone else; and these are things that Goethe himself does not know yet.

He writes to Charlotte quite unconcernedly, as though it were simply another harmless affair on the side. Immediately after his return he had told her not to take too literally his 'present distracted, I will not say torn, state'. In reality he is not in the least distracted or torn, he is very composed and sure of himself. Before there is any mention of the flower girl he writes that it is better 'to settle accounts amicably than always to try and assimilate one another'. This, her goal and her hope, fostered for so many years by him, he now expressly rejects, and this constitutes the final break. She can derive no consolation from the fact that in the same letter he acknowledges himself her debtor, asks her forbearance and closes with the words: 'Farewell and love me. From time to time I hope to tell you more about the beautiful secrets', of his experiences in Rome with 'Faustina', to whom she has listened with patience.

Almost in a state of agitation at being so misunderstood, when this last secret is discovered, he writes to her: 'And what sort of relationship is it? Who is going to be the loser through it? Who lays claim to the sentiments I bestow on the poor creature? Who to the hours I spend with her?'

He becomes harsh. The former intimacy could be restored and continue if she were disposed 'to talk about interesting matters' with him; but he cannot tolerate the way in which she now treats him, accusing him of coldness, supervising his every mien and gesture, finding fault continually, so that he is never 'at his ease' in her presence. All of which may well be true. Finally he puts the blame on her excessive coffee drinking, against which he has always warned her: it intensifies hypochondria. Perhaps the waters will effect an improvement.... A few days later he asks her: 'Look at the matter from a natural point of view, allow me to have a calm, sincere word with you about it, and I have hopes that everything can be put right between us.'

To see their very unnatural relationship from a natural point of view is no easy matter. They part, and remain estranged for many long years. The flower girl comes and goes in the garden-house. It is not only Charlotte but the whole of Weimar society that is up in arms, and this is not only due to gossip mania and self-righteous narrow-mindedness, though both of these play their part. As Schiller noticed, with surprise and annoyance, on his first visit to Weimar, opinion there had surrounded Goethe with a halo of admiration that bordered on idolatry; he was regarded as some higher form of being. Now, at one stroke, he appears coarse and earthly, common and living in a common liaison with a very common person, who can scarcely read and write; with a girl who speaks broad Thuringian, has a head covered in a mop of untended curls, and who wears a linen smock over her plump and sturdy body, a body that may be all right in bed but not anywhere else. His 'bedfellow' is the name Goethe's mother gives her in her blunt way, though without any disparagement, when some years later she learns for the first time of this Mamsell Vulpius. Far from complaining, she is pleased that her darling Hans is now so well off, that the material needs of his bed, his kitchen, his cellar and his household are now so well cared for. She remains unshaken in this view even when, as subsequently happens, reports constantly reach her that this Vulpius woman is so pleasure-mad that she drinks and dances all night with young students in Goethe's absence: 'Enjoy your dancing, my dear young thing, I like gay people!'

Very possibly it was just this gaiety that was a cause of annoyance to the frequently depressed citizens of Weimar. For Goethe, who also often suffered from severe hypochondria, it was an invaluable counterpoise. The first years with Christiane Vulpius are crowded with feelings of joy, peace and relief. He writes his lightest, gayest verses. He writes in her arms, inspired by her body; and out of this double experience, with Faustina and Christiane, he creates his *Römische Elegieen*, themselves the finest memorial to this new love. It is his pagan love, his love of the 'body in all its splendour', as he expresses it in one of his poems to her. Her intellectual equipment is small, and he enjoys this. He enjoys the warmth, the sheer love of living, the cheerfulness, the frank questions of an unspoilt mind that is by no means as silly as the society ladies make out, and the equally frank answers. He experiences a feeling of comfort, such as he had tasted in Rome, but which is now more lasting, more permanent. He has a quite insatiable need for the warmth of such comfort because he lacks it in himself; he can be charming, he can fascinate people, he can joke with them good-humouredly, but he is always surrounded by distance, respect, coolness. Christiane, herself, to the end of her days, never refers to him as anything but *'Der Geheimrat'*, and in Weimar they are convinced that even in bed she always addresses him respectfully as *'Sie'*. But this is beside the point; they understand each other, many words are not necessary. Goethe writes a letter in verse, in the old familiar style, to Karl August, who is plagued by boring relations, and ends it:

> *Indes macht draussen vor dem Tor,*
> *Wo allerliebste Kätzchen blühen,*
> *Durch alle zwölf Kategorieen*
> *Mir Amor seine Spässe vor.*

(And meanwhile just outside the door, where most enchanting catkins bloom, there play for my delight the whole twelve categories of *Amor*.)

The sour comments of Weimar society have been supplemented in the intervening years by discussions as to whether Goethe did not deserve some other, better, nobler woman, or, Christiane having been chosen as his life partner, by attempts to turn her into something finer and nobler than she was. All such conjectures are love's labours lost. Goethe makes and leads his own life according to the needs of his mind and body; the difficulties and burdens of this relationship are his and have little to do with Weimar society. In Weimar he lives as a guest and in this love affair, too, he lives as a guest: he comes and goes as pleasure or necessity dictates, sometimes he is away for several months, even half a year, at a time; he also has his other loves. He has his interests, his writing, of which Christiane understands next to nothing. He talks to her about his work when the spirit moves him; he even asks her advice from time to time, and is delighted by her common sense, which often catches the essential point where more educated minds would miss it. But he needs his independence, and this is something he insists on always, even when, having put her to the test for eighteen years and she has proved her staunchness in the calamities of the war of 1806, he later marries her and gives her his name. In his will of 1797 he describes her as his 'friend and domestic companion of many years', and, in his letter to the pastor who is to marry them, as 'my little friend who has done so much for me', and whom he now wishes to acknowledge formally and legally as his wife.

Until their marriage Christiane is known as Demoiselle Vulpius, or 'die Vulpia'. To begin with Goethe, drawing on antiquity, calls her his 'little Erotikon', and in these early days he does not contemplate any lasting union. Caroline Herder, who has just read the newly published *Egmont*, speaks of his *Klärchen*. To the Duke Goethe refers to his 'undergraduate streak', of which he has no cause to be ashamed, and Karl August shows complete understanding of his friend's behaviour, even providing Goethe and Christiane an apartment in one of his houses; when, at Christmas 1789, a son is born, the Duke stands godfather to him. Afterwards when Goethe and Christiane move to his large town house her step-sister follows, then her aunt, and for a time her brother too. Goethe now finds himself surrounded by a whole family, and the numbers would have increased had not a melancholy fate intervened. Medically this has never been properly explained, owing to inadequate data, but four further confinements all end unhappily, the children being either still-born or dying immediately after birth. Only the eldest, named August after the Duke, survives, and he grows into a sturdy child; he too, as it later transpires, is heir, both physically and mentally, to some dark strain and dies prematurely before his father.

This house of Goethe's is a strange establishment. He grows more and more attached to the little creature whom, as he puts it in one of his poems, he has dug up with all her roots and transplanted into his garden. He takes care of her and she looks after his comfort. Often she seems indispensable to him and he will return hurriedly from a journey. In 1790 he writes to Herder from Silesia, where he is staying with the Duke:

> There is nothing but trash and trumpery everywhere, and I shall certainly not pass a single pleasant hour until I have dined with you and slept at the side of my lass. So long as you retain your affection for me, a few good people remain my friends, my lass is faithful to me, my child lives, my big stove heats well, there is nothing else I want.

On one occasion he speaks of his 'passionate love' when, during an absence, he commends the girl and his child to the care of his friends. It is an expression he uses all too often, and often it does not fit, as here in the case of Christiane. The natural combination of home, child, stove and bed comes nearer the truth. And yet we should not underestimate this feeling of warmth. Goethe never knew it elsewhere. And who will presume to say that he did not love this girl, in his own way and in her way? The many fine threads of their daily life together, twining round him like tendrils, become a threat and a burden, that he is soon to lament in his Elegy *Amyntas*. Here, reverting again to the comparison with nature, he indulges in one of his gross overstatements: his beloved is like ivy that sinks its thousand tendrils into his life stream, draining him of his very marrow, of his soul; he feels himself withered up already, 'It is only her I feel, she alone entwining me, all I have are these fetters, this deadly ornament of alien foliage round me.' Between this lifelong fear and feeling of alienation, and the feeling of warmth and intimacy, Christiane has her role to play in Goethe's dual nature. After twenty years of living together Goethe says, as though in surprise and almost absentmindedly: 'Who would believe that this person has lived with me for twenty years? But this is just what appeals to me in her, that she abandons nothing of herself and remains as she was.'

She remains gay, and this cannot always have been easy for her. Goethe does indeed look after her, and the whole Vulpius clan who establish themselves in this house. He sends presents when he is away and asks after her health, particularly during her many pregnancies for which, in their private language, they use the curious and untranslatable word *Krabskrälligkeit* which, with all the mortality, has a somewhat bizarre sound about it. But time and time again he leaves her alone in the large house. Immediately after the birth of the first child he goes away for nearly six months, first to Italy and then to Silesia with the Duke; and so it goes on. For many years when there are guests Christiane does not eat with them; it is only intimates who see her. Five years elapse, and his son August is already a lively little boy, before he tells his mother of Christiane's existence, but she receives the news with far more generosity and grace than did Weimar society. She promises Goethe at once to write 'to his sweetheart', and performs this duty with dignity and warmth. In the whole of his correspondence with Schiller, with whom after a long estrangement he has now formed a friendship, Goethe does not mention Christiane, and Schiller makes only one passing reference to her, although he spent several weeks in Goethe's house, and although he makes sympathetic reference to the tragic outcome of the various pregnancies. To his friend Körner Schiller only mentions Goethe's 'miserable domestic situation, which he is too weak to change'.

In itself a free relationship of this kind was by no means unheard of. His Britannic Majesty's Professor Lichtenberg in Göttingen lived with a simple girl, and Hamann, the 'Magus of the North', lived with his father's maidservant. Schiller arrived in Weimar openly with his mistress, Frau von Kalb, and then, after he had decided in favour of the von Lengefeld family, lived for a time in a rather hazy relationship with the two daughters until he finally married the less beautiful, but gentler and more homely one, in preference to the other who was more fiery and passionate. Every lady of Weimar society, who was not hopelessly unattractive, had her romance. Charlotte von Stein's sister had married a Herr von Imhof, who was considered to be immensely rich, a 'Nabob', and had two young blackamoors as a bodyguard. He had been in military service in India, where he had amassed his wealth, not from his military career but from the sale of his first wife, an extremely pretty sergeant's daughter, to Warren Hastings. Imhof was a gambler and a spendthrift, and the indemnity paid by Hastings may not have been as high as rumour put it; however this may have been, the second Madame von Imhof had to make several journeys to London to seek help from her predecessor, now Mrs Hastings. Her sister Charlotte's only comment on her brother-in-law's change of wives was that 'living in foreign parts extinguishes moral concepts'. In his letters to Charlotte Goethe refers, with a touch of admiration, to one of her friends, the wife of a Weimar Court Chamberlain, who had fallen in love with another gentleman. Withdrawing to a distant country estate she feigned death, had a dummy buried in her stead, and met her lover in Tunis; there they tried unsuccessfully to prospect for gold, soon quarrelled, and then turned up together again in Weimar. 'To die!' wrote Goethe. 'To go to Africa, to start the most extraordinary romance only, in the end, to get divorced and marry in the ordinary way! I found it most amusing. In this workaday world one cannot accomplish anything out of the ordinary.'

No one in Weimar saw anything out of the ordinary in the fact that the Protestant Weimar Superintendent Herder travelled to Italy in the company, and as the guest, of a rich Roman Catholic dignitary, the two of them sharing the carriage with this devout gentleman's mistress. She was the daughter of the President of the Chamber of Finance with whom Goethe had stayed on his first arrival in Weimar, a very lively little creature and a widow, following her 'extremely gay and jolly marriage' with one of the gentlemen at Court, not unlike Philine in *Wilhelm Meister*.

This is the Weimar stage, no more frivolous than that of other princely Courts, but far more unrestrained, at least outwardly, than that of bourgeois Frankfurt. The age of bourgeois supremacy has not yet dawned, the age that later tried in vain to find an appropriate formula for Goethe's relationship with his Christiane, shamefacedly calling it a *'Gewissensehe'*, a marriage of conscience, or deploring it as an unaccountable lapse, or else pleading its final legalization. It is, and remains, a very free relationship; only thus was it tolerable to Goethe. In the letters between the two there are innumerable references and allusions to the word *Äugelchen*, casting eyes, which has now replaced the former *Misel* and which often has scarcely any deeper meaning. It is only when Goethe goes a little too far with casting his eyes, when Christiane hears disturbing reports of beautiful ladies on his visits to the spas – almost invariably undertaken without her – that she grows uneasy and sad, and he has to console her. But he assumes that he lets her eyes wander too, within reason. He has no objection to her dancing, going for drives, enjoying herself with a few friends on trips into the country, even though people in Weimar make nasty insinuations, and students pass scathing remarks about Goethe's mistress dancing her shoes out at village balls. He takes no notice of the rumours that she drinks too much; he himself likes to drink wine, sometimes heavily. Almost the only companions she has are actors, and they are no more accepted by society than she is; Goethe, on the other hand, welcomes this company for her because, with her charming pleasant ways and her clear little head, she can help a lot in smoothing out difficulties. Later, when he takes over the direction of the Court theatre, she becomes his most important assistant in the difficult problem of personal relations. These stage people turn up at Goethe's house with all their bags and baggage, for most of them are married, and Christiane looks after the children, who play on her lap as though they were her own, whom she has lost. When she feels lonely she works in the garden, which is her pride and sanctuary.

One can observe the most curious touches. After they have been living together for a decade, and the excitement in Weimar must long since have died down, Goethe, who has once more withdrawn into his bachelor life at Jena, decides he wants to pay Christiane a visit. Secretly, furtively, like a lover, he slips into his own house at dead of night so that no one shall see him, no one must know of his visit. On another occasion she begs him to come home soon, she yearns for him; she promises not to come to his bed in the morning and disturb him without being asked, and the child will not bother him....

She knows from long experience what an exceptionally sensitive vessel this strong, powerful body is. He has to be protected from all unpleasantness, above all from death, of which he refuses to see or hear anything. Christiane's step-sister, who has been living in the house with her for many years, dies of consumption. So far as possible all news of her illness has been kept from him, and now no one, not even Christiane's brother, has the courage to tell him of her death; it is only later, long after the funeral, that he learns what has happened.

Rather early in life Christiane gets stout and fleshy, then fat and heavy, and finally she becomes almost helpless. Her undiminished gaiety is a source of increasing embarrassment even to their close friends, and in her constant dancing and driving about there is an element of despair. Even housekeeping, which in the early days she looked after so splendidly, gets beyond her as the size of the household assumes ever larger proportions. Her great moment comes in the war days of 1806 when French marauders burst into the house and she places herself resolutely between them and the *Geheimrat*. Goethe legalizes their relationship in a quiet, private wedding, and next day takes her, as *Geheimrätin* von Goethe, to a reception; not one given by a member of Weimar society, it is true, for those ladies continue their resistance for a long time yet, but by a foreigner, a rich widow from Danzig, named Schopenhauer. Frau Schopenhauer, mother of the philosopher, who writes novels, declares gallantly that, if Goethe gives the woman his name, one can surely offer her a cup of tea. And it is this cup of tea, a gesture on the part of Frau Schopenhauer that Goethe never forgets, which confirms Christiane in her new status. Gradually the other Weimar ladies follow suit; in their letters they continue their slander, saying that Goethe's 'fat half' is a secret drinker, and that she is leading her son on the downward path by encouraging him to drink before he is old enough, but they come to tea or dinner at her house.

Christiane suffers an early death, at the age of 50, after painful illnesses and vain attempts to fight her increasing stoutness by cures with Eger water, that only aggravate her condition. The helplessness of the doctors and the total lack of palliatives turn her end – she dies of uraemia – into a ghastly two-day struggle of constant crying and screaming. Meanwhile Goethe lies in his own bed, suffering from a catarrh which, as often with him, may well have been an escape. He never saw his wife again, his only news of her was what others told him. The only person with sufficient courage to enter the screaming woman's room and hold her hand was an actress, mistress of Karl August, her own position now regularized as Frau von Heygendorff, the Duke's 'second wife'. In his diary Goethe notes: 'Approaching end of my wife. Final terrible battle of her constitution. She passed away about noon. Emptiness and deathly stillness in and around me. Arrival and festive entrance of Princess Ida and Bernhard. Hofrat Meyer, Riemer. In the evening the town brilliantly illuminated. At midnight my wife taken to the mortuary. Myself in bed the whole day.'

There could be no question of laying out the body; it was taken out of the house the same evening and buried in the early hours of the following morning. Goethe notes:

> My wife buried at 4 a.m. Various letters. Fragment from the Ramayana to Major von Knebel. Documents put together. Rehbein, Huschke and Kämpfer. In the garden. Consideration of what is to be observed next. Colour experiments prepared. Midday with August. Engravings to Peron. At 3 o'clock received list [i.e. of those sending condolences] for my wife from von Voigt. English journals. Hofr. Meyer. In particular the building of the castle wing.

For him the most important of these is 'what is to be observed next', referring to his observations of colour phenomena. One likes to assume that this is just the mask he normally wears in the presence of death. But it may also be the face of stone, which often stares at us out of Goethe's life and out of his personal testimony, and which can only be interpreted in terms of the sentimental and commonplace by imagining that behind his coldness he wishes to hide some particularly deep emotion. For such things Goethe had no time.

Twenty-seven years he spent with Christiane, and the question arises as to whether this association was of any deeper significance, aside from the early years of 'Erotikon' and the comforts of home, sweetheart and child. Christiane underwent no development, she remained the same, as Goethe remarked after twenty years, and for which he praised her. Indefatigable as he was in his urge to educate, he achieved virtually nothing in her case. He did not even succeed in teaching her to write legibly and tolerably correctly, although this was a matter of almost symbolic importance to him. To form the letters correctly, clearly and beautifully, to arrange a page of writing in an orderly manner, had seemed to him, since his student days in Leipzig, the first and most essential step in acquiring a good education. But he only smiled when Christiane put down on paper one of her scribbled and half-smudged notes, translating her broad Thuringian dialect into written symbols. He does not mind in the least if she gets other people to write, or even to compose, her letters, and later on, when the correspondence on his side begins to strike a deeper note, he addresses his letters not so much to Christiane as to the rest of the household, or else he simply sends his diary notes, which are to be carefully preserved for some future use. There now begins, too, a still more delightful game and one very much in keeping with his nature. Christiane's companion, Demoiselle Ulrich, of whom we shall have more to say later, writes the most delightful letters in Christiane's name, and vaguely on her instructions. Goethe answers ambiguously, with both Christiane and the charming *Nebengeschöpf* – complementary creature – in mind. In fact he is writing over the head of Christiane to Fräulein Ulrich.

This is how he often behaved, and only someone like Christiane would have been able to put up with it. If one were to eliminate from these twenty-seven years all the complementary creatures, his life and work would shrink considerably. The breadth and richness of his existence is due to the fact that he is able to project himself and extend his activities into every sphere and also, very substantially, to the fact that he is then able to find rest and quiet once more at Christiane's side. It is customary to see in the *Römische Elegieen* the justification for this otherwise somewhat scandalous relationship, but its importance goes far beyond this; Christiane is a decisive element in his life, the element of relaxation, rest and compensation. If the bed is the leading factor here, let us not underestimate this. Goethe's sensuality, or the joy he derives from the senses, is his strength and not something to be accepted, if need be, as a regrettable extra. It is this that gives his works their incomparable tension and span; a Faust, consisting only of philosophical ideas, would be a phantom, a phantom, admittedly, whose construction has been attempted often enough. Only the freedom of this relationship with Christiane could give Goethe the freedom to treat eroticism so naturally, and in all its variations, in all 'twelve categories of amor', down to the coarsely earthy, in verses which he showed only to intimates and which were long kept hidden away, and in which he goes very far, making extremely daring play between the sexes. Elsewhere he soars equally high to the most delicate and tender stirrings of life itself, as when, in taking his beloved in his arms, he feels the first faint heart-beats of the unborn child, and out of this experience creates a whole world.

There is no lack of grotesque touches in the relationship, for the girl is often only a receptacle for his thoughts and interests. When he is struggling with his world-shaking concept of metamorphosis, a word that cannot possibly mean anything to her and which she vainly tries to copy in her Thuringian dialect, he comes to her and asks her to listen. He has summarized his theory in simple Greek hexameters, making it easy to understand, so that a child, a dear little child, will be able to grasp it at once: '*Dich verwirret, Geliebte, die tausendfältige Mischung Dieses Blumengewühls über dem Garten umher?*' (Does the thousandfold medley of this throng of flowers spread out over the garden confuse you, my love?) He unfolds to her the eternal laws of botany, of growth, which he has discovered: seed, germ, division, crenature, calyx, variety. Pairs with an affinity come together, hymen floats by, the pair unites in harmony, for he has now passed to the animal kingdom, to the human race.

She understands him while the learned gentlemen hesitate or shake their heads. He speaks of the growing embryo in the mother's womb, or of the germ of acquaintance, of sweet accustom, which grows into friendship, till finally *Amor* begets blossom and fruit – 'rejoice in our day!' It is a veritable rejoicing on his part, the joy and pleasure of having at least one human being who can share his jubilation over the mighty discovery of the organic relationship of all creation.

Many poems, not only those expressly inspired by her body, and many drawings testify to his love for Christiane. Perhaps the most beautiful and tender of these latter is a sketch showing her asleep on the sofa, in a full skirt, her face surrounded by loose curls. He also describes her thus in a poem, equally light and tender; watching her asleep for a long time he silently places two oranges and some roses to greet her when she wakes:

> *Seh ich diese Nacht den Engel wieder,*
> *O wie freut sie sich, vergilt mir doppelt*
> *Dieses Opfer meiner zarten Liebe.*

(If once more this night I see my angel, Ah! to see her joy will be the twofold wages of my tender love's oblation.)

Strangest of all, perhaps, is an almost surrealist portrait sketch: the sturdy head, with hair falling down over the forehead and eyebrows, and out of the curls two more curly heads growing, one smiling and roguishly gay, the other cast down in thought and sadness. Even this simple creature cannot be summed up in a simple formula, and Goethe knew, or at any rate sensed this early in their relationship.

266

# 26

# *Collected Works*

It is as an artist in the full sense of the word that Goethe returns from Italy. After an interval of ten years he now begins to appear before the public as an author again. He has almost been given up as lost to writing, although his early works are still read and publishers still continue their reprints and pirated editions. No fewer than seven different pirated editions of his *Collected Works*, all in three or more volumes, have been published during these years, in Switzerland, Berlin, Amsterdam, his home town of Frankfurt and Reutlingen. One pirate pirated the others. The most popular edition was that of the Berlin pirate, Himburg, with charming engravings by the favourite illustrator Chodowiecki. Criticized from various quarters because of this continued piracy, he even offered Goethe a small compensation: a service of Royal Berlin porcelain for his table. This factory, later to become so famous, had great difficulty in marketing its wares, and Frederick the Great had decreed that every Jew, on contracting a marriage for his child, had to buy a service as a special levy. Thus it was that later generations of the old Jewish families of Berlin had collections of the most beautiful 'Old Berlin', until in course of time they saw it destroyed in the new Berlin. Goethe declined the impertinent offer. The piracy continued.

In German countries this piracy had its political aspect. Every ruling prince, in line with the mercantile concepts of the day, wanted to protect his country's industry, and if the theft of intellectual property brought work to his paper mills and printing presses he encouraged it. The Emperor, on the other hand, did go so far as to grant, against a suitable fee, an Imperial Privilege which was valid for the whole Empire; but it had little effect, and, in Vienna in particular, he protected his own pirates. His Court printer, Trattner, who embellished his stolen wares with charming little rococo ornaments called *Röslein und Zieraten*, built himself a stately palace and acquired the title Edler von Trattnern out of the proceeds. One can see from this state of affairs alone the extent to which the Holy Roman Empire had become a mere fiction. Goethe found himself unable to wax enthusiastic either over the Empire or over its reforming Emperor Joseph, who decreed that books and cheese were products of equal value – from the standpoint of commercialism a perfectly logical view.

Attempts on the part of authors to publish their own works always ended in financial loss, as it did in Goethe's and Merck's venture with *Götz*. Joint undertakings of this type, such as the *Gelehrtenbuchhandlung* in Dessau, were complete failures. Subscription lists helped a little, but these entailed a lot of work and often degenerated into begging. Goethe's long silence was partly, though not wholly, due to these conditions.

Goethe was by no means without business acumen. When, shortly before his Italian journey, he received a serious offer for an authorized Collected Edition of his works, he made exacting demands: two thousand *thalers* in gold, paid in advance, the most careful printing, and full compliance with all his requirements as regards contents, arrangement and publication. The publisher was a young man in Leipzig, who had just founded a firm with the help of Schiller's very speculatively inclined friend, Körner. His name was Georg Joachim Göschen, and he was to become the first great publisher of the German classics, of Schiller, of Wieland first and foremost, of Lessing, of Klopstock; he was the only one who printed not only much but beautifully, and in the grand style, with de luxe editions for which he obtained the type from Didot, the master printer, in Paris. Goethe was his first author of note, but the partnership was of short duration; Goethe soon grew dissatisfied and Göschen saw him go without much regret. For this first authorized edition of Germany's first poet, in eight small volumes, proved a striking failure. Of hitherto unknown works it contained *Egmont*, *Iphigenie*, *Tasso*, *Faust* as a fragment, and the first collection of his poetry: but the public remained cool. In addition to the ordinary edition, Göschen hopefully announced one on Dutch paper for connoisseurs and princely patrons. Chodowiecki's copperplates – 'wretched stuff' as Göschen wrote – were replaced by better illustrations, and, as a particularly subtle stroke, he reprinted his own edition in a cheap one of four volumes so as to be able to pounce on the expected pirates. But no pirate showed his head, and this was the surest sign of the public's indifference. The cheap edition remained unsold, the ordinary one sold only slowly, and the printing of the de luxe edition never got beyond the first few volumes. In vain did Göschen split the volumes and try to dispose of single plays, with new title-pages. He continued trying until his death, but some still remained unsold. Göschen's son went to England and became a banker; the grandson became Disraeli's Chancellor of the Exchequer and Viscount Goschen. The great-grandson, Sir Edward Goschen, British Ambassador in Berlin before the first world war, was still able to buy the volumes from the original stock at a shilling each.

Still more significant is the list of subscribers, printed in the first volume; it comprises three hundred and three names, only very few of which are of any intellectual importance. Wieland is among them, one of the grand total of two from Weimar, the 'Athens on the Ilm' as it liked to think of itself. There are six names from Frankfurt, three of them booksellers, and one from Munich, a Prussian secretary of the legation; the great Leipzig book-sellers are completely absent. Whole countries and provinces in Germany are unrepresented, as are all the great Courts. To Goethe the general picture must have seemed bleak and barren, not least in his own immediate vicinity. His great solitude is beginning.

Indeed it has already begun, and Goethe must take his share of the blame for this development, which hurts him the more because he is so spoilt and pampered. On the appearance of his first works he was idolized, adored, made the object of a cult; every little skit or operetta, scribbled down over a bottle of wine, was snatched out of his hand, the very summit of achievement was prophesied for him. Now he submits these great, serious, important works, and not an echo does he hear. To his contemporaries things appear in a different light: the author of *Götz* and *Werther* has discarded his fame like a piece of tiresome clothing and plunged headlong into Court life as favourite, *Geheimrat* and minister. This is all that is known of him, except that he is said to have written masques and other entertainments for the amusement of the Court. And indeed these entertainments occupy a quite astonishing place even in this extremely serious and important collection: the slightest stuff cheek by jowl with a *Faust* or a *Tasso*. Moreover, the volumes appear only gradually, complete publication lasting from 1787 till 1790. Originally Goethe had announced, in a rather off-hand manner, that the later volumes would contain only fragments and sketches, and this frightened intending purchasers away. Only after urgent representations from his friends, from the publisher, and from his admirers in Karlsbad, did he decide to take these fragments with him to Rome where, under constant pressure, he completed them. We may safely assume that without the pressure of this fateful *Collected Edition*, Goethe's *œuvre* would have been deprived of these powerful middle period works on which, later, his fame was substantially to rest.

In abandoning works and in leaving them incomplete Goethe surpasses all other great poets. Strictly speaking not one of his works is really finished. *Werther* he intended to continue, and he appended some Swiss travel sketches as the basis for a second part, *Iphigenie* passed through various forms, *Tasso* was later transformed into an un-tragic play, *Wilhelm Meister* was never finished; one could almost complete the list. There are even total reversals of an original conception, as in the case of *Stella*, which Goethe later ended with the three-fold suicide of the chief protagonists instead of with their marriage. Above all there is the constant changing of the main characters, most typically in *Faust* where Mephistopheles becomes at times the dominant personality, with his lord and master only a rather weak companion. There is the ceaseless transformation of the characters in his plays and novels who, in the process of writing and re-writing over the years, take on more and more of the traits of his own changing opinions and feelings. Nowadays we can follow this protean game, which has an immense fascination, through the whole range of his work. His contemporaries had to content themselves with what was available, and their frequent confusion and coolness was not mere obtuseness and lack of judgment.

In addition to this there is another point of material importance: it is not only his characters that Goethe changes, but his style as well, and this not once or twice but over and over again. And there is nothing more difficult for a public than to have to re-orientate itself to a new idiom, when it has only just, and with difficulty, assimilated a previous one. Goethe was fully aware of the fact that, as an author, he would have done better to write another dozen plays in the style of *Götz* and four or five more novels like *Werther*. Instead of which he now appears in strictly classic garb, excluding every noisy word and every violent gesture, writing chamber music of the most exquisite sensibility. Scarcely is he established in the minds of his readers as the poet of *Tasso* and *Iphigenie*, however, than he shocks the more delicate of them with the naked sensuality of his neo-Roman *Elegies*. Immediately following these comes a novel of theatrical life and then, with *Hermann und Dorothea*, the story of a German couple whose conduct could not be more domesticated or more morally rewarding to the German public. It is easy for us to-day to see the significant unity in all this; in his own day it was difficult to grasp.

And so it leads to a serious break, which is to have lasting consequences. Goethe now enters a period of hatred and contempt, uttering his most bitter words against the German people. He was never greatly concerned over questions of 'taste', although good and bad taste – whatever this may imply – was the absolute and dominating criterion of the century. Now he frees himself completely from such considerations. He no longer writes for his 'dear Germans', who have become blockheads and dullards, but for himself. He pays no attention to the demands of the stage, just as in life he pays none to those of society. And here again his contemporaries had difficulty in reconciling the Goethe of *Tasso*, the author of the precept that one should enquire of noble women as to what is seemly, with Goethe the lover of the sturdy Christiane. But the impression he makes on other people is a matter of complete indifference to him. He followes his star and is convinced that his *'dunkler Drang'* – his deep, mysterious impulse – is leading him on the right path. It is not for nothing that he has chosen the morning star for his coat-of-arms.

The characters in the plays he now publishes in the Collected Edition of his works are children of fate. What do people want with fate asked Napoleon, when the two of them met later, it is an antiquated concept; 'politics is fate' he said, referring to himself. In *Egmont*, Goethe makes an attempt to write a political drama. Schiller, in a sharply critical review of the play on its publication, puts his finger squarely on the vital point; he is a political thinker and a great dramatist. Is not the intention of the play to present the portrait of a hero, he asks. In their fight for freedom the people of the Netherlands have centred their whole love on this Count Egmont; they look to him to liberate them from the Spanish yoke. But in what respect has the amiable Count earned the right to our sympathy? What are his merits? But of these we hear next to nothing; it is only his weaknesses that are paraded for us. In what way does he prove himself the nation's last support? What great deeds does he do? He is vacillating, carefree, his love for Klärchen is more important to him than the affairs of State. And when the prudent Oranien warns him, he merely feels annoyed: 'and there is still a pleasant remedy to cleanse the brooding furrows from my brow' – a visit to his mistress. We do not bestow our sympathy on such a man, says Schiller; if he cannot be bothered to show any interest in saving himself from the scaffold, the noose may as well be slipped over his head. As though out of personal enmity towards Goethe, to whom at this time he is still hostile – and a trace of this hostility remains beneath the surface even of their subsequent close friendship – he quotes *Egmont*'s words on love, with which he is overwhelmed from all directions: 'In general it is vouchsafed only to those who do not seek it. ... Had I but done something for them! They love me of their own accord.' And so it is with Goethe, in Schiller's eyes; the people love him even though he does nothing to deserve their love.  Goethe is concerned in *Egmont* with his intensely personal problems and needs. The concept of the play goes back to his *Werther* days; its prime motivation was Goethe's horror at the uncertainty of fate, at the gods' demoniac toying with men, as well as his own indecision in love and in life. The unheroic hero's wavering is Goethe's own wavering; Klärchen, faithful, constant, inviolable, is the image of his own yearning for these virtues, he in whom there is so little faithfulness. Because of this, with no recognizable model, she develops into one of his most vivid and vital characters, and even her heroics at the end cannot efface what has gone before. *'Jeder Jungling wünscht sich, so geliebt zu werden'* (Every young man wants to be loved like that), says Goethe of *Werther*, and it is equally true of *Egmont* and his Klärchen.

It is, however, a play intended for the stage and Goethe trailed it round with him for eighteen years. The love scenes, which are among his finest, he did not want to discard, nor could the role played by politics be dispensed with without jeopardizing the whole. And so, with many interruptions, he works at the parts of the Count's opponents. Increasingly they acquire traits of Goethe's own character. Oranien, with his warnings, becomes Goethe the diplomatic advisor; the cold, merciless dictator, Alba becomes the representative of rational state government, in the inevitability of which Goethe believes. These characters grow and, as a result, the hero becomes weaker until finally, as Schiller says, he almost deserves his death. Goethe is driven still further by his need for compensation, his 'conciliatoriness' as he once called it, a fatal quality in a dramatist: he has to add a human note of conciliation to the dictator Alba's *coup de main*. The gloomy Spaniard's own son fervently espouses the cause of the doomed man. With this stroke the tragedy is almost resolved in harmony. Goethe never again attempted tragedy, with the single exception of the so-called Gretchen-tragedy, which is something contained within the total framework of *Faust*.

*Tasso* too, originally conceived as a tragedy, succumbs to this urge for metamorphosis, which is deep laid in Goethe's nature and which often clashes with the most obvious artistic requirements. Conflict with the outside world, the inner conflict of genius with itself, and the danger of being destroyed by this conflict: this is the original theme and, like Egmont, its inception goes back to the days of *Sturm und Drang*. It was another member of this movement, Wilhelm Heinse, who first had the idea of treating the Tasso theme, and in so doing he provided the stimulus for Goethe. At that time the figure of the unhappy Italian was the prototype of the poet menaced by his own genius and plunged by it into misery and disaster. Since then we have become very much more accustomed to madness in literary and artistic genius, and eventually the idea gained support that without a touch of madness the ultimate achievements of genius were not to be expected. This was not how Goethe's contemporaries saw Tasso. He was a special case, a particularly unhappy one, for whom there was no parallel among the other great poets. He was regarded as fundamentally healthy; his fits of melancholy were part of the poetic image and, like Dante, he was dogged by adversity. The morbid, ailing genius had not yet become the ideal. It was not only when he grew old, but even as a young man Goethe turned his back with almost ruthless impatience on those who came to grief, who 'did not know how to take themselves in hand', as he said of the gifted baroque poet, Günther, who had seen his life as well as his poetry seeping away. Even with his 'little younger brother' Lenz he showed not the slightest forbearance. Very little was known in those days of Rousseau's persecution mania; he was only the great genius who was hounded and persecuted by others, by the Philistines.

Likewise with Tasso who, as portrayed by Heinse, is the great poet against whom everything unites to stifle his innate genius: he is in love with the Princess at the Court of Ferrara, and she refuses him; the Duke, misled by intriguers into believing him mad, whereas he is only lovesick, imprisons him; it is the seven years' incarceration that turns him mad and causes him to see phantoms. The poet, however, refutes the charge of madness in his poems and proves that 'certain feverish attacks are among the attributes of great geniuses'. He escapes and, after many wanderings, dies in Rome at the very moment when he is to be crowned on the Capitol as *poeta laureatus*, his end coming 'as gently and serenely as though, in some sweet dream, he could no longer breathe for rapture'.

Tasso's true story is different, a political element lies at its core. Tasso, brooding, constantly haunted by religious doubts, voluntarily confesses his religious scruples to the Inquisition. The Duke, fearful lest the poet betray the existence of heretical, calvanistic tendencies at Court, particularly in respect of his wife, has him confined to prison as insane. He is no mild, enlightened Prince, as Goethe portrays him, but a cold-blooded despot. The love story is legend; the air that surrounds the historical Tasso is the cool, sharp air of the counter-reformation.

The setting of Goethe's play is nowhere and never. His *Tasso* has only borrowed the name of a great poet, and is destined to trail in its wake a flood of plays written round famous artists; his Court society consists of idealized figures such as never walked in Ferrara or Weimar. Nevertheless Goethe has not spent ten years at Court in vain, and in many of the passages we can read a homage to Weimar, the finest and noblest ever paid to a Court. It is thus, perhaps, that a circle of such nobility should, or even would, appear. It is already much that the earthly figures of Weimar should have provided the incentive for such unearthly transcendence, and among these Frau von Stein and her school of good manners can claim a well-deserved place. But it is vain to seek her or any other individual among the characters. They are created out of longing: these are the people Goethe longs to have round him, noble to a man, even down to the former intriguer, each a genius in his understanding of the others and in particular of the poet, whom they all wish to help, each in his fashion, but whom it is impossible to help, if for no other reason than that he is a genius. This alone is threat and danger enough. Goethe's *Tasso* does not, like Heinse's, suffer from 'certain feverish attacks' from time to time; he is permanently, incurably, ill, with an illness for which there is no palliative. He must, inevitably, founder. By writing the play Goethe has exorcised this spectre from his own life. The lines, *'und wenn der Mensch in seiner Qual verstummt Gab ihm ein Gott zu sagen was er leidet'* (and when a man is speechless in his pain there is a God to help him tell his agony), he used often to quote as a basic experience of his life when faced by important turning points, such as the torment and confusion of his last love affair at Marienbad.

Goethe treats his theme, as always, in a highly personal way. He is not concerned in leading his public through 'fear and horror' to a catharsis, as demanded by the traditional view, attributed to antiquity. He wants to clarify his own mind and liberate himself. He is really his own audience, and it is only much later, after Goethe has become a national possession as it were, that the play begins to reach a wider audience and exercise a deeper influence.

The work, of course, has other virtues. Goethe attempts to create an ideal society, the most difficult problem a poet can set himself. His society is aristocratic, a small circle. The masses, whom he has already found suspect in *Egmont*, are deliberately excluded. His Countess Sanvitale says, when they are talking of Florence: *'Das Volk hat jene Stadt zur Stadt gemacht, Ferrara ward durch seine Fürsten gross'* (This city is the people's monument,

Ferrara's greatness is its Princes' gift). The community consists of a few noble spirits. They constitute the Fatherland; *'die Menge macht den Künstler irr und scheu'* (the masses cause the artist doubt, dismay). And yet the artist does not want to be alone. He needs friends, helpers, and everybody wants to help him. Each is right: the Duke with his wisdom as a ruler, the Princess with her reticence, the courtier Antonio with his solid masculine counsel, and even Countess Sanvitale, the most worldly of them all, who tries to lead the poet out of the magic circle of his confusion. None is successful because Goethe does not want to be liberated. He wants, in this play, to drain to the last drop the cup of *Weltschmerz*, of his world-weariness as a poet. He wants to see his Tasso perish in order to save himself, Goethe.

*Tasso* is Goethe's greatest work of art, a piece of chamber music, a quintet in which each voice is of equal importance and in which the voice progression is of the utmost sensitivity. His most marvellous achievement is to have given to each voice, in spite of muting it down to the softest pianissimo and even beyond that to the barely audible and unexpressed, so much 'body' that, in a good performance, all the voices become effective on the stage. The characters are idealized and they live. The whole imaginary and improbable society of his dreams has even become, in the course of time, a sort of Tasso community. Hugo von Hofmannsthal, in a beautiful essay, has conjured it up once more in another dream in which the characters correspond with no more reality to the Vienna of 1906 than did the originals to the Weimar of 1790. But dreams such as these are also reality.

As with almost all his works Goethe wanted to change his creation with the changing conditions of his own life. When, after twenty years, the work finally reached the stage he adapted the play for performance, cutting out the passages which show Tasso as 'overwrought, sensitive and unjustly violent', cutting out even Tasso's despair, until in the end hopes of approaching recovery replaced the threatening catastrophe of the original. One of the critics, also mollified, said of this version that Tasso now recognized the fact that mere indulging in fantasies was not enough, that if he wanted to feel happy in this world it was necessary for man to act as well. Even this, his most intimate and personal creation, Goethe cannot allow to end in tragedy – it is a play.

Like Greek tragedy the work has its aftermath of satire. The play has just been completed and sent to Göschen, with more careful and detailed corrections than are to be found in any other of his works. Immediately following this the other side of Goethe's nature comes into evidence. He writes his most pungent verses, his most uninhibited erotic poetry, some of which, to this day, remains excluded from all editions of his works. He writes his bitterest words about the German people, and even about the German language, from which he has just elicited its finest and its subtlest tones. Goethe has escaped once more, from his ethereal dream society into the world of jugglers and harlots, and he enjoys the change. He is 'audacious', as he himself calls his epigrams – and why not? His poems are only the headings, the world is writing the chapters of his book. The world comprises both purity and impurity, filth too, dark passages, low company. It is a genuine explosion, a release from the excessive tension and self-control, comparable to the coarse jokes of his *Werther* days.

Goethe published some of these poems as *Venezianische Epigramme*, dedicating them to the Dowager Duchess Amalie, who was notably liberal-minded. Although omitting the most audacious poems, the collection nevertheless contains a number of extremely unconventional things, as well as more harmless ones interspersed among them to prevent the volume as a whole from being too controversial.

He returns once more to Italy, in March 1790, on semi-official business: he is to escort Anna Amalie in Venice, at the end of her long visit to Italy. The contrast on this occasion to his rapturous first love of the country is as marked as was his reaction from the *Tasso* mood. Goethe can never repeat an experience. Everything that had enchanted him before now seems wretched. He complains about the weather and the cheating of foreigners, the ancient ruins are now only 'scattered bones', Venice is a 'hole of stones and water', he is less tolerant of the 'Swinish life of this nation than the previous time'. The truth is to be found in another passage in one of his letters: 'Not that in any sense things have gone ill for me, why should they? But the first bloom of affection and curiosity has worn off.'

He is in one of his periodic moods of anti-climax. He has been up too high and now he has to descend, and, as with everything, he does not do it by halves but completely. In one of the epigrams his sweetheart at home, with their newly born son, is referred to as a 'little pearl', which he has found on the beach. He charges those at home to take care of her, but he remains away a good six months in this strange year of 1790. A 'Klärchen' is inadequate to satisfy his needs during such a period of reaction. He requires stronger stimulants and unhesitatingly sees that he has them; moreover, he speaks and writes quite openly about it. The restraints of society, imposed on him by his association with Frau von Stein, have been broken down first by his stay in Rome and then by his relationship with Christiane. Now they are discarded completely. He feels like a Greek, pagan and free, and in the metre of antiquity he writes of his lightest and freest experiences and presents the verses to his Duchess. So great has his prestige become that even this is permitted him, and perhaps even savoured; the aristocratic society of the rococo era, to which Anna Amalie belonged, was free from prejudice.

The name *Epigrams*, which Goethe chooses for his little collection of poetry, is an arbitrary one. The collection does contain a number of sharply pointed, dialectically treated, satiric verses, but he was not suited to this kind of writing; the verses are weak or else merely ill-tempered. He airs his anger at the French Revolution, which had just begun, and at the princes who, in his opinion, are no better than the demagogues. The 'Franks' annoy him; the Germans no less, and their language is a clumsy vehicle in which he has the misfortune to have to travel.

It is only when he writes epigrams that are not epigrams at all, but elegies in the style of his *Römische Elegieen*, that he once more becomes the poet. Venice, for him, is not all ill-humour and discontent, 'I have not found Faustina again', he says, but there is a Bettina to take her place, a girl from a troupe of jugglers, light, nimble, boyish. He amuses himself with all 'twelve categories of *amor*', and not merely with one partner. The great days of the Venetian courtesans are long past, as, indeed, are the great days of Venice itself. Apart from this, however, a visit to one of these grand and expensive ladies, who observed a strict code of etiquette, would generally have been a very solemn and boring affair, an essential educational feature of the Grand Tour, like the museum visits of later times; and the difference between the two was not great. Goethe is in a lazy mood. *Lacerten* is his name for the girls who scuttle across the squares like lizards, disappearing into some corner; he saunters after one of them down dark alley-ways into a den or coffee-house, 'and it is she who is the active one, not you'. He toys with homosexual feelings, and sees the boyish Bettina as a Ganymede watched by himself as Jupiter; he also remarks that attraction for boys was not unknown to him and that it was, in any case, as old as the human race. Everything in these weeks in Venice, in this old city that is nearing its end, has an aura of twilight; at the age of barely 40 Goethe is old, and in his pleasures youthful, high-spirited debauchery finds no place. It is almost as though he feels the need to exhaust the whole catalogue of knowledge before it is too late.

He feels old, too, in relation to the younger generation of writers now in vogue. Schiller, in *Die Räuber*, he finds particularly unsympathetic for his revival of *Sturm und Drang*, and with a power it never knew before. Goethe has outgrown it and has no desire to see it in others. Heinse, the companion of his younger days and now the same age as himself, has just published *Ardinghello*, a passionate novel of genuine and violent talent, which has been enthusiastically acclaimed. This is how people imagined Goethe would have described Italy, the Goethe they remembered from his early works. But Goethe saw Rome in a totally different light from Heinse's neo-Renaissance, and consequently he finds the book odious, an offence against good taste. He severely censures Heinse's 'sensuality', and it is a paradox that Goethe, who has just celebrated love in all its nakedness, down to the happy rhythmic creaking of the bed, should be outraged by Heinse's much more harmless bacchanals. He sees in this highly gifted man a rival, almost a rival in love: his descriptions are grotesque caricatures; this is not how to make love, above all not to art, it is more like a rape of the sanctity of art. The climax of the novel is a bacchanal held by the German artists in Rome, an orgy at which Goethe's fellow lodgers, Tischbein, Schütz and the rest – called by the painter Möller 'love-lorn starvelings' – would certainly not have felt at home: garlanded with ivy, the artists dance and revel with their girls and models, who finally throw off their scanty clothing and continue the revelry naked; 'reaching deeper and deeper into life, the feast became holier ...'. Goethe likes to celebrate his love feasts alone. What disturbs him in Heinse is the same thing that later disturbs Schiller in Goethe: the over-physical sense of touch that permeates everything, especially the frequent descriptions of works of art. Heinse's feeling for painting was very much stronger and more direct than Goethe's, and his aesthetic ideas enjoyed a wider and more lasting influence, one that extended into the Romantic era and even into the *Junge Deutschland* movement of the next century. He also had a very much stronger feeling for Italian music than Goethe; it formed the subject of another of his novels. Baroque and Romantic elements are combined in him; but Goethe has just arrived at the period of his Classicism, which makes everything in Heinse antipathetic to him.

It is the very things in Heinse that come so near to his own qualities and inclinations that irritate him; it is like seeing his own portrait in a distorting mirror. In fact Heinse's sensuality is a whole remove away from that of Goethe: there is a luxuriance about it, a restless flickering rather than a true fire, and it is never based on the solid rock of a mighty personality that embraces the erotic as an essential, though not the only, element of its whole nature. Heinse is very daring in the manner of what was then considered to be the Renaissance, in his heroes and heroines who rage like Nietzsche's 'blond beast', and yet he always remains, to some extent, the poor pastor's son from Thuringia, the poor tutor and companion – the fate of all the talents of his day – and at the end of his life he has to knuckle under as reader to an enlightened Roman Catholic archbishop, who enjoys his Boccaccio and his Aretino, as well as the conversation of a highly cultivated man.

We should not assume, however, that the success won by his contemporaries leaves Goethe indifferent. The days of his Olympian detachment are still far off. He is never jealous in the ordinary sense, but he is very sensitive. He expects everyone, always, to participate in his transformations, and he feels threatened in his very existence when the others go their different ways.

So sensitive is he in these years following his return from Italy that he seriously thinks of throwing 'all that' up – meaning poetry, writing, authorship. There is no similar example of a great artist repeatedly regarding his most particular vocation with such indifference, as though it were a matter of a 'whim', which he has followed for some time with considerable success, and which he can now relinquish. That his fame as a poet can involve any obligation on his part, or that the ideals he has just proclaimed in *Iphigenie* and *Tasso* might be worth fighting for, are ideas that never occur to him for an instant. These works, scarcely out of the womb, are already total strangers to him. He casts them out like foundlings; it is up to them to see if they can survive. He is almost surprised when they do survive and grow up.

Another 'whim' – *eine Grille* is his expression and he uses it over and over again – now has him in its grip; it might even be called an illness. He constantly makes use of the simile of 'being inoculated'. In those days inoculation was still a dangerous, brutal business, and not the universally accepted custom of to-day. It was a risk and involved surrendering oneself to fate, and it was thus that Goethe understood it. A germ has been planted in him. It grows and proliferates. It produces a fever, not just for a short while but recurrently, a lasting illness that torments him for decades. This is his own interpretation. He also finds expressions of purest bliss for this condition.

Hitherto observation of nature has been a pleasure, the landscape a stage for his sufferings and joys, nature a maiden. Now he starts to search, to think; he speaks of 'mother nature'. He believes he has discovered nature's eternal laws, which he is to announce. In this urge to announce, to preach, is to be found the religious element in his new passion. He has found a new faith for himself and seeks disciples for it. Only a few, very few, join him and so begins a long period of alienation from mankind. His discovery of the little bone he has kept to himself, revealing the secret only to a chosen few. Now he starts to publish his discoveries. In small, thin pamphlets he submits his results, or rather his first thoughts. These pamphlets, too, belong to Goethe's *Collected Works*. They did not find many readers during his lifetime and still fewer in the century that saw the great flowering of the exact sciences. They were then re-discovered, and subjected to all the usual misunderstandings surrounding such a renaissance. Attempts were made to fit his interpretation of nature and its phenomena into the main stream of scientific development, to demonstrate that Goethe had already foreseen this or that important development, or even that, in his universality he had known, divined or indicated the whole field of natural science. It is true that some of his ideas have had a wide and productive influence. But he is not a scientist, he is an artist.

# 27

# *Interpretation of Nature*

During his weeks in Venice in 1790 Goethe, in the company of his young servant Paul Götze, makes an excursion by gondola out to the Lido, where, in unconsecrated ground among the dunes, the rather neglected Jewish cemetery is situated. Wandering about, Götze finds a broken, weather-beaten skull, which he shows to the *Geheimrat*. Goethe takes it carefully in his hands and announces that it is not the skull of a human being but of a sheep. He knocks the earth out and, turning it this way and that, looks again and again into the cavity. His eyes sparkle and he radiates happiness, as though he had made some momentous discovery; it is a long time since Götze has seen his master like this.

In this Italian light – it is not without significance that he is surrounded by the brightness of the southern sun – Goethe has had his second vision, his second confirmation of an earlier presentiment. Three years previously and at almost the same time of year, in the spring, he had seen the primal plant, the *'Ur-Pflanze'*, in the botanical garden at Palermo. Now, in the Jewish cemetery, he sees the primal form of bone structure. As he has long suspected the vegetable and animal kingdoms follow the same structural plan. In the plant everything develops from the original primal unit, the leaf; in the animal organism the primal unit is the vertebra. Just as at Palermo he had seen the primal plant growing and developing before his eyes – sprouting, subdividing and branching – so now he sees the vertebrae developing and branching into the several parts of the broken sheep's skull, whose sutures fate has so skilfully revealed to him through the process of weathering. The transition from bone to bone and the resulting formation of the whole skull is incontestible. This is metamorphosis indeed, the trans-formation of the hitherto merely suspected primal principle into the com-pletely formed phenomenon of nature. *Natura non fecit saltus*; gently and consequently one thing merges into the next, rising stage by stage up to the ultimate stage of man, up to himself, Goethe, who at this moment is seeing all this for the very first time on this strange earth.

It is a question of seeing and holding these things in one's hand, out of doors and not in the study. Then, if one looks and feels properly, one may receive divine inspiration, which is like a *coup-de-foudre* in a love relationship. With his intensely personal use of language he calls this kind of brain flash an *aperçu*, for Goethe – and this has increased the problem of reconciling his ideas with science and even of understanding them at all – creates his own terminology. The expression 'metamorphosis' had, indeed, long been current quite apart from Ovid who, in his youth, had once been Goethe's favourite poet, until Herder dismissed him as a Roman imitator of the much more original Greeks and drew the young man's attention to *Ur*, or primeval, poetry. Voltaire, in his philosophical dictionary, had remarked caustically that the world was full of metamorphoses. Linné, of whom Goethe was a keen student, had expressed ideas which, in their wording, were almost identical with Goethe's own concepts of metamorphosis, though the poet regarded the great Swedish botanist merely as a forerunner whose ideas he had to develop further. He had the very highest regard for Linné, whom he grouped with Shakespeare and Spinoza as one of the three great masters to whom he was most indebted, adding 'except in botany', but without indicating where his indebtedness lay. Elsewhere he says 'dividing up and calculating was not my way of doing things', and 'what he tried to hold apart by force had, according to the innermost necessity of my being, to strive towards unification'. This, of course, is only Goethe's interpretation of Linné whom he regarded as having the characteristics of other naturalists and scientists: they were all men dedicated to division and separation, whereas he saw the whole. This whole was the unity of nature, to which he applied the religious term *Gott-Natur*.

In Spinoza he had found phrases that strengthened him in this belief, a belief which, though unformulated, had been active in him almost since childhood. We use the word phrases because Goethe had read Spinoza only in short sections; the philosopher's system as a whole, *more geometrico* demonstrated, was unsympathetic to him, and it is very doubtful whether he had ever read it in its entirety. In the first instance he did not read Spinoza in the original at all, but in the fairly extensive article on the philosopher in Pierre Bayle's *Dictionnaire*, the leading work of the early days of enlightenment. In the course of the century the influence of Spinoza had grown, as the momentum of 'heresy' and free-thinking gathered force. Goethe had questioned the traditional concept of God at an early age; in *Dichtung und Wahrheit* he describes, in poetic language, how as a boy he built his own altar to nature out of his father's natural history collection, surmounting it with a candle, which he lit when making his devotions. Spinoza, with whom he became more familiar through Herder, later confirmed him in these feelings. *Deus sive natura* was the phrase in Spinoza which provided this confirmation, and this was really all he needed.

He expresses this *Gott-Natur* poetically in verse and prose, as well as in conversation. A young Swiss visitor to Weimar, Tobler, noted down a fragment of such conversation – 'On nature' – in which the thought is expressed in rhythmic prose of strong contrasts, almost like an antiphonal psalm.

When this came to light again and was shown to Goethe in his old age he recognized it only in part; he felt that in the intervening years he had outgrown such things. He called it a stage, a 'comparative' that had since developed into a 'superlative': in it 'one sees the tendency to a form of pantheism in which an inscrutable, unconditional, humorous, self-contradictory being is conceived as the basis of phenomena, and which may well pass for a game, a game played in deadly earnest'. The strange, and again completely personal, use Goethe here makes of the word 'humorous' also serves to indicate his way of thinking.

His difficulties begin, not in the realm of poetry and hymn where he moves effortlessly and with the greatest boldness, but as soon as he tries to communicate his visions and revelations in realms in which certain conventions of expression already exist. Everything he sees seems simple to him and, at the same time, not new: 'However much I find that is new, I find nothing that is unexpected, everything fits and agrees because I have no system and seek nothing but truth for its own sake', he remarks on making his first botanical observations. 'Everything is so clear, I do not reflect on it, it all comes to me, and the vast kingdom [of the whole of nature] becomes simplified within me so that in a short time I can read off the answers to the most difficult problems.' Neither scruples nor doubts exist for him; the fundamental laws of creation can be reduced to a few easily grasped basic ideas, and these constitute 'truth'. He has seen it, it has been revealed to him.

It is over the communication of his ideas – and he is anxious to spread his gospel – that he finds himself up against the barrier of clumsy words and expressions, just as in government he was confronted by the inertia of the people. The real answer, as he wrote later, would have been to invent a new language in which the ideas could have been expressed unmistakably; this is a problem which, on a mathematical basis, has since occupied people's attention right up to the experiments of modern logistics. But mathematic, like philosophic, thinking is a closed book to Goethe. Of his discussions with Herder he complains: 'I was more interested in the sensuous observation of nature than Herder, who was always eager to reach his conclusion and had grasped the idea almost before I had started my observations.' Schiller irritates him at their first serious meeting, when Goethe explains his primal plant as an 'experience' and even tries to make a sketch of it; 'that is not an experience, it is an idea', comments Schiller, shaking his head. Goethe, as he tells us, controls himself with difficulty as he replies: 'It is very nice to know that I can have ideas without knowing it, and can even see them with my eyes.' The dividing line between them, says Goethe, was thus very sharply defined. It is also the dividing line between Goethe's viewpoint and that of everyone else.

What he, in good faith, calls 'seeing' is really the vision of his imagination. Science is concerned with what is universally binding, although this does not preclude the scientist from having similar experiences and using them as his starting point. But he must then demonstrate his thesis and submit his proof to the scrutiny of his peers of the republic of the mind. Goethe's *Gott-Natur*, however, is a faith, which is to be submitted to no further scrutiny. For him it is the truth, once and for all. All that is left is to discover, in individual phenomena of nature, especially clear pieces of evidence in its support, in the same way as every faith requires its witnesses. We shall see later how, in the course of time, his faith takes on a theological form, and how in the end Goethe, with no compunction at all, makes use of the old ecclesiastical terminology; one pupil, who deviates from his gospel, he calls a 'heretic' and angrily shows him the door.

At first he is gentler and very polite. He still believes he can insinuate himself into the general path of scientific progress. He publishes his *Versuch die Metamorphose der Pflanzen zu erklären*, his enquiry into the metamorphosis of plants, as a slim pamphlet. Even its title is modest. In the text he calls the booklet a 'discourse', hinting at future publications and mentioning the names of contemporary naturalists; in sober language, and in one hundred and twenty-three short sections, he sets out what he has to say. It is his finest work on natural history and it exerted a wide influence on future thinking, although not immediately.

The leaf, this is his hypothesis, is the fundamental organ of the plant, from which all others, up to the stamen, develop in advancing protean transformations. 'Everything is leaf. And this simplicity makes possible the utmost variety.' Such an hypothesis is open to argument. But to Goethe, the moment he states it it becomes an 'experience', part of his life, the more so in that it accords so wonderfully with the essential viewpoint of his nature. Consequently every doubt, or even coolness, regarding this thesis is like an attack on himself, a threat to his very existence.

> Every living thing is not a single unit but a plurality: even in so far as it seems to be an individual, it nevertheless remains an association of living, independent entities, which are similar in idea and plan, but which, in appearance, may be like and similar or unlike and dissimilar.... They separate and seek each other again, and thus effect an endless productivity in every way and in every direction.

Union and fusion is his aim. Now he wants everyone else to share his way of thinking.

In an article on how he came to make his discovery he speaks of how 'in a childlike way I grasped the concept of the metamorphosis of plants and mused on it lovingly, with joy and delight, in Naples and Sicily'. With naïve confidence he submits his pamphlet to Herder and other friends, and sends it to scientists and to the learned journals. The public is taken aback by this new transformation of the author; it wants, as Goethe says, 'to be served well and uniformly', and it cannot raise much enthusiasm for problems of botanical development, nodulation or anastomosis. One journal, the *Göttinger Nachrichten*, does indeed acknowledge the 'outstanding clarity' of his pamphlet, but Goethe wants more than this; the support seems to him half-hearted whereas what he looks for is active help, enthusiastic agreement. His painter friend, Tischbein, in Rome, who believes that Goethe wants to teach painters how to create more and more beautiful and delicate flower forms from the simplest beginnings, is the only one to write to him in this strain. Goethe is intensely pleased by this because, throughout his work on natural history, his mind is always on its practical application; nothing would have given him so much pleasure later as to learn that painters were painting according to the doctrine of his *Farbenlehre*. The ladies of Weimar are 'far from satisfied with my abstract gardening', he says; what they want to hear about is the fragrance and colour of flowers, not phantom shadows. Goethe clothes his ideas in hexameters and dedicates the work to his Christiane, and this again causes astonishment in the Weimar circle: the flower girl and this philosophy of nature!

In his disappointment Goethe resorts to the strongest expressions; he speaks of 'radical evil in its ugliest form', of the envy and antagonism to which he is subjected. This reaction has a lasting effect on his attitude to his work on natural science. His work on the metamorphosis of plants is abandoned immediately, the sequels he announced are not written, and the whole subject is put aside for many years, to be taken up again only at a very late period in his life. He treats all his publications on natural science in the same way, with the exception of his *Farbenlehre*, to which he stubbornly devotes several years. This one work apart he publishes a fragment only at long intervals and would have preferred to confine himself to aphorisms.

As 'fragments of a great confession' is the way in which he wishes his complete *œuvre* to be understood; it is a claim to which recognition could be given only after the completion of his whole life and work. Even to-day when we have all these essays in front of us, collected, sorted and arranged, it is difficult to find our way through their many oddities to his main ideas and so to be able to assess their value. It is even more difficult to believe in the threats of 'despair', 'rage' and 'ruination' of which he complains. We can believe in his jubilation, however, and in his frequent fits of depression, which are often nothing but reaction following the tension of great happiness or great creative achievement. His bitter laments about lack of recognition and co-operation, again, we cannot accept; they are due, to a large extent, to the fact that he withdrew into himself, was 'thrown back on himself' as he expressed it, at the least sign of opposition, refused to listen to criticism of any kind, or to agree to any suggestions however well intentioned. For Goethe is wholly incapable of scientific collaboration, of team work. His assistants must be mere hewers of wood and carriers of water, unconditional yes-men, and even these have no easy time, as we shall see later. Doubts and scruples, which are among the scientist's sharpest and most essential weapons, he does not know; this is his weakness and his strength.

Without so much as a glance over his shoulder, he goes straight from plants to animals. He wants to write a 'metamorphosis of animal development'. As so often happens many distractions intervene; it is only thirty years later, and after much urging and encouragement on the part of friends and those who are interested, that he publishes his findings on the subject.

In the casualness of his procedure Goethe is the complete dilettante; he enjoys, in the true meaning of the word, the material and the problems while he is working on them, and so long as he is in the right mood, but lays them aside when something else engages his attention. The label of dilettante is one he by no means despises, and he undertakes a survey of other dilettanti, to demonstrate how often they have furthered and enriched science and technical development. His list makes strange reading. He cites medical men who have been interested in architecture, business men who are passionate readers of fiction, serious fathers of families who prefer a farce to any other entertainment, pointing the moral that human life consists of work and play; only the man who holds a balance between the two can be called wise and happy, and this further emphasizes the polar contrasts of work and play in his own nature.

He could have given far more impressive examples. His day was still an era of free movement between the various branches of knowledge, of easy transfer from one science to another, and of highly important discoveries by non-professionals in the field of scientific progress. There was Joseph Priestley, the nonconformist preacher, who in his tiny private laboratory discovered oxygen and ammonia, and was one of Lavoisier's most important forerunners; his book on the history of optics was later one of Goethe's main sources. There was Rousseau with his work on botany, and John Dolland, the London optician, who invented the achromatic telescope. Sir William Herschel, an organist by profession, became one of the great astronomers of the day, and Benjamin Franklin, a printer, discovered the lightning conductor. The Montgolfier brothers, who were paper manufacturers, made the first balloon ascent, while Count Rumfort, the politician and social reformer, with some of whose optical aphorisms Goethe found himself in heated opposition, made significant contributions to the theory of heat. In addition to these discoveries there is a mass of dilettantism as well as a large body of popular literature. This last includes writings by the leading authors of the age, such as that by Voltaire on Newton, as well as alchemistic tracts in the most ancient cabbalistic style and multi-volume compilations on 'natural magic', in which the latest discoveries in galvanism are mixed up with recipes for preparing secret inks and producing gold from lead.

This is the world in which Goethe lives. Many traces of the old school of alchemists, whom he had studied so eagerly with Fräulein von Klettenberg, remain unconsciously active in him throughout his life. The urge to discover, which he sees at work all round him, is infectious, and he sees no reason why, with his 'good brain', he too should not make one of the great discoveries of the century. He is on the track of one. The world of colour has never yet been adequately described or understood; he is about to reveal it.

Chance plays its part. In the course of his various experiments Goethe has borrowed some prisms from one of the Jena professors and put them away in a drawer. Growing impatient, the professor sends a servant to recover his property and Goethe hands over the prisms unquestioningly. At the very last moment, on the doorstep itself, he takes one of them in his hand. He has a vague childhood recollection that by looking through it one can see the prettiest and most varied play of colours, and he remembers reading somewhere that Newton claimed that, by means of a prism, it was possible to divide light into individual colours. He turns the prism in the direction of the wall, which has been newly whitewashed, and lo and behold there is no play of colours; against the whiteness of the wall he sees only white. Like a flash the thing is clear. Newton's theory is wrong; light cannot be divided up and separated, it is one and indivisible, 'the simplest, most elementary, most homogeneous existence we know. It is not composed. Least of all of coloured lights.' This is what he writes shortly afterwards, in terse statements, at the head of his 'experiences'. At the moment he is in the grip of a still stronger emotion, the thought that he has made a fundamental discovery: the scientific dividers and separators, long odious and suspect to him, are wrong. Newton, for a century the leading authority, observed and concluded falsely. When, on a cardinal point such as this, one can demonstrate that the whole world of academic scholarship is thinking wrongly and seeing wrongly, one has achieved a Copernican feat; like Columbus one has discovered a new land. And it is with Columbus that he later compares himself.

From this doorstep experience begins his decades' long, and increasingly bitter, fight against Newton, against the establishment, against the priests of science. This 'discovery', and not the many and often valuable observations he makes in the course of his investigations, is his 'find'. It is this exposure of a century-long error that is his mission. His whole subsequent work, resulting in the two volumes of the *Farbenlehre*, serves this end; the polemical section is only a part of it and could really be left out, as Goethe says, because the whole work is one long polemic.

There is no longer any question of returning the prisms, and he sends the servant back with a friendly apology. 'A decisive *aperçu* is like an illness with which one has been inoculated: one is not free of it until one has fought one's way through it.' The fight begins with his very first conversation with a professional, a physicist, who cautiously points out to the *Herr Geheimrat* that Newton did not in the least maintain that, looking through a prism against a white wall, one would be able to observe the division of light into separate colours. On the contrary, he had postulated quite definite conditions for his experiment: the light had to pass through a very fine aperture, the prisms had to be placed in a certain way, and a whole series of strictly formulated precautions had to be observed. Goethe grimly enumerates these conditions under eleven headings and remarks naïvely: one only has to alter these conditions, and make the aperture large, 'and the beloved spectrum cannot and will not appear!' He dismisses the whole thing as 'hocus-pocus'. The very simple and fundamental requisite for a scientific experiment, that it must be subjected to certain clearly defined conditions which cannot be arbitrarily varied, he sees merely as a convention of the scientists' guild, and with that he refuses to have anything whatever to do.

Goethe creates his own poetic and picturesque language for his fight against Newton's hated spectrum. Reverting to the original Latin meaning of the word he calls it the 'spectre', the spectre in its dark cavern, whereas he stands in the open and sees the sun and the light, in its unity and allness, with his open eyes. According to Newton the sacred light is to be 'tortured' through a tiny hole and then untwined. Nature is to be 'put on the rack' until it confesses its secrets. The priests of this nonsense-faith communicate their mysteries in secret and abstruse signs like Egyptian hieroglyphs. One copies the other, repeating parrot-like the old formula, and everyone who is not a member of their guild is rejected, nay persecuted. In one of his epigrams he claims that they would like to burn him 'at the stake like Jan Hus'.

But Goethe does not stand in the open and look at the sun. He imprisons himself in the cavern with the spectre. He wants to 'set free the seven-coloured princess', as he puts it. He manipulates the spiteful little pieces of cut glass, and also constructs to his own design a large garden prism out of panes of window glass, mounted on a wooden frame and filled with water, to enable him to get out into the open. He draws, paints, and cuts plates out of cardboard, onto which he sticks his patterns. And at once, before delving more deeply into the matter, he starts publishing his experiences. He is in an indescribable hurry: his impatience knows no bounds.

He makes a few more half-hearted attempts to get advice from professionals, but all he really wants is confirmation. He writes to Johann Christoph Lichtenberg, who holds the chair of natural science at Göttingen, and is one of the finest minds of the day. Lichtenberg answers in a long, very respectful and detailed letter. He finds Goethe's essay excellent, the experiments striking, the whole thing a splendid beginning. Of 'rejection', as Goethe later described it, there is not a trace; Lichtenberg merely draws attention to some of his own observations and to further literature on the subject which he thinks might be useful.

Goethe has the books, he assures Lichtenberg, he has either read them or is going to read them. They are 'nothing in particular'. Moreover, and this is the critical sentence in Goethe's reply, 'however ready we may be to listen to doubt and disagreement, our nature is much too prone eagerly to seize on what is in agreement with our own way of conceiving things.' Lichtenberg soon abandons the attempt to enlighten the difficult *Herr Geheimrat*, or to collaborate, as he had offered to do in the first place. Goethe in turn drops the stubborn expert. Later he remarks, in angry scorn, that in his new edition of Erxleben's standard manual on physics Lichtenberg did not even mention him. To be left out of Erxleben caused him more distress than did neglect of any of his literary works.

Undeterred he puts out his pamphlets, planning a whole series of them. Only two appear, however, under the title *Beiträge zur Optik*. As he says in the announcement he is not writing only for experts. He hopes the fair sex, 'which has such a keen eye for colour relationships', will be interested, as well as artists, teachers, for whom he is providing a pleasant means of instruction, and amateurs of physics; at the end of his list he mentions the professionals. He strides vigorously on, convinced that people have only to follow him to reap undreamed-of knowledge.

The style is quite different from that of his metamorphosis of plants. He writes with a poetic verve that sometimes sounds as though he were telling fairy tales. Italy, with the harmony of its pure deep blue sky, is a fairy tale; regretfully he says he must leave the lovely picture of this southern landscape and take a calmer view. Calm, however, he is not; hidden anger is stirring within him. He is dealing with an abstract theory and the experiments are difficult. He has been told that it is impossible to understand and solve optical problems without a knowledge of mathematics. To this view he opposes his 'pure experiences'; the word 'pure' recurs again and again, in the sense that theologians speak of their own doctrine as pure while all others are impure. He says he has made up his mind to deal with light and colours 'free from any other consideration', which means without regard to the formalities of mathematics. In optics one doctrine has held stubborn sway for a century without ever being put to the test; he is now going to test it. This doctrine stands in his way like a 'fortress', a 'Bastille'. His first pamphlet appears in the year of the French Revolution and Goethe, who in other respects hates it, draws attention to the fact that they are living in an age 'when obsolete age-old rights are subjected to doubt and attack'. He is going to take this fortress by storm, this den of rats and owls, and free the prisoners. Newton, though already his arch enemy, he still refers to with caution as a 'thoughtful man'; before long he is referring to him as 'Bal Isaak' and calling him a conscious fraud. He speaks of the 'delicate empiricism' with which it is necessary to proceed, of his 'intimate contact' with phenomena. His attitude is determined by the polar opposites of love and hate, and the principle of polarity becomes the dominant factor in his interpretation of the world.

In order to understand the difficult problems with which he is going to deal the reader must provide himself with instruments; prisms are necessary, and tables of illustrations which Goethe intends to supply with the pamphlets. In a local playing-card factory he has cards made for these and packed in small cases. The booksellers, unfortunately, do not like such supplements and the cases of cards get lost or are simply not sent off. Goethe further requires a huge folio plate mounted on stout cardboard; as this can be neither folded nor rolled it too is almost never included and is put away in some drawer or other and disappears. Before long, in one of the countless paradoxes of his life, Goethe himself no longer possesses one; only in very recent years has a single copy come to light. The prism that Goethe asks the reader to buy he hopes also to include with subsequent issues. Thus armed the reader needs only to compare the little playing cards and the large plate with the text and carry out the prescribed experiments with the prism. Goethe visualizes earnest groups of people doing this; these are his public. He has already severed himself completely from the earth and its troublesome obstacles. For the outside of the little card case he has designed a woodcut; like some masonic symbol it shows a solitary and gigantic eye, probably his own. Beneath lowering eyebrows, and surrounded by a rainbow, it looks out on the world like that of some father god. Victorious sunbeams spread in every direction, dispelling the darkness; on the ground, discarded, lie the prism and mirror of the Newtonians who, with these artificial means, imagine they can grasp the mysteries of light. Goethe looks over and beyond all this; with his naked eye he sees light – eternal, pure and indivisible.

'Light and darkness wage constant war with one another', he writes, dividing everything, like a father god, into black and white. What lies between these two extremes he calls, again using a term coined by himself, *das Trübe*; this is a term that even in German, at least so far as physics is concerned, has no equivalent in normal usage and signifies that which is turbid, cloudy, semi-opaque, obscure. It has theological overtones and is intimately connected in his mind with his general approach to life: 'Human beings should be regarded as *trübe*', he notes; or 'Love and hate, hope and fear are only different states of our *trübe* innermost being.' Among the pietists the '*trübe Jammertal der Erde*' (earth's dark vale of tears) was a common expression and almost equivalent to the Slough of Despond. 'If we look out through this *trübe* organic world around us towards the light, we feel love and hope; if we look towards the darkness, we feel hate and fear. Both sides have their charm and attraction, for some, indeed, the sad more than the cheerful.' Both were present in him, and the dark side was often stronger than the bright. His interpretations of nature can always only be understood in the light of his fundamental outlook and philosophy of life.

The scientific value of his pamphlets cannot be examined here, because this would involve scientific discussion, and would, moreover, have to be assessed in relation to the physics and optics of his day. But Goethe's *Farbenlehre* stands outside the main stream of scientific development. It is no mere theory of colour, but a Goethe doctrine, a faith; it is autochthonous and autocratically conceived, created by himself for himself. One can accept it as a follower and disciple, or else one can attempt to understand it biographically as an important side of his nature.

The polarity of his nature is revealed here more clearly than ever, and with it the innumerable contradictions, which he does not see as such at all. For years on end he is engaged in the use of a delicately cut scientific instrument, the prism. Simultaneously he declares solemnly that the greatest calamity of modern physics is that 'it attempts to understand nature solely through the evidence of artificial instruments'. He is oblivious of the fact that in the last resort instruments also serve the human spirit to explore nature better and more deeply; yet he himself makes the freest use of them, using the microscope when he is interested in the micro-life of *infusoria*, the barometer as a daily and indispensable instrument for observing the weather, or electrical apparatus when electrical phenomena claim his attention. Astronomy, on the other hand, for which complicated equipment and his hated mathematical calculations cannot very well be dispensed with, he leaves alone. He maintains that man is the most sensitive and perfect instrument. Although he sometimes uses a lorgnette, he hates glasses, and a visitor wearing them has little hope of being received. Contradictions of this kind can be multiplied indefinitely. He possesses a complete physical laboratory containing some of the most up-to-date apparatus available; the finest piece, the latest development in polarization equipment presented to him by admirers in Munich, who had heard he was interested in this problem, he puts quietly away, unused, in his collection.

With all his talk of 'wholeness' he nevertheless leaves untouched whole sections of the problems on which he is working. In his research on plants he refuses to look at anything below the surface of the ground. Roots, which do not fit easily into his explanation of the leaf as the primal form of plant life, he dislikes intensely and tries to relegate to the realm of shadows: 'They did not really concern me at all, for what interest have I in a formation that can manifest itself only in fibres, cords, bulbs and tubers, and even thus limited only in some displeasing change.' One can see his disgusted expression at having to describe such mis-shapen objects. In physics he reads and hears about rays, and thunders: 'We hear now of experiments with refracted and reflected rays, with deflected, dispersed and decomposed rays, and as a final achievement they claim to have observed invisible rays!' One can feel a physical revulsion in the very words to such things as refraction and decomposition. As for invisible rays, they are entirely a professional conjuring trick by the 'guild'. The ultra-violet rays are discovered on his own doorstep, in Jena, by the extremely gifted private scholar Ritter, with whom, over a short period, he has some talks and whom he describes as a 'veritable galaxy of knowledge'; a year previously the infra-red rays had been discovered in London by Herschel. Herschel used a thermometer to measure the heat reaction, Ritter employed a photo-chemical means of verification; both extended the range of the spectrum beyond the vision of the human eye. But Goethe wants nothing to do with the spectrum, with the 'spectre'; everything connected with it is suspect and odious.

Nevertheless all this is forced on his attention and he has to contend with it; and in contrast to his attitude in other fields he sticks at this problem with quite unusual tenacity. He might have voiced his vision of the sun and indivisible light in great hymns, or in a didactic poem on the model of Lucretius, and he did in fact think of doing so. He might have written of colour as applied to art, which is what he had originally intended in Italy. All this fades away, however; a new experience has entered his life: he has made a discovery. It is contested and he has to fight for it.

> The thinker's sole possession are the ideas which spring from within himself; and just as every *aperçu* that is ours spreads a special feeling of well-being in our nature, there is a natural wish for others to recognize it as ours, since only in this way can we seem to be anything. It is for this reason that controversies over the priority of a discovery are so animated; strictly speaking they are controversies over existence itself!

These words were spoken of Newton, but they apply much more aptly to Goethe himself. He fights for his existence as a thinker. He invents a mythical enemy with whom he has to struggle. Often using lawyer's methods he conducts his 'case of Goethe versus the spectrum', as it has been called. Later we shall see the result of the case.

At first everything seems to him excessively simple. He has separated light and darkness and placed *das Trübe* between them. He nominates two colours, blue and yellow, as the only two which 'give a completely pure concept'; combined they produce green. Blue and yellow are his *Werther* colours.

The problems in which Goethe has involved himself, however, are by no means so simple. The word colour has to suffice for three different phenomena: pigment such as is used in paints and dyes, colour sensation which comes within the province of physiology and psychology, and the physical colours that appear in the spectrum as coloured light. The spectrum with its diffraction of light in the dark-room, as described by Newton, is for Goethe the great error, the deception, the lie, which has to be exposed once and for all. Whether he likes it or not, however, he is forced to concern himself with the spiteful little prism, which, like a story-teller, he presents in his pamphlet as something held in great esteem in the East, adding that in China its ownership is the Emperor's prerogative. Now he finds himself in the world of angles and triangles, and his attention is drawn to the fact that mathematics is indispensable to optical research. This he denies at once: mathematics has no place in physics and optics. We observe, we look through the little piece of glass, and this is sufficient. This is 'pure experience'; figures – he always refers to mathematics as *die Rechenkunst* – only get in our way.

The physiological aspect of colour sensation, in which, as his work progresses, he is to make his most valuable observations, is of less importance to him at first. Only after his contact with the anatomist Sömmering, who gives a warm welcome to Goethe's experiments, does this field begin seriously to interest him. Before long he is writing to tell Sömmering that he has penetrated so far into the world of colours 'that I can almost no longer see the place from where I started. I experiment ceaselessly.' Once everything has been reduced to its simplest form, a successful assault on Newton's theory will be possible, 'and then you will marvel and rejoice to see how it vanishes into thin air ... as it is it is only maintained by tricks...'.

Goethe reads everything he can find on the subject: the oldest books in Greek and Latin, the huge compilation on 'the great art of light and shadow' by the learned Jesuit Kircher, who, in Rome in the seventeenth century, had amassed a vast collection of material in every branch of knowledge and created a veritable factory of encyclopaedias, with volumes on volcanoes, music, and China. It seems to have been from Kircher that Goethe took his obscure term *das Trübe*. He reads the latest physics journals and the revolutionary Marat's book on colour; this last he takes up at the time of Marat's murder in Paris, an event that does not engage his attention for a moment – he is only interested in whether Marat is a victim of the Newtonian error. There is another Bastille to be stormed. Goethe buries himself in his dark-room, goes into the garden with his water prism, makes drawings, experiments with coloured glass, with candlelight and with coloured shadows. In his *Annals* he writes at the beginning of his entry for 1791:

> A quiet year spent within the confines of my home and the town! The detached position of the house, in which I was able to install a spacious dark-room, and the adjoining garden, in which every kind of experiment could be arranged in the open air, caused me seriously to devote myself to chromatic research.... [Then he adds:] So that I should not neglect the poetic and aesthetic side entirely, however, I was delighted to assume the direction of the Court theatre....

This year of 1791 is one of the most disturbed and portentous in world history. Not a single word does Goethe vouchsafe about what is going on 'out there' on the world stage. He is enveloped in a calm. He observes colour phenomena, the blue on the mountain sides, and notes: 'Light and darkness wage constant war with one another.'

291

# 28

# *Revolutionary Days*

For Goethe the French Revolution did not begin only in 1791 or 1789; with his hyper-sensitive organism he felt the earth tremors earlier than did others, and, for this reason and after his own fashion, he was also finished with it earlier. It is characteristic of him that he is not concerned with the political ideals, and still less with the catchwords, of the day; his starting point is people and events. Freedom, and its counterpart tyranny, have little significance for him, and he scarcely ever uses the words; when his companions of *Sturm und Drang* used to indulge in wild outbursts on these themes, he merely smiled ironically. The people, as a concept, is something he regards with complete indifference. In his wanderings he has gained a great respect for the 'simple people' that he has met, and in the course of his government activities he has learned to view with alarm the fact that the Court, of which after all he is a member, is in reality consuming the very 'marrow' of the country. Occasionally he talks for hours at a time with the bookbinder, whom he has engaged to bind the volumes of his correspondence. In this way, in direct contact with them and in individual cases, he can understand the people; but for the masses, the *hoi polloi*, he has no sympathy, and regards them as a menace.

We must remember, however, that he knows the masses only from hearsay. In Weimar there are no masses, but only very clearly detached little groups: the aristocratic and Court society, the citizens, who have their own association and keep, or are kept, quite separate from the aristocracy, and the 'humble people', who do not count and who have no cohesion at all. A self-conscious bourgeoisie with claims of its own does not exist in Weimar; a large proportion of those 'engaged in trade' live off the needs of the Court. Bertuch, the sole employer and 'capitalist' in the town, and indeed in the whole country, is a former writer, whose main undertakings are his illustrated periodicals, fashion journals, and children's books; he also publishes maps and geographical works, and was the publisher of Goethe's *Optische Beiträge*.

The whole town of Weimar, moreover, including Bertuch and his four hundred employees, could easily have been accommodated in a single side street of one of the Paris faubourgs. This is where the masses made their appearance, in processions and demonstrations; they armed themselves, stormed the Bastille and Royal Palace, dragged back the escaping King and beheaded him. They had their National Assembly, their factions, their great orators and tribunes. To Goethe, in the circle in which his life revolved, all this was alien. The four divisions of the Duchy, it is true, had their *Stände*, their diets, but these were seldom convened and had virtually no say in the affairs of Sachsen, Weimar and Eisenach. If asked for their opinions it is unlikely that they would have been motivated by anything except their own self-interest, for they consisted overwhelmingly of representatives of the nobility. Of orators and speeches not a word reached Goethe's ears. In Weimar the business of government was carried on by the pen; proposals were submitted in writing, briefly discussed in the *Conseil* and then forwarded to the Duke for his signature. There was no public opinion in Weimar, nor was there any press, apart from an official news sheet; there were no meetings and not even, as in many other German towns, a reading-room, where foreign papers and pamphlets could be seen.

These reading-rooms played a very important role in Germany at the beginning of the revolutionary era. They were the cells, or clubs, in which the new ideas first circulated and could be discussed. They did not exist everywhere but only in those territories where the government was less strict, or where the Prince was broadminded or simply lazy and disinterested. In these reading-rooms the splintering and dissolution of the Empire are very sharply spot-lit, above all its lack of any centre or capital; Berlin and Vienna stand in hostile opposition and all that lies between them is either wavering or seeking painfully to maintain an independent existence. There is no nation, there are only territories, and in the eighteenth century these are in such a constant state of flux that only a map with movable frontiers could show them.

In France, however, the nation now appears as a self-contained unity with a high degree of self-assertion. A National Assembly is formed, and a National Guard. The Nation acquires a Constitution. Simultaneously the rights of men are proclaimed beyond its own frontiers, in a charter based on the ideas of Rousseau, the Encyclopaedists, and the American revolutionaries. This is the first phase of the Revolution.

In Germany the beginning of the new age has a very mixed reception. The younger generation and the intelligentsia, for the most part, are enthusiastic; others are timid or mistrustful. Klopstock praises the summoning of the States General as the 'greatest act of this century', and asks his fellow Germans: 'France free – and you hesitate? Are silent?' Schiller and Herder welcome the new age hopefully. The young Hölderlin, a student in Tübingen, writes his *Hymn to Freedom*; his friend Hegel is considered by their fellow students a 'stout Jacobin'. Lafayette is hailed as the new Timoleon, Mirabeau as the new Demosthenes; reminiscences of the classics abound everywhere, even in Paris, where Brutus, Solon and Cato replace the Kings' heads on playing cards. In the German reading-rooms, in so far as they exist and are allowed, the Paris *Moniteur* is eagerly read and discussed.

What of the Courts and the governments? They too, at first, are by no means so united in their hostility as their subsequent attitude, and simplified historic legend, would lead one to suppose. They do not grudge the 'lesson' being given to the proud and dangerous Court of France which, since the days of Louis XIV, has considered itself superior to all others. Very frivolously they also hope for a protracted weakening of France through such disturbances. Even the dynastic solidarity behind the threatened Royal Family only makes itself felt at a very late stage. But among the petty princes something like panic reigns. A south German Prince of Wallerstein, more far-seeing than most people in his position, has had a premonition for years that time is running out for him and his kind: he borrows money from the more foolish of his princely colleagues, converts all his income into cash or valuables, pays the salaries of his officials in small instalments, consoling them with the promise of more to come and, in short, mortgages his country 'up to the hilt' so that, at the first sign of real danger, he can disappear and live abroad. There were numerous princes who, for different reasons but mainly because they were so bored at home, had their principal residence abroad. This costly way of life was frequently financed by the sale of their subjects as mercenaries to the greater powers.

In principle every country traded in soldiers, either by hiring regiments from abroad, buying recruits, or simply stealing them. To protect his own subjects by hiring foreign mercenaries was the sign of a considerate monarch. In France a large proportion, both of men and officers, in every regiment consisted of Irish, German and Swiss; even in the Revolution the Swiss allowed themselves to be hacked to pieces for their masters. The Dutch had Scottish brigades. In Prussia a large proportion of the army was recruited from impressed Saxon prisoners of war, or from personnel collected, by more or less honest means, in Thuringia and the other neighbouring provinces. The seizing of 'vagrants', who could just as easily be poor students making their way to their university, was common practice everywhere. The nationality or origin of the recruits was a matter of no consequence, although the Prussian army was careful to enlist a hard core of its own nationals. The corps of officers was just as motley a crew. Germans served in France, Frenchmen in Germany; one of Frederick the Great's favourite marshals was the Scotsman Keith, and of the famous generals of the later War of Liberation only a very few were native Prussians. A British admiral commanded the Neapolitan navy, and in the Russian army German officers for a time formed the dominating higher echelon. Transfer from one army to another was easy and was only considered dishonourable if undertaken in special circumstances, such as during a campaign. War was a craft.

It was very different for the common soldier. For a long time even the enlightened bourgeoisie regarded the principle of hiring soldiers, or even of impressing them, as beneficial: in this way the otherwise useless elements of the population were skimmed off; 'those who will not obey their fathers and mothers must follow the drum' was the usual formula. Gradually, however, a change took place; people grew more sensitive, and sensitivity and the sentimentalists played no small part in the change. People were shocked at the barbarous punishments, the constant floggings, running the gauntlet. The idea of 'human dignity' was one of the noblest concepts of the much maligned Age of Enlightenment; the time had come, it was felt, to apply it to these poor wretches of soldiers.

In *Kabale und Liebe*, the most powerful of his early plays and the one in which he is most intensely critical of his time, Schiller has written the best known scene on this traffic in soldiers: the Prince has made his mistress a present of a casket of diamonds; they 'cost nothing', the Prince's servant assures her, 'yesterday seven thousand of our countrymen left for America – they will pay for everything'. Goethe only touched on the theme casually, in the second version of his *Die Mitschuldigen*, where the inquisitive landlord wants to know what is going on: Is Frederick ill again? Nothing from America? 'From Hesse, is that still going on? are more going?'

The Landgrave of Hesse-Kassel was the most notorious of the princely merchants. The Duke of Brunswick, closely related to the Court of Weimar and well known to Goethe, also furnished some regiments of mercenaries, and tried to put the difference between the higher British and the Brunswick pay into his own pocket; there were long negotiations over it.

Next to the traffic in soldiers, as the subject of bitter debate, came the activities of the mistresses at the Courts, both great and small. Local historians later tried to play down this rather awkward subject by spotlighting some of the more magnanimous of these ladies and the services they rendered; even Schiller portrays his Lady Milford, for whom no historical model has been found, as a noble creature. Franziska von Hohenheim, mistress of Schiller's former sovereign, the Duke of Württemberg, is said to have tamed and reformed the extremely questionable behaviour of her master in later life, and to have led him on to better ways. Most of these ladies were feared as intriguers, a role they played in international politics as well, where even the most serious historians have to heed their machinations. Some were mere victims of family politics, like the pitiable Fräulein von Schlotheim, who was handed over to the Prince of Hesse in Hanau, and when she escaped was recaptured by her relatives and brought back again; she had twenty-two children by him, 'all born without love', as she told people. These children of princely blood had to be maintained as befitted their station, and at each birth the salt tax in the county of Hanau was increased by a *kreuzer*. In most countries these bastard children entered the ranks of the nobility, with some high-sounding title; it was only

Karl August who, having enough poverty-stricken aristocrats around him without these, dispatched his sons to serve among his keepers and foresters. Scarcely a novel of the day describes the wretchedness and misery of these mistresses, though such novels deal at length with the countless acts of violence, rape and blackmail perpetrated on the nation's women. In many cases the harems far exceeded in size those of the fabled East, and a hundred or even, as in the case of August the Strong of Saxony, three hundred and sixty-four bastards were recorded. International politics again touched on these problems of the petty princedoms: the solicitude of the Elector Karl Theodor of the Palatinate for his illegitimate children – he had none by his marriage – lay behind the events that led to the Bavarian War of Succession, which nearly caused a new European conflict.

Into this landscape, which, in spite of the strict censorship, is described with fair accuracy in the German literature of the day, the fanfares from beyond the Rhine now sound their alarm. The situation is discussed in the reading-rooms. The poets write their odes and hymns. People look for an improvement, somehow, somewhere. It is significant that even the Brutus worship and tyrant hatred of the *Sturm und Drang* never dared to mention a name, or to give any precise indication as to who was the object of admiration or hatred.

Now things are given names. Individual people enter the scene. It is necessary to take a stand. Fronts are formed; but on which front are the Germans to take their stand? They have not so much as a frontier. They have an Emperor only in name. They themselves have scarcely a name. It is characteristic that the poets, seizing on the ancient name of the myths, speak of *Germania*. The French people are addressed as the 'New Franks', the younger brothers, or else as the 'patriots'. For years to come in Germany a patriot means exclusively a French revolutionary; only gradually does the word become more generally adopted and acquire its present meaning. No one dares to speak of a German nation; it would be disloyal, indeed treasonable, to one's sovereign. But neither is it possible to speak, for instance, of a Sachsen-Weimar nation. One can only profess loyalty to one's hereditary prince, provided he does not change his heritage for some other territory, as frequently happens. There is no common flag, no German national hymn.

It would be very superficial to underestimate such symbols. The tricolour becomes a force, more powerful than all the manifestos and pamphlets, and its power reaches far beyond the frontiers of France. In Mainz, hitherto the quiet residence of an archbishop-elector, a very active group is formed, a 'Club', under the sign of the tricolour. A new symbol arises: the tree of liberty dressed with ribbons and crowned with the Phrygian cap. People dance in the open and sing the wild revolutionary songs such as the *Ça ira*, *les aristocrates à la lanterne* and the *Marseillaise*. Elsewhere, where the surveillance is stricter, they whisper together in small groups or pass on the pamphlets that come from Paris. In Göttingen one student teaches the choristers to sing carols to the tunes of the revolutionary songs, and at Christmas time sends the boys out to sing them from door to door, until the pastors catch him out. The reports of those just back from Paris are listened to with rapt attention; Goethe's friend Merck is one of these and has been introduced into the Jacobins' Club. He shed tears over a play, *The Storming of the Bastille*, and thought that 'Goethe himself could not have done better'.

This is the first flush of enthusiasm; it is short-lived. For most Germans it ends with the execution of the King. The French National Assembly had bestowed French citizenship on seventeen famous foreign personalities, the deed being signed by Danton: Joseph Priestley was the first, and others were Jeremy Bentham, Thomas Paine, Washington, Klopstock, and in a supplement, the 'publicist Gille', by whom is meant Schiller. But now, after his initial enthusiasm, Klopstock begins his series of Odes, with their warnings, reproaches and anger; in the poem *Die Verwandlung* (The Transformation), the child, liberty, is transformed by the two furies, ambition and revenge, into a monster. Schiller considers a petition in favour of the King, but soon gives it up. The Revolution marches on, devouring its own children; the wars, which are to last for twenty years, have begun.

These events find Goethe unprepared. His attitude is not to be understood by labelling him 'conservative'; he was an enthusiastic admirer of Napoleon. But for mass movements he had no sympathy whatever. He used occasionally to say: '*Zuschlagen soll die Menge, dann ist sie respektabel – Urteilen gelingt ihr miserabel*' (Sudden action is for the masses, thus they command respect – in judgment they are pitiful). Nor did he ever show much respect for deposed monarchs: '*Warum denn wie mit einem Besen Wird so ein König hinweggekehrt? – Wären's Könige gewesen, Sie stünden noch heute unversehrt!*' (To take a broom and sweep him off, is this the way a king's displaced? Had they been worthy of a king's name, their thrones had stood inviolate). It is always to the personality that he looks: a king who is a king is right in his eyes; a sovereign who, like the unfortunate Louis XVI, is a good-natured simpleton can go. What he looks for, above all, in everything is *Gestalt*, clearly defined form; the Revolution seems to him a wild confusion, a clamour of many voices, all fighting among themselves. One should add that he has just won his way to, and decided on, a very definite ideal of quiet, progressive cultural development, which he now sees endangered. He believes himself on the way to building a kingdom, which has nothing to do with the Holy Roman Empire or its member states, with France or any political unit, and even less with political catchwords and tendencies. He inhabits vast expanses, stretching far into the future and far into the past. At this moment the realm of nature is of far greater importance to him than the world of human beings, the play of colours between the extremes of light and darkness than playing with the tricolour. The quiet growth, before his eyes, of some plant cell from the *Ur-Pflanze* to its full flowering means very much more to him than any political cells, which may grow or which may be trampled under foot.

Certainly he saw in Napoleon the great creator of order, as did most of his contemporaries. He saw in him too, with the eye of an artist, the clearly defined figure of the great demon, a living *Ur-Pflanze* of the will for power as it were, which developed superbly before his very eyes and flowered unimaginably, until once more it had to wither and die, an eventuality accepted calmly by Goethe as a matter of destiny.

Long before the outbreak of the Revolution, before Goethe's departure for Italy, one of the pamphlets dealing with the notorious affair of the necklace had reached Weimar. People read it, discussed it, and were hugely amused by this exposure of the proud French Court. Goethe was far from amused. He went round like a man distracted; he felt as though the Gorgon's head were staring at him. His friends thought him slightly mad. After all, what had happened? A clever swindler had duped the frivolous Marie-Antoinette. All Paris was laughing, the Court at Versailles was laughing, the King's own brothers gleefully participated in the humiliation of their foolish brother and his wife. They were playing with fire, but no one suspected it.

The story of the necklace was a true comedy, and Goethe, with very inadequate means, tried to put it on the stage in his play *Der Gross-Kophta*. The Gross-Kophta, or Grand Master of an obscure order, is the self-styled Count Cagliostro, who was no more a count than was Casanova a chevalier; he was a simple Balsamo from Sicily. Goethe had found and visited his family in Palermo, and had tried to help them a little. Rogues and swindlers have always exercised a fascination over poets and writers of a completely opposite nature, releasing their secret anarchistic feelings, which have no outlet in real life. In Cagliostro we find focused in one man, as in a burning-glass, all the characteristics which gave colour to the period immediately preceding the Revolution: self-assured social bearing, cabbalistic nonsense, mysticism, freemasonry, bold speculation and the ability to raise hopes of immense gains in his victims, erotic opportunism, high politics and the basest instincts.

When Goethe learns that Cagliostro is mixed up in the necklace affair, he feels the ground shake beneath his feet. He sees these events as portending the self-destruction of the rulers, their self-abandonment. Later, during the preparation of his memoirs, he dictated a strange fragment in which he traces this self-destruction far into the past:

Precedents of the mighty, leading to sansculottism. Frederick severs himself from the Court. In his bedroom stands a luxurious bed. He sleeps in his camp bed alongside. Contempt for lampoons, which he orders to be displayed again. Joseph [Emperor Joseph II] discards outward forms. When travelling, instead of sleeping in the luxurious beds, he lies down by the side, on a mattress on the floor. Disguised as a courier on a hack he orders the Emperor's horses.

Maxim: the Regent is but the first servant of the State. The Queen of France [Marie-Antoinette] eschews etiquette. This mode of thought continues until the King of France considers himself an abuse.

The note is exceptionally characteristic of Goethe's feeling for forms and formality; he sees, in the juxtaposition of a luxurious bed and a camp bed, the incompatibility of regal demands and purely personal inclination. The famous saying that the King is the 'first servant of the State', which is later to be quoted in every school and college textbook, has no validity for him. The ruler is there to rule, not to serve. Even in the most superficial aspects of its representation he must preserve the dignity of his position.

It is a real life comedy played by living characters in the open-air theatre of Versailles. The principal actors are the Queen and Cardinal Rohan, who plays opposite to her; the same Cardinal Rohan whom Goethe had seen in Strasbourg celebrating mass for the young Dauphine on her arrival on French soil. For some reason or other, perhaps out of mere caprice or perhaps because he is arrogant and stupid, Rohan is out of favour with Marie-Antoinette and is openly cut by her, a fearful situation for a courtier and one that threatens to shatter his very existence. A clever trickster parading under the old and noble name of de la Motte, who has succeeded in getting the *entrée* to Court society on the strength of her noble lineage, recognizes in the duffer of a Cardinal a potential victim. A fabulous diamond necklace is circulating among the Paris jewellers. The Queen, suggests de la Motte to the Cardinal, would like to buy it but is afraid her husband might object; State bankruptcy is already round the corner. If he were to acquire it secretly and present it to the Queen, Rohan could be restored to favour, and might even win further favours. Completely out of his senses the Cardinal buys the necklace, the trickster having put into his hand a forged receipt giving the Queen's consent. There follows a scene in the garden. De la Motte has engaged a little strumpet from the Palais Royal to play the part of the Queen, by night in front of a shrubbery. The Cardinal appears, kisses the hem of her skirt, and the girl runs off in a panic. The whole affair explodes. The Queen is furious, and with reason, for stupid though she is, she knows she has been made a laughing-stock, and in Paris this is deadly. She demands that Rohan be arrested and brought to trial. The court, a tribunal composed of his peers, acquits him, adding the rider that he is 'without blame', to spite the Queen. De la Motte is branded and sent to the Salpetrière prison for life. The whole of Paris society visits her there and it becomes good form to have been seen at 'de la Motte's'. She is allowed to escape to London where she starts sending out poisonous letters and pamphlets, whitewashing herself and slandering the Queen. Marie-Antoinette is exposed as a Messalina, a Fredegundis, a monster. It is the first great press murder in history, and it leads to physical murder: excited sexual psychosis is the main factor in the subsequent trial and execution of Marie-Antoinette.

At the same time it is the most characteristic episode in the long drawn-out process of the aristocracy's self-destruction. This preliminary phase, oppressive and frivolous, with its corrupt Court society, its swindlers and its mystics, might be material for a comedy. Goethe first makes an opera out of it, and then re-writes it as a play, inventing a conciliatory ending. He employs the time-honoured specifics of dramatic art and, which is worse, of politics, 'well-tried prescriptions' that might possibly serve someone else, but not Goethe.

The reason he writes the play at all is that he has taken over the directorship of the Weimar Court theatre. He proceeds very cautiously in compiling his repertory because he knows he cannot expect too much from his public. *Singspiele*, operettas, the usual theatrical wares, form the mainstay, and continue to do so for a long time to come. Into this basic repertory he intends to insert some plays of his own, his original plan being three or four a year. He writes, or dictates, them with a light touch, often completing them in a few days. But he also wants to educate and instruct. So in his *Gross-Kophta* he combines the subject of the 'Grand-Master' of an 'Egyptian' society on the lines of the freemasons – Mozart's *Die Zauberflöte* had just swept the operatic stage and brought such masonic effects into vogue – with that of the Court intrigue surrounding the necklace. He sets the scene in an anonymous petty state, and adds a pair of lovers after the well-worn formula of the youthful lover and the *ingénue*. The play ends gently and quietly: the Cardinal, a prebendary in the play, is not arrested but merely banished temporarily from the sight of his Princess, the tricksters are conducted secretly over the border, the *ingénue*, replacing the strumpet in the role of the impostor in the garden, goes in penitence to a convent whence, after an interval, her youthful lover will rescue her and bring her back to the world. The *Gross-Kophta* utters some grandiloquent words about the spirits whom he will call to his aid, and is unceremoniously thrown out by the soldiers. A stage direction to one of the central scenes reads: 'On the right of the stage they form a handsome group, in which the two Swiss must not be forgotten.' Such playing with handsome groups, which owes its origin to amateur theatricals, engaged Goethe's attention frequently; but drama is concerned with action.

Goethe tries his hand a second time at a play with a contemporary theme, and on this occasion proceeds even more casually. A playlet, *Die beiden Billets*, has recently had a great success; the work of a writer named Wall, it is based on a French original by Florian, who had revived the harlequinade and the semi-arcadian rustic setting; Marie-Antoinette, whose taste was for more piquant attractions, called Florian's plays 'milk and water'. Assuming his public to be familiar with Wall and Florian, Goethe uses their plays as a starting point for his own. The characters are stock figures of the stage: a nice young village couple in love, with the girl's father, an old grumbler, providing a mild contrast. Into this idyll bursts the Revolution in the person of the village barber, whom a Jacobin propagandist has supplied with a sword, a cockade and a cap of liberty; thus attired, he poses in front of the old father Märten as the 'Bürger General', the citizens' general. He demonstrates the great tirades of the Revolution in kind: taking a pot of fresh cream from the old man's cupboard, he rubs bread, the aristocracy, into it, sprinkles sugar, the clergy, over this, stirs the mixture and tries to make a feast of it. The terrified peasant calls his son-in-law; there is fighting, shouting, the magistrate appears, and finally the local squire as the *deus ex machina*. The squire, the model of a wise and fine aristocrat, considers that the little incident should not be exaggerated:

> Children love one another, tend your fields and run your house well – let foreign countries look after themselves and don't watch the political skies except perhaps on Sundays and feast-days…. In a country where the Prince holds aloof from no one, where all classes think fairly of each other, where no one is prevented from using his gifts in his own way, where useful knowledge and information is distributed everywhere – in such a country there will be no factions. What goes on in the world will attract attention, but the seditious thought of whole nations will have no influence. We shall be quietly grateful that we can see a clear sky overhead, while disastrous storms are ravaging vast areas with their hail.

'It is so nice listening to you!' says the peasant girl.

We are not so foolish as to imagine that this was Goethe's real view, but that he thought he could educate and warn people with milk and water such as this seems strange. A few years earlier he would have laughed such stuff to scorn. More important is the fact that his fellow countrymen had no need of such warnings; they really did watch the political sky only on Sundays and feast-days, and continued to do so even after Goethe's day. Goethe made two other attempts to treat the great themes of his day: both remain fragments.

With this comes to an end not only this series of attempts 'to write something for the stage', but the whole series of Goethe's dramatic works that can be considered as works for the theatre. What he wrote subsequently was intended for special or solemn occasions, or else was in the form of lofty poetic conceptions in which there was no longer any thought of stage or scenery. It is a curious but significant fact that in almost thirty years of intimate association with the Weimar theatre Goethe, after these first unsuccessful attempts, did not write a single stage play. When possible he even left the adaptation of his own plays to others, and his own adaptations, including plays by Shakespeare, inhabit those regions of his mighty *œuvre* in which even his most ardent admirers hide their faces in shame.

His quarrel with the Revolution, however, is not yet over. It continues for a long time and leads from these nether regions up to works of great distinction, to his epic poem *Hermann und Dorothea* and the unfinished trilogy *Die natürliche Tochter*. Before he arrives at these, it is necessary

for him to learn more about events than he can by listening to travellers'
tales or stories of barbers posing as citizens' generals. He has to approach
closer to the spectre itself, although he would prefer to wrestle with that
other spectre, the spectrum. A war of intervention is planned to liberate
the King and put an end once and for all to all the uproar in Paris. Karl
August, as commander of a Prussian regiment of cuirassiers, has to take
part. He wants Goethe to accompany him, but Goethe is very reluctant to
leave his home, his Christiane, and above all his vital research into the
theory of colours. Everyone assures him the campaign will be over in a few
weeks: after all, to see the famous city and its splendours might be worth
a few uncomfortable nights on the way. So Goethe packs his notes on
Newton, his prism and Gehler's dictionary, orders a fine chaise with four
horses, and follows his Duke.

# 29

# *Goethe at War*

'Here and now a new epoch in world history is beginning, and you will be able to say you were present at it', declared Goethe to his companions on the eve of the bombardment of Valmy, in Champagne, on September 20, 1792. We cannot be certain that these famous words were actually uttered in their present form; Goethe's account of the French campaign was written late in life, as the last part of his memoirs, under the title *Campagne in Frankreich*, and in compiling it he refreshed his memory from old diaries, letters, memoirs, and by listening to the talk of his old servant Paul Götze. But his saying is true. Miserably planned and even more miserably conducted the campaign marked a turning point in world history: it decided the fate of the French Revolution. As the first great war of intervention undertaken for ideological reasons it also pointed to the future.

Goethe's description of it, although written in his old age, has a special charm of its own. It is carefully composed, with a nice interplay of themes and an effective mixture of serious and lighter episodes. Much of it is personal, and in the midst of battles and bombardments his *Farbenlehre* always remains more important to him than the war itself: 'Happy the man whose breast is filled with a nobler passion!' he exclaims on one occasion. His recovery, in the hospital at Trier, of Gehler's *Dictionary of Physics*, which he thought he had lost, was for him complete compensation for the defeat and for all the hardships it involved. An historical account of the campaign his description is not. For this purpose Goethe was too hampered by consideration for living people and friendly powers, and in any case history, which he always regarded as a 'hodge-podge of error and brute force', was not his *métier*.

Seldom has this concept been so catastrophically realized as in this campaign. If we accept a simplified view, and the legend that has grown up, the explanation is easy: on the one side the Revolution, on the other the forces of reaction which invade France and whose armies of mercenaries suffer ignominious defeat at the hands of the enthusiastic volunteers of the young republic. On the one side a new faith, uniting the whole people in the defence of their threatened country, on the other a coalition of the powers of the old régime. The events, it is true, embrace these contrasts, but they are enormously more complicated and fascinating than would appear from such formulas.

To begin with war is declared, not by the coalition but by France, the unhappy Louis XVI being forced to sign the declaration; to distract attention from the dangerous situation at home by switching it across the border – an oft-repeated recipe – seems to the men of the first Revolutionary government the best way out of their troubles. The declaration of war itself is a cautious, half-hearted document, and is addressed not to the German Emperor but to the 'King of Bohemia and Hungary'. The Holy Roman Empire stands expressly aside, and the troops of the Empire take no part in the campaign.

Prussia, on the other hand, does take part, although barely two years previously it had massed its troops on the Austrian frontier; it was on this occasion that Goethe had accompanied his Duke to Silesia, when the Duke's regiment took up its position on the Bohemian border. This antagonism is now forgotten in the face of greater problems; an alliance is concluded. The main problem is not France but Poland, now ripe, in the opinion of its neighbours, to be finally carved up.

And so, after fairly lengthy deliberations, Prussia declares herself willing to give Austria armed assistance. She provides the Commander-in-chief for the combined undertaking, putting forward for this post the Duke of Brunswick, generally regarded as the greatest soldier of the day. Of all species of fame, military fame is the most unaccountable; it has been bestowed on complete mediocrities and on total failures. In the case of Karl Wilhelm Ferdinand of Brunswick, the legend of his fame ultimately led to tragic consequences: he it was who was responsible for the Prussian débâcle at Jena and Auerstädt in 1806, losing his native land and ending his life, blinded in battle, a fugitive. As a young cavalry commander he had served under Frederick the Great in the Seven Years War – all the Brunswick Princes were Prussian generals – and by so doing earned the reputation of having been trained in the greatest military school of the day. The legend of *Fridericus rex* was current not only in Prussia but in England and France as well. Not a single battle did Karl Wilhelm Ferdinand ever win. He was a cautious strategist, and in the police action in Holland, in 1787, cautious manœuvring – the supreme wisdom of the old school – brought him success. Now he is to command the allied forces. He goes to Potsdam for a council of war.

So great was his reputation, however, that just prior to this, an emissary of the French Revolutionary government had visited him in Brunswick, with the object of persuading him to take over the command of the French army, re-organize it, and lead it to new deeds of glory. The strange story does not end even there. The rebellious Belgian patriots also approached him and asked him to place himself at their head; there was talk of a reward in the form of a new territory to be created out of provinces like Limburg, Geldern and Luxembourg. The confidence placed in the Duke on all sides was literally boundless.

Not without misgivings he attends the council of war at Potsdam, turning over in his mind the various offers he has received; and he is enough of a strategist not to underestimate the difficulties of such a campaign. He knows the chain of French fortifications, built by famous masters in the art; he knows the French army, weakened perhaps by political events, but still basically intact, and commanded by first-rate officers of the old school. He knows that, because of the Polish question, he will have very inadequate forces at his disposal; Austria is to provide a mere bagatelle, Russia nothing at all.

He is overruled. Opposite him stands another man of destiny, King Friederich Wilhelm II, nephew of Frederick the Great and heir to his famous army. He, likewise, cannot be summed up in a simple formula. Tall and well-built, in contrast to his uncle who was small almost to the point of deformity, full-blooded and maintaining an establishment of mistresses; a bigot into the bargain, he forbade his philosopher, Kant, to write on religious subjects. He was popular with the men, with whom he chatted easily and whom, unlike his uncle, he did not regard as mere cannon fodder. He was brave in the face of the enemy, and in pouring rain would ride without a cloak, which made the pampered French *émigré* princes groan because, in obedience to etiquette, they were forced similarly to expose their own delicate bodies. His head, large but intellectually not very strong, was filled with all kinds of progressive and reactionary ideas, but he was incapable of thinking them out or putting them into practice. Because of this he listened to all who had advice to offer and attracted the most unsuitable advisers. He had given sanctuary in Berlin to a large number of French *émigrés* and these described to him the situation in Paris in the rosiest terms. The campaign would be just an outing, they said, the whole spectre would vanish into thin air in face of the world-famous Prussian army. The King urges 'on to Paris!' without delay.

The campaign, then, opens late, in August. The Duke with his regiment of Prussian cuirassiers is in the van of the advance; his own Duchy of Weimar, as one of the member states of the Holy Roman Empire, remains neutral. Before his departure Karl August bestows a princely gift on his friend: the house on the Frauenplan with its garden, a large, fine, comfortable residence. He also gives permission for the invaluable Meyer to come to Weimar, to assist Goethe with his artistic interests. In the light of favours such as these the poet can hardly refuse the call to accompany his master. Reluctantly he packs his trunks. With a sigh he entrusts the household to Meyer's care and climbs into his carriage. He travels in considerable comfort, accompanied by his servant, Vogel, because during the ensuing 'outing' he intends to be very busy dictating the results of his work on the theory of colours.

Trier is the army's base camp, but the troops have already been launched across the frontier. Here Goethe meets the columns of *émigrés*, who constitute the third important factor in the failure of the campaign. Since the edict of Louis XIV, which drove Goethe's grandfather out of Lyon, French refugees had won a good name for themselves throughout Europe. But these *émigrés* of 1792 are of a different stamp; they are led by the King's brothers, gamblers and intriguers, who care little for the fate of their brother and still less for that of his detested wife. There are the aristocrats, shaking with fury over the treachery of their peers who have voluntarily relinquished their sacred privileges and thrown in their lot with the rabble. There are the ex-ministers, who claim to have been right with their warnings, who are now working out new financial measures, and have constructed a mobile factory for counterfeiting assignats, the paper money issued by the Revolutionary government – later, during the retreat, Goethe sees the huge wagons containing this factory. And there is also a whole group of ardent young Royalists, ready to take up arms in defence of their rights; Goethe sees them, in their camp outside Trier, watering their own horses because they have no grooms. In one of the columns is a young Vicomte de Chateaubriand. There are also a few troops of soldiers, men of long service, highly disciplined even in retreat.

As a whole they are undisciplined and irresponsible. Goethe is struck by the sight of the small group of soldiers, overshadowed by the vast mass of vehicles; carriages filled with wives, sweethearts, children, lady's maids and servants, and wagons loaded to the skies with trunks and hat-boxes. He is struck, too, by the scene at the post-house, where these people drop untold quantities of letters into the posting box, in full expectation that in a matter of days or weeks they will reach their relations in Paris.

The *émigrés* are not the only ones to draw out of the town with mountains of baggage, the strictly disciplined Prussian Army also moves off with a huge baggage train. There is a host of princely personages, and this means a huge staff of quartermasters, cooks, personal servants, grooms, orderlies and staff-officers, these last called the 'fowls', from the waving plumes of feathers on their enormous hats. In addition to Goethe, who has no other task than to follow his Duke, the allies have a complete diplomatic staff attached to them, and this again means further personnel, as well as special and superior provisions. Following the old practice, whereby the civilian population must not be penalized, the victualling is all done from stores in the rear, and this involves large supply columns. Finally there is an army of camp-followers in the form of catering women and whores; Goethe describes one of the former, an experienced old 'mother courage', who ruthlessly commandeers whatever she wants, ferreting out the most carefully hidden stores, and who insists on making room for some pregnant whore, be it in the midst of advance or retreat, so that she can bring her child into the world.

The unequal proportion of fighting soldiers to the vast mass of supply personnel and camp followers, common to all campaigns, must on this occasion have reached a point that is almost beyond anyone's power to estimate. Brunswick believes in waging war methodically in the time-honoured manner.

At first this strategy succeeds. The fortresses of Longwy and Verdun fall in quick succession. The allies are exultant. The road to Paris is clear, Brunswick, cool and calculating, hesitates. His entire army consists only of forty-two thousand Prussians, a weak Austrian contingent of fourteen thousand with a promise of another detachment from Holland later, and five thousand Hessians under the personal command of the Landgrave. Brunswick wants to attack the remaining frontier forts, and then go into winter quarters and negotiate. He is overruled. King Friederich Wilhelm urges him to advance, he wants a big victory before the year is out. The *émigrés* exert their pressure.

They have presented to Brunswick a very foolish and very ill-fated manifesto, to which he has put his signature. It consists of fearful threats: Paris is made responsible for the safety of the Royal family, each individual inhabitant, the mayor of every district, every deputy, is answerable with his life; anyone opposing it will be treated as a rebel and his house will be burned. This manifesto is the first step to defeat. Far from undermining the French, it unites them; even the old troops of the line and their Royalist officers feel an upsurge of patriotism in the face of threats such as these. Volunteers flock to the recruiting depots in their thousands. The first result is that not a single deserter appears in the allied lines; whereas the *émigrés* had declared that, once the frontier was crossed, the whole army, including its officers, would rush to the allies with outstretched arms. No one comes. In Paris, where the press continues to treat Brunswick with respect and admiration, as indeed it does throughout the whole campaign, the papers declare that unquestionably the manifesto has been foisted on him; such a 'liberal', enlightened prince could never have written such words.

The manifesto has a further consequence: it is issued on July 25, and on August 10 the Tuileries Palace is stormed. The Royal family is held prisoner in the Temple; the National Assembly debates the King's deposition. The National Convention declares the abolition of the Monarchy and the establishment of the Republic. General Lafayette, the standard-bearer of the Revolution in its early days, quarrelled with the government over this very point and, after vainly trying to prevent the 'second revolution', takes to flight. His successor as commander-in-chief, Dumouriez, is an unknown quantity to the allies. The situation is still wide open and no one knows what course the Revolution will take. This is the position at the end of August when Goethe overtakes the army in their camp behind Longwy, arriving in his four-in-hand. The picture that presents itself to him is deeply disillusioning. He sees a waste of tents on a muddy, churned-up plain; everyone has crept under cover out of the rain; not even sentries are posted, as his unmilitary eye observes with dismay. It is only with difficulty that he is able to enquire his way to the Duke's regiment, the 6th Prussian Cuirassiers. Here at last he finds some familiar faces, and a large comfortable tent in which he listens to stories of the march to the Rhine, of amusing adventures in Westphalian convents, with 'memories of many a pretty woman', and of complaints of fearful toils on the mountain roads behind the frontier.

The splendid uniforms – those of the cuirassiers are yellow, their tunics kept fresh and bright with daily applications of chalk – have already suffered with the damp and the dirt. Discipline is poor. The troops begin to plunder, requisitioning what they want against worthless scraps of paper to be honoured by Louis XVI, or simply robbing; orders from above are without effect. The provosts in the Prussian army are for the most part badly paid invalids, looking like convicts in their grey uniforms, and despised by the men, who refuse even to sit round the same fire, let alone drink, with them; they are not respected even by the wagoners, the catering women and the whores. The soldiers swear: 'Why the devil should we spare these people? They are damned patriots aren't they? It's their fault we have to put up with all this.' They kill the sheep belonging to the peasants, skewer the meat on their sabres and roast it over the open fire. The officers boast of the men's behaviour: 'This is the way to show them! Word will spread throughout France – this is what the Prussians do! This is how the Prussians plunder! This is how the Prussians knock the stuffing out of the people! And in three weeks the whole patriot bogey will have vanished!'

In conquered Verdun the famous liqueur, called *baume humain*, is sampled. Goethe sends home by courier a box of the well-known dragées, small spiced sweets shaped like little cylinders, addressed to Demoiselle Vulpius in Weimar. The whole campaign has a pleasant look about it. After all, what does the opposition amount to? Goethe attends the discussions at Karl August's headquarters. He learns that Lafayette, who commanded great respect – his deeds in the American War of Independence and his friendship with Washington were well known – has fled and passed through the allied lines, and that he has been replaced by a new man of the name of Dumouriez, who has been Minister of War for a short time; he will not give them much trouble.

Dumouriez is a name forgotten to-day, and yet he, too, is one of history's men of destiny. Goethe long remembered him, and recommended him to Schiller as a sort of French Wallenstein; but Dumouriez is not a man of the Friedlander's stature, nor does his life have the same dramatic ending. He is not a great Commander-in-chief, but he is an able general, as this campaign is to prove; he is also a very competent intriguer, and this brings his career to a somewhat inglorious end. As a young officer he fought with courage in the Seven Years War, and then took part in various adventures in Corsica, Poland, Spain and Portugal. He undertook secret diplomatic missions on behalf of the *secret du roi* and, as a result of some dark and mysterious intrigues, found himself imprisoned in the Bastille. On his release he understandably feels himself in sympathy with the new order of things. His great plan, which proves successful, is to shatter the coalition by separating Prussia from Austria. It is Austria, not Prussia, that he hates, and his ambition is to conquer the Austrian Netherlands for France. In this, too, he is successful, as indeed he is in almost everything he undertakes in this one great year of his career; he fails only in one point – ability to continue the gamble for high stakes. He jumps off the wagon too soon, loses his gamble and ends his life as a fugitive, with an English pension, a schemer against Napoleon and a writer of memoirs. In the words of one of his contemporaries, he was, within the space of six months, 'large-scale planner, minister, royalist, constitutionalist, Girondist, Jacobin, republican, general, victor, fugitive and outcast'. This is the man who now opposes the allies, and without a knowledge of his secret schemes the campaign is incomprehensible.

As they take their course the events are well-nigh incomprehensible to the participants themselves, on both sides. The French have as little plan of campaign and as little trace of any clear-cut policy as the allies. In one thing only are they united and that is in their patriotism. No one wishes to see a foreign army on French soil. No one wishes to see a foreign power determine the fate of their country. It is only the *émigrés* in the allied camp who dream of a return to feudalism, and in France these people are hated very much more than the King. Brunswick also has a low opinion of them; in his manifesto he had originally intended to include the explicit assurance that the Constitution, and what had been achieved in its name, would remain inviolate. With his usual vacillation he was persuaded to delete this, and by this stroke he played into the hands of the radical elements in Paris.

It is these elements, with Danton at their head, who now come to the fore, and the 'Terror' begins. Only during the course of the campaign does the Revolution become truly revolutionary in the modern sense, with mass murder of prisoners, mass executions, bitter and bloody feuds between individuals and factions, and the release of enormous funds of energy both at home and abroad. Paris is the stage, the testing ground, where the battles are fought; it is there that the new, hitherto unknown factor makes its appearance: the masses, armed, thronging the streets in numbers never before seen in the course of European history. Paris is a city of six hundred thousand inhabitants; when the invading army threatens, the people shout in scorn: let them into the town; they will be torn to pieces on the pavements of the Faubourg Saint-Antoine! Brunswick, who knows Paris, has considered this possibility too, and feels very little inclination to lead his small army into the witches' cauldron.

The shouting of the newspapers and orators is largely empty boasting.

The government is already contemplating a withdrawal to some town in the south, but its members hesitate to take the step for fear of losing their influence, and possibly their heads as well, because from now on every failure spells disaster for those responsible. Hence the decision to defend Paris at all costs. The army must be made responsible for this, but at the moment it is split into three widely separated groups, one of which has advanced towards Belgium, one towards the Ardennes, and the third towards the German frontier. These are now recalled, with orders to stop Brunswick's advance. Dumouriez, who, as Minister for War, was responsible for the declaration of war, is given command of the operation.

Manpower they have in abundance; three hundred thousand men have been called to the colours. What is lacking, however, is equipment and, above all, discipline. The latest batch of volunteers terrorize their officers, indulge in politics, desert in their scores and plunder as ruthlessly as the allied soldiers; at every reverse they cry 'treason', and sometimes run away in whole battalions. It is the earlier volunteers who form the patriotic core of the army; they have assimilated themselves with the old regiments of the line, learned the craft of soldiering from them and imbued them, in their turn, with the new patriotic enthusiasm. These are the motley ranks, ill-led by generals who are suspicious and jealous of each other, that oppose the allied thrust. The invasion may well succeed, and more than once the scale is in the balance.

Between Verdun and Paris there is only one natural obstacle of any consequence, the forest of the Argonnes. Brunswick's plan is to manœuvre, and to do so in such a way that the campaign will be quoted in future manuals of strategy as a masterly achievement carried out with the minimum losses. And he is determined never to lay himself open to the accusation of leaving his flank unprotected. An army, under the Alsatian Kellermann, is approaching from the Rhine to join forces with Dumouriez; Brunswick's plan is to strike at them both together and thus finish the campaign at one stroke.

And so they press forward, along bad roads, in the rain. The villages they pass through are almost empty, the few inhabitants sullen. Goethe makes some observations on the play of colours on a fragment of pottery in a pool of water. He dictates the results to his secretary in the tent, with the rain dripping through the canvas on to the paper. On another occasion, when he is in the Princely *entourage*, he stands on a piece of rising ground and notes how richly large masses of cavalry fill the landscape, and longs for a Van der Meulen to paint it: 'Some of the villages ahead of us were in flames, but smoke does not make a bad effect in a battle scene.'

They enter Champagne. Brunswick has manœuvred cleverly; one of the most important roads through the Argonnes has been penetrated and, by means of further manœuvring, he now wants to checkmate Dumouriez from the rear. But the King has received news that the enemy is going to try to make good his escape. He wants the decisive battle, and the glorious victory, now. He orders a turning movement to the right, in order to attack the enemy from the front and so defeat him. Brunswick gives way, against his better judgment. At dead of night – seen by one of the combatants, a Prussian major, as symbolic of the strategic eclipse – they advance. Goethe mounts his horse. He has been told that in warfare the best place is with the fighting troops, and so he takes his place among his Duke's Life Guards and rides off into the greatest adventure of his life.

Having joined forces with Kellermann, Dumouriez has taken up a well-chosen position on high ground at Valmy, in a sort of wide amphitheatre, as Goethe described it. At the foot of the hills further protection is afforded by small streams and gullies. Beyond these is a wide, empty, chalky plateau, and across this the Prussian army advances in two lines, slowly and in perfect order. The highest point of the plateau is a farm, called *La Lune*, to which, at first, neither side pays any attention. The Duke of Weimar, with Goethe at his side, forms the vanguard of the advance. The battle commences with a big attack by his cavalry, three regiments strong. Karl August's military talent, not held in very high esteem by his brother officers, now appears in a strange light. The compact mass of his cavalry moves into the attack in a curtain of mist and light rain. There has been no preliminary reconnaissance of the ground, and there are only a few hussars to indicate the approximate position of the enemy. No one knows against what part of the enemy line the attack is directed nor how far it is to go. They cross a highway along which run lines of poplar trees that remain in Goethe's memory. As he puts it, they storm on and on towards the west. Suddenly they come under fire from their flank, from *La Lune*, where, at the last minute, Kellermann has succeeded in establishing an advanced battery. The advancing cavalry stall, turn tail and gallop for home.

It was the strangest cavalry attack imaginable and with it Karl August's active participation in this famous day comes to an end. One of Brunswick's *aides-de-camp* rides up and gives him orders to take up his position further to the rear, behind the line of the farm, which is about to be taken by a Prussian mounted battery standing at the ready, a surging mass of finely disciplined horses and men, as Goethe observes. There is still firing from the farm, but the shots are falling short and are only throwing dirt over the cavalrymen. The standard, held by a good-looking young ensign, waves above the turmoil: 'His charming face brought to my mind at this awful moment, strangely though quite naturally, his still more charming mother, and I could not help thinking of the peaceful moments I had spent at her side.' Another order arrives and the Duke's cuirassiers ride further down the slope 'with great discipline and calmness', as Goethe remarks, to take up a reserve position. The total losses of the entire cavalry division at the 'Battle' of Valmy amounted to one horse.

In the meantime the main army has drawn up, also in impeccable forma-

311

tion. It is the farewell performance of this parade-ground manœuvring of the days of Frederick the Great that, up till the King's death a few years previously, had struck admiration and terror into the heart of all Europe. It is midday before the deployment of the army is complete. The chalky plateau resounds to the noise of commands and the beating of drums; the famous old regiments draw up with their flags flying, *aides-de-camp* gallop hither and thither, the commanders take up their positions in front of their men, and in front of them ride the Duke of Brunswick and the King, accompanied by their plumed staff officers. The *La Lune* farmstead, which might have spoilt the whole splendid pageantry of this deployment, has duly been captured by the mounted battery and a section of hussars; it is the only position that is seriously contested.

The army advances to the point where it comes under fire from the French positions on the twin hills of Valmy. The range is about fifteen hundred yards and most of the shots fall short, but some find their way into the dead straight ranks of the soldiers. The troops double up, an action that is still regarded as cowardice and against orders. The King on his charger, and in the full splendour of his majesty, takes up his position in the forefront and bellows at the men to watch him, he is a much better target than they are! The old soldiers mutter: he can well talk, he is bulletproof, only a silver bullet could touch him! Why, old Fritz has taken whole handfuls of lead out of his pockets in a battle, and not a bullet has grazed his skin! Some parts of the line begin to waver but are soon brought into formation again. They stand where they are, because they have to. The artillery has now taken up its positions ahead of the main army and begins to fire at the twin hills ahead. The mist has lifted. The bombardment starts.

Brunswick and the King, armed with field glasses, ride out to the edge of the plateau to reconnoitre. For the first time they see what they are up against. Until this moment they have had to rely on the reports of the hussars – brief, imprecise and contradictory. Now they realize that they face a well-organized army occupying good, indeed excellent, positions. Their own position is only moderate, if not downright bad. The two hills of Valmy, where there is a windmill, and Yvorn are heavily defended in depth by French infantry and dismounted cavalry. The French artillery is firing without a pause, and Brunswick observes with what speed and precision the gunners man their guns. In the valley on the right flank strong detachments of French cavalry are visible, well protected by infantry in the villages. The cavalrymen, dismounted, are quietly feeding their horses although they are within range of the allied cannon fire. On Valmy, alongside the windmill, Kellermann can be seen on his horse; he is waving his hat on the end of his sabre and shouting, while his men answer him with wild cries. The regimental band is playing the *Ça ira* and the *Marseillaise*. Brunswick is unable to detect the slightest trace of confusion in the French ranks, in spite of the bombardment which surpasses anything seen for fifty or a hundred years. The French are answering shot for shot.

The whole 'battle' is really less of an artillery duel than a duel between two systems, a battle of nerves as we should say to-day. After four hours Brunswick, suddenly very decided and prepared to brook no opposition, declares: 'Here we do not attack!' At his side the King has been making his own observations, and he is sufficient of a soldier to be able to draw conclusions. He has been lured into an adventure. The brothers of the French King, who are in his *entourage*, urge him to attack: the Prussian infantry, the most famous in the world, is standing there ready for battle, and they do not advance a step! Friedrich Wilhelm has no mind to hurl his best regiments into this fire; he will remain master of the battlefield, and thus preserve his honour. He agrees with Brunswick. During the afternoon the bombardment begins to die down.

What has Goethe been doing meanwhile? He has been off on a reconnaissance of his own; sitting among the reserves bored him. He wants to observe the phenomenon of battle nerves. And so the solitary *Geheimrat*, in his brown civilian overcoat, rides over the battlefield, up to *La Lune*, and over the rising ground beyond. He meets some officers, who want him to turn back with them, but obstinately he rides on. The shots are mostly falling short, hitting the ground with a dull thud. He is aware of a certain heat, which suffuses his whole body, and, being preoccupied with his colour theories, imagines that the earth takes on 'a certain reddish brown tint' during the bombardment. He hears the noise of the cannon balls as a mixture of the hum of a top, the gurgling of boiling water and the whistling of birds, and in hearing it has the experience of which he has heard so much. Slowly he rides back to join the Life Guards.

In the evening orders are received to camp on the battlefield. There are to be no fires. Goethe stands in the darkness with a group of officers. The atmosphere is bad. No one knows what to say about it all. Goethe rallies his companions by pointing out that they have taken part in a great occasion, which can have incalculable consequences; this, or something like it, will have been the origin of his famous saying: 'Here and now a new epoch in world history is beginning....'

The wind drops, it starts to rain. There are no tents, and no shelter is in sight. Someone suggests digging in. They borrow spades and shovels from the artillery, dig out the light, chalky soil, and lie down in their 'premature graves'. This evening also sees the burial of the campaign, the allied war plan, the reputation of the Prussian military system and the old order in general. It takes a little time for people to realize this, but Goethe was right, Valmy is the beginning of a new era.

Seldom, if ever, has a decisive battle in world history been fought with so little bloodshed. The Prussians had one hundred and eighty-four killed and wounded, though most of the wounded died for lack of any adequate medical service. The French losses were one hundred and fifty killed and two hundred and sixty wounded. Some thirty-five thousand men on each side took part. The indecisive battles of our own day in the same area, in Champagne and on the Somme, tell a different story. Nevertheless Valmy heralds a period of twenty-five years of war, which is also to devour several millions of men. And even this campaign, so economical of life in battle, ends in disastrous losses – half the army perishing during the retreat, from dysentery, typhus or exhaustion.

Almost everyone on the Prussian side was agreed, however, that after all his mistakes Brunswick now showed his real mettle and saved his army. It was still a fearful defeat, but without Brunswick's cool diplomacy it would have ended in unconditional surrender or complete annihilation. He starts negotiations with Dumouriez. Having very quickly recognized Dumouriez' cherished plan of dividing the allies, he now deludes him into thinking that an alliance between Prussia and France might be possible. He out-gambles the gambler.

Brunswick is friendly and non-committal, and leaves everything open; his own concern is to extricate his army from the trap. He wants to save his colours and his cannon, the symbols of unimpaired military honour, and he succeeds in bringing them home.

Although scarcely a shot is fired, the retreat is a fearful disaster. They camp for a whole week on the bare battlefield, for reasons of prestige and because Dumouriez cleverly protracts the negotiations. There is a shortage of bread and of water; the men collect the rain water from puddles. 'Lousy Champagne', as it is called in later campaigns as well, produces lice by the million, and this in its turn leads to a general deterioration of discipline. There is no lack of the usual stupid orders from headquarters in an attempt to preserve discipline: the men are to lay in an adequate supply of chalk to whiten their uniforms, is one that Goethe notes. Officers, lousy and filthy like their men, who have to take reports to the relatively comfortably housed and fed staff headquarters, are sharply reprimanded for their slovenly appearance and return seething with anger, half 'Jacobins' already; a mood of criticism, scepticism and even mutiny, that infiltrates into the ranks of the generals too, remains for many years. Later it gives rise to the reform movement in the Prussian army, whose members are for long described by the old school as Jacobins, and who then adopt for themselves the former term of opprobrium, 'patriots'.

Goethe organizes his own retreat, just as he had undertaken his own reconnaissance at Valmy, and he organizes it well. Surrounded by depression and ill-humour he preserves his own good humour and heartens his companions: think what we shall have to tell the ladies when we get home! He exchanges his own four-in-hand for the Duke's heavier and more comfortable kitchen waggon drawn by six horses, where he reads the third volume of Gehler's *Dictionary of Physics*. When the waggon gets stuck, he mounts his horse. He tells stories of successful foraging in the plundered villages, of finding his carriage and luggage again, including the precious manuscript of the *Farbenlehre*. In addition to his faithful Paul Götze he acquires another servant in the person of a clever hussar from the Life Guards, a French-speaking native of Luxembourg, who introduces his master everywhere as a relative of the King of Prussia and thus gets him accommodation when no one else can find any; he is a jovial scamp, hail-fellow-well-met with everyone, and thanks to him Goethe survives the ordeal in good spirits and, comparatively speaking, without mishap.

He has seen enough. The sick and wounded are left behind, in field hospitals or simply by the roadside. Exhausted men collapse on the march and are run over by the columns of vehicles, which refuse to stop. There are wild rumours, such as that of twenty thousand peasants gathered at Rheims intent on massacre. Marauders and stragglers follow the main army in droves, as they did in the Thirty Years War, and treat the villagers in the same way as Wallenstein's soldiery. Horses collapse, are butchered and thrown into the ditches. An order is received: riders are to dismount and harness their horses to the guns, which must be saved at all costs; then yet another order comes from Karl August that all cavalrymen are to take the saddles from their mounts and carry them, no cavalryman is to return without his saddle. The long columns stretch far into the distance on the soft, narrow roads; endless baggage waggons, with the kitchen and service waggons of the twenty different Princes at their head, the elegantly lacquered carriages of the *émigrés* with their ladies and their footmen, and the enormous two-tiered coach of the Prussian minister Haugwitz towering over everything and housing a complete nonentity. Goethe's sense of orderliness derives huge satisfaction from a few old soldiers among the *émigrés* who step carefully to avoid the dirt and the puddles, and who, as soon as they stop for the night, wash their leggings and brush them. But the whole thing is a flight, unmistakable disintegration. A new catastrophe threatens: the French general, Custine, who had been left in the rear of the advancing allied army, has struck in the Rhineland. Speier, the main supply depot for the entire invasion army, has already fallen, Mainz is threatened, Frankfurt is alarmed. Custine is expected in Coblenz at any moment, and there are reports that some sections of the population are eager to welcome him. In four weeks the climate of the world has changed, and the 'reddish' tone that Goethe thought he observed in the landscape during the bombardment at Valmy has become a reality.

Goethe, with his hussar and his servant Götze, pushes his way on to the fortress of Luxembourg, the former seeing to it that he gets good accommodation. He unloads his luggage from the carriage. 'First of all I put the papers concerning the *Farbenlehre* in order, always bearing in mind my earliest maxim: to enlarge my experience and purify my method.' He gets himself shaved and his hair carefully dressed; he has seen himself in the mirror with a shaggy beard and hair down to his shoulders.

He drives on to the Rhine, where he meets his Duke with his regiment of cuirassiers. Yellow chalk is found to clean their tunics. Senior staff officers draw up a balance sheet of the campaign: scarcely a thousand men lost in action, but nineteen thousand lost on the march. The régime they set out to save has been overthrown, the King is a prisoner, the Republic has been proclaimed and its armies are on the march everywhere. The coalition that undertook the crusade is on the point of dissolution. The army is demoralized and racked with sickness, the hospitals are overcrowded, the death roll mounts. The army surgeons are rogues and brutes, the orderlies mostly cripples, old and stiff. The patients are robbed, or else left to fend for themselves; they manage to drag themselves to the latrines, and there they die. The ditches are filled with corpses.

Goethe also has a mild attack of the universal sickness; he refers to it very reticently. He is finished with the whole adventure now, finally and for good. But instead of hurrying back to Weimar, to his sweetheart and his son, to the comfort of his home, he escapes in the opposite direction, down the Rhine, to his old friends the Jacobis, at Pempelfort near Düsseldorf. He makes his way leisurely down the river by boat. He has to consider a proposition he has received from his mother: his uncle Textor, the senator, has died, thus leaving the way open for him, according to the city rules, to enter the government service of his native town of Frankfurt as a *Ratsherr*. His mother clearly thinks that in such uncertain times, with thrones tottering everywhere, such a position in the Republic of Frankfurt might be more secure than his ministerial post in the Duchy of Weimar. Goethe does not consider for one moment exchanging his independent, pleasant position in Weimar for the old-fashioned, stuffy, rigid conditions of Frankfurt. And in addition there is the problem of his sweetheart and his child; how would they fit in to the bourgeois society of his native town?

For a further two months Goethe continues his wanderings. He visits the Jacobis and then moves on to Münster, where there is another group of his admirers. This group centres round Princess Gallitzin, rich, devout, a convert to Roman Catholicism, and a friend of the philosophers Hemsterhuis and Hamann. The Princess shows him her valuable collection of Greek and Roman gems and cameos, with their finely cut mythological figures. Goethe, as he notes in his diary, enjoys interpreting these enchanting pagan subjects for the benefit of this devoutly Christian circle. As his own confession of faith he recites a poem in which the youthful *Amor* begets a new *Amor* with the Venus Urania, the child whose 'charming arrow creates the love of art'. The Princess hands him her casket of gems to take back to Weimar to study and Goethe, overjoyed at the thought of taking this treasure home, decides to return to his sweetheart, having spent the last weeks forgetting the campaign and all its misery in a round of pleasant talks and discussions.

Goethe reaches Weimar shortly before Christmas. Christiane and the indispensable Meyer have seen to it that all the alterations are complete. Goethe is received with shouts of joy. There are none of the promised gifts from Paris, but he has Princess Gallitzin's beautiful collection. Carefully he bears the casket to the room that is to house his collections of antiquities; he will have much to discuss with Meyer about his treasure. He intends to devote himself once more, for a time, to the study of the ancients, as the present has proved so unfortunate. He turns to Plato, perhaps to the passage in which Socrates, in his defence, talks of his 'daimon', the voice which, since childhood, has given him counsel and advice, and which, 'whenever it speaks, tries to dissuade me from doing what I want to do, but never encourages me to do it. It is this voice which always opposes my intention to meddle in affairs of State.' Natural science is not to be neglected; he has managed to save all his notes and papers, even the ones that got soaked with rain, and his thoughts are crystallizing themselves more and more clearly into irrefutable propositions. A few more years of undisturbed work and he will be ready to present to the world this greatest of all his achievements.

His diary of the campaign he has destroyed in Düsseldorf.

# 30

# *The First German Republic*

History is not going to allow Goethe this rest. In January 1793 he learns that Louis XVI has been executed, sentenced by a majority of only a few votes in the National Assembly. The guillotine has been in action for six months, working at ever-increasing pressure, for the traitors and the guilty are legion. Before it comes to a halt several thousands will have been executed, including the traitors Danton and Desmoulins, who had led the storming of the Bastille, the Girondists who had unleashed the first Revolutionary war, the extreme radicals, and finally the traitors Robespierre and Saint-Just; to these can be added numerous Revolutionary generals such as Luckner, Custine, poets like André Chenier, men of learning like the great chemist Lavoisier, aristocrats, crooks, idealists, conspirators and little seamstresses. Goethe hears only a faint echo of these events and of the sinister intrigues of ambitious personalities engaging in mutual denunciation and murder. The jumble of high-minded idealists and ruthless careerists becomes more obscure to him every day. The innocent are slaughtered like rabbits while the cunning ones slink off like foxes and triumph.

At the beginning of the year the old tale of *Reynard the Fox* falls into his hands and strikes him as a true mirror of the times. The fable had been fashioned by medieval monks, with their own cause secretly in mind; the head, the intelligence, is what matters, not brute force. Reynard with his cunning proves himself the master, superior to all the heraldic and noble beasts, to the wolf, the bear and the noble but foolish lion, their king. He triumphs even in combat and solemn ordeal with his enemy Isegrim, who relies solely on the weapon of his teeth, and he triumphs through cunning: he shaves himself and rubs grease on to make himself more slippery, uses his tail to beat dust into his enemy's face and blind him, seizes him from below by his genitals and tugs at him until the wolf rolls bleeding in his own excrement. Reynard has triumphed and all his many crimes are forgotten. The monks changed the fable to suit the standards of the day: in the rough tenth century the fox is exalted, in the gentler thirteenth century the Dutch poet Willem has him outlawed in the end; soon he is the conquering hero again, round whom everyone throngs. In his epic poem, *Reineke Fuchs*, Goethe writes: 'It is always like this in the world ... each wanted to stand next the victor and preen himself. Some played the flute, others sang, or blew the trumpet and beat drums in between.' There is not much to be added to the old tale; Goethe transcribes it almost word for word, using a prose version made by Gottsched.

No models are necessary, they are provided by the times; the whole history of this year, down to the individual figures involved, is a living illustration of the old fable which, once and for all, had created eternal types and a cynical wisdom that was constantly being proved anew. Goethe is still at work on his cantos when the Duke summons him once more to active service. He has been able to enjoy the warmth and comfort of his home, his fire and his sweetheart for barely three months. Meanwhile much has happened. While the allied retreat was still in progress, Custine had marched boldly into the Rhineland. His forces are always called 'armies', but in reality they were small detachments of men, eighteen thousand in all, operating on their own, without plan of campaign or instructions from Paris, where no real High Command or other stable authority existed. Custine is given free rein, so long as he is successful. All the Revolutionary generals are *condottieri* or war-lords. Each has his own plans, his own style. Custine, ex-Marquis, wears an enormous moustache, the mark of a free man; his men call him *le général moustache*. He likes to make powerful speeches and thunder revolutionary phrases; he despises the Paris orators as babblers. Nevertheless he uses the slogan coined by the deputy Merlin de Thionville: 'War to the palaces, peace to the cottages.' Danton has called for world revolution. All the liberated peoples should rally to the French nation as the standard-bearer of liberty. They should form free republics or, still better, join the great universal republic.

Custine's soldiers are a rough lot, often in rags. At first they are laughed at. Goethe makes fun of them too: dwarf-like in stature and like a band of robbers is how they appear to him, in contrast to the tall cuirassiers of his Duke with their carefully powdered pigtails – still worn by Goethe too – their beautifully whitened collars, and top boots reaching to their hips. But these *sansculottes* go about in shoes and trousers, or even barefoot. They stick their spoons through holes in their hats which, in the Rhineland, earns them the name of 'spoon soldiers'. Their general, Custine, uses a large spoon to skim off the surplus so carefully stored up by these rich, sleepy old Imperial towns. Levies are the new method of financing war; the general also takes his share.

Like a wolf Custine pounces on the gentle flocks of sheep along the so-called *Pfaffenstrasse*, or priests' way, with its string of rich archbishoprics, abbeys and Imperial towns. Hitherto the Empire has remained neutral in the war of intervention, but such formalities have no meaning any more. Speier, although a free city, has been the allies' main depot; the city council had protested and then given in: reason enough for Custine to occupy it. Koblenz and Mainz have become centres of *émigré* conspirators; reason enough to take them. The Imperial city of Frankfurt has no special debt to pay but might become an enemy strong point, so Custine extends his advance to include this too. Goethe's mother has her first experience of war and occupation; the inhabitants have to pay a levy of two million francs. Custine delivers one of his addresses in the market place and reminds the people of the coronation of the Emperor Franz a few years previously: 'Have you seen an Emperor here since?' he sneers. 'You will never see one again!'

After a short time Custine has to withdraw; Prussian and Hessian troops are advancing. In Mainz, where he was greeted enthusiastically and fêted, he has established a strong base. The plan is to form a free Rhenish Republic, as a nucleus for an uprising of the whole of Germany. The finest minds in Germany have issued a call to freedom from the yoke of tyranny. Now the moment has come. All that is necessary is enthusiasm for the new idea of nationhood, in which the Neo-Franks have already shown the way, and the chains will fall away.

The Germans, however, are not a nation. Their Emperor, as King of Bohemia and Hungary, is at war, but his troops – Pandours, Croats, Czechs, Slovenes – rarely understand German. Prussia is about to increase its population by a third of Poland. There are principalities with names like Sachsen – Weimar – Eisenach – Jena, bishoprics, abbeys and counties. There is supposedly an army of the Empire, though it is seldom seen in the field, and at Regensburg there is an Imperial Diet without power or influence. The Germans feel a deep attachment to their hereditary rulers, provided they do not change too often; in the ecclesiastical principalities they change at every election of an archbishop or abbot. The Germans cling to their ancient rights and liberties, where these still exist, and to ancient forms of bondage, to which they have grown accustomed.

In Mainz the ruler is Archbishop von Erthal, though in reality it is Madame de Coudenhoven, a charming, cultured lady. Goethe makes her acquaintance when the catastrophe is over and calls her *la parure du château*. She on her part praises the people of Frankfurt, saying they had behaved better than the fickle population of Mainz, and had proved themselves true citizens. She would like to be a citizen of Frankfurt, she says. 'Nothing easier', replies Goethe; 'you have only to marry the one in front of you'.

The Archbishop, High Chancellor of the Empire and head of the Electoral College, is reputed to be the wealthiest prelate in Christendom. His territories extend far and wide; in the Middle Ages they had reached as far as Prague, and they still include possessions like Erfurt, in the midst of Protestant Thuringia, where the Governor, Dalberg, is the friend and trusted adviser of the nearby House of Weimar. Erthal loves pomp; the castle and park near Mainz, named by him *La Favorite*, is one of the finest of its day. He has revived the old university, his secretary is the great historian, Johannes von Müller, his librarian Forster, the world traveller and companion of Cook; his theatre is famous.

The ideas of the new age have penetrated Mainz. Sartorius' reading-room is the meeting-place of professors, officials, students and businessmen. The Archbishop's personal physician is to be seen there, as is also his superintendent of police. They read the French newspapers, discuss the petticoat government at Court and the financial situation – in spite of his vast income the Elector is deeply in debt. They are enthusiastic about the great tribunes and orators in Paris and about the constitution, but complain of the apathy of their own people, of their lack of spirit, dreaming away their lives under the pastoral staff. They discuss the peasants, whose dreams are not so happy and who pay the taxes to finance the extravagance. They write manifestos, and are convinced that bold action on the part of a few brave men will bring about the collapse of the whole outmoded structure, as it did the feudal splendour of Versailles. They are waiting only for the great moment, and it is at hand.

Custine is approaching. The garrison of this great frontier fortress of Mainz, as it nominally is, would need to number thirty thousand men if its wide bastions and ramparts were to be defended; in fact it numbers two thousand, mostly Austrians and Prussians. The Elector's forces, another few thousand strong, have had a short encounter with the French and been taken prisoner, with very little shooting. The citizens are summoned to man the walls. Custine's men have reached the meadows beyond the city walls, where the town's washing is still lying out to dry. 'The French were so polite, they called the women to remove the washing so that it would not get dirty', an eye-witness relates. The French artillery fires a shot over the thickly manned ramparts, 'the gentlemen ran right and left along the *terreplein* and in less than five minutes there was not a citizen to be seen'.

Thus it begins as a farce, but the end is serious enough. On Custine's entry the reading-room forms itself into a Club, the 'Clubbists' as its members are called. The tree of liberty is erected, and there is dancing and singing; it is a great festival of freedom and brotherhood.

Custine summons the city elders and corporations and lays three questions before them: Do they accept the new French Constitution? Do they want one of their own? Do they want to retain the old one? The city officials protest their great respect for France but declare that their position and – immortal answer – their 'natural phlegm' do not permit them to take a stand on such bold proposals. A modified monarchy, they think, might be the best solution.

The 'Club' intervenes and assumes the leadership. There are genuine idealists among its members, men like Georg Forster, who has travelled round the world with Cook and been to Tahiti with him, is a great naturalist and a correspondent of Goethe's, the friend and teacher of Alexander von Humboldt and one of the best German prose writers of the day; his fate and early death in Paris long remained in the public memory. Then, from one of the neighbouring villages, there is Adam Lux, the 'peasant philosopher', a young man with long flowing hair, grey eyes and a sensitive mouth, the figure of a Hölderlin rather than a revolutionary. He began with a dissertation *On Enthusiasm* and is to end, an ecstatic defender of Charlotte Corday, under the guillotine in Paris, where, with Forster, he goes to present the message from the First German Republic to the National Assembly, but where, within a few weeks, he finds himself disillusioned and in despair, distributing pamphlets with exhortations to unity, to universal brotherhood, not tyranny. Goethe has raised a small memorial to him in *Hermann und Dorothea*, where he is described in the person of Dorothea's first fiancé: 'a noble youth who, in the first ardour of the lofty idea of striving for noble liberty, went to Paris where he soon met a terrible death; for there, as at home, he fought against despotism and intrigue'.

In Mainz the first ardour of lofty ideas soon turns to despotism and intrigue. The 'Club' itself is already split; alongside the idealists are busybodies and place-seekers, as well as some able men who are later to hold high administrative positions. There is antagonism between the local people and 'those from outside', who are not natives of Mainz. Custine is disappointed. He is under urgent pressure from the capital, where they are not interested in independent republics but only in complete integration.

Merlin de Thionville arrives in Mainz and dissolves the 'Club'; he appoints a new one. Custine has already declared: 'The Rhinelanders want to be slaves!' Forster comments bitterly: 'They have to be ordered to liberty!'

Mainz has become a drab town. Trade is almost at a standstill, the craftsmen have little work. In the country there is ravaging and requisitioning; the contributions are often collected two and three times. The old taxes have gone, the new ones are just as bad. Fear is present too; there is constant talk of reverses being suffered by the Revolutionary armies. Under very uncertain auspices the deputies of the Rhenish Republic meet in March, at the Knights' Hall of the Teutonic Order in Mainz. Once more hopes are high. They vote for a free and independent State, comprising all territories on the left bank of the Rhine; these consist of archbishoprics, twenty small principalities, counties and baronies.

Custine is not satisfied with this, and after further deliberations – in which the deputies express their hope for future independence – it is unanimously decided that 'the people of the German Rhineland wish to be admitted into the French Republic'. Forster, Adam Lux and a third deputy are dispatched to Paris to lay the resolution before the National Assembly. A salvo from thirty guns announces the creation of the First German Republic.

But the people can already hear the Prussian cannon fire from across the Rhine. They are forced to take the oath of allegiance to the new régime;

non-compliance means banishment and confiscation of property. In the squares the tree of liberty is joined by four gallows. Entrenchments are dug in the fields outside the town. *La Favorite* disappears with all its summer-houses and parks. Custine, too, has vanished; appointed Commander-in-Chief of the Army of the Rhine he has gone to Landau, where he is rumoured to have suffered severe rebuffs. He calls for reinforcements from Mainz; Prussian, Austrian and Hessian troops are closing in on all sides. The great coalition, on the point of collapse after the catastrophe in Champagne, has been patched up and even extended: the Holy Roman Empire herself is now at war, whether she likes it or not, and England, Holland and Sardinia have joined in. In April Mainz is surrounded by the Allies.

At the end of May Goethe arrives in camp to join his Duke and the 6th Prussian Cuirassiers, the latter quite unsuited to the siege of a fortress. He has brought with him his work on the *Farbenlehre* as well as the draft of *Reineke Fuchs*, writing simultaneously at his hexameters on the old animal fable and his optical propositions.

He has comfortable quarters at Marienborn; for the Princes, again strongly represented in this campaign, the most delightful pavilions, summer-houses and grounds are being constructed by the soldiers and peasants – almost a second *La Favorite*. Nor is there any lack of favourites. Friedrich Wilhelm II spends most of his time in Frankfurt with Fräulein Bethmann, of the great banking family, who has hopes of contracting a morganatic marriage with him. Prince Louis Ferdinand has formed a liaison with the lovely *émigrée* Madame de Contades. For the men, who must also be looked after because Friedrich Wilhelm is the soldiers' friend, brothels are established in tents at prices ranging from eight to forty-five *kreuzer*.

Visitors come to the camp from far and wide to watch the great bombardment. Goethe notes 'the heavenly appearance' of the Princesses of Mecklenburg, the future Queen Luise of Prussia among them; they once stayed at his mother's house. The neighbouring peasants and their families, in Sunday attire, stroll by to have a look; for a tip the sentries let them up to the forward positions, with the warning to 'duck' when they see the flashes from the cannon on the other side. As they 'duck' the cannon balls pass slowly over the earthworks.

It is a strange war, waged with humour and traces of chivalry. One night a French officer leads a sortie across the Rhine and surprises a village where Prussian troopers are dancing with the village girls; he takes the troopers prisoner and apologizes to the girls for taking their partners away. The sentries shout abuse at one another: 'Murderers of your King!' – 'Miserable slaves!' and then exchange presents.

One French commander, leading his troops in a skirmish, exchanges pistol shots with a Prussian officer, and then proposes a duel with sabres. 'Fine,' says the Prussian, 'but supposing I meet you as a friend?' 'Suits me,' replies the Frenchman, and they shake hands and embrace; others join in and they arrange a picnic the next day between the lines. Senior members of the two sides take part as well: on the Prussian side Prince Louis, and on the French the two delegates from the National Assembly. Champagne is served and, to show how well stocked the fortress is, the French bring partridges and pies. The Prussians are fascinated at seeing Merlin, one of the legendary figures of the Revolution, one of the men responsible for the murder of the King, and the man who shouted, 'War to the palaces'. He is small, thick-set and very agile, his face almost black and with long matted hair down to his shoulders. He wears the uniform of an ordinary artillery-man, his cap is without braid, and he trails an enormous sabre casually behind him. He is known to be the moving spirit behind the defence, his soldiers call him 'dare-devil', and above all he is a powerful man in Paris. Prince Louis has a long talk with him.

Recent political developments lie behind this strange picnic. In Paris Danton has adopted a new line: having issued the call to undermine the thrones of Europe by propaganda, he now orders no interference in the internal affairs of other countries! Like his friend Dumouriez, who has already fled, he wants to negotiate with Prussia and split the coalition. The plan is smuggled into the Allied headquarters through diplomatic channels; Goethe hears of it when it is being discussed. Once more he feels how senseless this whole territorial bargaining is and how worthless the Holy Roman Empire, which is to be sold and then bought back piecemeal by its own members. The Prussians, however, listen very attentively to these proposals, and two years later, at the Peace of Bâle, they become a reality.

At the moment they are still fighting. The wily Merlin knows that a new storm is brewing in Paris. He knows that even the all-powerful tribune Danton is faltering, that the merciless Robespierre is in the ascendant. He decides it will be better not to capitulate too soon. The National Assembly is easily frightened, and this means death to those held responsible.

In the meantime the Allies have brought up more artillery. The devout Bishop of Würzburg has lent his 'twelve apostles', heavy mortars. They push their entrenchments and parallels nearer the fortress. There are fierce skirmishes for defended positions and villages. Prince Louis is wounded by a ricochet, though not severely, and tells his *aide* to inform the King: 'I beg him to send me to Mannheim, to Madame de Contades.'

Amidst all this Goethe carries on with his own siege, against Newton's fortress, the *Bastille* of superstitious physics. He is well provided with ammunition. Some years previously the physician and writer Marat, now in Paris the most violent of all the Revolutionaries, had published a tract, *Discoveries in Light*, which Goethe has brought with him. He wants to discover if Marat is also an enemy of Newton. He compares them, and notes down his own 'experiences' alongside. Two days before he puts his signature to the page, 'Marienborn, July 15, 1793', Marat is stabbed in his bath by Charlotte Corday – a scene immortalized on canvas by his friend David –

but Goethe cannot yet have heard the news. He formulates his thesis in monumental phrases: 'Light is the simplest, most undivided, most homogeneous element we know. It is not compounded. Least of all of coloured lights.' All previous experiments, he declares, are wrong.

He goes further, and drafts an appeal for a large society, or academy, to follow up his theses and to carry on the war against the priests of the old heresy. As in one of his Court entertainments, he makes everyone pass across the stage: the chemist, the physicist, the instrument maker, whose job it is to invent the new apparatus, painters and historians, who are to find new historical evidence. Finally he appears himself: he finds the trail already blazed, his task is to eliminate from the truth what is false and complicated, and to assume the unpleasant duty of defending the pure gospel against all who try to deface it. He asks for support, and demonstrates from his own experience how beneficial such research 'can be, especially in our times, in distracting the mind from other obtrusive thoughts'.

As this document shows, he feels very remote from the conflict of the day. What he wants is a republic of the mind, an empire of culture; the German Rhenish Republic and the question as to which portions of the Holy Roman Empire Prussia or Bavaria may snatch are matters of complete indifference to him. After the experiences of these years his approach to all world events is to be that of a quiet observer, ironic and sceptical, even during the war of liberation of his own people. He does not want to be engaged in them. In this world of politics he feels himself to be only a guest, as he does in Weimar. He has constructed his own world.

Meanwhile the entrenchments and parallels have been pushed far enough forward for the bombardment to be effective. The 'twelve apostles' set fire to the cathedral and other churches. After three weeks the fortress surrenders. The garrison is given honourable terms: free withdrawal, with their colours and their arms, on condition that they do not take part in any action against the Allies for a year. The members of the 'Club', a difficult point in the negotiations, are to be exchanged for hostages, whom Custine has taken from among the leading citizens of the town and sent to Belfort.

Goethe watches the withdrawal, which takes two days, from the window of a house overlooking the route. He observes the *sansculottes* with amusement; a motley crowd, small of stature, they are not in the least downhearted but sing, shake the Prussians by the hand, and wave to the people. At their sides, their bundles in their hands, walk girls of Mainz who have decided to return to France with them: 'Hey, Lieschen,' the people shout, 'do you want to see the world too?' 'Won't you soon walk through your shoes? Happy journey!' Then come the soldiers of the line and, finally, the *chasseurs à cheval*, with their band playing the *Marseillaise* in slow time. 'It was moving and awe-inspiring,' writes Goethe, 'and a solemn sight to see the horsemen approach, tall, thin men, no longer young, their carriage in keeping with the slow strains of the music; singly one might have compared them to Don Quixote, *en masse* they made an impression of intense gravity.' Bringing up the rear come the delegates, with Rieffel, the Colonel of the Clubbists, at Merlin's side. The populace hurl themselves at him. Merlin bellows: 'You know who I am! I am the nation's representative! I will avenge every insult. You have not seen the last of me here!' Prussian soldiers with fixed bayonets intervene. Merlin and the uniformed Clubbists march on.

The next day brings wilder scenes. The first column had comprised the *élite*, the second consists of less disciplined hordes. In the meantime the inhabitants who had fled, or been driven out, have started streaming back; they are in a rage. Merlin has only taken with him those Clubbists who played an active part in the defence, the others he has left to their fate. They try to escape in carts and carriages but are dragged out and beaten; some are killed. Goethe, from his window, puts a stop to one of these scenes; in a thundering voice he orders them to stop. No violence! The King has granted a free withdrawal, the people's only role is as peaceful onlookers! The crowd falls back.

Most of the Clubbists are seized; in some cases the French volunteers give away those who have infiltrated into their ranks. The crowds run wild in the city, plundering and smashing up the houses of known sympathizers. The military intervene, tardily, and arrest the survivors. Their situation is parlous, they are forsaken by everyone. The French army of the Rhine refuses to recognize the capitulation. No exchange of hostages takes place. The Clubbists have to spend two years in custody, until 1795 when the Peace of Bâle cedes the left bank of the Rhine to France and finally sets them free; as a result, for twenty years Mainz becomes a French provincial town.

The refusal of the army of the Rhine to recognize the capitulation had its reasons, because a sorry chapter of intrigues now begins, with Merlin in the role of Reynard the Fox. The leaders of the French armies, which were to relieve Mainz, are the first to see the danger they are in. Going into the attack before they themselves are attacked, their representatives hasten to Paris and demand court-martial for the 'traitors', whose duty was to hold out until help reached them. The National Assembly orders the arrest of the guilty Mainz officers. Merlin races to Paris. Dirty, unshaved, he storms into a meeting of the Assembly and mounts the rostrum. He rushes over to the Jacobin Club, where he talks and lies, saying that the fortress was reduced to starvation, they ate rats and cats, there was no more surgical equipment, the guns were worn out. His friends come to his aid, one boldly declaring the garrison had killed thirty thousand of the enemy – in fact the Allied losses in killed and wounded were three thousand. The Assembly rescinds its order. Now Merlin goes into the attack and demands court-martial for the leaders of the army of the Rhine. When this fails he comes to an agreement with the army's delegates: Custine shall pay the debt.

'Monsieur de Custine' he calls him in the Committee of Public Safety, and the title itself is his death warrant.

Merlin has judged the situation rightly. Danton is finished. Robespierre takes over. He declares Custine to be the nation's murderer, no further proof is needed, no complicated procedure: in Mainz he gave himself up to luxury and dissipation and demoralized the troops, the army is riddled with evidence of his intrigues.

The first victor of the Rhineland and of the fortress of Mainz, the creator of the First German Republic, is sent to the guillotine, together with his son, his aide and his wife, a few days before Adam Lux, the delegate of the German Rhineland, mounts the scaffold. The cunning Merlin, who must clearly escape from the inflammable situation in Paris as soon as possible, plays a final masterstroke: he gets himself appointed as commander of the capitulated army, which is being sent to the Vendée; out of action for use against an outside enemy, it can be used to suppress local risings of peasants and aristocrats in the provinces.

Goethe soon leaves the ruined city but, following his procedure after the previous campaign, he does not return home. He goes to Mannheim to visit Prince Louis, and then on to Heidelberg to see his old friend Fraülein Delph. In Mannheim he meets his brother-in-law Schlosser and discusses with him, as an experienced man of the world, his great plans for a universal academy and association of scientists to carry on his work on the theory of colours. Schlosser smiles and taunts him with his childish enthusiasm for such absurd ideas; does he really envisage a great, combined German undertaking, and at a time like this! ...

Goethe takes deep offence, grows biting and sarcastic, and leaves in a temper; he never sees his brother-in-law again. He takes this lack of sympathy as symbolic: nowhere can he look for help, all he can expect is scorn and arrogance. The French Revolution, Goethe declares, has stirred up people's minds and aroused in every private citizen the presumption that he is fit to govern. He must tread his path alone, there will be no friend at his side.

At the end of August, in ill-humour, he returns to Weimar; but even the comfort of his home, with his sweetheart and his son, cannot hold him for long. At the end of the year he goes to Jena, where he lives in a small bachelor flat. Since he can find no response in men, he turns once more to the quiet, grateful world of plants; a botanical garden is being established at the university. Even the restless Karl August has resigned the command of his Prussian regiment and is going to devote himself for a time to the government of his four little principalities.

As Goethe summarizes it later, a single day at headquarters in Champagne and a single day in ravaged Mainz are for him symbols of contemporary history, and of the terrible collapse of all institutions. An active and productive mind will be forgiven if it devotes itself to quiet study and clings to it 'as to a plank of wood after a shipwreck'.

# 31

# *Two Masters*

1793, the forty-third year of his life, marks the end of Goethe's active participation in world affairs. During his remaining forty years he stays within the narrow confines of Weimar, leaving the little town only for his annual visit to one of the Bohemian spas, or for short journeys to the Rhine or the Main. He takes cognizance of contemporary events only in so far as it is absolutely necessary. In the twelve years of his correspondence with Schiller, who now becomes his great friend and colleague, even the name Bonaparte, which is one everybody's lips, is scarcely mentioned; anyone expecting to glean a picture of the times from the six volumes of these letters will be sadly disappointed. They are concerned with quite other matters. The fundamental problems of poetics are discussed: rules and laws for it are to be drawn up; epic and dramatic poetry are to be kept distinct and separate. A new classicism is to be created, co-equal with that of the ancients. Above all the two men practise the most searching self-analysis; the correspondence is a dialogue, with no other participants, carried on in solitude, on a high and lonely plateau where neither tree nor shrub is to be seen. If colleagues are mentioned they are for the most part literary hacks or insignificant mediocrities; if there is any mention of the public, of the Germans, it is in terms of utter contempt.

Looking back on it, Goethe calls the state of German cultural life at the time one of 'aristocratic anarchy'. He compares it to that of the Middle Ages, 'which was advancing towards a higher culture'. To Goethe and Schiller falls the task of creating this higher culture, and in this task they succeed.

Schiller had lived in Weimar for seven years before having any close contact with Goethe. On his arrival in July 1787, filled with high hopes of the 'Weimar giants', of the *Musenhof*, the author of *Die Räuber* and *Don Carlos* suffered bitter disillusion. Herder's reception of him was friendly but he had read none of his works: 'His attitude to me was that to a person of whom he knew nothing beyond the fact that he was considered to be someone.' Wieland had read some of his writings but found them lacking in taste and refinement; Anna Amalie did not like them. On a visit to Knebel, Schiller established the fact that Goethe's spirit had moulded all those within his circle: contempt for all philosophy and in its stead an exaggerated veneration for nature, 'in short a certain childlike *naïveté* of reasoning characterizes him and the whole of his following here. They are more interested in looking for plants or pursuing mineralogy....' In Weimar Schiller found 'so many families, so many separate snail-shells from which the owner scarcely emerges even to sun himself'. Very sure of himself, he felt superior to this little world around him: 'I am really too much the worldling in their midst, they are altogether lacking in experience.' In fact Schiller was a very gifted diplomat, and Goethe said later that he would have been as pre-eminent in the councils of state as he was at the tea-table. He planned his output with foresight and realism: 'I have to live by writing and so must keep my eye on what is profitable.' After entertaining a variety of projects, which he discussed exhaustively with his friend Körner, he married the daughter of one of the old aristocratic Thuringian families, and thereby acquired far-reaching social contacts. It is only with Goethe, who holds himself severely aloof, that Schiller is unable to make any contact. At their very first meeting he finds him stiff and uncommunicative. It annoys him that Goethe, while charming and captivating everyone, always maintains his independence 'like a god, without giving anything of himself – this appears to me to be a consistent and systematic method of procedure aimed entirely at satisfying to the utmost his own self-love. People should not allow themselves to be imposed on by this kind of behaviour.' He soon finds that 'this person, this Goethe, stands in my way, and he reminds me often that fate has dealt harshly with me. How easily his genius has been borne along by his fate, and how hard I have had to fight, up to this very minute.'

Schiller never frees himself entirely from this mood, even during the years of his closest intimacy with Goethe. Friendship is an inadequate word to describe this relationship, however pleasant it may be to visualize the two poets hand in hand, in perfect unity, as they are represented on their Weimar monument. The facts, however, are different; their relationship is much more like a truce between two great powers that have the deepest respect for one another and open their common frontier for purposes of communication; many of their letters read like an exchange of diplomatic notes. Schiller is constantly forced to play the diplomat in dealing with his extremely difficult partner, and for a long time Goethe makes things very difficult for him. Goethe's eulogies of Schiller came after the latter's death; it was only then that he fully realized the magnitude of his loss.

Schiller has to woo him like a coy damsel, and on one occasion his masculine impatience drives him to the drastic remark: ' I look on him as a haughty prudish woman whom one wants to get with child.' He manifests an altogether unusual combination of love and hate, the feelings of a Brutus for a Caesar, 'I could kill his spirit and then love him again with all my heart.' He wants to surround Goethe with spies, who are to report back to him, because he does not want to question him personally about himself and run the risk of being cold-shouldered, a fate he has suffered only too often.

Goethe resists for a long time. He finds Schiller physically unsympathetic; tall and somewhat haggard, he is never well and his cheeks are always flushed. The mere suggestion of illness is anathema to Goethe, as are Schiller's constant smoking and snuff taking, and the yellow tobacco stain beneath his sharp aquiline nose. Schiller's way of life is the complete anti-thesis of his own: unmethodical to a degree, he rises late, often not until noon, works far into the night and, in order to keep awake, is forced to resort to a wide variety of stimulants, such as coffee, punch or the famous rotten apples which he keeps in a drawer. Catching their aroma one day, Goethe flings open the window in horror and fills his lungs with fresh air. The man's writings, which are arousing an enthusiasm in Germany comparable only to that evoked by his own early works, strike him as confused, abstruse or, in the case of the philosophical works, perverted and even dangerous. That this particular man should establish himself in Weimar and become, to some extent, a power in the land, he finds extremely disagreeable. He cuts him for as long as he can without causing an open scandal. Finally Goethe hits on the idea of appointing Schiller as a lecturer at the University of Jena. It is not much of a post, there being no salary attached, and Schiller thinks hard before accepting it; he finally does so to avoid causing bad feelings in Weimar. Karl August gives his consent, 'especially as this acquisition involves no expenditure'. Schiller receives no salary, being paid only the students' fees, and after the initial burst of enthusiasm, when the students storm the lecture room to catch a glimpse of the author of *Die Räuber* and serenade him with music with three *vivats*, the attendance falls to thirty, not all of whom pay their fees. Eventually, with downcast face and lowered voice, the Duke grants him a salary of two hundred *thalers*, which is the very most he can offer. On the strength of this salary Schiller is able to marry. But it is from far-away Denmark, not from Weimar, in the persons of the Crown Prince of Holstein and one of the ministers, Schimmelmann, that he receives an annual allowance of one thousand *thalers*, which relieves him of serious financial worry for several years. The financial story of the 'Weimar giants' of the classic age forms a very sorry chapter; it was over this question that Goethe's long friendship with Herder came to grief, and in later years there was a veritable exodus of the wretchedly ill-paid Jena professors.

They were all dependent on what additional income they could earn by writing. Schiller supplemented his earnings by journalism in these years, and showed that he had the makings of a great journalist. Here his rhetorical and political gifts show to advantage, as does his breadth of view, and his capacity for clarifying big issues and presenting them with verve and imagination. His historical works, which for many years provided him with his living, are great journalism; his history of the Thirty Years War appeared in Göschen's *Damenkalender*. He never engaged in historical research and said himself, when preparing his lectures, 'many of the students probably know more history than their professor'. He began his course with a large-scale survey of the whole of history and this was the only part of his work from which he derived any pleasure; the rest was a matter of duty, and he gave it up as soon as he could. He published a very large number of purely bread and butter works, and to-day only the Schiller collector knows such items as the series of volumes he edited on the 'most curious rebellions', the historical memoirs, or the series of crime stories based on the great French collection of Pitaval. Among other things he contemplated a German Plutarch, which might have been a fine work. The great publisher and industrialist, Cotta, who was just starting out on his career, wanted to engage Schiller as editor-in-chief of the new daily paper he had founded on the model of the great English and French dailies; under the name *Augsburger Allgemeine* this later became for nearly one hundred years the most influential German newspaper.

Schiller, however, now has other plans. He wants to withdraw, like Goethe, from daily politics into the realm of ideas. He prepares a draft prospectus for a journal that is to employ the best brains in the country and create a new epoch. Going boldly ahead, before even finding a publisher, he prints his draft, with the statement: 'a publisher in every respect worthy of this undertaking has already been found . . .', and then, having made a contract with him, he proceeds to insert in his beautiful flowing handwriting the name of Cotta. He announces that the most celebrated authors have already formed themselves into an association, while he is still sending out letters in all directions with urgent requests for collaboration. He plans to win Kant, Herder and Goethe for the project, for which he has devised the classic-sounding title, *Die Horen* – the *Horae* or the 'Hours'. Everything of merely current or passing interest is to be excluded. There is to be nothing about religious matters or political institutions; the journal is to be devoted to the world of *belles lettres* and the world of scholarship, to the free investigation of truth and the fruitful exchange of ideas.

Armed with this project he once more approaches Goethe and now at last, after many long years, he is successful. Their conversation about the *Ur-Pflanze*, on the door-step of Schiller's house at Jena, provides his first real contact with the unapproachable. In the course of it Goethe realizes, despite his annoyance, that he is face to face with an equal. The boundary line between them is established at the outset; across it conversation will now be possible. Schiller is of a philosophical turn of mind; well and good says Goethe, he himself is not. But philosophy, so everyone tells him, has become a powerful force. The name of Kant crops up everywhere; Jena is full of it, the professors swear by him and declare that with Kant a new epoch has begun. He is the *Alleszermalmer*, the universal pulverizer, who has swept away all previous speculation once and for all, the author of a turning-point in the history of the mind, as important as the French Revolution. The Germans are to be 'the nation of poets and thinkers' – religious matters and political institutions they can leave to others. This is a programme that Goethe finds both sympathetic and plausible. He does not read books on philosophy but he wants to be informed, and conversation is his favourite method of learning. This Hofrat Schiller, well versed in Kant's ideas, will be able to tell him something about it. The man talks well and with spirit, in spite of his ugly Swabian dialect and his unpleasant voice. He shows great respect and seems to be a good listener. He was destined for medicine and may have some feeling for natural science; perhaps one might be able to enlist his interest in colour and the *Farbenlehre*, provided it is made clear to him that this is a field for 'observation', not for so-called 'ideas'. And lastly, so he hears on all sides, Hofrat Schiller knows how to woo the public. Everything he undertakes is successful. His plays are staged everywhere, his writings are discussed by everybody, he is the darling of the booksellers, a favourite with the readers; even Karl August, who seldom reads, thinks highly of him. For almost fifteen years now Goethe has had no success with the public at all. His *Collected Writings* are still sitting on Göschen's shelves, and no one has shown the slightest interest in his pamphlets on natural science. A new edition of his works, on which a different publisher, Unger of Berlin, has recently embarked, has so far had a very poor reception; the first volume contains *Der Gross-Kophta*, which has been a universal disappointment. Goethe feels the time has come to take the stage again; he has been hearing for too long that he is a spent force. For several years now he has been planning a new novel; he has already written a preliminary version, and laid it aside. It is to have a theatrical setting, a subject in which the public is always interested, and is to portray a young man's cultural development, which could have far-reaching educational significance; Wilhelm Meister is to be the young apprentice's name. Goethe is jealous of this idea of his, which he believes to be particularly promising, and when he hears that his old friend Merck is contemplating a book on similar lines he expressly forbids him to proceed, claiming the theme as his own exclusive property. At the same time he knows how slowly he works and how dependent he is on a favourable wind; he recalls, too, what a salutary effect the pressure of a publisher's contract had on the completion of *Tasso* and *Iphigenie*. For this reason he has already made an agreement with his new publisher over *Wilhelm Meister*, although the book is still little more than a project. The novel is to form the centre-piece of his *Neue Schriften*, and will probably occupy two, three or even four volumes.

And so Goethe accepts Schiller's very respectfully worded invitation to collaborate on *Die Horen*. Schiller has spoken of a group of people whose admiration for the master is boundless, and has mentioned the names of Fichte, Wilhelm von Humboldt and the historian Woltmann. Goethe is a little uneasy about Fichte. The man is gruff, proud and difficult; newly appointed to the Chair of Philosophy at Jena he has already caused an upheaval. Of his importance as a scholar there can be no question, his position is that of Kant's heir apparent; his book *Kritik aller Offenbarung*, which appeared anonymously, was accepted as a work of the master's until Kant himself named the author. On this ground he would have been a satisfactory replacement for his predecessor, Wieland's son-in-law Reinhold, likewise a great Kantian, who has exchanged his poorly paid Jena professorship for a better post at Kiel. Fichte, however, has issued some extremely disturbing political pamphlets, attempting to refute erroneous opinions about the French Revolution, and demanding back from Europe's princes the freedom of thought they have suppressed. He has used harsh and arrogant words in speaking of the princes, saying they 'were brought up, for the most part, in slothfulness and ignorance', and 'are always behind the times by at least the length of their reign'. He has been expressly told by the faculty that he is not to introduce politics into his lectures. They are annoyed because Fichte has an unprecedented attendance at his lectures. The clergy complain that he lectures even on Sundays. The troublesome man retorts that his lectures do not touch on politics; furthermore he did not apply for the post, he was asked to come, and they should have known about him. As for the theologians, he says bitingly, 'I should be free to lecture on the most sacred festivals, provided it was to empty benches!' The whole thing is nothing but academic jealousy.

In his capacity as Karl August's adviser on cultural matters, all this comes under Goethe's jurisdiction. The University of Jena is, in any case, a bugbear to him. For almost a hundred years its students have had a reputation for the worst kinds of drinking and brawling, for the coarsest code of behaviour, for the most extreme kinds of students' associations; he himself, on behalf of the Duke, has repeatedly had to quell disturbances there. For some little time now, however, a more civilized tone has prevailed, and suddenly here are new disturbances breaking out.

On the other hand Fichte appeals to him as a man of energy and ability. He may be somewhat uncouth, and is said to come from the very poorest circumstances, from a simple weaver's family; but perhaps a little fresh blood among the professors will be quite a good thing. Fichte has also sent him the proofs of his latest work, an inquiry into the whole structure of scientific knowledge, and with them a letter of homage couched in the most flattering terms and ending with the words: 'It is to you that philosophy rightly turns. Your feeling is its touchstone.'

No philosopher has ever spoken words like this to Goethe before, and they are good to hear. Apparently admirers do exist here and there among men of superior intellect. Baron Wilhelm von Humboldt, now living in

Jena, has been mentioned to him by Schiller as another great admirer. Dalberg, the Governor in Erfurt, has told him about the Baron who, through his wife, has large estates in the vicinity. Dalberg is a fine and highly cultured ecclesiastic, and he and Humboldt have fought splendid philosophical battles together in Erfurt. The latter has written on the limits of state effectiveness, in privately circulated pamphlets and in certain magazines. One of these writings contains a sentence that conforms to Goethe's own ideas of the moment:

> It seems to me that the human race has now reached a stage of culture from which it can only advance further through the development of the individual; and therefore all institutions that hinder this development and crowd people together in large masses are now more pernicious than formerly. [Or again:] The true purpose of man is the highest and most perfectly balanced cultivation of his powers in order to form a complete whole.

To the state, which everywhere is being accorded a quite undue importance as though it were a new religion, Humboldt assigns a very limited sphere of influence; what really matters is the most manifold development of the individual. All this is in complete accordance with Goethe's own views. He welcomes Humboldt into the circle of his friends.

The Baron's brother, Alexander von Humboldt, a mining expert in service in Prussia's Ansbach territories, and a friend and pupil of Georg Forster – who in the meantime has met his death in Paris – might also be an interesting addition to his circle, he feels. He has been trained in Freiberg under the great master Werner, whom Goethe considers the leading authority on geology, principally because he explains the origin of geological formations as the result of gradual, gentle precipitation in the sea. Neptune is the god of this school of geologists, whom their opponents, the believers in Vulcanism, scoffingly call 'Neptunists'. Goethe is an out and out Neptunist, and his hatred for the 'Poltergeist' school is something he cherishes for the rest of his life. Like his brother, Alexander wants to give up government service and undertake extensive travels in the New World, and like his brother he enters the circle of Goethe's acquaintances. And so, to maintain the analogy of Neptunism, we see the formation of the first strata in the broad Goethe landscape that is ultimately to surround him like a huge mountain chain. His ties with the two brothers remain. In the bare year of his activity as leader of Prussian educational life, in 1809, Wilhelm becomes the founder of Berlin University, and the originator of the German classical 'Gymnasium', which is to incorporate the cultural ideals, based on the development of the individual, that he has acquired in Jena through his association with Goethe and Schiller. With iron tenacity he remains true to his youthful goal, the cultivation of personality, and it is the very lack of any creative capacity in himself that fits him so outstandingly to externalize his activities, to recognize the widely divergent forces of German intellectual life, to appreciate and attract both Schiller and Goethe, and even their antipodes, a Fichte, a Hegel and many others. Thus he is able to create in the minds of others the ideal of a cultured man, and to found a whole system, a whole school. This is his service to history; to him, more than to any other man, is due the wide influence of the German classics in the following century.

His brother Alexander, on the other hand, is to become the last great universalist in the field of natural science. He is like Goethe in his attempt to probe the secrets of the whole universe; in his eighties he published the four volumes of his *Cosmos*, the synthesis of his lifelong researches. Alas, the work appeared too late; it was greeted enthusiastically by cultured people and given an honoured place on their bookshelves as a compendium of the natural sciences, but scientists accorded it only the respect due to a message from the spirit of a bygone age. In science, universalism had given way to specialization, to specialized fields of activity, team-work and research; but Humboldt was venerated as a founder and pioneer. His work in every field has had its sequel, whereas that of Goethe has remained the solitary vision of an individual. Humboldt had his disciples, and opened up wide fields of research in climatology, botanical geography and oceanography; in the field of meteorological research he founded an international organization for the establishment of observatories, which still exist and enjoy an importance undreamt of in his day. Humboldt is unlike Goethe in that he ranges into the infinite not merely in thought but in action: with only the lightest equipment and with no mountaineering experience he climbed Chimborazo to a height of almost 18,000 feet; he was the great re-discoverer of Central and South America of his day, and even as an old man he travelled to Central Asia. The first volumes of his great work on his travels describing his explorations at the turn of the century were published in Paris in 1814, in the middle of the war; comprising thirty folio volumes, with two thousand copper plates, it is the most gigantic publication ever undertaken by a single natural scientist, and on it Humboldt spent the greater part of his considerable fortune. Study of the vast wealth of his observations in botany, zoology, geology, astronomy, anthropology, and even in economics and politics, has still not been exhausted. During his lifetime Humboldt's fame, which grew steadily throughout his ninety years, was equal to that of Goethe, and was to overshadow it in the subsequent decades, with their idolatry of the natural sciences. Like Goethe he had two sides to his nature, and the great cosmopolitan, who had spent the decisive years of his life in extensive travelling or in Paris, later wanted to play a political role in the narrow circle of the Prussian Court, as Goethe had done in Weimar. There is a sad and grotesque picture of this world-famous figure standing in the ante-room of the Palace, where behind his back he is known as the 'encyclopaedic cat', and being accosted by some impudent field-marshal with a slap on the shoulder and the words: 'Well, little Mr Know-all, how are you?'

The close personal contact between the two giants lasted only a short time, though subsequently it was renewed from time to time. Goethe marvelled at Humboldt's many-sidedness: 'Whatever one touches on he is familiar with, and he overwhelms us with the treasures of his mind.' In his own views, however, Goethe refused to be shaken, and he was careful not to discuss with Humboldt his *Farbenlehre*; the ideas of the great explorer of volcanic phenomena about these 'Poltergeists' were highly suspect in his mind, and he once said to his friend Müller that one day he intended to write a fearful *exposé* of 'that nonsense' in hexameters. To Goethe, Humboldt was above all an inexhaustible source of stimulating knowledge, 'a fountain with many jets, under which one only has to hold receptacles, and whose waters play for us refreshingly and inexhaustibly'.

Humboldt, for his part, was deeply under the spell of Goethe's mind. Recalling their Jena discussions during his great American travels he confessed to having experienced great elation from Goethe's view on nature, 'like being equipped with new organs'. He dedicated his *Ideen zur Geographie der Pflanzen* to the author of the *Metamorphosis*, providing it with a title-page by Thorwaldsen. So we see that even with two natures as opposed as these the radiation of Goethe's mind makes itself felt, no matter how its rays may have been bent in the prism of Humboldt's own mind.

Incomparably more profound, however, is the mutual exchange of ideas between Goethe and Schiller which now begins in Jena. Hofrat Schiller takes Goethe by storm; this is the task he has set himself, and he achieves it. Goethe's agreement to collaborate on *Die Horen* is immediately followed by a long letter from Schiller, an essay rather than a letter, and the most astonishing piece of analysis ever received by one great poet from another. 'A summing-up of my whole existence', Goethe calls it. Schiller is never greater than when summing up like this in bold strokes. His handwriting alone, which in its broad, powerful sweep reflects this, made a strong appeal to Goethe, who was very influenced by such visual impressions. In this letter-essay Schiller employs the most lofty phrases. He describes Goethe as a Greek, whose Greek mind has been *geworfen* – cast, a word that has been adopted by Martin Heidegger – into the Nordic world. Tactfully he hints at the difficulties facing even the greatest genius as a result of this fate, and offers himself as a guide through the maze, a Virgil, as it were, to Goethe's Dante.

Gratefully Goethe accepts this offer. It seems to him 'as if, after such an unexpected encounter, we must continue our way together'. He is well aware that there is much about which he is not clear, and that he often hesitates too long: Schiller will stimulate and encourage him. This is what he has always felt the need of. Herder has been a disappointment in this respect, even in his Strasbourg days; he would give an initial impetus and then let go, or else would become bitter and sarcastic. Women, such as a Charlotte von Stein, can listen and be receptive but, by their nature, have had very little to offer. Now for the first and also for the last time he meets a man, cast in a big mould, with high aspirations, who is prepared to recognize his unquestioned superiority – which Herder, with his jealousy, was never quite able to do – and who, at the same time, can make a worthwhile contribution of his own to the relationship.

A certain amount of caution will be necessary. Hofrat Schiller is too eager, too impetuous; he has a sense of hurry because his health is bad, and he may not live long. Goethe, on the other hand, from his early days, when Lavater said to him 'you behave as though we intended to live to be three hundred', has counted on long life and unlimited space. And now he writes to Schiller saying he has a very strong feeling that his undertaking 'far exceeds the measure of human powers and their earthly duration'. Therefore, in this undertaking, 'he would like to deposit something and thereby not merely support it but also give it vitality'.

The word 'deposit' epitomizes his attitude exactly. His most important work, the novel *Wilhelm Meister*, he does not intend to deposit; to Schiller's intense chagrin, because he had counted on it for the paper, Goethe retains it for himself. They discuss the work thoroughly together, and Schiller writes the most detailed and enthusiastic appreciations in his letters, but Goethe refuses to part with it. Instead he gives him a little collection of short stories, or tales, about German *émigrés, Unterhaltungen deutscher Ausgewanderten*. It is a *Rahmenerzählung*, a collection of stories within a larger framework, in the manner of Boccaccio, but instead of the plague the framework is the Revolution, the plague that has driven families from their homes on the left bank of the Rhine and brought them together. They are not exactly Goethe's 'most exquisite' pieces, as Schiller, in his annoyance writes to his friend Körner. The Hofrat is forced to recognize how difficult it is to lure anything out of Goethe, and in what a very strange way such a 'naïve' genius works – 'naïve' is Schiller's term for him, as distinguished from his own genius which he calls 'sentimental'. With Goethe nothing is really planned, although he drafts out many 'schemes' – these are disconnected sketches which he jots down. Everything depends on the happy inspiration of the moment, on catching a favourable wind to fill his sails; if the breeze dies down he waits, or escapes into some other activity, or complains of the intolerable distractions of his outward life. Schiller's approach to his work is fundamentally different. He commands his muse. He plans, makes his dispositions, and carries them through with the full force of his powerful will. Being of a philosophic cast of mind he boldly formulates requirements and aesthetic laws, and then has no scruples whatever in annulling them equally boldly and adducing excellent reasons for doing so. Goethe, on the other hand, frequently drives him to silent despair by the tenacity with which he clings to a principle, or to use his own word an 'experience', once he has arrived at it. He can be stimulated, and even driven, but he will never change his mind. He always remains the man he was and is, and at times he disengages himself from Schiller's hold with almost feminine artifice.

Thus it is a battle rather than a friendship, a vastly productive contest, like the *agon* of the Greeks. From it both gather the richest harvest. Schiller writes his great dramas, the most important part of his *œuvre*. Goethe completes his novel, and under Schiller's stimulus writes his great ballads for his friend's almanachs, as well as his epic poem *Hermann und Dorothea*; *Faust* too, virtually discarded, is taken in hand again. Having wanted to give 'all that' up, he once more becomes a poet. After this meeting with Schiller he never again contemplates taking flight from his greatest gift and vocation. This friendship, coming in the middle of his life, is a true turning-point. Among all his numerous metamorphoses this is the one that transforms him most deeply. He is unable to slough it like a snake's skin, as he has done with all the previous stages in his development. For the rest of his life his skin remains coloured by these years with Schiller.

It is a strange sort of friendship. Goethe never addresses Schiller with the intimate *Du*, as he does so many of his lesser acquaintances, nor does he ever refer to him in his diaries otherwise than as *Hofrat* Schiller. Schiller, for his part, during the whole twelve years of their correspondence, mentions Goethe's Christiane only once, and then with a single word in the margin. To others he writes of Goethe's 'wretched domestic circumstances, which he is too weak to alter'; and he blames these circumstances for the fact that Goethe does not work enough, 'altogether he is producing too little at present, rich as he remains in invention and realization'.

To exhort, to warn, to stimulate, this is Schiller's office. He exercises it with the whole range of his diplomacy: by careful criticism, by suggestions for the remaining chapters of the unfinished novel, by the presentation of a great philosophic system of classical aesthetics. Goethe acquiesces in everything, up to a point; in this relationship the feminine side of his nature becomes more marked than ever. Schiller is the man; he is sharp and even biting at times, although never towards Goethe, whom he always treats with the greatest forbearance, and the weaker sides of whose nature he even vigorously defends against outside attacks. It is Schiller who lays down formulas, categorical imperatives, dogmas, laws. For a hundred years the classical aesthetic of Schiller and Goethe continued to engage, and sometimes dominate, people's minds in Germany; even to-day it is a rewarding academic study.

The idea is to establish rules, a canon. Antiquity, conceived summarily as a unity and posited once and for all as 'the model', the eternal truth, is to provide the standard. But which works of antiquity? Throughout the century the problem of 'the beautiful' or 'the sublime' has continued to beget a spate of pamphlets and essays in France and, above all, in England.

In all this 'the ideal of beauty' varies radically with the personality and circumstances of the beholder. Hogarth, whose book the *Anatomy of Beauty* was translated by Lessing, claimed with one stroke of his pen to have found the ideal in a serpentine line, and introduced it like an heraldic device in his self-portrait. The weak and mediocre painter, Rafael Mengs, who had an international reputation as the greatest painter of his day, commended 'an intermediate arrangement of one part perfection and one part attractiveness'. On Winckelmann's recommendation Goethe devoted some time and study to Mengs and even listened without scorn to his 'artist's tavern talk', as Benedetto Croce called it. Winckelmann, again, approached the problem from the point of view of art connoisseurship, which he possessed in rare degree, and postulated for the recognition of beauty an inner sensitiveness, which he did not attempt to define. His interest was centred primarily on ancient sculpture and, as he presupposed this to be uncoloured, he wanted, as far as possible, to exclude colour and relegate it to a secondary place. It was in form and line that beauty really manifested itself. His views continued to exert a strong influence on Goethe all his life.

Now Kant, the greatest philosopher of the day, enters the discussion, in the third and last of his three great *Critiques*, the *Critique of Judgment*. His knowledge of the visual arts was minimal: as he never left Königsberg in his life, he never saw a painting or sculpture of importance, and his knowledge, like that of Lessing, was derived solely from engravings. His reading of poetry was also very limited; his point of departure had been the natural sciences. His aesthetics can only be understood in relation to his theory of knowledge as a whole and this, like all strict philosophic thought, was a closed book to Goethe. Kant's *Critique of Pure Reason* he laid aside unread; in his copy of the *Critique of Judgment* he marked a number of passages which seemed to support his own views. As earlier in the case of Spinoza, Goethe read only what was familiar to him; the 'system' never interested him. Kant's system, had the philosopher written it down, would only have alarmed him; there was something almost sinister about the man, in whom he felt a nature diametrically opposed to his own. He only bothered about him at all because philosophy, with Kant as its most distinguished representative, was constantly being represented to him as a power of the greatest importance in the history of the mind. An epidemic of philosophizing had swept Germany; the more wretched the material situation the more passionately did people try to escape into the world of ideas. Philosophy in Germany has always sounded a different note from that in England or France: in these countries one hears the voices of men of affairs, of a Bacon, who was Lord Chancellor, of a Locke, who was Secretary of State, of men with a knowledge of the world like Shaftesbury or Hume or, in France, Montaigne; in Germany, with the sole exception of Leibnitz, philosophy has always meant *Kathederphilosophie*, philosophy of the lecture room. This was completely alien to Goethe's whole nature. Nevertheless, he was forced to see how deeply stirred everyone round him was. Herder adopted a bitter, and extremely unfortunate position in his antagonism to Kant. Young men like Heinrich von Kleist broke down over the writings of the Königsberg professor, and felt 'annihilated' by his reasoning. Reinhold, Fichte's predecessor in Jena, a quiet almost timid man, told Schiller ecstatically that in a hundred years' time Kant's reputation would be equal to that of Jesus Christ. In the Berlin salons Kant was discussed by clever and discerning Jewesses. In Königsberg the officers of the garrison attended his lectures and took them down. One professor in Würzburg solemnly declared that the French Revolution could be traced to Kant's philosophy and its subversive influence.

Goethe fights hard against this influence. There are times when he sees Kant as a second Newton, 'a menace, a stronghold from whence enlightened excursions into the field of experience are to be contained'. Kant's teaching of the radical evil in man angers him to such an extent that he declares the mantle of philosophy, which Kant has cleansed of so many slovenly prejudices, has now been 'wantonly beslobbered with the shameful stain of radical evil'. He considers that Kant over-stresses the pathological element in man, and he explains this as being due to early impressions: 'There is an inescapable something about him, as there was with Luther, reminiscent of the monk who, although he has thrown open the door of the monastery, has nevertheless been unable entirely to eradicate its traces.' He recalls Kant's origin in the poor saddler's family, his long impoverished years as tutor and lecturer before becoming a professor, at the age of almost 50. Stories he has heard from Herder and others who have known Kant probably make him think of Kant's truly monastic life in his modest room in Königsberg, his gaze fixed for the last forty years on the same church spire that provides the focal point of his thinking. Goethe knows nothing about the younger Kant, who led an extensive and cultivated social life, was known as a lively and witty guest, and who, in intercourse with people from many lands in the rich trading centre of Königsberg, acquired a considerable knowledge of the world. The main thing that repels him, however, is precisely Kant's essential gift, that of acute analysis and critical elimination: 'When philosophy applies itself pre-eminently to separating and dividing, I cannot come to terms with it, and indeed I can say it has done me an injury thereby, in that it has disturbed me in my natural progress.' It is only acceptable to him when it 'enhances our original feeling of being at one with nature, consolidates it, and transforms it into a deep, quiet contemplation'.

This is the philosophy Spinoza taught him, or so he believes. Now Schiller, vehemently absorbed in Kant, wants to build a new classical theory of art on the basis of his philosophy. Goethe is willing to listen, he accompanies Schiller for a certain distance, but that is all. Later he shakes his head when he looks back on the 'unhappy time of those speculations', the 'unspeakable confusion', the harm that was done to Schiller's poetry by his philosophic outlook, 'for through it he came to regard the idea as higher than all nature and, indeed, through it to annihilate nature. What he was able to conceive had to come to pass, were it in accordance with nature or opposed to it. It is distressing when one sees such an exceptionally gifted man tormenting himself with philosophic modes of thought that cannot be of any help to him.'

Goethe said this in 1823; but we are still in 1795 and the new doctrine is resolutely brought into existence. A code of rules, as Schiller expressly stipulates, is to be laid down – in France at this same time the foundations of the Code Napoleon are being laid. The young art critics, in the eyes of the two *Dioscuri*, are at odds with themselves, they should be in possession of a clearly established canon. Critics and artists are to be trained, divided into classes as at school. A critical platform, an arena, is to be established in *Die Horen*. The two of them are in a very belligerent mood, especially Schiller. They begin to write their most biting satiric poems, calling them *Xenien* – gifts presented to guests – after the model of the ancients. A literary conflict develops, which has been honoured with a somewhat melancholy notoriety. A vast amount of ammunition is expended on all sides, a great upheaval takes place, and then everything remains as it was. At the end of it only one thing has changed: the two *Dioscuri* now stand together, united, invincible. They have made themselves feared far and wide. They are listened to, their words carry more weight than previously, more weight than their works. There is something sad about this, but great controversies have always interested the public more than a beautiful poem or a fine piece of writing. Whole chapters of literary history are filled with such controversies and many names owe their renown to nothing else. In the case of Goethe and Schiller it remains an episode, painful and unpleasant, but to some extent redeemed by the achievements that follow.

The conflict is touched off by the failure of *Die Horen*. The journal, announced with such high hopes and famous names, does not catch on. It is criticized, and not entirely without justification. Apart from the *Unterhaltungen* Goethe's contributions consist mostly of translations. Other articles, interesting to the editors in their discussions, are of little interest to readers. Goethe becomes quite disproportionately excited. Some hack writer in a Berlin paper complains of the lack of outstanding prose works in Germany. Goethe writes a fierce counter-article under the title *Literary Sansculottism*. He gives a very informative and excellent survey of the difficulties that face German writers: they have no social centre, no cohesion, their public is scattered, the author is often forced to undertake work he despises in order to earn a living. And yet, thanks to the example of men like Wieland – on whom he lavishes high praise – German literature to-day stands much higher than formerly, and the young writer enters a much larger and more enlightened circle than did his predecessors. Style to-day is better than ever it was, 'almost everybody writes well'. The critical news-papers and journals give proof of a 'consistently good style'. Thus a fair-minded German sees 'the writers of his country on a splendid level' – let us rid ourselves of the ill-tempered, carping critic who only causes mistrust in the mind of the public.

This should really have been the end of the matter, but Goethe is still angry. He writes some more stinging verses; the critical opposition journals deserve a few knocks. Schiller joins in the fray, both write epigrams, and suddenly the 'splendid level' of contemporary literature is transformed into a fair-ground of mediocrities and pathetic impotence. In the tones of the fair-ground the *Dioscuri* cry out their wares. They scatter their leaflets indiscriminately. Goethe castigates almost all his old friends: Stolberg, Lavater – now a 'rogue', Reichardt – his favourite composer, his brother-in-law Schlosser, Heinse, Jung – Stilling, Forster, Kant, the young Friedrich Schlegel, who, as the leader of the rising generation, is about to rally enthusiasm for Goethe in a passionate essay – no one is spared. The octogenarian Gleim is ridiculed mercilessly because he 'no longer possesses the elasticity of his youth'. Goethe adds some silly epigrams on Newton, which are incomprehensible to anyone not knowing his *Farbenlehre*. Schiller, using a mighty weapon, does battle with some little schoolmasters in a remote province, who have translated Tasso badly, and massacres a crowd of real mediocrities. There is political wisdom too: 'Tell me, where do we find the *Sansculotte* in Germany? In the middle – At the top and the bottom everyone has what he wants.' It is a pitiful output, made all the worse because not one of the verses is redeemed by wit, pungency or striking expression, and in not a single case has an epigram been handed down to posterity as a caricature of the object of attack. All that remains is the memory of a great storm, which was later interpreted as though German literature had been cleansed by a mighty cataclysm.

The affair has one beneficial result: never again does Goethe take part in a similar venture. He continues to pillory his opponents in biting verses, mainly in his far more successful Hans Sachs style, but he keeps them in a drawer and shows them only to close friends. It is only in the polemical section of his *Farbenlehre*, foreshadowed here in the lines on Newton, that we once more meet the angry, irritable, unrestrained Goethe, a side of his nature that also has its place in the complete picture of his personality.

The game very soon loses its charm for the *Dioscuri*. Schiller, who at first was filled with such drive and energy and who even declared that they must 'hound that insect Reichardt to death', is the first to grow cautious – because of his position as editor of the *Musenalmanach*. He declines Goethe's proposal to continue the slaughter in the next almanach. Goethe, in his Mephistophelian vein, draws up a balance sheet of the counter-attacks against them:

> If I am to be honest, the people's behaviour conforms entirely to my wishes; for it is a policy too little known and practised that everyone, who aspires to a degree of lasting fame, should force his contemporaries to unleash everything they secretly harbour against him. He will always eradicate any impression this makes by his presence, his life and his work.

# 32

# A German Idyll

It was in living and in working that Goethe's friendship with Schiller made its great contribution. Goethe described these years as a renewal of youth. The 'Xenien' conflict and its fair-ground atmosphere, provided we adopt a benevolent attitude, can be regarded as a belated outburst of youthful high spirits, comparable to Goethe's earlier satire *Der Jahrmarkt von Plunder-sweilern*. But now these two men have to meet the challenge of justifying by their work their claims to leadership, and it is a challenge met triumphantly by each of them.

The rules and regulations so painstakingly worked out are relegated to the sphere of academic discussion, where they long hold sway. It is for the visual arts, above all, that the 'classical ideal' is heralded as the model and proclaimed with such tenacity, but, at any rate in painting, it gives rise to nothing of lasting value. In poetry a powerful new undercurrent is already at work, unknown to the law-makers; it is later given the name 'Romantic movement'. *Das Märchen*, the first work of importance which Goethe includes in his *Unterhaltungen* in *Die Horen*, is already in the grip of this current, and it exerted a strong influence on the Romantics, who saw in the *Märchen* form a means of expression suited to them. Out of it they created the *Kunst-Märchen*, a *genre* that often degenerated into artificiality, though in the brothers Grimm the ancient heritage of fairy-tale and legend was reborn. Goethe's *Märchen*, however, is something different. It is the first work in which he consciously employs the element of ambiguity; it is intentionally 'incommensurable'. His tale is far removed from the gay transparent fairy-tales of the eighteenth century. It is intentionally obscure, leaving open many possibilities for the stimulation of further thought and reflection. 'One cannot help looking for a meaning in everything,' writes Schiller, carefully refraining from giving his own interpretation. Goethe too, often as he was pressed to do so, steadfastly refused to provide an explanation. People tried to connect it with the French Revolution; he remained silent. They imagined that in the snake, the giant and the lily they could see 'the mutual working together of various forces'; Goethe smiled, saying there were a hundred different interpretations. Three of the solutions sent to him he set down side by side and distributed to other admirers.

Goethe's attempt, with Schiller, to establish a clear distinction between all the different *genres* of poetry – in this field Goethe is not in the least opposed to dividing up and separating – leads him to try his hand at a wide variety of traditional poetic forms. They have been discussing epic poetry, so an epic it shall be, with Homer as the eternal ideal. Goethe begins an epic, *Achilleis*, that is to come between the *Iliad* and the *Odessey*. He wants to be a mere disciple of Homer. He goes so far in his classicism that he wants to follow the ancients even 'in the things for which they are reproached, indeed I must adapt myself to the things I myself don't care for; only thus shall I be in a degree certain that I am not completely missing the right sense and note'. He wants to eliminate everything that is subjective or 'pathological' – two words he regards as almost synonymous. He devotes himself with the utmost energy to works on archaeology, late Latin authors and lexikons, forgetting the wise words he spoke relative to his *Iphigenie* that it is lack of detailed knowledge that stimulates the creative faculty. Only fragments come of it all, written in beautiful language and yet reading like translations from some poet of Alexandrine times.

Another epic poem, originally also planned as an exercise, is more successful. 'In addition to Hero and Leander I have a domestic idyll in mind, because I must have done this kind of thing too,' he writes to Schiller. He had come across an old newspaper cutting about the Salzburg emigrants: in 1731 the Archbishop of Salzburg had banished from his territories all the Protestants who refused to renounce their faith. In a great trek, with their wagons, their cattle and their household belongings, they made their way right across Germany to East Prussia, where they were settled by the Prussian government. In a similar, though far more terrible, trek their descendants two hundred years later returned to the west. The old newspaper contained an edifying story about a Salzburg girl and the son of a well-to-do family in some little town on their route. The young man falls in love with the girl and presents her to his parents, who give their consent to his marriage with the penniless exile. When he puts the engagement ring on her finger, she puts her hand into her bosom and brings out a little bag with two hundred *ducats* in it – her dowry.

Out of this simple tale, and in a very short space of time, springs Goethe's epic idyll; Schiller is lost in admiration at how 'Goethe only has to shake the tree gently for the ripest fruit to fall into his lap'. It is almost the only one of his larger works that he completed at a single stroke and never altered or thought of continuing. He enjoyed reading it aloud, which he always did with deep emotion and a sense of wonder that out of this banal, *petit bourgeois*, story he had been able to create a picture of noble idealism.

> I have tried [he said] in the crucible of an epic poem to separate the purely human element in the life of a small German town from its dross, and at the same time I have endeavoured to reflect, in a small mirror, the great movements and changes of the world stage. The time of the story is approximately

last August (1796), and I was not aware of the boldness of my undertaking until the greatest of its difficulties had been surmounted.

The world stage refers to the Revolutionary wars. So far Weimar has been spared, but from the Rhineland there is a constant stream of fugitives, either singly and in little groups or in droves. Goethe had already witnessed the misery and distress of the *émigrés* in the retreat from Champagne; but then it had been confined to the French, whose behaviour often alienated sympathy. Now his fellow countrymen arrive. He is sent jewellery and bonds from the threatened areas for safe keeping; he hears of all kinds of experiences. It is characteristic that he is much more deeply affected by the fate of a family or an individual than by the great trends and watchwords of the day. In a group of these fugitives he sees a microcosm, a world in miniature, in a form he can grasp and understand; he sees primeval conditions of human existence, as in the days of the patriarchs: disorder, strife caused by their unhappy lot, people of outstanding character and ability, a young girl who takes charge and assists a woman in childbirth, an old sage, like one of the Old Testament judges, who restores peace and order. This is the kind of world he can re-create, just as he can the familiar world of a small town like Weimar or Ilmenau, or one of the places through which he has passed on his visits to Karlsbad.

He chooses hexameters. Voss, the translator of Homer, has made the ancient metre popular through his much admired rustic idyll *Luise*, with its homely parsonage among the lime trees, the visit of the bridegroom, the wedding and the abundance of good things at the wedding feast. Goethe places his accents with great skill: the girl, as the dominant and most powerful character, makes her entrance comparatively late so as not to overshadow the young man who, in spite of the bold trait in his character, is hesitant and repressed. The main charm of the poem lies in its colourful picturization, and no other work of Goethe's has been so often illustrated or become imprinted on the mind of the public pictorially rather than verbally. The hexameters have proved an obstacle to readers and, with the exception of the opening lines, not a single verse of *Hermann und Dorothea* has become a popular quotation, as have such countless numbers of his rhymes.

In spite of this the idyll proves to be Goethe's most popular work, even more popular than *Werther*, which made its appeal to a higher stratum of society. 'Tailors, seamstresses, servant girls – everyone is reading it', writes Goethe's mother delightedly; the clergy, hitherto not among his warmest admirers, shower blessings on the author, while booksellers recommend it in the most glowing terms as a wedding present. The German bourgeoisie sees its own virtues mirrored in the work. People feel uplifted and see their way of life confirmed; there are no disturbing or surprising elements, as in almost all the poet's other works. Everything is comprehensible and familiar, culminating in an ideal marriage and even in patriotic hope: if war should threaten now or in the future, says the young man, he will take up arms and Dorothea herself shall hand him his weapon, 'and if everyone were to think as I do, force would be met with force and we should all enjoy peace'. There was comfort in these words in an age when no one took a stand, when the very foundations seemed to be tottering and the Holy Roman Empire was finally torn to shreds by its own members. The work appears at the end of 1797, in the same winter that sees the Congress of Rastatt and the burial of the old Empire.

When this Congress opens Goethe is in nearby Stuttgart; a delegate from Weimar is attending the negotiations, which are to decide the fate of the individual German territories. Goethe, the Weimar minister, takes not the slightest notice of these proceedings; in his letters to Schiller the word Rastatt does not appear. He speaks only of a traveller who brought back 'many pleasant and amusing stories' from England and France, who had been in Paris 'on the 18th *Fructidor* [the day of Bonaparte's first *coup d'état*] and so had witnessed many scenes both serious and funny'. Goethe does not mention the name of this general, nor does he make any further reference to this hour of Germany's and Europe's destiny.

Goethe intends to travel again, back to Italy once more, although hidden forces are at work within him militating against this plan. He has just finished *Hermann und Dorothea*, with which he grew impatient at the end, and is on the look-out for a new subject: 'The kind of poetry we have been writing recently is altogether too serious an occupation.' Schiller agrees. It has become clear to him, he tells Goethe,

> that it is not possible to give the people, taken as a whole, a sense of ease through poetry, rather the opposite, and it seems to me if we cannot achieve the one we must pursue the other course. We must harass them, destroy their complacency, cause them anxiety and astonishment. Poetry must confront them in one of two guises, either as genius or as a spectre. Only thus will they learn to believe in the existence of poetry and acquire respect for poets.

They wink at each other like two augurs, and Goethe answers:

> If, like conjurors, we poets could rely on no one being able to see how the trick was done, the game would be won, just as anyone who takes advantage of the public by swimming with the stream can count on his luck. In *Hermann und Dorothea*, so far as the subject matter is concerned, I have given the Germans what they wanted, and they are abundantly satisfied. I am now wondering whether, in exactly the same way, one could not write a play that would find its way onto every stage, and be declared excellent by everybody, without the author himself necessarily being of the same opinion.

They speak in the same satirical vein of Goethe's *Faust*, which refuses to fit in with the high classicism of the theories they have just promulgated. Goethe has taken out his old *Faust* scenes, which have long remained tied up in a parcel, and has rapidly sketched out a short scheme: 'It only needs a month of peace and quiet for the work to rise from the soil like a large crop of mushrooms, to the astonishment and horror of everybody. If my journey comes to nothing, my entire hope is pinned on these drolleries.'

It is difficult to see who or what can disturb Goethe's peace: no one bothers the minister, Mamsell Vulpius sees that his life is spacious and comfortable, and his friend Schiller is at hand to provide mental stimulus. Scarcely is the *Faust* scheme noted down, however, than Goethe's inner restlessness drives him away. Once again, face to face with a big task he takes flight into a simpler one. The idea is to go to Switzerland to meet Meyer, who has been collecting drawings and other material in Rome; from there they may go on to Italy together. Goethe's energies are now diverted still further afield; he plans a giant undertaking, a comprehensive description of Italy, for his new travel book, embracing art, economics, politics and social conditions, and provides himself with files and 'pouches', already listed under the various headings. A whole staff of assistants would have been necessary for such a task and we can only be thankful that it never came to fruition.

A whole caravan proceeds to Frankfurt: Goethe, Christiane, their son, and a secretary; on the way newspaper cuttings and theatre programmes are sorted out and filed. Goethe, who has set out to discover facts and realities, very soon tires. His native town, with its thirty thousand inhabitants, seems enormous, confusing and detestable; he wants 'nothing more to do with all this wide empirical horizon' he writes on arrival. His mother, whom he is seeing for the last time, he does not even mention. The people of Frankfurt 'divide all their time between earning and spending'. The merchants in the narrow lanes look as if they want to grab the customers by the sleeve. The famous town-hall he sees as a former warehouse 'whose vaults, during the fair, still offer the vendor of faulty goods the advantage of a dark corner'. There is no interest in the arts or in poetry, and the theatre itself is only a means of diversion. His eye is caught, however, by the settings of an Italian stage designer named Fuentes, and under the stimulus of these he drafts out his ideas on stage design in the classic manner: the background must form a 'tableau', and the fundamental principles are to be those of architecture, which, for Goethe, means Palladio. Karl August, to whom he sends his observations, remarks: 'Goethe writes me reports which could go into any journal; it is really funny how solemn the man is becoming.'

The fact is Goethe has already lost his desire to travel and engage in combat with the hydra of empiricism; he would prefer to return to Weimar and 'bring forth phantoms of every kind' from the depths of his own being. He continues the journey only because he has started on it. Travelling by way of Stuttgart he reaches Switzerland, and there, at last, he meets Meyer. He climbs up to the St Gotthard once more, but quickly turns his back on its 'barren summits'. Meyer's Italian collections are to be digested in the peace and quiet of Weimar. Italy is given up. In an old Swiss chronicle he has found an idea for a new epic poem on Wilhelm Tell; but he soon passes it on to Schiller. He visits his old friend Knebel in Nuremberg, where he now lives, and has long talks on old Nuremberg art, as well as some discussions 'on the political situation'.

In Frankfurt Goethe was visited by the young Friedrich Hölderlin, so far author of some poems which had appeared in his countryman Schiller's almanachs and which Goethe had criticized as 'drawn with neither sensuous nor inner perception', though containing some 'pleasant German imagery'. The rather weakly young man, tutor to a rich merchant's family, struck Goethe as modest, and he advised him to 'write small poems, selecting for each a subject of human interest'. It is not Goethe, the minister of state, but this youth Hölderlin, innocent and lacking in any worldly experience, who is a witness at Rastatt of the liquidation of the Holy Roman Empire in a deplorable, underhand business transaction. He has gone there with his friend Sinclair, an official at the little Court of Hessen-Hombury, and, in his novel *Hyperion*, he has left a description of the character and ways of the German people, as he saw them at this time. Unlike Goethe's and Schiller's laments his words are not directed to a literary public but to all Germans: there is no nation more torn and divided, 'you see craftsmen but not people, priests but not people, thinkers but not people, lords and servants, young men and mature, but not people – is it not like a battlefield where dismembered hands, arms and limbs are all lying about together ... ?'

The idyll of *Hermann und Dorothea* and this outburst of Hölderlin's stand side by side in this same year, Goethe's journey in search of art and this Congress, which was to put an end to six years of war but which, instead, gave rise to wars for a further fifteen years.

Let us look at this world of *Rastatt,* at this carnival fair in which, for the last time, the entire old-Germanic disorder passes before us in procession, masked in its ancient splendour. At the last coronation in Frankfurt, seven years earlier, the potentates had been represented by delegations of hundreds, or even thousands; now they have sent smaller delegations to fight desperately for their very existence. The Chancellor of Mainz wears the expression of 'a bitten badger who, in his secret fury, would himself have liked to bite once more', writes one of the best chroniclers of this carnival. The whole thing is colourful; magnificent uniforms, church dignitaries in satin and taffeta, Knights of Malta in scarlet, the French delegates in the splendour of the Directoire; there are delegates from the Rhineland counts, the Hanseatic towns, and from the larger, more effective, powers. The Congress was originally called to consider the question of indemnities for the territories on the left bank of the Rhine, the possessions over which Goethe had wandered in his Strasbourg days, and the integrity of the Empire is proclaimed once more, with full pomp, by the envoys of the Emperor. In the meantime, however, much has happened. Paris has seen four successive revolutions, French armies are on the Rhine, in Italy and in the Netherlands. Frankfurt has been bombarded; the house of Goethe's grandfather Textor is a heap of rubble, and a considerable part of the fortune inherited from his tailor grandfather has been lost in levies, to which his mother has been forced to subscribe. Prussia has made its peace with the Revolution at Bâle, the first great power to do so; subsequently, but only after heavy defeats in Italy, Austria has done likewise at Campo Formio. Goethe celebrated the peace with a Court masque: 'The long-awaited peace once more approaches, and everything is garlanded, bedecked; here fury lays down all its keen-edged weapons, the victor's helmet ev'n is cast aside.'

The victor, in fact, plants his helmet more firmly on his head. 'They hasten to unite in harmony', writes Goethe, whereas in fact they are all hastening to plunder, intrigue, conclude secret pacts and commit treachery; it is an orgy of the most brutal and short-sighted self-interest and power politics. The indemnities for the territories on the left bank of the Rhine must be found from among the archbishoprics, bishoprics and abbeys on the right bank, the French delegates declare tersely. This is the signal for rape and plunder, and for the final annihilation of what remains of the 'unity' of the Empire. 'Each larger princedom had its plan to grab some bishopric or scrap of one, each smaller to grab an abbey, and the obscurest nobleman some sheep-pen or other.' The spiritual lords fall out among themselves: the archbishops are ready to abandon the bishops, and the bishops the abbots, in the hope of getting something for themselves; finally the Archbishop of Mainz wants to abandon everyone in the pious hope that they will at least let the Patriarch and Primate of all Germany remain. Prussia intrigues against Austria, and Austria against all the rest. The French delegates stare in amazement at the spectacle provided by the representatives of legitimism and the German nation. The Congress ends in further declarations of war, but it, and not the formal liquidation some years later, marks the real break-up of the Holy Roman Empire, in which Goethe has spent the first half of his life. The immediate conclusion to the Congress is more anarchic even than the Congress itself: Austrian hussars, on secret instructions from Vienna, waylay the returning French delegates, drag them from their carriages, and murder them.

So much for the world stage. Goethe ignores it to an extent that we, to-day, find hard to understand. In his *Annals*, in which year by year he notes down events, there is not one word about contemporary history until the catastrophe of 1806, ten years later. The entries concern the Weimar theatre, natural science, and actors he has engaged, of whom he gives detailed characterizations, but there is no mention of the actors on the European stage. On his first visit to Goethe, Jean Paul describes this godlike aloofness of the Olympian, as, at the age of forty-six, he already is to his contemporaries. The young novelist had been warned: 'He was depicted by all as completely cold towards every person and thing on the earth.' Charlotte von Kalb had said: 'He no longer admires anything, not even himself ... only things to do with art still warm the cockles of his heart.' Even the house, the only one in Weimar decorated in the Italian style, seems cold, like a mausoleum of pictures and statues. The visitor is stifled with apprehension. 'Finally the god appears, cold, monosyllabic, aloof. Knebel says: the French are entering Rome. – Hm! says the God.'

This 'Hm!' or 'Hm! Hm!' is a common experience. Often it is the natural reaction of a great man in the face of tiresome visitors who, since the days of *Werther*, have pestered him with silly questions and demands. It was still the custom in Goethe's day to call on famous men, and no one, however famous, could refuse to see visitors, who came in the hope of hearing some memorable remark. Jean Paul, too, shares the common expectancy: 'At last not only the champagne but the talk about art, the public, and so forth, began to kindle and – we were at Goethe's. His talk does not pour out in a flowery stream like Herder's, it is clear-cut and quiet.' Finally Goethe reads one of his unpublished poems 'and then his heart burst through the icy crust in flames'; it is not reading but acting, 'a deep thunder mingled with the gentlest murmur of falling rain; there is nothing one can compare to it.... He considers his career as a poet is finished.'

His appearance at this time is described by Karl von Stein, the elder brother of his former pupil Fritz:

> His gait is exceedingly slow, his stomach pendulous, like that of a woman in the last stages of pregnancy, his chin drawn right down onto his neck and tightly enveloped in a roll of fat; his cheeks are fat too and his mouth is half-moon shaped; only his eyes are turned heavenwards, though his hat is even more so. His whole expression conveys a kind of complacent indifference, but he does not look really happy. He moves me to pity, this fine man, who once expressed himself so nobly in his body!

A portrait by his friend Meyer presents a similar picture, a Goethe heavy, massive and gloomy. Only gradually did the splendid, radiant old man emerge from this formlessness, from this unhealthy state that, after numerous disorders, led to serious illnesses.

Like his body, Goethe's life is now expanding. His literary productiveness he regards as a thing of the past; *Faust* has been parcelled up and laid aside again, despite constant pressure from Schiller and new offers from the publisher Cotta. In these latter negotiations Schiller assumes the role of intermediary, a task that is far from easy.

> To put it bluntly, [writes Schiller to Cotta] it is not possible to strike a good bargain with Goethe, because he knows his own worth and puts a high value on himself, and the hazards of the book trade, of which he has but a vague notion, do not enter his considerations at all. Hitherto no publisher has maintained relations with him; he was satisfied with none of them and some may not have been satisfied with him. Generosity towards his publishers is not his habit.

351

Cotta continues to persevere and eventually becomes the sole publisher of Goethe's major writings. The first part of *Faust* appears in 1808, in a new Collected Edition of his works, further Collected Editions follow and, in the last years of the poet's life, Cotta embarks on the great undertaking of a Complete Edition in sixty volumes, including the second part of *Faust*. He publishes singly everything that Goethe offers him, though with no great success, even the *Westöstliche Divan*, the greatest achievement of Goethe's later years, remaining largely unsold until the beginning of the present century. With the Collected Editions, however, he fares better; the German public of those days had a passion for long, complete series of the writings of its favourite authors, and it is quite extraordinary how many 'complete' or 'collected' works of minor, and even very minor writers were marketed in fifty, sixty or even more volumes.

This connection with a great and enterprising publisher – he also had large printing, manufacturing and newspaper interests, and later established the first steamship company on Lake Constance – is also an important factor in Goethe's more expansive way of life. After long years he is now receiving substantial fees, the highest ever paid to a German author up till that time, and he is in need of money. He has become a great collector of engravings, coins, *majolica* and autographs; his house is turned into a museum. He attaches importance to fine *cuisine* and an elegantly appointed table. When his old friend Madame de la Roche comes to Weimar on a visit, he gives a dinner party for her, to which he also invites Charlotte von Stein: it is an evening of sentiment, with rare flowers for each guest, each guest's place at table marked with his name, the seating thoughtfully arranged to ensure conversation; when the dessert, consisting of fruit and cakes made by the Court pastrycook, is reached, soft music is heard from an adjoining room. His wine cellar is well stocked and still contains precious bottles, with famous years on their labels, from the legacy of his tailor-wine-merchant grandfather. He keeps a carriage and coachman; he seldom rides any longer. He even acquires a country estate and, exhibiting a strange lack of business acumen, concludes the agreement without even seeing the place; he has to raise money to pay for it, it is poorly situated and far away, the buildings are in bad repair. He leases it to a tenant, who remains in arrears with his rent, and after a few years, barely having seen his property, Goethe sells it. The reason for the whole transaction was Goethe's anxiety to give Christiane a higher and more respected position, Weimar society still not having resigned itself to 'that woman'. From time to time the innate brutality of these cultivated ladies and gentlemen bursts out, as in a scene, described by Karl von Stein, when at a ball a high Court official says to Goethe: 'Pack that hussy of yours off home. I have made her drunk!' Stein adds: 'So Goethe goes over to poor Vulpia and indicates that she had better go home, although she has remained quite sober.' Even the Jena romantics, whose own lives are completely unbridled and promiscuous, cannot stomach the fact that Goethe, whom they revere like a deity, is tied to this extremely earthy creature: 'To-day I spoke again with Frau Schiller', writes Karoline Schelling, 'asking why in heaven's name he had not at least brought back a pretty Italian girl.'

Most visitors feel uncomfortable in his presence. The great actor Iffland, who has been playing in Weimar, remarks: 'There is something unsettled and suspicious in his whole demeanour, which prevents anyone feeling at ease in his presence. I have the feeling I cannot sit still on one of his chairs. Outwardly he is the most fortunate of men. He has genius, he is honoured, he lives in comfort, he can enjoy the arts. And yet I would not be in his position even for an income of three thousand *thalers*.' The broader the basis on which Goethe orders his life becomes, with parties, intimate gatherings and recitals of his works, the more wide-spread and deep-seated is the feeling against him. He tries to form a court of love, after the model of the Minnesingers, with meetings once a week at his house; it is to be a sort of picnic – since the 'lady of the house', Christiane, cannot be present – with the ladies bringing the food and the gentlemen the wine. The old friends are not there; Goethe has found new ones. In spite of all the riddles, poems, and pairing off of 'loving couples', it develops into a somewhat chilly affair.

In a small group of two or three people, and especially if he can relax in the soft comfort of his dressing-gown, he can be charming and delightful; under these conditions he displays all his gifts. He himself once observed that people considered him greater in conversation than in his writings. But he is unable to hold a large group of people together; this is something Schiller does much better, and people flock to his house, where they feel vastly more at home than with the Olympian Goethe.

Even Schiller, the greatest of his friends, finally becomes irritated. Writing to Wilhelm von Humboldt, he says:

> It is unfortunate that Goethe allows his habit of sauntering such free rein and, because he tries his hand at everything in turn, concentrates his energies on nothing.... If Goethe still had faith in the possibility of doing something worth while, and if there was any consistency in his actions, there is much that could yet be achieved here in Weimar, in the arts generally and in the drama in particular. Something would emerge from it, and this dreadful deadlock would come to an end. Alone I can do nothing. I often feel like looking round for somewhere else to live and work. If a reasonable opportunity were to present itself I would go (17.2.1803).

This is the picture of the 'Athens on the Ilm', as seen from the inside, during the golden age of German classicism, its families living in their individual snail shells – as Schiller described them when he first arrived – its heroes disillusioned, embittered and estranged: Herder with his almost morbid fault-finding, Knebel an ill-humoured recluse who, late in life, marries his mistress, a young actress, and makes her life miserable, Wieland only managing with difficulty to preserve his reputation, Karl August taken up with his new mistress, the singer Demoiselle Jagemann, who rules not only the stage but the whole theatre. Even Anna Amalie's *Musenhof* has turned against her former favourite, Goethe, his place being taken by the ubiquitous Kotzebue, who uses some of his many talents to intrigue against the *Dioscuri*. It is a small world and it is easy to understand Schiller, now at the height of his powers, longing to free himself from it. More difficult to understand is Goethe's endurance of it.

Goethe is in the grip of something like a paralysis of his powers, following his great creative exertions. He shrinks before the task of completing *Faust*. For the next ten years – the second such ten-year interval in his life – he publishes only minor works, with the single exception of *Die natürliche Tochter*. He accepts his Duke's commission to translate Voltaire's *Mahomet* and *Tancred*, and fulfils the task dutifully; Karl August much prefers the French stage to the plays of his 'classics'. For his own pleasure he translates the autobiography of Benvenuto Cellini, entertaining both himself and his readers with this coarse and colourful slice of sixteenth-century Italian life. He translates Diderot's writings on painting for the private journal, *Die Propyläen*, which he edits with Meyer. Goethe and Meyer want to enlarge their sphere of influence, and they institute painting competitions, with prizes, under the name *Die Weimarer Kunstfreunde*; using the modern sounding abbreviation *W.K.F.*, they propose impossible subjects, mostly chosen from antiquity – after a few years the undertaking comes to an end. The evaluations of the works submitted are accompanied by detailed criticisms and proposals for further entries; the longest of these essays is an attempt to reconstruct the paintings of Polygnot at Delphi, known only from contemporary Greek descriptions. The idea that studies of this kind provide the best preparation for aspiring young artists shows Goethe at the summit of his classicism, remote from the world and from living art. His chief advice to young painters is to draw as much as possible from Greek sculpture, or from casts of it, and to follow this with the study of anatomy and perspective. Contours are to be drawn carefully and precisely with a pen and not with chalk, which is less precise and even ambiguous. If paintings are used as models, then it should be those whose clarity and purity of form are most marked.

These are monologues, or dialogues with Meyer, who is always at hand to listen and supply new material. Goethe lives on an island. It is touching to see with what care and devotion he handles the pitifully weak paintings and drawings submitted for the *W.K.F.* competitions and how he packs them up again with his own hands, 'rolled on a rod of adequate length', to send back to the artists. He is convinced that the whole artistic life of Germany will be affected by his theories, whereas in fact very different movements are beginning to sweep over Europe. His theories have never given rise to a single painting or sculpture of any serious pretensions. His influence sprang from his poetry, and it is part of the strange colour-blindness of his nature that he did not want to admit this. He was convinced he could teach in every field of art and science, and form men according to his own image.

Only in this sphere of forming or re-creating humanity do his schemes acquire any real shape. Winckelmann, who is the great teacher behind all this classicism, is extolled by Goethe in an introduction to his letters. The reputation of the founder of art history is already on the wane; something has to be done to dam the flood of the new romanticism. Goethe treats Winckelmann as a Greek. Daringly for his day he touches on his 'Greek leanings' towards homosexuality, and mentions his somewhat easy-going conversion to Roman Catholicism, a step which, according to Goethe, caused Winckelmann few pangs because he was basically a complete pagan and quite devoid of interest in either of the two denominations. This observation gives him an opportunity to emphasize his own paganism, and indeed the whole essay is in many respects a self-portrait and a confession of his own artistic *credo*. Antiquity is the golden age when everything was focused in the 'active present', when everything worked together for a common purpose, when no one lost themselves in wild schemes as the present younger generation was doing. Beauty was the ideal, and beautiful man nature's ultimate achievement in its constant advance from the lowest to the highest. This summit of achievement, in life possible only at a single moment, is still further enhanced by art until it exists as a work of art in 'ideal reality'. Such a work contains in itself all that is glorious and venerable, and elevates man to something higher than himself, nay more, it 'deifies him for the present age, and this includes the past and the future'. Such were the feelings which overcame the Greeks when they saw the statue of Jupiter at Olympia. The god had become a man in order to raise man to the stature of a god. The people perceived supreme excellence and were inspired with a feeling of supreme beauty.

This is Goethe's doctrine, with himself as the Olympian Jupiter. He writes – and he is writing under the impact of a severe threat caused by illness and premonitions of death – an apotheosis of Winckelmann and his early death. 'The decrepitude of old age and the decline of mental power are experiences he did not know. He lived as a man, and in the fullness of his manhood he departed. Now he enjoys the advantage, in the eyes of posterity, of appearing to possess eternal vigour and strength because in the image in which a man leaves the world he continues to walk among the shadows.' The task of those left behind is to continue his work.

This is how Goethe feels that he, too, should be seen, were he to depart at this moment – in an aura of beauty, after 'a brief fright, a quick pain', as he says of Winckelmann's death. He passes lightly over his great master's passing, because he never wants to hear mention of death. In reality Winckelmann's end was far from beautiful, nor was there any question of any Greek youth: a squat, thick-set rogue, a cook, a thief and a pimp, with whom he spent his evenings in Trieste on his way to visit his home, murdered the great scholar for the gold medals which he had been showing him. It was no brief fright: the mortally injured man staggered round with the strangler's cord still about his neck; in answer to his cries for help, servants sent for a priest instead of a doctor, and the dying man was subjected to the added cruelty of a long examination by the police. He died lonely and in agony, a traveller among strangers. In his luggage were found a copy of Homer, an interleaved copy of his *History of Art* which he was preparing for a new edition, a silver magnifying glass and a Roman measuring rod – truth writes with a symbolic power no author can ever achieve. And for Goethe's approach to art no more compact formula could possibly be found: Homer and the Roman measuring rod. These are the two waymarks he would wish to be found one day among his own effects.

# 33

# *Goethe's Theatrical Mission*

*Wilhelm Meisters Lehrjahre* or, as it is usually called in English, *Wilhelm Meister's Apprenticeship*, the main work produced by Goethe during the years of his friendship with Schiller, appeared in 1795 and 1796 in four small stout volumes; published by Unger in Berlin, it introduced to the public for the first time a new and beautifully cut Gothic type. The idea originally occurred to him at the time of *Werther*; during his first ten years in Weimar he wrote a first version and called it *Wilhelm Meister's Theatrical Mission*; ten years later this was completely recast into the *Apprenticeship*. After a further twenty years the *Wanderjahre*, his hero's years of wandering, was published as 'Part One', implying a further continuation. During the last years of his life Goethe handed it over to Eckermann to enlarge under his supervision. Even this was not the end. In 1910 the early *Theatrical Mission* came to light, and was christened the *Ur-Meister*. This manuscript, a copy made by Goethe's old friend Barbara Schulthess, was found among her papers by a schoolboy, who took it to his teacher. No other world-famous novel has had a similar creative and editorial history, extending over one hundred and twenty-five years. Nor is any other so unequal in its various parts. Side by side with great artistic maturity, freshness of invention and life in rich variety, we find laziness of a kind that almost no other great writer has ever permitted himself. For the final edition of his works the publisher asked Goethe for 'more copy' for the *Wanderjahre*, to make its two volumes equal in size, and Goethe instructed Eckermann to search the archives for further material. This material, in the form of 'meditations', maxims, reflections and poems, was then used to swell the volumes to the size required. The novel contains some of Goethe's most beautiful characters, his Mignon, his Philiene, as well as shadowy allegorical figures of which the author himself tired so that he thought of abandoning the *Lehrjahre* and leaving it to Schiller or someone else to finish. No true *finis* was ever written; Goethe's own death was the only end.

The whole *Meister*-complex is a fantastic production. It mocks every rule. Goethe himself often made fun of it, especially of the continual efforts of his 'dear Germans' to discover in it some guiding 'idea'. 'The work', as he says, 'is among my most incalculable productions and even I am almost

357

without a key to it. People look for some focal point, and this is difficult and at the same time not even good. I should have thought that a rich and varied life passing before our eyes was something in itself, without any specific tendency which, in any case, is only a theoretical concept.' He is speaking to Eckermann, and in order that the disciple should not go away empty-handed he adds: 'Basically the whole work seems only to be trying to say that, despite all the stupidity and confusion, man, led by a higher hand, eventually reaches a happy ending.'

Naturally it is only Goethe who can speak like that. He also calls his hero Wilhelm a 'poor specimen', and then elsewhere identifies him with himself. On one occasion he speaks admiringly of Sir Walter Scott, who has all the splendour of the three British kingdoms and their history at his disposal, whereas he has only what lies between the forests of Thuringia and the sandy wastes of Mecklenburg, 'so that in *Wilhelm Meister* I was forced to choose the most wretched material imaginable, strolling players and poor gentlefolk, merely to get some movement into my picture'.

Strolling players – this is the beginning. The *Theatrical Mission* was to have been a novel about the life of these people. There were many precedents; the theatre was a popular theme for novelists. The Frenchman Paul Scarron had written his *roman comique* and Venice, the El Dorado of the theatre, had produced a whole series of books on the subject. It was the picaresque novel of Spain that had fathered these offspring, and in Goethe's day the acting troupes still belonged to the world of rogues and rascals. In his famous engraving Hogarth has shown us the glory and misery of one of these troupes, their own rags and the splendour of their costumes, the naked legs of the actresses, their revealing eyes.

As a student in Leipzig he had heard about the legendary Frau Neuber; how under Gottsched's tuition she had tried to put an end to the old, coarse, fair-ground style of acting, with its unbridled improvisations, and with the harlequin as its chief attraction. There was already some idea of a 'mission', though with Gottsched rather than with Frau Neuber, who was no crusading missionary, but a full-blooded actress. She soon broke off relations with the dry professor, and ridiculed him on the stage; but it cost her the sympathy of the public who had become tame and decorous. Poor, half-forgotten, enmeshed in a series of wretched love affairs, she died. Frau Neuber's circle also provided another basic theme of *Wilhelm Meister*: the student who leaves home for the theatre or for a literary life. Her husband had done this, and so had the nineteen-year-old Lessing, whose first play she had produced, to the horror of his devout parents at home in their parsonage. Students were the playwrights for the strolling companies, acting with them and wandering round with them until they either found something better or succumbed. As distinct from the other actors, who were recruited from the ranks of fire-eaters, acrobats and tumblers – as was the great Schröder himself, whom Goethe used as a model for his theatrical manager in *Wilhelm Meister* – these students and academic men brought with them some higher ideas and aims: Germany might not be a nation, but at least she ought to have a national theatre and a national literature. This latter now came into existence and the repertory, which hitherto had consisted of hack plays, was enriched with works by Lessing, Goethe and Klinger. The national theatre had to wait; in fact it has never fully materialized.

This was Goethe's starting point: a young man from a good bourgeois family runs away to join the players, with whom he wants to fulfil his 'mission'. Frau Neuber, with her latter-day love affairs, he turns into Madame de Retti, the manageress of the troupe: a masculine woman, deeply versed in all the tricks of her profession except how to make money, she is constantly in debt and is infatuated with a thick-set, stocky member of the company. Goethe treats this man like a personal enemy, calls him a lout, a blockhead with a croaking voice, a simpleton. He ruins the performance of a play, *Belshazzar*, by Wilhelm Meister, the hero – in fact it is Goethe's own youthful play in disguise – the audience goes mad, storms on to the stage, tramples down the decorations and tears the whole booth to pieces. Madame de Retti escapes with her lover, leaving the company in debt.

This buffoonery is, more or less, the first germ. But Goethe in Weimar is no longer a student, and he must strike a higher note. He already sees himself in a biographical-historical light, a trait that developed early in his life. So he begins his 'Mission' with a long and detailed account of his hero's – in fact his own – youth, with many vivid memories of his home in Frankfurt; all of which is of greater value for the story of Goethe's early life than for a novel about the theatre. The book becomes an *Entwicklungsroman*, an account of his own development, with reminiscences of books he has read, discussions on aesthetics and reflections on contemporary literary events.

A romantic element, and a connection with the theatre, is provided by the hero's love affair with a young actress Mariane. The novel looks like becoming a love story, but soon after finding lodgings with the rich merchant who keeps the girl as his mistress Wilhelm leaves her, and Mariane disappears from the story, never to return. The journey into a higher and more cultivated life now begins, although the book is already half over. Wilhelm's company, however, is of the lowest; wretched as people and indifferent as actors, constantly engaged in fighting, drinking and brawling, they are treated as outcasts and deserve little better.

The world into which Goethe sets out to introduce his hero is that of the aristocracy. The troupe is invited to play at a castle belonging to some Count. 'Thrice happy those whose birth alone lifts them above the lower stations of mankind', we read, and he continues, with no trace of irony: 'From this higher standpoint it follows that their outlook is universal and

correct.... What comfort, what ease comes if one is born to wealth....
Hail, then, to the great ones of this world! Blessed all those who draw near
to them.' This apotheosis of the aristocracy is, in part, a reflection of his
association with Countess Werthern, when she was Karl August's mistress;
to Goethe she epitomized the great world and high society, and his admiration for her knew no bounds.

Life with the great at the castle amounts to an invitation from the Count
to Wilhelm to act as playwright and producer for some of the performances.
The way in which the officers carry on 'with the actresses is not of the
most delicate ... and very soon couples are trying to creep off into dark
corners'. Wilhelm, too, gets involved in a few flirtations, and then the
troupe is dismissed and has to go on its way. In a wood they are set upon
by robbers and the book looks like developing into an adventure story.
They are rescued, however, and finally reach a large town where Wilhelm
meets a theatrical director of a different calibre. Together they want to
establish a German national theatre and so fulfil the 'mission'. Wilhelm
learns that in the meantime his father has died, and with a solemn 'Yes!'
he pledges his loyalty to the new venture. With this vision of the future the
*Theatrical Mission* ends.

If there were no more to the book than this it would take its place
among Goethe's minor works. But from among the lesser characters there
emerge some who have a strange life of their own. They give the novel its
element of mystery. From the world of the jugglers a child springs into
being: Mignon, a hybrid, sometimes he and sometimes she. In the language
of the day the name Mignon meant a homosexual or a mistress, a pet child
or simply something very charming. Goethe's Mignon is all of these, and
more. The child is a sort of elemental being, like a fairy, though mischievous
and naughty too, and unaccountable; one moment tenderly solicitous for
her 'master', Wilhelm, the next moment hysterical; a will-o'-the-wisp she
suddenly becomes firmly practical. Blindfold she dances her intricate egg-
dance for Wilhelm, a secret symbol that, like an abstract pattern, reveals
the complex structure of her being. Mignon is an extremely romantic
character, and she cast her spell over the Romantics who tried in vain to
create something similar. She lived on in Ambroise Thomas' opera, in a
second Romanticism amid the cynicism of the Second Empire. Even there,
despite a routine libretto and facile stage music which are an abomination
to all Goethe admirers, the flames break out at the end of the second act
into one of the most effective finales in operatic literature. It might well not
have been unacceptable to Goethe himself, who welcomed every effective
impact of his works with a smile, great though the deviation from his own
intentions might be.

With Mignon, however, there is no original intention; the character
overwhelms Goethe. Into her he pours his longing for children and out
of her he forms a little family, with an old harpist, another mysterious

figure, and with his Wilhelm. Into her mouth he puts his songs of longing for Italy. Mignon has boyish characteristics, which are later eradicated. Goethe portrays her quite realistically, even referring to 'her skin spoiled by paint', and then lets her recede into mystery once more. At one point, when he is working on the novel in its later form, Goethe thinks of developing her into a fully grown woman; he writes a scene in which the reader is left to surmise that she steals into bed with Wilhelm. Unaccountably he then allows himself to be persuaded to discard the idea, possibly by Schiller, and provides the more 'fitting' solution that the nocturnal visitor was not Mignon, after all, but the frivolous Philine. In a higher sense Goethe may have been right; an elemental being cannot grow up. She dies a child-wife and is buried to the accompaniment of a solemn funerary celebration in the style of the *Magic Flute*. In the completed novel he finally destroys the element of fantasy and mystery in the character by adding an explanation in the most conventional novelistic style: Mignon, of noble Italian family, was the incestuous child of the mysterious harpist. This addition is one of the 'cogs', as he called them in his letters to Schiller, to enable him, in the proposed continuation of the novel, to take his hero to Italy.

The frivolous Philine is the other character with a life of her own, and she leads us back to the original subject of the theatre. She is an actress, and personifies the whole easy-going world of the theatre. Goethe is constantly on his guard against this creation of his. He never tires of showering derogatory expressions on her, once going so far as to call her 'impure'; it hurts him to see a person like this in the presence of so idealized a figure as the beautiful Amazon, who comes to the rescue of the actors when they are attacked in the woods by robbers. And yet, in one of the strangest creative manifestations in all literature, this little creature triumphs victoriously over the repugnance of her author. Her slippers tap their way charmingly throughout the whole length of the story. She plays her role far over the poet's head, just as in that mysterious night she lay close to him without his knowing who she was. Nothing Goethe does can prevent her from becoming one of the most entrancing and vital figures in his whole *œuvre*.

These two, Mignon and Philine, are already in existence when Goethe starts to re-write and extend the novel. The theatre drops out of the title, and the 'Mission' becomes the *Apprenticeship*, Wilhelm's years of learning. The style changes. Goethe now writes with great composure and with a richness of expression that he never again attains in prose. He uses irony too: when Wilhelm tries to tell his fair Mariane the whole story of his boyhood, so elaborately presented in the first version, the girl dozes off. The hero now starts out on his cultural journey at the end of his love affair, and the strolling players, though still a poor lot, are drawn more sympathetically. At the Count's castle Wilhelm makes the acquaintance of Shakespeare, not the actor and great playwright but the Shakespeare of the written word. Goethe writes a long essay on *Hamlet*; later in his life he even committed the vast error of declaring that the greatest of all dramatists was intended to be read and not acted. Wilhelm's reading of Shakespeare marks the beginning of the transition; the whole business of the theatre is seen as a mistake, it cannot further the hero's cultural development, and it is discarded. Higher powers watch over Wilhelm's progress to 'master' and guide his life to a happy ending. Their 'Society of the Tower' is a kind of freemasonry; its presiding genius is an *abbé*, 'an unpleasant fellow whose clandestine supervision grows wearisome and ludicrous', as Novalis said.

Living in an age when such secret societies flourished Goethe was repeatedly attracted to the idea. The central idea of his fragmentary epic poem, *Die Geheimnisse*, was to have been an order of spiritual knights led by a *Humanus*, who, in his person, united into one humanitarian religion the religious ideas of the various faiths. Goethe himself was a member of the Weimar Freemasons' Lodge, to which he dedicated some masonic songs. Here in the novel the 'Society of the Tower' is an allegory symbolizing 'society'. Social life is only possible within the framework of a communal existence, and this requires the leadership of superior people. Goethe's viewpoint is aristocratic, and to promote his hero's further development he chooses for him a somewhat vague existence as a guest on the estates of the various aristocrats in the neighbourhood; these latter, however – and this is one of the most serious shortcomings of the novel – are a bunch of 'pitiful gentlefolk', as he himself called them later. They travel about, indulge in love affairs, wait hopefully for some lucky speculation or the death of an uncle to put their finances in order, or even contemplate going to America, a lifelong dream of Goethe's that turns up again at the end of the *Wanderjahre*.

The 'Society of the Tower' gives Wilhelm a single task to perform; to this end he is handed a letter of indenture, his *Lehrbrief*, with the precept: '*Wo die Worte fehlen, spricht die Tat*' (Action speaks when words are lacking). The task is the education of his little son, Felix, his child by Mariane, now dead and forgotten. But before he begins seriously to start on this, Wilhelm's mind is already on its way to Italy where his great journey is to continue.

It is only the women that save the novel and its hero, who, as the story nears its end, becomes more and more the 'poor specimen' of Goethe's description. Neither Wilhelm nor Goethe can decide whom he is to marry. Is it to be the capable Therese – or the more beautiful Natalie, the rescuing Amazon of the scene in the wood? Both characters are drawn with great love and affection, and this is significant of Goethe's own partiality for having affairs with two women at the same time. Only when he is forced to at the end does he pair them off, like an operatic *finale*, and by then it is almost impossible to take the characters seriously any longer. The gay

Friedrich storms in and, *presto prestissimo*, we have the final tableau: Wilhelm gets Natalie, Therese gets Wilhelm's friend Lothario, and Friedrich the enchanting Philine.

Goethe's treatment of his characters can only be explained by the fact that he never regards the book as finished; he reserves the right to develop them further at some later stage, in a journey to Italy or in some other way. Later, in the *Wanderjahre*, he announces with the wisdom of his old age that Wilhelm must relinquish his dreams of improving his mind in the higher realms of society; he is to become a modest and useful citizen as a simple surgeon.

With Goethe we can never quite free ourselves of the suspicion that he may be speaking with his tongue in his cheek, seeing the whole thing ironically, as a 'play'. The very word 'mission' may, though it need not, have an ironic overtone. The book is full of such overtones, and we are not always aware of them. We find great riches in obscure places and apparently meaningless passages; as often with Goethe these can be very deceptive and be far more significant than they seem to be at first sight. The work is 'incommensurable', as it was intended to be, and is open to many interpretations. It is possible to concentrate on the colourful scenes and omit the didatic sections, as many readers have done; one can single out the Shakespeare essay and use it as a theme for further exegesis, or one can do any number of other things. This was all inherent in Goethe's 'idea' in publishing the book as it stood.

Let us now turn to Goethe and the theatre – he was director of the Weimar *Hoftheater* at the time he wrote the *Lehrjahre*. When he took it over the Court theatre was in a very poor state. During his first ten years in Weimar the amateur performances had been given in a variety of places, in Tiefurt or some other village, in the woods, or in a hall in Weimar, the stage being erected each time by the Court carpenter Mieding. Then for some years a mediocre company was engaged under the direction of a man named Bellomo. In 1791 the Court theatre was opened, but with equally mediocre actors: Weimar was poor, and was to remain so. Leading actors could at best only be invited for a guest performance. The theatre building was erected as a speculation by a former Court servant; the Court granted a modest subsidy, but otherwise the man was responsible for making his theatre pay. The building was called *Das Redouten-Comödienhaus*, and the balls and 'redouts' were the chief attraction and the main source of income. Goethe wrote many masques, devoting much care and attention to them. The form of the *Maskenzug*, with its procession of symbolic or allegorical figures, was a constant preoccupation with him, far into the second part of *Faust*; it played a greater role in his work than did the classic forms of drama which he discussed so assiduously with Schiller.

This barn-like structure, which from the outside resembled the better class of bourgeois house and inside was equipped with reception rooms and restaurant facilities, now became the famous Weimar Court Theatre where Schiller's great plays, as well as some of Goethe's, received their first performances. The repertory had a modest look about it; it included plays by Kotzebue and Iffland, drawing-room plays and, above all, *Singspiele* and operettas by Dittersdorf and, sometimes, Mozart. They played everything that the other smaller theatres played or that was offered by the travelling companies. The players were expected to be versatile, with enough voice for operetta and sufficient poise and address for the drawing-room plays; most important of all they were expected to live quietly and peaceably among themselves. Goethe, with his unquestioned authority as minister and friend of the Duke, had to keep the kindergarten in order. This he did with severity. Recalcitrant members were threatened with immediate arrest, and one actress, who had given a guest performance in Berlin without his knowledge, found herself under house arrest with a sentry posted outside her door. If during a performance the audience laughed, at a moment he considered unseemly, he would rise in his box and thunder, 'No laughing!' At the end of one of Schiller's plays some students from Jena, an important section of the audience and indispensable to the catering side, broke into a *'Vivat!'* Hussars were ordered to arrest the culprits and it was only with difficulty that the incident was settled. Newspaper criticism of any kind was unwelcome. When Professor Böttiger, something of a busybody but for years Goethe's collaborator in artistic matters and metrical problems, wrote an unfavourable review of Schlegel's *Ion*, Goethe immediately demanded withdrawal of the article and censorship of all future articles. In the end Böttiger had to leave Weimar.

As a kind of Code Napoleon for the stage Goethe drew up his 'Rules for Actors'. In these the actors' gestures are described in the minutest detail: 'The fingers must be partly bent, partly straight, but above all not clenched. The two middle fingers should always be kept together, the thumb, forefinger and the little finger being somewhat curved'; the upper arm must be held close to the body, the lower arm can be more flexible. The delivery is to be 'idealized', the 'ideal etiquette' always observed; 'the fashionable habit of putting the hand in the pocket when wearing long trousers is completely ruled out'. In order to ensure the correct articulation and scansion of the verse Goethe held rehearsals at which he beat time with his hands or even with a baton.

All this, of course, applied only to Weimar, and even there only for a certain period. Goethe wanted to establish a classical theatre playing verse drama, and this was hated by the actors and was strange to most of them. He was director of a Court theatre and had to insist on proper manners on the stage: no one was allowed to turn his back on the audience, which might include the Duke or his family. Devrient, the chronicler of the German stage, has described the Weimar theatre of Goethe's day as a 'theatre of Court *dilettanti*', and another great theatre director, Heinrich Laube, has said that Goethe never rid himself of the amateur stage.

Later concepts of the theatre, and far less our own, are not applicable here. Goethe's public was very small, his actors indifferent; his ideas were great, indeed vast. With Schiller he wanted to create a national theatre, to educate his public, his actors, to set an example for the whole of Germany. He wanted to experiment, too, and performed Plautus with the old classical masks. His directorship produced no lasting results. Despite the respect inevitably paid to the name of Goethe, the 'Weimar school' enjoyed a somewhat dubious reputation among theatrical people of the day for the monotony and pathos of its declamation and the stiffness of its acting. The great actors and traditions were bred elsewhere, in Hamburg, Berlin and Vienna where a very different public existed.

Goethe was no man of the theatre. He lacked the passionate devotion, the obsession for the stage without which no theatre can succeed. For him the stage was merely one interest among many, and not the most important. He gave his public farces when they wanted them, as they frequently did, and he gave Karl August his French classics. When he took over the directorship he thought that he would be able to contribute two or three lighter plays himself each year; his attempts are among his weakest works. He also produced important works, plays by Shakespeare, Calderon and Schiller, and was careful not to impose his own. He adapted Shakespeare's *Romeo and Juliet* in a version that even his greatest admirers cannot defend; it is a living monument to his thesis that 'Shakespeare is not really suited to the stage.' Finally, he very soon tired of his directorship. After five years he was already asking to be relieved, a request he continued to repeat. That in spite of this he held the post for twenty-six years is merely an illustration of the complete freedom of his position in Weimar. Christiane took over a great deal of the business of dealing with the personnel, and a competent *Kammerrat* Kirms took over the 'mechanical' side of the work.

Nevertheless Goethe devoted endless time and energy to this task, rehearsing the casts himself, sometimes with friendly words of advice, sometimes in more peremptory tones: 'This is how it is done!' The personal behaviour of his actors was a matter of deep concern to him: 'An actor who neglects himself is, for me, the most objectionable creature in the world!' He took an active interest in the smallest details of their lives, their holidays, their salaries and, as most of them got into debt, advances on these; their salaries were paid weekly, on Fridays. The actresses made their own costumes and most of them earned a little extra by dressmaking for the ladies of Weimar. The costumes were used over and over again, and an old curtain borrowed from the Court might serve as a coronation robe. Goethe was careful not to become involved with any of the actresses, 'I was passionately attracted to some of them, and occasions were certainly not lacking when they came half-way to meet me. But I took a grip on myself and said "no further"!'

His Duke was less particular. He chose the last and most enduring of his mistresses, Karoline Jagemann, from among them; she was a gifted person, with a well-developed figure and rather prominent eyes, a good actress and singer, and a skilful intriguer. She got the already ageing Karl August well under her thumb; after she had borne him a number of children she was given the title of Frau von Heygendorff, with a useful little fortune. She liked to appear on the stage proudly wearing the jewellery the Duke had given her, with 'five thousand *gulden* round her neck', as the unbejewelled and impecunious Weimar ladies bitterly observed. Goethe held out against her for a long time, but she finally brought about his downfall. A silly play, in which a trained poodle was supposed to appear, was the immediate cause of this: Goethe did not want the animal and Karoline Jagemann did; not that she was particularly interested in the animal, probably, as she was a tragedienne, but she wanted to have her own way. Shortly afterwards Goethe was dismissed by Karl August, and never entered the building again.

Only once after this did Goethe have any connection with the theatre; it was in his old age when, after frequent reconstructions, the building was burned to the ground. In conjunction with his friend Coudray, the architect, he prepared plans for a new theatre, but once again Karoline Jagemann intervened and Karl August accepted the design of another architect. Goethe's comment was: 'In the last resort a new theatre is only a new funeral pyre, to which sooner or later some accident will set light again. That is my consolation.'

Close association with the theatre is generally accepted as the only school for a dramatist. In Goethe's case its effect was the very opposite; it brought his dramatic works to an end. Only one further play did he produce, *Die natürliche Tochter* (The Natural Daughter), written when his discussions with Schiller on the drama and epic poetry were at their height; it remained a fragment, planned as the first part of a trilogy. It is quite remote from the stage, an exercise for the reader's imagination, on which it makes great demands, too great for most readers. Goethe wanted a serious vehicle in which to express his ideas on the French Revolution, hitherto treated only on the level of farce, in his *Gross-Kophta* and *Bürgergeneral*. He intended to create a new form for this purpose, stricter even than that of classical French tragedy – the symbolic drama. The characters were to be stripped of all connection with historic reality, they are called simply King, Duke, Eugenie; no period is indicated, and the setting is indeterminate, a wood, a room, a harbour looking over the sea. The language, written in blank verse, is laden with significance, rich in the most subtle stylization. The plot is well-nigh incomprehensible, hinting at some future that is never realized.

The occasion for the play was a book of memoirs published in the sixth year of the Revolution and written by a French lady, who claimed to be the natural daughter of Prince Conti-Bourbon and the Duchess of Mazarin. According to her story she had tried to get the King to legitimize her as a royal princess, but had been frustrated by her mother and legitimate brother, who had kidnapped her, taken her to a convent and then, having first drugged her into unconsciousness, married her to a bourgeois notary. In vain she had tried to get the crime punished and to obtain recognition for herself. Research seems to corroborate her story of the crime; she died in 1825, in penury. Although it follows the main lines of this sordid story, Goethe's play has almost nothing to do with the intrigue. His king is not Louis XVI, but simply 'a king', his heroine, Eugenie, is not a lady fighting for recognition at Court, but an 'ill-fated and unhappy woman'.

The problem of illegitimate birth was no strange one to Goethe; he had to fight for the recognition of his own son. When he showed his play to Herder the latter could not refrain from the joke: 'I prefer your natural son to your natural daughter', and this remark ended the twenty-year-long friendship between the two. Princely offspring of this kind existed everywhere, in Weimar, Prussia and elsewhere, and the claims of princes and princesses, who had been passed over, could disturb even world politics. Usually they were suppressed more brutally than by incarceration in a convent and forced marriage to a bourgeois notary; Catherine the Great simply had such claimants murdered. In Rome Goethe had been invited to dinner by the illegitimate daughter of the Pretender, Charles Stuart; he did not go, but his conscience pricked him for his excessive caution. All this, in part *chronique scandaleuse* and in part of more sinister significance, formed the background to Goethe's feeling that all order was in dissolution. In his play the Duke says: 'Our times, alas, are fearful in their portents, the lower orders rise, the high sink lower.' In the story of the necklace Goethe had already sensed this changed atmosphere.

These portents of the times Goethe transmutes into symbolic runic ciphers, which reveal little connection with the problems of the day. Occasionally we find a reference to some well-known contemporary circumstances. When, for example, the unhappy Eugenie is threatened with banishment to one of the fever islands and inevitable death from the 'tortures of the heated mists', the allusion was obvious to Goethe's contemporaries. They all knew it referred to the 'dry guillotine', by whose means several thousand further victims were dispatched when Paris became sickened with the real guillotine and its rivers of blood. Again, when the heroine is pursued step by step on her downward course by a mysterious letter from the King, denying her rescue or help of any kind, everyone could see a reference to the well-known *lettre de cachet* of French royal practice. These, however, are isolated examples. The main characters are allegorical, the King representing the power of the ruler and Eugenie the innocent victim of all arbitrary power. The real opposing character, the legitimate brother who wants to destroy his sister, does not appear in the play at all. He represents unlimited greed and lust for riches: 'to own enough would be to famish', says his secretary interpreting his views. 'All is demanded, all! Extravagance unbounded makes unrestricted wealth desirable.' It is a play of blind political power, of the operation of dark and brutal forces. The noble Eugenie is slowly destroyed before our eyes, after at first being offered the hope of reaching her goal. Up to this point Goethe is justified in calling the play a tragedy. But he recoils before the tragic ending on which a dramatist *pur sang* would have seized: the bourgeois notary, in the memoirs the guilty instrument of criminal conspiracy, is transformed into a lover. He offers Eugenie his hand and thus saves her from banishment to the fever-hell. But the play does not end with a conventional bourgeois marriage. Eugenie consents to go to the altar with him only on condition that he then leaves her, to wait patiently for the possible day when she may send for him. Resignation is the solution.

How Goethe would have developed this theme in the two remaining plays of his trilogy we do not know. He dictated some sketches, but these are open to many interpretations. Goethe loved his Eugenie and the character bears many traces of his affection. In his old age he said that the characters used often to visit him, 'returning like restless spirits, who sigh imploringly for their redemption'. The truth would seem to be that he grew increasingly disinclined to accept the implications of tragedy, both in life and in poetry, and that consequently he could find no solution for so essentially tragic a subject. Nor did he ever find an answer to the problem of the Revolution. His sketches for the trilogy contain phases that are not preliminary drafts of scenes but attempts to find a formula for the great events of the day. 'The masses become absolute. Drive out those who waver. Crush those who resist. Humble the exalted. Exalt the humble. To humble them again.' He sees despotism as being 'without any real supreme head', and losing itself in its subordinate parts, with their numerous 'ganglia'; he sees the mania for appropriation, with its resultant oppression.

Having long held aloof from world events Goethe is now about to see the storm break over him. In the *Natürliche Tochter* we seem to hear a foreboding of this in the words of the Duke: 'How hated what endures, how hated too to me the sight of pride in permanence. How welcome change and flow. Roll on you floods, tear down the dams, transform the land to sea.... Spread out afar, advance you warrior ranks, and on the bloodstained fields pile death on death!' For Goethe this now becomes reality.

# 34

# *The Days of Napoleon*

Looking back over the fateful year of 1806 Goethe speaks of the 'interim hopes' with which 'for many a year we had already buoyed ourselves, like Philistines.... The world was in flames from end to end, Europe had assumed a different form, on land and sea cities and fleets were in ruins, but central and northern Germany still enjoyed a measure of fitful peace, in which we surrendered ourselves to a dubious security.'

Goethe's private life in these years before the storm follows a strictly ordered pattern. The journey of 1797, which was cut short in Switzerland, was his last attempt to undertake a major journey; after that he stayed at home, alternating only between Weimar and Jena. His house in Weimar becomes more and more of a museum as his collections grow, with their busts and paintings and his rooms devoted to natural history. He has his own carriage and coachman, his servants and secretaries, and he keeps a well-appointed table, reinforced by his excellent wine cellar. For this last orders are dispatched far and wide; even his fees are sometimes paid direct to a wine merchant. One bookseller in Bremen, wanting a contribution from Goethe for his new almanach, accompanies his request with a case of fine Hock, and Goethe, pleased by this 'obliging form of invitation', sends him what he wants. One would imagine that peaceful Weimar was quiet enough, especially as Goethe did not take his Court responsibilities too seriously. But his exceptionally sensitive nature reacted to the slightest disturbance. Even at this period of his life he could be driven completely out of his mind by dogs barking. Falk tells the story, perhaps a little improved in the telling but substantially corroborated by Goethe himself, of how, disturbed in his thoughts by barking in the street, Goethe rushes to the window and calls out to the dog: 'Do what you like, you spectre, you won't get the better of me!' There are numerous instances of his silly petitions against disturbances of the peace; the construction of a skittle alley, for example, which he tries to prevent by every means at his disposal. Then there is a weaver, the noise, or if not the noise the vibration, of whose loom upsets him. In his distress he writes to his ministerial colleague Voigt: 'Delicate experiments are necessary to show how severe the vibration is. If one were to place, e.g., a vessel of water in the room occupied by Professor Meyer the slight movement of the surface would reveal the persistent vibration.'

So, particularly when he wants to work – and in spite of his ceaseless activity Goethe works only in short bursts and at long intervals – he retires to Jena, to a sort of bachelor life. Christiane has to see that provisions are sent from Weimar and, from time to time, is allowed to visit him. But Goethe finds a new family circle in Jena, in the home of the bookseller Frommann, and a new love. Goethe, now almost sixty, conducts his love affair with Minna Herzlieb, the Frommann's eighteen-year-old ward, with the greatest circumspection. In very regular sonnets – the bookseller has just published a new edition of Petrarch's sonnets – he makes play with the girl's name, and a new love legend, immediately taken up and spread by his admirers, is established. It was not only with the rise and dominance of the middle classes that all the discussion over Goethe's countless 'loves' originated, although it was they who enlarged on them with sickly sentimentality or, still more grotesquely, developed them in strictly philological dissertations on the 'influence' of this or that sweetheart on his various works. Goethe smilingly gave his consent to the legends and occasionally even encouraged them. Pressed to reveal his feelings he confesses to loving the girl, known to her friends as Minchen, *mehr als billig*, more perhaps than is seemly, and so leaves the affair open to any and every interpretation. The only interesting thing about this Minna is that, once again, she is a nun-type, transformed now into a 'little daughter'; her later life closely resembles that of Goethe's adored and never forgotten sister Cornelia. Minna, too, shudders at the thought of marriage; she attempts it nevertheless, becomes engaged to a thoroughly nice professor and at the last moment, to everyone's horror, refuses to marry him. Goethe writes to one of her friends: 'Remember me to Minchen; I always thought there was more loyalty in the little soul. But one must beware of trifling with the whole race....' The sequel is even sadder: she eventually marries another professor, but the experience of physical union is so repugnant to her that she becomes mentally deranged and ends her life in a home. Like Cornelia, the only solution for her would have been to become an 'abbess'.

Goethe chooses these shadowy and 'untouchable' natures because they provide an assurance that the relationship will not get too passionate; at the same time they are welcome, and sufficiently charming to find their way, in enhanced form, into his poetry. It is quite possible that, in addition to inspiring the sonnets, Minna may have contributed to the character of Ottilie in the *Wahlverwandschaften*. Otherwise Goethe's reference to her as the 'little soul' defines the relationship very aptly.

At the turn of the century, and to a far greater extent than Weimar, Jena is the intellectual capital of Germany, with a wealth of talent and famous names it would he hard to match anywhere: Schiller, Humboldt, Fichte, Hegel, Schelling, the two Schlegels, Brentano, Tieck, Voss, as well as a host of names distinguished in science and medicine. Goethe has a room in the old castle, a very modest and dilapidated building; later he moves to an inn, or sometimes a room in the Botanical Garden. His position in Jena is a strange one. In the first place he is the minister responsible for the University, an extremely complex institution. He has no authority to issue orders and instructions, as his monarchal nature would like to do, not even as the representative of the Duchy of Weimar; the University is responsible also to the other Thuringian principalities. The means are extremely limited, and almost all scholars of note confine themselves to very short visiting appointments. In spite of all his efforts Goethe is unable to alter this. Even Hegel has to eke out his existence for six years living on the students' fees for his lectures, and his lectures are sparsely attended; his title of Professor brings him only an *ex gratia* payment of one hundred *thalers*, but no salary. 'Should Hegel need money you may give him up to about ten *thalers*', writes Goethe to his old friend Knebel. In despair Hegel applies for a vacant professorship in botany, with free lodgings in the Botanical Garden, offering, as evidence of his suitability, the collection of plants he made in Switzerland when he was a tutor. In the end he goes to Bamberg as editor of a paper, then to Nuremberg as headmaster of a school until, with professorships in Heidelberg and Berlin, his fame spreads as one of the leading spirits of his age. Ritter, a scientist of genius with a flair for experimenting and the discoverer of ultra-violet rays, whom Goethe called a 'veritable galaxy of knowledge', has to live without any official position at all; after a few years he leaves for Munich. Academic life in Jena is a *misère*; but it is a very fruitful misery, and all the heavily endowed and elaborately equipped institutions would be hard put to it to show anything comparable. Goethe can hardly be held responsible for the poverty of this intellectual Benjamin of his; he does all he can, even using his influence on behalf of the private lives of his staff. Since he is unable to offer adequate salaries, he does his best to get professors whose wives have means; he even attempts a little match-making on these lines. He devotes much valuable time to work that should have been done by subordinates: the arranging of a large library, left to the University by one of the professors, occupies him for years. A mineralogical society gives him the opportunity to enlarge his knowledge of geology. Such institutions are semi-private, established and maintained by small groups. Goethe's own interests are dictated largely by his personal tastes and, while centred on anatomy, geology and physics, are almost universal, excluding only history, theology, and everything to do with politics or economics.

Goethe's ideal of a university, like that of Wilhelm von Humboldt, who was able to put his ideas into practice on a broader scale, is the formation of independent personalities of wide and liberal culture. He is sensitive to all disturbance, from within as well as from without, and protects himself against it with every means in his power; one has to bear in mind that Goethe was living in a defenceless, poor and tiny country exposed to constant pressure on every side. Very soon, having seen Jena 'at the summit of prosperity', as he notes in 1797, he has to abandon the realization of his ideal. Six years later there is a veritable exodus of professors to Halle or Würzburg; Fichte, accused of 'atheism', had already left, having defended himself with 'violence and stubbornness', as Goethe puts it. Jena's heyday, like all heydays, is short-lived.

So long as it lasts, however, Goethe can indulge in Jena his unbounded zest for knowledge. For botany he has the Botanical Garden, for anatomy Professor Loder, who also leaves and goes to Moscow, and for every one of his interests he can find a helper. With Schelling he discusses natural philosophy and, for the first and only time in his life, comes into immediate contact with a philosopher of real distinction; the result is a fruitful exchange of ideas, of more consequence for the philosopher than the poet. Goethe is attracted by the young man whom Schelling's friend Caroline calls 'Granite'. Goethe even thinks of entrusting to the young philosopher the composition, under his guidance, of a great epic poem on nature he is planning.

Caroline is always at Schelling's side to spur him on and encourage him. She is the moving spirit among the Goethe admirers in Jena, and of the group later known as the 'older Romantics' but at this time consisting of very young people. Caroline herself is no longer young; she is in her forties when, after previous marriages to a man named Böhmer and to August Wilhelm Schlegel, she marries the twenty-eight-year-old Schelling. Goethe helped to smooth over these matrimonial complications. Caroline's letter to Goethe on this occasion shows that not everyone saw in him merely the cold, statuesque Olympian: 'You exercise the same influence over him [Schelling] that nature herself would, were she able to speak to him in a voice from heaven. Give him your hand in nature's name. It asks for little more than you are doing already....' And to Schlegel she writes: 'He loves you like a father, I love you like a mother – what wonderful parents you have! Do not disappoint us.'

The group is riddled with matrimonial and amorous complications. The spirit of Romanticism manifests itself in this way long before it finds expression in literature or is turned into a literary programme. An adequate description of this labyrinth of relationships, often changing from month to month or even within the pages of a single letter, would require a graph, and all the charm would then be lost. It must suffice that Goethe stands aloof from this maelstrom, a calm observer noting the strange activities of these people. They are all highly gifted, the women no less so than the men, the women often more masculine than the men. It is the energetic Caroline who introduces the weakly August Wilhelm Schlegel to Goethe. His brother, the more headstrong Friedrich, undergoes his own evolution in regard to Goethe, from idolatry to estrangement; having developed his own theory of 'the poetic', he soon finds Goethe 'insufficiently poetic'. Romantic irony ordains that the two brothers' admiration for Goethe is at its zenith at the time when they themselves are mostly purely classicist; a true 'Grae-comania', Schiller calls it. In the face of Schiller's warning, who prophesies a 'total defeat', Goethe produces their two weakest works, the dramas *Ion* and *Alarchos*, at his Court theatre. Schiller is proved right. 'It is an illness on his part', writes Schiller to his friend Körner, 'that he should adopt the Schlegels while at the same time he bitterly reproaches and reviles them.' In retrospect Goethe described the brothers as 'hot-house talents', unhappy men all their lives who, wishing to appear more gifted than they were, caused a great deal of mischief both in literature and art.

In these Jena days, however, they cause no mischief. They spread Goethe's fame abroad. They proclaim him not only Germany's leading poet, relegating Schiller to second place, but one of the four or five greatest names in world literature. And it is Goethe's genius for language and the wealth of expression derived from it that enables Schlegel, in these Jena years, to make his translation of Shakespeare, the first great German master-piece in this most difficult of all spheres of literary activity. Translations of Dante and Calderon follow. These years bring Goethe into closer contact with world literature, and it would be very unjust to overlook the part played by the Schlegels in this – or to overlook their importance as writers – by judging them on the strength of ill-tempered remarks made by Goethe in later life.

Goethe lives alternately in Weimar and Jena; each year, in addition, he goes to some spa, usually Karlsbad. Here he sees new faces and feels even freer from domestic ties than in Jena, contriving little love affairs and flirta-tions with complete unconcern. 'At all events', he writes to Schiller in 1795, 'I have started a little romance on the spur of the moment, something that is very necessary to lure one out of bed at five o'clock in the morning. Let us hope we can restrain our feelings and conduct events in such a way as to spin it out for a fortnight.' As a famous writer he is well received, but there are disappointments too; an 'enchanting little creature' goes into raptures over his latest novel – alas, it turns out to be by his old friend Klinger. One admirer complains that his attitude to women 'who do not behave with strict circumspection is unrefined, and he is lacking in all tenderness and charm'. It seems he has been reciting his works with devastating mime and the terrified lady has seen him as *Faust*, riding through the air on a barrel, 'and then I thought the devil would carry him off on the spot. Oh Goethe, how your great spirit roams.... Now it hovers between heaven and hell.' There is no question here of the sedate *Geheimrat*. In Karlsbad Goethe descends from his pinnacle and allows himself free rein.

Goethe has made the acquaintance of two pretty Berlin Jewesses, daughters of a rich merchant named Meyer. The elder of the two, Marianne, is for many years his closest friend on these visits to the spas; she is the morganatic wife of a Prince Reuss, and after his death lives in Vienna as Frau von Eybenberg. On one occasion he meets her clandestinely in Dresden, and he keeps up the most lively and charming correspondence with his 'Mariannchen'. She is elegant, much sought after and clever, with tender lips and a sharp tongue, as Goethe says. She is a delightful companion and he responds to her; at their very first meeting he regales her with stories of his Roman adventures and with detailed commentaries on his Roman elegies. He writes in her album and on her fan, and sends her his manuscripts. Marianne sends him chocolate from Vienna and, on one occasion, four jars of caviare; she sends him Greek and Roman coins for his collection, and pesters him in the most charming way to continue his *Faust* 'of which I have heard so much that, like the children, I cry more, more! And I can hardly wait for an opportunity to see or hear something of yours.' She gets the lightest and airiest letters and notes from Goethe, whose style now is otherwise very official: 'What did you say, dear friend, to my running off like that! In fact I was abducted and am now held prisoner. Live and let live! Go and let go! Seem to me two important maxims, although neither is exactly diplomatic....' Thus he writes from Franzensbad, where he is relaxing a little from the exertions of life with Mariannchen in the company of another pretty friend, Silvie von Ziegesar, the 'daughter, friend and sweetheart' of his poem.

This is certainly not one of Goethe's 'great loves' which, in any case, are not so numerous or profound as the tireless commentators on his relations with women would have us believe. Marianne has not been put into any of his writings, but she helped substantially to turn the word *heiter* (cheerful or serene) which he often uses only in defiance and desperation, into a reality for him.

Not insubstantial, either, was Goethe's debt as an author to Marianne and her friends. It was not only in their passionate singing of his praises that this debt lay – and verbal recommendation has always been more effective than written, even when the latter is from the pen of a Friedrich Schlegel – but above all in Goethe's awareness that he now had an audience of readers who understood and valued him, even in his more difficult works. This was something he had long lacked. The extent of their understanding he did not bother his head about; he had no great opinion of the understanding of the essayists either, knowing quite well that they praised him only to support some thesis of their own, or to disparage someone else by the use of his name. Goethe never attempted to appeal to the public at large; if his works had a great success he accepted the fact, or scoffed at it. Yet he had no desire for solitude. The small communities of readers which now began to spring up were his public. In truth he has never had any other, the great name being something quite different – just a name.

The strongest Goethe movement started in Berlin, and its moving spirits were the Berlin Jewesses. At a time of social change they created the first literary salons in Germany, a Henriette Herz or a Rahel Varnhagen. It was a very short period. The Romantic era brought a reaction, with fiercely anti-semitic clubs and societies making their appeal to the 'true Christian' and old Germanic heritage of the Middle Ages. It was only for a decade or two, prior to the civic emancipation of the Jews, and of the German bourgeoisie in general, that the Jewish *salons* prospered; intellectually very active and socially very free, they were, for the most part, under aristocratic protection and patronage. Henriette Herz' husband was a physician and philosopher, regarded as 'Kant's representative' in Berlin, and it was with his pupils that she started her *salon*; some form of cultural activity was the only means the Jews had of gaining a degree of respect and social acceptance. In her attic rooms in the Jägerstrasse Rahel Levin, later Varnhagen, received all the well-known or rising authors and publicists, Friedrich Schlegel, Tieck, Jean Paul, the two Humboldts, Prince Louis Ferdinand, as well as diplomats, junkers and actors. If one can speak in terms of class at all, it was to the actor class, who also still had to fight for social recognition, that the Jews belonged; both were beyond the social pale and were regarded as questionable company. For this very reason they were more attractive than 'good society'. In one of his epigrams Goethe says: society 'is called good when it does not provide occasion even for the slightest poem'. Goethe was Rahel's idol, her solace and counsellor. 'Listen to Goethe,' she writes to one of her friends, 'it is with tears that I write the name of this great mediator, recalling great affliction'; he is to be read as one reads the Bible, she continues, he has been her unfailing companion throughout her life. Women, as we saw in the case of Caroline Schelling, felt this aspect of Goethe's nature far more keenly than the aesthetic.

While it would be foolish to ascribe to these circles a monopoly in their reverence of Goethe, it would be equally foolish to underestimate it. Goethe, at any rate, did not do so, although he was by no means the philosemite Lessing was; he was no more in favour of state recognition or civic equality for the Jews than he was of freedom for the press.

Goethe's visits to the spas, however, are not monopolized by his literary admirers; his time is constantly taken up with 'waiting on' some prince or other, and whole pages of his diaries are filled with lists of gracious lords, ladies and gentlemen. It all contrasts strangely with these Napoleonic days. In conversation with diplomats and those in high places one can occasionally feel a gust of keener air. Goethe's reaction is seldom more than the 'Hm!' recorded by Jean Paul when the poet was told of the French entry into Rome. In 1803 the Holy Roman Empire comes finally to its end, an end even more inglorious than that of the old Roman Empire. The so-called *Reichsdeputationshauptschluss* – the findings of the deputations sent to bargain over the liquidation – is, in the very enormity of its name, a symbol of bureaucratic haggling over territories and peoples of the most lamentable kind, and it completes the destruction begun at Rastatt. The Emperor Franz, the last to be elected in Frankfurt, lays down his old crown and now calls himself Emperor of Austria. Goethe, on his way home from Karlsbad, says he finds a quarrel on the driving seat between his coachman and his servant of more interest than the end of the Holy Roman Empire, which had been something impossible to grasp, a mere empty concept. And something impossible to grasp it really was; this structure which, at the time of its dissolution, still numbered a *reichsunmittelbare* member for every year of its existence, some eighteen hundred in all – kingdoms, principalities, both temporal and spiritual, independent counties and baronies. The exact number was not known, any more than was the number of inhabitants; at the Congress of Rastatt some enterprising publicist had scribbled down a few statistical tables, which were then published for the guidance of the delegates.

Since the campaign against France Goethe has allowed numerous wars to pass by him; before long details of these become confused even to contemporaries. For ten years Prussia maintains a friendly neutrality towards France and finally, just before her fall, even becomes her ally. Austria is fighting in south Germany, Italy and Switzerland, and is always defeated. Russian contingents are fighting in the Alps. There are short-lived peace treaties and coalitions. The only constant factors are the rise of Napoleon and England's stubborn resistance to his plans for world conquest. Goethe remains quite untouched by all this. To a Swiss pedagogue, who is thinking of going abroad, he writes: 'In our times the most unlikely things are possible, and for any thoughtful, resolute man, in whom there is a degree of independence, there is no alternative but to preserve the courage and ability to transplant himself. At a moment when people everywhere are busy creating new fatherlands, the impartial thinker, the man who can transcend his time, finds his fatherland nowhere and everywhere' (15.3.1799). He censures a critic in his Jena *Literaturzeitung* for his severity towards the consuls in Paris: 'Let peoples and governments see how to manage their own affairs! Only when their squabbles are on paper have they a place in a literary journal, and a true literary man can thank God that he is entitled to treat world affairs historically.'

Wars are still essentially the business of the armies concerned. People travel to Italy even when famous battles are being fought, and unless their carriages get entangled with the marching columns, and scarcely even then, they are not molested. Goethe visits the Bohemian spas and learns of troop movements in the neighbourhood, of fights and defeats; wounded officers come on leave and tell of their experiences. Scholars travel to scientific congresses in Paris, even from England, which is at war with France; on making enquiries beforehand they are informed slightly indignantly that of course scientists are free to come and exchange ideas. The battles themselves have become grim enough since the introduction of general military service made manpower cheap, but they are short, a matter of hours, and are accepted as verdicts of destiny. The campaigns are short.

The map changes from year to year. New revolutionary republics appear, with classicist names like the Batavian, Cisalpine or Helvetian Republics.

A kingdom of Etruria, a well-nigh archaeological title, is created by the Consul Bonaparte, and soon disappears again. The South German Princes form a *Rheinbund*, to-day they would be called satellites. Very soon still more fantastic creations appear, headed by members of the Corsican family clan, by marshals, army chiefs and staff officers.

Of the year 1806 Goethe writes in his Annals: 'The great Empire in the west was founded, its roots and branches spreading in all directions.' It is as a natural scientist that he looks on all this; the *Farbenlehre* is his chief preoccupation at this time. With his hyper-sensitive organism he can feel the gathering storm, even though he wants to have nothing to do with it. The vital thing, so far as he is concerned, is to bring this most important of his works safely to its conclusion. Since the beginning of the century he has undergone a number of serious illnesses, with the result that physically, too, he feels severely shaken. Schiller's death in 1805 has meant the end of an epoch for him. A new and unexpected epoch is opening.

This begins early in 1806 with Prussian troops marching through Weimar. With Riemer Goethe goes through the manuscript of *Faust*, which he now intends to finish. He goes to Karlsbad again, where he spends a great deal of time making drawings for a little book of 'travel, diversion and solace' for the ailing young Princess Karoline. It is a strange production, an escape to southern landscapes with classical monuments and grottoes, a Palladian villa, and recollections of the Swiss mountains. Suddenly a light explodes, like some mightly aurora borealis; when at last it dies down he adds sketches of the battlefields of Jena and Auerstädt.

He goes to Jena to unpack and catalogue the specimens of minerals he has collected in Karlsbad. The castle where he is living fills with Prussian staff officers. One of them, a colonel, has written an impassioned manifesto against Napoleon. Goethe, pressed by the printer and the city authorities, who already fear a French victory, stops its publication. He does so under the frigid gaze of a tall Prussian aide-de-camp, who stands in amazement at this 'daring of a civilian', a symbol of the inflexible Prussianism that events were now bringing to an end.

A Major von Marwitz describes Goethe at table: 'a tall, good-looking man in embroidered Court dress, powdered, with a bag-wig, and wearing a dress sword, who was always the minister and maintained the 'dignity of his office well, although he lacked the free and natural bearing of an aristocrat.' Another Prussian, Prince Louis Ferdinand, visited Goethe in Weimar while the troops were assembling; he wrote to his mistress, one of his many: 'Now I have really got to know Goethe; late last evening he came home with me and sat by my bed, while we drank champagne and punch, and he talked really splendidly. At the end he unbuttoned his soul and gave his spirit free rein; he said a great deal, I learned a great deal and found him completely natural and charming.' Karl August, who had retired early, noted later: 'the others spent the whole night drinking vast quantities, vying with one another: Goethe was by no means outdone, he could drink terribly.' In Jena Goethe again meets the Prince who, in the eyes of the younger generation, was Prussia's great hope. He was adored by women and esteemed by musicians; his chamber music, published posthumously with the Prussian eagle on the title-page, received even Beethoven's commendation: 'far from princely, but excellent!' He was unpopular at Court, because of his endless debts, and with senior officers of the old school, by whom he was regarded as undisciplined and reckless. He was the first casualty of the Battle of Jena, Goethe noting on October 10: 'Action between Saalfeld and Rudolstadt. Prince Louis fell.'

This was the prelude. Goethe had foreseen disaster. The Duke of Brunswick, his original reputation still unshaken, was once again Commander-in-Chief; among his staff there was the same dissatisfaction and hostility that had existed during the campaign of 1792. Goethe noticed the 'vanity of authorship' among the Prussian staff officers, who were in fact constantly writing articles and pamphlets, and either publishing them or preparing them with a view to publication. He could not foresee that all the great figures of the future campaigns against Napoleon already held high positions during the present catastrophe. Scharnhorst was chief-of-staff to Brunswick; a week before the battle he wrote: 'I know what should be done; what will be done the gods alone know.' They all still had a lot to learn, and they received a terrible lesson in practical, as opposed to theoretical, warfare.

Goethe, who has been in charge of provisioning in Jena, returns to Weimar as the army takes up its positions on the field of Auerstädt. On the eve of the battle there is a performance of Kapellmeister Himmel's operetta *Fanchon das Leiermädchen* at the Court theatre. Next day the distant roar of the artillery comes over in waves. Goethe sits down to lunch in a depressed mood. The bombardment ceases and there is a slight feeling of relief. Suddenly shots from very close at hand pass over the roof and they have to leave the table. Fleeing Prussian troops in complete disorder dash through the streets shouting, and disappear down the road to Erfurt. Once again there is a lull. Then some French patrols feel their way forward. Goethe tells his secretary Riemer and his son August to take them some wine and beer. More French troops arrive. Goethe goes to the castle with one of the officers; it is half deserted, only the Duchess Luise has remained behind. This is her great hour, as it is Christiane's. Goethe sends a message home telling them not to worry; Marshal Ney is to be quartered with them and, apart from some hussars of his escort, no one else is to be admitted.

The hussars arrive, most of them Alsatians. They are given billets in the servants' quarters; too exhausted to eat, they accept only a little beer and fall straight to sleep. Christiane has the table laid for the Marshal and his staff and prepares their rooms. The emergency reawakens the housewife in her, a side of her nature that had lain somewhat dormant; she is constantly busy, getting things done and giving orders. But there is no sign of the Marshal, and more and more troops pour into the town.

They start to plunder, breaking in doors and windows. Fires break out in several parts of the town. Anyone resisting gets badly manhandled; Goethe's old friend Kraus, the painter, dies from his injuries. Charlotte von Stein's apartment is completely stripped and broken up, as is that of Goethe's brother-in-law, Vulpius. Goethe, back from the castle, goes upstairs to his room to bed. During the night two tirailleurs, tired of camping out in the square, bang on the door with their muskets. They are let in and given food. Goethe comes downstairs in his voluminous dressing-gown, his 'prophet's mantle', majestic and awe-inspiring. The soldiers pour him out a glass of wine and touch glasses with him. He goes upstairs again, while they continue to drink; then they follow him, intent on plunder. They threaten to knock him down. With the help of one of the hussars, as Riemer tells us, Christiane rescues him, chases the marauders out of the room and locks the door. They go into the rooms prepared for the Marshal and lie down on the beds. In the morning the Marshal's aide-de-camp, who has come to inspect the quarters, beats them out with the flat of his sword. Marshal Ney appears. A sentry stands before the door.

For Goethe this marks the end of the danger. Henceforth he has only marshals as his guests, one after the other: Lannes, son of a groom and now the Duke of Montebello, Augereau, son of a fruiterer and now the Duke of Castiglione. Goethe receives an object lesson. These men are very different from the officers he has known, very different from the cold and vacillating Brunswick, now wandering round without a country, blinded in battle, and soon to die in some remote corner of Northern Germany. The French marshals are men in their prime, famed for their bravery; Lannes is the victor of Arcole, who in spite of three serious wounds raced back to his troops, placed himself, banner in hand, at the head of the 'devils' brigade' and was first across the Adda. They are great robbers; Augereau, an adventurer, has enriched himself vastly in Italy. None of this disturbs Goethe unduly. These men are soldiers first and last, and nothing else. They have no ambitions to shine as authors, like the Prussian officers; their only ambition is to win victories, and this they do unceasingly. Goethe sees them as perfect examples of their type and as well-chosen servants of their master, the most perfect example of the species. With the defeated Prussians he has little sympathy; he warned his Duke against throwing in his lot with them, and he has been proved right.

And now Karl August's untimely resumption of his Prussian command – he played no part in the battle, having been sent off on a senseless diversion in the direction of Franconia – threatens to bring about the complete destruction of the Duchy of Weimar. Neighbouring Brunswick, related to Weimar by family ties, is wiped off the map by a stroke of Napoleon's pen. Weimar's fate hangs by a thread. Napoleon arrives, gloomy, uncouth, sinister. As no one else is left – even the ministers having fled – he asks the Duchess imperiously: 'Where is your husband?' Quietly and with dignity she replies that he is at his post. Napoleon is impressed, or pretends to be. He continues to rail for a while; in fact he has long since decided to incorporate Weimar among his Rhineland vassals. He is in constant need of new recruits; a French historian has called the new empire the *Empire de recrutement*. He grants his pardon, with a gesture towards the pale Luise. None the less Weimar has to pay the enormous levy of two million *francs*. The Weimar contingent is ordered to join the French forces immediately, and soon finds itself in action against the Prussians at the siege of Kolberg. The Duke has to resign his Prussian commission and, in the general confusion, the King of Prussia accepts his resignation immediately. For three months Karl August wanders round trying vainly to present himself to his new liege. It is early in the following year before he returns to his capital; in the meantime his wife, who has stood in the background for so long, has been hailed as the saviour of her country.

Karl August is not the only one to collapse ingloriously. The defeat of Jena – soon to be the subject of bitter recriminations in an endless war of words – starts a chain reaction. The real catastrophe is not the battle but what follows: the surrender of the vital fortresses without a fight, the confusion, the cowardice, the abandonment of every position, moral as well as military. Within a few days Napoleon is in Berlin, at Sanssouci, where he appropriates Frederick the Great's sword, which he carries with him to St Helena.

Although his personal safety is guaranteed by his distinguished guests, and by a specific order of the French town commander, a native of the Palatinate who had studied at Jena, Goethe also wanders round in a daze. He is afraid he will have to leave Weimar; his whole position, everything he has so carefully built up, is in jeopardy. Christiane is his support during these days. She looks after the house and its guests, she helps her now destitute brother and his family, as well as other victims of the catastrophe. Goethe writes asking the Court chaplain to arrange a quiet wedding in the sacristy of the Court chapel; his secretary Reimer and his son August, now seventeen, are the only witnesses. Goethe has the wedding ring engraved with the date October 14, the day of the Battle of Jena, the day he regards as beginning a new epoch in his life; everything prior to this he calls the 'antediluvian' time.

The waters subside, leaving their residue of slime. Goethe's much criticized way of life has gone on for so long that his marriage sets the pens in motion. A report appears in the paper run by his publisher, Cotta; it is worth mentioning only as an illustration of the crudeness and pitiful standards of writing and of the press at this time: 'Amid the thunder of the battle Goethe married his housekeeper of many years standing, Demoiselle Vulpius, who thus became the only one to draw a winner when many thousands were drawing blank.' A further report, still more shabby, takes as its butt Goethe's brother-in-law Vulpius who, with his story of robbers, *Rinaldo Rinaldini*, has become one of the most popular writers of light fiction: 'Our celebrated novel manufacturer V-s also came within an inch of his life, and his wife was ravished; but sad as it is to experience such things, it is a joy to hear him describe the scene. In those moments the womb of his mind, from which so many robbers and monsters have emerged, will certainly have become pregnant again with a dozen similar creations, which will be grunting around like young porkers at the coming fairs.'

It is not some small local paper that publishes these articles but one of the most respected papers in Germany; this collapse is worth recording too. Goethe defends himself with great dignity. He writes to Cotta, with whom he has just reached agreement over a new Collected Edition of his works, to say that he demands to be taken seriously: 'I have led a serious life and still continue to do so.' So far as his brother-in-law is concerned, he goes on, this is surely no time to attack someone who has been robbed of everything or to use as an occasion for criticizing *Rinaldo Rinaldini*; 'and, to speak frankly, where are those articles that serve the booksellers best?' In conclusion he says: 'We know very well that peace, like stagnant water, produces vermin of this kind, but their appearance in wartime is truly loathsome.'

Such personal experiences serve only to strengthen his general feeling that it is useless to devote his time and energy to the struggles of peoples and governments. He turns to his *Farbenlehre*.

# 35

# A Galaxy of Kings

Goethe's work on natural science is only 'interrupted for a few days', as he notes in his *Annals*. He is referring in the first instance to his *Farbenlehre* which Cotta, still with his eye on *Faust*, is now prepared to publish, though undoubtedly with some misgivings. But Goethe does not neglect his University, and prepares a memorandum for Marshal Berthier. He draws the Marshal's attention to the international benefits conferred by his institutions, and mentions the school of drawing 'under the supervision of Geheimrat von Goethe, who is of the opinion that the arts will continue to decline unless they are placed at the service of the crafts'. He also refers to the modest art collections and to his art exhibitions.

To French eyes the local treasures must look poor indeed, but this has its advantage: little Weimar and little Jena ·are left with their collections intact. Elsewhere it is different. In the wake of the occupying forces Vivant Denon appears; known to Goethe from Venice, he spends some weeks as a guest at the house on the Frauenplan. Goethe has some lively talks with this extremely cultured man, who had accompanied Bonaparte to Egypt as his draughtsman, and who has now been promoted to the post of Superintendent of Museums and Collections in Paris. With a cultivated and sure hand he organizes, throughout Europe, the greatest theft of paintings, sculptures, manuscripts and art treasures of every kind known to modern times. As Denon soon realizes, there is nothing to be got out of Weimar. In nearby Brunswick, Henri Beyle, a protégé of his cousin Daru, the great Quartermaster-General of the army, is installed to scrutinize the treasures of the famous Wolfenbüttel library, amassed during the Thirty Years War by a passionate ducal collector, and to select valuable things for removal. Fortunately Beyle is a very lax official; he prefers to study the social life of the town and, by night, the soul of the German people, in the person of a girl with the very German name of Knabelhuber. Later Goethe read some of the novels written by this man who, in honour of Winckelmann's birthplace, assumed the name de Stendhal. He found him to be an author with great powers of observation and psychological insight, though he considered his women characters too romantic.

There is, and long remains, plenty of cause for anxiety in Weimar. Karl

August is careful to fulfil his duties as a Rhineland vassal correctly. The tiny Weimar 'army', so drastically reduced by Goethe in his active ministerial days, is brought up to strength again and sent to Spain, where tribes of rebellious and half-wild natives are resisting Napoleon's world empire. It is here that the word 'guerilla', or 'little war', is coined, although it is by no means a little war and absorbs many divisions. Goya's etchings portray this fighting in all its brutality.

Goethe shocks his friends by his strange cheerfulness and by his admonitions not to oppose the invincible demon Napoleon. Often they even avoid speaking to him. 'I cannot be frank with him,' says Schiller's widow, 'sometimes it is as though he were crazy, and I am not the only one to get this impression.' His melancholy, which breaks through from time to time, seems to her pleasanter 'than his unnatural gaiety'.

Goethe has worries of his own. Karl August, likeable in his indiscretions, is secretly supporting Prussian war comrades, while he helps Blücher with a loan and finds positions in Weimar for demobilized and wounded Prussian officers. A small spy ring is formed, a fact that does not remain unknown to Napoleon's own extensive and highly organized espionage system. Complaints and threats follow. Goethe is disturbed, fearing the annexation and disappearance of the Duchy of Weimar.

The supervision of the French authorities, and the strict censorship which was now introduced everywhere, were no mere illusion. In the neighbouring town of Erfurt, immediately converted into French territory and into their chief fortress against the East, a very strict account was kept of what went on in Weimar. Some time prior to the catastrophe Madame de Staël had visited Goethe in Weimar; she flew like a stormy petrel in front of Napoleon's armies spreading the reputation of his brutal methods of oppression. One of the great forces in literature and politics, she had been among his first victims. She had many children by many men, and many men in the most varied walks of life, politicians, artists, writers and straightforward robust lovers, a Catherine the Great of literature holding court at Coppet on the Lake of Geneva. Goethe had a high opinion of her as a writer and had translated part of one of her works. He was reserved and ironical when she visited him on her triumphal tour of Germany, on which she was received like a princess. He did not like being questioned, and was afraid of the notebook in her hand. Nor did he consider ultimate problems suitable for social conversation. But this was the very strength and intention of the imperious lady who, on arriving in Germany, had conceived the idea of describing this strange, poverty-stricken, musical, philosophic and elusive people to the greater European public, which knew nothing about them. She carried out her plan on a grand scale in her three-volume *De l'Allemagne*, the first book to present the German poets and thinkers to the world. Napoleon banned the book at once. There is a story of Savary, his Minister of Police, reporting to him on new publications. He mentions a three-volume work on Germany by Madame de Staël, adding that he has read it and found nothing objectionable, the Emperor's name is not even mentioned. 'A three-volume work in which I am not mentioned is to be banned immediately', snaps the demon. The facts are not precisely these, but in substance the anecdote is true, as a letter from Savary to Madame de Staël testifies.

In Weimar, after a few trying days with the lady, Goethe retires with a diplomatic cold. Time and time again, however, he had heard with what stubborn hatred Napoleon had pursued this opponent of his and how dangerous it was to cross the demon's path. Madame de Staël could afford to indulge her role of the persecuted free thinker. In addition to her fame as the most celebrated authoress of the day, she could fall back on the huge fortune she had inherited from her father, the banker and minister Necker, which gave her an income at least twice that of the Duke of Weimar. She could hold court on her princely estate in Switzerland, presiding over an international circle of well-known writers and a Garden of Circe, in which August Wilhelm Schlegel found a niche as tutor to her children, receiving an opulent salary against a promissory note declaring himself the eternal slave of his mistress. Unlike Madame de Staël, Goethe has no such possibilities for a free and independent life. He is bound to a country whose future is in the hands of the demon, he has lost a large part of his inheritance through the war, and, despite an increased income from his literary work, he is still dependent on his salary as minister. At Napoleon's headquarters Weimar's fate is under review.

Since his coronation in 1804 Napoleon, once the son of the Revolution, has become a legitimist. Having no children of his own he is making provision for his family by putting them on the thrones of Europe: his brother Joseph in Naples and then in Spain, Louis in Holland, where he is soon dismissed because his rule is too mild, while for his favourite youngest brother he creates a Kingdom of Westphalia with its capital at Kassel. Here the charming boy sits enthroned as *König Lustik*, the Merry King, no better than the German potentates he has replaced. An illegitimate daughter, Jenny von Pappenheim, one of the many offspring of his numerous love affairs with the ladies of his Court, later turns up in Weimar and becomes a favourite 'little daughter' of Goethe's in his extreme old age.

At first, however, the main concern in Kassel is not its gay life. The frontiers of the new State are not yet fixed. From the start Napoleon has cast his eye on the Thuringian States, Weimar amongst them, with a view to incorporating them into Westphalia. Karl August hurries off to Dresden to try to enlist the help of Saxony, Napoleon's most faithful ally. In the end he is spared, not because he is considered important, but for dynastic reasons: his son, the heir, is married to a Russian Grand Duchess and, for the time being at any rate, Napoleon wants an understanding with Russia.

Goethe does not learn of all this from the newspapers. In Karlsbad he has made the acquaintance of Karl Friedrich Reinhard, Talleyrand's distinguished colleague, whose remarkable career and personality fascinate him. Trained at Tübingen as a theologian he had gone to Paris at the time of the Revolution, and was the only one among the many German enthusiasts there who did not succumb. His persistence and his Swabian efficiency enabled him to rise in the administrative service to become Talleyrand's colleague and even, for a time, head of the French Foreign Ministry under the Directoire; although always a man of the second rank he was repeatedly sent by Napoleon on important diplomatic missions, when hard work rather than brilliance was needed. He survived all the changes of régime until finally, under the Restoration, he was made a Count and a Peer of France. This man now becomes Goethe's unofficial ambassador in Paris, and is one of the few friends of Goethe's later years with whom he carries on a correspondence until his death. As Goethe's ambassador he also submits reports to the court on the Frauenplan; they are as reliable as the official reports of which Napoleon thought so highly.

Equally reliable is Reinhard's description of Goethe at their first meeting in Karlsbad in 1807. He had imagined him differently, he writes to a friend.

> He is tall of stature and gives an impression of slimness, because one can see that he has lost *embonpoint*. The colour of his face is dark, almost like night. A certain hardness in his features, which are very alive, almost prevents one recognizing any longer the beauty there used to be in his face and still is in his look. Only his eye remains, as of old, a hidden beam of light which shines the moment he smiles, and then the rogue in him peeps out unmistakably as well. His manners are not exactly elegant. To me they seem rather shameless and, for this very reason, to have a quality amounting almost to a lack of preciosity. When he wants to be merely polite he lapses into a kind of affectation which does not suit him, because it is artificial; but I have seen him glow with warmth and heard the seething of the riches within, and so I recognize the lion by his claws.

Napoleon sends Reinhard as Ambassador to Kassel, to keep an eye on his silly brother Jerome. The political news in his letters to Goethe is carefully worded, for even the highest officials of the Empire must anticipate censorship of their letters. Thus Goethe learns from Reinhard of one of the demon's boldest and most unscrupulous strokes in phrases comprehensible only to a student of Homer: 'Zeus has now gone to the pious Aethiopes.' This means that Napoleon has gone to Bayonne where, in April 1808, he lures the Spanish King and his son into a trap, negotiating with them while his troops are occupying the country, and thus forcing them to abdicate; he orders his brother Joseph to leave Naples and ascend the Spanish throne in Madrid. The throne in Naples passes to Murat, a cavalry general, because he is married to one of Bonaparte's sisters; and with these two steps Napoleon, at the zenith of his power, starts to prepare his downfall. At the farthest outposts of his Empire he now comes up against the people, the very element that, in France, had carried him to his first great successes. It is the people who are fighting him in Spain, and in Calabria they fight him in the mountains; in the mountains of Tirol, too, the peasants fight him stubbornly. Everywhere the people are stirring.

Napoleon ignores these signs. The Emperor plans to hold a giant summit conference of Emperors, Kings and Princes at Erfurt in the autumn of 1808, and it is here that Goethe meets the mighty demon in person. This encounter remained one of the great experiences of Goethe's life. He made a secret out of it, and only late in life did he put down anything on paper. Other eye-witness reports exist, but they too are not very reliable.

It is the point at which the Goethe legend and the Napoleon legend meet, and in this meeting of the great man of action with the great man of letters it is tempting to see an impressive 'tableau', such as Goethe liked on the stage, with instant recognition of genius for genius. Something of the kind moreover, though simpler and more practical, was in Napoleon's mind. Side by side with world politics he wanted to engage in cultural politics in Erfurt. The *Empire de recrutement* was to be reinforced by the enlistment of German intellectual forces. There was no lack of willingness in Germany. Kassel was to become the new German capital. Johannes von Müller, the greatest living German historian had already been enrolled for the scheme; Frederick the Great's eulogist was now to perform a similar task for Napoleon the Great. Jakob Grimm had been appointed librarian and Beethoven was to be the Kapellmeister, a plan that fell through only because a group of Viennese aristocrats persuaded him to stay in Vienna by the offer of an annuity for life. The German philosophers, with Hegel at their head, saw in Napoleon the embodiment of the *Weltgeist*. The publicists paid homage to him. Poets and writers, a not inconsiderable force in Napoleon's calculations, were to join in. In France the writers had failed him; a Madame de Staël and a Chateaubriand had proved intractable, and the Emperor's directive on this state of affairs to his Minister of the Interior, 'see that it improves', had been ineffective. The Germans would be easier to manage. He had been given the names of Wieland and Goethe as the two most important in German literature. The name of Goethe was familiar to him from the days when, as a young lieutenant of artillery, he had tried to write novels himself; he had read *Werther* at that time, and the book was in his field library. His informant was Darn, his Quartermaster-General, who had sent him the two names from Berlin where, with his usual efficiency, he was collecting the huge Prussian levies – *le bon bœuf pour le labour*, as his master called him – and where, in his spare time, he moved in literary circles. It seems he confused Goethe with Schiller, because he recommended the former to his master as the leading German dramatist. This was exactly what Napoleon wanted. During the negotiations with the Czar over the division of the world into spheres of interest, Erfurt was to stage a great festival of drama. The theatre was to be a main attraction of the Congress.

Everything had been prepared in advance, down to the smallest detail, in long conversations with the Director of the Comédie Française: 'No comedies, they don't understand that kind of thing beyond the Rhine!' ordains the Emperor. They must be given classic tragedies. Corneille's *Cinna*, for example, in which conspiracy is followed by a scene of great imperial clemency, the sovereign stretching out his hand in forgiveness over the heads of his abject opponents. There are significant lines as well:

> All these crimes of state committed for a throne
> Heaven forgives – a crown is heaven's gift alone;
> Guiltless the man who thus can reach this lofty aim,
> Inviolate his life, whate'er his deeds proclaim.

Rehearsals have taken place with the great actor Talma, who is said to have taught Napoleon how to wear a Roman toga like Caesar. He has been given instructions which passages are to be played up and which played down, for these classical plays are full of political dynamite. Voltaire's *Mahomet*, for example, is a play Napoleon does not like, and says so to Goethe who had translated it; a few years later there are to be loud demonstrations in Vienna at the lines, in Goethe's translation: 'Upon your lips are words of peace, of which your heart is ignorant.' But *Mahomet* belongs to the classical repertoire, which is to be given in its entirety at Erfurt, and it does, after all, contain the very apposite words: 'Who made him lord? Who handed him the crown? T'was victory!' So Napoleon decides that *Mahomet* shall be performed.

For weeks there have been columns of wagons on the road bringing furniture, carpets and statuary from Paris, so that modest Erfurt can be decked out in the style of the new Empire, a style described by Talleyrand as a mixture of European and Asiatic, as 'scholarly luxury', the mantle of the Caesars and the tradition of the *ancien régime*. In every house where there are to be guests Savary, the Minister of Police, has placed Court officials, who are secret police as well. For behind the scenes another great play is being enacted. Talleyrand, Napoleon's principal adviser, warns the Czar and the Austrians against believing in his master's protestation of peace. He plays the traitor or, as one might also put it, he tries to put a halt to the coming catastrophe while there is still time.

World shaking plans are afoot. Napoleon wants to marry a sister of the Czar, a move that would relate Weimar to the demon. He wants to split up Turkey and hand over a part to Alexander. He wants a land route to India, where he intends to settle his score with England, being unable to attack her by sea; he has already sent a general to Persia to reconnoitre the route. To Erfurt he has summoned a galaxy of Kings, Grand Dukes and Princes, most of them owing their new titles to him and related by family ties to his own family clan or to his marshals. His finest regiments of cavalry stand by to parade – and as a demonstration. A salute is fired only for the Czar, who, since Tilsit the year before, has been Napoleon's uncertain ally. He is the only one to be greeted at the door by Napoleon, on whom all the other Kings have to wait attendance. At the theatre he receives a bow from Napoleon when the actor presents the line from Voltaire's Oedipus as though on a plate: 'A great man's friendship is a present from the gods!' Alexander plays his part too. He clasps the hand of the Emperor who implies, by expressive Italian gestures, that he is scarcely worthy of such a favour. At the next lines, 'not conqueror alone, nor man of victory, but hero of the peace his name henceforth shall be!' he nods significantly.

Meanwhile, however, the negotiations hang fire, either because of Talleyrand's warnings or because of Alexander's constant indecision. The treaty, by which Napoleon hoped to persuade the Russians to march against Austria and so enable him to withdraw his own troops to fight in Spain, is not signed. His marriage plan makes no progress. It is time for a cultural *intermezzo*. Herr von Goethe is summoned to an audience.

Goethe, busy with China and with his *Farbenlehre*, has gone to Erfurt much against his will. But the Duke has every reason to ingratiate himself with the Emperor by displaying all the forces his tiny, threatened land can muster. In the drawing-room of a lady from one of the Baltic states, who spends her time travelling, seeing places and meeting people, Goethe is introduced to Maret, formerly editor of the *Moniteur* and now Minister of the Interior. Maret informs the poet that Napoleon wishes to see him at his *déjeuner*. Goethe climbs the familiar steps of the Palace, formerly the residence of Dalberg, the Governor, who, as the only surviving spiritual Prince in Germany, is now doyen of the *Rheinbund* with the title Prince-Primate and is soon to become the Grand Duke of Frankfurt, another new creation. Goethe notes in his diary: 'The old scene with new faces.'

The new faces are legion. It is not a formal audience. The Emperor is having his breakfast; Goethe has to stand. He is not the only visitor, Napoleon has other business to attend to. Talleyrand comes and goes. Daru appears and presents his accounts of the Prussian levies. A general brings news of Poland, where there is growing unrest because Napoleon, having promised the country its freedom, is now hesitating. Goethe has time to take stock of his surroundings: 'The old wallpaper. But the portraits on the walls had disappeared. Over there is where the portrait of the Duchess Amalie used to hang, in ball-dress with a black mask in her hand....' That had been the old world of rococo. Now he is face to face with the new, with the soldier Emperor in the close-fitting green uniform of his *garde chasseurs*. With abrupt gestures of his small feminine hand, which in conversation he hides inside his white waistcoat, he rules the world before Goethe's eyes. For one brief hour of his life Goethe stands on the great stage of world affairs, at the centre of events. He sees how the fates of nations are decided, with a wave of the hand, a word of command. He is fascinated, and remains so for the rest of his life.

His scene comes too: Napoleon, 40, already fat and heavy, his chin reminiscent of Nero rather than of the Augustus of his youthful portraits; Goethe, 60, in full Court dress, his face brown, his hair carefully dressed, upright and very imposing. The Emperor is impressed; turning to his suite he says, *Voilà un homme.*

Napoleon begins with stereotyped questions: How old are you? 60? You are well preserved (*Voilà un homme*). Your family? Children? The Duke? He speaks of Karl August as though he were a naughty schoolboy who has been corrected. Goethe defends his master, saying he is a patron of the sciences and of poetry.

This brings Napoleon to his subject. He speaks of the theatre, and invites Goethe to the performance the same evening. The Prince-Primate will be there, he adds, and will fall asleep on the King of Württemberg's shoulder. Has Goethe seen the Czar yet, he asks; not yet, is the reply, though he hopes to be presented. He ought to write something about the Congress, and dedicate it to Alexander. Goethe excuses himself saying he has never done anything of that kind. Napoleon reminds him of the great writers of the time of Louis XIV. Goethe remains evasive.

Napoleon wants to win this imposing man. He speaks of *Werther* and claims to have read it seven times, adding that he even took it with him as far as the pyramids on his Egyptian campaign. What he does not tell Goethe is that on board his flagship on the voyage out he found his generals reading novels; one was reading *Paul et Virginie*, another, his future cavalry commander Bessières, *Werther*. 'Stuff for servants', snapped Bonaparte, and ordered all novels to be locked away: in future only works on history were to be issued, manly food for heroes treading in the footsteps of Alexander the Great.

Even now he cannot refrain from criticism, from regarding literature 'like a criminal judge', as Goethe says. He is critical of the fact that in *Werther* the two motives for suicide, thwarted ambition and unrequited love, are confused. To his mind they are two completely different spheres: ambition on the one hand, love on the other. Goethe defends himself by flattery: no one has ever noticed the fault before.

Napoleon now comes to his point. The theatre can become the school of the nations. There is a lack of great plays. He cites Voltaire's *Mort de César*, which pays insufficient homage to its hero. Voltaire should have made it clear that had Caesar been given time to carry out his vast plans, he would have brought happiness to mankind. Even on St Helena Napoleon still continued to harp on this theme. In Goethe, described to him as Germany's leading dramatist, he thinks he has found the tool he needs. He makes a direct approach: 'Come to Paris. I ask it expressly of you.' Only in Paris can such plans be realized.

This is a great moment. It is easy to understand that Goethe could not forget it. He may have recalled Napoleon's statement that had he been alive he would have made Corneille a Prince. What Goethe's answer was we do not know. Probably it was evasive.

The conversation continues, amid the coming and going of high ranking officials. The reports are presented piecemeal and assembled afterwards. Napoleon enquires about the mood of the people. Are they content. Are they happy? They have great hopes, replies Goethe guardedly. As fresh visitors continue to arrive Goethe asks, through the Chamberlain, if he may withdraw. Napoleon, bent low over reports from Poland, nods. The poet takes his leave.

At the theatre they have managed to find a place, among the many crowned heads, for the prince of the mind. The order of seating is strictly according to dynastic and military priority: in front of the orchestra, on a dais, sit the two Emperors and the Kings of Bavaria, Saxony and Württemberg, appointed by Napoleon. Then come the Princes and Dukes, followed by the Marshals as the leading military representatives. Further back come the Ambassadors, and at the very back the Ministers. Among the Russian dignitaries is the Ambassador in Paris, Count Tolstoi, who is later to give a younger member of his family some detailed impressions of the Congress and Napoleon; in *War and Peace* the beautiful Countess Helene scintillates in the drawing-rooms of Erfurt, and the Emperor's portrait, based on direct family tradition, is drawn with malicious precision, down to his fat, well cared-for body that always emits a strong scent of eau de Cologne.

The populace remains outside. They are required to demonstrate their loyalty by illuminating their windows and hanging out banners. A transparency carries the legend: 'Lived there amongst us still God's son, his name would be Napoleon.' The great masquerade proceeds to Weimar, where Karl August has arranged a great hunt; during this a magnificent stag is driven to within five paces of the short-sighted Czar and is happily killed. A hare shoot is organized, as though to commemorate the Battle of Jena, to which the Prussian delegate, Prince Wilhelm, is tactfully invited. A large marquee is erected in which models of the battle are displayed. Napoleon rides over the field with Alexander, to whom he points out the positions of two years previously, and demonstrates the art of defeating a famous and invincible army.

A Court ball is given at the castle in Weimar. Napoleon, who does not dance, takes the opportunity to approach Goethe and urge on him yet again his thesis of tragedy as the superior man's university. He utters his words about fate: 'What do people want with fate? Politics is fate!' Most of his conversation is with the aged Wieland, who holds himself well in spite of his great age. Wieland has prepared himself for this in advance, in an exchange of letters with Johannes von Müller, who has warned him that Napoleon will probably bring up the subject of Tacitus, 'the slanderer of the Caesars', his pet aversion. The subject duly comes up and Wieland has the temerity to defend him, in beautiful French, even giving Napoleon to understand that he is taking the liberty of speaking as one author to another. Had not His Majesty, when he was General Bonaparte, been a member of the Institut de France? Had not this distinction taken pride of place on the Commander-in-Chief's notepaper? Napoleon nods graciously, it pleases him to hear this. The Weimar notables standing round are proud of their venerable master in his black skull cap.

Others, too, receive a moment's attention, the physician Dr Stark, and the Burgomaster of Jena, who bemoans in moving terms the sufferings of his city, ingratiating himself by a tirade against the English who are the real cause of the world's misfortunes. Napoleon promises the city of Jena an emergency grant of three hundred thousand *francs*; as Goethe notes in his diary these 'somehow did not arrive'. He gives an assurance that the Weimar contingent will be spared active service in Spain, whither they are shortly due to depart. With Karl August he has one further short conversation, on one of the hunting expeditions, and it reveals more closely than do the great political discussions the great demon's secret. The Duke apologizes for the simplicity of the little house in which they are staying, for the bareness of its plain whitewashed rooms. Napoleon, his hat on his head, replies that on the contrary he likes it, it makes him feel at home, like the soldier he has been since his boyhood. In Paris, in his sumptuous apartments, he is bored; he cannot stand the life there. It is only in war that he feels at ease.

He returns to Erfurt and brings the Congress to an end with a lavish award of presents and decorations, of Grand Crosses, Knights Crosses and Crosses of the Legion of Honour. The bulletin contains the announcement: 'By an order of to-day the Cross of the Legion of Honour is bestowed on Messrs von Goethe, Privy Councillor to the Duke of Weimar, Wieland, ditto, Stark, Senior Staff Physician in Jena, Vogel, Burgomaster of Jena.'

On October 14, carefully chosen as the anniversary of the Battle of Jena, Napoleon leaves Erfurt for Paris and Spain. He forgets Goethe and does not refer to his proposal again. He now has to pursue his campaign against the 'pious Aethïopes'; in the following year it is against Austria, and after that against Russia. On his flight from Moscow, travelling incognito, as secretary to his own Foreign Minister, he stops for the night in a small town. 'Where are we?' – 'Weimar, Sire.' – 'Convey my greetings to Monsieur Göt.'

# 36

# *Exploits and Sufferings of Light*

At the time of the Erfurt Congress Goethe was putting the finishing touches to the main section of his *Farbenlehre*, dealing with the conflict of light with darkness. Colours he calls 'exploits and sufferings of light'. Since the catastrophe of 1806 he has been working feverishly on it, sending everything to the printer as soon as it is ready, in constant fear that the times may put an end to his life's work. For it is as a basis of his existence that he regards his doctrine and not merely as a modest contribution to scientific research. Only in this light can the book be understood. It is not science but a doctrine of life, based on his highly personal fundamental viewpoints. These he formulated more specifically, in a conversation with Schiller, as the polarity of all things and the principle of enhancement. Goethe's own nature is composed of polar opposites; his own enhancement, his own constant development, is his aim. His problem is to find examples and proofs of this in the world of natural phenomena.

Goethe was predominantly a man of vision; his eyes, powerful, penetrating and commanding, were his most arresting feature, a fact that struck every visitor. His other senses were not underdeveloped, far from it, but often they were merely sensitive and defensive. His nose was hyper-sensitive; even as a boy the smell of the riding-school used to nauseate him, and the smell of tobacco produced an almost feverish reaction. Noise affected him in the same way, the barking of dogs driving him almost to despair. He was exceptionally sensitive to changes in temperature and, in his later years, surrounded himself with barometers and thermometers, with which he took the most careful readings. He even invented a theory to fit his concept of inhalation and exhalation: the gravitation of the earth was not constant but variable and pulsating. To this he attributed the changes in atmospheric pressure and the variation in atmospheric tension.

These organic reactions cause him to maintain a 'suffering' attitude towards the phenomena of nature. His eyes alone are commanding and dominant. He re-writes an old Greek aphorism:

*Wär nicht dein Auge sonnenhaft,*
*Wie könnt' es je die Sonn erblicken?*

*Wes'te nicht in uns die eigne Gotteskraft,*
*Wie könnt' uns Göttliches entzücken?*

(Were there no sunshine in thine eye, how could it e'er perceive the sun?
Were God's own power not inherent in ourselves, how could Divinity enchant us?)

He took this from Plotinus, the last great philosopher of antiquity. Goethe declares that the Greeks were already 'familiar with everything that we recognize to be the basis of the theory of colours'; his original intention had been merely to re-write the little book by Aristotle's pupil, Theophrastus. Both in art and science the Greeks represent for Goethe the golden age and the eternal example. The *Farbenlehre* belongs to the period of his avowed classicism.

Really he should have treated the subject like a Greek, in poetic language; only occasionally, however, does he do so. The ancients, so he maintains, had perceived all the essentials but had not advanced to the point of refining their experiences and assembling them into a whole. 'And their experience was like that of a treasure seeker who, by means of the most potent formulae, has raised the glittering vessel filled with gold and jewels to the very edge of the pit but, overlooking a single detail of the magic spell, sees all his hopes, at the moment of realization, sink back again to the accompaniment of clatter and clamour and demoniac mocking laughter.' For centuries it has been lost and Goethe's task now is to raise the treasure again. A new obstacle has arisen: Newton has erected a stronghold, a Bastille, which stands astride the path of all true research. Nothing could be simpler than to take it by storm: 'For there is no question of a lengthy siege or an uncertain challenge. We find, on the contrary, that this eighth wonder of the world turns out to be a deserted relic, on the point of collapse, and we begin straightway and without further ado to tear it down, starting with the gables and roof, so that at long last the sun can shine into the rat-and-owl-infested hole.' This makes good reading, as do many sections of the work, which is full of human wisdom and adroit and witty comparisons. It is also full of barren polemics and arid theory, and of laborious attempts to explain complicated phenomena. It contains many practical instructions for carrying out experiments, the apparatus for which has to be procured, or made, by the reader. The *Farbenlehre* is to be practised and not merely read, as he says later.

His faithful Eckermann attempts this. In the course of his study, the sorcerer's apprentice discovers a passage in which he thinks his master may be wrong. Bravely, if uneasily, he stammers out his tale, only to be greeted with a fearful outburst. 'As though you had discovered it!' thunders the Olympian. 'That goes back to the fourteenth century, and what is more you are engulfed in a maze of dialectics.' Then he continues, a little more gently: 'My experience with my *Farbenlehre* is the same as that of the

Christian religion. One thinks one has faithful followers and before one knows what is happening they go off and form a sect. You are a heretic, like the others, and you are not the first who has left me!' As he slinks out through the door Eckermann hears the word 'heretic' being hurled after him. The episode is not without its significance; it can be supplemented by other remarks of Goethe's claiming this work as his greatest achievement:

> I do not pride myself in the least on any of my poetic achievements. There have been excellent poets in my time, there were still more excellent ones before me and there will be again after me. But that I am the only one in my century to know the true solution to the difficult science of the theory of colours – on this I do pride myself, and because of it I have a consciousness of superiority over many people.

On another occasion he compares himself with Luther, who had to overcome the darkness of the priesthood, 'and to my lot fell the error of the Newtonian doctrine'.

The fight against this arch-enemy is his main task; it is a fight in which his hatred leads him into the most grotesque insinuations and distortions. Among readers unfamiliar with the whole story he often finds a sympathetic audience. On the one hand we have the visionary, the poet, with the all-embracing viewpoint – on the other the cold, calculating man of figures. On the one hand the man of unfettered outlook, his head held high, his gaze searching the blue infinity of the firmament – on the other the man glued to his study and his apparatus. In our day mistrust and dislike of the 'exact' sciences has grown since the activities of scientists have become increasingly sinister, and scientists themselves are often unable fully to comprehend them. Faith in unlimited progress has been replaced by doubt and fear. Thus it is tempting to look back on Goethe as a father-figure in a vanished golden age, an age of 'completeness', such as he saw in the Greeks. These people forget that in Goethe's world of colours, in his world as a whole, all was not crystal clear and golden, but muddy and clouded – *trübe*, to use his own favourite term. They forget that it was a world of strife and that, while he was indeed a complete man, he was torn this way and that by the polar opposites of his nature to a degree that would have destroyed any other man.

Of the endless diversity of characters which constitute the man Goethe it is the crass party member, the demagogue, who comes to the fore in this fight against Newton; as one facet of his nature it also has its place in a complete portrait. The phrenologist Gall once described Goethe's skull as that of a public orator, a tribune of the people; this sounds strange, but here it is, in a measure, substantiated. In his scorn he hammers on his pulpit like a Luther, and thunders:

> And if in the lecture rooms and bookshops as many devils oppose me as there have been ciphers and figures squandered over the last hundred years in

support of the false doctrine, they will not stop me professing aloud what I have once recognized as true.... What is this freedom of the press, for which everyone cries and sighs so insistently, if I am not to be allowed to say that Newton deceived himself as a young man and then spent his whole life perpetuating this self-deception!

No one ever tried to stop Goethe publishing his writings, even when they contained abuse such as this; he himself, on the other hand, did not hesitate to exercise the right of censorship when he possessed it. Bismarck was quite wrong in saying that Goethe could not hate. He could hate. He hated Newton as a personal enemy who had thwarted his life, and he hated him with a bitter lifelong hatred; moreover, he used every means in his power to denigrate him both as man and scientist.

In martial tones he declaims that Newton's method of investigation must 'astonish, indeed horrify, everyone who is not demoralized'. He conceives the idea of sketching a whole gallery of characters – he has the rogue Cagliostro in mind – who have deceived themselves and others by means ranging from the most obvious villainy to mere vague suspicion of what they were doing; 'so no one would blame us if he found Newton among the rest, for he certainly had a dim presentiment of his wrong'. In his old age Goethe once said with grim complacency to his friend Müller: 'Oh, I can be beastly too, and I am a very good hand at it'.

He is fighting a shadow. His picture of Newton's character is wholly and completely out of drawing. He introduces him as a 'well-organized, healthy, placid man, without passions, without desires'. Healthy? Delicate as a child, Newton was later constantly afflicted with the most severe nervous crises. Placid? Newton was shy and irritable, again almost morbidly so. It was his friends who, after long demur on his side, first published his most important discoveries.

Newton, according to Goethe, was in too much of a hurry. In constructing his theory he excluded everything that could damage it, and 'the more rational a man is the more deceitful he becomes as soon as he goes wrong'; he becomes 'false to the world and, in order to be true to himself, declares reality a lie'.

Newton is the exact opposite of Goethe's portrait of him. He is cautious almost to the point of timidity, constantly stressing the provisional character of his ideas, so averse to all dogmatic hypotheses that his colleagues continually reproach him with the fact. His most significant ideas are presented in the form of queries. Above all he is in no sense the mere 'man of figures' that Goethe wants to see in him. On the contrary he is, in the highest degree, a man of intuition.

Furthermore Newton is incomparably more modest than Goethe. He stresses the fact that if he has been able to see further than others it is due entirely to his great predecessors, on whose shoulders he has been able to stand. This is also the formula for his own influence: his successors, up to the present day, have stood on his shoulders, even though they may have re-modelled his ideas or abandoned them altogether.

Certainly this has involved calculations and measurements, as well as the use of lenses, mirrors and prisms, of which Goethe also tried to make use, though in a simpler way. It is one of the paradoxes of Goethe's life that, while stressing the 'purity' of his experiments, he worked with impure prisms, which resulted in many false conclusions, and in preparing his illustrations used muddy and impure colours, which were often at variance with his text. But it can hardly be maintained that modern instruments, made of purer quartz, and the results they give do not belong to 'nature', which does not begin by moving from one's room out into the garden. Here again no one has yet drawn a line between what is 'natural' and what is 'unnatural'. Goethe admittedly tries to draw such a line. He states categorically that there is an *Ur*-phenomenon which cannot be explored and before which one must halt in reverence and awe. But he never defines the point at which this *Ur*-phenomenon begins and ends, or the point at which the halt is to be made. He only indicates in mystical, poetic language the point at which he, Goethe, calls a halt and regards his cycle as closed.

The world of colours he sees as a closed cycle. This cycle has validity for him, for his life and thought. It has had no influence, no sequel. No artist has painted according to his theory, which is what he so longed to see, no dyer has used his ideas; no physicist has been converted, a development Goethe hoped for and expected. There was only a small sect of followers and even these had no easy time with their leader. The young Schopenhauer listened to his teaching and for a short time Goethe thought he had found a docile pupil. But, like Eckermann, he began to work things out on his own – with no more success than his master – and was condemned as an heretic; in the second part of *Faust* he is lampooned as an 'impudent young know-all'. The physicist Seebeck in Jena assisted Goethe for a time, and is extensively quoted in the *Farbenlehre*, but he too fell away. Schopenhauer, who visited Seebeck in Berlin, caustically told his pupils afterwards that Seebeck secretly acknowledged Goethe to be right but lacked the courage to proclaim it to the world; 'He has since died, the old coward', added Schopenhauer.

Schopenhauer's judgments on his opponents are nothing more than the utterances of a powerful and unrestrained temperament. In this he is like Goethe. The tone adopted by the 'Goethe-sect', as it came to be known by contemporaries, in this decades-long battle, was painful even to Goethe's most devoted admirers, such as Achim von Arnim. It was not a factual debate over scientific questions – which always remain questions – but, as in the theological disputes of earlier centuries, the opponent was condemned out of hand as malicious and deceitful, a juggler, a conjurer, a charlatan who fobs off the public with tricks and hocus-pocus. These are Goethe's own words, repeated times without number, even in his 'maxims and reflections', about Newton and the whole tribe of mathematicians and physicists.

It is very seldom that a poet feels any affinity with mathematics; Paul Valéry is the rare exception. Goethe's knowledge of mathematics was scant in the extreme. As a boy he learned a certain amount of geometry, and immediately used the 'experience' to construct little cardboard 'pleasure-houses', as he relates in *Dichtung und Wahrheit*. For years after that he never used the word. It only enters his orbit again, this time as a warning, when he begins his optical experiments. Mathematicians he always refers to with deliberate contempt as *Rechenkünstler* (calculators). The surveyor, needing some geometry for his practical work, is Goethe's mathematician. He was once visited by one who brought 'to my table mathematics, the most alien thing that can enter my house; but we made a pact that figures were to be mentioned only in the last extremity'. It is unlikely that the last extremity was reached.

He is perfectly right when, on another occasion, he says he is dependent on words, language and imagery as means of expression, and is totally incapable of coming to terms with signs and figures. This is not a poet's business. In the *Farbenlehre*, however, he goes further and labels mathe-matical formulae, which are beyond his grasp, as 'stiff and clumsy'. In an essay on mathematics and its abuse he goes still further, so far in fact that the editor of the most complete recent edition of his works has felt com-pelled to exclude the essay in the interest of 'the dignity of mathematics'. In it the mathematicians are summarily dismissed as 'dishonest'; enemies of progress, they are preys to obstinacy, presumption, jealousy and other 'abominable passions'. By involved means they try to make simple things difficult, and Goethe goes on to compare them with an instrument maker who invents a complicated apparatus for drawing corks, when it can easily be done by hand. His only good word is for 'simple geometry and what is closely related to it, because it is nearer to ordinary commonsense'. It was also the only branch of mathematics that was to some extent accessible to him.

But why, one asks oneself, this furious onslaught on Newton and mathe-matics – synonymous terms so far as Goethe is concerned – and why these expressions, which are certainly not going to imperil the 'dignity of mathe-matics'. This conflict is the central point of the *Farbenlehre*, and it cannot be disposed of in a few embarrassed asides and marginal notes, which is the usual custom. The polar opposites in his nature demand an adversary, an enemy. He sees himself, with his god-like eye, as light; his adversary he sees as darkness. He intends – and these are his own words – to pursue him into the cavern, wrestle with him, overthrow him and free his prisoner, the 'seven-coloured princess'. He is battling with a spectre. Mathematics, as it is scarcely necessary to repeat, is not mere calculation, as Goethe implies when he says: 'Its whole certainty is nothing but identity. Twice two is not four but simply twice two, which we call four for short. But four is no new thing.' Goethe's age produced men like Euler, Lagrange and Laplace but it never seems to have occurred to him that mathematics involves creative imagination, new ideas, great changes, and that it has a beauty of its own. In fact the universality of the language of mathematics should have appealed to his sense of the universal. Once, and in yet another of the countless paradoxes of his nature, he does refer to this; tormented by the inadequacy of language to describe complex processes he says that perhaps one should copy algebra and use symbols like $x$ and $y$ ..., but he quickly lets the subject drop again, as though he had burned his fingers on it.

His fight against mathematics, as typifying his polar opposite, is also capable of a different explanation. The preceding century, up till the time of his own youth, had been in a very real sense the century of the mathematician. Leibnitz had reduced 'the essence of things to numbers' and wanted 'to establish a specific calculation to account for every truth'. This developed into a game, one Dutch mathematician even attempting to describe the physiognomics of the human face in terms of algebraic formulae. The whole European public took part in this new fashion; at the Courts the reigning families, especially the women, were Leibnitz's correspondents. Every Prince had his Court mathematician; in Weimar there was one by the name of Erhard Weigel, who produced a giant 'celestial mirror'. Through mathematics, so it was believed, the confusion in the world had been reduced to order; by it the Age of Enlightenment was inaugurated. Against this the age of the young Goethe, under Herder's leadership, rebelled. They wanted nothing more to do with figures and lines, let alone with calculations, and they disliked the wide, echoing vaults of the heavens, which seemed to them empty. Nature was to be experienced directly, closely and intimately. And it is thus, in the sense of this directness and intimacy of his youth, that Goethe wants his *Farbenlehre* to be understood. The opposition of the 'old school' provokes him to polemics which, as they become more and more intemperate, come near to overwhelming everything he has so laboriously gathered together.

He has gone to great pains. For this single work he has read, or thumbed through, more books and journals than in the whole of the rest of his life put together. He has made endless experiments, with the spiteful prism, with lenses and coloured pieces of glass, with plants, candles and mirrors. He has also cast his eyes about him, and to such observations we owe his most valuable results. For eighteen years he has worked on the book and now, under pressure of war and upheaval, it has to go to the printer, in two thick volumes of over thirteen hundred pages and a third volume of plates, the bulkiest work Goethe ever published. Even this was only a fragment, and was meant to be continued. He calls it *Zur Farbenlehre*, a contribution to the theory of colours, and he divides it into three parts: a didactic, a polemic, devoted to his battle against *Bal Isaak*, and an historic.

He begins with what he calls the 'subjective colours', or the physiological. They are 'irresistibly fleeting, swiftly vanishing', and they form the basis of his whole theory. Already known, they were usually called imaginary colours, visual deceptions, optical illusions, although they belong to the phenomena of healthy sight. To Goethe they are the 'required' colours: 'When darkness is presented to the eye it requires light; it requires darkness when brought into contact with light, thereby demonstrating its vitality, its right to apprehend the object, since it generates from within itself something that is opposed to the object'. In this he sees the 'silent opposition which every living thing is forced to express when confronted with some predetermined situation. Thus inhalation presupposes exhalation, and *vice versa.*' With these colours we are dealing with the very basis of his sense of life, 'it is the eternal formula of life'. These 'contrasting colours' do in fact exist, and Goethe's observations on the subject have been taken up and developed in physiological optics. He describes an evening in a smithy when he stares for a long time at the glowing red-hot iron on the anvil; he turns away and looks into an empty coal shed. A huge purple image floats in front of his eyes, and on switching his gaze from the darkness to a light-coloured boarding the colour appears half green and half purple; this then gradually disappears. A person blinded by snow sees purple. Strolling in his garden at dusk he observes some poppies; they seem to 'flash', and the image of the flower appears in the 'required' blue-green colour. These colours, created by the eye, his sun-like organ, are his colours, the 'Goethe colours' as they have been called. They are fleeting, and vanish swiftly; they can only be described, they cannot be captured or reproduced. Many, indeed most, people have never observed them, and the experiments Goethe describes for their production contain an element of surprise for the majority of observers, and of difficulty too, because the colours do not always appear to order. When they do appear, they are exceptionally pure, like the colours of the spectrum. The purple described by Goethe is not contained in the spectrum, and can be produced by the physicist only by mixing red and violet, the two extreme colours of the spectrum. For Goethe this purple is the 'royal colour', on the analogy of the purple robes of the ancient kings. Here, however, he is creating a myth, because this colour, produced in ancient times from the juice of the purple snail, was violet.

In its way the whole thing is a myth. Goethe's light is not the light of the physicists, whether of his own day, Newton's day, or later; beyond physics, it is 'meta-physical'. He calls it 'the simplest, most homogeneous, most un-decomposed existence we know'. On the other side from light, on the night side, we have darkness. This again is not a concept of physics but an age-old theological inheritance, understood and condemned in many religions as the opposite of light, of the divine. In Goethe's religion it is not condemned. It is the equal partner of light, its counterpoise, in the same way as his Mephistopheles is the necessary counter to his Faust. The magnet gave Goethe his idea of polarity, and now he sees light and darkness, like the two poles of the magnet, in opposition to one another, each able to influence and repel the other, but never to overcome it. Between the two lies what Goethe, using a term entirely his own, calls *das Trübe*; this cloudy, turbid, opaque world – in German the word *trübe* has an overtone of sadness – is the world of colours. He nominates two colours, blue and yellow, as the 'pure' colours. Blue is darkness, brightened by the influence of light; yellow is light, obscured when influenced by darkness. On this basis he builds his colour cycle; blue and yellow combined produce green, yellow darkened becomes orange and then ruby red, blue darkens to violet. He puts his colour cycle on paper – for Goethe it is always important that his hands play a part – and it is a closed cycle, without the ends or fringes leading off into the invisible that characterize the hated spectrum. This self-contained cycle is his world, round and homogeneous, his Goethe-world.

Light and darkness he calls the *Ur*-phenomena, using the prefix *Ur*, meaning primal or aboriginal, which has a mystical, mysterious sound in German and has no counterpart in other languages. It has played a special role in Germany, and in Goethe research and philosophy; attempts have been made to distil, from the endless multiplicity of Goethe's nature and experiences, an *Ur-Erlebnis* or primal experience to fit his individual works. Goethe also calls the opposing poles phenomena; he sees them as an appearance. The contrasting images in his eye are examples of such phenomena. He 'sees' these *Ur*-phenomena according to the image they present to him, he sees their contrast, in much the same way as Michelangelo in the Sistine Chapel sees the creation of the world, the separation of light from darkness, in the form of huge contrasting allegorical figures. Goethe paints with words, and language, as he well knows, is incapable of even an adequate, let alone a precise, reproduction of such things. But language has the advantage of being equivocal, of being able to conjure up memories and associations, to stimulate the imagination. Thus Goethe's *Ur*-phenomenon remains subject to the most varied interpretations, according to the personality, background, and faith of the observer. The strict school of physicists will reject it, theosophists will welcome it, the theologian will be disturbed at darkness being given equality with light, the aesthete will find pleasure in it.

His colour cycle has an aesthetic significance for Goethe too. Its origins are in his Italian experience, in the visual arts. He is in search of 'harmony', and once again it is his own colour harmony, highly personal and very much conditioned by his time, that he proclaims. We have already seen how slight was his interest in colour in painting; it was form and subject-matter that interested him. His own drawings are only occasionally touched up with colour, and then in pale tones. He himself realized the inadequacy of what the uninspired artists whom he knew were able to teach him about colour; at best they talked about 'cold and warm tones'. The invaluable Meyer could provide him only with second-hand notes on the colouring of Italian painters or of antiquity; the brilliant colouring of Greek sculpture was not even suspected in those days. Goethe saw the temples and the sculpture as white, but for this very reason they were the light that illumined his path; all that came later was *das Trübe*. His aesthetic view-point was completely under the spell of his classicism.

Goethe also wants to investigate the 'ethical' significance of colour, and here he finds himself involved in a highly problematic subject. There is no doubt that certain colours do have an effect on people's moods and feelings; they can excite or calm, stimulate or depress. But these effects vary from age to age and from place to place, they are not universal. In the West the colour for mourning is black, in the East it is white, although Herman Melville's *Moby Dick* shows that even in the West white can have a sinister significance. Green, which Goethe declares 'neutral', has an extremely aggressive significance for Islam, where its effect can be just as 'inflammatory' as red in other parts of the world. A history of sensibility to colour has yet to be written. In this sphere, too, Goethe remains within a cycle of his own drawing.

In the third part of his book, following his polemics against Newton, he makes an attempt to approach the problem historically. He presents a broad survey of the theory of colour from earliest times to his own. It is the most readable and, so far as style is concerned, the finest section of the work. He is no longer concerned with phenomena and theories – 'doctrines' would be a better word, because his *Farbenlehre* is no mere theory but a doctrine of colours – but with personalities, with human beings. And so he paints Plato and Aristotle as Raphael painted them in his 'School of Athens' in the Vatican. It is Goethe's Plato, not the Plato who wanted to deny every non-mathematician entry to his circle. Goethe sees in Plato a

blessed spirit who deigns to sojourn for a while on the earth. He is not concerned so much with getting to know it, for he already presupposes it, as with wanting to communicate to it what he has brought with him, of which the earth is so sorely in need. He probes its depths, not so much to explore them as to fill them with his own nature. Every word he utters relates to an existence eternally complete, good, true and beautiful, and he tries to awaken a demand for this in every breast.

It is a self-portrait, and a description of his own procedure in the *Farbenlehre*. He always regards himself as a guest who deigns to sojourn for a while on the earth, *'ein trüber Gast auf der dunklen Erde'* (a mournful guest on this sombre earth) as he expresses it in his poetry, who has to enhance and realize his personality through *Stirb und Werde* (death and re-birth), through the battle between light and darkness. With Goethe the important thing is not to explore, but to re-discover and confirm what he already knows or has divined; it is a constant sense of anticipation that is an integral part of his life. And it is because he sees in such confirmation the justification of his whole being that he reacts with such violence to all opposition, even to the slightest deviation, seeing in it an attack on his very existence. The result is that even this fine, broadly conceived survey grows increasingly irritable and arbitrary the nearer it approaches the shadow of the detested *Bal Isaak*: everyone who doubts Newton is welcome, every follower is either confused or an adventurer.

In many respects the whole *Farbenlehre* is an adventure, and it is not for nothing that Goethe sees himself as the knight errant riding out to free the seven-coloured princess from the ogre. In spite of so much precise observation, so many careful experiments and so much that is valuable, the book remains, both in style and layout, a product of a bygone age, closer to the sixteenth century of Paracelsus than to the beginning of the nineteenth century. Goethe toyed with the idea of re-writing it as a novel, a baroque notion that had occurred to Leibnitz too, who thought of presenting his whole cosmic edifice to the public in the form of a giant novel. Goethe also considered writing a dialogue between a Newtonian and a pupil, an inversion of the scene in *Faust*, in which the pupil would put the master to shame by his clever arguments. Time and time again he carried on his war in epigrams, either against Newton or against other scientists, such as one by the name of Wünsch, whose bold hypothesis that all colours are derived from red, green and violet-blue is still the basis of physiological theories of colour vision; Goethe ridiculed this as 'cucumber salad'. Playfully and in jest, though with an underlying deeper significance, he wrote that we should try seeing man as *Trübes*: against a light background yellow, bright and clearly defined; against a dark background enveloped in blue haze, obscured. 'Blue haze is well-known; why not also yellow haze?' Sending a book to a friend he wrote: 'The blue author certainly takes life rather more seriously than the yellow one.'

In 1810 the work was presented to the public. It is understandable that the scientists did not know quite what to make of it. Goethe's intemperate complaints about their 'fiendish enmity', his epigrams declaring that had they been able to they would have liked to burn him at the stake or crucify him, are poetic exaggerations. In fact he received help and encouragement such as are rarely given to an outsider. The great libraries let him have whatever he asked for, and complained to the *Geheimrat* only in the most guarded terms when after several years their books had still not been returned. The reviewers treated him with the greatest respect, but they were not prepared to condemn Newton and abandon the spectrum. Schweigger, the editor of the leading scientific journal, presented him with a piece of very up-to-date and costly polarization apparatus. Goethe shrank at the idea of using it, gave one glance inside and then stopped – the same procedure as he demanded for his *Ur*-phenomenon: the use of such machinery might confuse the 'pure human understanding'. Perhaps the most significant episode in his research, it underlines the difference between his approach and that of the true scientist.

He finds another public. In Karlsbad he explains his new doctrine to the other visitors, and they grasp it at once. Gratefully he lists the many princes, diplomats and statesmen; time and again, as he notes, he finds that such people, used to receiving reports and grasping their 'essentials', are far more receptive to his ideas than the obdurate high priests of the guild. Literary people and philosophers are interested. Hegel, now a celebrity, writes to him a long letter which Goethe publishes. In it the philosopher praises the term *Ur*-phenomenon as 'simple and abstract', remarking that it can be turned to useful account in philosophy as well.

> When we eventually succeed in working up our Absolute, which at first is like an oyster – grey or black, whichever you prefer – towards the air and light, so that it becomes desirous of them, we then need window space in order to introduce it, fully and finally, to the light of day. Our phantoms would vanish into thin air were we to attempt to transfer them at one stroke to the motley confusion of a refractory world.

In such a predicament the *Ur*-phenomenon suits him admirably.

From Weimar Hegel receives a sort of private decoration, a yellow Bohemian drinking glass with the dedication, 'to the Absolute, with best wishes from the *Ur*-phenomenon'; inside the glass is a piece of black silk, through which the yellow appears as blue. Hegel finds it a more agreeable apparatus than a prism, 'the triangular glass cudgel which the satanic angel carries in his hand to strike the physicists'. He recalls Goethe saying at Jena 'that you wanted to nail the physicists to the table by their donkeys' ears'. A pupil of Hegel's, the jurist von Henning, lectured for a time at Berlin University on Goethe's theory. The physicists remained faithful to their glass cudgel.

To the end of his life Goethe remained sincerely convinced that he had made the great discovery of the century. He took an interest in later research in so far as it seemed to corroborate his own views, he ignored it when it ran counter to them. With one phenomenon, however, he never ceased to wrestle, because he could find no way of incorporating it in his system: the rainbow. Newton had offered some explanations, but Goethe would have nothing to do with them. He could not deny that in front of his eyes, not hidden in the dark cavern but displayed in the open sky, there appeared a play of colours which looked remarkably like the detested spectrum. There were times when he simply closed his eyes to it. When his friend Meyer decorated the ceiling of the new entrance hall of Goethe's house on the Frauenplan with a rainbow, he was instructed not to use the natural colours but to restrict himself to Goethe's ideal of the three principal colours blue, red and yellow. During the last weeks of his life Goethe was still wrestling with this problem, employing a glass cobbler's sphere, as Theoderich von Freiberg, the first classic of rainbow research, had done in the fourteenth century. He writes to his young friend Boisserée about it, and calls the rainbow the most complex example of refraction, still further complicated by the addition of reflection; he indulges once more in polemics against rays, an abstraction postulated by mathematics but having little or no significance. He concludes touchingly:

> But do not imagine that you will ever be free of this problem. If you have to struggle with it all your life, you must make the best of it.... I have always sought to apprehend what could most readily be perceived, known and applied, and in this I have gone a long way, to my own satisfaction and indeed to the approval of others. By this means I have reached what is for me the limit in such a way that I begin to believe where others despair, I mean those who make too great demands on knowledge and who, so long as they can achieve something of what it is given to man to do, regard as of no importance the greatest treasures of mankind. Thus we are driven from the general to the particular and from the particular to the general, whether we like it or not.

> Grateful for friendly interest,
> Desirous of continued patience,
> Hoping for further confidence,

> Weimar, February 25, 1832.

# 37

# *The Patriarch*

With the *Farbenlehre* Goethe has freed himself from the greatest burden of his life and from his only great enemy and opponent. Now he can breathe. His anger remains till the end of his life, and is vented from time to time in epigrams, letters and conversation, but these are only rumblings after the storm. One fact remains still to be noticed: Goethe wrote the book during the years when his physical condition was at its worst; he had grown fat and flabby and was often ill, twice, in 1801 and 1805, severely so, the first time with erysipelas, the second time with angina followed by kidney trouble. Out of this heavy body, with its paunch, its pendulous cheeks and its bags under the eyes, there now gradually emerges the much slimmer Goethe of the closing years, the very epitome of a splendid and magnificent old man; it is thus that he has been described and painted by the many visitors to his imposing house on the Frauenplan.

With the deaths of the poets and writers of the older generation, of Wieland, Schiller, Herder, Lavater and many more, Goethe is left as the only survivor of an age which, to the younger generation, has already passed into history. The Dowager Duchess Amalie is also dead – she died soon after the catastrophe of Jena – and her *Musenhof*, her Court of the Muses, has passed into legend. All that remains is Goethe's Court and this now assumes the features of a real Court. Dr Riemer is the major-domo or Court Marshal; having entered the household as tutor to Goethe's hitherto rather neglected son, August, he soon becomes indispensable as secretary and proof reader, empowered even to alter whole sentences and delete whole paragraphs, work which Goethe finds irksome. He is in charge of the Goethe protocol; anyone wishing to see the master must apply to him.

Riemer was a thick-set, rather unprepossessing man with a soft fleshy face and protruding eyes. He was lazy, and it was only later that he laboriously gathered together his *Mitteilungen* about the master which, along with extremely valuable material, contain a mass of unimportant notes. Like many in Weimar he stuck fast in the Goethe environment and although he was aware of this, he fought only half-heartedly against it. He was an accomplished scholar; in Rome he had seen something of society life as tutor in the household of Wilhelm von Humboldt, but he immediately fell in love with the mistress of the house and so put an end to this episode in his career. He left Humboldt's service with good recommendations, however, and thus came to Goethe with whom, except for intervals of teaching at the Weimar 'Gymnasium', he remained for the rest of his life. He became Goethe's Riemer; beyond that he achieved nothing. He chose service with Goethe in preference to all offers from outside, embittered and proud of his position. To an extent that is still hard to define he exerted an influence on the texts of Goethe's works; Goethe was constantly asking his advice and sometimes even left to him decisions on the most important points. Before long Riemer's letters refer only to 'we': 'we are now working on the *Wahlverwandtschaften*, or on *Dichtung und Wahrheit*. He wrote poetry a little, in Goethe's style, and, when his master was engaged elsewhere, flirted a little with the ladies of Goethe's acquaintance, as his deputy. Finally, after Christiane's death, he married the *Frau Geheimrat*'s companion, Goethe's charming *Nebengeschöpf* – his complementary creature, and perhaps even his secondary wife as well. Even to this Riemer had to be driven by friends; he did not want to stand in his master's way. Shortly before Christiane's death, during one of her illnesses, he discussed with the *Nebengeschöpf* what she was going to do after the death of the *Frau Geheimrat*; in his opinion she should unquestionably stay with Goethe. But what would people say, replied the girl – why naturally he would marry you, answered Riemer.

His veneration was boundless. And among his lazily recorded and slovenly compiled notes on Goethe are the most surprising flashes of insight. Of Goethe's illnesses, for instance, he says that they 'were mostly the direct result of repressed and suppressed agony of mind' – the concept of repression is not so modern as it is often supposed. Or there is the remark about tiresome visitors: 'One had to bring something, if one wanted to take something away', which is a fairly comprehensive summing-up of Goethe's attitude to his many visitors during the latter years of his life. Of Goethe's method of work, of which he had an intimate knowledge, Riemer says: 'He frequently waited, like a Roman augur with his flights of birds and omens, for something to happen, to unfold to him, to enter the house, that might serve to bring his work to a conclusion, and there were days when he went out in search of inspiration. Generally he was successful. ...' This is no mere copyist speaking. Riemer thinks too, and sometimes he thinks ahead of Goethe and has to be called to order. But he is indispensable, both to Goethe and to us.

The *Nebengeschöpf* in the patriarchal household is Demoiselle Ulrich, known as the 'little Chinese', or the 'mandarin', because of the slanting eyes in her delicate pretty face. Engaged as companion to Christiane when the latter grew fat and her health gave way, the girl's gay, lively nature has a beneficial effect both on her and on Goethe, with his frequent fits of depression. Goethe's letters to his wife are addressed to them both, and Fräulein Ulrich writes the answers on Christiane's behalf; often his letters, though written to Christiane, are addressed to Fräulein Ulrich. He dictates to her and she models her handwriting on his, while his own takes on some of the characteristics of hers. Goethe gives her a ruby ring and writes poems for her; to visitors she is introduced as the niece, and to his friends he refers to her as his guardian angel, the 'pretty child', the 'juvenile'. Before long there are tears and little scenes when she hears of Goethe's many other friends in Karlsbad. She has numerous offers of marriage, but she remains on in her extremely equivocal and often embarrassing position, and eventually marries Riemer merely in order to be able to stay near Goethe. As Frau Riemer she embroiders away her grief on beautifully worked little coverlets, lampshades and slippers, which she is allowed to present to the patriarch on his birthday.

The Goethe court now assumes an oriental air and becomes a sultanate. The *Westöstliche Divan* is in course of preparation. Riemer notes among other projects, never realized alas, one for a novel, *Der Sultan wider Willen*, in which a man is simultaneously attracted to four women; 'each in her own way is lovable; whichever one it is to whom his mood of the moment draws him, she alone is lovable, and he finds it incomprehensible that he could love another'. It is not only in Karlsbad with his Mariannchen, with Silvie von Ziegesar in nearby Franzensbad, or with the vivacious Pauline Gotter, later to marry Schelling, that the game with his *Augelchen* goes on; in Weimar too this 'casting eyes' is an incessant pastime. A Göttingen professor's wife thus describes the Goethe household:

> Wine, women, song, and even in the autumn of his life the two first inspire our friend, for whom there reigns an eternal spring, to the most wonderful songs. To be in love is the order of the house, everyone who enters or leaves it is in love; by the end I was genuinely worried lest the epidemic should claim us too. This summer in Karlsbad there was a love to whom he sang his sweetest songs, and these sonnets, all still unpublished, he recited to us.

They have since been published, together with exhaustive research into the possible subjects of the various poems; even in Goethe's lifetime there were heated arguments among the ladies as to who was who.

Riemer also notes a plan for a novel called *Der Egoist*, of which the essence, in Goethe's words, was 'that mastery was taken for egoism'. No reproach was more often levelled at Goethe than that he was an out-and-out egoist; it was a cry generally raised by people who wanted or expected something of him, and were disappointed. But when we come to the way in which he treated his only son, it is hard to acquit him of this charge. Sons of great men never have an easy time, even when they are abler and more gifted than August, who inherited from his father only his pedantry and some rather more questionable characteristics. Whatever Goethe's writings may proclaim as to his pedagogic wisdom, as a practical educator he had no success with any of his pupils. The idea that children should be brought up like the young Greek Hydriots, and taken on board and allowed to roam the ship and share in the plunder and booty, had already produced poor results in the case of Fritz von Stein. August, too, is taken on board the great Goethe ship and allowed to 'crawl around' wild on its sundry voyages, but little is done for his education or even for his mere existence. There are times when he does not even live at home, as though the large roomy house were not big enough, and he is lodged elsewhere. Occasionally old Charlotte von Stein takes care of the boy, commenting sadly that all he has got from his mother is his fatal taste for drink, which may be true enough. He starts drinking young, and he starts his love affairs young too. He grows up into a fine figure of a lad, though with rather unnaturally flushed cheeks and unsteady wavering eyes. Sensitive and shy, he has few friends, and is disliked by Weimar society to whom he always remains the son of Mamselle Vulpius. Away from home his life is a little happier, notably during his short time as a student at Heidelberg. Then he is ordered back to Weimar, where Goethe's powerful influence has got him a position as government 'assessor'; in fact he returns to assist his father as secretary, librarian, steward and accountant. In these capacities his energies are consumed, his life wasted.

In addition to his court at Weimar, Goethe has his ambassadors and correspondents all over the world. In Rome there is the Prussian ambassador, Wilhelm von Humbolt, in Kassel the French plenipotentiary Reinhard. In Berlin his agent and friend is the builder and musician Zelter, the only friend whom, in his later years, he addresses with the fraternal *Du*. Anyone picking up a volume of Zelter's songs will find him a disappointment as a composer; the wags in Berlin used to say he built his songs of bricks, though it would be truer to say they were constructed of light scaffolding. But this was exactly what Goethe liked about them; he did not want to see his songs obscured by the music. Zelter's real importance lay in another field. Energetic and socially inclined, he founded his *Liedertafel*, the first of the German choral societies, which soon spread throughout the country; on the lines of the English glee clubs, they cultivated the *Tafellied*, the drinking song and the humorous *quodlibet*. Goethe enjoyed contributing to these, and in this way some of his songs found their way into student circles.

He liked the man, with his rugged ways, although he could not bring himself to accept any of his numerous invitations to Berlin: 'there is such a foolhardy race of men there, that one would need to be a man of courage, and something of a boor, to hold one's head above water', as he wrote rather quaintly. His correspondence with Zelter provided one of the great entertainments of his later years, and Zelter writes excellently, with great life and vigour. He was also Goethe's musical adviser and, as such, had severe shortcomings, rejecting everything modern from Beethoven to Berlioz. Handel and Bach were his gods, and the first performance of Bach's Matthew

Passion, which his pupil Mendelssohn gave in 1829 – one hundred years after its composition – was the great experience of his last years. Like Meyer, he died a few months after Goethe.

Goethe's friendship with Zelter was the only real male friendship of his later life; it was a friendship strengthened in times of crisis, when Zelter would hurry over to Weimar to console his friend, and pleasantly cultivated in quieter days, when parcels of Teltow turnips, a great favourite of Goethe's, would arrive in Weimar, and drinking songs with the refrain *Ergo bibamus!* were sent in return. Nor was this all. After Schiller's death Zelter became Goethe's chief correspondent, and in these letters Goethe 'deposits' many of his ideas, in the same way as he did with Schiller. In the same way, too, the correspondence was done up in volumes and sent to the binder, in preparation for its publication as a supplement to the posthumous works; it gave the old man pleasure to see the collection grow – finally Riemer was able to publish it in six volumes. Zelter, of course, was a very different foil to Schiller; he had no original philosophic ideas and no claims in that direction, but he was a character, a personality, a *Natur* as Goethe used to call people with strongly defined individualities, a man with a keen eye for men and situations. Goethe, who in his protean way adapted himself to each of his correspondents, took care to pull himself together so as to appear as resolute as Zelter, and to discard his 'moaning and groaning', as he termed it in one of the *Tafellieder* he wrote for his friend. In spite of the gulf between them, Zelter exerted an educative influence over Goethe, not by advice and admonition like Schiller, but simply by his example.

From Frankfurt a will-o'-the-wisp turns up in the form of Bettina Brentano, daughter of the Maximiliane de la Roche, whose black eyes had replaced the blue ones of Lotte in *Werther*, and granddaughter of Madame de la Roche who, as a very old lady, once paid a visit to Weimar: she was accorded a solemn reception at the Frauenplan and entertained to a sentimental dinner; in her diary she wrote, in her incorrigibly literary style: 'Old Baucis, your playful dream now stands as reality before your eyes! You expected to see a feast of the gods in Weimar only from the threshold of the temple, and now you receive your own portion of ambrosia!' The grandchild, as enthusiastic a writer as her grandmother but a poet as well, is not satisfied with the threshold, she wants to enter the holy of holies, sit on the god's knee and throw her arms round him. She wants even more – she has greedy, impudent eyes and an ample, an over ample, bosom. She puts on the airs of a child, and it is as *Briefwechsel Goethes mit einem Kinde* that, after her idol's death, she publishes their correspondence; it is a book that combines the genuine, the imaginary and the spurious into an attractive whole, which can still fascinate us to-day. As a child she used to curl up at the feet of Goethe's mother, listening to her and writing down what she heard. 'Bettina spends at least two hours a day with Frau Goethe,' writes her brother Clemens, the poet, 'they cannot live without one another, and she has a large book lying there in which she takes things down from the mother's mouth ... in the latter's well-known pungent style'. The book has disappeared and of the pungent style nothing remains, for Bettina's style is romantic, its charms different. Bettina courts everything, nature, people, her own reflection in a mirror; the greatest sorrow of her childhood days in a convent was the absence of a mirror in her room. One day later on she stands in front of a mirror and recites Goethe's *Iphigenie*: 'My emotion, my spirit, deeply stirred by Goethe's spirit, were thus the means of enhancing my feelings for the dramatic; I was clearly aware of the enthusiasm of being enthusiastic.' This was the basic formula of her existence, and the enthusiasm was genuine; she exercised it on Goethe, Beethoven and many others. But simultaneously she began spinning legends, dreams and fantasies, always seeing herself as it were in a mirror and controlling what she saw, and in what she saw there was always a disconcerting erotic undertone. One of her later friends, Prince Pückler, remarked on her purely 'mental sensuality', which she turned on artificially and could switch at will from one object to another.

It is this creature, armed with childhood memories of his mother as a welcome gift for the master, who now appears in Weimar, intent on getting not only into Goethe's house but onto his knee if possible. Far from being a child any longer, she is now 24, with a fine head, dark Italian complexion and a pointed nose; she is small and plump but with curiously large, almost clumsy, hands. Without a trace of reticence she exercises her charms. Coming from his home town she addresses the Olympian straight away as *Du*, making constant allusions to his early love affairs, to her own mother Maximiliane, to the 'convenient little gardens' where he used to amuse himself with his other sweethearts, and to the barmaid in Offenbach. She holds forth about a marvellously handsome French officer, the son, or so she asserts, of Goethe's 'first true love' Lili, who fell in love with her, when he was stationed in Frankfurt with his regiment, and then galloped off into a hail of bullets – her own and Goethe's first love affairs united in a single episode. Goethe listens amiably; her chatter, with its familiar Frankfurt cadences, stirs all sorts of memories in him. Christiane, now *Frau Geheimrat*, looks with suspicion on this spoilt creature from the well-to-do family, whose dialect she can scarcely understand but whose restless, probing eyes she understands only too well. On her way to Weimar Bettina pertly told her friend Tieck, hanging on to the back of his chair: 'You know, Tieck, I have got to have a child by Goethe at all costs – why, it will be a demi-god!' This may only be an anecdote, but in her book she tells of a supposed clandestine visit from Goethe, who stole over one night to the inn, *Zum weissen Elephanten*, climbed three flights of stairs to her room and then clasped her in his arms on the sofa, covering her with his cloak. This cloak, sometimes dark and sometimes of white wool, recurs like a symbol throughout the fictional correspondence of the book.

On one of Bettina's visits a small catastrophe occurs; Christiane and Bettina come to blows, literally it seems, at an art exhibition. Achim von Arnim, now Bettina's husband, leads his pale and trembling wife outside. Goethe avoids the couple. Bettina, soon herself once more, spreads the story round Weimar, and elsewhere, that 'a raving black pudding bit me', a remark that is a success among those familiar with Christiane's now almost deformed figure. After Christiane's death Goethe again receives the Arnims occasionally, but after Bettina's last visit he notes: 'Frau von Arnim's advances repulsed.' His letters to her speak a different language. With her, too, he transforms himself and adopts her impudent, playful tone; the mercurial girl fascinates him with her combination of the genuine and the artificial. He is grateful to her for her stories of his youth, vague and imaginary though they are; his own memory of those far off days is dim, too, and he incorporates much of what she tells him in *Dichtung und Wahrheit*. Indeed it is largely due to the stimulation of her talk that he now decides to compile this review and survey of his early life.

His encounter with this arch-romantic, however, had no very favourable effect on his opinion of the Romantic movement as a whole. When Bettina's husband, Achim von Arnim, sent him a copy of the collection of old German folksongs, *Des Knaben Wunderhorn*, published by him and Clemens Brentano in Heidelberg in 1806–08, Goethe welcomed it with a long and friendly review, but of Achim as a poet he wrote only disparagingly, comparing him to a wine-cask on which the cooper had forgotten to fasten the hoops properly, 'so that the stuff runs out everywhere'. This is one side of Arnim's nature, but only one: how many of his writings Goethe had actually read is a matter of speculation.

Goethe very soon grew impatient with all these young people, with their lives as well as with their writings. Novalis he notices only in passing, and the weak and delicate young Hölderlin received the well-intentioned advice to write shorter poems on 'subjects of human interest'. With Heinrich von Kleist, who approached him 'on the knees of my heart', he clashed violently; in staging his *Zerbrochener Krug* in Weimar Goethe made a very unfortunate division of the play into three acts, and the result was a total failure. The poet's *Penthesilia* he rejected as unplayable. In writing to Kleist he offered the advice that young writers should not wait for a theatre of the future: 'Before every stage I would say to the true theatrical genius: *hic Rhodus hic salta*! At any fair, and on planks placed on barrels, I will undertake to give the greatest pleasure, either to a cultured audience or to the uneducated masses, with the plays of Calderon.' He wanted plays he could perform on his Weimar stage. None of the young Romantics provided him with such a play, except Zacharias Werner, whom he patronized for a time and whom he considered a 'very gifted man', until the restlessness of this most restless of all the Romantics became too much for him. After three marriages in twelve years, and after great successes on the stage with *Der 24.*

411

*Februar*, which caused a sensation in Weimar, and a play on Martin Luther, Werner became converted to Roman Catholicism in Rome – impelled to this step by Goethe's *Wahlverwandtschaften*, as he wrote to the poet. He ended his life as a popular preacher in Vienna.

It seems strange that Goethe, to whom personal impressions meant so much, should have been attracted to the grotesque figure of Werner, to this tall lanky man with his incessant fidgeting and playing with his handkerchief, his roving eyes and impossible manners: at one of Madame Schopenhauer's receptions in Weimar a maid, sent out to fetch the missing writer, returned screaming that he had tried to rape her; a story that is by no means improbable, as a glance at Werner's diaries will show. On Kleist's forehead Goethe saw only the mark of Cain and self-destruction, 'with horror and revulsion, as though a body, intended by nature to be beautiful, had been attacked by an incurable disease'.

The personal impression was also decisive for Goethe's attitude to Beethoven, whom he met in Teplitz. Beethoven played to him and Goethe was struck by the effort, energy and fervour in his face, qualities which the composer's advanced deafness must have rendered particularly impressive. Writing to Zelter Goethe speaks of Beethoven's 'unfortunately quite untamed personality which, indeed, is by no means wrong if he finds the world detestable, but it certainly does not make the world more enjoyable either for himself or for others'.

Bettina, ceaselessly weaving her legends, spread the anecdote of the two great men meeting the Emperor Franz and his family on the Promenade: Goethe, moving to one side, bowed in deep reverence, while Beethoven strode defiantly on through the Royal party; afterwards he rebuked Goethe for his subservience. What is true is that Beethoven, in a letter to his publisher, says the atmosphere of the Court appears to be more congenial to Goethe than is seemly for a poet. But Beethoven was no boor. In Vienna he mixed constantly with the high aristocracy, proud and self-assured, but without aggressive ill-manners; moreover, it was to these princes, counts and archdukes that he dedicated his works. If any such incident took place, it was probably no more than the fact that His Excellency's frequent bowing seemed to Beethoven overdone.

Of Beethoven's music Goethe knew next to nothing until the young Mendelssohn played him the *C minor Symphony* on the piano; Goethe never heard an orchestral performance of any of the symphonies. Even this piano version was too much for him: 'It is tremendous, quite mad; one could fear the whole house might collapse – imagine the whole lot of them playing it together!' He counted Beethoven among the 'modern technicians', of whom he asked Mendelssohn to give him some idea in the course of an historical survey of music from the time of Bach and Handel.

In his fear of being overwhelmed, Goethe reacted almost in the same words to the paintings of the Romantics. Philipp Otto Runge's illustrations of the various times of day, delicate and charming though they seem to us, almost frightened him: 'Look at the sort of stuff it is, enough to drive one crazy, beautiful and mad at the same time.' The visitor to whom he said this compared the paintings to Beethoven's music, which someone happened to be playing on the piano. 'Exactly,' said Goethe, referring to Beethoven as well as Runge, 'it tries to embrace everything and in so doing always loses itself in the elemental. ...' Of Runge, who had just died at the age of 33, he went on: 'But the poor devil could not stand the strain, he has gone already, and it cannot be otherwise; anyone standing on the edge of a precipice like that must either die or go mad, there is no mercy.' Caspar David Friedrich, the other great painter of the German Romantic school, he praises for the accuracy of his observation of the various types of tree and his industry in rendering their foliage; but he is doubtful about his mystical-religious tendency, and sharply critical of the fact 'that he either does not understand, or else despises, the art of light and shade, just as he does the use of colours, to the softening and harmony of which he pays no regard'. Here again we can see what Goethe understood by colour-harmony.

His rejection of this whole younger generation is almost complete. It can be traced to his views on art, which postulate 'softening and harmony', a gentle, strict classicism. His pagan belief in nature rejects the new religious piety as affectation. Lastly, and far from least, he is on his guard against all overpowering impressions, in the same way as he avoids all contact with over-beautiful women. He feels constantly threatened and has to husband his resources. The strong words he writes to Zelter, his calls for rugged and resolute behaviour, are addressed to the 'foolhardy race' in Berlin. Left to himself he prefers soft music, agreeable pictures, charming poetry; *artig* – well-behaved, nice, pretty – now becomes one of his favourite expressions. This kind of thing does not disturb him, it cheers him up and promotes, so he believes, what is right and true; those transgressing this principle are 'soon done for', like the 'poor devil' Runge.

Irony decrees that it is at this very moment that Goethe's *Faust*, the first part of which appears in 1808, falls into the hands of the younger generation, who acclaim it with tremendous enthusiasm. Here is no gentle, strict classicism, as taught by the *W.K.F.* and the master himself, no well-balanced compositions on archaeological themes, but wild, detached scraps of genius savagely thrown down on paper. Here is the Brocken of the *Walpurgisnacht*, not portrayed in terms of carefully executed foliage but with desolate, cleft giants of trees. Here is the very desire to 'embrace everything' that Goethe criticized in Runge and Beethoven: mysticism, medievalism, the old Germanic world, God and the devil, insanity, all that the Olympian tells the younger generation to avoid. Here is irony, satire and deep significance, not in classic hexameters but in the liveliest Hans Sachs verse and rhyme, with short couplets that get wafted all over Germany, like dandelion seeds, to become household words.

Nor is the enthusiasm confined to Germany; it spreads to France and England too, despite translations that are often pitifully bad, only extracts sometimes or even mere paraphrases. Matthew Lewis, author of the 'Gothic' horror novel, *The Monk*, which itself contained a sort of Faust-like ending, read some scenes to Shelley and his friends in Switzerland. Lewis did not understand much German but it sufficed to give his listeners an inkling that something gigantic had been written, something unprecedented, satanic, reeking of hell and brimstone. The philosophers – and in those days every German was something of a philosopher who liked to roam in higher spheres because his own was so constricted and miserable – seize on the book, or rather on the theme of *Faust*; since then they have never tired of subjecting it to treatment, or maltreatment. Goethe, so long known to the world as the author of *Werther*, now becomes the poet of *Faust*, himself a legendary Faust figure, with his limitless thirst for knowledge and investigation, some reports of which have leaked out, even if people are not prepared to study the three volumes of his *Farbenlehre*.

For Germans the times are deplorable, but at least now they have the consolation of possessing a great poet. No one can confiscate his empire as Napoleon has done with what was left of the Holy Roman Empire, taking a principality here and a duchy there to give to one of his marshals or relatives. They have to bow their heads, and this they do, deeply and from age-long practice. But now, in the realm of thought and poetry, they can hold their heads high. As 'the nation of poets and thinkers', they are a unity; a nation they are not. The young patriots dreaming of nationhood – be it under the leadership of Prussia or Austria, or in some other form – venerate the creator of this empire of the mind, however much they find to offend them in the Weimar *Geheimrat*, who never loses an opportunity to display his French decoration, and who keeps on telling people to be content with things as they are, to cultivate the arts and sciences, and to leave world affairs to those who understand them.

Goethe looks on at all this with grim composure; they praise his *Faust*, he writes, and whatever else they can find in his works that is stormy and violent:

> *Das alte Mick und Mack,*
> *Das freut sie sehr;*
> *Es meint das Lumpenpack,*
> *Man wär's nicht mehr.*

(The same old clap and trap, that they adore; the idiots think that I'm not I any more.

He is, but not in the way they mean. He stands outside physics and outside his time. He lives in other spheres. His mythical play *Pandora* – possibly intended for a peace celebration – is set before time itself, during the first stirrings of the human race, even the action taking place before sunrise,

414

in the earliest hours of morning; only at the end does Eos, the dawn, appear. The characters are given Greek names and the scene is imagined in the style of Poussin, but the characters are transformed in accordance with Goethe's own personal mythology. Pandora is not the Greek messenger of ill omen who secretes in her box – in Hesiod, the oldest version, it is a whole cask – and brings to earth all the ills and sufferings from heaven. Goethe changes her into a figure of light and love, she is the muse, art, who alone can stand against the warlike world of action. Prometheus, so close to the young Goethe, becomes the representative of power and action; his brother Epimetheus, the 'man of reflection', is closer to Goethe now.

A trilogy was planned but, as with the *Natürliche Tochter*, never realized. The play is a kind of oratorio, with recitatives and choruses; linguistically it is Goethe's most richly varied work, containing flowing verse of great splendour together with contrived experiments in ancient metres. 'Everything is wedged together', as Goethe said. The work is written for an imaginary stage; it cannot be performed, it can only be read like a musical score in which the complex voice progressions and wealth of thematic material can be followed by the eye and inner ear. One then takes part in an act of creation: the genesis of the first men, who embrace, in embryo, all that is later to stir and confuse the world. It is also the act of creation by which Goethe, in his maturity and resignation, attempts once more to bring order into his world.

This is now his chief preoccupation. Around him lies a world in disorder; nor is harmony the keynote of his own domestic life. His marriage is a relationship that is questionable and embarrassing not only to the Weimar Philistines but to his closest friends as well. His elegy *Amyntas* shows that he himself sometimes feels it as a heavy chain that binds him, almost endangering his life. Despite the strain to which it is exposed, his attachment to Christiane remains constant, out of genuine gratitude, but from defiance too, and perhaps from mere familiarity with the comfort of his home. The relationship is tolerable only because he reserves to himself the absolute right to freedom. Society and the public follow Goethe's well-known, and even celebrated, love affairs with interest, curiosity and, occasionally, criticism. He has now become a representative personality; he is expected to take a stand on the great problems of life. And now word has gone round that he is trying to solve, or at least to deal with, the problem of marriage as one of the cardinal issues in human relationships.

Goethe's novel *Die Wahlverwandschaften*, the Elective Affinities, grew out of his plans to continue *Wilhelm Meister*. One of these projects, intended for the *Wanderjahre*, became too big and important for that work, and he developed it into a separate novel. The unhappy Minna Herzlieb played a certain initial role in the creation of this, through her similarity to his sister and to others he had known; other figures from his experience were added, transformed beyond recognition, all being reduced or combined, to leave four main characters, a quartet. The novel, like his *Tasso*, which artistically it resembles, is chamber music. Originally, as Goethe wrote, it was intended for a small circle of friends who understood him and would know how to listen.

The book was written at extraordinary speed, and sent straight to the printer; as a result it has a unity rare in Goethe's work, the characters being given no time in which to change, as they so often do with him. They are established from the beginning; their fate is irrevocably determined, inevitably fulfilled. Goethe never wanted to write tragedies but in this novel – in reality an extended short story – he has written a tragedy, a tragedy, moreover, severely restricted to the small cast and single setting of classical French drama, of which he had recently seen great examples performed by Talma and his company at Erfurt. In its construction the book is like the plan of a building, its chapters measured off and symmetrically disposed like rooms.

The characters are so swathed in mystery that interpretations of the book have ranged between the most diverse extremes. Devout circles have branded the book as 'immoral', although it portrays the life of a saint and has a genuinely Roman Catholic ending that looks forward to a happy reunion of the ill-fated lovers in the hereafter. Others have seen as its central idea the conflict between duty and desire. Goethe himself, pressed for an opinion, quoted the Bible: 'Whosoever looketh on a woman to lust after her hath committed adultery with her already in his heart.' Always anxious to stress the continuity of his *œuvre* as a whole, he drew a comparison with his *Werther*, who was forced to shoot himself, 'after allowing sensuality to become his master'.

It is a love story and it deals with love seen as a terrible, life-destroying force of nature. 'To love is to suffer', Goethe says to Riemer, 'one can only bring oneself to it under compulsion [*natura*], that is one has to do it, one does not want to.' He also says, soon after publication of the novel in 1810: 'The greatest works of art are simply unaccommodating, they are ideals which can, and should, please only *approximando*, they are aesthetic imperatives.'

In this novel Goethe propounds an imperative compared to which Kant's categorical imperative seems tame. It demands renunciation of all sensuality, even to the point where the mere thought of sin leads to the death of the person concerned. Goethe carries through this idea with devastating logic, yet it is an idea that finds no support either in his life or in his nature. He never renounced sensuality, nor did he ever eliminate it from his nature – to the great good fortune of his work. But he did always feel love to be a thing of enormous menace, and he tried to avoid it by every means in his power, by flight, by spreading the danger over more than one love affair at the same time, or by its 'removal' into the figurative, into a work of art. And just as in his *Farbenlehre* each colour requires its contrasting colour, so here the strongest contrast demands expression: love as misfortune and disaster, the fate that ultimately destroys all love's participants. Nature is cruel and merciless, it does not spare even noble men, those who, 'however great the inner discord, always maintain outward decorum', as Goethe said to Riemer. The attempts of such noble people to observe decorum are what give the novel its inner tension. The end, however, is predestined, it has to be tragic. The closing sentences, not implied by the rest of the novel and its characters, testify only to Goethe's 'conciliatoriness', which even here, in his only true tragedy, has to sound a final note of hope and reconciliation.

The novel is an experiment, a psycho-chemical one. The title is taken from contemporary chemistry; the great Swedish chemist Torbern Bergman had used the term 'attractio electiva'. The four main characters, Baron Edouard, his wife Charlotte, the Captain, and the girl Ottilie are treated at first like chemical elements and are even given ciphers, A, B, C, D. In a discussion on chemistry the question is posed as to what would happen if the chemist, symbolizing the arbitrary forces of nature, were to bring opposing elements into contact – 'then God have mercy on them!' Starting from this formula, Goethe, as he had done previously in *Tasso*, endows these phantoms with such richness that they become credible as human beings, even though they scarcely move, merely drifting, as it were, in a steady catastrophic descent. They move blindly like sleep-walkers, and the heroine, Ottilie, is so named after St Odilia, the patron saint of Alsace, known to Goethe from his Strasbourg days. The saint, born blind and gaining her sight only with baptism, is the patron saint of the blind and of those who suffer from their eyes; her emblems are eyes, arms and a book. How much Goethe remembered of the legend, or of his visit to the Odilienberg convent, we do not know, but he calls his Ottilie '*Augentrost*' (consolation to the eyes) and at the final moment of catastrophe, as she lets Charlotte's child slip into the lake, he puts the book into her hand, as if she were in need of that emblem of the saint.

There is no consolation in Ottilie's own eyes however, and, like Goethe's sister or Minna Herzlieb, she refuses physical union with her lover, Baron Edouard. More than a mere reminiscence of these shadows, she is for Goethe an ideal, and ideals are only conceivable to him in the form of a woman. On one occasion he made the strange remark to Riemer: 'The sexual act destroys beauty, but nothing is more beautiful than what precedes this moment. Only in ancient art is eternal youth captured and depicted. And what does eternal youth mean other than never to have known a man or a woman.' Here he recalls his great prototype Leonardo da Vinci, who similarly rejected physical union of the sexes, and in much stronger language, though whether because of his homosexual tendencies or because of the very strong feminine element in his nature, more marked even than in Goethe, we do not know. In Goethe's case – and we venture this interpretation only with diffidence – the feminine in his polar nature may have been the 'cold', negative side, the side that shunned the act, and the masculine his positive, asserting side. If we are aware of these tensions many things in his life, and in his writings, become comprehensible, among them this character of Ottilie, which otherwise would be as artificial as the background of plot and action against which she is set.

Goethe has to call on all his art in order to make his predetermined ending plausible. The crucial chapter, which so shocked many of his contemporaries, is a scene of mental adultery: Edouard is dreaming, in his wife Charlotte's bedroom, of his beloved Ottilie, while Charlotte's thoughts are on her captain. The child born of this night has Ottilie's eyes and the captain's body. It has to die. Ottilie unintentionally lets it slip into the water as she crosses the castle lake. She too must die, although Charlotte is prepared to stand aside for her. Feeling guilty because she has 'strayed from her path', she mortifies herself, takes no nourishment and passes away; at her grave miracles take place. Edouard follows her into death.

It was as a great chemist that Goethe wrote this story, which conforms to his requirements for a short story – the description of an 'extraordinary event' – rather than to those for a novel. The book's unity lies in its style which, avoiding any purple patches, is rich in wisdom and innuendo, and in irony too. Each generation has sought to find its own interpretation. Goethe's contemporaries, with the exception of a few friends, remained for the most part bewildered, respectfully silent or indignant. If they were expecting a practical contribution to the problem of marriage, it is understandable that they found nothing to satisfy them in the book.

It is only with his autobiography, *Dichtung und Wahrheit*, that Goethe once more reaches a wider public. In his own eyes he has now become an historical figure, and he feels the time has come to describe the process of his development, before others step in and do it for him. His memory is 'like a sieve', as he says. His mother, who could have helped him so much in recalling his early life, is dead, bequeathing only some anecdotes to Bettina, who has translated them into her own language. But facts and events are not Goethe's chief concern; history, that 'hodge-podge of error and brute force', has never been a favourite subject with him. What he wants to portray is the life of a poet, unfolding like his *Ur-Pflanze* from the seed to the fully developed tree. Wisely he breaks off before his arrival in Weimar, and this allows his life to appear as a continuous, uninterrupted development. Nothing stops its flow; there are no hesitations or digressions into other spheres of activity: it is the life story of a poet from childhood to the first years of manhood.

Written as *Dichtung*, as the work of a poet, it was accepted as such. Unlike Rousseau, Goethe has nothing to 'confess'; he regards the whole of his remaining life and work as a single great confession. He does not try to surprise us with 'truths'. He does not try to surprise us at all, either by the exposure of vices and moral transgressions, or by psychological flashes throwing a 'new light' on hitherto unsuspected facets of his inner life, or least of all by striking references to world affairs and contemporary events. He is calm and self-assured; he has no need even to be vain – like most autobiographers. Fate has been kind to him, and that he sees as perfectly in order; in fact it is proof of the supreme order. Chance plays no part. There is order and purpose in everything; even his birth takes place under a favourable constellation of the planets. Everything comes his way at the right moment, his first love, his first sorrow, his first success; and at the end Apollo's chariot bears him off to new lands where, as the reader knows, his way will lead onward and upward.

There is a grandeur in this simplicity, even if at times it appears almost ingenuous and leaves much to be desired for us, who are children of another age. There is nothing about death, suffering or grief – significantly it is only in his last hours that 'grief' disturbs the dying Faust; there is no fear, no adversary, not even the enemy within, his severe hypochondriac inheritance. Everything unpleasant is left on one side. The book is to be *'heiter'*, serene and cheerful, and to create a sense of well-being. For Goethe this sense of well-being is an essential element of the novel, and in *Dichtung und Wahrheit* he has been more successful in creating it than in his expressly fictional works. In Germany it soon became almost a household book. Its characters became members of the family, even the poet's many loves being welcomed into the family circle, for *Dichterlieben* became a cult and after that an industry, whose looms still continue to turn even to-day. Lotte, Friederike, Lili joined his Klärchen and his Gretchen and, immortalized in woodcuts, engravings and coloured prints, were soon to be found on the walls of every home.

Goethe has succeeded in painting a picture in which a pleasing harmony prevails, as required by his aesthetic viewpoint at the time he wrote the book. The problematic side of his nature and even the problematic works like *Stella* or *Faust* are excluded. Mephistopheles makes no appearance; brimstone is not included in his palette. As a result the portrait not infrequently becomes tame and too well-behaved. There is something of the model boy about it, and only occasionally does the dangerous irony in his nature flash out and give a hint that, behind the pedagogic amiability, there lurks something of a very different order.

Thus the living Goethe writes the legend of his life and erects his own monument. Like the other monuments of his day its base is decorated with numerous reliefs and medallions, and these secondary figures are not the least of its charm. It is superfluous to draw attention to the riches of wisdom the book contains in its sayings, remarks and observations. Goethe puts into it the 'sum total of his existence', often reinterpreting his earlier years in the light of his experience and achievements. The return this yields is enormous. Once when people were discussing the vanity and pretensions inherent in every self-portrait, he said, very wisely, 'in reality the autobiographer is the most courteous of men ...'.

# 38

# *Awakening of the Sleeper*

Contact with these reminders of his youth has rejuvenated Goethe. He looks with astonishment at the old manuscripts of his *Satyros*, which his loyal, though often derided, friend Fritz Jacobi has sent him. 'A document of the divine insolence of our early years', he calls it. But it is not to be published for the moment, because it does not harmonize with the antique columns and architraves of his new teaching. Nevertheless Goethe grows pensive. Two lines keep running through his head: '*Wir sind vielleicht zu antik gewesen – Nun wollen wir es moderner lesen*' (Perhaps we have been too tied to antiquity – now let us try to be more up-to-date). However much he may regard himself as part of history, he is still very far from finished with his life; indeed he feels one of his new skins growing.

His rather flabby corpulence has disappeared. Just how is not very clear, for he is quite as fond of his food as ever; it is true he pays a little more attention to what he eats, but he does not resort to despairing fits of slimming like Byron. He continues to drink his good red wine, in its large bottles, as well as champagne and the heavy Würzburg '*Steinwein*'. He has lost his teeth, but perhaps this is just as well since, according to modern views, not a few of his rheumatic and other complaints may have been due to them. He takes a more lively interest in his surroundings; worldly objects come closer to him and are not looked upon merely as intangible '*Ur*'-phenomena. For whatever Goethe may have said about his 'pure' way of looking at things, he is, in his interpretation of nature, primarily a thinker and a poet, attempting to re-create the world. His many experiments are made, in the first instance, to re-discover what he already knows or has divined. But his thinking always has to be accompanied by physical contact, he has to feel the things under his hands. And so he always goes about with his little geologist's hammer, tapping the rocks round Karlsbad, deriving pleasure from some crystalline formation, or still greater pleasure from the 'thermal tuffs' which an old man in Karlsbad collects, cuts and polishes, and sells done up in pretty little boxes to the visitors. These 'Neptunist' products of long and gentle formation on nature's part are very much more to his liking than a disturbing phenomenon like basalt, which is constantly being held up to him – stubbornly, like the Newtonian error – as probably of volcanic origin. Basalt becomes another adversary, a fiendish black enemy: 'There's that damned basalt sticking up its blackamoor head again!' he mutters angrily, as he turns away to look at more conciliatory rocks. He wants nothing to do with these poltergeists, either in nature or in contemporary affairs, where all around him there are eruptions and streams of molten lava. The present is his concern, not some uncertain and perhaps even gloomier future.

But the present also means attractive, intelligent, stimulating women. Whatever Goethe may have said in his *Wahlverwandschaften* about marriage as the 'beginning and summit of all culture' and about the dark side of passion, his own life is that of an oriental patriarch, a 'sultan', to use the term he had in mind for the novel – *Der Sultan wider Willen* – he was planning simultaneously with the *Wahlverwandschaften*. He even makes use of the title of his great and tragic book in describing his little dietetic relationships: 'A small love affair,' he says to Eckermann, 'is the only thing that can make life at a spa tolerable; otherwise one would die of boredom. And I was almost always fortunate enough to find some little *Wahlverwandschaft* there. ...'

Karlsbad is a part of the Goethe landscape. He made twelve visits to the spa, the first before his flight to Italy, the last in 1820. The ailments that took him there he describes only in the vaguest terms. Illness, like death, was a thing he disliked referring to: he calls it 'the ailment' or 'the old trouble'; it was probably his kidneys. For Goethe the main attraction of the spa is always as a summer resort, where he can enjoy the social life and association with people other than the eternal Weimar set, where he can go for gentle strolls and study a little botany and geology.

'From granite through the whole of creation up to women,' wrote Goethe to Karl August on his first visit, 'everything has contributed to make my stay pleasant and interesting'. The spa, although the meeting place of elegant European society, would have seemed modest in the extreme to us. It had long been a favourite resort. A hundred years earlier Johann Sebastian Bach had gone there with his master, the Duke of Anhalt-Köthen, to entertain the guests on his cembalo, expressly brought for the purpose. In Goethe's day the half-timbered houses had not changed; they were closely packed together in the narrow valley of the Tepl. Trumpets announced the arrival of visitors, of whom the list shows a total of about five hundred; later, when the spa became a favourite with the Imperial Austrian Court, the number rose to a thousand. The inns still kept the old names, such as *Zur schönen Königin*, *Zum golden Elephanten* or *Zum grünen Papagei*; there were also pensions like *Zum roten Herzen*, the red heart, a name not without its significance.

It is a closed society, everybody knows everybody. The high aristocracy form the majority, and there are counts in business as hoteliers. French is the dominant language, but German, Italian, Russian and Polish are also heard; Karlsbad is an international oasis in an increasingly nationalistic world. At the balls they dance the polonaise, the dance of the Polish aristocracy, and Geheimrat von Goethe takes his place in the procession with the others, nodding friendly greetings to his fair acquaintances. In the evenings the men gamble, and the stakes are high; on one occasion Prince Lobkowitz, the Imperial Spa Commissioner, gambles away his elegant equipage, horses and all. There are excursions into the surrounding country and visits to a porcelain factory, there are the famous Bohemian glass cutters, from whom glasses can be ordered with views of the spa and the initials of one of the many *Äugelchen*; in all of this Goethe participates. He also works. He travels with a servant and his secretary, a tall, lanky, sullen fellow named John, who soon gets on Goethe's nerves, despite the fact that he writes an excellent, clear hand. 'He is pretentious, difficult about his food, has a sweet tooth, is fond of the bottle, speaks in a muffled voice, and never works at the right time.' It was very different with Riemer, now a teacher at the Weimar '*Gymnasium*'.

The dark and gloomy world always provides some obstacle to put in Goethe's path, but by and large he finds life pleasant in Karlsbad, living on an island with wars all round him. News of this outside world comes to him only from afar, as it were, in conversation with diplomats, ruling Princes, or army people; he notes down a few things, but most of what he hears he keeps to himself. Louis, the ex-King of Holland ignominiously dismissed by his brother Napoleon, is among the Spa visitors, under the modest name of Comte de St Leu, and is staying at the same inn as Goethe; they have long talks together. Goethe's admiration for the great demon does not prevent him applauding the gentle, pious disposition of this lesser brother, who had little alternative but to resign himself to his fate. A still higher favour now falls to Goethe's lot: the Empress of Austria, Maria Ludovica, appears. A slender, ailing woman, she is the third wife of the 'good Emperor' Franz who, in reality, is a narrow-minded and, towards his abler brother, insatiably jealous wretch, no less ailing than his wife, and popular with his loyal subjects only because of his sly, cleverly exploited *bonhomie*. With the pale Empress Goethe pursues a cult which surpasses even his cult of the pale Duchess Luise in Weimar. He writes to his friend Reinhard that the good fortune of having met this wonderful creature is so overwhelming that only 'the anxiety lest my strength be insufficient to bear it often brings to mind human frailty in the midst of my enjoyment'. To be vouchsafed such an experience towards the end of one's life makes one feel 'as though one were dying at sunrise, fully convinced with both one's inner and outer faculties that nature is eternally productive, divine to its very core, alive, true to type and not subject to age'.

Goethe's life in this Karlsbad society, and his poetry too, are in the old style; even Napoleon and those surrounding him adapt themselves with astonishing speed to the forms and ceremonies of the *ancien régime*. The demon's marriage to the daughter of the Austrian Emperor, Marie Louise, an entirely undemonic and ordinary person, is the crowning point of this process; all that is required of her is to produce an heir to the throne for the new Empire, and this she does with the accustomed Habsburg punctuality in such matters. With this act Napoleon's Empire appears to be dynastically assured for ever. In a long poem Goethe celebrates the Empress and her infant son, who as King of Rome is laid in a cradle of antique oriental design, as the gracious 'bride of peace'; in the new Empire she is greeted by the welcome of millions who from out of the darkness of night can now look forward to happier days. At the end he repeats his prayer for peace: '*Der alles wollen kann, will auch den Frieden*' (Who all can will, will also peace desire). The date is 1812, the eve of Napoleon's campaign against Russia.

Napoleon is a soldier, a man of war. As he told Karl August during the Erfurt Conference, it is only in war that he feels at ease; peace simply bores him. His intention is to go overland to India, there to get to grips with England, whom he cannot reach by sea. Russia bars the way of this new expedition in the footsteps of Alexander the Great, and must therefore be quickly crushed. Napoleon plans and calculates; he has at his disposal the greatest army of modern times. The Weimar contingent finds itself among the supporting troops, with Karl August now a French general; Spaniards, Italians, Prussians, Württembergers, Bavarians are also marching. King Ludwig of Bavaria later erects a black obelisk in Munich to commemorate the thirty thousand Bavarians who fell in Russia. The French soldiers are to be protected to the utmost; the country is exhausted, in twenty years of war almost two million of its young men have been lost. Men are beginning to desert, and no war history records the number of those who ran away or evaded service. Even the great marshals, who have earned their batons by rising from the ranks, are growing soft and half-hearted; they are millionaires now, Dukes, Counts, or Kings like Murat and Bernadotte, and they want to enjoy their fame and fortune. Marshal Lannes, Goethe's guest in 1806, is dead, killed in 1809 at Aspern, fighting against Austria who, since 1810, has been Napoleon's ally and relation by marriage. Napoleon paid a last visit to the cruelly wounded man on the battlefield, intending to take a great and moving farewell from his old comrade in arms, the Duc de Montebello. But the old stable-lad's son only cursed bitterly and despairingly, and in stable-lad's language, at his master and his eternal wars. Napoleon did not hear this warning of 'enough'. He put his trust in the formidable figure of four hundred thousand men, no matter what their flag, and in his star.

Goethe hears a great deal in his conversations with influential people at Karlsbad, but the resulting picture seems to him doubtful in the extreme. He sees a clash of personalities, not of peoples or ideologies. On the one side he sees the mighty demon, now certainly an oriental despot, but a man who knows how to command. On the other side there is the Emperor Franz, delicate, vacillating, epileptic, jealous of his more gifted brother Karl, who at Aspern had been the first to call a halt to Napoleon and was thereupon dismissed, and jealous of his other brother Johann, who had made common cause with the Tirolese peasants in their revolt and fell into lifelong disgrace. There is also the Prussian King, Friedrich Wilhelm III, a dull-witted martinet, speaking the clipped jargon of the Potsdam guards officers, who leaves on one side all men of talent and genius, the poet Goethe as well as Baron vom Stein, and surrounds himself with mediocrities whom he picks out with the unerring eye of a kindred spirit. Finally there is the Czar Alexander, another vacillating figure, good-looking with markedly feminine characteristics, and full of hazy ideas for promoting the happiness of his subjects, such as Goethe cannot stand; his Swiss tutor, La Harpe, had instilled into the boy some of the ideas of the Encyclopaedists. Alexander is half deaf, one of his eardrums having burst as a boy when, in order to toughen him, the great Catherine had ordered the batteries to fire a salvo outside his window. The good ear he lends to his constantly changing advisers who, like the great reformer Speranski, find themselves banished to Siberia the moment another counsellor gains the ear of the ever mistrustful autocrat. On top of all this he is short-sighted, and at Weimar had only been able to shoot a stag when it was specially driven to within five paces of him. He is short-sighted mentally, too, swaying between one extreme and another, between enlightenment and the crassest religious mysticisms; Goethe's Strasbourg friend Jung-Stilling turns up again as a sinister influence, together with a Baroness Krüdener from the same circle, who suggests to the Czar that he is destined to save the world from the apocalyptic monster.

These are the antagonists. Goethe does not confine himself to verses of devoted homage; he also writes trenchant epigrams, such as one he wrote in 1812, though it was not published till much later: 'Sind Könige je zusammengekommen, So hat man immer nur Unheil vernommen' (The outcome of every meeting of kings is always and only the evil it brings). Napoleon's greatest opponent he ignores. There is much talk of popular insurrections, in Spain, in Calabria, in Tirol; Bettina tells him in her letters of heroic deeds of the peasants in the mountains of Tirol, and of how she wants to rush to their side in doublet and breeches, 'waving the short green and white banner, far in front on the steepest pinnacle, with victory burning in my limbs'. Goethe regards this as emotionalism on the part of the romantic girl; when she tells him of the execution of Andreas Hofer, the peasants' leader, he sends her a few words of sympathy in her patriotic grief, and goes on, 'You must not let life with its capricious turns distress you too much. ...'

In this fateful year of 1812 Goethe's Annals contain notes on performances by visiting actors, an essay on Myron's cow, a book he has read on the digestive organs of insects, the discovery of fossilized bones in Bohemia; in Jena the Crown Princess Maria Feodorowna has graciously presented an air pump to the University physics institute. Meanwhile Napoleon has reached Moscow.

Reinhard is the first to tell him about the burning of the city. In his reply Goethe writes: 'The fact that Moscow has been burned is of no concern whatever to me. It will also provide history with something to write about.' In the draft of his letter he writes: 'And one really does not know where to find all the astonishment that these great events demand of us. Our imagination is incapable of grasping them, our intellect of ordering them. History is amassing great treasures at our expense.'

'*Das Volk steht auf, der Sturm bricht los*' (The people rise, the storm's unleashed) cries the young Theodor Körner, in a line that later became famous. His father, Schiller's friend, had sent Goethe his precocious son's first lyrics and plays: Goethe had praised them highly, saying that here was a young poet after his own taste, his verses distinguished by their 'facility', his plays short and easy to stage. 'What harm Schiller did himself', Goethe goes on, 'in attempting to treat his vast conceptions dramatically and theatrically. ...' In Körner he sees a hope for the rising generation of playwrights, a hope he would probably have fulfilled.

During a visit to Dresden, on his way to the Bohemian spas, Goethe learns that this exceptionally promising young man has enlisted with the Prussian volunteers, although his father, as a Saxon State official whose King is Napoleon's most faithful ally, is bound to suffer severely as a result; Goethe shakes his head at the news. At the Körners he meets another Prussian patriot, Ernst Moritz Arndt, who 'has made a name for himself with his writings', as Goethe writes home. He has not read the pamphlets but would certainly have disapproved of them intensely, for they are full of violent hatred of the French and were banned by the Royal Prussian censorship in Berlin, even after the French had withdrawn. Arndt describes this meeting in his memoirs, where he records Goethe's scornful remark: 'Rattle your chains to your heart's content; the man is too big for you. You will not break them.' Soon Goethe learns that the young Körner has been killed in a daring attack on a heavily guarded French transport column. A few hours before the engagement he wrote his last poem, a bridal song to his sword, ending with the lines: '*Der Hochzeitmorgen graut, Hurrah du Eisenbraut!*' (Now dawns the wedding day, Thou bride of steel, hurray!) to which is added the note, 'at the "hurray" everyone clashes swords'.

Only much later, when Körner, together with this whole period of the wars of liberation, had become a legend, did Goethe defend himself to Eckermann against the charge that he had stood on one side: 'Writing war songs sitting in my study! That would have been my way of doing it! Out there in the bivouac, hearing the horses of the enemy outposts at night – that I could have enjoyed. However it was not my life, not my calling, but that of Theodor Körner. ... Nor can we all serve our country in the same way, but we each do our best according as God has endowed us.'

Most of what has been written of this period in school books and history books is legend. The people do not rise. Nowhere are the fleeing remnants of the *Grande Armée* so much as molested, let alone attacked; on the contrary the tattered wretches, stammering of the fearful Russian cold, are objects of pity. The Prussian general, York, concluded an agreement with the Russian general, Diebitsch, at Tauroggen, which neutralized the Prussian corps, whereupon Friedrich Wilhelm immediately branded York a traitor and dismissed him, a step that can be explained by the fact that the King was still surrounded by the French forces of occupation; he never forgave his general his arbitrary action. Hesitatingly, reluctantly, the King sets the great 'uprising' in motion; it is the work of ardent reformers, 'Jacobins' as they are called by the still all-powerful old-school reactionaries. Auxiliary forces, the *Landwehr* and the *Landsturm*, are to be formed; the very word *Sturm*, storm, is suspect, it leads to 'complete anarchy and the overthrow of the Crown', as the Prussian Minister of Police explains in a memorandum. The King dissolves the Berlin *Landsturm* before the real fighting begins, and issues an edict against the 'misuse of the *Landsturm* weapon', as though he were dealing with partisans. He does not like the volunteers, who are formed almost against his will and with whom students are enlisting; they have to buy all their own equipment, wearing black uniforms that contrast strongly with the regulation blue of the regiments of the line. The King puts his signature to a manifesto, 'To my people', written by one of the reformers; he also promises constitutional reforms, and goes back on his promise the moment victory is won. 'This is no war of which crowned heads know ought,' sings Körner, in lines that undoubtedly the censor would have suppressed had they not been reserved for posthumous publication.

It is not a war of which the crowned heads know anything. They favour moderation, and negotiations with the demon, whom they still fear, and who is about to inflict on them a series of bloody defeats with a hurriedly assembled force of half a million men. As general he is almost never greater than in his last campaigns; as Emperor he is an adventurer, a gambler who stakes his all on a final stroke of fortune, refusing terms, however favourable, and playing desperately for a rift in the coalition. At first the new war moves uncertainly back and forth, and the Prussian and Austrian patriots – which has now become a term of honour – are often on the verge of despair.

At the first approach of the allied Prussian and Russian troops Goethe, under strong pressure from those near him, leaves for Bohemia and the spas. Christiane stays behind and makes the necessary billeting arrangements, with rather more difficulty than in 1806, for she has grown fat and heavy and is a sick woman. The reports which Goethe sends home to his wife and the *Nebengeschöpf*, Ulrich, are mostly about art and architecture and are more detailed than ever. In Dresden, where the Russians are in occupation, he finds himself caught up in the hubbub of war. He is awakened by a 'terrible apparition' as a group of soldiers, still in search of quarters, burst into the building by torch-light; they are pacified with beef, sauerkraut and schnaps. He visits the famous picture gallery, watches the Cossacks who have brought a camel with them, and sees the entry of the Czar and the King of Prussia into the illuminated town. A few months later the town is again illuminated for the 'invincible Napoleon', who once more enters Dresden; on his way back Goethe describes his arrival in Dresden in lovely weather, 'still in time to see part of the celebrations for Napoleon, which have been put off until to-day'. At the spa, Teplitz this time, he continues to dictate his memoirs and listens to the stories of wounded officers. One of these tells him of how, while fighting on the side of the Allies, he had been robbed by Russian stragglers and had then been taken prisoner by the French, who had robbed him again and severely beaten him; he wants to recuperate and then rejoin the Prussians. 'He is one of the many thousands who are straying in the wilderness, not knowing to which saint to dedicate themselves.'

Goethe is very sure of his way. He even makes a bet with an official that Napoleon will win; the following year he pays his debt in Rhine wine, 'now that they're fighting beyond the Rhine', as he says in his accompanying poem. 'Whenever something of an appallingly threatening nature arose in the political world, I would fling myself stubbornly to the farthest corner of the earth.' And so on his return from Teplitz Goethe devotes himself to the study of Chinese history and geology.

In October Napoleon's military might is brought to an end by the Battle of Leipzig; in the previous June his political fate had been sealed in his decisive conversation with Metternich. 'I have won two battles, I shall not make peace,' he says to the Austrian statesman, who has offered him the Rhine as a frontier; 'in October we shall talk together in Vienna.' Metternich reminds Napoleon of the state of his army; he has seen the soldiers himself, they are children, an 'anticipated generation'. 'You are not a soldier,' Napoleon shouts back, 'I have grown up on the battlefield, a man like me does not bother his head about the lives of a million men.' Metternich suggests opening the doors so that all France can hear his words. Napoleon, now completely beside himself, says the French have no reason to complain of him, he has protected them; it was the Germans and Poles he sacrificed at the gates of Moscow, and even though there were three hundred thousand casualties, no more than thirty thousand of these were French. 'You forget, Sire, that you are speaking to a German,' replies Metternich. His final words are: 'You are lost, Sire.'

With Leipzig the collapse begins. The Princes of the Rhineland desert the Emperor and set about saving the thrones he gave them while there is yet time. His brother-in-law Murat deserts him in order to remain King of Naples, his former Marshal Bernadotte has already gone over to the Allies; in the end, with very few exceptions, his remaining marshals make their peace with the victors to save their titles and their fortunes.

In December 1813 Goethe has a memorable conversation with the young historian Luden. The energetic Bertuch wants to publish a political journal in Weimar; it is to be called *Nemesis*, and Luden is to edit it. Goethe advises strongly against it. His advice to Luden is to return to the study of history and 'to let the world go its way and not to meddle in the disputes of kings, in which your and my voices will never be listened to'. Luden defends his point of view courageously: hitherto the average German has thought only of himself, eating his dumpling and contentedly wiping his mouth – it is just this that has brought all the misery on the fatherland. In Jena, he goes on, he talked to one man who said: 'Well, my friend, what do you expect? The French have gone, the parlours are scrubbed. Fine! Now the Russians can come if they want to.'

Goethe speaks quietly, and with a wisdom far beyond his time. A journal to fight Napoleon? But there are many points to the compass. 'You will find yourself up against the thrones. ... You will have everything that is great and distinguished in the world against you, for you will be representing the cottages against the palaces, and championing the cause of the weak against the hand of the strong. ... They are not pleasant people to deal with. You have nothing to put against their weapons.'

He emphasizes that he is not indifferent to the concept of the fatherland.

> I have often suffered bitter anguish at the thought of the German people, who are so admirable as individuals and so wretched as a whole. A comparison between the German people and other peoples awakens in us painful feelings, which I try to overcome in every possible way, and in science and art I have found the wings that enable one to rise above them, for science and art belong to the world and before them the barriers of nationality disappear.

If Luden reports him correctly, Goethe then adds that nevertheless this is but poor consolation and cannot replace the awareness of belonging to a strong and great nation. It is in the future, therefore, that our hope must lie. No one can foresee when this time will be. When Luden speaks of the nation's awakening, Goethe says:

> Are the people really awake? Do they know what they want and what they are capable of? The slumber has been too deep for even the severest shaking to bring them back to consciousness so soon. And is every movement an uprising? Does someone rise up who is forcibly roused up? We are not speaking of the thousands of educated youths and men, we are speaking of the masses, of the millions. And what has been achieved? You say liberty, but perhaps we should do better to call it liberation – liberation, not from the yoke of the foreigner, but from one foreign yoke. It is true I no longer see Frenchmen, no longer Italians, but in their place I see Cossacks, Bashkirs, Croats, Magyars, Cassubians, Samlanders, brown and other hussars. We have long accustomed ourselves to turn our eyes only to the west and to expect every

danger to come from that direction, but the earth also extends far to the east. ...

Luden does not venture to note down the rest of the conversation which, so he says, grew increasingly pointed and outspoken. In Goethe's words he sees only pained resignation, and the mistake people have made in accusing him of having no faith in the German people.

More casually, and in his earlier rococo style which still breaks through from time to time, Goethe writes to an old friend: 'Our young gentlemen find nothing easier than to march off and make things as unpleasant for others as other people have made them for us: and it is a very tempting occupation since one passes as an established patriot at the same time.' He expressly forbids his son August to join the Weimar volunteers; he cannot prevent his Duke, as a Russian general, from commanding a detachment. In his letter he adds:

> But to those of us over 60 nothing remains but to flirt with the ladies, so that they do not completely lose heart. But how are we to set about it? With the older ones I play cards, and to the younger ones I try to teach something. *Vivat sequens.* May heaven preserve your sense of humour! I have no ambition beyond wanting people to say to me: you are the merriest undone Man in Europe. [This last phrase is written in Goethe's quaint English.]

In the following year, when there is talk of a 'moral and literary union', he says, in more serious vein, 'let us private individuals, as is right and proper, leave to the great, the mighty and the politically experienced', the union of the German Empire in the political sense. Even a cultural union is conceivable only as a result of a miracle, 'namely if it should please God to bestow overnight on all the members of the German nation the gift of being able to judge one other on their merits'. In analysing this failing he says it derives from a virtue: nowhere else are there so many outstanding individuals.

> But because each individual of significance has his hands full completing his own cultural education, and because each younger generation takes its culture from its own day, which is foreign to the previous generation and the one prior to that, and since the German recognizes nothing positive and, without ever becoming a butterfly, is in a constant state of flux, there arises such a series of cultural differences, not to say levels, that the most conscientious etymologist cannot trace the origin of our Babylonian idiom, nor can the most accurate historian trace the course of a cultural development that is eternally self-contradictory. A German does not have to be an old man to find himself abandoned by his pupils, he has no one to follow him. Each of us who feels his worth starts from the beginning....

In April 1814 the news reaches Weimar that Paris has been occupied by the Allies. Napoleon abdicates and goes to Elba. Goethe receives an invitation from Berlin to write a play for the victory celebrations. He refuses, withdraws his refusal, and writes his allegorical play *Des Epimenides*

*Erwachen*; the intention is to perform it on the King's return. The theatre hesitates; the play, with its highly personal symbolism, makes an unfavourable impression. It is only out of respect for the great poet that finally, a year later, they decide to stage it. The performance takes place on March 30, 1815, the anniversary of the fall of Paris. At the self-same moment Napoleon, having escaped from Elba, re-enters his capital again in triumph, while in Vienna the Congress dances, the great struggle over the spoils of victory has begun, and it is only with difficulty that a new war, this time between the Allies, is averted.

Works written for official celebrations of great occasions seldom bring out the best in great poets, or great artists of any kind. Although in some respects anticipating the *Ninth Symphony*, Beethoven's Cantata, *Der Glorreiche Augenblick*, written for the assembly of crowned heads in Vienna, is also a strange work, composed to painfully loyal words by a local poet. It closes with a pious chorus, for it is a Holy Alliance that is being consummated: '*Und die alten Zeiten werden Endlich wieder seyn auf Erden*' (And once more the olden days will come again upon this earth). It has a very topical significance for the glorious moment.

For his play Goethe chooses antiquity and a severely classical style, with a Greek seer Epimenides to represent himself. This is not the first time his interest has been aroused in the figure of this Greek sage of the legendary days of pre-history, before the advent of 'philosophy and science, whom for long years the gods keep protected from the world in a silent cave. While asleep in the cave he acquires mysterious powers which, on returning to the world, he exercises in making great prophecies. Travelling from place to place as a priest he establishes expiatory measures for serious crimes on Delos and in Athens, and acts as peacemaker between the factions of the people. In Greek mythology Epimenides sleeps for fifty-seven years. Goethe does not record the length of time, but uses this mythical sleep to explain his own absence during the years of fighting and revolt. Epimenides, awakened from his sleep, expresses his shame for his long hours of rest and his admiration of those who have suffered. For the rest the play is an allegory, ending in a final chorus extolling the liberation.

Goethe's original instinct to refuse the commission was right. The impact of Napoleon, one of the greatest experiences of his life, was by no means over; the demon of war he presents in this play is a wholly un-Napoleonic figure, frightened by shadows and phantoms. Neither at this time nor later did Goethe ever create a man of action. It is in *Dichtung und Wahrheit*, however, and without mentioning the Emperor by name, that he speaks authentically of the demoniac, of which he sees Napoleon as the most complete embodiment:

> Every philosophy and religion has tried to solve this riddle in prose and in poetry and to dispose of the matter once and for all, and may well continue to do so in time to come....

But the demoniac is to be seen in its most terrible form when it is overwhelmingly manifested in some one individual.... Such people are not always the most outstanding, either in mind or talents, and rarely commend themselves through kindness of heart; but a titanic force emanates from them and they exercise an incredible power over every creature and even over the elements, and who can say how far their influence will extend? All the moral forces put together are powerless against them; it is in vain for the more enlightened section of humanity to brand them as deceived or deceivers, the masses will be attracted by them. Rarely if ever do their equals exist at the same time, and nothing can overcome them but the very universe against which they declared battle....

# 39

# *The Oriental Divan*

Goethe's awakening is very different from that of the Greek seer, Epimenides, in his cave; with it, and with this play, his period of strict classicism comes to an end. Once more he undergoes a change and dons a new mask. North, South and West are splitting into fragments, thrones are bursting asunder, and so he makes his escape in order to 'taste the atmosphere of the patriarchs in the purity of the East', as he writes in the introductory poem to his *Westöstlicher Divan*, the great collection of verse which he signs as 'the occidental author'. Napoleon's great march to the East in the steps of Alexander the Great is at an end, and his Empire is now reduced to the little island of Elba. Goethe is only just setting out on his own journey to the East. One should really live in a tent, he said some years later under the stress of the constant restlessness of his nature, a restlessness he is only able to curb by the strict regularity of his life in the small triangle of Weimar – Jena – Karlsbad. He is a guest on this gloomy earth – *auf der trüben Erde* – and now he wants to live in oases as the guest of the herdsmen. riding over the desert by night with 'only the stars above my head'. The East, which he has never seen, has nevertheless been a familiar landscape since childhood through his reading of the Bible; he has always wanted to write an epic on the passage of the Children of Israel through the desert. He has read parts of the Koran and now the old Persian poet, Hafiz, has come into his hand, translated by a Herr von Hammer of the Court Chancellery in Vienna; Hammer was a many-sided and industrious man who knew ten languages, none of them very thoroughly, and who translated indefatigably from the still more or less unfamiliar Oriental literatures. He edited a beautifully printed serial work called *Fundgruben des Orients*, which contained contributions from a number of authors; Goethe had looked at it and found it rather too scholarly and difficult. It is Cotta, his publisher, who sends him Hammer's translation of Hafiz, and in spite of the specialists, who find much to criticize and who point out hundreds of mistakes, Goethe is moved by the old poet; he recognizes him as a kindred spirit, a fellow poet who lived through strangely similar times. He reads of Court life, of empires in flux and collapse, of a meeting with the great conqueror, Tamerlaine; there are songs of the nightingale and the rose, of wine and love. There is also, so he is told, a deep mysticism beneath the light sounding verses, and perhaps love really signifies faith and wine the spirit. He can almost believe that half a millennium earlier he had lived and walked in the gardens of Shiraz.

He is stimulated by other things too, things that satisfy his need for direct sensuous contact. One of the unlucky Weimar contingent, who had to go to Spain to fight for Napoleon, has brought back a leaf from an old Arabic *codex*. Goethe's pleasure in the beauties of calligraphy is awakened by the fine flowing hand in which the manuscript is written. The Russian regiment of Bashkirs stationed in Weimar holds Mohammedan services in the 'Gymnasium', and Goethe hears the murmuring of *suras* from the Koran, magical incantations to his ear; the men give him one of the ancient bows and arrows they still carry, and he hangs the weapon over his mantelpiece, fascinated by this symbol that also speaks to him like a handwriting. A collection of oriental books has been acquired by the University of Jena, and he already refers to it as a 'camel load' of volumes. His vocabulary acquires strange words. He reads of the six famous pairs of lovers of oriental tradition: of King Solomon and Queen Balkis of Sheba – the brown one, familiar from the Bible like so much in Islam – of Medsnun and Leila, and of the pair he chooses for himself, Joussouph and Suleika. These last are none other than Joseph, son of Jacob, and Suleika, wife of Potiphar; Goethe adopts Suleika as his oriental love.

He does not only read. Goethe was no orientalist, and in Germany the study of the East was still in its infancy. France already had its distinguished scholars, and to the greatest of these, Baron de Sacy, Goethe pays tribute at the end of his book. To France too, to Napoleon's Egyptian expedition, can be traced the re-discovery of the Orient. The Egyptian hieroglyphs, that riddle of the centuries which had fascinated Goethe when he came upon the abandoned obelisk in Rome, had now been deciphered, and the exploration of a world, hitherto known only from reports of missionaries and travellers, had begun. Fashion succumbed to the trend, and the Court of the Grand Sultan Napoleon decorated its furniture with sphinxes and Egyptian palmette motifs. Romanticism discovered Spain, with its strong Arab influence, and India was brought nearer by Friedrich Schlegel's first bold 'enquiry into the language and wisdom of India'. In Brighton, Nash built a veritable nabob's palace for his friend the Regent, whose oriental style of living was not confined to architecture. Byron travelled in Greece and Albania wearing Turkish costume, with turban and sash. The Near East which, until the days of Goethe's own youth, had so long been the great and dreaded menace to the West, now became the happy hunting-ground for adventurous young noblemen, serious archaeologists, and painters in search of new and stronger colours.

Goethe drifts in this current. In theory, and frequently with angry words, he fights Romanticism, which seems to him undisciplined and unstable, as indeed it often is, especially as exemplified by the lives of its representatives. To Riemer he says: 'The romantic expression is not a natural, original one, but something artificial, contrived, exaggerated, and bizarre to the point of distortion and caricature.' And yet he cannot extricate himself from the waves that wash round him. The severe, plastic forms of the Greeks, which he has always held up as the eternal model, now weary him and he wants, as he puts it in one of his poems, to feel the waters of the Euphrates and let his hands play in their fluid element. But it is to be no mere playing: '*Schöpft des Dichters reine Hand, Wasser wird sich ballen*' (Water, pure-drawn by the poet's hand, forms a crystal globe).

Most important of all is the fact that he feels young again, in the enjoyment of one of his 'recurring puberties' as he calls them; it is the greatest creative period of his later life. During the summer of 1814 he re-gathers his strength at the little spa of Berka, near Weimar, in wonderful weather. He has long conversations, far removed from the deserts of Arabia, with his friend Wolf, the great Homeric scholar, who had shattered the Homer image by dividing up the *Iliad* into songs by individual rhapsodists. Logically Wolf should have been as unsympathetic to Goethe as Newton, but the poet is in a very conciliatory mood. The local organist, a stout and vigorous man, plays Bach to him on the piano; the great composer has just been rediscovered and Goethe is particularly attracted by a 'little trumpet piece' – there is no question yet of any profound knowledge of Bach – the *Capriccio* Bach wrote on the departure of his younger brother. Goethe never tires of the piece, with its final '*Aria del postiglione*', in which the sound of the horn, after being heard repeatedly, is turned into a fugue where it is drowned by the sound of the departing coach.

Perhaps the coachman's horn recalls to Goethe the postillion, sent to carry him off to Weimar and a new life, who blew his horn so insistently outside Fräulein Delph's door in Heidelberg. At any rate he once more decides on a journey. Weimar has become too narrow, too flat. He wants to travel eastwards, to the camel drivers and the patriarchs; instead, following his star, he goes west, back to the land of his youth. In Berka, having finished his festival play for better or for worse, he has started writing poetry again, in the new-old style. The classical style, with its columns and capitals, is finished and done with. He begins from the beginning, as it were, with the story of creation – the Bible story, not the story of Greek myth. '*Hans Adam war ein Erdenkloss, Den Gott zum Menschen machte*' (Old Adam was a lump of earth, which God made into man), he writes in Hans Sachs style. He surveys the 'elements' out of which the poet has to create his song: love, the clinking of glasses, and the clash of weapons too. It is as though he were planning the chapters of some future book. He is still very much under the influence of Hafiz.

The journey now begins. Goethe travels in comfort in a fine carriage, his 'little house on wheels' as he calls it. On the box beside the coachman sits his servant, a wide-awake youngster named Stadelmann. Like his predecessor, Philipp Seidel, he apes his master in many ways, even copying his interest in geology; he flirts with the kitchen-maids and writes lively letters to his friends, telling them of his own and his master's adventures. The weather is magnificent, a word that recurs constantly throughout the journey. On the outskirts of Erfurt, a centre for nurseries and market gardens, the poppy fields catch Goethe's eye, and at once become Persian carpets or pleasure tents for a vizier's wives. Walking among the market stalls in the town he is reminded of little pleasures of long ago, a baker's daughter, a cobbler's wife: 'That one never was a kill-joy, this one knew life's pleasures too.' The cobbler's wife has even been identified as a well-known beauty of the town named Frau Vogel; Goethe sees them both as houris in Mohammed's paradise. In Eisenach he recalls the days when the strings of his psaltery vied with the rays of the morning sun; from the woods he hears hunting horns, like a last echo of the postillion's horn in Bach's *Capriccio*. He sees the first rainbow and lo, in the mist and haze, it does not appear in the puzzling colours of the hated spectrum, but white, a white rainbow. Delightedly he writes the lines:

> *So sollst du muntrer Greis,*
> *Dich nicht betrüben,*
> *Sind gleich die Haare weiss,*
> *Doch wirst du lieben.*

(Oh happy man, thine age need bring no sorrow, white-haired thou still canst know love's sweet to-morrow.)

His house on wheels is furnished with writing pad and pencil, and he notes down his impressions in verse as he goes along; they grow into a booklet, into a book almost, which he divides up into sections. The evenings are spent making fair copies. He looks contentedly on what he has already produced: 'If the poet's mill is turning, do not stop its wheel.' Writing poetry is an '*Übermut*', a feeling of high-spirited abandon. He recalls an old dream he had in Italy: he is sailing towards the coast of an unknown island, the whole boat laden with pheasants, whose shimmering tails hang down over the side, sparkling in the sunlight.

He welcomes everything, down to the dust on the roads, just as he did on his arrival in Italy. A storm breaks and settles the dust, the thunder rolls, the whole sky is lit; a strange mysterious feeling of growth pervades the air as he smells the fresh green after the rain, standing up in his carriage to survey the 'All-Leben' around him. The last poem, written on his arrival in Wiesbaden, brings this first new creative period to a close with the symbol of death in flames:

> *Keine Ferne macht dich schwierig,*
> *Kommst geflogen und gebannt,*

*Und zuletzt, des Lichts begierig,*
*Bist du Schmetterling verbrannt.*

(Aware of neither toil nor distance, as thou fliest on, decoyed, till yielding to
the flame's insistence, butterfly, thou art destroyed.)

Not to know this 'death and re-birth' is to be but 'a mournful guest on this
sombre earth'. It is as a guest that he always sees himself, but at this moment
the earth is not sombre. It is bright and clear and joyous; generally he uses
the word '*heiter*' as a challenge to himself, now it falls easily from his lips.

At Wiesbaden he enjoys a small flirtation with one of his 'little daughters',
does some sketching and goes for walks. The girl runs too quickly up the
terrace of a vineyard. Goethe tries to chase and catch her, and he falls; he is
no longer as agile as he was. A 'Hafiz' has no business running about, he
should sit comfortably on a cushion and be waited on by fair maidens, confining his activities to tousling their hair and feasting his eyes.

At this predetermined moment he is confronted with this very temptation
in the Wiesbaden casino. An old family friend, the banker Willemer, comes
up to speak to him; at his side is a pretty, well-proportioned, curly headed
creature, described in his diary as 'Demoiselle Jung'. In the second entry she
is 'Willemer's little companion'; after that she is already Marianne. She has
become immortalized as Suleika, she herself contributing both to the poetry
and to the love relationship. Of all Goethe's partners she is the only one who,
for a brief moment, reaches his own heights as a poet. The history of
literature shows many examples of productive powers released by association with a genius, of active collaboration, of independent writing of poetry
or fiction, but scarcely another example of a dialogue at the highest poetic
level. It becomes a duet between the two of them; they have the same ideas,
use the same words, speak in the same rhythms. It is kept a secret, a very
personal secret between the two of them. No one else knew of it until long
after Goethe's death, and then it became known only because Marianne, in
her old age, disclosed it to her young friend Herman Grimm, son of the
famous Jakob Grimm. No philologist would have dared to ascribe some of
the finest poems in Goethe's *Divan* to a little former dancer.

Demoiselle Jung was about 30 when Goethe met her. Her position in
Willemer's house was similar to that of Christiane in Goethe's in the early
days, and in her outward appearance she may have reminded the poet of his
*Erotikon*. She was from the Austrian theatre world, but her origins are
obscure; her father is unknown, the date of her birth doubtful, and even the
name of Jung was a stage name taken by her mother, who played minor
roles in the Vienna suburbs. At the turn of the century mother and daughter
appeared in a theatrical company in Frankfurt, the former as one of the
company servants, the latter last but one on the list of stage personnel. She
sang in the chorus and took small male parts such as a kitchen boy or a
dwarf; her greatest moment came in a ballet, *The Birth of Harlequin*, when,

an egg having been passed from hand to hand growing bigger all the time, Marianne finally broke the shell, stepped out and performed a few steps.

It was in these conditions that she was found by Willemer, banker, senator, twice a widower, and financial agent in Frankfurt of the Prussian Government, by whom he was decorated with the title of *Geheimrat* for his services. A busy man, Willemer had numerous literary interests; writing political and educational pamphlets, as well as plays for the Frankfurt theatre. Rich enough to be independent, he paid little attention to the opinion of Frankfurt society, with whom he often found himself in opposition, the clergy taking exception to his free mode of life and to the brilliant suppers he gave for the actors, while his fellow senators had misgivings about his connections with the Prussian government. He quite simply bought Marianne, giving her mother two hundred *gulden* for her, and a small annuity on condition that she returned to her native Austria.

A strangely confused life now began when Willemer took the girl to his country house, the *Gerbermühle*, an old mill on the road from Frankfurt to Offenbach, and introduced her as 'another sister' to his daughters, who were the same age. He gave Marianne a good education, with lessons in French, Italian, Latin, drawing and singing; from time to time she took part in a concert, but otherwise was rarely seen in public. The young poet Clemens Brentano had a short love affair with her, and in his early romances she appears as 'Biondetta', held prisoner in a tower by a wicked sorcerer. After fourteen years Marianne finally consented to marry Willemer and there was a quiet wedding, held at Willemer's house because she was unable to produce a birth certificate, or documents of any kind. Willemer was 54 and Marianne 30, mature, experienced in many of the ways of life, exceptionally highly cultured, and a woman whose heart so far had always been on the defensive. It was at this moment that Goethe met her.

Goethe is in love with love; as we saw, this was true even in his Leipzig days when the real object of his love was never merely a Kätchen, a Lotte, or whoever else it may have been. So here it is Suleika whom he loves, a figure already distinctly formed in his imagination and now conjured up before his eyes in desirable reality. But Marianne is no mere literary phantom, she represents closeness, warmth and comfort, and becomes his willing partner in playing out the love story of a new youth. Goethe contentedly allows himself to be spoiled, and in a subtler, more charming way than ever before. Everything is symbolic in this love story, and Marianne knows how to give to the simplest things of everyday life a deeper, symbolic meaning.

It is in his white woollen dressing-gown, his 'prophet's mantle', that Goethe feels most at ease; in it he can stretch and relax his limbs, which now become stiff when he has to appear at dinner in formal dress. Marianne swathes his head in a turban of the finest muslin, and later makes him a pair of Turkish slippers. They evolve a complete oriental ritual for themselves, with words and expressions they alone understand. *Hudhud*, for instance, which is the Arabic name for the hoopoe. It was a hoopoe that acted as messenger between King Solomon and the Queen of Sheba, and in the Koran it still had the solemn mission of winning another kingdom to the true faith. Soon, however, it became the love messenger of the fairy-tales, and in folk tradition it carried in its beak a magic herb that had the power to discover buried treasure; its feathers, placed on the head, were a cure for headache. Between Goethe and Marianne it flies back and forth causing new heartache, at any rate for one of them.

For Goethe this short episode is only one of many such in his long life, although it stirs him to the very depths of his being. For the woman it is her single great experience: 'Once in my life', she said in after years, 'I was aware of feeling something noble, of being able to say things that were sweet and heartfelt, but time has not so much destroyed as effaced it all'.

Their first meeting, in the summer of 1814, is only fleeting, and Marianne's very recent marriage creates a sense of distance between them. Nor is it only with Hafiz in mind that Goethe has travelled south; there are other contemporary influences at work in him which also have their place in the universality of his nature. He makes an excursion to Bingen, where the chapel of St Rochus, destroyed during the wars, is to be re-consecrated. The traveller in the desert, who calls God Allah and quotes the Koran, here joins a procession of Roman Catholic pilgrims. He has always preferred the more colourful and popular rites of the Roman Catholic church to the austere severity of the Protestant churches and their sermons. Even on the way to the chapel his eye is caught by the Italian pedlar holding his tray of images, not 'the colourless figures of gods and heroes one sees in the north, but brightly painted saints that harmonize with the gay and cheerful landscape'. It is in bright colours, too, that he paints the festival and the rich landscape with its famous vineyards of Hattenheim and Rüdesheim; with the other pilgrims he drinks the good wine from brown stoneware mugs decorated with the name of the patron saint. It is one of the rare occasions when we see Goethe at ease among the people, sitting side by side with them at a long table, discussing the merits of a Hochheimer or a Johannisberger, and deciding that the 1811 is the wine of the century, a fact that Goethe is later to celebrate in a poem. It is also his most reassuring encounter with the times: everyone believes in the recent peace, in reconciliation, in the smoothing out of religious and political differences. On his return to Weimar he has a painting made of the saint, which he presents to the chapel.

Another contemporary trend is also brought to his notice in the course of this rich summer. A young collector and enthusiast, Sulpice Boisserée, attempts to convert the 'determined pagan' and prophet of antiquity to the devout Middle Ages. With his brother and another companion Boisserée had amassed a large collection of paintings by old German and Dutch masters; his family came from Brabant, and a big textile firm in Cologne, founded by his parents, had provided him with the means to do this. A great deal of money was not necessary, because the wars and revolutions had scattered the art treasures, many of which could be picked up literally in the street. The Boisserées obtained one of their most famous pictures by stopping a cart that was carrying it off to a rubbish dump. Another collector found a van Eyck in the fishmarket at Ghent; a fisherwoman was using the oak back of the painting for cleaning her fish. Within a few years the Boisserées had a whole gallery of old masters on the walls of their rooms: to-day it is the pride of the Pinakothek in Munich. They were dilettanti, but in any case there was no serious study of earlier art in those days. They gave their pictures names that have suffered the same fate as their theories of the history of art, one of which was that 'Byzantine' art in Europe lasted until the end of the fourteenth century. They were devout Roman Catholics seeing in medieval art a true piety. Being born into their religion they had a fairly tolerant outlook on questions of faith, and it was because of this that the wise diplomat Reinhard introduced them to Goethe; he knew how intensely Goethe disliked the fervour of converted Catholics. The Boisserées transported their collection to Heidelberg, the centre of Romanticism, where their house became a place of pilgrimage. To this bastion of the new movement, which otherwise he finds so distorted and bizarre, Goethe makes his way from Frankfurt in this relaxed, conciliatory summer and early autumn of 1814.

He has received a very warm and pressing invitation from Sulpice Boisserée, whose first attempt at conversion, during a visit to Weimar some years earlier, had not been a success. At that time Goethe was suspicious, and references to his passionate youthful essay on the Strasbourg Minster and Erwin von Steinbach had left him quite unmoved. He looked upon that outburst as 'idolatry', and if then he had praised the Minster as the embodiment of German power and splendour, he now shook his head over a German patriotism 'that would like to regard this Saracen plant as springing from its own native soil', as he wrote to Reinhard. Nevertheless he was attracted to this heavily built young Belgian, his fleshy face bursting with energy and enthusiasm, whose manner was so serious, whose purpose so whole-hearted. And if any cognizance at all had to be taken of the disagreeable and perverted Romantic Movement, this young man would be the representative of his choice.

And so in the autumn of 1814 Goethe decides to go and see these art treasures in Heidelberg, staying with the Boisserées at their house. The pictures, about two hundred in all, are stacked against the walls of three medium-sized rooms, because there is no room to hang them. One after another the pictures are put on an easel for Goethe to see. His hosts stand round expectantly, waiting for him to be overwhelmed by all this splendour. Goethe is not overwhelmed. He proceeds cautiously, telling them, as Boisserée notes down, that they have introduced him to a new and hitherto unknown world of colour, which has 'forced him' off the old tracks of his artistic viewpoint. 'How very differently artistic life must have flourished in van Eyck's day: now the evil of luxury is devouring everything.' The brothers' hopes are raised when he says of the old masters: 'These fellows were different to us, damn it, so let us praise them and praise them again!' Goethe promises to write something about their collection, and they think they have won him over to the cause. He writes one article, but that is all; in attempting a second he finds himself stuck, unable to go on.

The writer Helmine von Chezy gives the most vivid account of Goethe's impressions:

> For three years now I have been pestered about the pictures here. They come and babble to me about Hemmlink [Memmling] and van Eyck until I see all the colours of the rainbow. The fools come and drive me crazy, and then a man of perception comes and his praises cause me to reflect. Finally Frau von Helwig comes and waxes so poetic in her description that I feel nauseated. I decide that I must see them for myself and put an end to the business; and now here I am. What really pleases me is that all these rascals have failed to see the right things, it is I who have seen them.

The old masters of Germany and Holland are 'before his time'. As soon as he gets back from Heidelberg he immerses himself in his Italian memories, and there he finds 'few mistakes to regret'. He writes sarcastically to Boisserée, agreeing with his 'Byzantine' theory and saying he is now convinced that the 'whole cycle of the Christian Olympus' derives from that source, as indeed it must if one wants to express 'the characteristic difference between the greater and lesser gods'. He stays with his Greek Olympus. Only in some very non-committal lines does he once place 'Hans van Eyck' and Phidias on the same pedestal: 'This is art, this is the world, the charms of each in turn unfurled.'

From his pilgrimages to the old masters and to the Chapel of St Rochus, Goethe returns to the Willemers. Marianne is wearing the 'old German', or neo-Gothic, dress so keenly advocated by her husband in one of his pamphlets; it is the anniversary of the Battle of Leipzig, and the great victory over Napoleon is being celebrated by bonfires on all the hill tops, an idea suggested by Ernst Moritz Arndt. The custom was short-lived, because the German governments regarded this playing with fire as politically dangerous, and it was soon replaced by official military parades; but now, in October 1814, the bonfires flare and flicker. Goethe, with Marianne at his side, watches the 'little lights' animatedly; for him they have a significance other than the patriotic. He enjoys the naturalness of the young woman's conversation, as she points out to him the various hills round Frankfurt – he himself has quite forgotten his native town and its surrounding countryside. He likes her quick intelligence, and as she is not sparing in her criticisms, he calls her his 'little critic'; when she gets a little more insistent in her attacks she becomes his 'little Blücher'. The distant bonfires he can enjoy, but this fire at his side is too hot, it frightens him. He withdraws and leaves for Weimar, promising to return again next year.

Back in Weimar, however, he feels its narrowness, as though he were 'wedged in between walls, flues and chimney stacks'. He longs for the open windows of the *Gerbermühle*, with their view over the broad river. He already has enough verses to make a little book. For Marianne the name of Suleika has been decided on, but for himself he now chooses, instead of Hafiz, the less famous name of Hatem, which can be traced back to two ancient Persian poets, Hatem Thai, he who 'gives everything', and Hatem Zograi, he who 'lives most fully'. Goethe delves eagerly into oriental sources and travel books, in which the name Tamerlane, the great Mongolian conqueror, constantly recurs. With Napoleon in mind he plans to devote a special section to him, a *Buch Timur*. In the end only one poem is completed, because just as he is starting on the work news arrives, in the spring of 1815, that Napoleon has escaped from the island of Elba and landed on the coast of France. The Congress in Vienna has a rude awakening from its round of entertainments, balls and dinners, and from its protracted negotiations which, because of the bitter struggles over the spoils, have nearly resulted in a war between the Allies. The common danger compels the coalition to join forces again. The great war against Napoleon begins afresh.

Goethe travels to the Rhine once more, to Wiesbaden, his carriage repeatedly crossing the marching columns. He continues to deny himself a reunion with Marianne, the 'little Blücher', as the great Blücher presses on ever more impatiently for the decisive encounter with his opponent. Goethe pursues his geological studies with a mining friend, while his keen young servant, Stadelmann, also fishes pebbles out of the river Main and notes down his own and his master's observations on them.

Goethe still continues to avoid Frankfurt. He accompanies his mining friend on one of his official journeys and, in Nassau, meets the great statesman Baron vom Stein. He invites Goethe to travel with him to Cologne, and, when the poet hesitates, simply packs him into his carriage and drives off. The small, gruff Baron, with the powerful nose and granite features, who for a short time was Napoleon's great counterpart in Europe, is now almost at the end of his career. The King of Prussia, who in any case had only granted him a temporary role in his government, wants nothing more to do with his reforms and his plans for a German Empire. The Czar, who had offered Stein asylum when he was outlawed by Napoleon, still retains him as his nominal adviser at the Congress in Vienna; but Alexander is now dedicated to new and mystical plans. The smaller Princes hate Stein, and he returns their hatred with the pride of a former independent Baron of the Empire, who regards himself as equal to them in birth and superior to them in his conceptions. This journey to Cologne is an escape for Stein, too, an escape into the past. He wants to see the Cathedral, the great ruin of a still greater past; there is talk of rebuilding it, as a symbol of the rebuilding of the German Empire. It is a quiet journey. Stein is careful to speak only to the poet in Goethe; he is aware of his strongly differing political views. He even softens the razor edge of his voice and warns his companions, when they complain about Goethe: 'Gently, gently, children, keep away from politics, he does not like it; we cannot exactly commend him for this, but all the same he is too great a man.'

At last, in August, Goethe is at the Willemers again, at the *Gerbermühle* in its setting of tall trees, with the broad river in front of him and Marianne at his side. In the mornings, at ten o'clock, he takes his wine from a silver goblet. For luncheon he dresses formally in his tail coat, wearing his decorations. Although Napoleon is already on his way to St Helena, Goethe still continues to wear his *Légion d'Honneur*, as well as the Russian Order of St Anne, with which he was also decorated at Erfurt, and the Austrian Order of Leopold bestowed on him after Waterloo. In the afternoons he goes for walks and observes the cloud formations, a new and favourite interest. His guide in this study is to be the Quaker, Luke Howard, a quiet persistent man, originally a druggist and to Goethe's great satisfaction no 'priest of the guild'. Goethe later pays tribute to him in some fine poems, and to the classification of clouds described by Howard, still in use to-day; Goethe then adds one class of his own, which has not been adopted by the meteorologists.

In the evenings, dressed in his white 'prophet's mantle', Goethe is completely relaxed and at his ease. Marianne sings his ballad *Gott und die Bajadere*, in which the initiated see an allusion to her own story, to the 'sweet lost child' who, in her dancing days, was probably not much more than a little courtesan. Appositely she sings of how busy she is looking after her visitor, Mahadöh, the God, of the awakening of her love beneath her painted cheeks, of the sudden death of her guest whom, like a loyal widow, she follows with outstretched arms into the fiery death, and who carries her up to his heaven with arms of fire. Goethe is moved and once more takes flight from the flames of this love. Willemer lends him his town apartment in Frankfurt, and now begins Goethe's poetic dialogue with Marianne.

For a short time she now becomes a poet, although it is not her first attempt at writing verse. Goethe begins by turning to the proverb, opportunity makes the thief, and says that Marianne has stolen all the love that remained to him: '*Dass ich nun, verarmt mein Leben, nur von dir gewärtig bin*' (My life impoverished, in thy hands lies my whole expectancy). Marianne answers in the same tone, but gives it a fuller ring; she does not speak of remains and poverty, she is ready to hand over her whole life to him: '*Macht uns nicht die Liebe reich? Halt ich dich in meinen Armen Jedem Glück ist meines gleich*' (Are we not enriched by love? When I hold thee in my arms, no one knows a greater bliss).

Goethe goes once more to the *Gerbermühle*, to say good-bye; he has already made arrangements to go on to Heidelberg. In the evening Marianne sings. Boisserée, who has come to fetch Goethe, is with them and they spend a long time together; Willemer falls asleep in his chair. At one o'clock Goethe goes off to bed, but even now he cannot sleep. He goes out on to the balcony with Boisserée: it is full moon. With the aid of a candle he tries to demonstrate to his young friend 'the phenomenon of coloured shadows'. Marianne watches the two of them from her window.

The next day Goethe leaves for Heidelberg. Marianne follows him, but at first only in verse: '*Was bedeutet die Bewegung? Bringt der Ostwind frohe Kunde?*' (What the meaning of this movement? Brings the east wind news of joy?) Then she follows him in person, with her husband and his daughter. They have two more days together with more walks, another night under a full moon, more poems. Goethe writes the lines: '*Unter Schnee und Nebel-schauer, Rast ein Ätna Dir hervor*' (Amid the snow and mist and rain, an Etna bursts forth at thy feet) in strange contradiction of his lifelong aversion to all volcanic phenomena. There is no stream of molten lava, but Goethe feels a 'threatening ailment', as he puts it in a letter, and then ' I felt an ache in my chest, which might well have gone to my heart', a remark with an intentional double meaning; the letter is addressed to Willemer's daughter, who had already left for Frankfurt. Goethe leaves it to us to decide whether or not this ailment was the 'natural result of the draughty Heidelberg air'. He goes on to speak of the deeper meaning that lurks behind everything the outward senses take in: 'From which I conclude, too hastily perhaps, that one would do best to write something quite incomprehensible, so that friends and fond people would be left entirely free to supply a true meaning. ...'

The two lovers never meet again. It is in the poetry that the lava flows, a whole *Suleika* book comes into existence, the core of his *Divan;* so far as his life is concerned, a quiet, private, cult is established, with the hoopoe, *Hudhud*, to carry messages over long distances. Marianne has the bird carved on the handle of a walking-stick, and sends it to Goethe, secretly hoping that he may use it for another walk by the Main. The poet puts it beside his writing desk, where it remains till he dies.

The journey back had been a disturbed one; Boisserée, who accompanied him, tells of Goethe's unrest, of his feeling ill and wanting to make his will, until eventually he recovered in the carriage. Goethe takes his leave of Willemer in a letter in which he speaks of seeing him again: 'When? How and where? ... And now I hurry home through Würzburg, soothed only in the knowledge that I am following my prescribed path, unforced and un-hindered, and thus can let my longing rest the more purely on those I have left behind.' He adds a request, knowing that some pain and sorrow still remain: 'You, who understand the heart of man, will know how to alleviate this.'

The rest of the correspondence consists of letters written in a complicated cipher, of letters that have been destroyed – and of poetry. The *West-östlicher Divan*, as Goethe now christens the book, is born; for another four years, until the work's publication in 1819, a constant stream of poems is added. But it is only a preliminary version; he continues to write additional poems, or lyrics 'in the style of the *Divan*'.

When she gets her copy of the book, which contains her poems as well, Marianne writes to Goethe:

> If my nature and my inner being have become as clear to you as I hope and wish, indeed as I feel sure they have, since my heart was open to your gaze, no further description is needed, and in any case it would be an extremely unsatisfactory one. You feel and know exactly what went on inside me, I was a riddle to myself; at once humble and proud, ashamed and delighted, the whole thing seemed to me like a blissful dream in which one sees one's portrait embellished, indeed ennobled, and willingly approves of all the lovable, praiseworthy things one says and does in this exalted condition.

For the most part Goethe's contemporaries were disappointed when the book came out, and it was long regarded as a somewhat cold work of his old age. Its oriental garb puzzled rather than attracted readers. Single lines were quoted, but torn from their context. When the secret of their collaboration was discovered, a Marianne cult was added to the many other cults of Goethe's 'loves'. Later the book's oriental content, its German content, the author's mysticism, all became subjects for commentators; it was interpreted as a *Gesamtkunstwerk*, a 'universal mirror', which is what it was intended to be, although only fragments of this all-embracing scheme remained. Goethe's religious belief was discovered in some of the poems and interpreted, each interpreter accusing his predecessors of 'not digging deep enough'. In none of Goethe's works, however, has such surveying, whether upwards, downwards or on the level, so little point as in the *Divan* – Goethe himself often protested at such searching after a 'deeper meaning'. The book forms a rich and colourful carpet. The 'slightest' poems are often the most beautiful, the most fleeting lines the most charming. Even the hastiness in some of the writing has its charm, such as the line he ends with the Anglo-German hybrid, *Kriegesthunder*' because he needs the rhyme, or his inclusion of the names of Cupid and Mars in his Arabian imagery. He wears the oriental mask lightly, in spite of his frequent use of Arabic words that need an explanation; a supplement containing notes and digressions is appended, but it succeeds only in creating new difficulties, adding new beauties, or providing a bare list of chapter headings of some book he has read.

The book is not the 'universal mirror' it was intended to be; it is a Goethe mirror and this, in itself, is a world. The work's unity does not lie in its composition; 'the poet looks upon himself as a traveller', says Goethe in announcing its publication. It is a lyric travel book, and the author does not only pitch his tent among the Bedouin; he travels back to his youth, to the poppy fields at Erfurt, to the Rhine and the Main, and then to the houris in Mohammed's paradise who, in turn speak in the metre of Hans Sachs, as he says with a smile. The unity of the work lies in its language, which extends from this coarse old German doggerel style to the most ethereal flights, in which he explores regions almost beyond the reach of words. Goethe does not entrust his words to paper, or to leaves of oriental silk, he entrusts them to dust, as he says in one of the later poems, with the wisdom of old age. It is in the dust that they are inscribed, where the wind passes over them and they are gone. 'But the power remains, tied spellbound to the soil, reaching to the centre of the earth'; the wanderer, the lover will come and on finding the place his limbs will feel the shock of this power: 'Here before me loved the lover ... I love as he loved, feeling him!'

And thus, amidst all the dust that has fallen on this book, we can feel Goethe's heart beating for those who love. It is a restless heart, often confused, always in danger of losing itself, and always held in check by supreme artistic understanding, or by his own impenetrable faith, which comprises all the symbols of East and West from Islam, denoting 'surrender', to sturdy Frankish folk-lore. Even now, following this greatest of the creations of his old age, it finds no rest.

# 40

# *The Wanderer in Weimar*

THE journey to the East and to the river Main was Goethe's last considerable undertaking. In the summer of 1816, a year after his parting from
Marianne, he decides to make one further attempt to see her, and he sets
out with Meyer, but the carriage comes to grief on the still appallingly
neglected Weimar roads; Meyer is cut about the head, and they turn
back.

Goethe is an old man now. The biblical reckoning of threescore years
and ten for ordinary mortals still holds good in Goethe's day; it is only
patriarchs who are permitted an almost indefinite span. But it is precisely
as one of these that Goethe thinks of himself. He never wants to hear of
death, let alone meet it face to face, and when one of his friends does, even
so old and trusted a friend as his ministerial colleague Voigt, Goethe's
steadfast confidant in all the affairs of government, he shuns a final meeting
with cruel and solemn determination. Voigt sends a note across, begging
him: 'Ah, dear Goethe, let us be close to one another', and 'perhaps to-
morrow then', but Goethe hesitates with his answer. Then he writes excusing
himself: 'When those dearest to us prepare to leave on a journey we oppose
the idea. Should we not also set ourselves against it in the most serious
case? Permit me then my fondest hope....'

Goethe's loneliness is of his own making. It is allied to his complaints
that people leave him alone. On one occasion he makes the almost desperate
suggestion to his friend Müller that social gatherings should be organized
in his house during the winter to 'stimulate me and cheer me up'. 'Each
guest could come and stay as long as he liked and would be free to bring
guests of his own. The rooms would be open and lit from seven o'clock
onwards, with ample tea and refreshments. People could make music, play
cards, talk, or read aloud as they felt inclined. I would come and go as
the spirit moved me.... Help me, I beg of you, to put these preliminary
ideas into practice!' There is something touching about this desire of
Goethe's, but he overlooks the fact that such gatherings cannot very well
succeed without a hostess, and that the coming and going of an Olympian
figure, who simply vanishes when the spirit moves him, would scarcely
be likely to help matters. His son is married now, it is true, and he has a

daughter-in-law in the house, but it is useless for him to look to her; she might easily leave in the middle and go off to the theatre, or to some other party, as in fact she does. Goethe is not surrounded by family life in his old age; nor has he been at any age.

August's marriage was arranged by Goethe, but his attempt to order his son's marriage turned out no more happily than did his earlier attempt to educate him. The boy's 'indolent sensuality' had long been a trial to him, as he admitted himself, both because of his excessive drinking and because of his wretched affair with a soldier's wife, who boasted of the relationship all over the town and took the money home to her hussar. Goethe had obtained the position of 'assessor' for August and had persuaded the Duke to grant him the title *Kammerrat*, but apart from subordinate appointments on various government committees, his principal occupation was as steward and secretary to the Goethe household. During the war his father had forbidden him to join the Weimar volunteers, as a result of which August became involved in some unpleasant incidents. A challenge to a duel was hushed up through Goethe's influence, and this did further damage to August's reputation. In the imposing but prematurely stout figure of August Weimar society saw only the 'son of that Vulpius woman', and was able to note with satisfaction that such an association had produced such an offspring. Goethe felt that marriage to a lady of suitable standing would help to improve August's position. The marriage was not solemnized until after many obstacles had been overcome, including long-drawn-out and unpleasant financial negotiations with the girl's family.

The bride Goethe selected for August was a creature of the most varied and changing hues; she would not have made a success of any marriage, let alone of one under the irregular conditions of the Goethe household. Ottilie von Pogwisch had a very entangled family background. Her mother, daughter of a Countess Henckel von Donnersmarck, had married a poor Prussian army officer, whom she divorced because they could not afford to live 'as befitted their rank'. She then became a lady-in-waiting in Weimar, where her mother held the position of Mistress of the Robes; a prolonged affair with one of the gentlemen-in-waiting, who eventually made a better match for himself, formed the background of her rather wretched life in Weimar. The Henckels were poor, the Pogwisches even poorer, and the Court appointments in Weimar were poorly paid. Ottilie and her sister lived in an attic room somewhere in the castle, and later with their grandmother, taking their meals with various Court officials who had pity on the neglected girls; contact with their mother seldom went beyond listening to her tales of woe. Ottilie had a father complex, as we should say to-day: the picture of the vanished Prussian hero was always before her eyes; during the war years she was a zealous patriot, and for a while she lost her heart to a Prussian officer, who had remained for some time in Weimar. Ottilie was a small, dainty person, with restless blue eyes, beautiful hair, a loose mouth and a ready tongue. She sang, drew a little, was sentimental, and shrewd beyond her years. The clumsy and pedantic August, who worshipped and fought her in turns, could mean little to her. In Goethe she found her father hero again. It was his courting that decided the marriage. Her Countess grandmother, very proud of her noble lineage, insisted that the wedding must wait until the death of 'Mamsell Vulpius', otherwise she had no objections; *Kammerrat* August seemed a good match, the Goethes were rich and, after all, had a title, even though it was of very recent origin.

In his letters to Goethe, Zelter paints, though somewhat prematurely, the rosiest picture of the life that is now about to begin for him. He speaks of the 'able August' and of the girl 'who is loved and acclaimed by town and country'. Then, he goes on, 'the young wife comes and strokes the old gentleman's beard, and scratches behind his ears, and makes herself scarce at the right moment, and tastes his soup, and pries into the corners and picks up the specks of dust with her fingers'. Nothing of the kind ever happens. The young wife has no idea whatever of keeping house and no intention of picking up specks of dust; the large house, with its numerous servants, gets dustier and dustier, so that Goethe himself has to complain when his servant brings the portfolios of engravings. Ottilie dispenses money with both hands, either on silly trinkets or because she does not know how to use it. In the early days of the marriage Goethe enjoys the new feeling of cheerfulness that pervades the house. Ottilie's sister Ulrike soon joins them, as Christiane's step-sister had done before her. Goethe likes Ottilie's readiness to learn; she is good at languages, being especially keen on English, and is an admirer of Byron and of his young English followers who come to stay in the now famous Weimar. She likes the theatre and looking at Goethe's engravings and other collections. She also writes poetry a little, such as these two lines on her relationship with August: 'Two flames that never merged in one, two rings that never formed a circlet.' The marriage, ill-conceived from the beginning, very soon goes to pieces. There are two sons, whom Goethe lives to enjoy as lively boys, but whose later development he is fortunately spared; after an interval of ten years a daughter, Alma, is born. But the two parents go their own ways, Ottilie not merely going but almost charging into one affair after another, with great anguish and emotion, and even offering herself indiscriminately to the various young visitors who come to the house. After Goethe's death her later life became a constant journey from one lover to the next; in Vienna, far from Weimar where life had become impossible for her, she found a small circle of friends but by then she had exhausted her capital, financial as well as emotional, and had even mortgaged her son's inheritance. She was forced to return to Weimar, to the old house on the Frauenplan, now covered in dust and in bad repair, where she died in her old attic room. The two sons – the daughter had died young – came to even sadder ends: morbidly shy, friendless, unsociable, unmarried, barren in every respect, they refused the house in Weimar to every visitor and died, far from home, on a journey that was like an escape from a heritage they were unable to bear. With their deaths the Goethe family came to an end; one of them once described himself as a 'remnant of the house of Tantalus'. It is a dark heritage, this Goethe heritage, with Goethe's father's elder brother an imbecile, his own sister unhappy and ill-fated, his other brothers and sister incapable of survival, as were four of his own children, his surviving son weighed down by this hereditary burden, and his grand-children's lives consumed by nervous crises or fading out in a sunless twilight. And in Goethe himself, in whom the whole strain bursts forth, as it were, in a single huge and over-brilliant flower, there are many dark streaks. He, too, has a constant fight against severe hypochondriac crises, he, too, has his periods of brooding and drifting, which he transforms into the restless activity of collecting, classifying his material, and supervising his archives; nor was all this confined to his later years. To overlook these traits is to underestimate the great achievement of his life's work.

The restless Ottilie, who is not worthless but who is utterly lacking in stability, is Goethe's choice as a support for his closing years. It is as though a single element in his nature had sprung to life in her, growing wild and rank, whereas his own sensuality is only one of the many sides that form and round off the whole man. Looking at her he could have been looking into a distorting mirror, but he prefers to close his eyes, only blinking good-humouredly or complaining when his 'little daughter' neglects him too obviously. In his son others of his own characteristics are dangerously distorted and developed, but here too he prefers to welcome his taste for pedantry and officialdom, and for leading a free life.

After the war years Goethe lives in greater style than ever before. Weimar has also grown, the town as well as the country; at the Congress of Vienna it had become the Grand Duchy of Sachsen-Weimar. Karl August, it is true, had not been able to lay claim to any great distinction there. He had been a Prussian commander during the 1806 catastrophe, then he had been a member of the *Rheinbund* and a French general, a rank he continued to hold even after Moscow. The Duke had only been persuaded to enter Russian service by a Cossack colonel who, arriving with the first Russian cavalry detachment, had brought news of the victory of Leipzig; Goethe disapproved strongly of this over-hasty decision. But the other Princes of the *Rheinbund* did the same and the King of Saxony, the only one of the kings created by Napoleon to remain loyal to his Emperor, had to pay dearly for his loyalty, losing half his country to Prussia. Nor did Karl August shine in Vienna through his social graces, and these were of great importance in the glittering life of the Congress; on the contrary his un-polished behaviour earned him the nickname of the 'eternal student'. At his side, however, he had a very able minister in Gersdorff, and, most important of all, he held a trump card in the dynastic game: his son and heir was married to a Russian Grand Duchess. And so he became the Grand Duke Karl August, his country was almost doubled in size, and he could now call himself 'His Royal Highness'; from Frankfurt Goethe sent his solemn congratulations, saying he looked forward to seeing *Höchstdieselben* again soon. There was a solemnization ceremony, at which Goethe, as the oldest servant of the Grand Duke, stood next the throne, that now replaced the modest chair of former days. The Order of the White Falcon was created, and the star of the Grand Cross pinned on Goethe's breast; in 1901 the Grand Duke of Weimar could still say, from his own childhood memories, 'it suited him well'. A formal Ministry was now established, replacing the old *Conseil,* and Goethe bore the official title *Staatsminister*, previously used only unofficially in speaking. Karl August entrusted to him the 'supervision of the institutes of science and art' and, not least, granted him an increased salary. And to complete the list of these official honours – by no means unimportant to him – Goethe was permitted to retain and wear his beloved *Légion d'Honneur*. King Louis XVIII, who as Comte de Provence had been with Goethe in the campaign of 1792, had decided to retain the decoration out of respect for the many veterans of the great battles; he was not quite so simple-minded as the Napoleonic legend would have liked to paint him. He had also decided, with considerable tact, that Napoleon's portrait on the medal should be replaced by that of Henri IV, and not by his own. Goethe wrote to his old friend Reinhard, now chief of chancellery under the Bourbons, and received the welcome news of the revival of the order. He did not content himself with this, however, and asked Reinhard whether it would be possible to take this opportunity of converting his 'silver Henri' into a 'golden Henri', the next class in the order. This metamorphosis, too, was successfully achieved and he received his golden Henri. He was careful to enquire of Reinhard as to the proper form in which to convey his thanks to the Chancellor of the Order and the French Prime Minister. We saw how seriously Goethe took such matters of form, even at the age of thirty; it was part of his sense of order.

The question also arises now of putting his papers in order for, despite all his posts and decorations, Goethe is after all really a writer, *eigentlich doch ein Schriftsteller,* as he noted in his diary in his active ministerial days. And in his true profession, after half a lifetime of very disappointing financial results, he is now extremely successful, thanks in the first instance to his connection with Cotta, his eminently capable publisher, now also the possessor of a title, that of Freiherr von Cottendorf. The *Westöstlicher Divan,* the only one of Goethe's books that Cotta published with any degree of style and taste, has remained largely unsold, but the Collected Editions are in great demand, the constant reprints increasing from twelve to twenty and then to twenty-six volumes; these, poorly printed and containing many mistakes, are printed in double issues with further mistakes and corrections. Goethe's fees are the highest ever paid to a German author up to this time: 10,000 *thalers* for the first and 16,000 for the second Collected Editions, and 2,000 for each of the volumes of his memoirs; he keeps a strict reckoning and August, competent in this capacity, acts as his accountant. Goethe does not intend to allow his hard-earned income to be depleted by heavy taxes, so he writes a detailed memorandum to the authorities pointing out that he has now become a 'public person', the recipient of a very large number of letters from every quarter, which he has to answer at the cost of much time and money. Consequently 'it will not be taken amiss if I flatter myself in the hope of receiving some relief from the State to the modest extent requested'. His request is granted. The taxes paid by Goethe on his annual income of seven, eight or even ten thousand *thalers* amount to one hundred and fifty *thalers*. In his native Frankfurt the authorities are merchants and treat him less generously. To his great annoyance he has to pay heavy taxes on the income he receives from the remaining mortgages inherited under the estate of his grandfather the tailor. Because of this he petitions for release from his bond of citizenship; his petition is granted immediately. On his last visit the Frankfurt paper *Oberpostamtzeitung* had hailed him as 'the last surviving great hero of German literature'; now there is only a short entry in the margin of the old city burgess-roll, mentioning the fact that the *Geheimrat* has 'settled his affairs with the worshipful Incomes Commission'. By this act 'the name of the said *Geheim Raht* was erased from the Roll of Burgesses. Thirty *kreuzer* were charged as fee.' A firm stroke of the pen through the old entry of 1771 completes the formalities, under the date March 2, 1818.

This is the outer framework of his life. As regards Goethe's inner feelings, there is a significant sentence in the draft of a letter to Wilhelm Grimm, who had approached him regarding a project for a cultural union of all German territories. In this Goethe says he has 'always been a restless, homeless wanderer, never settling anywhere'; the sentence was omitted, however, in the letter as sent to Grimm.

It is as a wanderer that he makes his way through the Weimar landscape, now considerably changed since the day he first arrived, when the town gate had to be opened and his carriage inspected before he was allowed to proceed. There is no inspection any more, the walls have been opened up, and parks, which Goethe helped to design, have been laid out everywhere.

Weimar has grown into a cultural centre and the inns, improved now, house visitors from England, America, Poland and Russia. The wealthy Russian Crown Princess has brought a certain opulence to the little country that was formerly so poor; the Castle, which in Goethe's early years was a burnt-out ruin, has been gradually rebuilt. The town has nearly ten thousand inhabitants.

The main attraction for the visitors is not the Prince who, even as a Grand Duke, can play only a very modest role and has to feel his way among the greater powers. In these post-war years he soon makes himself unpopular in Vienna, Berlin and St Petersburg because his native honesty prevents him quite forgetting the promises made to the people during the patriotic 'rising'. He grants his country a constitution, he permits freedom of the press, in fact he does all the things that his *Staatsminister* Goethe dislikes or openly disapproves.

It is the Goethe shrine, the Goethe residence, that is the chief attraction for the visitors. When they have climbed the wide stair-case, flanked with casts of antique sculptures, they are received in audience. Standing there in his long dark coat, which conceals the shortness of his legs, and with his hands behind his back, Goethe has something of the air of a piece of statuary himself. They feel themselves in the presence of the unapproachable. On taking leave he sometimes holds out his hand, but only when a visitor has awakened his sympathy. This does not happen often; why should he feel any sympathy with the merely curious, with these visitors who come to see only their pre-conceived idea of the Olympian 'Jupiter'? They rarely bring anything – as Riemer pointed out was necessary – they merely want to take something away, something for their album, some words of wisdom. Goethe develops his own technique for getting the people to talk, so that at least he can find out something, though preferably nothing about literature or art. The Bavarian, Lang, describes one of these audiences in which he is received by the 'old, ice-cold Imperial City Syndic' who, after a long silence, finally asks him: 'Tell me, you must have a fire insurance company in your Ansbach district, have you not?' He wants to know the procedure when there is a serious outbreak of fire in one of the villages: 'We shall permit, if we may, the place to burn completely to the ground!' Lang, who, besides being a witty chronicler, is a senior official of the district, lets the fire rage: the next day the damage is assessed, plans for rebuilding the village are drawn up, and the report and plans are sent to Munich, where they lie around for a long time; all of which is familiar, and of great interest, to Goethe. 'I thank you,' he says when Lang has finished. The only other thing Goethe wants to know is the population of the district of Ansbach. 'A little over 500,000,' is the answer. 'Well, well,' mutters Goethe under his breath, as this is almost twice the size even of the new Grand Duchy of Weimar. 'Hm, hm, that is quite a figure.'

There are still a great many outbreaks of fire in the Grand Duchy, although most of the houses now have tiled roofs. There are fires in Jena, too, in the heads of the students. On his victorious entry into Berlin in 1815, King Friedrich Wilhelm III of Prussia had turned angrily to his minister Schuckmann: 'Who has dared to illuminate my own buildings, my arsenal even, without my permission?' and it was only with difficulty that he was restrained from ordering the lights to be extinguished. The custom of lighting bonfires on the hills to commemorate the Battle of Leipzig had soon been brought to an end, but the fires continue to smoulder in the minds of the younger generation. Although some have more revolutionary ideas, their demands, for the most part, are modest enough; 'constitution' is the great watchword. Students form the spearhead of the movement, and Jena is their rallying point. As 'supervisor' Goethe has to deal with these matters and he does so in his own highly personal way, warning the students against their activities and at the same time being secretly pleased when the young people show their mettle.

Secret societies and conspiracies he does not favour. The secret societies he envisaged in his epic poem *Die Geheimnisse,* and in *Wilhelm Meister,* were associations of superior beings, men of wisdom and maturity. Government, in his view, should be left to those who are qualified for it and understand it. And freedom of the press? Of this he is extremely doubtful; he feels it might easily degenerate into intolerance of those who think differently. He is by no means opposed to censorship, and when his direction of the Weimar theatre was under criticism, he introduced his own supervision of the press. On the other hand he is quite ready to respect opposition, if it is sufficiently apparent and forceful. 'If I had the misfortune to find myself among the opposition', he says, 'I would rather stir up revolt and revolution than spend my days in the depressing atmosphere of eternal criticism.' Mere carping criticism irritates him; moreover, one must not forget that he is still under the spell of 'enlightened absolutism'. Intelligent, satirical, witty opposition on the lines of the French Encyclopaedists he is prepared to accept, even considering it beneficial in enabling one to acquire the ability and the mental weapons to defend oneself in battle.

Of such weapons he sees little sign among the younger generation. With them *Turnerei,* gymnastics, is all the rage. It is a new form of gymnastics, with apparatus such as parallel and horizontal bars, invented by *Turnvater* Jahn, who has grown a long Teutonic beard and wants to introduce a new old-Germanic language of his own. A *Turnplatz* is set up in Jena, the gymnasts wear clothes made of unbleached linen and address each other as *Du*; one of the unbleached youths even addresses His Excellency von Goethe as *Du,* a pleasantry that is very ill received. Nevertheless from time to time Goethe enjoys watching the agile and graceful movements of the young athletes, regretting that his old body prevents him taking part. In the manner of long ago he says: 'Alas one is not young enough to take this opportunity of snatching a sweet kiss.'

This was not the way of the gymnasts and students. They advocated rough manners, virtue and chastity; their leaders had been recruited from the *Tugendbund,* the League of Virtue, of the war years. Many of these were the leaders of the students' movements, and some very radical, calling themselves *die Unbedingten,* those who were not prepared to make any concessions. There was a great deal of singing, and one of the students declared: 'Give me a good gymnasts' song and you can have the whole of Fouqué and Goethe.' Another student wrote a gymnasts' chorus with the lines: 'The tyrant's head hacked off! The knife of freedom drawn! Hurrah for the dagger that slits the throat!'

The students want the fires lit again on the hilltops, and in October 1817 they decide on a great demonstration to celebrate the three hundredth anniversary of the Reformation. The scene of the celebration is to be the Wartburg at Eisenach, where Luther had fought with the devil, and from Jena the students, joined by many delegations from all over Germany, make their way up to the old castle. Goethe advises against the demonstration, Karl August gives his consent. In fact it proves to be a very orderly affair, recognized by the authorities and with the Jena professors and other officials taking part in the procession. A veteran of the wars, with the Iron Cross pinned to his breast, gives the address; prayers and the singing of a Hymn of Praise conclude the ceremony. One of those taking part records that afterwards, in the Knights' Hall of the Wartburg, 'friendships were formed, sealed by kisses and solemn oaths, and compacts made that were to last till the end of time. There was much talk and discussion as to what should be done in honour and praise of the German nation.' There is a toast to Karl August: 'Our Duke, we hail Thee in Thy land, Thou gavs't Thy word, Thy word did stand; the constitution – this alone can shield the people and the throne.'

No fire is lit until the evening, when they light one to commemorate the Battle of Leipzig. Recalling Luther's burning of the bull of excommunication they also throw writings by well-known reactionaries into the flames, such as Haller's *Restoration of Political Science*, pamphlets by the hated Schmalz in Berlin, who denounces all students' associations, and books by the German playwright and Russian Councillor of State Kotzebue, who sends secret reports to Russia. They add a corporal's stick and a corset – an allusion to the corsets of Prussian guards officers – with the lines: 'Behold the Uhlan hero-knight, enveloped in his corset tight; it keeps the good man's heart at ease, which else might sink down to his knees.'

It is more like a students' rag than a revolution and, at first, Goethe takes it all with easy good-humour. Kotzebue's intrigues have given him a lot of trouble, however indispensable he may be to the Weimar theatre, where almost a third of the plays are his. He is pleased at this busy-body being given a lesson; he writes a poem in praise of the young men who came from far and wide to throw his books into the fire: 'St Peter, too, is pleased about the flames.' The governments in Berlin, Vienna and St Petersburg are not pleased. They see the Wartburg fire as a revolutionary beacon. The Prussian Chancellor arrives in Weimar, as well as an envoy from Vienna. The tiny country, so recently elevated to the status of a Grand Duchy by the great powers, suddenly finds itself a political focal-point and extremely unpopular. Even Karl August's new-won title is in danger. Goethe tries to think of some sedative for his 'dear little hot-heads' – he has no idea what is happening.

The theology student Sand travels to Mannheim, where Kotzebue edits his magazine, writes his special reports for the Russian Government, and has just finished a comedy, *The Straight and Narrow Path is the Best* – the last of his more than three hundred plays. To the younger generation he is an intriguer and informer, one of the chief agents of reaction. Sand, who takes literally the line, 'The knife of freedom drawn', kills him with his dagger.

It was an act of insanity, a godsend to the forces of reaction. The governments of the great powers now had a pretext for decisive action. They banned the students' associations, and placed the universities and press under strict control; their ministers met in the pleasant surroundings of Karlsbad and worked out their plans in an atmosphere of convivial dinner parties. The 'Karlsbad Resolutions', as they were called, provided for a central office of investigation to combat 'demagogic machinations'; spying and informing on a huge scale resulted, arrests followed. Many of Goethe's 'little hot-heads' went to prison, often for years, to think over their reckless plans for a constitution; many were forced to go abroad, to Switzerland, England or America. The period of Russian dominance over Prussia had begun. In the same year as the Wartburg demonstration the Czar had discovered a secret society in his own country; known as the 'Society of the True Sons of the Fatherland' it demanded a constitution, a *duma*, or diet, spread other similar and monstrous revolutionary ideas, and was ruthlessly suppressed. Prussia, with its close ties, followed Russia's example; and for decades followed its every nod; its *élite* guards regiments carried the Czar's name on their shoulder straps and their bands played the *Alexander March*; in Potsdam a Russian colony sprang up with Russian log houses built in the old Russian style. In the rest of Germany the 'era of Metternich' began, the era of the grand seigneur from the Rhineland, the Austrian Prime Minister, who, with his slender elegant hands and his many unofficial ambassadresses at the various Courts, directed central European politics. Metternich was another of the great figures Goethe met at Karlsbad, a 'gracious lord' as he called him.

There is no gracious treatment for Weimar, which is virtually placed under supervision by the great powers. As a first warning Prussia, Austria and Russia forbid their nationals to study at Jena University. Karl August, no demon but a decent, honest man, receives one instruction after another with which he has to comply. He is forced to suppress newspapers and magazines, such as Professor Luden's *Nemesis*, the *Oppositionsblatt*, and others. He has to appoint a 'curator' for the university and wants Goethe to take the post. Goethe refuses, and withdraws once more to devote himself exclusively to his own work.

Political papers are banned, but no one has any objection to the great poet and sage producing his own newspapers. As a vehicle for his rich store of notes, aphorisms and ideas he starts a private journal called *Zur Naturwissenschaft* (Contributions to Natural Science) with copperplates, poems, epigrams, and with the significant sub-title: 'Experiences, teachings and conclusions, knit together by the events of a lifetime.' Another publication, *Kunst und Alterthum*, is devoted to art, topography and archaeology; Meyer is his chief collaborator in this magazine, which carried on until Goethe's death. Goethe becomes the editor and administrator of his own legacy; to his young admirer Schubarth who is planning a work on Goethe, he writes: 'Persevere in the study of my legacy.' He finds it very gratifying that young people should study the unfolding and development of his life, because this is the best means for them to cultivate their minds. He regards this development as symbolic.

Goethe's dissatisfaction over his own attempts to collect and sift his literary legacy breaks out occasionally. Writing to Boisserée he says: 'I will not deny, and why should one boast, that I am in a state bordering on despair, as a result of which, in seeking a diversion, I have adopted the most utterly wrong means, and for the simple reason that for the time being I could see no prospect of producing anything.' Thus he looks through his old papers and notes, 'where, along with some pleasant surprises and things that may be useful, there is also a mass of ore to be smelted, which would need a fearful amount of fire and forging to extract the small quantity of metal it contains'. The fire is lacking, the forging not attempted. So he does his editing 'as well as I can', as he writes to his friend. He edits his *Italienische Reise*, using old letters cut up into small strips, on which he writes in pencil 'done with'; he edits his *Campagne in Frankreich* from old diaries, and finally he dictates the two volumes of his *Annalen*, the dry, year by year annals of his life. Scattered among these last are entries of great value and interest, but they contain no mention of the most important events and people in his life; the word 'important' recurs constantly however, being applied to such things as a distant relative's marriage or the appointment of a new librarian. Only a few episodes maintain a certain interest, the longest of these being a somewhat picaresque account of his visit to a Professor Beireis at the University of Helmstedt. Beireis was like a caricature of Faust. Doctor of all the faculties, as his visiting card proclaimed, and known for his secret and marvellous cures for illness, he was also the inventor of artificial substitutes for the costly carmine and indigo dyes, from which he made a fortune; this fortune he used to buy paintings, and the walls of his bedroom were lined with dozens of genuine or faked Raphaels, Titians, Dürers and Correggios. He also invented ingenious *automata*, like the duck which ate and digested its food, although when demonstrated to visitors it usually suffered from indigestion. Beireis was the possessor of a fabulous diamond, the size of a goose's egg, which he produced like a conjuring trick from his trousers pocket; Goethe, examining it carefully at the window, decided it was a fine piece of quartz. The demoniac old man entertained Goethe and his party of ladies to a meal of giant crayfish served off Chinese porcelain, keeping up a constant stream of pleasantries throughout, addressing 'the mothers as though once upon a time they had had tender feelings towards him, and their daughters as though he were about to offer them his hand there and then'.

This is not very different from the way Goethe behaved during his visits to the Bohemian spas; in the winter he used to feel he was buried in a 'badger's burrow'. This is when he had his attacks of hypochondria, and completely lost interest in everything: 'Man is a strange being! Since I have known how the world goes round, nothing interests me any more. The good Lord could certainly put us in a quandary if he were to reveal to us all the secrets of nature; we should not know what to do with ourselves for lack of interest and boredom.'

He becomes more and more of a mystic, writing a poem *Orphische Urworte*, in which he translates the Orphic doctrines of the Greeks into his own mythology. 'Demon' is man's native indestructible individuality, transformed by 'Tyche', chance and fate, tormented by 'Eros' with escape and recurrence, compelled by 'Ananke' to obey the law, and finally liberated by 'Hope': '*Ihr kennt sie wohl, sie schwärmt durch alle Zonen, Ein Flügelschlag, und hinter uns Äonen!*' (You know of her, she roams through all infinity, a single wing-beat, and behind us lies eternity).

He includes the poem in his periodical *Zur Naturwissenschaft*, which is intended to supplement his memoirs by presenting Goethe the thinker, the naturalist, the natural philosopher. His original plan was to express his ideas in the form of aphorisms, like one of the Greek sages, and often – fortunately very often – they have survived in this form. Here we find many of the ideas that have exercised the greatest influence on posterity; his concept of *Gestalt*, for example, which has so deeply influenced modern Gestalt theory. The scientists have adopted his 'morphology' and developed it, and in the heyday of Darwinism Goethe was hailed as a forerunner; subsequently Monism claimed him, and there have been many later stages of development. Goethe also battles with the insoluble problem of the *Ur*-phenomenon, which gives him no peace; ultimately he has to accept resignation, confining himself to enigmatic statements. The theory of 'higher' and 'lower' states of the soul he refuses to accept; the terms higher and lower, he maintains, can no more be applied to the human spirit than they can to the universe, everything being connected with equal right to a common centre, which manifests its hidden existence through the harmonious relationship of all the parts to this centre.

But there are times when, instead of this harmony, Goethe feels himself growing increasingly inflexible and cold, and he fights against it. He does not want to rest, he always wants to feel renewed wonder and astonishment; '*zum Erstaunen bin ich da!*' (to marvel I am here). This is, perhaps, the finest side of his character, here he is eternally young and flexible: '*und umzuschaffen des Geschaffne, damit sichs nicht zum Starren waffne, Wirkt ewiges lebendiges Tun*' (anew to re-create creation, and thus resist its numbed stagnation, is living's ever-active role).

Writing in his morphological essays of bark and skin, of the outer husks that die and grow again, he speaks of 'skins, eternally detaching themselves and being cast off, abandoned to lifelessness, behind which new skins continually form, beneath which again, nearer or further from the surface, life brings forth its creative image'.

# 41

# *Trilogy of Passion*

For Goethe the year 1823 begins with a severe attack of pericarditis, his first serious illness for twenty years. He feels lost, and scoffs at the doctors: 'You can try all your tricks but you will not save me!' Then mystically he says: 'For three thousand years I have suffered under such a weight of illness. ...' In the intervals he exults in the acuteness of his sense of taste, which has detected a slight trace of anise in his medicine. He learns with satisfaction that he is to be given arnica, and immediately proceeds to deliver a lecture on the flower, of which he had found splendid specimens in great profusion in Bohemia.

He recovers, but questions whether his torn and tortured body will ever be restored as 'a new unity'. Soon he is able to get about in the garden. Mentally he is more vigorous than before, and says he has to restrain rather than drive himself. Physically, too, he feels better than before his illness, an illness he has been unable to prevent, although very well aware of its approach.

His recovery is celebrated by a special performance of his *Tasso*, at which his bust in the theatre is garlanded with a laurel wreath. Throughout Germany there is widespread emotion that he has been spared, and people think he may be ready to undergo some measure of heart-searching and reformation. His youthful sweetheart, Auguste Stolberg, whom he has never seen and who is now white-haired and the widow of Count Bernstorff, the Danish Minister, writes him a moving letter recalling 'the Songs of Old Times', as she says in an English allusion to his letter-lyrics of forty years earlier. She begs him to renounce the vanity of the world and to turn his gaze towards the eternal. She has often noticed questionable things in his writings, 'with which you so easily cause hurt to others – Oh, make amends while there is yet time!' She prays for him.

Goethe answers her in an equally fine letter. Of family matters, about which she has asked him to write, he does not wish to speak. 'Allow me to remain in the realm of the general ... to live long means to survive much, people, loved, hated or indifferent to us, kingdoms, capitals, even forests and trees that we planted when we were young. We survive ourselves, and feel grateful indeed if some even of the gifts of the body and mind are left to us.' To her attempt at converting him he replies that he has always had honest intentions and directed his gaze 'toward the highest', and therefore he is not concerned for the future; in our Father's house are many mansions and perhaps one day it will be possible to meet face to face in the life to come, and love one another. 'May all be re-united in the arms of the all-loving Father. ...'

All attempts, by others as well, to win or claim Goethe for a particular faith remain unavailing. In his youth he listens to the pietists, to Lavater he describes himself as a 'decided non-Christian', and in his essay on Winckelmann, more outspokenly, as a 'pagan'. He has always continued to write blasphemous verses and in conversation his blasphemies sometimes go so far that those to whom he is talking do not dare put them on paper. He speaks of *Gott-Natur*, of the gods, of the 'Christian Olympus'. He treats Roman Catholic saints like Filippo Neri or Rochus with respect and sympathy. He praises Luther, while at other times he reviles him. When the question of protesting arises he becomes a Protestant – he is a Protestant in science and art. Thus in 1817, the jubilee year of the Reformation, he protests vehemently in the name of the *W.K.F.*, the *Weimarer Kunstfreunde*, against the modern German religious tendencies of the young painters, who want to dedicate themselves to a devout and cloistered life in Rome, forming a fraternity and turning their backs on all that is frivolous. In this same Jubilee year he even tries to write a Reformation *cantata*; but as he is still living in the oriental world of his *Divan*, he falls to trifling and, in the opening song, Shulamith sings of her love for Solomon 'by night and day', in the style of Suleika. This was scarcely the appropriate text for an audience of strict churchmen in long black gowns who were gathered to hear of Martin Luther the great Reformer, the founder and model of true German family life. And so the work remained a fragment.

On the subject of family life Goethe is not in a position to speak, either to Auguste Stolberg or to an audience such as this; in his own household he is surrounded by darkness and confusion. Even during his recent severe illness the constant round of hectic amusement in the attic rooms over his head scarcely abated. Goethe himself had told August and Ottilie not to let themselves be put out, and to continue going to Court and the theatre as usual. To Müller he expressed the opinion that Ottilie's life was empty and hollow, without passion, inclination or real interest, and having as its only motive a craze for excitement. He also mentioned the fact that he could not stand Weimar any longer and thought of going elsewhere, perhaps to Frankfurt where, as he was aware, a welcome awaited him. Even the German newspapers spoke of his intention to leave Weimar.

He hopes a visit to a spa will do him good and provide him with recreation and more cheerful faces. In Bohemia, too, he will have his beloved granite; contact with this *Urgestein* always gives him a renewed sense of power, now more necessary to him than ever. Some years previously he had exhausted his favourite Karlsbad as a geological hunting ground; with his hammer he had knocked on every rock, he had described and sent home specimens of everything. So he had turned to Marienbad, then just becoming fashionable, and had at once started on a mineralogical catalogue of the district. The *Kammerberg* near Eger exercised a fascination over him; he was unable to form a definite opinion as to its structure and called it 'problematic'. An expert had explained it as volcanic, but Goethe, with his Neptunist viewpoint, declared that the whole of Bohemia must once have been an inland sea in which, as the waters receded, the mountains had been deposited. Then he grew dissatisfied with this explanation and retracted it; finally, unconcerned about any particular theory, he wrote: 'As a result there arose in me a gentle, one might say a versatile, mood, such as produces in us the pleasant feeling of swaying between two opposing views, without having to persist in either. In this way we double our personality. ...' His geology and his love-affairs follow the same life-rhythm.

Marienbad has been his choice as a spa since 1821. In his catalogue of the local minerals he makes special mention of his host, Herr von Brösigke, a former Prussian officer, who runs a comfortable pension in the town. Brösigke shows Goethe a precious document, the letter in which Frederick the Great had consented to stand godfather to him. Goethe's sense of orderliness is shocked at the condition of the letter, with its damaged edges and dog-eared corners, and he takes possession of it; Brösigke, knowing of Goethe's passion for autographs, is convinced he will never see it again. But the following year he gets it back, carefully mounted and with a dedicatory poem from Goethe on a second sheet of paper, the two documents being bound together in a blue case; blue is Goethe's heraldic colour.

Brösigke possesses yet another magnet that draws Goethe to his house. His daughter is a Frau von Levetzow, whom Goethe had met in Karlsbad, in the fateful year 1806, and whom he referred to in his diary of the time as 'Pandora'. She was then 19 and recently, though not happily, married; divorced soon afterwards, she married a second member of the same family, who was killed at the Battle of Waterloo. Now, at 35, she is a charming widow with three daughters in their teens. She does not live as a widow, however; her friend is a Count Klebelsberg, who has rich estates in Bohemia and the prospect of a high position in the Austrian Government. Marriage is out of the question as the first Herr von Levetzow is still alive and Klebelsberg is a Roman Catholic; but in Austria things can be 'arranged', and the two appear in public together. It is Klebelsberg who has built her parents the house in Marienbad where Goethe stays. The house has a terrace in front, looking over a large lawn, and Goethe, spoilt by the whole Brösigke-Levetzow family, finds here the happy family atmosphere, care and stimulation, that he lacks at home in Weimar. The three daughters provide him with the freshness and vitality of youth. Amalie, the second one, is a tomboy, and the youngest, Bertha, promises to turn into a beauty; Ulrike, the eldest, is also very attractive, slim, with large blue eyes, fair hair and a shapely nose. She has just returned from a finishing school in Strasbourg and she is full of it. The 73-year-old Goethe enjoys chatting to this girl of 17 and hearing about the town where he spent his own student days; he has described and published these in *Dichtung und Wahrheit*, and the *Sesenheim Idyll* has become a favourite with the public, but the young Fräulein von Levetzow knows nothing of this, she has never read a word of Goethe. She does not even know he is a poet. She calls him the 'great scholar', a description she still uses sixty years later; his talk is so learned and instructive. He gives her a copy of his newly published *Wilhelm Meisters Wanderjahre*, the great repository of the wisdom of his old age and not exactly easy reading for a young girl. From references it contains she gathers that 'there must have been something before it'; Goethe agrees that there is another *Wilhelm Meister*, but it is not suitable for a girl of her age. So he makes extracts, in a new version, to tell his 'little daughter'.

The great scholar is very taken up with other things. He compiles a detailed chart of the barometric changes at Marienbad. He spends much time in the surrounding countryside, tapping the rocks with his hammer and bringing specimens home. He tries to explain about these to his 'little daughter': 'This is a piece of flesh-pink granite with a predominant quartz content, this one is a detached biparous crystal, a very rare piece, my child, and perhaps the only one so far discovered here.' The child cannot make much of the stones. Noticing this the old man slips a piece of chocolate in amongst the specimens: it is soon picked out with delight. After this Goethe brings her flowers, instead of stones, from his expeditions.

He is back at the Brösigke's the following year; the year after that, 1823, he stays across the road at the inn *Zur golden Traube*, because Karl August has gone to the Brösigke's, the best and most elegant lodgings in Marienbad. They all meet there on the terrace. There is a busy social life and, despite his recent illness, Goethe takes part in everything. He is still 'morbidly sensitive', as he writes to Zelter, but he also tells him of the many acquaintances he has made: 'Older relationships make common cause with new ones and a past life permits belief in a present one.'

He goes back over his memories. Strasbourg recalls Friederike, and Lili too, who went to live there as Frau von Türkheim. Lotte and Wetzlar have also been recalled to him by the original publisher of *Werther*, who wants to issue a Jubilee Edition of the novel and has asked Goethe to write some verses as a preface. A son of Lotte's, one of her twelve children and now established as head of some record office, is on the list of the spa guests and Goethe will have to say a few words to him. Charlotte von Stein, now reconciled with Goethe, still lives in Weimar. He has dedicated a fine poem to her, *Einer Einzigen angehören* (to belong to one and one alone), in which he places her on a level with Shakespeare, a star of stars:

'I owe to you two what I am.' The old lady, 80 now, impoverished, disillusioned, and still living in the apartment over the stables where Goethe was once her daily guest, knows the significance of these lines that relegate her to the distance of the stars.

He promenades constantly, attends the receptions and goes to the balls, where he leads the Polonaise and where, once more, the prettiest girls are served up to him. He sits on the Brösigke's terrace, and it becomes a stage, where the whole of Marienbad comes to look at him, jealous of little Fräulein von Levetzow, who is clearly his favourite. Only through her is it possible to get an introduction to the great man, and people exploit the opportunity ruthlessly. Goethe consents to everything she suggests, merely asking sometimes: 'Are you satisfied now, my child?'

Then he is to be seen alone once more, or with a single companion, walking off up into the hills carrying his little geological hammer. He is given the nickname 'old Merlin', after the magician whose legend the Romantics have revived. His companion tries to convince him that the structure of the whole mountain can be deduced from two sites where slate is present, to which Goethe answers: 'Because a girl kissed me on the first and third days, it would not be right to assume that she kissed no one else on the second day.'

He writes poems, as is expected of a poet, on the beneficent spring, Hygeia, that has so many ways of alluring and confusing us, through playing and dancing and through our affections; '*so wird von Tag zu Tag ein Traum gedichtet*' (and thus from one day to the next a dream is born). A remote sound as of a harp whose strings are touched by the wind reaches his ears, and tears well in his eyes; he is in a very tender mood, the tears come easily and he feels better for them.

Great music plays its part. There are concerts by famous artists: Frau Milder sings, and for once in his life Goethe hears a voice of the first rank; a beautiful Polish pianist, Madame Szymanowska, plays and Goethe feels himself 'opened out' like a hand that has been closed. He asks to be introduced and they go for walks together; he is enchanted by her, quite losing his heart to this attractive creature with her slanting eyes and black eyebrows, her delicate clear-cut mouth and slightly turned-up nose, and with her easy fluent conversation, although this is a little difficult for him as she speaks only French. But they understand each other, even if they do not understand each other's every word.

Maria Szymanowska, Court Pianist to the Empress of Russia and acclaimed by Cherubini and Rossini as the leading woman pianist of her day, came from a Warsaw family of the name of Wolowski. They belonged to a somewhat strange Jewish sect called the Frankists. Its founder, Jakob Frank, fluctuating between Judaism and Christianity, and suspect to both, led a wandering life; in the course of it he spent some time in Offenbach, where he held court in the grand style, to the astonished admiration of the local people who called him the 'Polish Prince', until one day he disappeared. Maria, a prodigy, married a member of the same sect named Szymanowski; their daughter later married the great Polish poet Mickiewicz. Maria soon obtained a divorce and, with her sister, set out on her great concert tours of Europe; these developed into a triumph, due not least to her personality and charm. She was also a composer who, in addition to *salon* pieces like *Le Murmure* which became a great favourite, composed some fine *études* that anticipated those of Chopin; Schumann called them 'the most important music so far produced by a woman composer', and praised the 'delicate blue wings of her music'.

Goethe enjoys the company and admiration of this charming person, who is no 'little daughter' but a woman, and a very famous one at that, elegant, a woman of the world and a fine musician. Her playing was not so overpowering as that of Beethoven, which forced Goethe on the defensive and which he could bear only for a moment or two; very probably the main item in her concerts was *Le Murmure*, or one of her delicate blue-winged *études*. But Goethe feels 'opened out'; for two years he has heard scarcely a note of music and consequently, as he writes to Zelter, this organ has become 'closed'. Now 'suddenly and at the hands of great talent this heavenly thing descends upon us and exercises over us its whole power, comes fully into its own, and awakens the sum total of slumbering memories'. He feels as though he has been taken out of the world and lifted above it.

Madame Szymanowska is too much, her music-making disturbs him too deeply. He seeks safety in his little daughter and the terrace overlooking the gentle lawns. His demon has reserved for him a last violent emotional upheaval. The day-to-day dream becomes reality.

In his diary he notes down 'conciliatory dreams', but they do not remain wholly dreams. His relations with the Levetzow family as a whole remain the same: Amalie, the second girl who is something of a tomboy, he takes seriously in hand, and with Bertha, the youngest, he reads one of Sir Walter Scott's novels, warning her to speak carefully and distinctly, pitching her voice low at the beginning of a phrase and then gradually raising it. With the mother he shares common memories of Marienbad and Karlsbad in the old days. But Ulrike begins to step out of the dream into reality. She has an easy confidence in the 'great scholar', and she is undoubtedly proud of her unexpected role in society; hitherto she has been simply a young girl of no importance, and now everyone wants to meet her, to get an introduction to 'him'.

At the balls Goethe watches her as she dances past, light in her movements, unaffected, always a little serious; 'serene but not gay' as her mother says of her, not without misgivings. Sitting on the terrace, he watches her on the lawn in her becoming tartan dress – the fashion in Sir Walter Scott has spread to the dressmakers as well. To please the great scholar she bends down to pick up a few stones to take to him: 'a new addition to the hundred attitudes in which I see her', as he later writes in all innocence to her mother. It is something very different from the hundred classical attitudes Emma Hamilton had displayed in Naples; this is the present, quite un-classic, and it lives and breathes.

Goethe is lured into strange thoughts and still stranger actions. In the words of Thomas Mann it becomes a story of 'gruesomely comic and highly embarrassing situations, at which, nevertheless, we laugh with reverence'. Mann intended turning the affair into a novel, but finally trans-formed it into the 'Tragedy of Mastery' in his *Tod in Venedig*.

Goethe consults a doctor to find out whether, at his age, marriage might be detrimental to health. The doctor puts his mind at rest, probably sup-pressing a smile with difficulty. Goethe next takes into his confidence his old friend Karl August, who simply laughs at him: 'Girls, girls, even at your age!' Goethe assures him he is serious, and the Grand Duke is moved by the sight of this white-haired old man, desperately begging him, like some youth, to act as his intermediary, a wild, insane look of hope in his dark brown eyes, those eyes that normally are so dominating and that have often caused him so much trouble. The situation intrigues the Duke, and probably appeals to his sense of mischief: if the Olympian wants to make himself a laughing-stock, why should he try to stop him? On the other hand the Levetzows might be a welcome addition to Weimar society, and that is certainly more than Goethe's children have been.

So Karl August pays a formal call on Frau von Levetzow and presents his friend's offer of marriage. At first the lady takes it for a joke; the Duke's sense of humour is known for its lack of subtlety. Karl August, however, promises Ulrike a large pension in the not too improbable event of Goethe dying before her. The mother expresses her anxiety at the almost certain opposition of the Goethe children and the consequent bad atmosphere in the house; this, too, can be arranged, Karl August assures her, as he will place a house opposite the castle at the disposal of the 'young couple', Goethe and Ulrike. The mother stresses the age of her 'child', but Ulrike is 19 and at this age she herself was on the point of divorce. Finally Ulrike has never shown the slightest interest either in marriage or in men in general. At least she must be consulted. The offer is certainly an excep-tionally honourable one.

Karl August's mission is now completed and, whether it is he or Frau von Levetzow who talks, the affair is known at once. Letters fly in all directions. Goethe himself writes to his daughter-in-law hinting at the possibility of their domestic difficulties being overcome by the addition of 'a third or fourth' person.

All we know of what passed between Frau von Levetzow and her daughter is the account Ulrike gave in her old age. She is another in that long line of Goethe's 'abbesses' that began with his sister. Neither at this time in Marienbad nor later did Ulrike ever show any interest in any man. She died just before the beginning of the present century, almost a hundred years old, a lonely Sister of Mercy 'of the Holy Sepulchre', living on one of her stepfather Klebelsberg's estates, who on the death of the first Herr von Levetzow had been able to marry Ulrike's mother.

'It was far from being love,' the old lady once said when she was pestered by inquisitive people. She then declared that 'her reason for refusing was consideration for Goethe's family, although apart from that she did not like the idea of being separated from her grandparents, her sisters and her mother. Finally she had felt no desire whatever to marry. So far as Goethe was concerned she had loved him like a father, and she might have married him if she could have been 'of use' to him. In any case he himself had never said a word about marriage, either to her or to her mother.

There is still a postlude to the affair. In order to escape the unpleasantness of the situation the Levetzows go to Karlsbad. Goethe goes to spend a few days at Eger. While there he writes to one of his naturalist friends about the relationship to him of 'very good people': 'All of a sudden [that is, after leaving Marienbad] the peace of God came over me, and it was powerful and gentle enough to set me right with myself and the world.' To this he adds: 'Just as all the higher things in science and elsewhere have an immediate ethical effect and thus result in great moral benefit.'

The peace does not last. He must see the girl again at all costs, so he follows the family to Karlsbad, where he takes rooms at the same inn, just above them. The next twelve days pass decorously enough. On his birthday Goethe receives a cut glass goblet, engraved with the date and the initials of the three daughters – the mother makes a special point of this. Each year now all three daughters have to send Goethe congratulations on his birthday, in wording carefully chosen by their mother, to recall the 'day of the open secret'; all Karlsbad, of course, knew of the secret of the goblet. 'Continued gaiety' notes Goethe in his diary, and on another occasion 'delightful mistakes over the stars' – coming home late in the evening the lights of the town deep down in the valley twinkle like fallen stars. Hopefully he notes: 'New plans. We stayed long together.' Then the time comes to pack. It seems it is Frau von Levetzow who first decides on this. The affair is honourable in the extreme, and in future it continues to be treated with the utmost discretion, but it is beginning to get impossible. 'General, somewhat tumultuous leave-taking', notes Goethe. Ulrike runs once more up the steps for a parting kiss; then Goethe walks down the street to the inn, where his carriage is waiting. It is still early, nine o'clock, on a bright September's day. Goethe knows that for him it is evening. He never sees the girl again. For a long time he still continues to hope and to write letters that are full of discreet hints; once there is a half-despairing, 'Oh, that my longings may find yours! Oh, that nothing, nothing shall prevent their fulfilment and success!'

As soon as he is in his carriage he realizes that this is the final parting. This realization shakes him to the depths of his being. But with the agony comes exaltation in the knowledge that he can find expression for it. In Marienbad he had started a poem for Madame Szymanowska with the words 'Passion brings its suffering', but the 'Twin happiness of music and of love' with which it ended was conciliatory. There is no question of conciliation now. Each night he copies out the lines he has scribbled down on his writing-pad during the journey. By the time he gets to Weimar the long poem is finished. He takes out nine sheets of the finest paper and in his most careful hand – which still shows the schooling of his old *magister artis scribendi* in Frankfurt – he copies it out. With his own hands he encloses the work in a binding of blue cardboard, his heraldic colour, in the same way as he had bound Frederick the Great's letter, which he had smoothed out and restored so carefully for Ulrike's grandfather.

These lines, too, are carefully smoothed and polished; they are the most powerful, most magnificent, lines he ever wrote. In his poem he finds himself again, deep as the wound has been. At the opening he quotes his own *Tasso*: '*Und wenn der Mensch in seiner Qual verstummt, Gab mir ein Gott zu sagen, was ich leide*' (and when a man is speechless in his pain, there is a God to help him tell his agony). The form itself of his stanzas shows consummate artistic skill; it is close to that of the Italian stanza, but shorter, simpler. He employs every artistic device. He lets his loved one speak as though she were taking part in a semi-dramatic scene; at the end he himself addresses unseen friends: 'Leave me now!' He wants to be alone and rids himself of all companionship, even his beloved natural science brings him no consolation and is discarded: 'Observed, explored, its every detail probed, we stumble still in search of nature's mystery.' He feels utterly lost; he who was once the darling of the gods has now been subjected by them to this sore trial: '*Sie drängten mich zum gabeseligen Munde, Sie trennen mich, und richten mich zugrunde*' (They drove me to these lips so rich in blessing, they tear me from them now to my destruction). And thus, without hope and in the most merciless final lines he ever wrote, he ends the poem.

In full consciousness of what he had written, he looked upon this poem as a sacred thing; only specially chosen people were allowed to see and hear it. His servant, Stadelmann, had to place lighted candles on the table; when he had withdrawn Goethe would begin to read in his deep, resonant voice.

The whole of Weimar is in a state of excitement over Goethe's homecoming; people take sides, and most take his part, because August and Ottilie are showing themselves at their most unfeeling and cruel. August threatens to take Ottilie to Berlin if the marriage plan materializes. The other Ulrike, Ottilie's sister, joins in and one can only conjecture the unkind or even downright rude things that may have been said, or the bluntness with which August may have expressed his material anxiety over his inheritance. For the first time in his life Goethe learns what it means to be surrounded by scenes, anger and hatred. These are things he has always studiously avoided and now, in his old age, he is beset by them in his own home circle. 'The whole household was in despair,' writes Schiller's widow, 'this is not the way to soothe his heart. It is in his nature that opposition hardens him. I do not know how it will end!'

In November he experiences a last excitement and pleasure. Madame Szymanowska has accepted an invitation to play in Weimar. There is a dinner in her honour, which Goethe attends. A toast to 'the memory' is proposed. Goethe is on his feet in a moment, launching into a passionate speech that revokes in prose the words of his poem:

> I suffer no memory in the sense you mean [he cries into the hall], that is but a clumsy way in which to express oneself. Whatever enters our life that is great, or beautiful, or important is not to be remembered merely from without, hunted down as it were, but from the outset it must be woven into the very heart of our being, united with it, so that it may create within us a better self and thus live on in us eternally active. There is no past for which we have a right to long, there is only what is eternally new, formed from the expanded elements of what has gone before; true longing must always be productive, must always create something new and better. [Pointing to Madame Szymanowska he goes on:] Have we not all experienced this for ourselves during these last days? Do we not, all of us, feel refreshed, improved, expanded within ourselves through this charming, noble creature who is now about to leave us again. No, she cannot vanish from our sight, she has become part of us, she lives on in and with us, and try as she will to escape me, I hold her forever fast within me.

Madame Szymanowska pays one more visit to Goethe at his house. She brings him presents she has worked herself. She thanks him in fine, well-composed phrases that sound like a study in good breeding and that, animated with feminine sympathy, mirror Goethe's own words to her. In leaving him she feels rich and comforted: 'You have confirmed my faith in myself, I feel better and worthier for having your esteem.' Goethe looks aghast at the charming figure before him; she has come in deepest black because she has to pay a call at Court, which is in mourning for some princely relative. To Goethe the colour is symbolic; it disturbs him, he can find nothing to say. Her carriage is at the door, and before he realizes what has happened the woman and her sister have gone. Suddenly he cries out passionately, bring her back to me, bring her back! He urges them, begs them, and they rush out to catch her. She comes once more. Silently he takes her in his arms. The tears run down the great brown wrinkled face. He watches her as she walks away through the long vista of his reception rooms. It is no 'very last' kiss he has taken, it is the very last, irrevocable farewell from life.

Madame Szymanowska, too, he never sees again, he even survives her. She died in 1831, still a young woman, a victim of the cholera epidemic that swept the whole of Europe, and that also killed Hegel at the height of his fame.

The two partings in Karlsbad and Weimar have completely exhausted Goethe's newly awakened, though somewhat deceptive, fullness of power and vigour, to use Zelter's phrase. His illness returns, or else he escapes by taking to his bed, as Riemer suspected he did during such crises. Goethe is weak, he has no resistance, and around him rages only further disturbance and hatred, for the marriage project has by no means been abandoned. Friends arrange for his old servant Paul Götze to be sent for to look after him; Götze is now Inspector of Roads and Rivers, and is responsible for damming and dyking the uncanalized rivers against flooding. He makes no bones with his *Geheimrat*: 'You see, Your Excellency,' he says, 'we can't keep up the Polish style any longer!'

Another resolute, blunt man hurries by special coach to Goethe's side. No one is at the door when Zelter arrives; a woman's face appears at a window and disappears again. Stadelmann, the servant, appears and shrugs his shoulders.

> I stand at the door [Zelter writes in his diary] wondering whether to go away again. Is there death in the house? Where is the master? – Doleful eyes. – Where is Ottilie? – Gone to Dessau – Where is Ulrike? – In bed. – August comes: Father is not well, ill, very ill. – He is dead! – No, not dead, but very ill. – I approach closer and marble figures stand and watch me. I climb the stairs. The easy treads seem to withdraw beneath my feet. What shall I find? What do I find? Someone who looks as if his body is racked with love, all the love of youth with all its agony. Well, if that is what it is he will get over it! No! he must keep it, he must burn like quicklime!

Zelter is not merely blunt, he understands psychological family medicine. The poet shows him his Marienbad Elegy, and Zelter reads it aloud three times, one after the other. Says Goethe: 'You read well, my old friend!' – 'That was quite natural,' Zelter wrote to a friend, 'but the old fool did not know I was thinking all the time of my own sweetheart.' The doctors shake their heads over the musician's natural remedies, but Goethe recovers surprisingly quickly. Satisfied that all is well, Zelter departs. He has 'commanded' Goethe's recovery, as he puts it, and leaves him in 'full vigour'.

Goethe sets to work. The *Elegy* retains its special place, but now it is to be set in a frame. The artistic problem of writing a trilogy is an old one for Goethe, and one that he had failed to solve both in 'Pandora' and in *Die Natürliche Tochter*. Now, in poetry, he succeeds. He prefaces the *Elegy* with five stanzas on the subject of *Werther*; ironic, bitter verses about the 'oft regretted shadow', that smiles sentimentally, having left its author behind: '*Zum Bleiben ich, zum Scheiden du erkoren, Gingst du voran –*

*und hast nicht viel verloren*' (I to remain, thou to depart wast chosen, in going on thy loss has been but slight). This reunion after fifty years awakens the memory of another meeting, another parting, and at the end there awaits the final parting – *Scheiden ist der Tod*. There follows, as the centre piece of the trilogy, the *Elegy* with its merciless closing lines. The poem to Madame Szymanowska forms the conclusion, with its final 'twin happiness of music and of love'. Goethe gives the whole work the title *Trilogie der Leidenschaft* (Trilogy of Passion).

'I wonder only whether this unity, so torn and so tortured, will be able to assume the form and appearance of a new unity', he had said a year earlier, as he began to recover from his illness. In his poem this new unity has been achieved, in what is perhaps the most marvellous of all the metamorphoses of this man who refuses to die, who will not grow old, who fights with all his might against the parting that is death.

# 42

# *Conversations with Goethe*

Seen merely from the outside the last ten years of Goethe's life are spent in the narrow confinement of his home; for his mind it is a period of extensive exploration into the measureless regions of the infinite. He ceases to travel; even nearby Jena becomes remote. Every corner of the big house on the Frauenplan is filled with records of his life, with gifts, diplomas of honour, his natural history collections, his art treasures. Even during his lifetime it becomes a museum, an archive, a chancellery from which every day countless letters are dispatched to every part of the world. It is also the scene of splendid receptions; on formal occasions visitors are expected to wear full evening dress 'with decorations'. His table is superb. At one of his suppers, by no means a great occasion, the tutor to the Weimar Princes, a young man from Geneva named Soret, notes, as contrasting somewhat with the homely fare he is used to in Calvinist Geneva, cups of strong cold *consommé* (taken at first for chocolate by Soret), caviar, cold meat and venison, three or four dishes of salads and sandwiches decorated with anchovies and lampreys, all these courses accompanied by three kinds of wine; for dessert pickled fruits, and, to end up with, large fruit tarts. Goethe still drinks freely even in his old age, and he enjoys serving wine to his guests from the large squat wine bottles of the day.

Visitors come from every country and are seldom turned away, provided they have an introduction of some kind; among them are students and great statesmen, inquisitive ladies and budding poets. On his way back from a walking tour through the Harz mountains, of which he intends soon to write a description, the young Heinrich Heine, a student at Göttingen, presents his card and is received. After talking of this and that Goethe asks him: 'What are you working on at the moment?' – 'On a *Faust*' – 'Have you no other business in Weimar?' asks the Olympian. 'Having set foot over Your Excellency's doorstep my whole business in Weimar is completed', replies the impudent young man and takes his leave. The Austrian dramatist Grillparzer, 35 years old and already famous, also finds Goethe cold on his first visit, when he is received in audience as though by a monarch: 'It was not as though my vanity had been hurt, on the contrary Goethe treated me with more friendliness and consideration than I had expected.

471

But to see my youthful idol, the poet of *Faust, Clavigo* and *Egmont*, as a stiff minister dispensing the blessing of tea to his guests, disillusioned me completely. I should almost have preferred it if he had been rude to me and thrown me out of the house.' The next day the Olympian is transformed. He takes Grillparzer in to dinner with him, speaks in high terms of his *Sappho*, asks about Vienna society, and even urges him to come and live in Weimar. Grillparzer, who all his life was suspicious and inhibited, is so overwhelmed by this that he cannot bring himself to accept Goethe's further invitation; had he done so he might have seen Goethe completely at ease in his white woollen dressing-gown, a large bottle of red wine in front of him, with another for his guest, dispensing immortal sayings such as could never be vouchsafed to mass receptions or inquisitive strangers.

These, more or less, are the three different ways in which Goethe shows himself to visitors; there are others, of course. Since the world fame of his *Werther* every visitor has written down the poet's every word. They have eulogized him in those intolerable phrases which, to this day, render a large part of Goethe literature unreadable. They have stared open-mouthed, like Gretchen in his *Faust: 'Du lieber Gott! was so ein Mann Nicht alles, alles denken kann! Beschämt nur steh ich vor ihm da, Und sag zu allen Sachen ja'* (Good Lord! I've never heard or read the things this man has in his head, ashamed I stand there in distress and say to all he utters yes). They are disappointed if he does not conform to their preconceived idea of him. If he appears wearing all his decorations, as he likes to do, they see in him a 'courtier', or, if they happen to be courtiers themselves, they remark in a self-satisfied way that His Excellency's manner never has the ease and poise of a true man of the world. Most visitors reveal more of themselves than of Goethe, and in every 'conversation with Goethe' it is necessary first to examine the credentials of the speaker, who he is, where he comes from, the extent of his intellectual qualifications.

It is rare to find an acute observer. Soret, trained in the natural sciences, is an exception. During a conversation on the *Farbenlehre*, about which he is sceptical, he looks carefully at Goethe's eyes: 'The iris is composed of three different colours; round the brown centre of the iris there is a large blue ring which, together with the deep black of the pupil, results in three concentric circles and this creates a strange impression.' Seldom does a visitor contribute anything; the majority only want to take home some words of wisdom. Goethe likes to get information when he talks to people, no matter if it is only trivial; the deaf Beethoven's conversation books also contain more about actors, singers or food than they do about the *Ninth Symphony*. Goethe does not want to talk about things around him; he shows little interest in German literature, and none whatever in aesthetics, the favourite topic of the younger generation in Germany. But he is always interested to hear about what is going on in England, France, or distant America, in Russia or China. He hears of great projects, of proposed canals at Panama and Suez, of plans for huge harbours. In his old age his thoughts roam far over the sea, of which he has had only one brief glimpse, on his visit to Italy. In the second part of *Faust* Thales sings of the ocean: '*Du bist's, der das frischeste Leben erhält*' (Thou it is maintains life at its freshest).

An octogenarian's life cannot very well be fresh, but Goethe's vitality is still amazing. He is surrounded by his staff of secretaries and copyists and, on a higher level, by his advisers and specialists, his 'living encyclopaedias' as one visitor calls them; it is they to whom he turns when he wants to know anything. Riemer is the authority on antiquity and the classics, Meyer on art; an architect named Coudray, who has been appointed Director of Buildings in Weimar, is his architectural consultant. Goethe prepares numerous plans with Coudray, though few are realized; one of these latter is a 'princes' vault', in which Goethe is to lie side by side with Schiller. Apart from this, death is seldom mentioned. Goethe can still be very passionate in his talk, magnificently unjust, magnificently wise; 'then the abuse started', notes Boisserée. Müller, the Chancellor and Minister of Justice, to whom we owe the most accurate transcriptions of Goethe's actual words, says of one conversation about freedom of the press: 'On this subject one simply cannot argue with Goethe, he is much too one-sided and despotic in his views.'

Müller is Goethe's social equal, ennobled like him; an adroit political negotiator, and adroit socially as well, he is in no sense a subordinate; consequently Goethe talked much more freely with him: 'Oh, I can be beastly too,' he confessed happily on one occasion. He would pull the most famous names to pieces mercilessly: 'And then he scrutinized the greatest of our men with epigrammatic trenchancy and biting criticism' – unfortunately Müller did not record the epigrams. He saw clearly Goethe's 'protean disposition to transform himself into every shape, to play with everything, to adopt diametrically opposite viewpoints and approve them'. He was also well aware of Goethe's consciously developed contrariness. They were speaking once of large industrial undertakings; when Goethe dismissed them all as futile, and Müller reminded him that formerly he had thought quite differently, Goethe was completely unconcerned: 'What! have I reached the age of 80 merely to think the same things all the time? On the contrary I do my utmost to think something different, something new, every day, so that I don't become boring. If one is not to stagnate, one must be constantly changing, regenerating oneself, growing young again.' It is a cardinal passage, giving us a beautiful picture of this very old man; but it is one that is highly embarrassing to all those who want to provide a comprehensive summary of what Goethe 'really' thought about this question or that. Müller has also left a fine description of Goethe the sage and prophet, looking out over centuries and peoples, and composing for himself a kind of 'alphabet of the *Weltgeist*'. Afterwards he takes leave of his companions, who have been with him on a short expedition to the hills near Dornburg Castle, and goes down the hillside to his beloved minerals:

> After such a conversation it is fitting for old Merlin to renew his friendship with the *Ur*-elements. Moved and very happy we watched for a long time as, wrapped in his light grey overcoat, he made his way solemnly down to the valley below, stopping here and there at some rock or some individual plant, and testing the former with his mineralogical hammer. The mountains were already casting long shadows in which gradually he disappeared from view like a ghostly apparition.

Silence is often his favourite companion now: 'Stones are silent teachers; they force silence on the observer, and the best that one learns from them cannot be communicated.' Occasionally he sits among his faithful followers silent like a rock. A Jena mining expert, with whom Goethe likes to talk, receives an urgent summons to Weimar by special messenger, the carriage is to call for him in an hour's time. The man hurriedly changes into his good clothes and drives post haste to Weimar. On entering Goethe's room, so his son tells us, there were

> Riemer, Eckermann, etc., sitting round the table, the old gentleman was wearing his green shade over his eyes, no one spoke a word, each had a bottle of red wine in front of him. As my father was about to go up and ask His Excellency in what way he could be of service, Riemer whispered to him: His Excellency is thinking! Finally at ten o'clock Goethe rose and pronounced his well-known, 'I wish my friends good night.' The following morning His Excellency had no recollection of the invitation.

The chief witness to these years, however, is no silent one. It was with a sure eye that Goethe selected Johann Peter Eckermann from the many young men who offered him their services; having chosen him he held on to him, firmly moulding and pressing him into shape, until finally, and only on his death, he released him to perform the single task of his life: to compose and write, from the notes he had made, his *Conversations with Goethe during the Last Years of his Life*. The book is Goethe's last great work, deliberately planned as a new means of expression, at his great age the only one still left to him. It makes no difference that Eckermann, as has been proved, changed a great deal, added things, is 'unreliable'. There are other charges that can be levelled against him: he is often servile, he is vain about his gift for putting the right words into the great man's mouth, not infrequently he is unable to distinguish between important and unimportant works, his education is deficient, being improved only through his contact with Goethe. Like Boswell he has a sense of humour, but his humour has a touching quality entirely lacking in the Scot. His later life, like that of Riemer, makes pathetic reading: badly paid, fobbed off by the Court with the worthless title of *Hofrat*, he stays on in Weimar; when the windows of every house in Weimar are illuminated to celebrate the centenary of Goethe's birth, his remain dark.

There is a shining light in his work, but it is not the light of the sun; like a moon that gets its light from Goethe's sun, he creates and brings to completion one single work. Never at any time does he produce anything else of note. His reward – the rest of his remuneration is not worth mentioning – is a taste of immortality, posterity's usual consolation in such cases; in his life he drinks the cup of bitterness.

It is a bitter life and a bitter childhood. As a boy he has to help his father, a hawker, to carry the heavy bales of cloth. Until he is 14 he has no schooling. Small, and with a weak chest, the trade of tailor is thought the most suitable for him, but he manages to get a little education, finds work as a copyist and eventually becomes a minor official in Hannover; at the age of 24 he wants to learn Latin. People help the gifted boy and enable him to go to the 'Gymnasium'. He writes poetry, and becomes engaged to his Hannchen, who is as penniless as he is; they have to wait thirteen years before they can get married. With a small grant he goes to Göttingen University to study law; instead he studies literature and philosophy. After three terms he gives this up too and retires to a small village near Hannover, where he writes *Contributions to Literature, with Particular Reference to Goethe*. In this he criticizes the 'folly of mistaken originality', in other words the Romantics, and sets up antiquity and Goethe as his models. The manuscript is sent to the master, who receives it well and persuades his own publisher, Cotta, to publish it. The author himself is also well received when he arrives in Weimar to see his god. Young only as a writer, Eckermann is a man of 30, his lean, prematurely care-lined cheeks surrounded by long strands of pale hair. Goethe dislikes hair worn long like this, in the 'old German' style favoured by the young people of the day, and tells Eckermann he should go to the hairdresser and have his hair cut and curled, as he has been doing for the last fifty years; the old man, his Olympian head swathed in curls, beams radiantly on the indigent young man. There is no radiance in Eckermann's eyes, which are narrow and introspective; he is a dreamer, and, like many people from Lower Saxony, is gifted with second sight. He saw Goethe in a dream before he set out on his pilgrimage to walk to Weimar, and wrote to his Hannchen:

> Last night I dreamed I was at Goethe's. I had a long talk with him. I kept on catching hold of his legs but he was wearing thick underpants; he said he could no longer keep warm otherwise. He was already very old, but took a great liking to me, he brought me a whole handful of pears out of his room and peeled them, but only down to the stalk; he wanted me to eat them all, but I said I wanted to take two of them home to my Hannchen in Hannover....

Hannchen has to wait a long time for her pears. It is not until the last year of Goethe's life that they are able to marry, and even then their marriage brings no happiness; she is too old, and dies shortly afterwards in her first confinement.

Eckermann is not only a dreamer; he has the tenacity common to quiet people, as well as a certain discretion in fulfilling his mission. His approach to Goethe is carefully prepared through correspondence with those surrounding the master; in the end it is Riemer, the senior of these and now grown lazy, who helps the younger man, until finally he is able to stand in the presence of his idol: 'He talked slowly and at his ease, as one would expect an aged monarch to speak.' Goethe happens to be in need of a helper, and has been looking out for one; the younger men, however, all want to make conditions and are not prepared to come to Weimar without a reasonable salary. Eckermann asks nothing. He is content to serve. In fact he receives almost nothing, apart from occasional little gifts of pocket money; for years even the penniless Hannchen has to help him out with small sums.

Goethe behaves like a monarch, and at once, 'quick and resolute as a young man' as Eckermann says, enrols the young adept for editorial work. He lays on the table two thick volumes of the *Frankfurter Gelehrte Anzeigen* for 1772–73, containing the first reviews Goethe ever wrote, and sets Eckermann the task of identifying these – an impossible task that has since defeated even skilled philologists. The young man goes to work with a will. What he really wants, however, before starting on his duties, is to see something of the world, but Goethe will not hear of this; 'if one is able to treat one subject clearly,' he tells him, 'one will be capable of doing many other things as well'. Nevertheless he sends him on a short visit to Jena, to stay with his friends the Fromanns, whom he has asked to give the young man a little social polish; at present he is far too inexperienced and awkward to be allowed to appear in public at the Goethe Court. In Jena, Eckermann reads Goethe's letters from Italy: 'The fresh air of a great life is wafted from their pages ... had I but seen the half of all that I should be satisfied, but as it is I have a great thirst for life!'

Goethe decides that Eckermann is to make an index for *Kunst und Altertum*. On his departure for Marienbad, he says paternally: 'I hope to find you quietly at work when I get back, for when all is said and done that is the surest and purest way of acquiring experience and an insight into the world!' On his return he announces: 'I wish you to remain in Weimar with me this winter.' Eckermann remains and never gets away again. To live on he has the fee for his book and the small amounts of pocket-money Goethe gives him, but no salary. He is asked by foreign magazines to write about Weimar, now internationally famous, but Goethe warns him against dividing his interests in that way. He is anxious to publish the master's sayings as soon as possible. This, too, is forbidden him; it is too soon. Goethe hints that if he waits there will be further, and still more important, sayings. And to this not exactly merciful game that Goethe plays with his adept we owe many of his last and wisest utterances. Eckermann shows an almost indiscriminate enthusiasm for everything to do with the master: 'He collects my single poems together like an ant, without him I should never have done it, but it will be very nice,' writes Goethe, 'he collects, sifts, sorts, and in his great love is able to make something out of the things ... he takes an interest in what no longer has any interest for me.' Eckermann writes down his first short draft of his conversations with the old man. Goethe glances through it: 'You are on the right track. You cannot do anything on the spur of the moment and perfunctorily, you must be able to penetrate quietly to the heart of your subject; but in this way the highest results will be achieved.' Eckermann achieves the highest results of which he is capable. In a higher sense Goethe's attitude has been right.

With Eckermann, Goethe creates the legend of his closing years, the myth of the *Vollendete*, of the completed and perfected man, poet and sage, that for a century dominates the image of Goethe's life. Everything which might disturb this image or raise problems is omitted, so that the whole may flow uninterruptedly and consequentially to its goal. Eckermann has noted down a wealth of invaluable sayings, even though we need to be on our guard against his constant polishing of the marble. *Eckermann* is the monument Goethe erects to his old age, just as *Dichtung und Wahrheit* is his monument to his youth; for the intervening years of his manhood, for the most important years, there is no monument.

Eckermann's great achievement is that he has succeeded in making Goethe talk, and he has done this by every conceivable means: by respectful queries, by hinting at interesting subjects, by historical allusions to works of Goethe's which the master himself has forgotten, and even by naïveties, which he utters in the most solemn Goethean manner and which cause Goethe to enlarge on the theme far above the head of his disciple. We hear Goethe speak, though always selectively, and always and infallibly making the right point. The word 'despair', so often used by Goethe, finds no place in Eckermann.

Eckermann himself must often have had cause for despair. He is silent on the subject. He serves, reveres, and writes his notes. His Hannchen, in her almost widow-like engagement, grows impatient and asks why Goethe, who loves her Peter so dearly, does nothing for him. Peter chides her. He lives in a small furnished room in Weimar; there is no question of his becoming a member of the Goethe household, like Meyer. His room is filled with birdcages. In the market he buys birds of prey, kestrel hawks, sparrow hawks, wild, daring birds; in the end he has forty of them and his room must have smelled like a menagerie. He practises archery and wants to become a marksman; he borrows Goethe's Bashkir bow and notes in triumph that an arrow which buried itself in the shutters of one of Goethe's windows could not be pulled out. He has a great 'thirst for life'; he sees himself as a poet and writes some poems as a result of a hopeless love

affair with a tall handsome actress, who then marries an equally tall handsome actor. Looking back on his ten years with Goethe he says that at the
beginning everything was wonderful, but 'now the world has changed me a
little, inoculating me with attacks of mistrust like an illness'. His book
reveals nothing of this, only unswerving trust and unlimited veneration,
which Goethe rewards with precious gifts. Eckermann is allowed to see the
drafts of the second part of *Faust*, and the Marienbad *Elegy*. Since a man
without a title is a solecism in Weimar society, Goethe bestows on him the
title of Dr Eckermann and introduces him as such to his friends; when, on
the fiftieth anniversary of Goethe's appointment as minister responsible,
Jena University offers him two honorary doctorates to distribute as he
wishes, Eckermann receives the official diploma from his master's hands.
Goethe also entrusts to Eckermann, in association with Riemer, the editing
of his posthumous works: the remuneration of approximately eight hundred
thalers, for work that takes him many years and embraces twenty volumes,
is meagre in the extreme. Eckermann lives by giving private lessons; occasionally he teaches the Princes, for which he receives a small compensation.
In the end he is even forced to part with his birds of prey, which Goethe has
heard about with some annoyance, but never seen. He has to renounce his
great 'thirst for life'. Once he sets out on a great journey, to Italy, as companion to the unfortunate August, but when half way to Rome they quarrel
and Eckermann turns back. His life is incomplete, but he has created a
complete work, and one that takes its place in Goethe's *œuvre*.

Eckermann is not a secretary; Goethe does not dictate to him because his
handwriting is poor. Goethe now employs three copyists. Of these a local
man, Theodore Kräuter, is the most competent; the ideal staff-sergeant for
the great Goethe staff-office. He has left a description of the Spartan
simplicity of this office, with its plain pinewood shelves and cabinets, its
hard chairs, and its small reference library containing the *Konversationslexikon* that Goethe often uses when his 'living encyclopaedias' are not at
hand. The quill has to be cut neither too long nor too short, and above all
with no plume. The ink-pot must never be too full. The quill must be dipped
carefully, there must be no inkstains. No sand is allowed for drying the ink,
the master prefers to hold the page in front of the stove. For sealing, small
squares of paper have to be used, to prevent the wax damaging the letter.
While these things are being done Goethe mutters ceaselessly: 'Softly,
quietly!'

When he is dictating he either stands still or paces up and down, his
hands behind his back. He dictates as unhesitatingly as if he were reading
from the book. If the barber or some messenger comes, he stops; afterwards he goes on again where he left off. Often Goethe stops in his stride
to group his images together: 'With his hands outstretched, and his body
inclined to one side or the other, he would bring the object of his
thought into balance, so that it was properly disposed. When he had

succeeded in doing so, he usually said: "Now it's right! Absolutely right!" '

We owe this last description to Schuchardt, another of Goethe's secretaries, who was also responsible for the collections, housed in their innumerable drawers, folders and cases, and for preparing the catalogues to the various sections. Goethe had long since divided up his own writings into separate bundles, paper bags and folders; important correspondence such as that with Schiller or Zelter was given to the bookbinder. In common with all bureaucracy these Goethe archives had an inner disorder of their own, which even to-day has not been entirely unravelled, despite the work of generations of philologists. Sometimes important things were in the wrong place; sometimes very important ones were missing altogether, and it is amusing to see Goethe's attempts to buy his own first editions at book auctions. Even his beloved engravings, which he liked to show to friends and visitors, were often covered in dust, and he had constantly to speak to his servant Stadelmann about it.

Stadelmann is a good servant, but he drinks. He apes his master in his walk, his manner and his interests. 'Here in Jena', he writes to Kräuter, 'professors simply crawl between one's legs: this one is a mining expert, that one a chemist, there goes an artist, here comes a technologist, and God knows who else; I have to dance about with these people all day long, and in the process I have learned something from each of them.' It is Goethe through the eyes of Sancho Panza. Stadelmann apes his master in other ways too; again writing to Kräuter he says:

My dear good friend! Oh, Lord, quick, quick! Oh, I am so out of breath! Harness the horses! Get out the carriage! Pack your things! Jump in! Hurry here to Jena! Because you have no idea how heavenly it is here. Everything white! Everything white! Warm! Sunny! Magnificent, divine, heavenly is muck in comparison. I am exhausted. Don't you want to join us and taste some sweet fruit for once? Don't put it off too long, otherwise you will be too late. Good night!

Stadelmann does some research into the theory of colours, and one day, taking a wine glass – which has not come into his hands by accident – a candle and a piece of paper he asks if he may demonstrate his experiments to His Excellency. 'Let's see, Stadelmann, let's see', says Goethe. Stadelmann takes the wine glass and places the piece of paper underneath; when he holds the candle above it the light, passing through the wine, produces on the paper an image of 'three suns', or of a rainbow. 'Stadelmann is a genius who rivals nature,' says Goethe; 'now leave us the glass and your three suns, so that we can have a closer look at it.' Stadelmann goes off, muttering that he could make much more important discoveries, if only he had the time. But he plays too much with the wine glass, and has to be dismissed. Goethe tries to find him a job in Jena, in one of the institutes, but there, too, he drinks too much and is dismissed. He ends up in the poor house.

After Goethe's death he remains completely forgotten until the unveiling of the Goethe memorial in Frankfurt in 1844, when his existence is discovered and he is invited to attend as one of the few surviving members of the Goethe circle. He arrives in an old coat of Goethe's, and is given a seat of honour in the front row. A collection is made for him and he is promised a small annuity. Before receiving the first instalment he indulges in a heavy bout of drinking, goes up to the attic of the poor house and hangs himself. He seemed to be smiling, so the people said who found him, 'his face was clean-looking, with a faint touch of colour'. Out of respect for the name of Goethe he was not handed over to the dissecting room but was given a proper burial.

Such a fate has its place in the Goethe circle, which is not all quiet light and perfect order. Goethe's son August drinks no less heavily than Stadelmann, although he keeps his attic rooms scrupulously clean and tidy, 'like a ship's cabin'; Goethe calls them the 'little ship'. August collects Napoleonic relics to spite the people of Weimar, who have not forgotten the role he played in the war; he is also an enthusiastic admirer of Schiller, to spite his father. He has no friends in Weimar; it is only foreign visitors who befriend him, out of pity or because they imagine they see hidden traces of genius in him.

The noise and fighting that go on over Goethe's head, and throughout the house, as well as the disorder and neglect, sometimes get so bad that the old man escapes to his garden house for a few weeks in the summer. Here he can breathe again. He strolls reflectively beneath the trees he had planted fifty years earlier. The trellis of roses has grown up to the roof and is full of linnets' and hedge-sparrows' nests. After only a week he notes in his diary: 'Tackled the main business and brought it to the right point.' The main business is the last acts of *Faust*. In the evenings his lamp casts a light across the lawn. A young French admirer, son of the great physicist Ampère, walking along the river bank with Eckermann, looks up and cannot take his eyes off this quiet peaceful light.

After these weeks of peace and quiet Goethe has to return to the large house and its noise. Ottilie, rushing all over the place, falls from her horse and suffers severe cuts to her face; her sister, dancing like a mad woman, falls down and sustains lasting injuries; the staff becomes rebellious and has to be changed, there is quarrelling and stealing, the expenses mount and mount. The grandchildren crawl about the decks of the great Goethe ship like their father before them, and like him they are subjected to but scant discipline. Goethe, at this very moment, is writing the section of his *Wanderjahre* in which he describes his ideal of a 'pedagogic province', where the strictest education is enforced and where the three stages of veneration, involving special gestures and deep bowing, are taught. Nothing of this respect is to be found in the Goethe home. The grandchildren's tutor complains that the boys will not get up in the morning; they spend half their lives in sleep and somnolence as well. Goethe tells him to say to the boys that it is their grandfather's wish that they should get up. A few days later he asks what the result has been. Embarrassed, the tutor says he did as Goethe told him, 'but it made no difference whatever'. With a 'Hm', as his last word in practical education, Goethe turns away.

The little ship above his head rocks so dangerously that Goethe decides on a last attempt to set his son on a straighter course. The idea of Italy comes into his head; perhaps this could be the solution. August writes poetry in secret, which he does not show to his father, and in it there are some clumsy lines of dark foreboding: he no longer wants to be kept on leading strings, and he speaks of his torn heart, 'destruction is its certain fate'. Flushed with wine he blurts out his despair to a friend from abroad: 'You think I am drunk? I am never drunk unless I want to appear drunk! None of you knows anything about me! You take me for a wild, superficial kind of fellow – but here, inside me, it goes so deep! If you threw a stone down you would wait a long time before you heard it fall!' With Eckermann, the most unsuitable companion imaginable, he is finally dispatched, well supplied with money and letters of introduction. The German artists in Rome are anxious to greet him. Their meeting place is a tavern *The Golden Bell*, near the theatre of Marcellus, where in the old days Goethe is supposed to have told his Roman mistress when he could next see her by writing down the date clandestinely in spilled wine. A green tree stands outside the entrance to the large room with its bare black stone walls, its rough tables and benches. Here they take their places and their president reads aloud the *Römische Elegien*; they sing, and drink the master's health. Wilhelm Müller, the poet of the *Müllerlieder*, reads his song of the great poet who lived there and, in the full flush of living, extracted earth's deepest joys and sorrows without losing a single drop.

In November 1830 these German artists accompany the funeral procession that takes the body of August von Goethe to the little Protestant cemetery at the Pyramid of Cestius, near the San Paolo gate, where Keats and Shelley had been buried before him. 'Here lies one whose life was writ in water' – how much better would the epitaph Keats wrote for himself have fitted Goethe's unhappy son. Fate was merciful in ending his life as it did, after only a short fever; the autopsy revealed 'deformities in the brain'. Goethe receives the news with resignation: 'I knew I had begotten a mortal.' To Eckermann, who had slunk slowly back to Weimar after leaving August in Genoa, Goethe says not a word of his son's death. The only apparent sign of the shock he has suffered is a haemorrhage some weeks later; but this, too, is overcome by his will to live.

The 81-year-old man, however, is now forced to bring a little order into his house. The housekeeping has become so slovenly that a young American visitor notes in his diary that the grand old man's clothes do not look very clean. Goethe asks for all the keys; he puts the key to the woodshed under his pillow every night. In future the bread is to be weighed and portioned out. It is as well for us to keep this background in mind, in the same way as it was in his Frankfurt years when he lived in the next room to his father's crazy lodger; in those days he was writing the first scenes of his *Faust*, now he is at work on the last. Ottilie is no housewife, as Goethe had hoped she would be; she was no wife either, and now she is no widow. She is a hungry, restless, dissatisfied woman who is not without artistic gifts: she sings well, reads well, and even edits a small private magazine for her own intimate circle and for the wider circle of her young English admirers. Its title, *Chaos*, symbolizes her whole existence.

In his own sphere Goethe has always managed to preserve a degree of tranquillity and to pursue his own quiet cults. Letters and presents pass between him and Marianne; he sends her myrtle and laurel accompanied by verses, in memory of hours of bliss and happiness and 'as a symbol of a couple that competed, like Hatem and Suleika, in love and poetry'. On her these act as a 'tonic for my heart'; her heart needs tonic, she is often ill. Goethe recalls her nickname of 'little Blücher', her charming insolence and high spirits; but there is no gay insolence any longer, there is to be no more meeting. Only the cult remains, with all its sadness: at full moon they think of each other in memory of the night at the *Gerbermühle*. Shortly before his death, when he is sorting out the 'endless papers' that have accumulated, Goethe puts her letters apart, seals them in a bundle and returns them to her, with the request that she leave them unopened till some unspecified time: pages such as these 'give us the happy feeling that we have lived'.

Another, more literary cult is devoted to Lord Byron. Goethe never met him, and it is very open to question whether a meeting between the two men would have been a success. Byron could be enchanting, but he could also be insufferable; moreover, he could not speak a word of German, beyond a few oaths he had picked up from the coachman. He knew, or at any rate knew of, *Werther* and had read a French translation of *Die Wahlver-wandschaften*; he had heard Matthew Lewis read from *Faust* and, in his short-lived paper *The Liberal*, had published Shelley's translations from the *Walpurgisnacht*. He was a careful reader of the great English reviews, in which the name of Goethe was beginning to be discussed, though not always very favourably, and he felt a sympathy with this 'idol of his countrymen' who, at the same time, seemed to have powerful enemies. Byron also heard about Goethe from travellers. The young American, George Bancroft, had been to Weimar, where he wrote in his diary that Goethe chose prostitutes as the heroines of his novels, and that he missed in Goethe that 'purity of thought and loftiness of soul' that was the poet's special prerogative; if he repeated this to Byron it may well have attracted the poet more strongly to Goethe. On the other hand Byron had also heard stories of Goethe's cautiousness, and he sometimes made sarcastic remarks about 'the old fox' who preached moral sermons from his hole, from which he never emerged. For all that, Goethe was unquestionably the greatest name in European literature, and Byron decided to dedicate one of his works to him. A little carelessly and with a number of corrections he wrote out a solemn dedication, intended for his *Sardanapalus*, and sent it to Goethe to ask his permission: in it he refers to himself as a stranger who offers the homage of a literary vassal to his liege lord, 'the first among living writers, who has created the literature of his own country and illuminated that of all Europe'.

Goethe was overwhelmed. This was not some minor dedication, of which he had received many – the list of books dedicated to Goethe is a series of unimportant names – it was a flattering recognition by the most famous contemporary poet. He had lithograph facsimiles of the page made immediately, and sent them to his friends; it hurt him to have to send back the original, but to his great joy it was returned to him after Byron's death by his executors. He put it in a precious morocco folder along with his few other souvenirs of the hero. Meanwhile there had been a whole comedy of errors: Byron's publisher forgot to print the dedication in *Sardanapalus* and, on the poet's angry remonstrance, printed a considerably reduced and watered down version of his own in *Werner*; to cover up the omission, dedication pages were pasted into the copies of *Sardanapalus* for Goethe, but they contained the wrong dedication.

The two poets corresponded only once, at the decisive moment of Byron's life. Goethe had been informed of Byron's pending departure for Greece by one of the young Englishmen in Weimar, and wrote him a poem in which he expressed his affectionate concern: '*und wie ich ihn erkannt, mög' er sich kennen!*' (and as I have seen him may he see himself). Byron, already on board the *Hercules*, received the poem when he put in at Livorno. He answered in a fine letter, taking the poem as a good omen and mentioning the possibility of a visit to Weimar 'in case I should ever return'. Byron's expedition was an escape and amounted almost to suicide; he was fully aware of what was in store for him in Greece, a country he knew better than the gentlemen of the 'Philhellenic Committee' who sent him out and then let him down. It was an escape from his last and most tiresome mistress, from women in general, from fame, and from his whole previous life, with its public parade of his melancholy and despair. He knew the Greeks were not the Greeks of old, though this was the belief of the classical enthusiasts in Europe, who saw in every brigand leader a Themistocles and in every Greek woman a Helen. He knew that what he was going to was a hard life, a hopeless struggle between factions, mutiny, fever and dirt; and it was from fever and dirt that he died at Missolonghi.

It was, however, a glorious, legendary end. The Greeks, it was said, had wanted to make him their King. Throughout the whole of Europe there was a wave of enthusiasm for the oppressed Greek kinsmen, new crusades were preached and some small expeditions went out. A German battalion of

'Philhellenes' had landed on the Peloponnese before Byron's death, and had been severely defeated by the Turks. The survivors, among them some Jena students, escaped to bring home stories of civil war among the Greek factions, of treachery, and of the great chief Odysseus, with the classic name, who sold himself and his men to the Turks. Goethe described the years of fighting for Greek independence as a time of 'grimmest anarchy', and grim and anarchic these years were, in common with all initial periods of liberation of peoples long oppressed.

Goethe observed these struggles with scepticism. Some of the leaders he knew, such as Count Capo d'Istrias, whom he had met in Karlsbad, when he was a Russian minister and diplomat. When Goethe heard that this man had been appointed chief of government of a still very undefined Greek State he said that in his opinion the Count would not be able to stay in power because he was not a soldier. 'We have no example of a man trained in cabinet government being able to organize a revolutionary State and sub-jugate the military and the commanders-in-chief. Sword in hand, at the head of an army, a man is in a position to command and make laws, and he can be certain of being obeyed, but without this it is a precarious business.' He was right; Capo d'Istrias was murdered in the struggle between chief-tains and factions.

This guerilla fighting meant little or nothing to Goethe; Byron was a figure he could grasp. In this last venture of his Goethe found 'something impure', that worried and disturbed him. But a great deal in Byron touched a chord in him, it was like the fulfilment of secret desires of his own which he had never been able to realize. He was a keen reader of his works, even attempting to translate and annotate them; he even read the hysterical Caroline Lamb's three-volume novel *Glenarvon*. He was always hearing about him; the whole younger generation was under his spell, and Ottilie was a fanatic admirer of the demon poet. In the calm that followed the downfall of Napoleon, the truly great demon, people longed for colour, adventure and excitement in a world that was growing tamer year by year. It was the heyday of the virtuoso. Paganini, of whom it was said that the devil himself tuned his violin, was feted everywhere with wild enthusiasm. And like a comet this English Lord flashed across the European stage, another virtuoso performing his own devil's trills and moving lamentosos on the G-string, until fate tore the instrument from his hands. Goethe's admira-tion for him was boundless, he looked upon him as his only peer. In *Euphorion*, in the second part of *Faust*, he has raised to Byron the most splendid monument erected to any poet of more recent times.

The completion of *Faust* is now Goethe's 'main business', and it is the greatest achievement ever accomplished by a poet of his years. He also tries stubbornly to bring some sort of completion to his many half-finished or abandoned works. He takes his memoirs up to the point he has planned; the material that cannot be included in the continuous narrative he notes down separately. Here he sees himself with sharper and more critical eyes than any of his commentators have dared to do.

I have never known a more presumptuous man than myself, and the fact that I say this shows it to be true. I never believed a thing had to be attained, I always thought I had already attained it. If someone had set a crown on my head, I should have taken it for granted. And yet just because of this I was only a man like other people. It was only the fact that having undertaken things beyond my powers I tried to carry them out, that having received beyond my deserts I tried to be deserving, which differentiated me from a truly insane person.

Everything becomes the subject of doubt, even his beloved natural science, which to the outer world he still defends with furious outbursts against the 'priests of the guild'. Reflectively he muses: 'All my research into nature has gained me no more than the conviction that I know nothing.' Eckermann copies the sentence down on the spot, but he does not dare to include it in his book. 'If I had not been so absorbed in stones, and had put my time to better use, I could now have the most beautiful collection of diamonds.' Eckermann writes this down, crosses it out, and finally appends it to Goethe's other regret that he had devoted so much time 'to things that did not belong within my real province. When I reflect on what Lopez de Vega did, the sum of my poetic works looks very small. I should have kept more to my real *métier*.'

Nevertheless even in this real *métier* there is plenty of material. Goethe wants to collect it together in a great final edition of his works, an *Ausgabe letzter Hand*, which is to be his last will and testament: forty volumes, with a further twenty volumes of posthumous works. It is also to serve as the first example of a German author being able to harvest the fruits of his labour, instead of merely feeding the pirates. Goethe's protracted and careful negotiations to protect this edition by privileges, in every possible way, also afford a picture of the contemporary political situation in Germany. At the Congress of Vienna, and with great difficulty, a 'German *Bund*' had been created; a very loose, unstable structure, it was really no more than a permanent conference of delegates, with its seat at Frankfurt. This substitute for an empire had no executive authority, it could only discuss and make recommendations, and the larger member States paid no more attention to these than did Prussia and Austria in the old days to the Diet of Regensburg. Goethe, therefore, has to approach each member State for a privilege. To this end he writes to friends and admirers and makes use of all his far-reaching connections. Long negotiations with almost a dozen publishers follow. Goethe demands the huge sum of one hundred thousand *thalers*, and finally Cotta, who has already proved his worth, wins the contract. It is almost like an auction, and it gives Goethe the satisfaction of seeing the extent of his fame and influence, of seeing the size of the Goethe

Empire that he has built up. It is bigger than the 'German *Bund*', and is to last longer.

Goethe lived to see the first forty volumes on his writing-desk: 'I did not think I should live to see it', he said in 1830. The first of the posthumous volumes contained the second part of *Faust*, further sections of his memoirs, his writings on natural science, many additions to the poems, and other works. Throughout this 'last will and testament' one can observe how strangely his sense of form and order becomes confused by the editorial requirements of the moment: it is desirable that in the posthumous volumes the public should become acquainted with important and hitherto unknown works, so that the interest does not flag. The result is that the production exhibits a lack of order and unity; shortly after Goethe's death, a newly arranged edition was necessary.

But this had little effect on its tremendous impact. In convenient pocket-size volumes Goethe's works spread throughout the country; Cotta also printed a larger and finer edition, but few people bought it. These small volumes were henceforth 'the Goethe' for the great majority of readers. It was from them that composers took their *Lieder* texts, and the German Lied from Schubert to Hugo Wolf is based to a considerable extent on Goethe's lyrics. Students of aesthetics turned to the volumes on art and literature, philologists – already at work in Goethe's lifetime – studied early versions of works, the German family now had its 'complete Goethe' in the bookcase, and sometimes even read it.

Goethe tried to complete his *Wilhelm Meister* for this edition, and *Wilhelm Meisters Wanderjahre* also develops into a kind of last will and testament, with the same mixture of wisdom and disorder as the *Works*. The colourful and varied life, which made the first Meister novel so rich, is so completely excluded from the *Wanderjahre* that the novel becomes deliberately grey, colourless and, in many parts, dark and sombre. With the 'wandering' of its title the book has little to do, or at any rate not in the romantic sense extolled in the *Wanderlieder* of the day. Goethe's characters move about and the scene changes, but all trace of naturalness, of high spirits, of freedom to roam from place to place is denied them. Their code of behaviour is based on service and renunciation; the book's sub-title is *Die Entsagenden*. They are to be educated, and a 'pedagogic province', an educational Utopia, forms the central section of the book. But with all Goethe's preaching of discipline and order, his novel displays the very opposite of these qualities. It is loosely put together from previously published short stories intended for another collection; some of them are of a high quality, others are poor. Goethe had his publisher send him a copy of the first version, interleaved with blue paper for additions and supplementary material; this was supplied by Eckermann from the drawers of the Goethe archives. The blue of the paper comes through everywhere and frequently it is not even covered. Maxims, reflections, and poems are scattered through the book. Goethe has lost all interest in his earlier characters; Wilhelm himself disappears almost completely, the charming Philine is relegated to honest housework and to knitting stockings, as though the author wanted to take a belated revenge on the character that had so worried him in the earlier book. Other characters fade off into allegorical shadows, or become so confused that the author himself loses his way and lets the threads fall from his hands. He then calmly addresses an editorial note to his public telling them that they must see what they can make of it all.

But Goethe is also a great magician and loves games. He enjoys doing conjuring tricks with his grandchildren Wölfchen and Walter; there are games, such as a 'magic *quodlibet*', magic squares and puzzles, and Marianne sends a box of such games from Frankfurt. A conjurer, addressed by the title of Professor, is invited to the house, and leaves with a poem from the Olympian in his pocket: '*Bedarfs noch ein Diplom, besiegelt? Umögliches hast du uns vorgespiegelt* (What is the need for a title as well? You have dazzled our eyes with your marvellous spell).

Goethe's Utopia is a magician's performance like this, a game with glass pearls, as Hermann Hesse saw it when, using Goethe's *Wanderjahre* as a starting point, he tried to emulate it in his *Glasperlenspiel*. Goethe's starting point is a dream, a fairy-tale. His fairy-tale, *Die neue Melusine*, which has absorbed him since his early days, is placed at the centre of the book. He records in his memoirs that he told the tale to Friederike and her family in Sesenheim; at that time, it had a hidden meaning. His Melusine is no mermaid, but a dwarf from the pygmy world; the thought of being imprisoned with her in her Lilliputian household, be it ever so charming, is his lifelong dream of fear, the dread of the 'marriage sack' that had tormented him as a student in Leipzig. 'What a sense of horror I felt when I heard the mention of marriage', says the hero of the story, whom the little princess entices into her tiny home. Secretly filing through the wedding ring that holds him prisoner, he grows once more to his former size, as he had seen himself in his dream: 'I had an ideal of myself, and sometimes in my dreams I saw myself as a giant.' The aged giant Goethe dreams a dream once more. He wants to transform the miniature world in which he lives. He wants to teach wisdom; the desire to teach has always been very strong in him, and now he wants to influence future generations, a future community. His goal is no longer the individual, as it was in the *Lehrjahre*, but the community. Nor is it an aristocratic society any longer, its members devoted exclusively to cultivating their minds. In his new community the people are expected to be active, modest, practical; his hero, Wilhelm, who in the *Lehrjahre* had been granted the title of nobility by one of his superiors of the secret society, now becomes a modest unassuming surgeon. There is no question, however, of any wider application to the state and society in general; even here Goethe can only envisage a small group, a band of brothers with common aspirations, who leave their homeland to settle in a new country, in America for example. Lili, his sweetheart of long ago, had once wanted to go with him to the New World.

The education of this small group, which he sees as a microcosm of mankind in general, to their new life of renunciation and worthy practical activity is outlined by Goethe in his Utopian 'pedagogic province', which, like all Utopias, is situated nowhere. Recalling his talks with Goethe on the subject, Riemer said that 'the Germans with their chronic passion for teaching' saw in this Utopia a practical proposal for some kind of boarding school, but this had not been the master's intention, who had printed an imaginary picture which, at the same time, he had surveyed with a serene good humour.

It is only thus, by regarding Goethe's image with a certain amount of humour, that this Utopia becomes tolerable. The theatre, once seen as the 'mission', is forbidden out of hand to its students: 'The drama presupposes leisured masses, perhaps even a vulgar mob, and such things do not exist with us', says the Principal; 'rabble of that kind if it does not leave indignantly of its own accord, is shown across the border.' The theatre is trickery and incompatible with the serious purpose of his scheme of education. Plato, with whom a reviewer compares Goethe, to the old man's great pleasure, banned Homer with equal joylessness from his terrible Utopian state. Even the imagination, a 'vague, unstable faculty', is to be excluded so far as possible: strict and formal discipline, such as is necessary in practising the piano, is recommended, rather than 'originality and independence'. Discipline and respect are to be studied, respect being paid 'even to what could be termed conventional – for what else is this other than that the most eminent people have agreed to consider that which is necessary, that which is indispensable, to be the best'. There is scarcely a single thing which the ardent, creative young Goethe, or even the man Goethe, did, thought or hoped, but that we find its exact opposite advocated here. Christ himself, alien to Goethe throughout his life, is now introduced as an active Christ, although the suffering Jesus is to be excluded, for the Cross has no place in this Utopia: 'we draw a veil over this suffering'.

A veil enshrouds the whole book and its characters, which are no longer characters but simply puppets that bear scrolls announcing Goethe's views. The work has no conclusion, but merely a closing scene: Wilhelm, the surgeon, rescues his son Felix from drowning; perhaps a new life awaits him beyond the confines of the novel, in common with the others who seek the New World. The community life is not shown or described: it is a doctrine, an aspiration, a challenge; as Goethe himself says, it is up to the reader to lift the veil and interpret his teaching. Then it will be said that 'Goethe already knew' what the future had in store. He speaks of the menace of industrialism, although, living in rural Weimar, he had no experience of industry; it is an intuition, a surmise, based on certain forebodings. There are many things in the book which would be more likely to draw the comment: 'Goethe could still say. ...' He stands on the watershed of the times and often has the feeling that with his life a whole epoch has passed which will never return.

The echo produced by this work is, not unnaturally, very conflicting and confused. Goethe is deeply moved by every sign of recognition on the part of his readers; he sees it as evidence of active co-operation in a difficult and ungrateful task. They are not satisfied merely to accept what he has done but invest it, 'out of their own charming fertility, with higher meaning and more powerful effect'. It pleases him to see the problem of his life, 'about which I myself could still well be mistaken, solved so plainly and clearly before the eyes of the nation; as a result I feel enlightened as to much that was puzzling, and quietened as to much that was disturbing'.

To these observations he adds a *Lebenslied*, a song of midnight, the sound of whose bells has accompanied him from childhood to the fullness of his manhood. Musingly he repeats the dark-sounding word 'midnight' at the end of each stanza; it is a warning of a last midnight that now draws near.

# 43

# *Faust*

The great marvel of Goethe's closing years is the completion of his *Faust*. There are many examples of great creative activity continuing into extreme old age. Sophocles wrote *Oedipus Coloneus*, the last of his one hundred and twenty-five plays, at the age of almost 90; at 80 Verdi wrote his first comic opera. Goethe liked to quote the case of Titian, who according to legend lived to nearly a hundred, saying that at the end he painted velvet only symbolically, 'the idea of velvet', a remark that has its significance for Goethe's own work on *Faust*.

In the last scene, Faust is a hundred years old when he dies. Perhaps Goethe thought he would reach that age. He heard of pious hopes in the ranks of his admirers, among them the romantic King Ludwig I of Bavaria, that this would be so. When told, Goethe recalled the great courtesan, Ninon de Lenclos, who reached the age of 90 'after having brought happiness and despair to hundreds of lovers until she was in her eightieth year'. Goethe by no means despised such comparisons. The great lovers and sinners among the women of the Bible and church tradition are among the circle of those who welcome Faust in Heaven. In the second part of *Faust* the Sirens sing: '*So herrsche denn Eros, der alles begonnen*' (Let Eros then reign, the begetter of all). *Das Ewig-Weibliche* (the eternal feminine) is his final word.

In his own life too, Goethe jests daringly about death. When his old friend Sömmering, with whom he had exchanged ideas on the *Farbenlehre*, dies at the age of 75, he cries scornfully: '75! what fools men are that they have not the courage to live longer than that!' He has praise for Jeremy Bentham, on the other hand, that 'great radical fool ... his health remains good, and he is some weeks older than I am'. Bentham is a fool for his ideas on parliamentary reform, and for his doctrine of 'the greatest happiness of the greatest number'; but it gives Goethe pleasure to hear that he has never had a day's illness in his life. He dies in the same year as Goethe.

Goethe does not let himself think of death. Around him the stage has grown bare, even those nearest to him, like Karl August and the Duchess Luise, are dead; the poets and writers of his own generation, and even younger ones like Kleist, Novalis and Byron, have gone too. The great musicians have died young: Mozart, Schubert, Weber. They all had to be 'ruined', as he said to Eckermann; they had fulfilled their mission and it was time for them to go, 'so that something should still be left for other people to do in this world ...'. Schiller's body has been exhumed, thirty years after his death, and re-buried in the new 'princes' vault'. Goethe held the skull, the 'dry shell', in his hands; it was 'as though a well of life were sprung from death', as he writes in his poem, 'A glimpse that took me to those surging waters, pouring forth enhanced and nobler beings.' *Steigerung*, constant enhancement and development, is his life-principle. For the end of his *Faust* he turns to the imagery of ecclesiastical tradition: 'The end was difficult to write,' he tells Eckermann; it could easily have become lost in vagueness 'had I not given to my poetic intentions a salutary restricting form and firmness through the use of the sharply defined figures and notions of the Christian church'. So far as he himself is concerned he scornfully rejects these notions; such things are for people who have not been successful in this life, or for pious women. These have examined him often enough, as Gretchen examines Faust: What about your religion? 'But I annoyed them by saying that while I should be quite ready to enjoy another life after this one was finished, I should want to insist on not meeting up there any of those who had been believers here below.' Even eternal bliss with an eternal Gretchen would have been disagreeable to him. He tells his friend Müller: ' I must confess I should not know what to do with eternal bliss, if it did not present me with new problems and difficulties to overcome.' There is no dearth of problems: 'We have only to look at the planets and suns, they will provide us with sufficient nuts to crack.' And to Eckermann he says: 'For me the conviction of our continuing existence derives from the concept of activity: for if I continue to be unremittingly active until my end, nature will be obliged to assign to me another form of existence when the present one is no longer able to endure my spirit.' It could not be expressed more proudly.

He sees himself as a continuously and permanently active unit of power that is indestructible. To express this he uses the philosophical term 'entelechy', used originally by Aristotle and transformed by Goethe for his own purpose; the principle of metamorphosis applies also to the terms he uses. For him the essential part of the word is *telos*, the goal, an infinite goal to which the *einmal geprägte Form*, the form once moulded, aspires. From Leibnitz he takes the term *monad*, by which he understands 'the stubbornness of the individual, and the fact that man discards what does not conform to his individuality'. This stubbornly preserved unity is immortal: 'I have no doubt of our continuing existence, for nature cannot dispense with entelechy; but our immortality takes different forms, and in order to appear in the future as a great entelechy it is necessary to be one already.'

Later it becomes the task of the philosophers to discuss the underlying philosophic content of *Faust* in their own idiom. The theologians debate the problem of God's mercy, also in their own idiom, while the lawyer disputes the question whether Faust lost his wager, knowing that his colleague will disagree, '*car tel est son métier*'. Literary research probes the sixty years of the work's genesis, pointing out the many flaws, inconsistencies and gaps, which undeniably exist. Some of the investigations are subtle and admirable, worthy of Goethe's own, many are mere scholastic exercises. We do not know Bach's 'intention' in writing *Das Wohltemperierte Klavier*, and we do not know Goethe's 'intention' in *Faust* – he himself expressly refused to define it. It is the work of a poet. Schubarth's attempts to solve the riddle by supplying his own solutions drew from Goethe the angry comment: 'The way in which I have ended my *Faust* is a matter you should leave to the poet!' What Schubarth had done was 'prosaically realistic', what he had done was 'poetically symbolic'.

Poetry and symbolism are open to many interpretations and, if we are to use the word at all, this is Goethe's intention. A poem should be 'incommensurable', he declares time and time again. In his old age he likes to express himself in the form of Orphic or Sibylline aphorisms, in 'secret oracles', or, as Rainer Maria Rilke has said, he 'deigns' to write. It is the form he uses intentionally for his *Märchen* and for his *Novelle*, which is really a legend. Sometimes we can see the augur's smile which he used to exchange with Schiller; after Schiller's death he rarely found another augur of equal standing. Above all Goethe believes in intuition – and in *Faust* more than anywhere else – in the happy inspiration, the *aperçu*, as he calls it in his writings on natural science. In the *Sturm und Drang* period of his youth it was *Dumpfheit*, unconscious divination. It is the spirit of holiness that possesses the seer, it is the Pythia of the ancients seated on her tripod above the crevice in the rock, enveloped in the mist that rises from the bowels of the earth.

In the second part of *Faust* this tripod becomes the symbol of poetic creative power. When Faust wants to conjure up Helen he has first to descend to the 'mothers', in the bowels of the earth, where 'some sit, others come and go, as the spirit moves them'; Goethe conjures up the picture as '*Gestaltung, Umgestaltung, des ewigen Sinnes ewige Unterhaltung, Umschwebt von Bildern aller Kreatur*' (Formation, transformation, eternal mind's conversation, and all around the images of every creature). The tripod stands there aglow. Faust has to touch it with the key that Mephistopheles has given him, it will find the right place of its own accord. In fact the tripod attaches itself to the key, following it like a 'faithful servant', an idea not easy to visualize; it is a symbol, a sign, almost a cipher, and would be an easy subject for a surrealist painter. The tripod is attached to the key like iron to a magnet, pole to pole, and with this magic sign Faust is able to transform the mist into gods and goddesses, and to conjure up Helen from the past. Faust is going to awaken her for his 'conversation'. Neither time nor space is stipulated for the 'mothers', and all attempts of later commentators to define or localize them, to interpret them as Goethe's *Urphenomena* or as manifestations of his concept of 'type', are vain. When Eckermann asks for an explanation, Goethe refuses to say anything; he only looks at him with his great eyes and quotes his own lines: '*Die Mütter, Mütter, s'klingt so wunderlich*' (Mothers, mothers, how strangely the word sounds). This in its turn may give rise to many new interpretations, if commentators wish to dig deeper in search of the 'mothers' and their images. But in one of Goethe's grandest inversions Mephistopheles says to Faust, before Faust descends to the 'very deepest' depths: '*Versinke denn! Ich könnt auch sagen: steige!* (Sink to the depths then! I could as well say: rise).

The almost strained silence with which Goethe greets his pupil's question has yet another significance. The word 'mothers' always comes 'like a blow' to Faust. He does not want to hear it, just as Goethe does not really want to hear his own mother's name mentioned. He dislikes being reminded of his origin. To him 'mother' represents the persisting, unchanging element of which he has a horror. This mother's womb is the darkness from which he came. What he wants is to rise to the light. Thus it is that in this passage he makes Mephistopheles speak of rising, of *hinauf*.

But we are concerned here with Goethe's life. A sense of horror, of secret anxiety, like that of Faust trying to awaken the shadows, repeatedly overcomes him in the presence of this work, and often causes him to hesitate. On a number of occasions he even thinks of giving it up entirely, of 'burying' it. On one occasion he writes an *Abkündigung*, giving the work 'notice', and declaring the whole First Part to be barbarism, a term he had invented with Schiller to denote everything that was not classical. What he has written hitherto has been born of a 'confusion of emotions'; now he has advanced on the road to clarity, and the 'limited circle with its magic' is to be closed for ever. Mephistopheles too, the representative of evil, is to disappear. But the work is more powerful than all aesthetic theories, and he is not going to be able to rid himself of his Mephistopheles until the end. The work is always clamouring for attention, bringing new doubts and a new creative urge.

The work has already been made very famous by the publication of its First Part, and even before the appearance of the Second Part the questions start.

What strange people the Germans are [Goethe says to Eckermann], they make their lives miserable by trying to find deep thoughts and ideas everywhere and to read them into everything. Just for once have the courage to surrender yourselves to impressions, to allow yourselves to be entertained, to allow yourselves to be moved, to be uplifted, yes to be instructed and to be kindled and encouraged to something great! But do not always think everything vain and empty unless it is an abstract thought or idea of some kind!

Now they come and ask what idea I have tried to embody in my *Faust*. As though I knew myself and could put it into words. From heaven through earth to hell – that might do at a pinch; but it is not an idea, it is the course of the action. And furthermore the fact that the devil loses his wager, and that there is a man to be redeemed who is constantly striving to escape from his mistakes and rise to better things – all this is certainly an operative and good thought that can explain much, but it is not an idea.... [No] the more incommensurable and the more impossible for reason to grasp a poetic creation is, the better!

Goethe's work on *Faust* lasted sixty years and had a previous history of three hundred years. Goethe did not invent the theme; its origins are in the dark soil of ancient folk tradition, in a very crude figure that nevertheless was predestined to grow into a world poem. The first *Faust* book, a bookseller's speculation, was compiled by a cleric with a ready pen, and published in Frankfurt in 1587. It is a tract, a collection of drolleries, and the story of a Dr Faust, an historical figure who had lived at the beginning of the century. He was a wandering scholar, a physician, astrologer, magician and braggart, whose real name was probably Sabellicus but who called himself Faustus, the fortunate one. He died poor, and totally lacking in fortune, somewhere about 1540, carried off by the devil, it was said. He is mentioned by Luther in his *Table Talk*; Melanchthon calls him an abominable beast, a 'sewer of all the devils', a trickster who went round accompanied by the devil in the form of a dog and boasted that his magic had led the Imperial army to victory in Italy. The book, however, presents Faust as a rather pitiful figure, a constant prey to his bad conscience.

Although he starts by announcing that he is going to take eagle's wings and explore every corner of earth and heaven, this *Faust* is hardly a man to storm the gates of heaven. He is a speculative creature who has studied too much in obscure languages, the cabbalistic arts and necromancy; books are his undoing and the magic book seals his fate. This book is really a book against books; it is no accident that Faust's name is mentioned so often later in connection with the invention of the art of printing, the 'black art'. It is a book directed against the scholars and the learned, or at any rate against such of them as stray from the path of honest orthodox Lutheran theology. It is a reaction against the proud and stormy age of the humanists, who had begun by rediscovering antiquity – Dr Faust also volunteers to produce the lost comedies of Plautus and Terence – and had then dared to explore the universe and to stretch out their hands towards the suns and the stars. Only mischief can come from such presumption. The author does his best to reduce the doctor to a small and pitiful figure, and to let him perish miserably. But he is unable to bury him once and for all, as no doubt he wished to do.

Quite to the contrary: this Dr Faust now grows as though by magic into an entirely different figure. The Reformation and the Renaissance have not resulted in enlightenment; people are more superstitious than before, haunted by fear of demons, by fear of sorcerers and, at the same time, by secret admiration for these all-powerful miracle workers. The trashy book becomes the best-seller of its day, is reprinted times without number, and translated into five or six foreign languages; it spreads over the whole of Europe. Scarcely a year after its first appearance, the first great *Faust* poem is written in London. At one stroke Christopher Marlowe restores the figure, darkened by the pious tract, to its original splendour, or rather he gives it its first true greatness. His play breathes a different atmosphere to that of the German book, with its stuffy scholar's study in a small Gothic town. Marlowe lives at the centre of things, close to the sea and close to a great port; his eyes are turned to the world into which Drake and the other royal pirates sail, to conquer an empire or to win unheard of treasure. His Faust wants to plunder India, the ocean of its pearls, to unite Africa with Spain. His Faust is the contemporary of Bacon, not of Luther or Melanchthon. He is already able to conceive the daring notion that Hell may be a fiction, 'trifles and meere olde wives' tales'.

Goethe did not read this work of genius until after he had written his *Faust*. But it was Marlowe's play that first gave stature to the Faust-figure and enabled it to live on, though in ever more stunted and ludicrous forms. On the stage this *Faust* survived in popular plays and puppet shows, and through these became familiar to Goethe in his youth. Parallel with this stage figure, and completely separate from it, the original tract begat a long series of further tracts, by further devout clerics, who continued to storm in the same spirit against the 'hideous and abominable sins and vices' of Dr Faust. The book became so swollen with pious additions that nobody read it any more, and finally it ended its existence cut up into dry-as-dust extracts in the manner of the eighteenth century. One of these tracts once came into Goethe's hands, but it is doubtful if he made any use of it; the stage *Faust* of the popular plays and puppet shows was his first inspiration.

The way in which this figure reached Germany was a strange one. The travelling companies of English comedians played Marlowe's tragedy, with additions and alterations by his successors, who debased it with clown scenes; in this form it reached the German public. Although these travelling companies acted in English, they were understood, despite the fact that scarcely anyone in the Germany of that time spoke English: the actors were superb mimes, who used enormously dramatic and violent gestures and effects; the principal attraction was the clown with his wooden stick, which he carried suggestively between his legs, like the phallic comedians of the Greek theatre. *Doctor Faustus* was first and foremost a performance in mime. The Courts patronized them, and in Brunswick Duke Heinrich Julius himself wrote plays for them in the latest prose style; the Duke ended his days in Prague as chief counsellor at the Court of the Emperor Rudolf II, in the weird Faust-like atmosphere of cabbala, sorcery, deep artistic understanding and brutal superstition that led into the witches' sabbath of the Thirty Years' War.

Duke Heinrich Julius of Brunswick, so modern in other respects, was extremely superstitious and a great burner of witches; stakes by the hundred, with their charred corpses, surrounded his residence of Wolfenbüttel. For it was only now, and not in the Middle Ages, that the really great and bloody days of demonism began. The Blocksberg, the Brocken, close to the Brunswick residence, became the secret meeting-place where, on Walpurgis-night, the witnesses were supposed to meet and worship Satan as 'Herr Urian'. Poisoned sexual imagination gloated on their obscene doings. Anti-feminism was the chief feature of the epidemic; woman and woman alone, not man, was the seat of all evil, it was from her womb that the devil spake. Learned scholars furnished the proof. Jean Bodin, a great teacher of political science still admired in the Age of Enlightenment, became the 'scientific' authority with his work *Demonology*; in this he appeals to Plato and to physiology to show that, by their very size, the internal organs of woman must give rise to insatiable desire, which in its turn leads to Satan. The book was printed, reprinted, and enlarged through the centuries; even around 1700 a Bodinus was published in Frankfurt, with additions by a learned German lawyer who expounded in detail, from the 'official records', what took place on the Blocksberg.

The 'ugly ways of devils and witches', as Goethe referred to them in his old age, nevertheless exercised a great influence over him. They were ugly enough. The women were supposed to smear themselves with ointment made from the fat of murdered new-born children and ride up the chimney and through the night on rakes, brooms and tubs to the Blocksberg. 'Up and away, on high and in the nowhere, in the name of the evil one!' On the Blocksberg there were lights and torches, countless people, great lords too, and knights and officers – as in Goethe's *Walpurgisnacht* – clergy, scholars and peasants. The witches had to present themselves to Satan, enthroned in the midst in the form of a he-goat, and kiss his hindquarters in adoration. This was also used by Goethe in a daring scene, which he then put away in his '*Walpurgis-bag*', where many things disappeared and only came to light again long after the poet's death. It was the logical climax of the witches' sabbath, with its song and stink of the he-goat. Satan instructs the assembly of he- and she-goats: shining gold and the resplendent phallus, these are the symbols of ultimate things. The chorus joins in: '*Er zeigt euch die Spur des ewigen Lebens, der tiefsten Natur*' (He shows you the way to eternal life, to the very heart of nature). Here once more is the magic word nature, which does not mean for Goethe mere pleasant landscape and the study of morphology. He has also treated the same theme in the Second Part of *Faust*, but in a more cautious, veiled form. It is a very essential part of the basic conception of the work; Goethe speaks here of elemental forces.

The dark world of magic and witches was still a reality in the early years of Goethe's own lifetime, and by no means only in books, or as a relic of the Middle Ages, as it was for the Romantics. The courts and popular 'justice' still examined witches and they were still drowned and burned at the stake, if not in masses, nevertheless in grim reality. At the fairs popular cheap books were on sale containing the story of Doctor Faust. *Fausts Höllenzwang*, his recipe for conjuring up Hell, circulated in manuscript copies; even the theologian Dr Bahrdt, satirized in one of Goethe's early parodies as an insipid modernist, relates in his autobiography how he once tried out the recipe. To the young Goethe all this was living reality, like the cabbalistic books on alchemy, or Swedenborg, from whom his *Erdgeist* is taken, or like the 'red lion' of his experiments with the sand-bath and 'virginal earth'.

Goethe's *Faust* does not derive only from books. Its background is old Gothic Frankfurt, and from the court records, which his father had had transcribed in many volumes to console his lonely hours, Goethe took the case of Susanna Margaretha, who had murdered her newly-born child. The case occurred in 1772, soon after Goethe's return from Strasbourg, where in one of the theses for his Licentiate, he had dealt with the problem of punishing such a crime, simply stating that the experts were divided on the subject. Later, when he was minister, he voted in favour of the traditional capital punishment. In the Frankfurt of his youth this was still carried out with grisly traditional pomp, and with the participants wearing their old colourful costumes, as a spectacle for the whole town. The girl, a poor soldier's daughter, had been seduced by a journeyman goldsmith who vanished soon afterwards. The accused maintains that her lover drugged her by putting something in her wine. She speaks continually of the devil, saying that Satan never left her side until the murder was committed. Deeply repentant she is sentenced to death by the sword; among those trying her are some of Goethe's relatives. The judge announces the sentence dressed in black and wearing boots and spurs; round his shoulders hangs a red cloak, from beneath which he produces the dreaded little red stick. Breaking this, he throws the pieces at the girl's feet. In prison the traditional last meal of many courses is served, attended not only by the executioner but also by the judges and members of the clergy; the pastors eat little, the girl takes a sip of water. Bound with rope and to the accompaniment of bells, the criminal is led in a great procession through the streets; '*die Menge drängt sich ... der Platz, die Gassen, können sie nicht fassen*' (the people throng ... the square, the streets, cannot contain them all) as Goethe's Gretchen sings in prison. The executioner leads the girl by the rope, finally mounting the scaffold, where she is placed on the executioner's chair. 'To the accompaniment of constant exhortations from the clergy the head was successfully severed at a single stroke', states the official record with satisfaction. Her sister has to sign a receipt for the girl's belongings: some clothes, a prayer book, and a little pearl necklace – perhaps a present from her goldsmith.

This Frankfurt episode – in his memoirs Goethe mentions only 'horrible scenes' – is, of course, not the whole 'Gretchen tragedy'. Infanticide was a common literary theme. The young Schiller wrote a poem on the subject, full of pathos and theatrical effect, in which he showed early evidence of the great playwright in contrasting the 'rose-hued lover's knot' with the 'black band of death' on the scaffold. In his *Phantasie an Laura* he also expressed the anxieties of every young man of the day concerning the 'snakes' coils of shame and remorse entwined round sin', the treacherous danger that was always lurking. Whether Goethe, after Sesenheim or on any other occasion, ever experienced such feelings of shame and remorse we do not know; the evidence we have of his life and letters speaks a very much more care-free language.

We know equally little of the sources from which his first *Faust* tragedy stems. Goethe himself made a secret of it. There were the puppet shows, the penny pamphlets on Doctor Faust, and the popular plays, one of which he may have seen in Strasbourg. But there were Faust figures peeping from every corner, even though Marlowe's daring firebrand of a doctor had degenerated into a travelling quack with the red nose of a clown. The public were ready to laugh at the mere thought of seeing a Dr Faust on the stage, and when Lessing thought of writing a play on the subject, well-meaning friends advised him against touching this popular figure of farce. In spite of this Lessing wrote his play, or possibly even two, but all that has survived is a published fragment of one of them. In any case, he intended to endow the character with a certain nobility and with the desire to seek truth. An angel was to dispute Hell's triumph: 'Deity has not given man the noblest of all impulses in order to make him eternally miserable.' There were other Faust plays as well; the painter Müller, whom Goethe met again in Rome, wrote some disconnected *Faust* scenes in the style of the *Sturm und Drang*, with realistic dialogue and a fine etching on the title-page which is the best part of the work. All of which shows only that the character seemed to be waiting to be brought to life again.

At first Goethe, too, only wrote down disconnected scenes on loose sheets and scraps of paper. He destroyed these early sketches. Fifty years after his death a copy of some early *Faust* scenes was discovered among the papers of the Duchess Amalie's hunchbacked lady-in-waiting, Fräulein von Göch-hausen; in the excitement over the great discovery this copy was optimistically christened the *Ur-Faust*. Since that day commentators have never ceased speculating about this 'very first', original *Faust*, about the various stages in the work's creation, and about the 'very last' posthumous *paralipomena*, which in fact are an assortment of fragments from the various stages of the work.

For twelve years after the first Frankfurt sketch almost nothing was added; then in Italy one scene was written, and after his return to Weimar Goethe added some more; in this form, and under the title *Faust, ein Fragment*, the tragedy appeared for the first time among his *Collected Works* in 1790. Under pressure of preparing a new *Collected Edition* Goethe finished the First Part and published it in 1808. Finally the preparation of the last great edition of his works stimulated him to the completion of the Second Part, which was published shortly after his death in the first volume of the *Posthumous Works*. These are the bare facts. The *Ur-Faust* was written by the young man in his twenties, the First Part by the man of 50, and the Second Part was completed when Goethe was over 80.

Once more he summons all those powers which he has so often dissipated, and they are still mighty powers. Once more he turns an external stimulus to account and publishes his *Helena*, as well as some scenes from the beginning of the Second Part, before the rest of the work in the first volumes of his last *Collected Edition*; he adds at the end 'To be continued'. He has the manuscript bound and plain white pages inserted for filling in the omissions; in a similar way Richard Wagner used to rule out and divide the blank sheets of his scores before he wrote down a single note. He keeps this folio volume by his side as a constant and imperative reminder. On July 22, 1831 he notes in his diary: 'All the fair copies stitched together.' In August he seals the parcel. In January 1832, a few weeks before his death, he breaks the seal again to note: 'New excitement over *Faust* in regard to more extensive treatment of the principal themes which, in order to finish the work, I had treated too laconically.' But he has to leave it as it is; perhaps it will do. It will do.

*Faust* consists of *Verwandlungen*, a German word meaning changes of scene but having also the deeper meaning of transformations. Goethe has changed and passed through many transmutations, as have also his characters. We have seen such changes take place in his other writings; the longer he spends on a work the greater the changes, and on *Faust* he spends sixty years. This sequence of metamorphoses, combined into a single whole, constitutes the work's unity. In his *Farbenlehre* Goethe defines the struggle between the two powers of light and darkness as a struggle between equals, these being none other than the two poles of his own nature; between the two we have the interplay of colours – and in his drama the colourful play of *Faust*. Mephistopheles, to begin with the traditional tempter and delegate of Hell, becomes in turn Faust's 'companion', partner and, later on, sometimes merely the *raisonneur* of the early stage plays; from time to time the poet forgets both his main characters and turns his attention to other figures. Subjected to constant questioning about his play and his intentions, Goethe says that the First Part is the product of a more constrained, more passionate individual, 'a semi-darkness that may still give pleasure to people'. The Second Part is intended to display a higher, broader, less passionate world, less 'specific' and more 'generic'. These are abstractions, answers to painstaking queries on the part of his disciples. Goethe is also constantly at work on the portrait of himself he wishes to leave to posterity; it is to show a continuous development from the highest level to still higher levels. Consequently each previous stage in his development is cast aside, often scornfully, as 'tomfoolery'. In the intervals, however, he sometimes recalls 'the sweet darkness of the senses', 'the golden sunlit hours of spring', in which this dream, this *Faust,* began. We find many contradictions – Goethe is a man.

The great contradictory figure of the play is called Mephistopheles; he is no mere evil principle, but a living person who is often more convincing than his partner Faust. He is not only 'the spirit that always says "no"'. As Goethe shows in one of his masquerades (1818) he also affirms life; Faust, lost in fruitless study and speculation, is rescued by Mephistopheles: *'Ich macht ihm deutlich, dass das Leben Zum Leben eigentlich gegeben'* (I made it clear to him that life is really given to be lived) and should not be spent in mere whims, imaginings and intellectual subtleties. In the Second Part Faust expresses the same opinion; even in the hour of his death he does not want to hear of the life to come. The prospect is barred to us and only a fool turns his eyes in that direction and imagines people like himself up there above the clouds, *'er stehe fest und sehe hier sich um!'* (here is his place, here let him cast his gaze). These are the words of the dying Faust, and of the dying Goethe too.

In his private life Goethe also speaks as Mephistopheles on occasion; Soret has preserved one such conversation. The subject is Jeremy Bentham, the 'radical fool', who is always wanting to introduce radical reforms. Surely, says Soret, if His Excellency lived in England he would not shut his eyes to reform?

> Goethe (assuming at this instant the paradoxical and ironic tone of his Mephistopheles, no doubt in order to avoid political discussion, which he dislikes): Do you take me for a simpleton? You imagine that in England I would have spent my time tracking down and exposing abuses? I should have lived off them and exploited them! Had I been born an Englishman – which, thank Heaven, is not the case – I should be a duke and a millionaire, or still better a bishop with an income of 60,000 pounds.

Soret tries in vain to point out that in the lottery of life one can draw a blank. 'Do you suppose I should have been such a fool?' counters Goethe. He works himself up into the role of a stout defender of the articles of the Anglican faith, as though he were already a bishop. 'In a word, I should have lied in verse and prose for so long that the 60,000 pounds could not have eluded me. If one does not want to be crushed, one has to rise above everything, and look down from one's eminence on the crowd, which consists only of fools and imbeciles.' One must turn their stupidity to one's own advantage and not leave it to others to do. The mention of fools brings

Goethe to the subject of the madhouse: Karl August once tried to lure him into a lunatic asylum, although he knew Goethe's dislike of seeing such things; but he saw the game in time and refused, saying, 'I have no need whatever to see the ones who are locked up!' The whole world is a madhouse, and only a fool does not take advantage of the fact. This is Goethe too. He cannot be split into halves. One cannot even take his Mephistopheles apart; he also is made up of 'higher' and 'lower' qualities.

In order to explain the play to the many who were asking for guidance, Goethe wrote first his 'Prologue in Heaven' and, when this did not suffice, he followed it with the 'Prelude on the Stage'. Both led to new misunderstandings, caused above all by lines being taken from their context. Because of Goethe's great mastery of the epigram – more marked here than in the poems expressly called epigrams – *Faust* became the most popular and most quoted work in German literature. And not to the work's advantage; one could even reconstruct from those lines which have become common usage a picture of German Philistinism: '*Hier bin ich Mensch, hier darf ichs sein*' (Here I am a man, here I can be myself) the good honest citizen would say as he settled down comfortably in his favourite beer-garden, or when he slunk off down some back street in search of pleasure. One could also construct a whole psychology of German scholarship, and this is said without arrogance, from the various interpretations and commentaries that have been written on *Faust*. The scholar's profession calls for resignation, and so we find Goethe's 'resignation' being constantly stressed.

Goethe himself does not practise self-denial or resignation. He has to forgo many things, more often in his old age than in his younger days, but he rarely does so voluntarily. To his very last breath he never gives up. He wants to continue the fight. This is also the essential characteristic of his *Faust* who, at the last, wants to defeat the elements. Activity, ceaseless endless activity, is the important thing, not 'the deed' itself; *Faust* is no more a 'man of deeds' than is Goethe. It is significant that, although Goethe adopted almost all the features of the old folk tale, he left out the episode of Alexander the Great, the man of deeds. One of the most grotesque distortions of *Faust* interpretation was to call on *Faustisches Streben* to explain the establishment of the Second German Empire in 1871, and to justify the expansionist policy 'of the Germanic or, if one prefers, the West Aryan family of peoples', to quote the phrase used shortly afterwards by a great Goethe connoisseur, whose official position was financial adviser to the House of Hohenzollern.

Activity is the task assigned by the Lord to Faust in the Prologue, because without it mankind easily grows lazy. The devil, *der Schalk*, the rogue, is to act as a stimulant and thus prevent him from succumbing to absolute inactivity, and the Lord speaks the often-quoted lines: '*Ein guter Mensch in seinem dunklen Drange Ist sich des rechten Weges wohl bewusst*' (A good man, though he gropes to find his way, is well aware the path he ought

501

to take). Flashes of intense irony play about this whole scene, even though it is introduced by the archangels in some of Goethe's most powerful lines. Mephistopheles refers to the Lord as 'the old man' who speaks 'with such a human touch even to the devil'. Goethe also refers to God as 'the old man' in his letters. Instead of 'the good man', he calls Faust 'the poor man' on another occasion, and this is not so very far removed from 'the poor specimen' that he applied to Wilhelm Meister. Goethe follows the most solemn and mighty lines, in which in a few strokes he describes the creation of the universe, with '*In jeden Quark begräbt er seine Nase*' (he sticks his nose in every mess he finds). It is in this play of colours, in this tension between the sublime and the commonplace, that the secret of Goethe's incomparable voice lies; to extract single lines from their context destroys this unity and leads only to pedantry and scholastic exercises.

To make his play still clearer Goethe brings the poet, the fool and the theatre director in front of the curtain. The poet announces his high aims, the fool his deep wisdom, and 'the old man' of the stage has the final word. He tells the poet that he has hesitated too long and must now command his muse and brew 'strong drink'; the whole theatrical universe is at his disposal: the planets, the great and small lights of heaven, machinery and the water and fire of *Die Zauberflöte*, the great model for the opera-like scenes. Thus within the narrow confines of the stage he will be able to make his way through the whole cycle of creation, 'from Heaven by way of Earth to Hell'.

To Hell; this was written before Goethe was clear in his mind about the ending. For a long time he was in doubt, and was very far from commanding his muse. Whether, to begin with, he had the traditional descent to Hell in mind we do not know. In any event he adopted the story of the pact with the devil. In the old sixteenth-century tract this pact is seen as a solemn obligation: when a monk tries to convert the doctor and promises him God's mercy, Faust declares that it would not be honest 'for me to forswear my letter and seal, that were given with my blood: the devil has been honest in keeping his word to me, and so I intend to be honest in keeping my word to him'. He has transgressed God's command, and for this he must atone. For Goethe this theology has no validity, and he wants at all costs to avoid a tragic ending. He has already rescued Gretchen, at the end of the First Part, from the judgment of his *Ur-Faust* and 'saved' her by a voice from Heaven. In the 'Prologue in Heaven' a happy ending is already foreseen as a certainty, for in it Mephistopheles is none other than one of the 'ideas of God' himself, a beneficent vitalizing spirit that is to be allowed to have his way with Faust so long as 'the good man' is alive. What becomes of Faust, or of his soul, when he is dead is of no concern whatever to Mephistopheles; 'I've never in the least enjoyed dealing with the dead', he says somewhat disconcertingly. The old Hell of traditional ecclesiastical belief is not mentioned at all.

In the first part, however, Goethe has placed the pact, the bond Faust signs with the devil, at the beginning; it is a pact made with the devil of popular tradition and countersigned according to ancient usage in Faust's blood. The conditions are clearly laid down: the devil will serve Faust here on earth; in the world beyond Faust will serve the devil. Faust agrees readily – he is not worried about the world beyond, a statement he repeats, almost in the same words, at the end of Part Two, immediately before his death. The only thing left uncertain is the precise moment at which the pact becomes redeemable. In the old tract the term was twenty-four years. Goethe now invents a new and original form of pact, which he calls a 'wager', and which is concluded almost lightheartedly with the *Topp* and *Schlag auf Schlag* of tavern betting. Faust is impatient, he wants unlimited pleasures, gold, women, honour; as to his higher aspirations, the 'poor devil' cannot understand them anyhow. Feeling quite certain that Mephistopheles will never be able to provide these pleasures to his full satisfaction, Faust tells the devil: *'Werd ich zum Augenblicke sagen: Verweile doch! Du bist so schön! Dann magst du mich in Fesseln schlagen, Dann will ich gern zu Grunde gehn!'* (If the moment provided by Mephistopheles would be so sweet that he could wish it to last for ever, he will willingly allow himself to be cast into chains and perish in Hell). With this pact the journey into life in all its variety can start; it leads to the Brocken the summit of sensuality, and to Gretchen, at which point the drama emerges from the alluring world of pleasure and adventure and becomes a tragedy of love.

It is above all thus, as a tragedy, that the First Part of *Faust* has exercised an influence, both on its readers and on the theatre-going public for whom the play was expressly intended. In the Second Part, however, the tragedy becomes a 'world poem', and the mere 'subjectivity' – to use Goethe's expression – of the First Part is raised to the level of the universal. Faust is to enter a 'broader, higher, brighter' world, where he is to gain honour and riches and lead his life in more exalted regions. The Gothic world disappears to make way for the Greek dream of the *Helena*. Mephistopheles is changed from the devil of popular tradition into the companion and partner, or into the mere speaker who at times even addresses the audience directly. The pact is often forgotten and for a long time is completely abandoned. At times Goethe thinks of calling his *Helena*, the central section of the Second Part, an *Intermezzo*, to separate it from the context of the whole. But an ending has to be found and Goethe turns back to the beginning, to the traditional devil and Hell. The old pact makes its appearance once more and causes Goethe considerable difficulties. To his commentator Schubarth, whose main interest was the problem of Faust's guilt, Goethe says a little ambiguously: 'And when Faust is left with only half the guilt, the old man's prerogative of mercy comes into play and leads the whole work to the most serene and pleasing ending' (1820). But Goethe is still far from clear how this is to be achieved. When the fatal words that end the pact are spoken, he first makes Faust say: '*Ich darf zum Augenblicke sagen: Verweile doch!*' (And now I *can* say to this moment: Oh, linger on!), and then he corrects it to: '*Zum Augenblicke dürft ich sagen ...*' (and now I *could* say to this moment ...) to which he adds the lines '*Im Vorgefühl von solchem hohen Glück, Geniess ich jetzt den höchsten Augenblick*' (Anticipating bliss so great as this, makes this the greatest moment of my life). And this, Goethe thinks, should suffice.

But it does not satisfy the commentators. They want to know in so many words whether the wager was won or lost. To Schubarth Goethe spoke of 'half the guilt', but can one wager half a soul or half one's stake? Since then every conceivable 'halfness' has been broached: in his pact Faust 'really' means something different from the devil, who takes the pact literally, whereas Faust understands it in a 'higher sense'. Or still further equivocation: it is not the moment itself that is for Faust the greatest moment, but only the anticipation of some future moment. Or more questionable still: Faust has not his own personal enjoyment or advantage in mind but, as his last wish, wants to create 'free land for a free people', a noble and desirable aim. Such an explanation loses sight of the fact that Faust does not achieve this noble aim by his own endeavour, but solely through the quick and easy assistance of the devil. It also loses sight of the fact that, although shortly prior to this he has said that he would like for once 'to banish magic from his path', he does nothing of the kind, and that Mephistopheles is to conjure the land from a worthless swamp. Moreover, as Faust's previous conquests of land have shown, this creation of new land is unlikely to be accomplished without great sacrifice of human life, although indeed many people believe that a high aim can justify even the greatest sacrifices of human life and the use of the most devilish means.

All such attempts at interpretation are questionable in the extreme. The justifications have much the same look about them as Goethe's attitude in his conversation with Soret, when he was willing to lend his full support to the articles of the Anglican faith in order to gain his bishop's mitre. Goethe plays with the idea. His *Faust* is also a play, and a wager, after all, is a form of playing; in this work he is playing with lofty thoughts and images. Faust's deliverance is eventually brought about by God's mercy, a traditional ecclesiastical concept which Goethe treats very freely and in which he does not himself believe. Hell is represented by a prospect, or a piece of machinery, at the side of the stage; the ironic stage direction says: 'the hideous jaws of Hell yawn on the left'. It is a picture taken from the old mystery plays in which this scene was one of the main attractions, the audience cheering wildly as the devil's agents seized the damned and, with wild gestures, cast them into Satan's gaping jaws. Here Goethe is even closer to the old plays than he had been in his youth, and he conjures up the devilry in an extraordinary display of grotesque scenes and coarse language. The struggle for Faust's salvation is waged by the most daring means, and the heavenly hosts are forced to resort to what is virtually a rape of Faust's soul. The great redeemed women sinners of church tradition, those who have sinned and loved much and been forgiven, provide from their experience in their lives of sin the flaming roses, which drive away the devils. Nor has Goethe the slightest hesitation in transforming the ecclesiastical concept of the treasure of grace, which the saints have amassed, and which is available for transfer to others. It is as though Goethe wants to let all that is left him of fire and passion flare up and burn out before Faust is transferred to higher and cooler regions which, at the end, are given the neuter name *Das Ewig-Weibliche*. His Mephistopheles, now changed back into the old devil who, traditionally, is always fooled in the end, is tempted by the enticement of angels who, offering every conceivable allurement, including that of homosexuality, are so 'appetizing' that the representative of the eternal 'no' says an emphatic 'yes' to the 'charming rascals' and wants to embrace them. In his stage direction Goethe says that at this point Mephistopheles is 'forced into the proscenium', in other words out of the action altogether.

The 'clearly defined figures of ecclesiastical tradition', as Goethe described them to Eckermann, now enter. The final scene on the stage is a tableau, of which Goethe was so fond, inspired by his memory of the great fresco in the Campo Santo at Pisa, with its strictly hierarchically arranged ranks and groups. It forms a 'handsome group' at the close of a gigantic masquerade. Goethe had a continuation in mind and drafted a 'trial of Faust's soul', of the kind familiar to him from the Middle Ages and the proceedings at the canonization of saints, in which the *advocatus diaboli* appeared; wisely he abandoned the idea. He could not very well present his Faust as a saint, and the devil's advocate would have been able to produce much evidence to the contrary. At best Faust was a 'good man in his vague desires'; even the epithet 'good' is questionable and is only to be understood as spoken with kindly irony by the Lord.

In the old mystery play, *Everyman*, 'Good Works' and 'Faith' accompany the dying man as his helpers. Goethe did not believe in good works as a justification, and at no stage of his long journey does Faust have anything of the kind to show. As he confesses: *'Ich bin nur durch die Welt gerannt, ein jed Gelüst ergriff ich bei den Haaren'* (I have merely sped through life, clutching by the hair each new desire). He seduces Gretchen and witnesses her end with horror, but without exhibiting any feelings of guilt or remorse; he forgets her at once and she reappears only at the gates of Heaven. He then turns to 'more exalted spheres', to the Court of the Emperor. As an *intermezzo* he conjures up Helen and lives with her in a dream world of Greek beauty. He also dreams of ruling, of owning property – *'Herrschaft gewinn ich, Eigentum'*; with the help of Mephistopheles' magic he wins a battle for the Emperor, and for himself, as a reward, a wide stretch of barren land by the sea, which he is to make fertile. A centenarian now he plans his greatest work: in this barren stretch he sees a place for millions to live, a free land for a free people; and thus, in anticipation of his greatest moment, he dies. His urge for activity reigns until the end, and beyond: the dying man sees himself as the one mind, ruling over the multitudes of his subjects. They are to be industrious, each day they are to earn their freedom anew. Fame will cast its light on him: '*Es kann die Spur von meinen Erdentagen Nicht in Äonen untergangen*' (The traces of my earthly pilgrimage will ne'er be lost though aeons pass). As a future ruler he sinks into his grave.

That Goethe should put into the mouth of Faust these words about a free land for a free people is a fine and heartening thing, and shows him, as often, to be superior to most of his contemporaries. But to read into the words a social theory is to labour the point: moreover Goethe has given no indication of the precise form such a community would take. If we consult his life, and for that matter if we consult his *Faust*, we find that what he sees is always the one mind controlling the teeming multitudes. And it is very much an open question whether the close of his poem is intended to convey the degree of hope that is commonly read into it, and that he himself indicated in his reference to the 'most serene and pleasing ending'. The aged Goethe, as distinct from the aged Faust, is gloomy and pessimistic about the future; a few days before his death he writes to Wilhelm von Humboldt: 'muddled teaching giving rise to muddled action holds sway in the world'.

All this is dark and gloomy, and justifies Goethe's choice of the word tragedy. Faust's salvation, an extremely problematic affair if we try to explain it in ethical or religious terms, is achieved by poetic mercy. The triumph belongs to Goethe's poetic creative power, and it is victorious over all interpretation. He has seen to it that his characters and images constantly provide new problems. His world is not a fixed immovable world of faith like that of Dante, in which redemption in paradise is a certainty from the beginning. Goethe is a modern man, who errs so long as he lives and strives. And if we accept as true his traditional last words, and this again is extremely problematic, his thoughts on his death-bed were not directed towards eternal rest in God, but to 'more light!' He does not solve the problems to which his work gives rise. When Eckermann asks him about the 'mothers', the secret behind the process of poetic creation, Goethe silently hands him the manuscript to read: 'See what you can make of it!'

Between the pact at the beginning and the end in Heaven the play passes over the stage in all its many transformations; we do not need to follow its course here. We can only indicate some features which have a relevance for Goethe's life and for his attitude to this particular work. His irony, his great medium of expression which he employs in *Faust* even more than elsewhere, renders the task far from easy; his own irony, too, has to be taken with a touch of irony. Goethe changes time and space, turns height into depth, the characters even question their own existence. There is no 'final word'. One can well believe that, had his life been still further prolonged, Goethe would have regarded the Second Part as superseded in the same way as he did the First Part. It is only death that writes *finis*.

After the love tragedy of the First Part Goethe wants to raise Faust to the loftier brighter world of Beauty. To this end Helen is conjured up, and with her Faust celebrates the 'marriage of the German spirit with the Greek'. The fairest of all women is portrayed in all her bodily splendour; the lovers sing a fervent love duet and live, for a time, in an Arcadian idyll, where the acorns are pregnant with sweet sap and honey drips from the hives: *'Ein jeder ist an seinem Platz unsterblich, sie sind zufrieden und gesund'* (And where he is is each of them immortal, they are content and they are well). There is even a child, named Euphorion. But all this, Goethe's lifelong dream, is suspect from the beginning, it is a *phantasmagoria*, as he called it; Helen, querying her own existence, describes herself as an 'idol'. The very lines, in long-rhythmed classical metre, are described ironically by the poet – in one of his Faust fragments – as 'long-tailed lines'; or expressing himself still more scornfully on the subject of solemn diction he says: *'Da spricht ein jeder sinnig mit verblümten Wort Weitläufig aus, was ohngefähr ein jeder weiss'* (In words profound, with subtlety disguised, each says at length the things we each already know). In this scene, too, Goethe has no hesitation in using the word boredom, a word that, in any case, is not rare in his writing. Enormously quick and intense in his thoughts and feelings, Goethe very quickly tires even of his greatest creations and experiences. The classical scene is forthwith transformed into a romantic setting: a medieval castle on the Peloponnese, round which play recollections of the contemporary fighting in Greece, and of Byron, who has just died; the scene is set from 3000 BC to 'the time of Missolonghi'. This develops into a sort of opera, 'conceived throughout with full-toned music'. Dancing is added, led by Euphorion who, untamed and wilful like the young English Lord, climbs higher and higher until, like Icarus, he plunges headlong. Helen is forced to follow him into the shadows, and Faust is left holding only her veil, the symbol of poetry.

Goethe finds himself alone with his dream of a Greek revival. He knows that with him a whole epoch is coming to an end. In his opinion the younger generation, with its romantic 'higher and higher' and 'wilder and wilder', can only come to grief. It is both a literary parody and a parable: every poet's dream must vanish. With Helen the whole Greek world disappears. And so Goethe turns to Faust's death.

He has come a long way and seen many things; many things he has had to forgo. What has become of Faust, or Goethe, the daring scientist? From all his research Goethe has gained only the bitter conviction 'that I know nothing'. Faust already says the same thing at the beginning of the play. He does not appear as a scientist again, he only observes natural phenomena from time to time; on one occasion he has a conversation with Mephistopheles on geology, which demonstrates yet again Goethe's furious hatred of Vulcanism. When the study and the laboratory are reintroduced in Part Two, it is not Faust but his pupil Wagner, the dry devotee of retorts and test-tubes, who has manufactured the *homunculus* of the old cabbalistic and alchemistic books. An artificial manikin, a human pre-existence, sexless, he is enclosed in a glass globe, like an artificial embryonic casing, in which he floats about giving rise to vague, confused interpretations. He is not clearly defined even in Goethe's mind; originally he thought of adding a 'nice little wife', an *homuncula*, to beget offspring from his creation, but the ingredients would not coalesce. The play of Goethe's irony here reaches heights of magic that leave far behind all later surrealist fantasies and attempts to marry the unmarriageable. The manikin knocks impatiently against his globe, which gives forth a mighty sound as though in secret travail. At another time he sniffs the soft sea air through the walls of his casing, a very Goethean touch but one that is hardly in keeping with the imprisoned *homunculus*. But who would wish to quarrel with a bubble? With a being that is yet to be born? Proteus puts the unstable creature on his back and carries it down to the sea, where it is dashed to pieces against the shell-chariot of Galatea, who is to show Faust the way to the Greek world of the Helen-dream.

But this is not the end of the manikin. While working on this scene Goethe read a paper by some naturalist on the phosphorescence of the sea, caused by millions of micro-organisms. Stimulated by this idea of development he transfers it to his *homunculus*, quite undeterred by the creature's origin in a retort in the tedious Wagner's laboratory. When the human pre-existence is dashed to pieces he lets it burst into phosphorescent fire, and then change into glowing corpuscles which are to develop stage by stage in the water, through untold thousands of forms, until finally man is reached. Were we to let them do so, these fireworks of Goethe's imagination might shed a strange light on his scientific viewpoint; but this is poetry, a poetic idea mirrored in the walls of a glass globe. '*Willst du entstehn entsteh auf eigne Hand!*' (If creation's your desire, create yourself) says Goethe to the *homunculus*; and so he is created, in fiery imagery, and is married to the ocean instead of to a little *homuncula*. This is Goethe's philosophy of nature, to re-create creation in poetic imagery. Here he attempts to solve the greatest secret of all, the age-old dream of mankind. It must remain an attempt. Goethe is not a god, he merely feels like a god.

Not being a god, he has to die. He gives Faust a life-span of a hundred years. It is a stroke of genius to wait until Faust is on his deathbed before introducing him to those great and sinister figures that normally accompany people through life, the four grey women: Want, Guilt, Affliction, Sorrow. Like Goethe, Faust has neither bothered about them nor been plagued by them. Goethe has had his own troubles, arising from the dark strains in his nature. He has had a hard struggle and, looking back on his life, he can see nothing but labour and toil, the eternal torture of Sisyphus, in strong contrast to the ideas of those who regard him as one of fortune's darlings. He has consumed people and worn them out – women, the hewers of wood and carriers of water, the 'poor devils' – and only poetic imagination can ascribe to him any feelings of guilt or remorse. He has denied himself nothing he wanted, he has only had to forgo from time to time a life of action and intervention in world affairs, or the attempt to teach the younger generation. He has been a guest, in Weimar, in Germany and in the world. He has lived only in his creations, and in these he has amassed and disseminated great riches. Like his Faust, he dies a rich man.

Even now, in his last hour, the grey women, Want, Guilt and Affliction, cannot reach the dying man; only Sorrow, the idea of death, breathes on him. Her breath turns him blind. As a blind man, in whom the inner light still shines, Faust now wants to accomplish his great deed. He summons his servants with shovel and spade, and sinks into the grave the lemures have dug for him in the treacherous swampy soil by the sea's edge.

This ending is composed of polar opposites, of darkness and light. The synthesis – for Goethe does not want a tragic ending – is not contained in the allegorical picture of ecclesiastical tradition; we have already given Goethe's views on this. It is indicated in the figure of Lynkeus, the warden of the tower, who surveys the plain from his lofty vantage point and sings: '*Ihr glücklichen Augen, Was je ihr gesehn, Es sei wie es wolle, Es war doch so schön!*' (Oh, fortunate eyes! All you have seen, whatever it was, how fair it has been.) He, too, after a short interval, no longer than a 'dash', has to witness fire, murder of the innocents, and the darkness of this world.

And yet this is not how Goethe wants to end. He believes in life after death. He employs mystical choruses. Even in the First Part Mephistopheles has been forced to admit that there is no way of destroying the 'damned breed' of animals and men: in the air, in the water, on the earth, thousands of seeds and germs are detaching themselves, '*und immer zirkuliert ein neues frisches Blut*' (and fresh new blood is always circulating). The naturalist in Goethe even sees these myriads of germs springing to life in the sea when his *homunculus* is dashed to pieces. The Goethe who dreams of deeds and action creates a new land and free people in the vision of the blinded Faust. When Euphorion dies the poet looks forward to new songs and a new life: *Denn der Boden zeugt sie wieder Wie von je er sie gezeugt* (for the earth once more begets what it's begotten from of old). Goethe, the man, believes in his morning star.

# 44

# *World Literature*

The completion of *Faust* is the great poetic achievement of Goethe's last years, but the influence of his creative personality extends beyond his own work, and this is perhaps his finest gift to posterity. 'People from the most distant countries will speak to one another and answer one another', says the aged Leonardo da Vinci in one of his riddles. The phrase sounds like a motto for Goethe's activity, which ranged far and wide into distant parts of the world, and continued to do so until his death. The aged Leonardo lived a solitary life in a foreign country. He, too, had his Eckermann with him, his faithful Melzi, who rescued his manuscripts and drawings for posterity. Leonardo, like Goethe's Faust, planned large-scale construction of canals and reclamation of wide areas of swamp land; he even designed units for prefabricated houses and drew up systematic ground plans for his settlements. On visits by the French Court he acted as *maître de plaisir*, as Goethe had done in Weimar, devising ingenious masquerades and clever mechanical contrivances. One of these was a lion that opened its chest to reveal an interior entirely in blue – Goethe's favourite colour; another was a heart which, when brought on to the stage, split in half to reveal the figure of 'cupidity' standing on a globe and divided into 'polar' opposites – the right side armed for conquest, the left side pale, in tears and in rags. But Leonardo was lonely and solitary. His greatest works perished in his own lifetime; when Goethe saw the *Last Supper* he lamented the fact that so inventive an artist should expose his painting so carelessly to decay. Goethe wants to make his influence felt in this life, in the here and now. He speaks to the world, and it answers him.

He speaks through his letters. People at close quarters he finds disagreeable, and only those who surrender their own lives completely can endure living with him. Even to Zelter, his best friend during the latter part of his life, he writes: 'There is something oppressive, limiting and often hurtful about presence – absence on the other hand induces freedom and naturalness, and leads people back to themselves', and this applies not only to his relations with men. Becoming still more pointed, he says: 'The absent person is an ideal person, in each other's company people appear trivial to one another.' And thus the more his fame grows the more estranged he becomes from his immediate surroundings. Members of the Ducal house still pay friendly, but formal, visits to the great adornment of their Residence, commemorative occasions are still celebrated, as 'Supervisor of the Institutions for Science and Art' he still composes memoranda in his gravest style – this, in broad outline, defines his relationship to the Duchy of Weimar. A few years before his death he paid his first visit to a Weimar school; it was a new building and, in his report, he remarked with pleased surprise on the bright, cheerful rooms, comparing them with the former dingy nooks and crannies that he had never seen. 'The teaching itself was too alien to me for me to be able to form a clear idea of it.'

In his fine obituary on Goethe, Soret, who was deeply devoted to the poet, describes the changes that had taken place in the Duchy during the last years of Goethe's life: 'Within a few years the face of Weimar has changed. New schools have been built everywhere, and elementary education has been everywhere improved, good almshouses have been put up to replace the miserable holes in which the poor used to eke out their existence, neglected and dirty.' He mentions institutions in aid of welfare, general education, farming and prisoners, none of which, it is evident, existed before. He concludes with the words: 'The fame of all this is not so brilliant as that of the preceding time, but it also assuredly has its value in the eyes of thoughtful people.'

When the first publications on Goethe's official career began to appear after his death, another great admirer wrote of his activities in connection with the University of Jena:

> For me it was depressing to have to see the whole ground of the unfortunate state of affairs that existed in former years – which one thought had been forgotten – gone over once again, and to have to see every note, as it were, of the universally recognized mistake made by the great man I loved so much played through again. In this field [administration] Goethe mistook his good intentions for principle throughout. He hated the *savants* because of his *Farbenlehre*; he thought he could get the better of them solely through the medium of ideas, without much substance, and he never understood the character of a university. Hence the appointment of so many unskilled and unqualified people, his stubbornness when there was some defect to remedy, and a certain illiberality, which he – *horrendum dictu!* – actually called his liberality!

The minister and *Geheimrat* are roles in Goethe's life, but they are minor roles. Much of his activity was mere bustling about, evasion of more difficult tasks, or relaxing after his great creative periods. Much that he did should have been left to others. He had no particular gift for organization; he was unable even to organize his own household properly. A born ruler, he was at the same time lazy and quick to show impatience. Detail, on which he set so much store, soon bored him and was left to subordinates. In keeping with his dual nature, however, he would sometimes meddle with extraordinary obduracy in petty details, and till his very last days there are countless documents and memoranda that bear his signature. The essence of the matter is contained once and for all in the letter he wrote to the Duke on his return from Italy: 'Accept me as a guest, at your side let me fill to overflowing the measure of my existence. ...'

In these last years governmental and administrative 'mechanics', a word he had used even in the early days, recede into the background and Goethe is left solely as the poet, writer and widely influential personality. He has coined the word *Weltliteratur*, and brought it into circulation. By worldliterature he understands not so much the treasure of great classic masterpieces as contact between the living, the international exchange of ideas, closer acquaintance between peoples and individuals. He has in mind direct personal contact through correspondence, through travel, through meeting people. He himself can no longer leave Weimar. The world comes to him in the form of representatives of every nation, including those, like the Czechs and the Serbs, who are only emerging into nationhood. Until the end of his life he seeks to understand and absorb new impressions; he wants to act as a mediator, too, like the 'Ombudsman' in Danish political life, who stands above parties and group interests. He is the object of boundless admiration, such as has been accorded few great men in their lifetime. His realm has become vast and comprises almost the whole civilized world; in his mind he embraces the Near and Far East as well.

This Goethe Empire grew from small beginnings, from tiny conventicles scattered here and there across the country, like the devout circles of the pietists. Larger groups attached themselves in Berlin, Switzerland and Vienna; then, mainly through the influence of Madame de Staël's book, there were additions in France, England and Scandinavia, while there were also admirers in Poland, Russia and America. As in all great expansions, the centre became weakened in this process. To the Germans, Goethe, in his last years, was an historic figure, the last survivor of a great epoch. To the younger generation he was often a burden; they showed him respect, grumbled secretly, or attacked him openly. To the nationalists he was not German enough, to others he was the sycophant 'courtier'. The German poets and writers, it is true, could rarely boast a single encouraging word from the grand old man. In the two hundred odd literary articles and reviews he wrote in the last twenty years of his life, German authors are virtually not mentioned, apart from some friendly asides. The 'latest German poetry' he dismissed, without mentioning any names, in a bare statistical table: 'gifted – embarrassing – skilful – disturbing'. In conversation and letters he was more specific, and his letters circulated widely: 'poor stuff', he wrote, 'the poets all write as though they were ill and the whole world were a hospital'. In the literary almanachs he can find only 'signs and interjections by well-meaning individuals', but nothing on matters of general or higher importance, and problems of church and state are avoided. In contrast he praises the young French writers, who never detach themselves 'for a moment from the life and passion of the nation as a whole', even though it means being in opposition. It is very open to question whether he would have treated the German opposition authors so kindly. Understandably he judges his own countrymen more harshly than foreigners; he is more keenly aware of their every fault, he regards as a threat every deviation from the 'right path' he has recently indicated; foreigners he does not expect to follow his instructions.

Even a supreme genius has not unlimited time and interest at his disposal. Goethe's interests, in any case, are very wide and he often picks out the authors of real worth with an astonishingly sure eye. In the Italian Alessandro Manzoni he recognizes a great writer, before he is generally appreciated in his own country, and he helps energetically in promoting his name. He makes mistakes too, and his admiration of Béranger is incomprehensible to us. The extent of his admiration for Byron can only be explained by the fact that he discovered him at a time when he was in need of a heroic, demoniac figure; the fact that this 'insolent darling of the graces', as he once called Aristophanes, was also a Lord, may have played a part too. But an analysis of the reasons why Goethe's interest was sometimes aroused and sometimes not is a matter of only historic interest. The essential thing is his great conception of mutual enrichment, of the development of one's powers through contact with others, which he emphasizes over and over again. The individuality of each national literature, he maintains, should be preserved and even strengthened by this; nothing is further from his thought than a colourless universal language.

He is fully aware of the imperfection of all translations, but he is equally aware of how indispensable they are. In one of his letters to Carlyle he observes:

> that the translator works not only for his own country but also for the country from whose language he has taken the work. For it happens more often than one imagines that a nation sucks the sap and strength from a work, and absorbs it into its own inner life, in such a way as to be able to derive no further pleasure, and draw no further nourishment, from it. This applies especially to the Germans, who assimilate all too quickly everything that is offered them and, in the course of transforming it by sundry repetitions, in a sense destroy it. Therefore it is of great benefit to them to see something of their own re-appear endowed with new life through the means of a successful translation.

Goethe observes with pride how the German language has been enriched by numerous translations, and has become a general market-place of foreign literatures. And in fact a wealth of masterly translations had come into existence in his own immediate surroundings: August Wilhelm Schlegel's Shakespeare and the Calderon of Johann Diederich Gries of Jena were achievements that had no equal in any other country at that time. The period in Germany when activity in translating and adapting was at its height, and at times it was almost limitless, was far from being detrimental to the country's literature; on the contrary it went hand-in-hand with the greatest productivity in its own intellectual life. In this other sense world literature for Goethe was not only a dream of his old age but a lifelong experience. He passed through various epochs: an English one in his youth, with Shakespeare, Sterne, Richardson and Goldsmith, a French one with Voltaire and Diderot, an Italian one with Tasso and Cellini; to these must be added his interest in the literature of Spain, Persia and the Arab world. The Indian 'Sakuntala' of Kalidasa gave him the idea for his 'Prelude on the Stage' in *Faust*, and even as a very old man he was still interested in the folk poetry of the Greeks and Serbs. In all this he took a very active part, and his own translations range from his boyhood exercises in Corneille and Terence to his late attempts to translate Byron and Manzoni. They comprise large undertakings like his translation of Cellini, a welcome labour to Goethe at the height of his classicism with its colourful vigorous life, and Diderot's *Le Neveu de Rameau*, which first appeared in Goethe's transla- tion, some decades before the French original. Other things again have become completely integrated in his own poetry, and can only be separated from what is really his own by a process of philological detection; they are to be found in his poems, in the *Wanderjahre*, and in the Second Part of *Faust*. All this Goethe included in the last *Collected Edition* of his works, and indeed it belongs very definitely to his *œuvre*.

Equally significant are the things that Goethe does not adopt and absorb into his work. The whole Nordic mythology, a dark mist of giant barbaric figures, remains foreign to him, as does German poetry of the Middle Ages, although, when pressed to do so, he tried unsuccessfully to interest himself in the *Nibelungenlied*. Dante, too, was 'before his time', as he had found Giotto and Cimabue on his Italian journey. From the continent of India it was only Kalidasa who had anything to say to him; the gods and myths he rejected, as he did Indian art. This last he knew only from the pathetically poor and flat engravings of the day, in which the sculptures, intended to be seen in full sunlight, looked like dried-out leaves from some herbarium. Seen like this he found them unbearable: 'The tiresome trunks of elephants, the coiling nests of crawling snakes, the age-old tortoise in its cosmic swamp, those kingly heads on a single trunk – such things will turn us mad unless the pure East swallows them up.' Sakuntala, Nala, Megha-Duta are his 'spiritual kin', and he cries: 'I should like to live in India, if only there had been no stone-masons there.'

Our outlook on painting and sculpture has changed, but because of this we have no right to criticize his viewpoint as narrow; in a hundred years' time our own will look equally strange and arbitrary. The weak Roman copies of Greek originals, the Apollo Belvedere, the Juno Ludovisi – pro- bably the head of a Roman empress – which Goethe worshipped as the in- comparable and eternal models of all art, as well as his whole world of faded, colourless antique art makes little appeal to us to-day. Not until he was a very old man did he even see a piece of authentic Greek art; this was a cast of one of the horses' heads from the Parthenon, and he marvelled at the plastic power of this *Ur-Pferd*, this primal horse, as he called it. Otherwise he remained a child of his times, the times in which he had grown up and formed his 'doctrine'. In this field his teaching proved very transient, being superseded even in his own lifetime. 'Each in his own way must be a Greek, but a Greek he must be!' he exclaims, including quite unconcernedly in this formula the Dutch painters he has just been discussing. For Goethe the 'classical' is simply the healthy, the beautiful, the true, while 'Romanticism' is the untrue and sickly. The whole dispute over these two concepts has become unimportant, greatly as it engaged people at the time; it was only a continuation of the interminable eighteenth century discussions about the precedence of the ancients or the moderns. In Goethe's own works the two are intermingled in the most delightful way; his *Helena*, conceived at the height of his classicism, develops into a 'classico-romantic *phantasmagoria*'.

In Goethe, traces of earlier stages in his development are constantly reappearing. The '*Chinesisch-Deutschen Jahres- und Tageszeiten*' of his extreme old age, inspired by travel books, is an echo of the Rococo Chinoiserie of his youth. Here, too, he breaks unexpectedly into his own style: '*Wohin mein Auge spähend brach, Dort ewig bleibt mein Osten!*' (Where'er my eye would penetrate, there reigns eternally my East). As in his Oeser days he continues to cultivate his little gems and cameos of antique, or pseudo-antique, workmanship, and how much he sees in these tiny figures, scarcely the size of a thumbnail! In a little essay on the 'tomb of a Greek dancer' he says himself that he may have read too much into the figures on the tomb, and that his interpretation should be regarded 'as a poem to a poem, a change of viewpoint that could well give rise to new enjoyment'.

Goethe's influence on the world at large is often like a poem to a poem. It depends only to a small degree on any close acquaintance with his works, which in the early days were almost always badly translated or appeared only in extracts. His lyric poetry, the greatest achievement in his *œuvre*, defied and still defies any attempt at translation. Abroad he has been admired for the most varied reasons, in which the mistakes have been as productive as 'true understanding'.

For the young French writers of his day the First Part of *Faust*, and Mephistopheles in particular, was the great romantic attraction. Goethe read the translation by 18-year-old Gérard de Nerval, not yet the poet who was to be re-discovered by the surrealists as their ancestor, with his *épanchement du songe dans la vie réelle*; such a spilling of dreams into real life would scarcely have appealed to Goethe. Nerval was a young man with a certain knowledge of German, though it was not very great; he made his translation in prose, interspersed with lyric passages. He was in love with a romantic Germany: 'Do you not already feel', he wrote, 'the pure, life-giving breeze that comes to us from Germany, impregnated with smells of the wild, across the Vosges, from the Ardennes, from over there beyond the Rhine, from still further away beyond the Taunus, where the eternal dark green of the forest reigns?' This smell of the wild in *Faust* attracted them like an 'exotic' charm. Another translation was presented to Goethe, with lithographs by Delacroix, an *édition de luxe*, whereas his own publisher had printed the work so poorly, indeed almost shabbily. Goethe was delighted by the format and by the fine paper; the illustrations he quite liked at first but soon came to have his doubts about them. He had heard unfavourable reports of the young painter, of the 'turmoil of his compositions', of their 'crude colouring'; now he found that Delacroix had 'ranged between heaven and earth, the possible and the impossible, the coarsest and the most tender' – which, one must admit, corresponds fairly closely to *Faust*. Goethe felt that the splendour of this beautiful edition was dulled by the illustrations, 'the mind is led from the clear lettering into a sombre world'. Meyer, the artistic authority in the Goethe household, may have been behind these judgments; the criticisms continue and Delacroix is reproached for his 'careless' drawing – the artist had worked in the then new technique of lithography, using full, sweeping strokes of his crayon. A German artist, according to Meyer, would have treated the subjects more delicately and smoothly, the figures in a 'more scholarly way'. That was the way of the German artists, such as Moritz Retsch, whose *Faust* engravings Goethe praised as 'clean and tidy'; to our eyes they are clean and empty outlines, turned almost into caricatures by the affectation of the gestures.

The inspiration for Delacroix' illustrations, moreover, was not Goethe's *Faust* at all, but a spectacular *Faust* play in London in which the part of Mephistopheles was turned into a starring role for the great comedian Daniel Terry, 'and everything in the deepest black imaginable', as the painter wrote. It was this deepest black that aroused the enthusiasm of the younger generation in France. Of the Greek *Faust* of the Second Part they were still ignorant; when the work was published they were disappointed.

Another young romantic genius, Hector Berlioz, submitted to Goethe his *Opus 1*, eight scenes from *Faust*, out of which he later developed his great *Damnation de Faust*. He addressed the master as *Monseigneur*, as though he were royalty; he had been reading *Faust* for years, and could not suppress a '*crie d'admiration*'. But Zelter, Goethe's musical adviser, condemned the work in the harshest terms, and so this admirer received no reply.

Goethe's relation to music is that of a poet; the words are the important thing, the composer must fulfil his task discreetly. Schubert, who sent Goethe his *Opus 19*, was also ignored; he died before Goethe, leaving behind him the greatest and most beautiful of all the collections of Goethe *Lieder*. They were never heard in Weimar and would have had no success there, being far too 'difficult' and full-bodied. Goethe held the view that music should be light, a social grace; he gave his own house-concerts. He liked instrumental music, played by a quartet in the next room, as a stimulus to his work – during his writing of *Iphigenie*, for example. At concerts he was bored, and when Weber gave a concert in Weimar, the Olympian was heard engaged in loud conversation. His admiration for Mozart was admiration for the phenomenon of his genius, less for the musical genius who had taken the world by storm with his *Zauberflöte*. Goethe continued this work with a second part – but to Schikaneder's libretto not to Mozart's opera. The operatic scenes in the Second Part of *Faust* are strongly influenced by this model, and at a change of scene in Goethe's libretto there is a stage direction: 'The scene changes to chaos, out of which emerges A Royal Hall', which could very well serve as a direction for parts of *Faust*.

The young Felix Mendelssohn, introduced by his teacher Zelter, was the only musician of rank with whom Goethe ever came into close contact. He reminded him of the child Mozart, whom he had heard as a prodigy in his youth. The boy Felix, 11 years old when he first went to Weimar, was accomplished and high-spirited, a little hobgoblin; he played everything the old Jupiter asked for, including a complete historical survey of music from Bach to the 'more recent technicians' as Goethe called Beethoven and his contemporaries. He played Bach, who had just been rediscovered, and on hearing the *Overture in D major* Goethe remarked: 'One really sees the ranks of elegantly dressed people as they descend a large staircase.' He is a man of sight. It is only by visualizing music that he can understand it. And it is in musical imagery above all that Goethe's *Faust* has lived on; each composer has written 'his *Faust*': Wagner, Liszt, Boito, who even added philosophic footnotes, and Busoni, who tried to revive the old puppet play. It is in the *Lied*, however – but a quite different *Lied* from the song Goethe envisaged for his lyrics – that his poetry has made its greatest impact on the world. The term 'the *Lied*', or '*le Lied*', was adopted by other nations. In France even the lyric poetry was stimulated by this influence and developed a new tone. Alfred de Musset speaks of the '*douce obscurité*' which came to France in this way.

Goethe's relations with England were quite different. German literature had for a long time been unpopular in England, and Goethe, in particular, was considered 'immoral' and irreligious, while the deeper qualities in his work were unappreciated. Even Coleridge and Wordsworth rejected him; Shelley was the only poet of stature to recognize him, and he translated some scenes from the *Walpurgisnacht* – largely because of his admiration for the atheist in Goethe. But now, in the closing years of Goethe's life, there appears a young man named Thomas Carlyle. He writes to the master from his home at Craigenputtock, which Goethe tries in vain to find on a map, sending him his translation of *Wilhelm Meister*, some articles he has written for well-known periodicals, and calls himself Goethe's disciple, 'nay a son of his spiritual father'. He writes: 'I have been delivered from dark-ness into any measure of light,' and 'Many saints have been expunged from my literary calendar since I first knew you.' In this letter from Scotland, Goethe hears a note that has not previously reached his ears. He has been acknowledged as a poet and a writer, but never before as a moral force, almost as a saint. The young Englishmen he has known have been of a different stamp. There was the young lawyer Crabb Robinson who, at the beginning of the century, had been a student at Jena and had later pub-lished translations of some of Goethe's poems in a London magazine, strug-gling hopelessly with the impossible task of turning the master's hexameters into a similar metre in English. There were numerous young visitors to Weimar, who often stayed a few months or even some years, among them the young Thackeray, still at that time thinking of a career as a diplomat or a lawyer. Well off, he was also a gifted caricaturist and made a sketch of the old master in a characteristic pose, leaning forward with his hands behind his back; later on a more elaborate version of this sketch, by Daniel MacLise, was published in *Fraser's Magazine*. Weimar was very popular among young Englishmen:

> The Court was splendid but yet most pleasant and homely [wrote Thackeray]. We were invited in our turns to dinners, balls and assemblies there ... we knew the whole society of the little city, and but that the young ladies, one and all, spoke admirable English, we surely might have learned the very best German ... Goethe's daughter-in-law's tea table was always spread for us. We passed hour after hour there, and night after night with the pleasantest talk and music. We read over endless novels and poems in English, French and German....

Goethe admires these free and easy young visitors enormously: 'Is it their origin, the soil, or is it due to the free constitution and the sound educa-tion?' he remarks to Eckermann. They are never put out 'and are as much at their ease as if the whole world belonged to them. It is also this that pleases our women-folk and it is why they cause such devastation in the hearts of our young ladies.... They are dangerous young people, but ad-mittedly it is this very fact that is their great virtue.'

How different, he continues to Eckermann, are his Germans! Even the children playing in the street are chased away when a policeman appears: 'With us everything is concentrated on taming our youth while they are still young, and on driving out all naturalness, all originality and all their wild spirits, so that finally nothing remains but the Philistines.' The young scholars who visit him are 'short-sighted, pale, with hollow chests...they are completely immersed in ideas and only the deepest problems of speculative philosophy are worthy of their attention. Of healthy feelings and sensual enjoyment there is not a trace.' If only they could be taught to have more energy and commonsense, like the English, and less philosophy and theory!

It is as just such a capable, vigorous and active young man that this Mr Carlyle in Craigenputtock strikes him – at first, until he finds out more about his background, Goethe calls him Sir Thomas Carlyle. With their correspondence a very close and touching friendship begins; Goethe sends the young couple many affectionately packed presents, a necklace for Mrs Carlyle, a medallion with the poet's head on it for the husband, a private decoration he used to bestow on selected recipients at the end of his life. In him Goethe wins a son, and a devoted missionary. Carlyle, being a lay-preacher both by nature and in his literary style, proclaims Goethe as the embodiment of the eternal 'Yes', the necessary antithesis to the eternal 'No', the 'whole man' the great conqueror, the hero. We know now how split Carlyle's mind was and how great was his need of making constant appeals to his own higher nature and to that of any hero he worshipped. If he saw in Goethe a Puritan after his own heart – Carlyle had the German word *Entsage* engraved on his seal – there were biographical reasons for this; it is not necessary to drag in Mrs Carlyle and her life of unendurable resignation. Carlyle, however, created a portrait of Goethe whose influence on thought throughout the world has continued until our own day; perhaps it was only in such a form that the poet could be introduced to the Anglo-Saxon world of that time. Rarely has a poet found such an evangelist. With his essays, translations and articles, as well as with works on German literature in general, Carlyle produce an *œuvre* in these early years, before he started on the large bulk of his own writings, that might well have been a life's work for another man. He immediately adopted Goethe's concept of world literature and enlarged on it, envisaging literature and its great writers as 'one universal commonwealth'. 'Literature is now nearly all in all to us, not our speech only, but our Worship and Lawgiving; our best Priest must henceforth be our Poet.' He hoped that one day even wars might be rendered obsolete through its influence.

Goethe takes up this idea in a review of Carlyle's *German Romance*, saying that for a long time the best writers of every nation have been directing their efforts towards universal humanity: 'And since in practical everyday life the same tendency prevails, and permeates all that is humanly coarse, savage, cruel, selfish and false, endeavouring everywhere to spread its mellowing influence, we may hope that the unavoidable strife will grow progressively less, that war will become less cruel and victory less arrogant, even though we cannot hope that it will bring universal peace.' Goethe has progressed from his former ideal of the development of the individual – who is necessarily privileged – to a more universal ideal. He proclaims it at a time of increasing nationalism, when people have very little patience with these wise words spoken by the old sage in Weimar.

In the early days of August 1830 very disturbing news of the political situation in Paris reaches the Weimar Court. It appears that the city is once more in the throes of a revolution, a spectre it was believed had been buried forty years previously. After lunch Soret goes at once to see Goethe.

'Well,' said Goethe, 'what do you think of this great event? There it is: everything is in flames! It is no longer a matter that can be dealt with behind closed doors – the volcano has erupted!'

'It is a terrible business', replies Soret. 'With such a miserable family there is little to be hoped for, and it is supported by an equally miserable ministry into the bargain! It will end by their being thrown out.'

'But I am not speaking of these people', says Goethe indignantly. 'What concern are they of mine! I am talking of the great dispute between Cuvier and Geoffroy!'

For him what matters is the heated discussion between the two great scientists in the Academy of Sciences; that is where the volcano has erupted. Soret is speaking of the Royal Family, who are indeed thrown out, of Charles X, who had been with the allied forces in the campaign of 1792 and whom Goethe had seen there in the company of the King of Prussia. At the moment this does not interest Goethe in the least. For months he has been following an entirely different struggle within the precincts of the Academy. The questions at issue appear to be highly specialized: the organic structure of molluscs and fish. Nevertheless Goethe is uncommonly excited; behind these specialized debates he sees once more a problem fundamental to his views on nature. Geoffroy de Saint-Hilaire represents the views of natural philosophy, Cuvier those of more analytical research. Geoffroy proclaims the *unité de composition organique*, a *grande harmonie et des rapports nécessaires* between all the phenomena of nature; Cuvier stresses the prime importance of observation and of the classification of the animal world. Questions such as these can, in fact, only be discussed behind closed doors, but the world has become more democratic and the public is now admitted to the Academy's meetings. The dispute between the two scientists finds its way into the papers and becomes a *cause célèbre*, in the midst of the struggle over the freedom of the press, which is threatened by the King, over the workers' associations, and the intrigues surrounding the formation of a new ministry. Goethe has decided to intervene. He is wholly on the side of Geoffroy, with his *grande harmonie* and the unity of all organic existence. At the same time he has to show respect to Cuvier, who is no mere 'priest of the guild', as he calls the German professors, but a great authority on the whole realm of nature, and a man to whom Goethe himself owes a great deal. Under Napoleon he had organized the whole French educational system, he is a man of the world and, in addition, had sent Goethe a copy, with a dedication, of his fine commemorative speeches on former members of the Academy. Goethe plans an essay in which he intends once more to state his own views, which seem to him to have been magnificently vindicated by Geoffroy. In his essay he tries to represent these two opponents as personalities, against their historical background, and not merely as advocates of a principle; he traces the whole course of scientific history in France over the previous fifty years, from the time of Buffon. Cuvier he sees, as it were, as the Newton and Geoffroy as the Goethe of scientific research. But he now regards the opposing viewpoints in a much more conciliatory spirit than formerly, almost – although not quite – as a necessary antithesis, as part of a dialectical process that will always be repeated. And even an observer looking back on this dispute of the revolutionary year of 1830 is forced to concede right and wrong to both sides; a scientific world consisting only of Cuviers, or only of Geoffroys, would soon atrophy and perish.

There is great political change in Paris in this year of 1830, although Goethe does not deign to notice these events. The problem is not the organic structure of the lower forms of animal life, nor is it Geoffroy's *grande harmonie*. In Paris a new class is on the move, the industrial workers, strongly represented in the capital and organized in *associations*, though without any effective leadership. New ideas are in the air; Count Saint-Simon, member of a famous Ducal house impoverished during the first revolution, has placed the idea of manual labour at the centre of his, as yet indistinct, social system, has called for a 'new Christianity', the canonization of labour, and the elevation to a higher level of the poorest and most numerous class. His disciple Bazard has already coined the famous phrase: 'Exploitation of man by his fellow men.' Goethe has heard of the Saint-Simon school; in 1830 they take over the *Globe*, which he used to read so carefully and which he now finds sinister. He warns his son, Carlyle, in far off Craigenputtock, who sees in these people a significant 'sign of the times' and who has been approached by them as a possible ally. He, too, is discontented with the times and thumps his pulpit angrily. He storms against the machine-age, foresees mechanical education, mechanical religion introduced by the steamship and the steam locomotive, and the mechanization of science and art. There will be no solitary creative minds any longer, only bustling societies and committees.

These views were published in the *Edinburgh Review*, which Goethe often read. He had numerous sources of information. His old friend Reinhard, the revolutionary of 1791 and now Talleyrand's colleague – Talleyrand, also after experiencing many changes, is now once more at the centre of affairs – writes to Goethe, a few months before this new revolution, about the 'determined but quiet attitude the country has adopted ... they have no desire for revolution, still less for counter-revolution'. This, however, was the precise aim of the stubborn King Charles, with his *ordonnances*, his suppression of the press, and his return to absolutism; the eruption of the volcano was inevitable, and not only in the Academy.

Goethe said little about all this, in general he disliked discussing politics, but he followed this last great political event of his long life closely. The Weimar Minister, Gersdorff, sent him the secret reports and dispatches, and kept him informed. The last book found at Goethe's bedside on the day of his death, a present from the French envoy in Weimar, was a description of the 'sixteen months' that shook Europe and the world. It was a colourless, watery affair by a Count de Salvandy, whose novels Goethe had read and reviewed. Saying little about the actual fighting, it contained many arguments about anarchy and disorganization, which had permeated everything, politics, literature, the press, the theatre, the streets, and even 'the circles of the propertied class'. It is doubtful whether Goethe read the book, but at any rate he must have been informed about it, for in his last letter to Humboldt he referred to it: 'Muddled teaching giving rise to muddled action holds sway in the world.'

The teaching and the action were both muddled. We have the reports written by the young Heinrich Heine, who shortly after the event, came to Paris and wrote his brilliant articles for the *Allgemeine Zeitung*, the paper edited by Goethe's publisher Cotta. Heine is jubilant: the Gallic cock has crowed for the second time! Paris, after a period in the shade, is once more at the centre of events, a shining example for every nation. At the *Salon* Delacroix has exhibited his large revolutionary poster, which Heine sees and describes: a fine sturdy young woman representing Liberty, holding the tricolour in her hand. At the same exhibition he also notes Ary Scheffer's two striking paintings of Faust and Gretchen, called 'snuff and soft soap' by the wits because of their dark colouring. A year later, as Heine remarks, the colour of the revolutionary poster has already faded. The fighters at the barricades have scarcely had time to mop their brows, before they learn that the arch aristocrat Charles has fled, and that his cousin Orleans has entered the scene. He too had been present at the bombardment of Valmy as Citizen General Chartres, standing by the windmill on the hilltop facing Goethe, beneath the tricolour which now once more flutters over his head. He has grown fat in the long years of waiting, and caricaturists soon nickname him 'the pear'. He strides through the excited crowds on foot, carrying an umbrella and shaking hands to right and left, even the calloused hands of the workers. His predecessor's prime minister Polignac, owner of large estates in Normandy with the largest flock of merino sheep in France, is replaced by Casimir Perier, a banker and owner of large ironworks, a bony vigorous man of whom the journalist Heine has great hopes. There are professors and scholars in the new government, like the small, tough Thiers, 'a man of the deepest indifference', as Heine writes, 'who, in the clarity, good sense and graphic power of his writing, understands so wonderfully the art of restraint, the Goethe of politics'. The *Juste Milieu* begins with the construction of railways, in which some of the most ardent disciples of Saint-Simon take part and become millionaires, with the building of factories, with trade, and with colonial expansion. In this same fateful year of 1830 Algeria is conquered by the

French; the fighting is long drawn out and does not come to an end until 1962.

There are many farcical touches to this revolution. The riots start when cowardly bourgeois tradesmen, hearing of possible unrest, take the precaution of removing the royal warrants from outside their premises, and thereby give the signal for the destruction of all the emblems of the hated régime. Vast crowds of people surge through the streets in the July sunshine, and Heine mocks: 'For a good mutiny one needs good weather!' The military strength of King Charles consists of a paltry handful of a few thousand men, of which Swiss mercenaries form the backbone; the troops of the line immediately fraternize with the populace. Only at a few places is there any serious fighting, and the first shot is fired by an Englishman out of his hotel window at a passing patrol. The small detachments wander helplessly through the narrow streets, not yet broadened by Napoleon III into the wide boulevards, which his artillery could command. Neither the revolutionaries nor the military have any military or political plan, and the whole thing ends in the compromise of the 'citizen King' Louis Philippe, to whom at first no one had paid any attention. And yet the effects of these three summer days of revolution were far-reaching. Sparks were set off and spread in all directions. To Goethe, reading Gersdorff's secret reports, it looked as if Europe was in flames from end to end. The patriots rose in Poland and were defeated in bloody fighting by the Czar Nicholas, who annexed their country by a simple ukase, cynically named the 'organic statute'. In Italy, Austrian troops suppressed risings in the Papal States, Modena and Parma, and the French fleet intervened in Portugal. Belgium freed herself from Holland. Everywhere there were threats of intervention; a new world war seemed imminent. Such was the political situation in the last year of Goethe's life.

There was disturbing news of Germany, too, in these secret reports, with riots in Dresden and Aachen. In Weimar's neighbouring Duchy of Brunswick the castle in which Anna Amalie had spent her joyless childhood was burned to the ground in the first and only wild revolutionary outbreak in German history. The Duke, a haughty, insolent young man, disliked even by his fellow Princes, fled his country and wandered round seeking asylum; despite his huge fortune, which he had prudently converted into diamonds, no one was willing to give him refuge. Finally, after a long time, the Republic of Geneva granted him asylum and, on his death, even erected a monument to the 'Diamond Duke' in gratitude for his legacy of some forty million *francs*.

Goethe was not the only one to be disturbed by what he heard and read. The great Roman historian Niebuhr, a cool and sober observer, wrote to him at the end of 1830, almost at his wit's end: 'I do not think you will find me mistaken, nor be in doubt yourself, that we are at the beginning of the most brutal and horrible barbarity.'

It is the end of an epoch, which Heine refers to as the 'period of the arts', the age of Goethe. And in his letter to Humboldt, written immediately before his death, the poet sees his work, which has just been completed with the Second Part of *Faust*, 'driven on to the shore, lying in ruins like a wreck, and covered for the time being with the sand and debris of the hours'.

In this 'for the time being' lies his inflexible hope. Goethe does not believe in complete destruction. The political outlook may be bleak, but in eighty years he has scarcely known it otherwise. He believes in values of a different kind. In his essay on 'epochs of social development' he has painted a picture of mankind's progress in culture and civilization as he sees it, from the small national society, through the 'social and civic epochs', to the general, and finally to the universal, when 'all foreign literatures arrive at equality with our own, and we are not outdistanced in the currency of the world'.

In a last, long talk with Soret he looks back once more over his whole life. His point of departure is a book on Mirabeau which has been severely handled by the Paris critics, who complain that the author has laid far too great stress on the debt owed by the great tribune to contemporary stimuli and to the ideas of others. Of course he owed a debt, says Goethe, and why not? 'The greatest genius would not get very far if he attempted to find everything within himself. What would become of a genius if one were to deprive him of the gift of using everything that comes to hand, of taking the marble to build his house from here, the bronze from there?' And he asks, as though looking at himself from a distance, 'Who am I? What have I created? I have taken and absorbed everything that I have heard and observed. My works have been nourished by thousands of the most diverse natures, fools and wise men, clear heads and dullards.' He has often reaped what others have sown. 'My work is that of a composite being, and it bears the name Goethe' (17.2.1832).

Goethe is not only magnificent in his calmness and serenity, he can still break out into scorn on the subject of theorists and dreamers:

> Absurd people! They are like certain philosophers among my compatriots, who shut themselves up for thirty years in their rooms and never take a glance at the world. All they do is to keep on sieving through the notions they have got out of their own wretched brains, in which they seem to find an inexhaustible source of original, great and useful ideas! Do you know what the result is? Empty phantasies, nothing but empty phantasies. For a long time I was stupid enough to get angry at these tomfooleries; now in my old age I amuse myself by laughing at them!

Goethe is wise and conciliatory in his messages to the world, but he does not deny himself the pleasure of giving free rein to his scorn and anger in talking to his few faithful friends. Even from these he keeps his little secrets. Before Soret's last visit Goethe has been playing a curious game of tops with some carefully punched out discs of painted cardboard. Only Eckermann, the unquestioning Eckermann, is allowed to know about it. As Soret enters, Goethe quickly puts it aside; the 'sceptic', the crystallographer, would not understand. Goethe is still haunted by his desire to free the 'seven-coloured princess'. The ever-hated Newton describes a coloured disc of this kind, maintaining that when spun it will produce 'white'; in fact the result is never a true white, because the pigments are never sufficiently pure. Goethe sees in this another proof that Newton was wrong, and calls the resulting colour 'dirt colour'. We have no idea what kind of 'pure phenomenon' he may have seen in his spinning discs. He still continues to muse constantly over the inexplicable mystery of the rainbow, and writes to Boisserée saying that a lifetime would not suffice to solve it.

Until the very last days of his life he maintains an active interest in every part of his universe, in natural science, mineralogy, and even in astronomy, with which, hitherto, he has hardly concerned himself. He sends a note to the observatory in Jena telling them to make preparations for observing the comet that is expected in 1834. He hears with satisfaction that, in the course of the excavations at Pompeii, one of the houses has been named *la Casa di Goethe*. The new edition of his *Metamorphose der Pflanzen*, in Soret's French translation, has appeared and has been received with great respect by the French Academy. He looks at drawings by young artists, and his grandchildren are old enough to go to the theatre now and tell him about it; he has not been inside the place since his dismissal. He reads Balzac's latest novel and some Plutarch. There is no apparent decline in his powers; on the contrary, the style of his letters is freer than in the preceding years. Those near him have no feeling that the end is near.

On his last birthday he even makes a small excursion to Ilmenau. He walks up the hillside to the little hunting lodge, in whose solitude, fifty-two years earlier, he had written his poem, *Über allen Gipfeln ist Ruh*, on the bare wood of the walls. He looks at his lines, now preserved under glass, for the hut has become a place of pilgrimage, and ponders the words *Warte nur, bald ruhest du auch*. But he also gazes out over the country round him, and writes to Zelter:

After so many years it was possible to survey the permanent and the transient. The successful things came to mind and brought cheer and comfort, the failures were forgotten and had melted away. The people still lived as they used to live, from the charcoal burner to the porcelain manufacturer. Iron was being smelted and manganese extracted from the mines, although at present it is not in such demand as formerly. Pitch was being boiled and the soot collected, the little huts for the soot being very artfully and painstakingly constructed. Coal was being hauled up at the cost of incredible toil, colossal trunks of primeval trees discovered in the mine during the workings ... and so it has gone on, from the ancient granite through the adjoining epochs, always giving rise to new problems, which the most modern creators of the world conjure out of the earth with the greatest ease. Throughout it all there prevails an admirable utilization of the surfaces and depths of the earth and the mountains.

In his years as an active minister he scarcely ever saw as much human toil and labour in one day as this. But he stands once again on his beloved granite, his *Urgestein*, that still, as always, gives him the feeling of being strengthened by direct contact with the earth. His view embraces both the dark green pine trees of the Thüringer Wald and the black primeval fern trees of the coal mines. Once again he resists the 'most modern' theorists, with their eruptions and revolutions, whether beneath the earth or above it. What he sees is activity, the 'admirable utilization' of the heights and the depths. '*Kein Wesen kann zu nichts zerfallen!*' (No being can decay to nothingness), he writes in his last great poem, his legacy.

After this he stays at home and puts his affairs in order. He discusses his will with his old friend Müller, making arrangements for the disposal of his estate, his collections and the posthumous works. He sends Marianne's letters back to her in Frankfurt, and he writes a last letter to Frau von Levetzow, when his eye is caught by the goblet from Marienbad on his writing desk, 'it takes me back so many years and brings to mind the fairest hours'. The chapter on Lili Schönemann for *Dichtung und Wahrheit* has been finished. He carries on his correspondence until the last days of his life, and at the highest intellectual level.

But his body is worn out. He is seen by one of his old friends under the trees of his garden house, grown very small now and bent with age; to us he seems more venerable thus than as the marble statue of the 'perfection of beauty', as Eckermann finely described him lying in state on his bier. The seasons have always played an important role in Goethe's life; Winter being the 'badger's lair', into which he crawled. Now, calendar in hand, he is waiting impatiently for the spring. In March 1832, although it is cool and there is a sharp wind, he orders his carriage to be made ready to take him for a short drive. He returns with a heavy cold and goes to bed. His physician Dr Vogel, for many years his colleague in the *Oberaufsicht*, reports Goethe's last illness as: 'catarrhal fever, pneumonia, failure of the lungs and heart'. He also describes with clinical objectivity – his report was written for a medical journal – the terrible fear of death which overcame Goethe; his account is incomparably more accurate and impressive than all the letters sent off by the old man's faithful companions, which speak only of a gentle falling asleep or of a mythical withdrawal into the poet's heaven. Round the death-bed of every great man gather the chroniclers, anxious to report a last-minute conversation or some deep and symbolic last word. And so Eckermann has written into his conversations a post-humous last talk, intended to clear Goethe of the charge of being an un-believer, and to present him as a true Christian, albeit in a free and personal form of his own. Others have circulated the much-quoted, 'More light!' as his last words – perhaps no more than a barely audible request to his servant to open the shutters, his eyes having already grown dim. Other similar sayings have been collected with embarrassing curiosity, and embarrassing too is Eckermann's description of the naked corpse, despite its fine portrayal of his master's divine perfection. Goethe's life was perfected and completed in a different sense; his body could be none other than that of an old man of 83. The body was laid out in state in a silk 'Petrarchian' shirt, with the golden lyre and laurel wreath at its head; the funeral was a solemn and festive occasion, the interment taking place in the 'Prince's Vault' where Goethe was laid to rest at Schiller's side. It was carried out according to the taste of the time and with the honour due to a Weimar citizen. The beginning and end of his life were brought together in a small symbolic detail: the coffin was placed on the old Gothic bridal rug, belonging to the Goethe family, which had been used at Goethe's christening in the *Katharinenkirche* at Frankfurt, when he was given the Christian names of Johann Wolfgang.

Goethe did not die easily. At the slightest sign of improvement his hopes would rise and he would ask his servant the date. When told it was March 22nd, he said: 'That means spring has begun and we can recover all the quicker.' He asked the doctor not to give him any more medicine, because movement in the open air would soon restore his strength. But the doctor had foreseen the end two days previously when he was called in the early hours of the morning:

> A piteous sight awaited me. The aged man, who had long been in the habit of moving only very sedately, was in the grip of a terrible fear and agitation which drove him at one moment to bound into bed, where he vainly tried to find relief through constant changes of position, and at the next to jump up into the armchair at his bedside. The pain, which became more and more localized in his chest, forced alternate groans and loud screams from the tortured man. His features were distorted, his face ashen, his eyes, sunk deep in their livid sockets, were dulled and feeble; in his look was the most hideous fear of death. The whole ice-cold body ran with sweat, his pulse, unusually frequent, quick and hard, was barely perceptible; the abdomen was very swollen, his thirst agonizing....

On March 22nd he died, in the armchair by his bed; it was noon, the hour of his birth. He continues to dream till the end: 'Observe the lovely woman's head – with its black locks – in magnificent colouring – against the dark background.' He is no longer able to speak and so he lifts his hands, as he used to do while dictating, those hands which, with their short un-aristocratic fingers, are more like a workman's hands. He still tries to establish some order, and traces patterns in the air, Then his arms grow heavy and he lets them fall. With his finger he writes on the coverlet round his knees. Still writing the great writer dies – according to those round him even observing the exact punctuation. The last letter he draws is a large W. We may take it as the first letter of his name, Wolfgang, or, in keeping with his last great thoughts on world literature and the mutual understanding of mankind, of World.

# *Postscript*

This book is a study of Goethe's life and times; it is not an analysis of his individual works, still less of his individual poems, let alone of individual lines – this has been done sufficiently often, and with very varying results. The book's aim is to give a picture of the man in his completeness, and of his wonderfully rich and full life. Goethe's stature as one of the master-minds in world literature received early recognition and his fame is undisputed, but he still remains something of an enigma. This is true not only of the world at large, to whom for the most part he is little more than a name, but of his own countrymen as well who have never ceased to worship the great 'Olympian', while often denigrating and even reviling him, and who finally succeeded in enveloping him in a haze of vague admiration that has little to do with the very earthy and very fascinating person he was. In this book Goethe is not portrayed as the *Vollendete*, the perfected eternally god-like figure, nor is the age in which he lived depicted as the 'golden age', as posterity has come to regard it. A man of contradictions and paradoxes, of 'polar' contrasts, to use his own expression, such as might well have destroyed a lesser figure, he yet achieves a synthesis, a unity in the end. Goethe's times, too, extending as they do from the old German world of peaceful, bourgeois life in 'Gothic' Frankfurt, through numerous wars, revolutions and social changes, present a highly colourful and varied picture. This changing picture I have tried to see not only through the eyes of 'old Weimar', which in fact was by no means so homely and peaceful as it is often represented, but in the wider context of European history as a whole.

A few words are necessary about the English edition of this book. The English version – it is not a mere translation from the original German – is the result of very close collaboration between my friend John Nowell and myself, although I would like to emphasize the predominant share he has taken in the work, with unceasing labour and diligence. I could not have wished for a happier collaboration.

The problems involved in any form of translation need not be stressed; they have been discussed often enough. In the case of poetry, they are insuperable, particularly in the case of Goethe, whose poetry so often deceives us by its simplicity and seemingly light or even 'superficial' appearance; this is also true of the poet's prose. Only where it seemed necessary or advisable have we attempted an approximation to the original rhythm and language; elsewhere we have used prose or simply a paraphrase. In order to achieve a greater unity we have avoided existing translations throughout – their different styles and aims would have presented a very incongruous appearance; moreover many of the quotations have not previously been translated into English. Attempts to translate Goethe's language, so rich in overtones as well as beauty, easily degenerate into impertinence, and in a few cases, such as *Über allen Gipfeln ist Ruh*, no attempt even at a paraphrase has been made. It is, perhaps, not superfluous to point out that even to his own countrymen many of Goethe's lines, and even whole poems and works, are still the object of widely differing interpretations. In the author's view those which proudly claim finally to have discovered the 'deeper', 'true' meaning are by no means the best. Goethe himself protested repeatedly and bitterly at the attempt of his 'dear Germans' to search for 'ideas' in his works, instead of simply enjoying the 'full, rich and very varied life' he had presented to them in his *Wilhelm Meister* or *Faust*.

It is this rich, full, varied life that is the subject of this book. Its description is a task that each generation must undertake anew. In his essay *Shakespeare und kein Ende*, Goethe points out that 'apparently nothing of value remains any longer to be said – and yet it is the characteristic of a great mind always once more to stimulate the mind'.

LONDON, NOVEMBER 1963           *Richard Friedenthal*

# Chronological Table

| | |
|---|---|
| 1749 | August 8, born in Frankfurt. Father Johann Caspar Goethe (1710–1782); mother Katharina Elisabeth, *née* Textor (1731–1808). |
| 1759 | Frankfurt occupied by the French (Seven Years War 1756–1763). |
| 1764 | Coronation of Emperor Joseph II. |
| 1765 | October till 1768, student at Leipzig University. *Buch Annette, Laune des Verliebten.* |
| 1768/70 | Frankfurt |
| 1770 | March–August 1771, in Strasbourg. Visits to Sesenheim, Friederike Brion (1752–1813). Becomes Licentiate of Law. |
| 1771/2 | Frankfurt. Short period of legal practice. *Frankfurter Gelehrten-Anzeigen. Von Deutscher Baukunst.* |
| 1772 | May–September in Wetzlar. Lotte Buff, marries Kestner (1753–1828). |
| 1773/5 | Frankfurt. Farces, Shrovetide plays, poems, *Clavigo*, beginnings of *Faust* and *Egmont. Werther.* Engaged to Lili Schönemann (1758–1817). |
| 1775 | May–July, journey to Switzerland. November, arrival in Weimar – at the invitation of the Duke, Karl August (1757–1828). |
| 1776 | Appointed member of the Council. Charlotte von Stein (1742–1827). *Die Geschwister.* Mining project in Ilmenau. |
| 1777 | November–December, journey to the Harz mountains. |
| 1778 | May, visit to Berlin. (Bavarian War of Succession, 1778–1779.) |
| 1779 | President of War Commission, Director of Roads and Services. *Iphigenie* in prose. September–January 1780, second journey to Switzerland. |
| 1782 | Granted diploma of nobility. Takes over financial affairs. |
| 1784 | Anatomy, discovery of the human *os intermaxillare.* |
| 1785 | Negotiations over the Princes' League. Studies in botany. |
| 1786 | September–June 1788, journey to Italy. *Iphigenie* in verse, *Egmont, Tasso.* |
| 1788 | Release from the day-to-day business of government. Christiane Vulpius (1765–1816). *Römische Elegien.* |

1789    December, Goethe's son, August, born (d. 1830), the sole survivor of five children.

1790    Completion of publication of *Goethe's Writings* in 8 small volumes. March–June, in Venice. *Venezianische Epigramme*. July–October, active service in Silesia. Studies in anatomy, botany, optics. *Metamorphose der Pflanzen*.
Assumes direction of the Court Theatre. *Gross-Kophta*. *Beiträge zur Optik*, 2 volumes.

1792    August–November French campaign. (First Coalition War, 1792–1797.) New writings start to appear (7 volumes).

1793    *Reineke Fuchs. Der Bügergeneral*. May–July, Siege of Mainz.

1794    Beginning of the close association with Schiller (1759–1805). *Wilhelm Meisters Lehrjahre* (completed 1796).

1795    *Die Horen. Unterhaltungen deutscher Ausgewanderten, Märchen.*

1796    *Xenien*, with Schiller. *Hermann und Dorothea.*

1797    *Balladen*. July–November, journey to South Germany and Switzerland. (Congress of Rastatt, 1797–1798.)

1798    Periodical, *Die Propyläen* (continued till 1800).

1799    *Achilleis*. – 2nd Coalition War, 1799–1802.

1801    Attack of erysipelas.

1803    *Die natürliche Tochter*. Visits to the Frommann family in Jena, at whose house, in 1807, Goethe meets Wilhelmine Herzlieb (1789–1865). (Reichsdeputationshauptschluss, end of the Holy Roman Empire.)

1804    Madame de Staël. *Winckelmann*. – Napoleon proclaimed Emperor.

1805    Serious kidney complaint. Death of Schiller. Friendship with Zelter (1758–1832).

1806    October 14, Battle of Jena. Occupation of Weimar. Marriage to Christiane Vulpius. (Formation of the Rheinbund.)

1807    Completion of the First Part of *Faust. Pandora.*

1808    Publication of the First Part of *Faust* in first Collected Edition of the Works in 12 volumes (1806–1808). Meeting with Napoleon at the Congress of Erfurt. (End of the Third Coalition War, 1805–1807.)

1809    *Wahlverwandtschaften*. Memoirs begun. (Napoleon's campaign against Austria. Risings in Tirol, Spain, Calabria.)

1810    *Farbenlehre.*

1811    *Aus meinem Leben Dichtung und Wahrheit* (6 volumes, 1811–1822).

1812    Meetings with Beethoven and the Empress Maria Ludovica of Austria. Napoleon's Russian campaign.

| | |
|---|---|
| 1813 | April till August in Teplitz. – Russia, Prussia, Austria join in war against Napoleon. October 16–18 Battle of Leipzig; April 1814 Napoleon's abdication; Napoleon exiled to Elba; Congress of Vienna. |
| 1814 | *Des Epimenides Erwachen.* Journey to the Main and the Rhine. Marianne von Willemer (d. 1860). |
| 1815 | Renewed journey to the Main and the Rhine; trip to Cologne with Freiherr vom Stein. Second Collected Edition of the works in 20 volumes (1815–1819). – The Hundred Days: Waterloo; Napoleon's banishment to St Helena. Weimar becomes a Grand Duchy. |
| 1816 | Death of Christiane. Periodical *Kunst und Alterthum* (continued till 1832). |
| 1817 | Dismissal from directorship of the Court Theatre. Marriage of Goethe's son to Ottilie von Pogwisch (1796–1872); grandsons Walter (1819–1885), Wolfgang (1820–1883), granddaughter Alma (1828–1845). Periodical *Zur Naturwissenschaft* (continued till 1824). – October, celebration on the Wartburg. |
| 1819 | *Westöstlicher Divan.* First performance of scenes from *Faust* in Berlin. |
| 1821 | *Wilhelm Meisters Wanderjahre*, Part One. |
| 1823 | Serious illness at the beginning of the year. Johann Peter Eckermann (1792–1854) comes to Weimar. June till September in Bohemia; meets Ulrike von Levetzow (1804–1899) in Marienbad. *Marienbader Elegie.* |
| 1825 | Work on Second Part of *Faust* resumed. |
| 1826 | Last Collected Edition of the works: 1826–1831, 40 volumes; 1833–1842, 20 further volumes of which volume 1 (1833) comprises the Second Part of *Faust.* Sees Schiller's skull, poem in terza rima. *Novelle.* |
| 1827 | *Chinesisch-Deutschen Jahres- und Tageszeiten.* |
| 1830 | Death of Goethe's son in Rome. Interest in the Cuvier–Geoffroy controversy at the Paris Academy. – July Revolution in Paris; beginning of the reign of Louis Philippe, the 'Citizen King'. |
| 1831 | Will. Completion of *Faust.* Last birthday in Ilmenau. |
| 1832 | March 14, last drive; March 16, falls ill; March 22, dies; March 26, burial in the Princes' Vault. |

# Bibliographical Survey

To give a full list of sources, especially of historical sources, would require a separate volume; I am, therefore, forced to confine myself to mentioning only some of these, and must necessarily omit altogether individual essays and contributions to periodicals and the *Goethe-Jahrbücher*, greatly indebted though I am to these. The specialist will observe, moreover, that I have made use of direct evidence almost throughout. As a guide to further Goethe study I refer the reader to the annotated edition published by Christian Wegner Verlag (Hamburg 1949 ff., 14 vols.) or to the *Goethe-Handbuch* (Metzler, Stuttgart 1958 ff., 4 vols.). The catalogue of the Kippenberg collection (Leipzig 1913, 2nd edition 1928, 3 vols.) was a constant and valuable guide to me, as was the information contained in the *Goethe-Jahrbücher*.

For Goethe's works we still have to rely on the 'Sophien' edition (Weimar 1887–1919, 143 vols.), the shortcomings of which are well known. The new critical edition of the Weimar archives as yet comprises only a few volumes, and work is still in progress on a very necessary Goethe dictionary. Supplementary volumes have been published on Goethe's drawings, his collections, and the *Amtliche Schriften* (vol. 1, Weimar 1950). The writings on natural science are now available in re-arranged form in the edition of the *Leopoldina* in Halle (Weimar 1947, 7 vols. to date, with comprehensive volumes of notes).

No full and scholarly account of Goethe's life exists, although the writing of a comprehensive biography was one of the tasks envisaged when the Goethe archives were opened in 1885. Existing 'biographies' seek to connect the course of Goethe's life with the interpretation – attempted with varying degrees of success – of his works. History, on the other hand, receives varying treatment in the biographies; the latest of these, that by Wolfgang Leppmann (*Goethe und die Deutschen*, Stuttgart 1963), observes that, in the judgment of 'noted scholars', the English life by George H. Lewes (London 1855) – in its day a considerable undertaking and one that found many readers in German translation – still remains the best introduction. Historical surveys of Goethe, however, have appeared repeatedly. The books by pedagogues like Karl Heinemann (1895) or Albert Bielschowsky (1904) were intended for the cul-

534

tured home or for scholastic purposes; even the biographies by Richard M. Meyer (1913) and Georg Witkowski (1932), both of whom were specialists and made valuable contributions elsewhere, do not go much beyond this. In the other works the so-called 'outward life' is pushed further and further into the background. Nevertheless it would be very ungrateful of me not at least to mention Konrad Burdach, Georg Simmel, Friedrich Gundolf, Ernst Cassirer and Hermann Korff, as well as the essays of Hugo von Hofmannsthal, Rudolph Alexander Schröder, Thomas Mann, Max Kommerell and Walter Benjamin. Among more recent works I have found those of Emil Staiger (*Goethe*, 3 vols., Bern 1952–1959), Barker Fairley (*A Study of Goethe*, London 1947), and the studies of Wilhelm Emrich the most stimulating.

In his *Essays um Goethe* (2 vols., 4th edition, Wiesbaden 1948) and in the volumes of the Artemis edition (Zurich, 24 vols., and to be continued), which he has edited, Ernst Beutler has made valuable biographical contributions. For the rest I consulted first and foremost the yearbooks and publications of the '*Goethe-Gesellschaft*' (since 1880), of the *Freies Hochstift* in Frankfurt (since 1902), of the 'English Goethe Society', the very informative yearbooks of the Kippenberg Collection (1921–35), commemorative works, catalogues of exhibitions and special publications. Somewhere and at some time almost everything has now been said about Goethe, often only to be forgotten again. The *Gespräche* (edited by Woldemar Freiherr von Biedermann and his son Flodoard, 2nd edition Leipzig 1909–11), as well as the collection by Heinz Amelung (*Goethe als Persönlichkeit*, Munich-Berlin 1914–15) and Wilhelm Bode (*Goethe in Briefen seiner Zeitgenossen*, Berlin 1918–23) are indispensable; for the conversations with Frédéric Soret I have used the original French (*Conversations avec Goethe*, edited by A. Robinet de Cléry, Paris 1932) and not Eckermann's translation. I omit individual references to the correspondence, some of which is available only in the *Goethe-Jahrbücher*. Walter H. Bruford is almost the only writer to deal with the sociological background in his *Germany in the 18th Century: The Social Background of the Literary Revival* (London–Cambridge 1935), *Theatre, Drama And Audience In Goethe's Germany* (1959), and *Culture and Society in Classical Weimar* (1962). *Goethe und seine Zeit* (Bern 1947) by Georg Lukacz enjoys a certain reputation as a 'Marxist' interpretation; about Goethe Lukacz speaks with subtle understanding, about his times only in clichés. Hans Eberhardt, in *Goethes Umwelt* (Weimar 1951), supplies exhaustive material on the 'social structure of Thuringia'.

THE TIMES: German history of the Goethe epoch is predominantly local history and the history of the various Princedoms; the broad outlines of the age are dealt with by Friedrich Christoph Schlosser in his *Geschichte des 18. und 19. Jahrhunderts*, 'with special reference to its culture' (Heidelberg 1836–48), and by his pupil Ludwig Häusser in *Deutsche Geschichte bis zur Gründung des Deutschen Bundes* (1854–57). In connection with earlier work I have made a more detailed study of some of these local histories, such as those of Brunswick, Hanover, Hesse and the Palatinate, but first and foremost I have relied on contemporary evidence, on periodicals like Ludwig Schlözer's *Staatsanzeigen Göttingen* (1783–93), the first German political organ of importance, Christian Daniel Schubart's *Deutsche Chronik* (Augsburg–Ulm 1774–77) written very vividly in the *Sturm und Drang* style, or the *Europäische Annalen* (edited by Ernst Ludwig Posselt), which were published by Cotta in Tübingen (1795–1806) and were read by Goethe and Schiller. Among the memoirs I would mention: *Memoiren des Karl Heinrich Ritters von Lang* (Brunswick 1842); Daniel Schubart's *Leben und Gesinnungen* (Stuttgart 1791–93); Joseph Anton Christ's stage memoirs *Schauspieler-Leben im 18. Jahrhundert* (Munich 1912); Johann Christian Brandes, *Meine Lebensgeschichte* (Berlin 1799); Eduard Genast, *Tagebuch eines alten Schauspielers* (Leipzig 1862–66); Karoline Jagemann, *Errinerungen* (Dresden 1926); *Friedrich Perthes' Leben*, by his son Clemens (Gotha 1848–55) who also wrote with thoroughness on *Deutsches Staatsleben vor der Revolution* (1845) and *Zustände zur Zeit der Franzosenherrschaft* (1862). *Christian Gottlob Heynes Leben*, by Arnold Heeren (Göttingen 1818) shows the rise of a great Greek scholar from circumstances of the extremest poverty; Karl Friedrich Bahrdt (*Geschichte Seines Lebens, von ihm Selbst Beschrieben*, Berlin 1790–91), who was mocked by Goethe, presents himself with great frankness as the type of the half-wastrel scholar. Heinrich Steffens, *Was ich Erlebte* (Breslau 1840 ff.). Memoirs of the War of Liberation listed in H. H. Houbens *Bibliog. Repertorium* (Berlin 1912). Of the numerous books of travel I shall confine myself to Charles Burney, *The Present State of Music in Germany* (London 1774); James Boswell, *Germany and Switzerland in 1764* (Yale University 1953); *Briefe eines Reisenden Franzosen* (Karl Risbeck), *Über Deutschland* (Zurich 1784); and Christoph Friedrich Nicolai, *Reise durch Deutschland und die Schweiz* (Berlin 1783 ff.). The *Almanach de Gotha* (since 1764) records the dynastic confusion; Hegel, in his masterly early work, *Die Verfassung Deutschlands*, 1802 (*Werke*, edited by Georg Lasson, vol. 7, Leipzig 1923), pronounces the final word – 'Germany is no longer a State' – and gives a brilliant survey.

GENERAL: René Wellek, *A History of Modern Criticism* (vols. 1 & 2, London 1955). Ernst Grumach, *Goethe und die Antike* (Berlin 1949); Humphrey Trevelyan, *Goethe and the Greeks* (London 1949). Contemporary literature on art is listed in Julius Schlosser's *Die Kunstliteratur* (Vienna 1924). Also of importance to me were the contemporary volumes of copper-plate engravings: James Stuart, *Antiquities of Athens* (London 1762–64); Robert Wood, *The Ruins of Palmyra* (London 1753); *The Ruins of Baalbec* (London 1757); Thomas Major, *The Ruins of Paestum* (London 1768). Benedetto Croce, *Estetica* 10th edition (Bari 1958), and his volume on Goethe (Opere, vol. 12, Bari 1960); Paul Frankl, *The Gothic, Literary Sources and Interpretations Through Eight Centuries* (Princeton 1961).

YOUTH: Ernst Beutler, *Briefe aus dem Elternhaus* (Zurich 1960), with extensive introductions on Goethe's parents and sister; the *Viaggio* by Goethe's father (Rome 1932); K. Knetsch, *Ahnentafel Goethes* (Leipzig 1932); *Labores Juveniles* (facsimile edition, Frankfurt 1932).

The Frankfurt city archivist, Georg L. Kriegk, has published important material on old Frankfurt from the city records: *Deutsche Kulturbilder aus dem 18. Jahrhundert* (Frankfurt 1874), which also contains extracts on Goethe as attorney. Kriegk quotes the secret chronicler Senckenberg in *Die Gebrüder Senckenberg* (Frankfurt 1869), though clearly with a degree of circumspection, as does Ernst Beutler later. I mention this only because so much concerning Goethe has been lost. He himself systematically destroyed the evidence of his youth, including the letters of Merck and Corona Schröter, among others.

*Goethes Beziehungen zu seiner Vaterstadt* (Frankfurt Exhibition 1895), produced by the 'Freies Hofstift'; and Friedrich Bothe's publication under the same title (Frankfurt 1949).

STUDENT YEARS: Julius Vogel, *Goethes Leipziger Studenten Jahre* (Leipzig 1923); Jean de Pange, *Goethe en Alsace* (Paris 1925); Ernst Traumann, *Goethe der Strassburger Student* (Leipzig 1923). The literature on Friederike Brion began appearing in Goethe's own lifetime: A. F. Näke, *Wallfahrt nach Sesenheim* (1822: published by Varnhagen, Berlin 1840); August Stöber, who knew Georg Büchner and gave him the idea for his *Lenz*, published two small volumes, *Der Dichter lenz und Friederike von Sesenheim* (Bale 1842) and *Der Aktuar Salzmann* (Frankfurt 1853); Stefan Ley, *Goethe und Friederike* (Bonn 1947). Heinrich Gloël, *Goethes Wetzlarer Zeit* (Berlin 1911); August Siegfried von Goué, *Masuren oder der Junge Werther* (Frankfurt 1775); the Jesuit F. Callenbach, *Uti Ante Hac – Auff die Alte Hack* (n.d., probably Nuremberg ca. 1714).

PIETISM: *Die Schöne Seele* (Fräulein von Klettenberg – edited by Heinrich Funck (Leipzig 1911); *Der Deutsche Pietismus* (confessions – edited by Werner Mahrholz, Berlin 1921), and *Deutsche Selbstzeugnisse* (vol. 7, *Pietismus und Rationalismus*, edited by Mathilde Beyer-Fröhlich, Leipzig 1933); Gottfried Arnold, *Unpartheyische Kirchen – und Ketzerhistorie* (Frankfurt 1700) and *Historie und Beschreibung der Mystischen Theologie* (2nd edition, Leipzig 1738); Carl Heinrich von Bogatzky, *Güldenes Schazkästlein* (Halle 1718); I quote the same author's *Geistliche Lieder* (2nd edition, Halle 1775).

ALCHEMY: John Ferguson, *Bibliotheca Chemica* (Glasgow 1906); Gustav Hartlaub, *Der Stein der Weisen – Wesen der Bildwelt der Alchemie* (Munich

1959); Will – Erich Peuckert, *Die Rosenkreuzer* (1928); Swedenborg: Immanuel Kant, *Träume eines Geistersehers* (Königsberg 1766); Martin Lamm, *Swedenborg, seine Entwicklung zum Mystiker und Geisterseher* (from the Swedish, Leipzig 1923).

STURM UND DRANG: *Klingers Jugendwerke* (edited by Kurt Wolff, Leipzig 1912–13). A monograph, *F. M. Klinger* (Weimar 1962), by Olga Smoljan includes new material in Klinger's life in Russia, but otherwise contains little that is not to be found in the earlier and very thorough volumes of Max Rieger: *F. M. Klinger* (3 vols. with letters, Darmstadt 1880–96). Lenz: *Werke* (edited by Franz Blei, Munich 1909); *Briefe* (Munich 1918). Merck: *Briefe von und an Merck* (3 collections, edited by Karl Wagner, Darmstadt 1835, 1838, 1847); *Schriften und Briefe* (edited by Kurt Wolff, 2 vols., Leipzig 1909); *Fabeln und Erzählungen* (edited by Hermann Bräuning – Oktavio, Darmstadt 1962). Heinse: *Werke* (edited by C. Schüddekopf, Leipzig 1902 ff.); the magazine *Iris* (Düsseldorf 1774–77); Heinse's translation of *Beffreytes Jerusalem* (Mannheim 1781) containing the *Leben Tassos*. Roy Pascal, *The German Sturm und Drang* (Manchester 1959); Friedrich Gundolf, *Shakespeare und der deutsche Geist* (2nd edition, Berlin 1914). *Portraits* (anonym., Leipzig 1779). Hamann I have purposely not included; he belongs in a different context.

WEIMAR: Biographies of almost all the members of Goethe's circle exist, and recently even a life of Bertuch has appeared: A. von Heinemann, *Friedrich Justin Bertuch* (Weimar 1955). Anna Amalie has been the subject of a number of books, among them *Amalie Herzogin von Weimar* by Wilhelm Bode (3 vols., Berlin 1907) and *Anna Amalie* by Otto Heuschele (1947). Bode's assiduous study of the local history enabled him to contribute much on the subject of old Weimar, in his *Charlotte von Stein* (Berlin 1910), *Goethes Sohn* (Berlin 1918), and in the many volumes of his Goethe biography (Berlin 1922 ff.). In addition I would mention only Willy Andreas, *Karl August* (Stuttgart 1955), and the other works on the Duke cited in this book; Fritz Hartung, *Das Grossherzogtum Sachsen unter der Regierung Karl Augusts* (Weimar 1923); Joseph A. von Bradish, *Goethes Beamtenlaufbahn* (New York 1937); A. Diezmann, *Aus Weimars Glanzzeit* (Leipzig (1855); Karl von Lyncker, *Am weimarischen Hof* (Berlin 1912); Karl August Böttiger, *Literarische Zustände und Zeitgenossen* (Leipzig 1838). A great deal of material supplied by Goethe's contemporaries – including Eckermann – is contained in the early editions of Brockhaus' *Konversationslexikon*, which was also much used by Goethe, and the supplementary series *Zeitgenossen*. There is also the annual *Nekrolog der Deutschen* (1794–1806) by Friedrich Schlichtegroll, who roused Goethe's anger by his contribution on C. Ph. Moritz, just after the latter's death, and who was lampooned in the *Xenien* as a 'carrion crow'.

ITALY: The *Italienische Reise, mit den zeichnungen Goethes, seiner Freunde und Zeitgenossen* (with 124 illustrations, Leipzig 1912); the diaries and letters, as well as the *Nachgeschichte* in *Schriften der Goethe-Gesellschaft* (vols. 2 and 5, Weimar 1886, 1890) and *Goethe und Tischbein* (*ibid.*, vol. 25); on the last named, Franz Landsberg, *Wilhelm Tischbein* (Leipzig 1908), and *Die Kunst der Goethezeit* (Leipzig 1921). The travel guide used by Goethe: J. J. Volkmann, *Historisch-kritische Nachrichten von Italien* (3 vols., Leipzig 1777) – 'compiled from the latest French and English accounts of travels and from the author's own commentaries', in the words of the compiler himself, who wrote a whole series of guides. Volkmann's predecessors, especially Jonathan Richardson, *An Account of the Statues and Pictures in Italy, etc.* (London 1754),who was held in high esteem by Winckelmann and who, with his similarly named son, influenced views on art for half a century. The travel guides, including those to individual towns, are listed in Julius Schlosser, *Die Kunstliteratur* (Vienna 1924); I looked at a number of these, particularly that by Giuseppe Vasi, the most celebrated Baedeker of his day, and his album of engravings *Magnifizenze di Roma* (Rome 1786). The guide used by Goethe's father – and by Mozart too – *Joh. Georg Keyssler, Neueste Reise durch Teutschland … Italien Usw* (Hanover 1740–41) contains much on Germany and Switzerland in its nearly 1,500 pages. Descriptions of travels and the history of the lure of Italy in general: Wilhelm Waetzoldt, *Das klassische Land* (Leipzig 1927); Carl Philipp Moritz, *Reisen eines Deutschen in Italien* (Berlin 1792–93). On C. Ph. Moritz: Eckehard Catholy, *K. Ph. Moritz* (Tübingen 1962), and Robert Minder (Berlin 1936). In addition J. W. von Archenholz, *England und Italien* (Leipzig 1787), which Goethe repudiated, and J. H. Baron von Riedesel, *Reise durch Sizilien* (Zürich 1771), which he praised. Henry Swinburne, *Travels in the Two Sicilies* (London 1785). Sir William Hamilton, *Campi Phlegraei* (Naples 1776–79), the most opulent collection of views of its day with engravings by Fabri, and now published in abridged form in facsimile (Milan 1962, with a bibliography of Hamilton's publications). Lady Emma Hamilton, *Attitudes after the Antique* (engravings in outline, London 1807). Benedetto Croce, *Goethe a Napoli* (Bari 1954). From the copious German literature I would mention only Friedrich Noack, *Deutsches Leben in Rom* (Stuttgart 1907), and H. Smidt, *Ein Jahrhundert Römischen Lebens* (reports of eye-witnesses, Leipzig 1904). The travel sketches of Wilhelm Müller, the poet of the Müllerlieder, *Rom, Römer und Römerinnen* (Leipzig 1820), form the most lively of the older travel books; it contains the poem on Goethe which I quote in recording the death of his son.

WAR AND REVOLUTIONARY YEARS: Arthur Chuquet, *Les Guerres de la Révolution* (11 vols., Paris n.d.). Chuquet was a rare combination of military professional (he was teacher at the Paris military academy) and connoisseur of German literature; his *Etudes d'Histoire* (7 vols., Paris 1903–14) and *Etudes de Littérature Allemande* (Paris 1900–02) contain, among others, essays on *Goethe en Champagne*, Klopstock, Adam Lux, Stolberg, Karl August. Friedrich Christian Laukhard, *Leben und Schicksale* (5 vols., Halle 1792–1802). *Briefe eines Preussischen Augenzeugen über den Feldzug des Herzogs von Braunschweig* (Hamburg 1794). The military almanach *Minerva* (Hamburg 1792 ff.), whose editor, Archenholz, sent out war correspondents in the modern manner. The *Revolutions-Almanache* (edited by Heinrich A. O. Reichard, Gotha 1793 ff.). Georg Forster, *Sämtl. Schriften* (Leipzig 1843; a new critical edition has just been undertaken by the Berliner Akademie). Franz Xavier Remling, *Die Rheinpfalz in der Revolutions-geschichte* (Speyer 1865). Helene Voigt, *Die deutsche Jakobinische Literatur* (Berlin 1855). Erich Weniger, *Goethe und die Generäle* (Leipzig 1942). Willy Andreas, *Goethe und Karl August bei der belagerung von Mainz* (publication of the Bayrische Akadamie, Munich 1955).

ERFURT: Talleyrand, *Mémoires* (Paris 1891–92); *Napoleons Hofmarschall* (*Jahrbuch Kippenberg*, vol. 5). Erwin Redslob, *Goethes Begegnung mit Napoleon* (Weimar 1944). *Goethes Briefwechsel mit Reinhard* (Wiesbaden 1957). The phrase '*empire de recrutement*' was coined by Gabriel Hanotaux.

Goethe's relations with the Romantics and the Austrian friends are dealt with in vols. 13–14 (Weimar 1898–99) and 17–18 (1902–03 of the *Schriften der Goethe-Gesellschaft*. Madame de Staël: Christopher Herold, *Mistress of an Age* (New York 1961). *Rahel Varnhagen*: Hannah Arendt, Rahel Varnhagen (Munich 1960). Hilde Spiel, *Fanny Arnstein oder die Emanzipation* (Frankfurt 1962).

NATURAL SCIENCE: I grew up in the house of a scientist; my father was a physiologist, Professor in Berlin, who counted Ernst Haeckel, Iwan Pavlov, Wilhelm Ostwald among his friends; he was certainly no 'priest of the guild' in Goethe's sense. In his bookcase stood the works of Albrecht von Haller and Johannes Müller, alongside his favourite Ariosto. The Heidelberg lectures of Rudolf Magnus (*Goethe als Naturforscher*, Leipzig 1906), who was a friend of my family, were my first introduction to this subject; they are still of value. Since those days this literature has become enormous (cf. Günther Neumann's bibliography: *Goethe und die Naturwissenschaften*, Halle 1940) and has frequently assumed mystic forms. Rudolf Steiner, *Goethes Weltanschauung* (Weimar 1897), is still worth reading in my view; the book by his disciple E. Lehr, *Man or Matter* (London 1958), appealed to me very much less. At the opposite extreme to this stands the sober work of the physiologist Sir Charles Sherrington, *Goethe on Nature and Science* (2nd edition, Cambridge 1949). The observations of great physicists like Werner Heisenberg or Max Born show how uncertain the further development of their science has become to its most distinguished representatives: whether this will open a way 'back to Goethe' is another matter. Carl

Friedrich von Weizsäcker rightly emphasizes, in the selection from the *Naturwissenschaftliche Schriften* (vol. 13 of the *Hamburger Ausgabe*), the connection between Goethe's scientific work and his writing and personality; the more specialized literature will be found listed in this volume. I have also consulted some of the works by Goethe's contemporaries: Joseph Priestley's *Geschichte der Optik*, Lichtenberg's *Erxleben* and his very informative *Göttingisches Magazin der Wissenschaften und Literatur* (Göttingen 1780 ff.). Georg Landgrebe's book *Über das Licht* (Marburg 1834) gives an instructive review of scientific work in the Goethe era; it also gives a full account of Ritter's discoveries. Ritter's *Fragmente* (Heidelberg 1810) are based in part on the posthumous writings of Novalis and lead on to the natural philosophy of the Romantics. Goethe's position in relation to the natural science of his day, which by no means consisted only of 'separating and dividing', remains still to be established. Novalis' observations on Ritter show how close the latter must have been to Goethe, who did indeed admire him though he soon rejected him. According to Novalis 'Ritter is always searching for the true *Weltseele*. His idea is to learn to read the visible and ponderable letters, and to explain the "composition" of the higher spiritual powers. All external processes should be comprehensible as symbols and final effects of internal processes.'

NEWTON: Edward Neville da Costa Andrade, *Isaac Newton* (New York 1950); M. Roberts, *Newton and the Origin of Colours* (London 1938); K. T. A. Halbertsma, *History of the Theory of Colours* (Amsterdam 1949); P. J. Bouma, *Farbe und Wahrnehmung* (Eindhoven 1951); A. Wolf, *A History of Science in the 18th Century* (London 1938). On the rainbow: Carl B. Boyer, *The Rainbow – from Myth to Mathematics* (New York 1959).

MORPHOLOGY: The botanist Wilhelm Troll, whose edition of the *Morphologische schriften Goethes* (Jena 1932) is copiously illustrated and annotated.

METEOROLOGY: Waldemar von Wasielewski, *Goethes Meteorologische Studien* (Leipzig 1910).

GEOLOGY: Max Semper, *Die Geologischen Studien Goethes* (Leipzig 1914) and G. Linck, *Goethes Verhältnis zur Mineralogie und Geologie* (Jena 1906). Alexander von Humboldt: *Studien zu seiner Universalen Geisteshaltung* (edited by J. Schultze, with contributions from three continents, Berlin 1959).

LEONARDO DA VINCI: Perhaps I may be allowed to refer here to my book *Leonardo da Vinci* (London 1960), which is concerned with similar problems of a universal spirit.

GOETHE AS AN OLD MAN: *Der Westöstlicher Divan* (edited by Hans-J. Weitz, Wiesbaden 1951); Eckermann's *Gespräche mit Goethe* (edited by Fritz

Bergemann, Wiesbaden 1955). Julius Petersen, *die Entstehung de ecker-mannschen Gespräche* (2nd edition, Frankfurt 1924); Heinrich Hubert Houben, *J. P. Eckermann* (2 vols., Leipzig 1925–28), the same author's *Hier Zensur* (Leipzig 1918), *Verbotene Literatur* (2 vols., Leipzig 1924), *Ottilie von Goethe* (Leipzig 1923). From the posthumous papers of Ottilie and her mother, which are now in America, Heinz Blum has published *Briefe aus der Verlobungszeit* (Weimar 1962) and *Tagebücher und Briefe* (Vienna 1913), supplementing the correspondence previously published in the *Schriften der Goethe-gesellschaft* (vols. 27–28, Weimar 1912–13). Lise-lotte Lohrer, *Cotta, Geschichte eines Verlages* (Stuttgart 1960). Bettina Brentano: *Briefwechsel mit Goethe* (edited by Fritz Bergemann, Leipzig 1927); there is now a new edition of her Works (vol. 5, Frechen 1961). Marianne von Willemer: Edwin Zellweker, *Marianne Willemer* (Vienna 1949); Hans Pyritz, *Goethe und Marianne von Willemer* (Stuttgart 1948); Bernard von Brentano, *Dass ich eins und Doppelt bin – Marianne von Willemer und Goethe* (Wiesbaden 1961); I have not yet had an opportunity to examine the new edition of the correspondence (Wiesbaden 1963).

ART: Richard Benz, *Goethe und die Romantische Kunst* (Munich 1940).

MUSIC: Hans Joachim Moser, *Goethe und die Musik* (Leipzig 1949); Romain Rolland, *Goethe et Beethoven* (Paris 1930); *Felix Mendelssohns Briefe* (complete edition in one volume, Leipzig 1899), and the very reliable essays by Max Friedländer in the *Goethe Jahrbücher* (especially the volume for 1916); also by the same author 2 volumes of Goethe's poems in settings by his contemporaries in the *Schriften der Goethe-gesellschaft* (vols. 11, 21, Weimar 1896, 1916).

BOHEMIA: Johannes Urzidil, *Goethe in Böhmen* (Zürich 1962); E. Hlawaek, *Goethe in Karlsbad* (2nd edition, Karlsbad 1883). Eliza M. Butler, *Goethe and Byron* (London 1956); Frederic Norman, *H. C. Robinson and Goethe* (English Goethe Society, 2 vols., 1930–31); Thomas Carlyle, *Essays* (4 vols., London 1839), and *Correspondence with Goethe* (London 1887). Gérard de Nerval, *Œuvres Complètes* (vol. 1, Paris 1868); Charles Dedeyan, *Gérard de Nerval et l'Allemagne* (2 vols., Paris 1957–58); Eugène Dela-croix, *Letters* (edited by Burty, Paris 1880).

1830 REVOLUTION: Eye-witness reports in the *Annual Register*; Narcisse Achille de Salvandy, *Seize mois ou La Révolution et Les Révolutionnaires* (Paris 1831; according to an entry by a previous owner the British Museum copy is Goethe's own copy). Maria Szymanowska, *Album mit Komposi-tionen* (facsimile edition, Cracow 1953); recently various accounts of her life and family have appeared in Poland, which I know only from report.

WORLD LITERATURE: Fritz Strich, *Goethe und die Weltliteratur* (Bern 1946).

# Index

Individuals mentioned are to be found under their family names (not under 'von' or 'de'). Dates of birth and death are given in the case of less familiar personalities, but not for persons of world-wide fame, such as Napoleon, Beethoven, or Lord Byron.